Wonders

Program Authors

Dr. Diane August
Dr. Donald Bear
Dr. Janice A. Dole
Dr. Jana Echevarria
Dr. Douglas Fisher
Dr. David J. Francis
Dr. Vicki Gibson
Dr. Jan Hasbrouck
Margaret Kilgo
Dr. Scott G. Paris
Dr. Timothy Shanahan
Dr. Josefina V. Tinajero

Mc
Graw
Hill
Education

Also Available from McGraw-Hill Education

ETS and the ETS logo are registered trademarks of Educational Testing Service (ETS).
TextEvaluator is a trademark of Educational Testing Service.

Cover and Title Pages: Nathan Love

www.mheonline.com/readingwonders

Send all inquiries to:
McGraw-Hill Education
2 Penn Plaza
New York, NY 10121

ISBN: 978-0-07-680477-1
MHID: 0-07-680477-1

Printed in the United States of America.

1 2 3 4 5 6 7 8 9 RMN 20 19 18 17 16 15   A

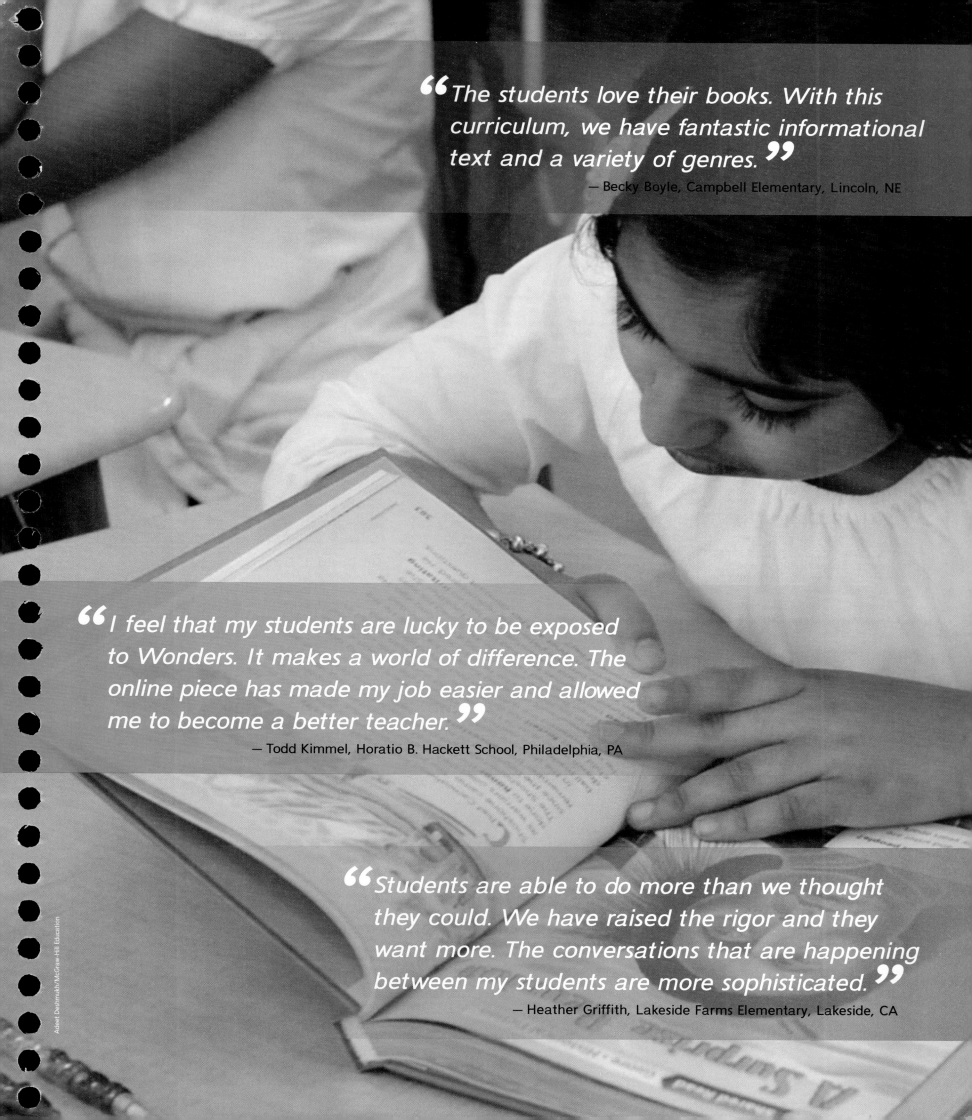

"The students love their books. With this curriculum, we have fantastic informational text and a variety of genres."

— Becky Boyle, Campbell Elementary, Lincoln, NE

"I feel that my students are lucky to be exposed to Wonders. It makes a world of difference. The online piece has made my job easier and allowed me to become a better teacher."

— Todd Kimmel, Horatio B. Hackett School, Philadelphia, PA

"Students are able to do more than we thought they could. We have raised the rigor and they want more. The conversations that are happening between my students are more sophisticated."

— Heather Griffith, Lakeside Farms Elementary, Lakeside, CA

PROGRAM AUTHORS

Dr. Diane August
American Institutes for Research,
Washington, D.C.

Managing Researcher
Education Program

Dr. Donald R. Bear
Iowa State University

Professor, Iowa State University
Author of *Words Their Way, Words
Their Way with English Learners,
Vocabulary Their Way,* and *Words
Their Way with Struggling Readers, 4–12*

Dr. Janice A. Dole
University of Utah

Professor, University of Utah
Director, Utah Center for Reading and
Literacy
Content Facilitator, National Assessment
of Educational Progress (NAEP)
CCSS Consultant to Literacy Coaches,
Salt Lake City School District, Utah

Dr. Jana Echevarria
California State University, Long
Beach

Professor Emerita, California State University
Author of *Making Content Comprehensible
for English Learners: The SIOP Model*

Dr. Douglas Fisher
San Diego State University

Co-Director, Center for the Advancement
of Reading, California State University
Author of *Language Arts Workshop:
Purposeful Reading and Writing Instruction,
Reading for Information in Elementary
School;* coauthor of *Close Reading and
Writing from Sources, Rigorous Reading: 5
Access Points for Comprehending Complex
Text,* and *Text-Dependent Questions,
Grades K-5* with N. Frey

Dr. David J. Francis
University of Houston

Director of the Center for Research
on Educational Achievement and
Teaching of English Language
Learners (CREATE)

Consulting Authors

Kathy R. Bumgardner
National Literacy Consultant

Strategies Unlimited, Inc.
Gastonia, NC

Jay McTighe
Jay McTighe and Associates

Author of *Essential Questions: Opening
Doors to Student Understanding,
The Understanding by Design Guide
to Creating High Quality Units* and
*Schooling by Design: Mission, Action,
Achievement* with G. Wiggins,
and *Differentiated Instruction and
Understanding By Design* with C.
Tomlinson

Dr. Doris Walker-Dalhouse
Marquette University

Associate Professor, Department
of Educational Policy & Leadership
Author of articles on multicultural
literature, struggling readers, and
reading instruction in urban schools

Dinah Zike
Educational Consultant

Dinah-Might Activities, Inc.
San Antonio, TX

Dr. Scott G. Paris
Educational Testing Service,
Vice President, Research Professor,
Nanyang Technological University,
Singapore, 2008–2011

Professor of Education and Psychology,
University of Michigan, 1978–2008

Dr. Timothy Shanahan
University of Illinois at Chicago

Distinguished Professor, Urban Education
Director, UIC Center for Literacy Chair,
Department of Curriculum & Instruction
Member, English Language Arts Work
Team and Writer of the Common Core
State Standards
President, International Reading
Association, 2006

Dr. Josefina V. Tinajero
University of Texas at El Paso

Professor of Bilingual Education &
Special Assistant to the Vice President
of Research.

Dr. Vicki Gibson
Educational Consultant Gibson
Hasbrouck and Associates

Author of *Differentiated Instruction:
Grouping for Success, Differentiated
Instruction: Guidelines for Implementation,*
and *Managing Behaviors to Support
Differentiated Instruction*

Dr. Jan Hasbrouck
J.H. Consulting
Gibson Hasbrouck and Associates

Developed Oral Reading Fluency Norms for
Grades 1–8
Author of *The Reading Coach: A How-
to Manual for Success* and *Educators as
Physicians: Using RTI Assessments for
Effective Decision-Making*

Margaret Kilgo
Educational Consultant
Kilgo Consulting, Inc., Austin, TX

Developed Data-Driven Decisions
process for evaluating student
performance by standard
Member of Common Core State
Standards Anchor Standards
Committee for Reading and Writing

National Program Advisors

Mayda Bahamonde-Gunnell, Ed.D
Grand Rapids Public Schools
Rockford, MI

Maria Campanario
Boston Public Schools
Boston, MA

Sharon Giless Aguina
Waukegan Community Unit School District #60
Waukegan, IL

Carolyn Gore, Ph.D.
Caddo Parish School District
Shreveport, LA

Kellie Jones
Department of Bilingual/ESL Services
Brockton, MA

Michelle Martinez
Albuquerque Public Schools Curriculum and
    Instruction
Albuquerque, NM

Jadi Miller
Lincoln Public Schools
Lincoln, NE

Matthew Walsh
Wissahickon School District
Ambler, PA

CONNECTED LITERACY TOOLS

Weekly Concept and Essential Question

The Keys to Unlock the Week

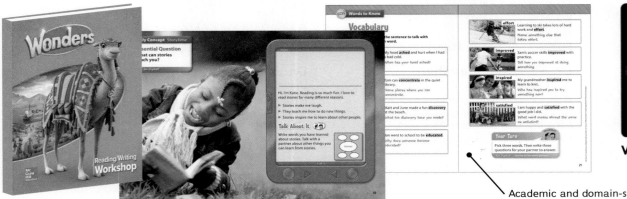

Weekly Opener Video

Reading/Writing Workshop

Academic and domain-specific vocabulary

Teach and Model

With Rich Opportunities for Collaborative Conversations

Collaborative Conversations PD

Reading/Writing Workshop

All building on the week's Essential Question

Practice and Apply

Close Reading, Writing to Sources, Grammar, Spelling, and Phonics

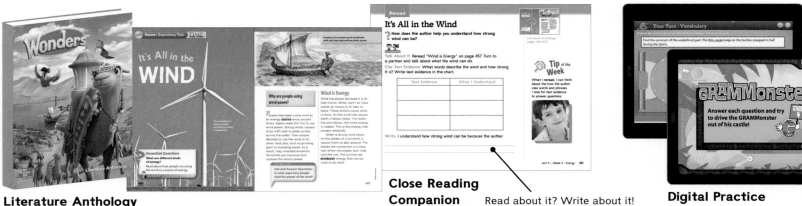

Literature Anthology

Close Reading Companion

Read about it? Write about it!

Digital Practice

Build Knowledge and Skills at Every Level

Differentiate to Accelerate

Move students ahead as soon as they're ready

Also available:
- WonderWorks
- Wonders for English Learners
- Wonders Adaptive Learning

Over 6500 more leveled readers online!

Nonfiction Leveled Readers

Fiction Leveled Readers

Adaptive Learning

Integrate Understanding

Writing across texts, research and inquiry

Performance task practice throughout the year

Writer's Workspace

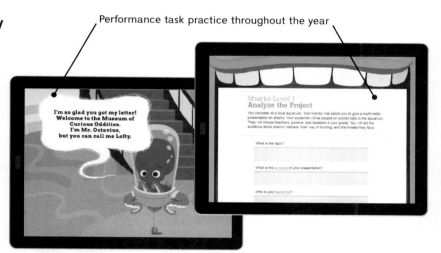

Inquiry Space

Assess

Specific skills and standards for every student, assignment, and class

Specific recommendations for every skill and standard.

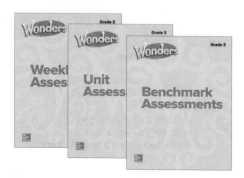

Weekly, Unit, Benchmark Assessments

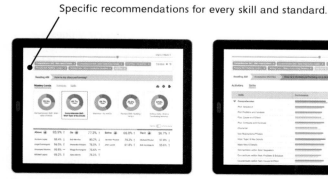

Data Dashboard

Proficiency Report

PROGRAM COMPONENTS
Print and Digital

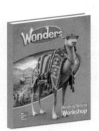

Reading/Writing Workshop

Literature Anthology   **Close Reading Companion**

Leveled Readers

Teacher Editions

Classroom Library Trade Books

Your Turn Practice Book

Visual Vocabulary Cards

Leveled Workstation Activity Cards

Sound-Spelling Cards

High-Frequency Word Cards

Response Board

Weekly Assessment   **Unit Assessment**   **Benchmark Assessment**

Additional Digital Resources

For You

 Plan
Customizable Lesson Plans

 Teach
Classroom Presentation Tools Instructional Lessons

 Manage and Assign
Student Grouping and Assignments

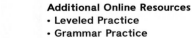 **Assess**
Online Assessments Reports and Scoring

Collaborate
Online Class Conversations Interactive Group Projects

School to Home
Activities and Messages

Professional Development
Model Lessons and PD Videos

Additional Online Resources
- Leveled Practice
- Grammar Practice
- Phonics/Spelling
- ELL Activities
- Genre Study
- Reader's Theater
- Tier 2 Intervention
- Instructional Routine Handbook

For Your Students

 My To Do List
Assignments Assessment

 Read
e Books Interactive Texts

 Write
Interactive Writing

 Words to Know
Build Vocabulary

 Play
Interactive Games

School to Home Support
- Activities for Home
- Messages from the Teacher

www.connected.mcgraw-hill.com

viii

Meet the Challenge

Unit Planning

Weekly Lessons

Genre Writing: Narrative Text

Writing Process

Extended Complex Text

Model Lesson

Close Reading Routine

Program Information

(t to b) McGraw-Hill Companies, Inc./Tonika G. Johnson; Jeff Greenberg/Alamy; Greg Winston/National Geographic/Getty Images; Unimedia Images/Unimedia International/Newscom; Ira Block/National Geographic/Getty Images

UNIT OVERVIEW

Week 1 CHOICES	**Week 2** SKILLS AND TALENTS	**Week 3** ADAPTATIONS

READING

Week 1 — CHOICES

ESSENTIAL QUESTION
What choices are good for us?

Build Background

ccss Vocabulary
L.3.6 *aroma, expect, flavorful, graceful, healthful, interrupted, luscious, variety*
Root Words

ccss Comprehension
RL.3.l Strategy: Ask and Answer Questions
Skill: Point of View
Genre: Folktale

ccss Phonics
L.3.4c /ü/ and /u̇/, Roots in Related Words

ccss Fluency
RF.3.4b Expression

Week 2 — SKILLS AND TALENTS

ESSENTIAL QUESTION
How can you use what you know to help others?

Build Background

ccss Vocabulary
L.3.6 *achievement, apologized, attention, audience, confidence, embarrassed, realized, talents*
Prefixes

ccss Comprehension
RL.3.l Strategy: Ask and Answer Questions
Skill: Point of View
Genre: Realistic Fiction

ccss Phonics
RF.3.3c Plural Words, Vowel Team Syllables

ccss Fluency
RF.3.4a Phrasing

Week 3 — ADAPTATIONS

ESSENTIAL QUESTION
How do animals adapt to challenges in their habitat?

Build Background

ccss Vocabulary
L.3.6 *alert, competition, environment, excellent, prefer, protection, related, shelter*
Sentence Clues

ccss Comprehension
RI.3.8 Strategy: Reread
Skill: Text Structure: Compare and Contrast
Genre: Expository Text

ccss Phonics
L.3.4c Variant Vowel /ô/, Greek and Latin Roots

ccss Fluency
RF.3.4a Intonation

Inquiry Space   **Narrative Performance Task** Write About: Frogs T38–T39, T102–T103, T166–T167

LANGUAGE ARTS

Week 1

ccss Writing
W.3.la Write to Sources: Opinion

ccss Grammar
L.3.la Linking Verbs

ccss Spelling
L.3.2f Variant Vowels /ü/ and /u̇

ccss Vocabulary
L.3.4c Build Vocabulary

Week 2

ccss Writing
W.3.la Write to Sources: Opinion

ccss Grammar
L.3.2f Contractions with *Not*

ccss Spelling
L.3.2f Plural Words

ccss Vocabulary
L.3.4b Build Vocabulary

Week 3

ccss Writing
W.3.2a Write to Sources: Informative

ccss Grammar
L.3.ld Main and Helping Verbs

ccss Spelling
L.3.2f Variant Vowel /ô/

ccss Vocabulary
L.3.4a Build Vocabulary

 Writing Process   **Genre Writing: Narrative Text** Fictional Narrative T344–T349

Meet the Challenge

Review and Assess

Week 4	Week 5	Week 6
FLIGHT	**INSPIRATION**	

Week 4 — FLIGHT

ESSENTIAL QUESTION
How are people able to fly?

Build Background

CCSS Vocabulary
L.3.6 *controlled, direction, flight, impossible, launched, motion, passenger, popular*
Context Clues

CCSS Comprehension
RI.3.3 Strategy: Reread
Skill: Text Structure: Cause and Effect
Genre: Expository Text

CCSS Phonics
RF.3.3d Homophones, *r*-Controlled Vowel Syllables

CCSS Fluency
RF.3.4b Accuracy

Week 5 — INSPIRATION

ESSENTIAL QUESTION
How can others inspire us?

Build Background

CCSS Vocabulary
L.3.6 *adventurous, courageous, extremely, weird*
Metaphor

CCSS Comprehension
RL.3.2 Genre: Narrative and Free-Verse
Skill: Theme
Literary Elements: Repetition and Rhyme

CCSS Phonics
RF.3.3c Soft *c* and *g*, Words with *-er* and *-est*

CCSS Fluency
RF.3.4b Expression

Week 6

CCSS Reader's Theater
RF.3.4b Focus on Vocabulary
Fluency: Accuracy, Rate, and Prosody

CCSS Reading Digitally
SL.3.2 Notetaking
Skimming and Scanning
Navigating Links

CCSS Inquiry Space
SL.3.5 Creating a Presentation
Speaking, Listening
Review and Evaluate

> **Unit 4 Assessment**
>
> **Unit Assessment Book
> Fluency Assessment**
> pages 152–161

Inquiry Space   Narrative Performance Task Write About: Frogs T230–T231, T294–T295, T330–T331

Week 4

CCSS Writing
W.3.2a Write to Sources: Informative

CCSS Grammar
L.3.1i Complex Sentences

CCSS Spelling
L.3.2f Homophones

CCSS Vocabulary
L.3.4a Build Vocabulary

Week 5

CCSS Writing
W.3.3d Write to Sources: Narrative

CCSS Grammar
L.3.1d Irregular Verbs

CCSS Spelling
L.3.2f Soft *c* and *g*

CCSS Vocabulary
L.3.5a Build Vocabulary

Week 6

CCSS Writing
W.3.6 Publishing Celebrations
Portfolio Choice

Writing Process **Genre Writing: Poetry** Poem T350–T355

UNIT OPENER

Reading/Writing
Workshop

Unit 4
Meet the Challenge

The Big Idea
What are different ways to meet challenges?

256

Meatballs on Wheels

Our meatballs roll from door to door,
    We go each week at half past four.
We deliver dinner on wheels,
    Bringing seniors hot, tasty meals.

Meatballs rolling from door to door,
Meatballs and a whole lot more.

— by Trevor Reynolds

257

READING/WRITING WORKSHOP, *pp. 256–257*

The Big Idea *What are different ways to meet challenges?*

COLLABORATE

Talk About It

Have students read the Big Idea aloud. Ask students to describe challenges that they have had to meet and overcome in their lives. Answers may include school projects, sporting events, moving to a new town, or starting a new school.

Ask: *What does it take it meet a challenge?* Have students discuss with partners or in groups, then share their ideas with the class.

Music Links Introduce a song at the start of the unit. Go to www.connected.mcgraw-hill.com
Resources Media: Music to find audio recordings, song lyrics, and activities.

Read the Poem: "Meatballs on Wheels"

Read aloud "Meatballs on Wheels." Ask students questions to explore the theme.

• What does the narrator do at half past four?

• Why do the seniors need meals brought to them?

• What challenge is the narrator meeting?

Figurative Language Ask students what they think the author means when he writes that the meatballs "roll from door to door"? How are the meatballs moving from place to place?

Rhyme Scheme Review that a poem's rhyme scheme can be shown by letters that stand for the end sound of each line. Ask students to identify the rhyme scheme in "Meatballs on Wheels."

Inquiry Space

Narrative Performance Task Each week students will complete one level of a six-week narrative performance task in a digital environment. Via a game-like interface, students are assigned a task and work independently to:

- plan and conduct research
- synthesize information
- communicate ideas in writing and presentation

Resource Toolkit At each level, a toolkit of resources is available to students. These point-of-use resources include a variety of animated tutorials, videos, and slide presentations that students can view (and review) to help them at each level. Tools are designed to be viewed independently, with the option to be utilized in small group instruction if needed.

WRITE ABOUT: FROGS

The narrative performance task is broken down into the following levels:

LEVEL 1 Research Plan, T38–T39 **(Week 1)**
LEVEL 2 Evaluate Sources, T102–T103 **(Week 2)**
LEVEL 3 Take Notes on Sources, T166–T167 **(Week 3)**
LEVEL 4 Outline and Draft, T230–T231 **(Week 4)**
LEVEL 5 Collaborative Conversation, Revise, Edit, T294–T295 **(Week 5)**
LEVEL 6 Publish and Present, T330–T331 **(Week 6)**
Speaking and listening reminders and rubrics and checklists for evaluating students' work are provided at the end of Level 6.

Presentation About Frogs

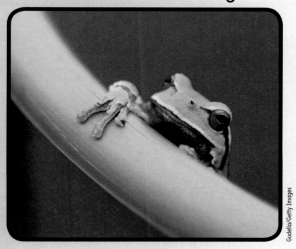

Gudella/Getty Images

WRITING

Analytical Writing **Write to Sources** As students read and reread each week for close reading of text, they take notes, cite text evidence to support their ideas and opinions, and write short analytical responses. After reading, students build writing fluency, analyze model responses, craft longer responses incorporating text evidence, and focus on writing traits. Each week, students first write to one source and then write to two sources.

WEEKLY WRITING TRAITS

Week 1 Voice, T28
Week 2 Ideas, T92
Week 3 Organization, T156
Week 4 Organization, T220
Week 5 Word Choice, T282

Writing Process: Focus on Narrative Writing

Over the course of the unit, students will develop one or two longer narrative texts. Students will work through the various stages of the writing process, allowing them time to continue revising their writing, conferencing with peers and teacher.

GENRE WRITING: NARRATIVE TEXT

Choose one or complete both 3-week writing process lessons over the course of the unit.

Fictional Narrative, T344–T349

Week 1 Expert Model, Prewrite
Week 2 Draft, Revise
Week 3 Proofread/Edit and Publish, Evaluate

Poetry, T350–T355

Week 4 Expert Model, Prewrite
Week 5 Draft, Revise
Week 6 Proofread/Edit and Publish, Evaluate

Go Digital

WRITER'S WORKSPACE
Ask students to work through their genre writing using the online tools for support.

Build Knowledge
Choices

? Essential Question:
What choices are good for us?

Teach and Model
Close Reading and Writing

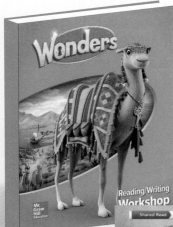

Reading/Writing Workshop

"Nail Soup," 262–265
Genre Folktale Lexile 580 ETS *TextEvaluator* 40

Practice and Apply
Close Reading and Writing

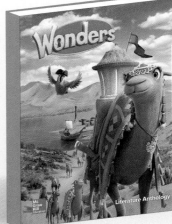

Literature Anthology

The Real Story of Stone Soup, 278–295
Genre Folktale Lexile 570 ETS *TextEvaluator* 26

"Healthful Food Choices," 298–299
Genre Expository Text Lexile 420 ETS *TextEvaluator* 10

Differentiated Texts

APPROACHING
Lexile 520
ETS *TextEvaluator* 20

ON LEVEL
Lexile 570
ETS *TextEvaluator* 29

BEYOND
Lexile 780
ETS *TextEvaluator* 39

ELL
Lexile 510
ETS *TextEvaluator* 11

Leveled Readers

Extended Complex Texts

Stone Fox
Genre Fiction
Lexile 550

Make Way for Dyamonde Daniel
Genre Fiction
Lexile 620

Classroom Library

Student Outcomes

Close Reading of Complex Text
- Cite relevant evidence from text
- Identify point of view
- Ask and answer questions

RL.3.1, RL.3.6

Writing
Write to Sources
- Draw evidence from literature
- Write opinion texts
- Conduct extended research on frogs

Writing Process
- Prewrite a Fictional Narrative

W.3.1a, W.3.8, W.3.10

Speaking and Listening
- Engage in collaborative discussions about choices
- Paraphrase portions of "Three Wishes"
- Present information on choices

SL.3.1b, SL.3.2

Content Knowledge
- Learn how organisms have diverse life cycles, but all have birth, growth, reproduction and death in common.

Language Development
Conventions
- Distinguish linking verbs

Vocabulary Acquisition
- Acquire and use academic vocabulary

aroma	expect	flavorful	graceful
healthful	interrupted	luscious	variety

- Use root words as clues to the meaning of a word

L.3.1a, L.3.1d, L.3.4c, L.3.5b, L.3.6

Foundational Skills
Phonics/Word Study
- /ü/ and /u̇/
- Roots in related words

Spelling Words

spoon	goose	booth	gloom
rude	tube	due	clues
true	chew	July	look
shook	notebook	could	

Fluency
- Expression

L.3.4c, RF.3.4a, RF.3.4b, RF.3.4c

Professional Development
- See lessons in action in real classrooms.
- Get expert advice on instructional practices.
- Collaborate with other teachers.
- Access PLC Resources.

Go Digital! www.connected.mcgraw-hill.com.

Ken Karp/McGraw-Hill Education

INSTRUCTIONAL PATH

1 Talk About Choices

Guide students in collaborative conversations.

Discuss the essential question: *What choices are good for us?*

Develop academic language.

Listen to "Three Wishes" and discuss the story.

2 Read "Nail Soup"

Model close reading with a short complex text.

Read

"Nail Soup" to learn how smart choices and sharing can benefit everyone, citing text evidence to answer text-dependent questions.

Reread

"Nail Soup" to analyze text, craft, and structure, citing text evidence.

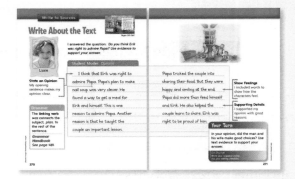

Write About "Nail Soup"

3

Model writing to a source.

Analyze a short response student model.

Use text evidence from close reading to write to a source.

4 Read and Write About *The Real Story of Stone Soup*

Practice and apply close reading of the anchor text.

Read

The Real Story of Stone Soup to learn how three brothers choose healthful foods to make a surprising soup.

Reread

The Real Story of Stone Soup and use text evidence to understand how the author uses text, craft, and structure to develop a deeper understanding of the story.

Write a short response about *The Real Story of Stone Soup*.

Integrate

Information about food choices.

Write to Two Sources, citing text evidence from *The Real Story of Stone Soup* and "Healthful Food Choices"

5 Independent Partner Work

Gradual release of support to independent work.

- Text-Dependent Questions
- Scaffolded Partner Work
  Talk with a Partner
  Cite Text Evidence
  Complete a sentence frame.
- Guided Text Annotation

6 Integrate Knowledge and Ideas

Connect Texts

Text to Text Discuss how each of the texts answers the question: What choices are good for us?

Text to Poetry Compare how the information in the texts read and the purpose of the poem, "The Vulture," by Hilaire Belloc.

Performance Task

Analyze the task and form a research plan.

DEVELOPING READERS AND WRITERS
Write to Sources

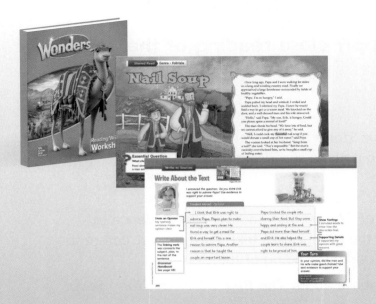

Day 1 and Day 2
Build Writing Fluency
- Quick write on "Nail Soup," p. T28

Write to a Source
- Analyze a student model, p. T28
- Write about "Nail Soup," p. T29
- Apply Writing Trait: Show Feelings, p. T28
- Apply Grammar Skill: Linking Verbs, p. T29

Day 3
Write to a Source
- Write about *The Real Story of Stone Soup*, independent practice, p. T25T
- Provide scaffolded instruction to meet student needs, p. T30

Day 4 and Day 5
Write to Two Sources
- Analyze a student model, pp. T30–T31
- Write to compare *The Real Story of Stone Soup* with "Healthful Food Choices," p. T31

Writing Process

Go Digital

Writer's Workspace

Genre Writing: Narrative Text

Fictional Narrative Expert Model

- Discuss features of narrative writing
- Discuss the expert model

Prewrite

- Discuss purpose and audience
- Plan the topic

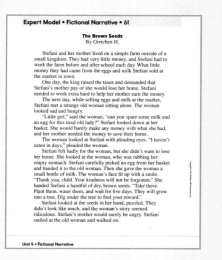

Expert Student Model

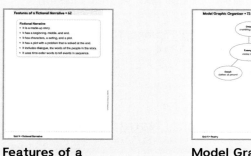

Features of a Fictional Narrative

Model Graphic Organizer

Graphic Organizer

Grammar and Spelling Resources

Online PDFs

Reading/Writing Workshop Grammar Handbook p. 481

Online Spelling and Grammar Games

Grammar Practice, pp. 76–80

Phonics/Spelling Practice, pp. 91–96

SUGGESTED LESSON PLAN

Whole Group

READING

READING		DAY 1	DAY 2
Teach, Model and Apply *Wonders Reading/Writing Workshop*	Core	**Introduce the Concept** T10–T11 **Vocabulary** T14–T15 **Close Reading** "Nail Soup," T16–T17	**Close Reading** "Nail Soup," T16–T17 **Strategy** Ask and Answer Questions, T18–T19 **Skill** Point of View, T20–T21 **Vocabulary Strategy** Root Words, T24–T25
	Options	**Listening Comprehension** T12–T13	**Genre** Folktale, T22–T23

LANGUAGE ARTS

		DAY 1	DAY 2
Writing Grammar Spelling Build Vocabulary	Core	**Grammar** Linking Verbs, T32 **Spelling** Variant Vowels /ü/, /ů/, T34 **Build Vocabulary** T36	**Write About the Text** Model Note Taking and Write to a Prompt, T28–T29 **Grammar** Linking Verbs, T32 **Build Vocabulary** T36
	Options	**Write About the Text** Writing Fluency, T28 **Genre Writing** Fictional Narrative: Read Like a Writer, T344	**Genre Writing** Fictional Narrative: Discuss the Expert Model, T344 **Spelling** Variant Vowels /ü/, /ů/, T34

Writing Process: Narrative Fictional Narrative, T344–T349   Use with Weeks 1–3

Small Group

Differentiated Instruction Use your data dashboard to determine each student's needs. Then select instructional support options throughout the week.

APPROACHING LEVEL

Leveled Reader
The Weaver of Rugs, T40–T41
"How to Weave Paper Mats," T41
Literature Circles, T41

Phonics/Decoding
Decode Words with Variant Vowels /ü/ and /ů/, T42 **TIER 2**
Build Words with Varient Vowels /ü/ and /ů/, T42 **TIER 2**
Practice Words with Variant Vowels /ü/ and /ů/, T43
Roots in Related Words, T43

Vocabulary
• Review High-Frequency Words, T44 **TIER 2**
• Answer Choice Questions, T45
Root Words, T45

Comprehension
• Identify the Narrator, T46 **TIER 2**
• Review Point of View, T47
Self-Selected Reading, T47

Fluency
Expression, T46 **TIER 2**

ON LEVEL

Leveled Reader
Why the Sea Is Salty, T48–T49
"All About Salt," T49
Literature Circles, T49

Vocabulary
Review Vocabulary Words, T50
Word Parts: Root Words, T50

Comprehension
Review Point of View, T51
Self-Selected Reading, T51

DAY 3	DAY 4	DAY 5
Close Reading *The Real Story of Stone Soup,* T25A–T25T **Literature Anthology**	**Fluency** T27 **Close Reading** "Healthful Food Choices," T25U–T25V **Integrate Ideas** Inquiry Space, T38–T39	**Integrate Ideas** T38–T39 • Text Connections • Inquiry Space **Weekly Assessment**
Phonics/Decoding T26–T27 • /ü/: oo, ew, u_e, ue, u, ui, ou; /ů/: oo, ou • Roots in Related Words	**Close Reading** *The Real Story of Stone Soup,* T25A–T25T	

Grammar Linking Verbs, T33	**Write About Two Texts** Model Note-Taking and Taking Notes, T30	**Write About Two Texts** Analyze Student Model and Write to the Prompt, T31 **Spelling** Variant Vowels /ü/, /ů/, T35
Write About the Text T30 **Genre Writing** Fictional Narrative: Prewrite, T345 **Spelling** Variant Vowels /ü/, /ů/, T35 **Build Vocabulary** T37	**Genre Writing** Fictional Narrative: Teach the Prewrite Minilesson, T345 **Grammar** Linking Verbs, T33 **Spelling** Variant Vowels /ü/, /ů/, T35 **Build Vocabulary** T37	**Genre Writing** Fictional Narrative: Choose Your Topic and Plan, T345 **Grammar** Linking Verbs, T33 **Build Vocabulary** T37

Writing Process **Writing Process: Narrative** Fictional Narrative, T344–T349   Use with Weeks 1–3 ➔

BEYOND LEVEL

Leveled Reader
Finn MacCool and the Salmon of Knowledge, T52–T53
"Brain Food," T53
Literature Circles, T53

Vocabulary
Review Domain-Specific Words, T54
• Root Words, T54
• Analyze, T54

Gifted and Talented

Comprehension
Review Point of View, T55
• Self-Selected Reading, T55
• Independent Study, T55

ENGLISH LANGUAGE LEARNERS

Shared Read
"Nail Soup," T56–T57

Leveled Reader
Why the Sea Is Salty, T58–T59
"All About Salt," T59
Literature Circles, T59

Phonics/Decoding
Decode Words with Variant Vowels /ü/ and /ů/, T42
Build Words with Variant Vowels /ü/ and /ů/, T42
Practice Variant Vowels /ü/ and /ů/, T43
Roots in Related Words, T43

Vocabulary
• Preteach Vocabulary, T60
• Review High-Frequency Words, T44
Review Vocabulary, T60
Root Words, T61
Additional Vocabulary, T61

Spelling
Spell Words with Variant Vowels, T62

Writing
Writing Trait: Show Feelings, T62

Grammar
Linking Verbs, T63

DIFFERENTIATE TO ACCELERATE

  Scaffold to **A**ccess **C**omplex **T**ext

IF ▶ the text complexity of a particular selection is too difficult for students

THEN ▶ see the references noted in the chart below for scaffolded instruction to help students Access Complex Text.

Qualitative — Quantitative
Reader and Task
TEXT COMPLEXITY

	Reading/Writing Workshop	Literature Anthology	Leveled Readers		Classroom Library
Quantitative	 "Nail Soup" **Lexile** 580 *TextEvaluator*™ 40	 *The Real Story of Stone Soup* **Lexile** 570 *TextEvaluator*™ 26 "Healthful Food Choices" **Lexile** 420 *TextEvaluator*™ 10	**Approaching Level** **Lexile** 520 *TextEvaluator*™ 20 **Beyond Level** **Lexile** 780 *TextEvaluator*™ 39	**On Level** **Lexile** 570 *TextEvaluator*™ 29 **ELL** **Lexile** 510 *TextEvaluator*™ 11	 *Stone Fox* **Lexile** 550 *Make Way for Dyamonde Daniel* **Lexile** 620
Qualitative	**What Makes the Text Complex?** • **Connection of Ideas** Make Inferences T17, T21 **ACT** *See Scaffolded Instruction in Teacher's Edition T17 and T21.*	**What Makes the Text Complex?** • **Prior Knowledge** Plot T25A–T25B • **Connection of Ideas** Prior Knowledge T25G, T25I, T25M, T25O–T25P • **Sentence Structure** T25E–T25F, T25J, T25O, T25Q • **Genre** Folktales T25K; Expository Text T25U–T25V **ACT** *See Scaffolded Instruction in Teacher's Edition T25A–T25V.*	**What Makes the Text Complex?** • **Specific Vocabulary** • **Sentence Structure** • **Connection of Ideas** • **Genre** **ACT** *See Level Up lessons online for Leveled Readers.*		**What Makes the Text Complex?** • **Genre** • **Specific Vocabulary** • **Prior Knowledge** • **Sentence Structure** • **Organization** • **Purpose** • **Connection of Ideas** **ACT** *See Scaffolded Instruction in Teacher's Edition T360–T361.*
Reader and Task	The Introduce the Concept lesson on pages T10–T11 will help determine the reader's knowledge and engagement in the weekly concept. See pages T16–T25 and T38–T39 for questions and tasks for this text.	The Introduce the Concept lesson on pages T10–T11 will help determine the reader's knowledge and engagement in the weekly concept. See pages T25A–T25V and T38–T39 for questions and tasks for this text.	The Introduce the Concept lesson on pages T10–T11 will help determine the reader's knowledge and engagement in the weekly concept. See pages T40–T41, T48–T49, T52–T53, T58–T59, and T38–T39 for questions and tasks for this text.		The Introduce the Concept lesson on pages T10–T11 will help determine the reader's knowledge and engagement in the weekly concept. See pages T360–T361 for questions and tasks for this text.

Monitor and *Differentiate*

✓ Quick Check

To differentiate instruction, use the Quick Checks to assess students' needs and select the appropriate small group instruction focus.

Comprehension Strategy Ask and Answer Questions T19

Comprehension Skill Point of View T21

Genre Folktale T23

Vocabulary Strategy Root Words T25

Phonics/Fluency Variant Vowels /ü/ and /ù/, Expression T27

If No → | **Approaching Level** | **Reteach** T40–T47 |
| **ELL** | **Develop** T56–T63 |

If Yes → | **On Level** | **Review** T48–T51 |
| **Beyond Level** | **Extend** T52–T55 |

Using Weekly Data

Check your data Dashboard to verify assessment results and guide grouping decisions.

Level Up with Leveled Readers

IF ▶ students can read their leveled text fluently and answer comprehension questions

THEN ▶ work with the next level up to accelerate students' reading with more complex text.

Beyond

T49

On Level

Approaching   T41   T59   ELL

ELL ENGLISH LANGUAGE LEARNERS

Small Group Instruction

Use the ELL small group lessons in the Wonders Teacher's Edition to provide focused instruction.

Language Development
Vocabulary preteaching and review, additional vocabulary building, and vocabulary strategy lessons, pp. T60–T61

Close Reading
Interactive Question-Response routines for scaffolded text-dependent questioning for reading and rereading the Shared Read and Leveled Reader, pp. T56–T59

Writing
Focus on the weekly writing trait, grammar skills, and spelling words, pp. T62–T63

Additional ELL Support

Use *Reading Wonders for English Learners* for ELD instruction that connects to the core.

Language Development
Ample opportunities for discussions, and scaffolded language support

Close Reading
Companion Worktexts for guided support in annotating text and citing text evidence. Differentiated Texts about the weekly concept.

Writing
Scaffolded instruction for writing to sources and revising student models

Reading Wonders for ELLs Teacher Edition and Companion Worktexts

→ Introduce the Concept

Reading/Writing Workshop

MINILESSON 10 Mins

Build Background

ESSENTIAL QUESTION

What choices are good for us?

Have students read the Essential Question on page 258 of the **Reading/ Writing Workshop**.

Discuss the photograph of the girl eating a carrot with students. Focus on the girl's choice and the healthful choices people make every day. Tell them that *healthful* means "good for your body and mind."

• We make a **variety**, or many different types, of decisions every day.

• Making smart choices takes a lot of practice.

• Smart choices help us lead healthy lives.

Talk About It

COLLABORATE

Ask: *What smart choice do we make every day? How do these decisions help us lead healthy lives?* Have students discuss in pairs or groups.

• Model using the Concept Web to generate words and phrases related to choices. Add students' contributions.

• Have partners continue the discussion by sharing what they have learned about choices. They can complete the graphic organizer, generating additional related words and phrases.

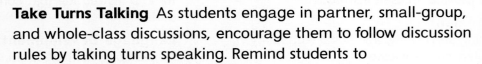

Collaborative Conversations

Take Turns Talking As students engage in partner, small-group, and whole-class discussions, encourage them to follow discussion rules by taking turns speaking. Remind students to

• wait for a person to finish before they speak. They should not speak over others.

• quietly raise their hand to let others know they would like a turn to speak.

• ask others in the groups to share their opinions so that all students have a chance to share.

Go Digital

Discuss the Concept

Watch Video

Use Graphic Organizer

Weekly Concept Choices

? Essential Question
What choices are good for us?

Go Digital!

Smart Choices

Some decisions are easy. This crispy carrot is my favorite snack, and it is delicious and healthy. Making good choices makes me feel good.

▶ We make many decisions every day.

▶ Smart choices help us live healthy lives.

Talk About It

Write words you have learned about choices. Talk with a partner about making smart decisions.

Smart Choices
↓
↓
↓

258 259

READING/WRITING WORKSHOP, *pp. 258–259*

ELL ENGLISH LANGUAGE LEARNERS SCAFFOLD

Beginning	Intermediate	Advanced/High
Use Visuals Point to the carrot. Say: *This is a carrot. A carrot is a healthful snack.* Demonstrate being healthy and strong. *It is a smart choice.* Point to your temple when you say *smart choice.* Have students repeat after you. Ask students to say a question that they have about carrots.	**Describe** Have students describe the girl's smart choice. Ask: *What choice did the girl make? How is this a healthy choice?* Encourage students to use Academic Language in their response. Elicit details to develop their responses.	**Discuss** Ask students to describe smart choices they make every day. Ask questions to help them elaborate: *What choices do you make every day? What is your choice for a healthful snack?*

GRAPHIC ORGANIZER 88

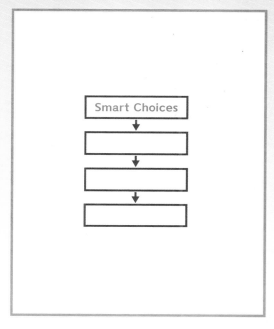

Smart Choices
↓
↓
↓

→ Listening Comprehension

MINILESSON
10 Mins

Interactive Read Aloud

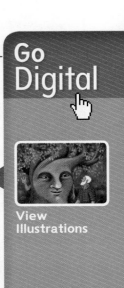
OBJECTIVES

CCSS Ask and answer questions to demonstrate understanding of a text, referring explicitly to the text as the basis for the answers. **RL.3.1**

CCSS Recount stories, including fables, folktales, and myths from diverse cultures; determine the central message, lesson, or moral and explain how it is conveyed through key details in the text. **RL.3.2**

CCSS Determine the main ideas and supporting details of a text read aloud or information presented in diverse media and formats, including visually, quantitatively, and orally. **SL.3.2**

• Listen for a purpose.
• Identify characteristics of a folktale.

ACADEMIC LANGUAGE
folktale, ask and answer questions

Connect to Concept: Choices

Tell students that it is important that we make choices that are good for us. Let students know that you will be reading aloud a passage about a woodcutter who is given the chance to make three choices. As students listen, have them think about how the passage answers the Essential Question.

Preview Genre: Folktale

Explain that the story you will read aloud is a folktale. Discuss the features of a folktale:

• often teaches a lesson

• may feature certain character types, such as people who are very wise, hardworking, clever, and so on

• may be based on the beliefs and customs of a region or country

Preview Comprehension Strategy: Ask and Answer Questions

Explain that readers can ask questions before, during, and after reading to help them focus on important story events. When reading a story, it is helpful to ask, "Do I understand what is happening in this part of the story?"

Use the Think Alouds on page T13 to model the strategy.

Respond to Reading

Think Aloud Clouds Display Think Aloud Master 1: *I wonder. . .* to reinforce how you used the Ask and Answer Questions strategy to understand content.

Genre Features With students, discuss the elements of the Read Aloud that let them know it is a folktale. Ask them to think about other texts that you have read or they have read independently that were folktales.

Summarize Have students determine the main idea and details of "Three Wishes." Then, have students briefly retell the story in their own words.

I wonder...

Model Think Alouds

Genre	Features

Fill in Genre Chart

Three Wishes

Once there was a poor woodcutter who set out one day to chop down a very old tree in the middle of the forest. As he drew back his axe to make the first cut, the tree spoke. "Sir, I ask that you spare my life. In return for this favor, I will grant you three wishes." **1**

The woodcutter thought about this. *With three wishes I might never be a poor woodcutter again!* So he agreed, put away his axe, and ran home to tell his wife of his great luck.

"Three wishes!" she cried. "What shall we wish for? Gold? Silk? A basket filled with jewels? We should think about it and wait until morning so that we can choose wisely. We wouldn't want to waste a wish!"

"That's a smart idea," said the woodcutter. "But for now, I'd like to have a lovely dinner. I wish we had a nice sausage." No sooner did the words escape his lips than a long sausage appeared on the table. **2**

"Fool!" cried his wife. "You've just wasted a wish on a sausage!" Now, the woodcutter did not like to be called names. Before he knew what was happening, he said, "Wife, I wish that sausage was on the end of your nose!" And there it was, a long sausage hanging from the end of his wife's nose.

Oh, did she scream and cry! The woodcutter felt terrible for causing his wife so much sorrow. He had no choice but to make his last wish.

"I wish . . . I wish . . . for the sausage to be back on the plate!" And, just like that, the sausage dropped from his wife's nose onto the plate. **3**

"This is terrible!" his wife cried. "You've wasted all three wishes, and for what? A sausage!"

"Well," mumbled the woodcutter, timidly taking a bite. "At least it is a very delicious sausage."

1 **Think Aloud** As I read I can **ask and answer questions** to help me better understand and remember story events. I can ask myself, "What important story event just happened?"

2 **Think Aloud** As I continue to read, I can check my understanding by **asking questions** about the choices the woodcutter and his wife are making. I know that he has just wasted a wish. I can ask, "Will he use his last two wishes wisely?"

3 **Think Aloud** After reading this paragraph, I can **answer** my previous question by stating, "No, he did not use his wishes wisely." I can also **ask**, "If I were given three wishes, what would I wish for? Would I use my wishes wisely?"

Stockbroker/SuperStock

→ Vocabulary

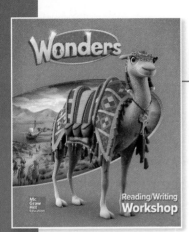

Reading/Writing Workshop

MINILESSON
10 Mins

Words in Context

Model the Routine

Introduce each vocabulary word using the **Vocabulary Routine** found on the **Visual Vocabulary Cards**.

Visual Vocabulary Cards

Vocabu
Define:
Example:
Ask:

Vocabulary Routine

<u>Define:</u> **Healthful** things are wholesome and good for your health.

<u>Example:</u> Sue chooses healthful foods at the market.

<u>Ask:</u> What is a good example of a *healthful* lunch?

Definitions

- **aroma**   An **aroma** is a pleasant or agreeable smell or fragrance.
                     Cognate: *aroma*

- **expect**   To **expect** means to think or suppose something.

- **flavorful**   When something is **flavorful**, it is tasty and full of flavor.

- **graceful**   Something that is **graceful** is beautiful or pleasing in design, movement, or style.

- **interrupted**   When something is **interrupted**, it is stopped for a time or broken off.
                     Cognate: *interrumpir*

- **luscious**   Something that is **luscious** smells or tastes delicious.

- **variety**   A **variety** is a number of different things.
                     Cognate: *variedad*

Talk About It

COLLABORATE

Have students work with a partner and look at each picture and discuss the definition of each word. Then ask students to choose three words and write questions for their partner to answer.

OBJECTIVES

CCSS Demonstrate understanding of word relationships and nuances in word meanings. Identify real-life connections between words and their use (e.g., describe people who are *friendly* or *helpful*). **L.3.5b**

CCSS Acquire and use accurately grade-appropriate conversational, general academic, and domain-specific words and phrases, including those that signal spatial and temporal relationships (e.g., *After dinner that night we went looking for them*). **L.3.6**

ACADEMIC LANGUAGE
- *healthful, variety*
- Cognate: *variedad*

Go Digital

healthful

Use Visual Glossary

Words to Know

Vocabulary

Use the picture and the sentence to talk with a partner about each word.

aroma

Carl smells the sweet **aroma** of the flowers near his house.

What is your favorite aroma?

expect

I see clouds, so I **expect** it will rain today.

What do you expect to do while it is raining?

flavorful

Jo and Tori eat lunches that are delicious and **flavorful.**

What are some of your favorite flavorful foods?

graceful

Katie is a **graceful** dancer.

What word means the opposite of graceful?

healthful

Sue chooses **healthful** foods at the market.

What is a good example of a healthful lunch?

interrupted

A small dog **interrupted** the soccer game.

How might you feel if someone interrupted you?

luscious

These strawberries are sweet and **luscious.**

What is another word for luscious?

variety

The bookstore has a large **variety** of books by my favorite author.

Where else could you find a variety of books?

Your Turn

COLLABORATE

Pick three words. Then write three questions for your partner to answer.

Go Digital! Use the online visual glossary

260

261

READING/WRITING WORKSHOP, pp. 260–261

ELL ENGLISH LANGUAGE LEARNERS SCAFFOLD

Beginning

Use Visuals Say: *Let's look at the picture for* healthful. Point to the vegetables. Elicit that another word for *healthful* is *good*. Ask: *Are vegetables good for you? Are they healthful?* (yes) Have students use the frame: *Vegetables are _____* (healthful). Correct students' pronunciation as needed.

Intermediate

Describe Have students describe the picture. Write the word, and cover the suffix with your hand. Say: *I know what* health *means.* Put your hand over *health* to show the suffix *-ful.* Say: *This means "full of something." What is* healthful *full of?* (health) *What does healthful mean?* (full of health; good for you) Have students write a sentence that uses the word *healthful.*

Advanced/High

Discuss Ask students to talk about the picture for *healthful* with a partner and write a definition. Then share the definition with the class. Correct the meaning in students' responses as needed.

Finally, challenge students to use each vocabulary word in a sentence. Provide support as needed.

ON-LEVEL PRACTICE BOOK p. 151

| flavorful | luscious | expect | aroma |
| variety | healthful | graceful | interrupted |

Finish each sentence using the vocabulary word provided.
Possible responses provided.

1. **(expect)** Each autumn we expect the leaves to fall from the trees .

2. **(flavorful)** I think the new recipe will make our meatballs more flavorful .

3. **(aroma)** My mother's perfume gives off a sweet aroma of flowers .

4. **(luscious)** It's the time of year when our garden produces ripe and luscious tomatoes .

5. **(graceful)** After many years of swimming lessons, she has become graceful in the water .

6. **(interrupted)** I started to tell her the roof was leaking, but I was interrupted by the phone ringing .

7. **(variety)** My brother eats the same cereal every morning, but I like to eat a variety of different things .

8. **(healthful)** As a snack, fruit is more healthful than candy .

| APPROACHING | BEYOND | ELL |
| p. 151 | p. 151 | p. 151 |

Shared Read | Genre • Folktale

Nail Soup

Essential Question

What choices are good for us?

Read about how choices helped a man and his wife learn a lesson.

262

Once long ago, Papa and I were walking for miles on a long and winding country road. Finally we approached a large farmhouse surrounded by fields of healthy vegetables.

"Papa, I'm so hungry," I said.

Papa patted my head and winked. I smiled and nodded back. I admired my Papa. I knew he would find a way to get us a warm meal. We knocked on the door, and a well-dressed man and his wife answered.

"Hello," said Papa. "My son, Erik, is hungry. Could you please spare a morsel of food?"

The man shook his head. "We have lots of food, but we cannot afford to give any of it away," he said.

"Well, I could cook my **flavorful** nail soup if you would donate a small cup of hot water," said Papa.

The woman looked at her husband. "Soup from a nail?" she said. "That's impossible." But the man's curiosity overwhelmed him, so he brought a small cup of boiling water.

263

READING/WRITING WORKSHOP, *pp. 262–263*

Reading/Writing Workshop

Shared Read

CLOSE READING

Lexile 580   *TextEvaluator™* 40

Close Reading Routine

Read   DOK 1–2

- Identify key ideas and details about making choices.
- Take notes and summarize.
- Use Ⓐ Ⓒ Ⓣ prompts as needed.

Reread   DOK 2–3

- Analyze the text, craft, and structure.
- Use the Reread minilessons.

Integrate   DOK 4

- Integrate knowledge and ideas.
- Make text-to-text connections.
- Use the Integrate lesson.

Read

Connect to Concept: Choices Tell students they will read about how smart choices and sharing can benefit everyone.

Note Taking Read page 263 together. As you read, model how to take notes. *I will think about the Essential Question as I read and note key ideas and details.* Encourage students to note words they don't understand and questions they have.

Paragraph 3: Read the paragraph together. Ask: *What does Erik's father do that provides a clue about how he is going to get them a warm meal?* Model how to cite text evidence. Erik's father winks at him, which signals that he may have a secret or plan.

Papa carefully took out a long, crooked nail and with one **graceful** motion, dropped it into the cup. He stirred the cup of hot liquid.

"This is beginning to smell wonderful," said Papa.

I smiled at Papa. He was clever and charming, and my admiration for him grew. He could do anything! Then I remembered something he taught me.

"Papa, it is impolite for me to eat nail soup without offering some to everyone," I said. "But there is such a small amount here."

"We can't let the boy eat alone," said the man to his wife. "We can spare more water."

The woman filled a big pot with water and put it on the stove. When the water boiled, Papa placed the nail into the pot, stirred, and sniffed the air. "The **aroma** is good, but it would be much more aromatic with an onion. Have you any old onions?"

The woman gave Papa three small onions, and he dropped them into the pot.

"Papa, remember how **luscious** nail soup was with carrots?" I asked.

The man jumped up and pulled four plump carrots from a large basket of vegetables on the floor. "How about some beets and cabbages, too?" he said. "I can spare a few of those."

"And here are some potatoes and green beans," the woman **interrupted**. "They are **healthful** and nutritious contributions. We grow them ourselves!"

Papa dropped the vegetables into the boiling water while the man grabbed a **variety** of spices and meats. "Here, add these, too," he said enthusiastically.

Soon the soup was ready, and we sat down to eat. I knew the man and his wife would enjoy nail soup.

"This soup is amazing," said the woman. "And all from just one nail and a pot of boiling water."

Papa pretended to be surprised by her amazement, but as usual, he had the perfect answer. "What did you **expect**?" he said. "I told you it would be flavorful."

The man and woman smiled. "We just didn't know that sharing a little of our great wealth would taste so good!"

Make Connections

Why is making nail soup a smart choice? ESSENTIAL QUESTION

How do you feel when you make good choices? TEXT TO SELF

264   265

READING/WRITING WORKSHOP, pp. 264–265

Paragraphs 4–7: Remind students that retelling events in a story helps to ensure that they understand what they are reading.

Papa greets the man, says that Erik is hungry, and asks if the man can spare any food. The man says "No." Then Papa asks for hot water so he and Erik can make nail soup. The man is curious, and Papa's trick has begun.

Make Connections

Essential Question Have partners discuss why making nail soup was a good choice. Use these sentence frames to focus discussion:

> *Papa made nail soup to . . .*
> *The man and his wife learned . . .*

A C T **Access Complex Text**

▶ **Connection of Ideas**

On page 264, Erik says his Papa is clever, then remembers something Papa taught him.

- *What does Erik do?* (He says it is impolite to eat all the soup without sharing but is worried there is only a small amount.)

- *What happens because of this?* (The man offers more water to make extra soup.)

- *Why is this clever just like Papa?* (It is clever because the man does not want to share, but Erik gets him interested in sharing by implying nail soup is delicious.)

Reread

→ # Comprehension Strategy

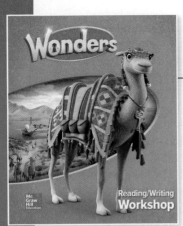

Reading/Writing Workshop

___

OBJECTIVES

 CCSS Ask and answer questions to demonstrate understanding of a text, referring explicitly to the text as the basis for the answers. **RL.3.1**

___

ACADEMIC LANGUAGE

• *ask and answer questions, folktale*

• Cognate: *folklórica*

View "Nail Soup"

MINILESSON 10 Mins — Ask and Answer Questions

1 Explain

Explain that when students read a folktale, they may come across a section they do not understand. Remind students that they can ask questions about the events they read about and then look for answers in the text.

• Students can look for details to support the answers to their questions.

• If students do not find an answer to a question, they can reread the text.

Point out that asking and answering questions about a story will help students understand it better.

2 Model Close Reading: Text Evidence

Model how asking and answering questions can help students understand why Erik admires Papa. Reread page 263 of "Nail Soup."

3 Guided Practice of Close Reading

 Have students work in pairs to think of a question to ask while they reread "Nail Soup." Suggest to students that they might ask: "Why does Papa keep smelling the soup while it cooks?" Have partners think about how clever Papa is while they answer their question.

Comprehension Strategy

Ask and Answer Questions

Ask yourself questions about "Nail Soup" as you read. Then look for the details to answer your questions.

 Find Text Evidence

Look at page 263. Reread and think of a question. Then read again to answer it.

page 263

Once long ago, Papa and I were walking for miles on a long and winding country road. Finally we approached a large farmhouse surrounded by fields of healthy vegetables.

"Papa, I'm so hungry," I said.

Papa patted my head and winked. I smiled and nodded back. I admired my Papa. I knew he would find a way to get us a warm meal. We knocked on the door, and a well-dressed man and his wife answered.

"Hello," said Papa. "My son, Erik, is hungry. Could you please spare a morsel of food?"

The man shook his head. "We have lots of food, but we cannot afford to give any of it away," he said.

"Well, I could cook my **flavorful** nail soup if you would donate a small cup of hot water," said Papa.

The woman looked at her husband. "Soup from a nail?" she said. "That's impossible." But the man's curiosity overwhelmed him, so he brought a small cup of boiling water.

I have a question. Why did Erik admire Papa? I read that Papa patted Erik's head and winked. He says he knows Papa will find a way to get a warm meal. Now I can answer my question. Erik admires Papa because he knows Papa will take care of him.

Your Turn
COLLABORATE

Reread "Nail Soup." Think of a question. You might ask: Why does Papa keep smelling the soup while it cooks? Reread the story to find the answer.

266

READING/WRITING WORKSHOP, *p. 266*

ELL ENGLISH LANGUAGE LEARNERS SCAFFOLD

Beginning

Understand Help students reread page 263 of "Nail Soup." Point out difficult words and phrases such as *admired, winked, nodded,* and *hungry.* Define them, and then guide students in connecting these words and phrases to text elements and ideas in the story. For example, ask: *Why does Eric admire Papa?* (because he knows Papa will get them a meal)

Intermediate

Describe Have students reread page 263. Ask: *Why does Eric admire Papa?* (because he knows Papa will get them a meal) *How does he know?* (Papa pats him on the head and winks.) Point out why this text is confusing. Erik knows what the pat and wink mean because he can infer it, or guess it, based on what he knows about Papa.

Advanced/High

Demonstrate Comprehension Have students reread page 263. Elicit from students why this text is confusing. Ask: *What does Papa do to make Erik think about how he admires him? Why does Erik think this? Turn to a partner and explain.*

Monitor and *Differentiate*

✓ Quick Check

Do students ask a question about "Nail Soup"? Do they reread the story to find the answer?

Small Group Instruction

If No → | Approaching Level | Reteach p. T40
| ELL | Develop p. T56
If Yes→ | On Level | Review p. T48
| Beyond Level | Extend p. T52

ON-LEVEL PRACTICE BOOK pp. 153–154

Read the passage. Use the ask and answer questions strategy to find details and answer questions.

The Turtle and the Box of Riches

Long ago there was a young fisherman's helper sitting on a
11 dock. As he waited for his boat to head out for the day, he heard
26 a group of children laughing under the dock. He peeked down
37 and saw them teasing and pushing a small turtle.
46 "Leave that turtle alone!" the boy shouted and jumped down.
56 The children quickly ran away. The boy picked up the turtle.
67 "Thank you," the turtle said.
72 The boy jumped. "You can talk?"
78 "Yes," the turtle said. "I am a very powerful turtle in my
90 land. Your act was an inspiration. I want to reward you for your
103 kindness. Go to sleep tonight, and when you wake up, you will be
116 in a wonderful place."
120 The turtle swam out to sea. The boy went to bed that night in
134 disbelief. Yet, the next morning he woke up in a beautiful palace.
146 "Welcome to our home under the sea," the turtle greeted him.
157 The turtle took the boy through the underwater palace. Large
167 windows showed many types of fish and plant life. Gold walls
178 and mirrored ceilings shined brightly. The boy met all of the
189 friendly turtles that lived in the palace. Later that day, they had a
202 big feast, and the boy ate more than he had ever eaten before.

| APPROACHING pp. 153–154 | BEYOND pp. 153–154 | ELL pp. 153–154 |

→ Comprehension Skill

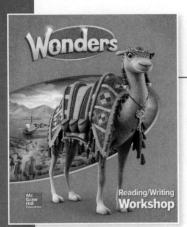

Reading/Writing Workshop

OBJECTIVES

CCSS Distinguish their own point of view from that of the narrator or those of the characters. **RL.3.6**

Identify the narrator's point of view in a folktale.

ACADEMIC LANGUAGE

• narrator, character, point of view, details

• Cognates: *narrador, carácter, detalles*

SKILLS TRACE

POINT OF VIEW

Introduce Unit 2 Week 5

Review Unit 4 Weeks 1, 2, 6; Unit 5 Weeks 1, 2; Unit 6 Week 5

Assess Units 2, 4, 5, 6

MINILESSON 10 Mins Point of View

1 Explain

Explain to students that what a narrator thinks about the events or other characters in a story is the narrator's point of view.

• To identify the narrator's point of view, students should look for details that show how the narrator thinks.

• Students should use the actions and reactions of the narrator or characters to infer their point of view when it is not directly stated.

2 Model Close Reading: Text Evidence

Model identifying details that help clarify the narrator's point of view. Then model listing the details in the graphic organizer.

 Write About Reading: Point of View Model for students how to use the notes in their graphic organizer to write a summary of the details that describe the narrator's point of view in "Nail Soup."

3 Guided Practice of Close Reading

 Have students work in pairs to complete a graphic organizer for the narrator's point of view in "Nail Soup," going back into the text to find more clues that show what Erik thinks about Papa. Remind them to use these clues to determine the narrator's point of view. Discuss each detail as students complete the graphic organizer.

 Write About Reading: Point of View Ask pairs to work together to write a summary of their point of view about Papa in "Nail Soup." Students' summaries should distinguish their own point of view from that of Erik, the story's narrator.

Go Digital

Present the Lesson

Comprehension Skill

Point of View

Point of view is what a narrator thinks about events or other characters in a story. Look for details that show what the narrator thinks to figure out point of view.

 Find Text Evidence

I read on page 263 that Erik, the story's narrator, nodded and smiled at Papa. Then he said he admired his Papa. This tells me he has a lot of respect and love for his father. He trusts he will take care of him.

Details
Erik smiles and nods. He knows Papa will get them a warm meal.

↓

Point of View

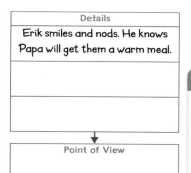 **Your Turn**

Reread "Nail Soup." Look for more clues that show Erik's point of view about Papa. List them in the graphic organizer. Then tell Erik's opinion of his father. Do you agree with Erik's point of view about Papa?

Go Digital!
Use the interactive graphic organizer

267

READING/WRITING WORKSHOP, *p. 267*

A C T Access Complex Text

▶ **Connection of Ideas**

Students may need assistance inferring Erik's point of view about Papa. Ask:

- *What does Erik think about Papa on page 263?* (Erik admires Papa and knows he will find a way to get them a warm meal.)

- *What does Erik think about Papa on page 264?* (Erik thinks he is clever and charming, and that he can do anything.)

- *What do Erik's thoughts tell you about how he feels about Papa?* (Erik's thoughts tell me he trusts Papa to take care of him.)

 **Monitor and** *Differentiate*

 Quick Check

Can students identify details that clarify the narrator's point of view? Can students distinguish their own point of view from the narrator's?

↓

Small Group Instruction

If No →	Approaching Level	Reteach p. T47
	ELL	Develop p. T57
If Yes →	On Level	Review p. T51
	Beyond Level	Extend p. T55

ON-LEVEL PRACTICE BOOK pp. 153–155

A. Reread the passage and answer the questions.
Possible responses provided.

1. What do the first seven lines of the passage tell you about how the narrator thinks about the fisherman's helper?

The narrator thinks that the fisherman's helper is a good person, who gets involved and helps when he sees someone in trouble.

2. Do you think the narrator approves of what the fisherman's helper does? Use text evidence to support your answer.

Yes; in paragraph 6, the turtle talks about the fisherman's helper's act as an inspiration and as kindness that should be rewarded.

3. What is the narrator's point of view about the fisherman's helper at the end of the passage? Does the narrator still think the same as at the beginning of the passage?

The narrator still believes the boy is a good person, but understands that the boy made a mistake by not taking the turtle's advice and opening the second drawer.

B. Work with a partner. Read the passage aloud. Pay attention to expression. Stop after one minute. Fill out the chart.

	Words Read	–	Number of Errors	=	Words Correct Score
First Read		–		=	
Second Read		–		=	

APPROACHING pp. 153–155	BEYOND pp. 153–155	ELL pp. 153–155

→ # Genre: Literature

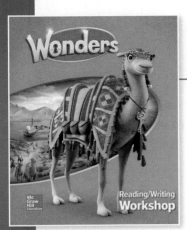

Reading/Writing Workshop

OBJECTIVES

 Recount stories, including fables, folktales, and myths from diverse cultures; determine the central message, lesson, or moral and explain how it is conveyed through key details in the text. **RL.3.2**

 By the end of the year, read and comprehend literature, including stories, dramas, and poetry, at the high end of the grades 2–3 text complexity band independently and proficiently. **RL.3.10**

ACADEMIC LANGUAGE

• *folktale, lesson, moral, problem*

• Cognates: *folklórica, lección, moraleja, problema*

 MINILESSON 10 Mins

Folktale

 **Go Digital**

1 Explain

Share with students the following key characteristics of a **folktale**.

- A folktale is a story that has been passed down orally from person to person. Folktales have been told over the course of many generations.

- A folktale usually has a message, lesson, or moral.

- In some folktales, the main character must find a clever way to solve a problem.

Present the Lesson

2 Model Close Reading: Text Evidence

Model for students how to identify the elements of a folktale on page 263 of "Nail Soup." Point out that there is a problem Erik and his Papa have to solve and that the story teaches the man and his wife a lesson.

3 Guided Practice of Close Reading

 Have students work in pairs to reread page 265 of "Nail Soup." Ask: *What lesson does the man and his wife learn?* Have partners discuss the lesson they learn, citing evidence from the text.

Genre | Literature

Folktale

"Nail Soup" is a folktale. A **folktale**:
- Is a short story passed from person to person
- Always has a problem the characters have to solve
- Usually has a message or lesson

🔍 Find Text Evidence

I can tell that "Nail Soup" is a folktale. There is a problem Erik and his Papa have to solve. The story also has a lesson. It teaches the man and his wife the importance of sharing.

In this folktale, Erik has a problem. He is hungry. Papa finds a way to solve his problem.

A folktale often has a message that is stated at the end of the story.

Your Turn

Reread page 265. What lesson does the man and his wife learn? Tell a partner.

268

READING/WRITING WORKSHOP, *p. 268*

ELL ENGLISH LANGUAGE LEARNERS SCAFFOLD

Beginning	Intermediate	Advanced/High
Clarify Reread page 263. Tell students that "Nail Soup" is a folktale. It has a problem, because the man and woman will not share, and the father wants to teach them a lesson. Have students use the frames: *"Nail Soup" is a ____ (folktale). It has a ____ (problem/problema). It has a ____ (lesson/lección).*	**Describe** Have students reread page 263. Say: *This is a folktale. What is the problem? What might be the lesson? Explain to a partner.* Then have partners describe the problem and lesson. *The problem is ____. The lesson is ____.*	**Discuss** Have partners reread page 263. Ask: *How do we know that this is a folktale? Turn to a partner and explain what details in the story show that it is a folktale.*

Monitor and *Differentiate*

✓ Quick Check

Are students able to identify the lesson by the end of the story?

Small Group Instruction

If No →	Approaching Level	Reteach p. T40
	ELL	Develop p. T56
If Yes →	On Level	Review p. T48
	Beyond Level	Extend p. T52

ON-LEVEL PRACTICE BOOK p. 156

Kyoto Frog and Osaka Frog

Two frogs lived in Japan. One frog was from Kyoto. The other was from Osaka. Each frog set out to see the other's town. They met halfway between Osaka and Kyoto. Both were very tired. Neither knew if he could go on. Then Osaka Frog had an idea.

"We should help each other stand on our hind legs. That way we can look out at the towns we want to visit. Then we'll know if we really want to keep walking," Osaka Frog said. Each frog faced the town he wished to see. Then each pushed the other up on his hind legs. But when they did this, their underbellies faced the town they wanted to go to and their eyes faced back home.

"Kyoto looks just like Osaka!" said Osaka Frog.

"And Osaka looks just like Kyoto!" said Kyoto Frog.

Each decided to go home rather than travel to a town that looked exactly like home. So each went home, not knowing that Kyoto and Osaka were as different as two cities could be.

Answer the questions about the text.

1. How do you know this is a folktale?

   It has a problem that the characters have to solve; it has a lesson.

2. What problem do the frogs have to solve?

   The frogs get tired before they get to where they want to go; they want to find out if they should keep going.

3. What do you think is the message or lesson of this folktale?

   Possible response: Think carefully before making important decisions.

APPROACHING p. 156	BEYOND p. 156	ELL p. 156

→ Vocabulary Strategy

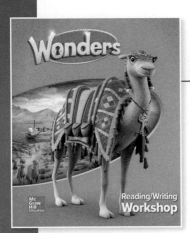

**Reading/Writing
Workshop**

OBJECTIVES

CCSS Determine or clarify the meaning of unknown and multiple-meaning words and phrases based on grade 3 reading and content, choosing flexibly from a range of strategies. Use a known root word as a clue to the meaning of an unknown word with the same root (e.g, *company, companion*). **L.3.4c**

**ACADEMIC
LANGUAGE**
root words

Root Words

1 Explain

Explain to students that a root word is the simplest form of a word.

- A root word is a word to which no prefixes, suffixes, or inflectional endings have been added.

- If students know the meaning of a root word, that can help them figure out the meaning of other words that use the root.

2 Model Close Reading: Text Evidence

Model identifying the meaning of the word *admiration* on page 264 of "Nail Soup" using the root word *admire*.

3 Guided Practice of Close Reading

Have students work in pairs to figure out the meanings of *aromatic* and *amazement* in "Nail Soup" by using the knowledge of root words. Ask partners to first identify and define the root of each word. Then have partners write definitions for the unknown words based on what they know about the root words.

Use Reference Sources

Dictionaries Have students check a dictionary, either print or digital, to compare the definitions of the root words of *aromatic* and *amazement* with their own knowledge. Have students note any differences between what they thought each root word meant and the precise dictionary definition.

Once students have determined the precise meaning of the root words and have used that knowledge to write definitions of the unknown words, have them clarify their definitions by using the dictionary to look up *aromatic* and *amazement*.

Go Digital

Present the Lesson

Vocabulary Strategy

Root Words

A root word is the simplest form of a word. When you read an unfamiliar word, look for a root word in it. Use the root word to figure out the unfamiliar word's meaning.

 Find Text Evidence

On page 264 of "Nail Soup," I see the word admiration. I think the root word in admiration is admire. I know admire means "to respect or appreciate." Erik had a lot of admiration for his Papa. That means he "has respect" for him.

He was clever and charming, and my admiration for him grew.

Your Turn

Find the root word in each word. Use it to figure out the word's meaning.

aromatic, page 264

amazement, page 265

Illustrator: B Gerardo Suzan

269

READING/WRITING WORKSHOP, p. 269

Monitor and *Differentiate*

✓ Quick Check

Do students use root words to figure out the meaning of the words *aromatic* and *amazement*?

⬇

Small Group Instruction

If No →	Approaching Level	Reteach p. T45
	ELL	Develop p. T61
If Yes →	On Level	Review p. T50
	Beyond Level	Extend p. T54

ENGLISH LANGUAGE LEARNERS SCAFFOLD

ELL

Beginning	Intermediate	Advanced/High
Understand Point out the word *aromatic*. Cross out the suffix. Define the root word, and explain that adding *-tic* changes it to mean "with aroma." Repeat with the word *amazement*. Use the words in sentences, and help them replace them with words they know.	**Define** Write the words *aromatic* and *amazement* on the board. Cross out the suffixes. Define the root words for students. Say: *Reread the sentence with the word* aromatic. *What does it mean?* Repeat with *amazement*. Then, have them work in pairs to write a sentence for each word.	**Write** Have students work in pairs to define the root words *aroma* and *amaze*. Have them find context clues to explain the meanings of *aromatic* and *amazement* and then use them in sentences.

ON-LEVEL PRACTICE BOOK p. 157

Read each sentence below. Write the root word of the word in bold on the line. Then write the definition of the word in bold.
Possible responses provided.

1. I am a very **powerful** turtle in my land.

   power; important or influential

2. Your act was an **inspiration**.

   inspire; someone or something that stirs a feeling

3. I want to reward you for your **kindness**.

   kind; friendliness or thoughtfulness

4. I have a lot of **admiration** for your home, but I must return to my home before morning.

   admire; a feeling of respect

5. The boy was filled with **appreciation** but could not help but wonder about the second drawer.

   appreciate; a feeling of being thankful

APPROACHING p. 157	BEYOND p. 157	ELL p. 157

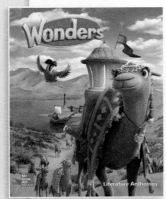

The Real Story of Stone Soup

Literature Anthology

Text Complexity Range

Lexile

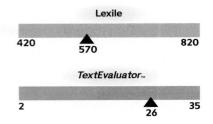

420   570   820

TextEvaluator™

2   26   35

What makes this text complex?

▶ **Prior Knowledge**

▶ **Connection of Ideas**

▶ **Sentence Structure**

▶ **Genre**

This selection is suggested for use as an Extended Complex Text. See pages T356–T361.

Close Reading Routine

Read   DOK 1–2

• Identify key ideas and details about making choices.

• Take notes and summarize.

• Use **A C T** prompts as needed.

Reread   DOK 2–3

• Analyze the text, craft, and structure.

• Use *Close Reading Companion* pp. 100–102.

Integrate   DOK 4

• Integrate knowledge and ideas

• Make text-to-text connections.

• Use the **Integrate** lesson.

Genre • Folktale

The REAL STORY OF STONE SOUP

by Ying Chang Compestine
illustrated by Stéphane Jorisch

? Essential Question

What choices are good for us?

Read how three brothers choose healthful foods to make a surprising soup.

Go Digital!

278

A C T Access Complex Text

▶ Prior Knowledge

If students are unfamiliar with the plot of the traditional versions of "Stone Soup," briefly expand on the summary given on the first page of this selection. Explain that a hungry soldier goes door to door, asking villagers for something to eat. Each refuses to give him something. The soldier has a pot of water and a stone. He goes to the center of the

*B*y now, you have probably heard the old folktale about stone soup. A hungry soldier tricks some stingy villagers into making him a big pot of soup. The truth is that stone soup was invented here in China, and without any sly tricks.

Here is the real story.

279

LITERATURE ANTHOLOGY, *pp. 278–279*

Tell students that they will be reading a folktale that may be similar to other stories they have heard or read. Ask students to predict how the selection will help them answer the Essential Question.

Note Taking:
Use the Graphic Organizer
Analytical Writing

Remind students to take notes as they read. Have them fill in the graphic organizer on the **Your Turn Practice Book** page 152. Ask them to record the narrator's point of view throughout the story.

1 Vocabulary: Root Words

Find the word *villagers* on page 279. How can you use the root word *village* to determine its meaning? (I know that a *village* is a small town where people live. *Village* is the root word of *villagers*. I think *villagers* are the people who live in the village.)

Build Vocabulary page 279
   stingy: not willing to give to others in need

---

village, puts the stone in the pot of water, and stirs. One by one, the villagers bring an addition, such as meat, vegetables, or salt for the soup. Soon, the soldier has a delicious soup and the whole village eats it. They learn that they can make something wonderful when they combine their resources.

Read

2 Skill: Point of View

What does the narrator think about himself? How do you know? Do you agree or disagree? Explain. (The narrator thinks he is the hardest working. He says he has the hardest job. I disagree. The boys appear to be working very hard while the narrator is relaxing in the boat.) **Add the clues and point of view to your graphic organizer.**

Clue
Even with three of them, I did most of the work.

↓

Clue
I kept the hardest job for myself.

↓

Clue
I steered the boat.

↓

Point of View
The narrator thinks he is the hardest worker.

Build Vocabulary page 280
troublesome: causing problems

It all began when I hired those troublesome Chang brothers to help me on my fishing boat. Nice boys, but lazy and, I'm sorry to say, somewhat stupid. The only good thing is I could get away with not paying them very much.

280

A C T Access Complex Text

▶ Connection of Ideas

Remind students to connect the ideas in the illustrations with the ideas in the text to help them better understand what they read.

- *What does the narrator say about the Chang brothers?* (He says they are stupid and lazy.)

- *What does the illustration show?* (It shows the Chang brothers working hard to bring in a net full of fish.)

- *How does the illustration connect with the text and help you make your own judgment about the brothers?* (The narrator says the brothers are lazy and stupid, but the illustration shows them working hard. It also shows the narrator relaxing in the boat. So, I think the brothers are hard workers and the narrator is lazy.)

Even with three of them, I did most of the work, and I kept the hardest job for myself. I steered the boat. **2**

STOP AND CHECK

Ask and Answer Questions What kind of person is the narrator? Use the illustrations and what you have read to find the answer.

281

LITERATURE ANTHOLOGY, pp. 280–281

STOP AND CHECK

Ask and Answer Questions What kind of person is the narrator? (The narrator thinks he is hardworking, but he is actually lazy.)

Reread *Close Reading Companion*

Author's Craft: Character Development

Authors do not always tell you directly what a character is like. What do the narrator's words and actions tell you about his character? (The narrator says that he can "get away with" not paying the Chang brothers very much. This suggests that the narrator is not very honest or fair. He knows he should pay the brothers more but will not. The narrator also says that he is working hard. But the illustration shows that he is being lazy while the Chang brothers do all the work.)

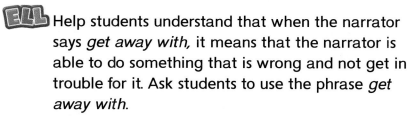 Help students understand that when the narrator says *get away with,* it means that the narrator is able to do something that is wrong and not get in trouble for it. Ask students to use the phrase *get away with.*

Have students look at the illustration. Ask questions to help them talk about it. Ask:

- *Who is working?* Students can point or answer.
- Point to the narrator. *The narrator is the person telling the story. Is the narrator lazy?* Help students elaborate on their responses.

Read

3 Skill: Point of View

When it is time to make lunch, what does the narrator think? How do you know? (He thinks he is going to have to do all the work. He says his work really began and the boys are too dull to know what to do.) Do you agree with the narrator? Why or why not? (I disagree. He is just giving orders. The boys have to do all the hard work.) Add the clues and point of view to your graphic organizer.

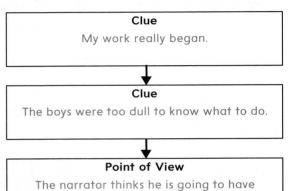

Clue
My work really began.

↓

Clue
The boys were too dull to know what to do.

↓

Point of View
The narrator thinks he is going to have to do all the work.

Build Vocabulary page 282

dock: bring the boat to shore and tie it up so it doesn't drift down the river

One summer day, after a full morning of fishing, I decided to stop early for lunch.

"Time to eat, boys!" I yelled. "Dock the boat."

After the Chang brothers got the boat tied up, my work really began. Those boys were too dull to know what to do. "Ting! Gather firewood. Pong! Prepare the cooking pot and clean the fish. Kuai! Get some fresh water."

"The cooking pot isn't here," **interrupted** Ting, the oldest, a troublemaker. He always talked back to his elders.

"What do you mean the pot isn't here? Where is it?"

They looked at one another and shrugged.

"You boys forgot the cooking pot? How could you?" I asked.

"It's your pot," said Ting. "You should have remembered to bring it."

282

ACT Access Complex Text

▶ Sentence Structure

Tell students that authors may use time-order words and phrases to show the order of events. Time-order words usually appear at the beginning of a sentence.

- *When do the boys start digging a hole?* (Right after the narrator asks, "With a hole in the ground?") *What phrase helps you know this?* ("No sooner had those words left my mouth")

- *Do Ting and Pong start the fire before Kuai starts digging, after Kuai starts digging, or at the same time? How do you know?* (At the same time; the word *meanwhile* means "at the same time.")

Point to the dash in the first paragraph on page 283. Explain that a dash is often used to show an interrupted thought or unfinished sentence.

Those stupid potato heads! What were we to do now? Pong, the middle one and the most well-mannered of the three, tried to apologize. "Sorry, Uncle. We left in a hurry this morning, and we—"

Kuai, the youngest, interrupted. "We don't really need a pot to cook lunch." He whispered something to his brothers. Kuai is always full of silly ideas.

"How are we supposed to cook lunch?" I asked. "With a hole in the ground?"

Those crazy boys must have thought I meant it. No sooner had those words left my mouth than they started digging a hole in the sandy beach.

"What are you doing?" I asked.

"Cooking lunch, of course," said Kuai. He began to line the hole with banana leaves. Meanwhile, Ting and Pong started a huge fire next to the hole.

283

LITERATURE ANTHOLOGY, *pp. 282–283*

Read

4 Strategy: Ask and Answer Questions

Teacher Think Aloud As I read, I **ask questions** and try to answer them to check my understanding. One question I asked myself is what the boys plan to do with the hole in the sand. To find the answer, I can reread the last paragraph on page 283 and paraphrase Kuai's answer. The boys are making a hole in the ground so that they can make lunch.

Reread *Close Reading Companion*

Author's Craft: Word Choice

What words does the narrator use to show his opinion of the boys? (The narrator uses the words *dull, stupid,* and *crazy* to describe the boys.) How does the author show that the narrator is wrong about how smart the boys are? (The narrator believes the boys are digging a hole only because he suggested it, but the boys also fill the hole with leaves and start a fire, which shows they have a detailed plan.)

- *Who is speaking the words before the dash?* (Pong)
- *What does the sentence immediately after the dash tell you?* (It says that Kuai interrupts.)

ELL Before reading, clarify the meaning of the following: *talked back; elders; no sooner had those words left my mouth.* Then help students talk about the events.

- *What is missing?* (the cooking pot)
- *Do they dig a hole?* (yes) *What else do the boys do? Do they start a fire?* Have students point to the illustration or text that gives them the clue.

Read

5 Skill: Point of View

What does the narrator think about the boys' plan? How do you know? (The narrator doesn't think it will work. He says, "Come now. Even you can't be foolish enough to believe—" He also says "The hunger must have gone to their heads.")

Do you agree with the narrator? Explain. (I agree. I do not think you can make soup from stones.) Add the clues and point of view to your graphic organizer.

Clue
He says, "Come now."

↓

Clue
"Even you can't be foolish enough to believe—."

↓

Clue
He says, "The hunger must have gone to their heads."

↓

Point of View
The narrator does not think the boys' plan will work.

Build Vocabulary page 284
blabbering: talking nonsense

"Now we need some stones," said Kuai.

"For what?" I asked

Kuai didn't answer. He picked up a nearby rock and held it to his ear. "This is a fish stone," he announced. Then he threw the rock in the fire.

5 "Come now," I said. "Even you can't be foolish enough to believe—"

"Shh!" Ting interrupted, holding a stone to his ear. "I need to hear what it is telling me. Aha! This is a fine vegetable stone." He tossed his rock into the fire, too.

I tried listening to a couple of stones. I didn't hear a thing. The hunger must have gone to their heads. "If you're so clever, what kind is this?" I handed a stone to Pong. He listened for a moment.

6 "Aha! Uncle, you are brilliant. You picked out a yummy egg stone." He pitched my stone into the fire.

I had no idea what he was blabbering about. But by this time I was hungry enough to eat anything, even stones.

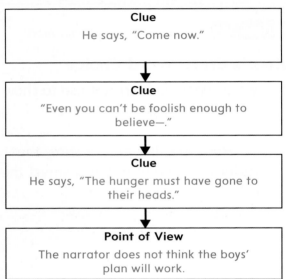

284

A C T Access Complex Text

▶ Connection of Ideas

Review with students that to understand characters' actions, they have to use their prior knowledge and what they have read to make inferences.

- *Do you think the stones can really talk?* (No)

- *What do you already know about the boys from what you have read?* (They are clever, even though the narrator says they are not.)

- *What do you think the boys are doing?* (They are pretending the stones can talk to trick the narrator.)

- *So far, the narrator has been lazy and has not done any work. What happens on page 285 to change that?* (Pong convinces the narrator to make bowls. The narrator agrees because he does not trust the boys with his ax.)

"We need something to carry water from the river and to eat the soup with," said Kuai.

"Oh, Uncle," said Pong. "Could you use your mighty ax to make some bowls from bamboo stalks?"

"Ai yo!" I grumbled. "I have to do all the work, as always!" But it was true that none of them could be trusted with my sharp ax.

With a few quick chops, I made four bowls from a thick stalk. The boys used them to fill the hole with water.

285

LITERATURE ANTHOLOGY, *pp. 284–285*

Read

6 **Strategy: Ask and Answer Questions** COLLABORATE

Teacher Think Aloud As I read, I remember to **ask questions** and try to answer them to check my understanding. What is a question you might ask yourself about what you have read?

Prompt students to apply the strategy in a Think Aloud. Have them turn to a partner and share their question. Then have them paraphrase the text that helped them answer it.

Student Think Aloud A question I asked myself is what the boys are going to do with the stones. They are tossing the stones into the fire, so they must be using them, somehow, to make lunch.

Reread

Author's Craft: Word Choice

Authors choose precise verbs so that readers can visualize the characters' actions. What effect does the word *grumbled* have on the reader? Why would the author choose that word instead of *said?* (It is a word that describes an unhappy mood and clearly shows that the narrator is complaining.)

ELL Help students use the illustrations to talk about the story. Point to the illustration on page 284. Ask:

- What is the narrator doing? Is he listening? What is he listening to? (The narrator is listening to a stone.)

- Point to the illustration on page 285. *What is the narrator making?* Help students use this sentence frame to respond in a complete sentence: *The narrator is making _____ (bowls).*

Read

7 Text Features: Illustrations
COLLABORATE

Turn to a partner and talk about the illustrations on page 286. What is one of the boys doing? How can you tell he is tricking the narrator? (The boy is dropping a fish in the pot. He has his hand cupped to his mouth to show that he is laughing because he is tricking the narrator.)

8 Skill: Make Inferences

Based on the narrator's words and actions, what do you think he is going to do with the stones? (The narrator thinks he is going to eat the stones. He says that he agreed to make the chopsticks because he was not stupid enough to eat hot stones with his fingers.)

Build Vocabulary page 287
purred: made a low sound like a happy cat

I shook my head at them. "Now we have a puddle and a fire. How do you **expect** to get the water over the fire?" I asked.

"Leave that to us," said Ting.

"Uncle, you made the best bowls in the village with nothing more than an ax," said Pong. "Could you use your **graceful** knife to make some chopsticks to go with them?"

"*Ai yo!*" I cried. "You lazy boys want me to do all the work." Nevertheless, I carved out some chopsticks. Unlike the Chang brothers, I wasn't stupid enough to eat hot stones with my fingers. **8**

286

A C T Access Complex Text

▶ Connection of Ideas

Remind students that in this selection, it is important to use the illustrations and their own knowledge to make inferences and connections.

- *What are the boys really doing to make the soup?* (They are putting in a fish without the narrator seeing.) *How does the illustration help you understand what is happening?* (It shows the boy

adding the fish. If you did not look at the illustration, you would not fully understand the trick the boys are playing.)

- *Why does the steam smell like fish when the boys drop the stone in the pot?* (When the hot stone touches the water, it makes steam. The steam smells like fish because a fish is in the pot.)

When I finished, I gave each boy a pair of my skillfully carved chopsticks. "How long does it take the stones to cook?" I worried that the stones might burn like potatoes. Then I couldn't believe what those crazy boys did next. With long sticks, Ting picked a stone out of the hot fire, and instead of offering it to his elder first, he held it before Kuai and Pong!

They didn't eat it, though. They whispered to it, "*Yú, yú, yú*" ("Fish, fish, fish"), and blew on it.

Then Ting dropped the stone into the hole. *Sploosh!*

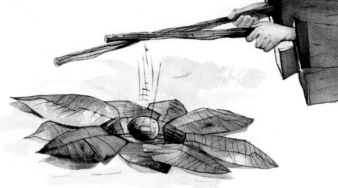

"*Ai yo!*" I yelled.

Bubbles of steam shot off the stone as it sank to the bottom. The steam carried a wonderful fish smell. I saw pieces of fish floating in the soup. Those boys had told the truth—it really was a fish stone! My stomach purred like a kitten.

> **STOP AND CHECK**
>
> **Ask and Answer Questions**
> Look at the illustration on page 286. Why are there pieces of fish floating in the soup?

287

LITERATURE ANTHOLOGY, *pp. 286–287*

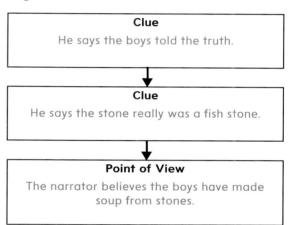

Read

9 Skill: Point of View

Does the narrator think the boys have made soup from stones? How do you know? (He says the boys have told the truth. He thinks they added a fish stone to the soup.) **Do you agree with the narrator?** (No; the illustration shows the boy adding the fish to the soup, so I know the narrator is not right.) **Add the clues and point of view to your graphic organizer.**

Clue
He says the boys told the truth.

↓

Clue
He says the stone really was a fish stone.

↓

Point of View
The narrator believes the boys have made soup from stones.

STOP AND CHECK

Ask and Answer Questions Why are there pieces of fish floating in the soup? (One of the boys put a fish in the soup.)

▶ Sentence Structure

Point out the italics in the second paragraph on page 287. Explain that words from other languages are often put in italics to set them apart. Then point out the parentheses. Ask:

- *What do you think the text in parentheses tells you?* (It explains what *yú, yú, yú* means. It tells you that it means "Fish, fish, fish.")

ELL *The boys are making soup. What is the boy putting in the pot?* (a fish) *Point to the picture that gives you a clue. Does the narrator see them put in the fish?* (no)

Explain that the expression *my stomach purred like a kitten* means that the narrator's stomach is grumbling gently because he is going to eat the delicious soup.

Read

10 Skill: Make Inferences

Why do the brothers talk about the soup as fit for a schoolmaster? (It is their way of saying the salt improves the soup's flavor. A schoolmaster is an important person, someone in a position of authority. So they are saying the salt would make the soup special, fit for an important person.)

11 Skill: Point of View

What is the narrator's point of view about Ting? (The narrator thinks he needs to teach Ting good manners.) Do you agree with the narrator's point of view? (Yes, I agree with the narrator. Even though the narrator is rude, Ting does not speak to him very respectfully.)

Kuai gently stirred the soup. "Hmm, this is turning into a tasty soup. If only we had a little salt, it would be a soup fit for a schoolmaster."

"Ting!" I said. "Get the salt off the boat."

"It's your salt. You get it," Ting said rudely. I was too hungry to teach him good manners. So I went to get the salt.

288

A C T Access Complex Text

▶ Genre

Explain that folktales often include repetition of words and actions. Help students identify examples of repetition.

- *Each time, how do the boys manage to add ingredients to the soup without the narrator noticing?* (They give him a task to do.)

- *What steps are repeated each time the boys add a stone to the soup?* (They chant the name of the ingredient three times and then blow on the stone before adding it to the soup.)

- *What do you think the boys are doing when they send the narrator back for sesame oil?* (They are adding another ingredient to the soup.)

As I returned with the salt, Ting picked up the second stone and held it before his brothers. *"Cài, cài, cài."* They whispered the word for vegetables three times and blew on the stone. Ting dropped it into the soup.

Shoosh! More steam leapt into the air. Surprisingly, I smelled vegetables! The **aroma** was so yummy, my stomach growled like an angry tiger.

Kuai stirred the soup again and sprinkled in a little salt. "This is a wonderful vegetable stone. If only we had a little sesame oil, this would be a soup fit for an emperor," said Kuai.

"Just a moment!" I cried. "I'll be right back with the sesame oil."

289

LITERATURE ANTHOLOGY, *pp. 288–289*

Reread *Close Reading Companion*

Author's Craft: Dialogue

How do you know that the narrator has been completely fooled by the Chang brothers? (the dialogue in which the narrator says, "I'll be right back with the sesame oil") **What clue does the dialogue give the reader?** (It shows that the narrator is eager to do whatever it takes to complete the soup.)

Author's Craft: Figurative Language

Personification is a type of figurative language in which human characteristics are given to things that are not human. The author says "the steam leapt into the air." **Why does the author describe the steam this way?** (To show how quickly the steam rose from the pot when the stone hit the soup.) **What is another example of figurative language?** (My stomach growled like an angry tiger.) **Why does the author use this description?** (To show how loud and forcefully the narrator's stomach is now grumbling.)

ELL Before reading, clarify the terms *schoolmaster* and *emperor*, pointing out that *emperor* is a cognate. *(emperador)* Explain that in the first sentence on page 289, *before* means "in front of," not "earlier."

Then invite students to tell in their own words or act out what the boys do each time they add a stone.

Read

12 Strategy: Ask and Answer Questions

COLLABORATE

What is a question you might ask yourself as you reread pages 290–291? Turn to a partner and share your question. If you reread to find your answer, paraphrase the text for your partner.

Student Think Aloud A question I asked myself is how the egg got into the soup. I know from what I have read so far that the boys are adding ingredients while the narrator is not looking. I think they added the egg while the narrator went back for the sesame oil.

When I returned with the sesame oil, Ting was holding up the last stone. All three boys yelled, *"Dàn, dàn, dàn!"* ("Egg, egg, egg!") Then they each blew hard on the stone, one at a time.

"Why are you shouting at that stone, you potato heads?" I asked.

"Egg stones don't hear very well," said Ting. He dropped the stone into the soup.

290

A C T Access Complex Text

▶ Connection of Ideas

Remind students that when they read a complex text, they should think about what they have already read to better understand characters' actions.

- *Ting says that he is shouting at the egg stone because egg stones do not hear very well. Do you think this is true?* (No)

- *Why is Ting really shouting at the egg stone?* (Ting is shouting at the egg stone to continue the trick he and his brothers began at the beginning of the story. By pretending to talk to the stones, the boys make the narrator believe the stones have special powers.)

Shoom! The hot stone brought the soup to a wild boil. I couldn't believe it when I saw threads of egg float to the top. A **luscious** fragrance filled the air. Even the monkeys came closer to get a whiff. **12**

Kuai drizzled in the sesame oil. More delectable smells! By now I was sure the sounds from my hungry stomach could be heard back in the village. **13**

291

LITERATURE ANTHOLOGY, *pp. 290–291*

Read

13 Skill: Make Inferences

What can you infer about the soup at this point in the story? How do you know? (I think the soup is almost done. The narrator says the smell of the soup is filling the air with delectable smells. Food usually smells delectable when it is almost ready to be served.)

Build Vocabulary page 291
  whiff: slight smell
  drizzled: poured a small amount
  delectable: very pleasant to taste or smell

Reread

Genre: Folktale

Remember that folktales often include repeated events. What details on page 290 give you a clue that this story is a folktale? (The Chang brothers follow the same procedure before adding the stone. They say the name of the ingredient three times, each blows on the stone, and one adds it to the pot.)

ELL Read from the first paragraph on page 291: *A luscious fragrance filled the air.* Have students repeat the sentence, focusing on pronunciation. Ask:

• *Does a luscious fragrance smell good or bad?* (good)

• *What is something you think has a luscious fragrance?* Help students list examples of foods, flowers, and other things that they think have a luscious fragrance.

Read

14 Skill: Make Inferences

Based on his actions, what can you infer about Ting? (He respects his elders after all. He serves the narrator first.)

15 Skill: Point of View

What does the narrator think about the soup? How do you know? (He thinks it tastes good. He has never tasted such a wonderful soup.) Add the clues and details to your graphic organizer.

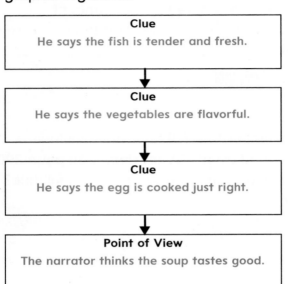

Clue
He says the fish is tender and fresh.

↓

Clue
He says the vegetables are flavorful.

↓

Clue
He says the egg is cooked just right.

↓

Point of View
The narrator thinks the soup tastes good.

Finally, Ting did something right. He filled one of the bamboo bowls with soup and served me, his elder, first. **14**

292

A C T Access Complex Text

▶ Sentence Structure

Help students figure out what "it" in the first sentence on page 293 refers to.

- *What can the narrator hardly wait to taste?* (the soup)

- *How do you know?* ("It" refers to the soup that the narrator is served in the last sentence on page 292.)

▶ Connection of Ideas

Tell students to think back to the plan Kuai whispered to his brothers on page 283. Ask:

- *What do you think Kuai's plan was?* (Kuai's plan was to trick the narrator by pretending to make soup from stones.)

I could hardly wait to taste it. I lifted the steaming bowl to my lips and took a sip. "Mmmmm . . . *Hǎo chí! Hǎo chí!*" ("Tastes good! Tastes good!") I must tell you that I have never tasted such a wonderful soup! The fish from the fish stone was tender and fresh. The wild mushrooms and onions from the vegetable stone were **flavorful**. The threads of egg from the egg stone were cooked just right.

Thanks to the bowls and chopsticks I had made, now the boys could enjoy the soup, too. The rest of the afternoon, they were happy and even worked a little harder. Not harder than me, of course.

15

16

293

LITERATURE ANTHOLOGY, *pp. 292–293*

Read

16 Vocabulary Strategy: Root Words

Find *flavorful* on page 293. How can you use the meaning of the root word *flavor* to find the meaning of *flavorful*? (I know *flavor* means "taste." *Flavor* is the root word of *flavorful*. I think *flavorful* means that something is full of taste or flavor.)

Reread

Author's Craft: Word Choice

Why does the author occasionally choose to use Chinese words and then translate them into English? (Using Chinese words makes the folktale feel more authentic. Translating the words into English removes any misunderstanding for the reader of what the words may mean.)

• *Were the boys able to fool the narrator? How do you know?* (Yes; the boys fooled the narrator. As he describes the soup, he talks about the fish stone, the vegetable stone, and the egg stone.)

ELL *The soup is ready to eat. Is there fish in the soup?* (yes) *What else is in the soup?* (mushrooms, onions, eggs) How do you know? Point to and read aloud the first paragraph on page 293, starting with *The fish. . .* Have students read with you.

Read

17 Skill: Point of View

Who does the narrator think invented the real stone soup? (He thinks he invented it.) How do you know? (He tells everyone the secret and demonstrates the steps. He does not know how others got their folktale.) **Do you agree that the narrator invented the real stone soup? Why or why not?** (No; you cannot make soup from stones, and if you could, the Chang brothers were the ones who came up with the idea.) **Add the clues and point of view to the graphic organizer.**

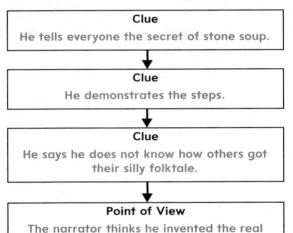

| **Clue** |
| He tells everyone the secret of stone soup. |

↓

| **Clue** |
| He demonstrates the steps. |

↓

| **Clue** |
| He says he does not know how others got their silly folktale. |

↓

| **Point of View** |
| The narrator thinks he invented the real stone soup. |

294

A C T Access Complex Text

▶ Connection of Ideas

Remind students to connect the illustrations with the text.

• *Look at the illustration on pages 294–295. Do the people believe the narrator when he tells his story? How do you know?* (No; the people in the illustration are laughing or pointing at their brains to show that they think the narrator is telling a crazy story.)

▶ Sentence Structure

Point out the italicized word *real* in the last paragraph on page 295. Explain that authors often use italics to emphasize a word that would otherwise not stand out.

• *Why do you think the author uses italics to emphasize the word* real*?* (To show that it is very important to the narrator that readers believe his version of stone soup is the true, correct version.)

From that day on, I always carried rocks in my pockets and told everyone the secret of making stone soup. I even demonstrated how to whisper to fish and vegetable stones, and how to yell at egg stones. But the truth is, I still haven't had time to make it. You know, I work too hard already.

And that, my friends, is how I invented the *real* stone soup. I don't know how people ended up with that silly old folktale. **17**

STOP AND CHECK

Summarize How did the brothers make stone soup? Tell the events from the story in order.

295

Read

Return to Purposes Review students' predictions and purposes for reading. Ask them to use text evidence to answer the Essential Question. (Choices that are good for us are choices that are healthy for our bodies and our minds.)

STOP AND CHECK

Summarize How did the brothers make stone soup? (They dug a hole and lined it with leaves. They put water in it. They built a fire next to the hole. They put stones in the fire. They put fish, vegetables, and eggs in the water. They took hot stones from the fire and put them in the water. This heated the water and cooked the soup.)

Build Vocabulary page 295
   demonstrated: showed by example

Read

About the Author and Illustrator

Ying Chang Compestine and Stéphane Jorisch

Have students read the biographies of the author and illustrator. Ask:

- How might growing up in China have inspired Ying Chang Compestine to write this story?

- Why are Stéphane Jorisch's illustrations an important part of this folktale?

Author's Purpose

To Entertain

Remind students that authors who write to entertain can also use illustrations to add humor and help them tell the story. Discuss how the author wanted to show that the boys were playing a trick on the narrator.

Reread

Author's Craft

Explain the meanings of *onomatopoeia* and *similes*. What examples of onomatopoeia and simile do you see in the story? How do they add to the story? (Answers will vary, but may include the onomatopoeia *Shoosh!* that helps the reader hear how the steam sounds going into the air and the simile, *"My stomach purred like a kitten,"* that describes how the author's stomach sounded.)

About the Author and Illustrator

Ying Chang Compestine says that writing keeps her close to China, where she grew up. Ying writes cookbooks as well as children's books. She travels around the world talking about her life and her writing. Ying says that traveling to new places lets her find the best food and the best stories.

Stéphane Jorisch lived near a big river in Canada as a teenager. He loved floating in boats of all kinds. Stéphane's father illustrated comic strips. That inspired Stéphane to become an artist. Stéphane also illustrated *Emily's Piano* and *Anancy and the Haunted House*. He now lives in Montreal, Canada.

Author's Purpose
Why are the illustrations an important part of this story?

296

© Ying Chang Compestine for Luc Normandin

LITERATURE ANTHOLOGY, *pp. 296–297*

Respond to the Text

Summarize

Summarize the main events in the story. Use the details from your Point of View chart to help you.

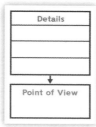

Details

↓

Point of View

Write

How does the author use dialogue to help you understand how the Chang brothers solved their problem? Use these sentence frames to focus your discussion.

> The author uses what the narrator says to . . .
> What the Chang brothers say is important because . . .
> The author helps me see how they . . .

Make Connections

Which healthful foods do the Chang boys choose to put in the soup?
ESSENTIAL QUESTION

What are some healthful choices that people make every day?
TEXT TO WORLD

297

Integrate

Make Connections COLLABORATE

Essential Question <u>Answer:</u> The boys put fish, onions, mushroom, and egg in the soup. <u>Evidence:</u> On page 284, they add fish. On page 289, they add mushrooms and onion. On page 290, they add egg.

Text to World Answers will vary. After students list and share people's healthful choices, have them discuss choices they make and how to make more.

Respond to the Text

Read
Summarize

Tell students they will use the information from their Point-of-View Chart to summarize the story. As I read the story, I collected the key details about the point of view. To summarize, I will reword these details in a logical way.

Reread

Analyze the Text

After students summarize the selection, have them reread to develop a deeper understanding of the text and answer the questions on **Close Reading Companion** pages 100–102. For students who need support in citing text evidence, use the Reread prompts on pages T25D–T25P.

Write About the Text

Review the writing prompt and sentence frames. Remind students to use their responses from the **Close Reading Companion** to support their answers. For a full lesson on writing a response using text evidence, see page T30.

<u>Answer:</u> The author uses dialogue to show that the Chang brothers easily trick the narrator into thinking that it is possible to make soup out of stones. <u>Evidence:</u> On page 284, the narrator refers to the boys as foolish, but the boys tell him he has "picked out a yummy egg stone." On page 286, the illustration shows the brothers putting a real fish in the soup. On page 289, the narrator's dialogue reveals that he is entirely fooled by the brothers' trick.

"Healthful Food Choices"

Text Complexity Range

Lexile

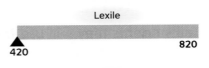

420   820

TextEvaluator™

2   10   35

What makes this text complex?
▶ **Genre**

Compare Texts *Analytical Writing*

As students read and reread "Healthful Food Choices" encourage them to take notes and think about the Essential Question: *What choices are good for us?* Tell students to think about how this text compares with *The Real Story of Stone Soup.*

Read

1 **Skill: Point of View** What is the author's point of view regarding healthful eating? (The author thinks that people should choose to eat a variety of healthful foods. He tells the reader that they need to eat energy-producing foods, such as vegetables, to get needed energy.)

Reread   *Close Reading Companion*

Author's Purpose What is the author's purpose for including the recipe for salsa? (The author wants to show the reader that healthful food can taste great and be easy to make.)

Genre · Directions

Compare Texts
Read about how people can choose healthful food to get energy.

Healthful Food Choices

Food Is Energy

What's for dinner? There are so many choices. Every time you go to the market you find a **variety** of foods to eat. Which ones do you choose? Why does it matter what you eat?

It matters because you move around and think all day long. You go to school. You play with friends. You do chores and homework. All that activity takes energy. You get energy from the food you eat. You need to eat energy-producing food because, unlike a plant, your body can't make its own food.

1

Energy from the Sun

Think about the tomato you ate for lunch. It began as a tiny seed. A seed contains just enough food to begin growing. The plant uses energy from the Sun. It changes water and air into food. It uses the food to produce tomatoes. A farmer picks the tomato and sends it to a supermarket.

Plants can make their own food from sunlight.

(l) Ingram Publishing (b) Peter Frank/Corbis

298

A C T   Access Complex Text

▶ Genre

Point out the headings. Help students use them to understand the key details in the text and how these details are connected.

* *Look at the first heading. How does it help you answer the question at the end of the first paragraph?* (Food is energy; you need to eat food that will give you energy.)

The next time you go to the market, what will you buy? You might choose a juicy red tomato for two reasons. It's **healthful** and delicious, and it's good for you, too. It gives you energy!

You can get many healthful vegetables at a grocery store.

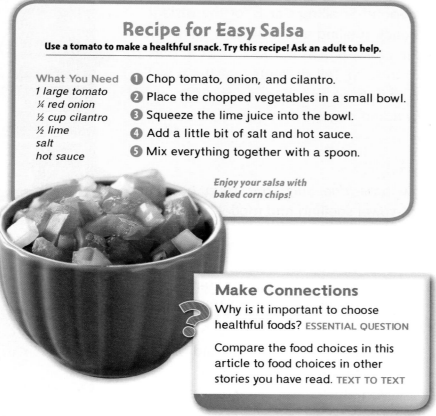

Recipe for Easy Salsa

Use a tomato to make a healthful snack. Try this recipe! Ask an adult to help.

What You Need
1 large tomato
¼ red onion
½ cup cilantro
½ lime
salt
hot sauce

1. Chop tomato, onion, and cilantro.
2. Place the chopped vegetables in a small bowl.
3. Squeeze the lime juice into the bowl.
4. Add a little bit of salt and hot sauce.
5. Mix everything together with a spoon.

Enjoy your salsa with baked corn chips!

Make Connections

Why is it important to choose healthful foods? ESSENTIAL QUESTION

Compare the food choices in this article to food choices in other stories you have read. TEXT TO TEXT

299

LITERATURE ANTHOLOGY, pp. 298–299

Read

Summarize

Guide students to summarize the selection.

Reread

Analyze the Text

After students read and summarize, have them reread to develop a deeper understanding of the text by annotating and answering questions on pages 103–105 of the **Close Reading Companion**.

Integrate

Make Connections

COLLABORATE

Essential Question <u>Answer:</u> Healthful foods give our bodies the energy they need to perform. <u>Evidence:</u> On page 298, I read that food gives our bodies energy, and our bodies cannot make energy on their own.

Text to Text Answers may vary, but encourage students to cite evidence from *The Real Story of Stone Soup* and other texts they have read.

- *How does the second section on page 298 connect to the first section?* (The first section tells us that food gives us energy. The final heading and paragraph on page 298 tell us that the energy in food comes from the Sun.)

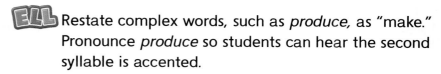 Restate complex words, such as *produce,* as "make." Pronounce *produce* so students can hear the second syllable is accented.

- *What gives plants energy to make food?* (the Sun)

- *Do tomato plants make tomatoes with the food?* (yes)

→ **Phonics/Fluency**

MINILESSON
20 Mins

/ü/: *oo, ew, u_e, ue, u, ui, ou;*
/u̇/: *oo, ou*

Go Digital

Variant Vowels

Present the Lesson

View "Nail Soup"

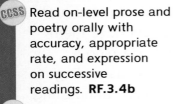

OBJECTIVES

Read on-level prose and poetry orally with accuracy, appropriate rate, and expression on successive readings. **RF.3.4b**

Use a known root word as a clue to the meaning of an unknown word with the same root (e.g., *company, companion*). **L.3.4c**

Rate: 82–102 WCPM

ACADEMIC LANGUAGE
• *expression*
• Cognate: *expresión*

Refer to the sound transfers chart in the **Language Transfers Handbook** to identify sounds that do not transfer in Spanish, Cantonese, Vietnamese, Hmong, and Korean.

1 Explain

Display the *Spoon* and *Book* **Sound-Spelling Cards** for the variant vowels /ü/ and /u̇/. Point to each spelling and provide a sample for each: *oo* as in *spoon*; *ew* as in *chew*; *u_e* as in *tube*; *ue* as in *due*; *u* as in *July*; *ui* as in *fruit*; *ou* as in *soup*. Tell students that the vowel sound /u̇/ can be spelled *oo* as in *book* and *ou* as in *could*. Point out the irregular spelling *ui* in *fruit* and *ough* in *through*.

2 Model

Write the words *spoon, chew, tube, due, July, fruit, soup, book,* and *could*. Underline each variant-vowel spelling and model blending.

3 Guided Practice

Write the following words on the board. Help students identify the variant-vowel spelling in each word. Guide students as they underline the variant-vowel spelling and pronounce each word.

loop	gloom	rude	should
true	shook	group	tooth
clue	hoop	hook	few

Read Multisyllabic Words

Transition to Longer Words Help students transition from reading one-syllable to multisyllabic variant-vowel words. Draw a T-chart on the board. In the first column write *hood, stood, fruit, gloom,* and *through*. In the second column, write *childhood, understood, fruitful, gloomy,* and *throughout*. Point to the words in the first column and explain that each word has a variant-vowel spelling. Underline the variant-vowel spellings. Model how to read each word and have students repeat.

Explain that the words in the second column include a word part with a variant-vowel spelling. Have students underline the variant-vowel spelling in each word. Point to each word in random order and have students read the words chorally. Have students add the irregularly spelled words to the word wall for review.

Roots in Related Words

1 Explain

Related words share a common root or base word.

- Readers can use their knowledge of root words to figure out the meanings of unfamiliar words that have the same root.
- The words *act, active, action, react,* and *actor* are related words. They share the same root word *act.*

2 Model

Write and say the words *company* and *companion.* Have students repeat the words. Model using your knowledge of the word *company* to figure out the meaning of *companion.*

3 Guided Practice

Write the related words *create, creative, creator, recreate; write, writer, rewrite, typewriter.* Have students identify the common root word in each set of related words and then use their knowledge of the root words to determine the meanings of the words.

Expression

Explain/Model Explain that part of reading with expression is emphasizing certain words to show emotion and understanding. Remind students that reading with expression will help them understand and enjoy what they are reading.

Model reading the first three paragraphs of "Nail Soup" on page 263, emphasizing the word *so* in the second paragraph. Point out how you used expression to show how hungry Erik is by emphasizing the word *so.*

Practice/Apply Ask one student to read the first sentence, then ask the next student to join in, then a third, repeating until all students are reading together. Remind students to use appropriate expression as they read. Offer feedback as needed.

Daily Fluency Practice FLUENCY

Students can practice fluency using **Your Turn Practice Book**.

Monitor and *Differentiate*

✓ Quick Check

Can students decode words with variant-vowel spellings? Can students determine the meanings of words with common roots? Can students read fluently?

Small Group Instruction

If No →	Approaching Level	Reteach pp. T40, T42
	ELL	Develop p. T58
If Yes →	On Level	Review p. T48
	Beyond Level	Extend p. T52

ON-LEVEL PRACTICE BOOK p. 158

A. Read each word in the box. Sort the words by writing each under the correct heading.

true	booth	look	glue
shook	tube	grew	should
would	spoon	flew	tune

oo as in *moon*
booth
spoon

ew as in *chew*
grew
flew

u_e as in *rude*
tube
tune

ue as in *due*
true
glue

oo as in *book*
look
shook

ou as in *could*
should
would

B. Related words have a common root or base word. Read each set of words. Circle the related words.

1. (metal)   (metallic)   melted
2. (company)   counting   (companion)
3. able   (action)   (actor)
4. (telephone)   totally   (television)
5. (reality)   (real)   railroad

APPROACHING p. 158	BEYOND p. 158	ELL p. 158

→ Write to Sources

Reading/Writing Workshop

OBJECTIVES

 Write narratives or develop real or imagined experiences or events using effective technique, descriptive details, and clear event sequences. Use dialogue and descriptions of actions, thoughts, and feelings to develop experiences and events or show the response of characters to situations. **W.3.3b**

ACADEMIC LANGUAGE

voice, emotions, personal narrative

Go Digital

U4W1 Voice: Show Feelings

DAY 1

Writing Fluency

Write to a Prompt Provide students with the prompt: *Tell what Erik's problem is and how Papa helped solve it.* Have students share their descriptions of the problem. *What was the outcome of the story?* Have students write continuously for eleven minutes in their Writer's Notebook. If students stop writing, encourage them to keep going.

COLLABORATE When students finish writing have them work with a partner to compare ideas and make sure that they both have a clear understanding of the story.

Genre Writing

Fictional Narrative pp. T344–T349

First Week Focus: Over the course of the week, focus on the following stages of the writing process:

Expert Model: Discuss the Expert Model found online at Writer's Workspace. Work with students to find the features of a fictional narrative.

Prewrite: Explain narrative writing to students. Teach the minilesson on sequence of events. Distribute the Problem and Solution Chart found online at Writer's Workspace and have students use it to start planning their own fictional narratives.

DAY 2

Write to the Reading/Writing Workshop Text

Analyze the Prompt Read aloud the first paragraph on page 270 of the **Reading/Writing Workshop**. Ask: *What is the prompt asking?* (to state and support an opinion) Say: *Let's reread to see what Papa did. We can note text evidence.*

Analyze Text Evidence Display Graphic Organizer 31 in Writer's Workspace. Say: *Let's see how one student, Lizzie, took notes to answer the prompt. She notes how Papa first asked the man and his wife to share a cup of hot water.* Guide the class through the rest of Lizzie's notes.

Analyze the Student Model Explain how Lizzie used text evidence from her notes to write a response to the prompt.

- **State an Opinion:** Lizzie clearly states her opinion in the opening sentence. Trait: Voice

- **Show Feelings:** Writers use their voices to show how they feel about a character or event in a story. Lizzie describes how the couple were "happy and smiling" at the end of the story. Trait: Voice

- **Supporting Details:** Supporting details provide reasons to support the writer's opinion. Lizzie includes supporting details in her paragraph. Trait: Ideas

For additional practice with voice and showing feelings, assign **Your Turn Practice Book** page 159.

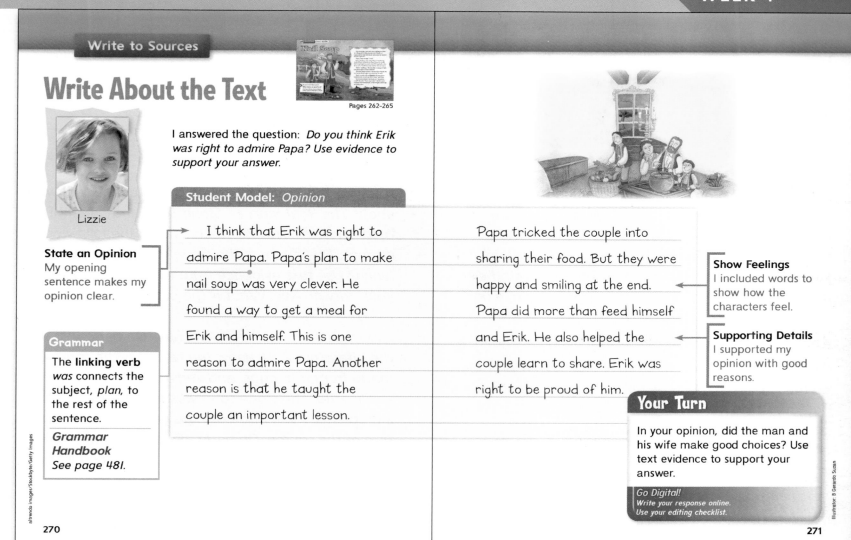

Write to Sources

Write About the Text

Pages 262–265

Lizzie

I answered the question: *Do you think Erik was right to admire Papa? Use evidence to support your answer.*

State an Opinion
My opening sentence makes my opinion clear.

Grammar

The **linking verb** *was* connects the subject, *plan*, to the rest of the sentence.

Grammar Handbook See page 481.

Student Model: *Opinion*

I think that Erik was right to admire Papa. Papa's plan to make nail soup was very clever. He found a way to get a meal for Erik and himself. This is one reason to admire Papa. Another reason is that he taught the couple an important lesson.

Papa tricked the couple into sharing their food. But they were happy and smiling at the end. Papa did more than feed himself and Erik. He also helped the couple learn to share. Erik was right to be proud of him.

Show Feelings
I included words to show how the characters feel.

Supporting Details
I supported my opinion with good reasons.

Your Turn

In your opinion, did the man and his wife make good choices? Use text evidence to support your answer.

Go Digital!
Write your response online.
Use your editing checklist.

270

271

READING/WRITING WORKSHOP, *pp. 270–271*

Your Turn Writing Read the Your Turn prompt on page 271 of the Reading/Writing Workshop aloud. Discuss the prompt with students. If necessary, review with students that authors of personal and other types of narratives make use of voice to express emotions.

Have students take notes as they look for text evidence to answer the prompt. Remind them to include the following elements as they craft their response from their notes:

- State an Opinion
- Show Feelings
- Supporting Details

Have students use **Grammar Handbook** page 481 in the Reading/Writing Workshop to edit for errors in linking verbs.

ELL ENGLISH LANGUAGE LEARNERS SCAFFOLD

Beginning

Write Help students complete the sentence frames.
First, the man and his wife ____.
Then they ____.

Intermediate

Describe *Papa asks the man and his wife to ____. After making the soup, ____.*

Advanced/High

Discuss Check for understanding. Ask: *What do the man and his wife do? Do you think this was a good choice? Why or why not?*

Write to Sources

DAY 3 For students who need support to complete the writing assignment for the Literature Anthology, provide the following instruction.

DAY 4

Write to the Literature Anthology Text

Analyze the Prompt Explain that students will write about *The Real Story of Stone Soup* on **Literature Anthology** pages 278–295. Provide the following prompt: *How does the author use dialogue to help you understand how the Chang brothers solved their problem?* Ask: *What is the prompt asking you to do?* (to explain how dialogue helps you understand the story)

Analyze Text Evidence Help students note evidence.

Pages 282–283 Read the pages. Ask: *What problem do the Chang brothers have?* (They have docked their boat for lunch, but their boss has forgotten the cooking pot and blames them for doing so.) *Why does the boss blame them?*

Page 289 Read the page. Ask: *How do the brothers get their boss to bring flavoring to add to the soup?* (They have him convinced that they are making soup from stones, so he goes to get flavorful ingredients because he is hungry and his stomach is grumbling.)

Encourage students to look for more text evidence. Then have them craft a short response. Use the conference routine below.

Write to Two Sources

Analyze the Prompt Explain that students will write about *The Real Story of Stone Soup* and "Healthful Food Choices." Provide students with the following prompt: *Do you think the stone soup was a healthful lunch? Use text evidence from two sources to support your answer.* Ask: *What is the prompt asking you to do?* (to state and support an opinion about how healthful the stone soup was) Say: *On page 293 of the Literature Anthology, the text says the soup was made from fish, eggs, and vegetables. So in my notes, I will write:* The stone soup was made from healthful ingredients. *I will also note the page number and the title of the source. On page 299 of "Healthful Food Choices," I read that energy-producing food is the most healthful. I will add this to my notes.*

Analyze Text Evidence Display online Graphic Organizer 32 in Writer's Workspace. Say: *Let's see how one student took notes to answer the prompt. Here are Lizzie's notes.* Read through the text evidence for each selection and have students point out the information that can be used to point out the benefits of a healthful lunch.

Teacher Conferences

STEP 1

Talk about the strengths of the writing.

You chose good examples of dialogue to support your topic. The writing stays focused and on topic.

STEP 2

Focus on how the writer uses text evidence.

All of the text evidence you cited supports your answer. Your points would have more impact if you used linking words to connect the ideas.

STEP 3

Make concrete suggestions.

This section is strong, but it needs more ____. Rewrite this sentence to add more supporting details.

DAY

5

Share the Prompt Provide the following prompt to students: *In your opinion, is it easier to make salsa or stone soup? Use text evidence from* The Real Story of Stone Soup *and "Making Healthful Choices" to support your opinion.*

Find Text Evidence Have students take notes. Find text evidence and give guidance where needed. In necessary, review with students how to paraphrase. Remind them to write the page number and source of the information.

Analyze the Student Model Review the prompt and Lizzie's notes from Day 4. Display the student model on page 160 of the **Your Turn Practice Book**. Explain to students that Lizzie synthesized her notes to write a response to the prompt. Discuss the page together with students or have them do it independently.

Write the Response Review the prompt from Day 4 with students. Remind them that they took notes on this prompt on Day 4. Have students use their notes to craft a short response. Tell students to include both titles and the following elements:

- State an Opinion

- Show Feelings

- Supporting Details

COLLABORATE

Share and Reflect Have students share their responses with a partner. Use the Peer Conference routine below.

Suggested Revisions

Provide specific direction to help focus young writers.

Focus on a Sentence
Read the draft and target one sentence for revision. *Rewrite this sentence by adding a linking word to connect _____.*

Focus on a Section
Underline a section that needs to be revised. Provide specific suggestions. *This idea is strong. I want to know more about _____. Try using dialogue to support this point.*

Focus on a Revision Strategy
Underline a section. Have students focus on a specific revision strategy, such as stating a clear topic. *Revise your first paragraph so it begins with your topic sentence.*

Peer Conferences

Focus peer responses on adding supporting details to support an opinion. Provide these questions:

- Is the opinion clearly stated?

- Are the writer's or a character's feelings expressed clearly?

- Do the details stated support the opinion?

→ Grammar: Linking Verbs

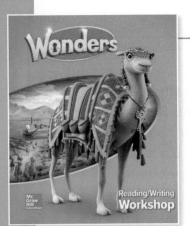

Reading/Writing Workshop

OBJECTIVES

 Explain the function of nouns, pronouns, verbs, adjectives, and adverbs in general and their functions in particular sentences. **L.3.1a**

 Form and use regular and irregular verbs. **L.3.1d**

- Distinguish linking verbs
- Capitalize and punctuate complete sentences correctly
- Proofread sentences for mechanics and usage errors.

Have students work in pairs to write four sentences using linking verbs. Ask students to include examples of singular and plural subjects in the sentences and check that each linking verb agrees with its subject.

DAY 1

DAILY LANGUAGE ACTIVITY

Misses Bell decorated her home. She hunged pictures and placed two book's on the coffee table.

(1: Mrs. Bell; 2: hung; 3: books)

Tuesday Grammar worksheet

ce Linking Verbs

on **verb** tells what the does.

g verb connects the to a noun or an adjective in the predicate. It tells what the subject is or is like:
    He **is** my brother.

- The linking verb **be** has special present-tense forms: *am, is, are*

- A subject and linking verb must agree. The verbs **am, is,** and **was** are singular. The verbs **are** and **were** are plural:
    The girl **is** dancing.
    The girls **are** singing.

Discuss linking verbs using page 481 of the Grammar Handbook.

DAY 2

DAILY LANGUAGE ACTIVITY

Leafs was falling from trees. The wind blowed and cold air moved in acros the Northeast.

(1: Leaves were; 2: blew; 3: across)

Review Linking Verb *Be*

Review linking verbs and subject-verb agreement. Review present-tense forms of *be: am, is, are*.

Introduce More Linking Verbs

- The verb **be** is the most common linking verb. It has special past-tense forms: *was, were*.

- Use the linking verbs **am, is,** and **was** when the subject is singular. Use **am** with the subject **I**:
    I **am** a swimmer.
    She **is** excited.
    She **was** excited.

- Use **are** and **were** with plural subjects and **you:**
    The runners **are** fast.
    You **were** fast.

 TALK ABOUT IT

COLLABORATE

USE LINKING VERBS

Ask partners to use linking verbs to talk about choices that are good for us. Students might discuss how choosing to eat fruit and vegetables over snack food is better for us. As they talk, students should listen to be sure they use linking verbs.

CHANGE THE LINKING VERB

Have groups write five sentences about making good choices using linking verbs. Then have each student read the sentences aloud, substituting a new linking verb in each. Students should keep the verb tense the same and ensure that it agrees with the subject.

DAY

I am taken this bag of plastick bottles to the recycling center. Amy and I cleened the park yesterday.

(1: taking; 2: plastic; 3: cleaned)

Mechanics and Usage: End Punctuation and Complete Sentences

- A statement and a command sentence end with a period.
- A question ends with a question mark.
- An exclamation and an exclamatory sentence end with an exclamation point.
- A complete sentence has a subject and a predicate, and shows a complete thought.

As students write, refer them to Grammar Handbook pages 474 and 481.

DAY

I asked Sarah, "Did you do you're homework!" ill help you study for the test said Sarah.

(1: your; 2: homework?; 3: "I'll; 4: test,")

Proofread

Have students correct errors in these sentences.

1. the children was ready to go to sleep. (1: The; 2: were)
2. He were so excited he yelled, "Yes" (1: was; "Yes!")
3. What is Sue Ellens' phone number (1: Ellen's; 2: number?)
4. quincy said he will be home at 5 o'clock (1: Quincy; 2: o'clock.)

Have students check their work using Grammar Handbook pages 474, 481–483, and 498–500.

DAY

You is lucky to have a friend like Valerie. she is the nices person I know.

(1: You are; 2: She; 3: nicest)

Assess

Use the Daily Language Activity and Grammar Practice Reproducibles page 80 for assessment.

Reteach

Use Grammar Practice Reproducibles pages 76–79 and selected pages from the Grammar Handbook for additional reteaching. Remind students that it is important to use linking verbs correctly as they read, write, and speak.

Check students' writing for use of the skill and listen for it in their speaking. Assign Grammar Revision Assignments in their Writer's Notebooks as needed.

See Grammar Practice Reproducibles pages 76–80.

STATE END PUNCTUATION

Have students in small groups each write down four sentences without end punctuation on index cards and place the cards in a pile. Students will take turns selecting a card and reading aloud the sentence, as the others guess what the end punctuation is.

PLACE THE LINKING VERB

Have students in small groups each write down five linking verbs on index cards and place the cards in a pile. Students will take turns selecting a card and reading aloud the linking verb, as the others use it in a simple or compound sentence.

ROLE-PLAY A SCENE

Have students reenact a favorite scene from a story the class has read about making good choices. As students role-play, be sure they use many linking verbs. As other students watch, have them listen for the linking verbs.

Spelling: Variant Vowels /ü/, /u̇/

OBJECTIVES

CCSS Use spelling patterns and generalizations (e.g., *word families, position-based spellings, syllable patterns, ending rules, meaningful word parts*) in writing words. **L.3.2f**

CCSS Consult reference materials, including beginning dictionaries, as needed to check and correct spellings. **L.3.2g**

Spelling Words

spoon	tube	July
goose	due	look
booth	clues	shook
gloom	true	notebook
rude	chew	could

Review coins, joyful, round
Challenge classroom, childhood

Differentiated Spelling

Approaching Level

loop	tube	soup
spoon	due	grew
gloom	true	chew
hoop	glue	look
rude	group	shook

Beyond Level

spoon	include	renew
gloom	clues	shook
booth	through	childhood
classroom	groups	notebook
tube	chew	could

DAY 1

Assess Prior Knowledge

Display the spelling words. Read them aloud, drawing out and slowly enunciating the /ü/ or /u̇/ sound in each word.

Model for students how to spell the word *gloom*. Segment the word sound by sound, then attach a spelling to each sound. Point out that the *oo* spelling is almost always found in the middle of a word.

Demonstrate sorting the spelling words by pattern under key words *booth, chew, due, book, would,* and *rude.* (Write the words on index cards or the IWB.) Sort a few words. Point out that the *ue* spelling for /ü/ usually comes at the end of a word.

Then use the Dictation Sentences from Day 5. Say the underlined word, read the sentence, and repeat the word. Have students write the words.

DAY 2

Spiral Review

Review the diphthongs in the words *coins, joyful,* and *round.* Have students find words in this week's readings with the same sounds.

Use the Dictation below for review. Read the sentence, say the word, and have students write the words.

1. These are rare old <u>coins</u>.
2. We were <u>joyful</u> over vacation.
3. Wheels are <u>round</u>.

Challenge Words Review this week's words, pointing out the variant vowels /ü/, /u̇/ sound spellings. Use this Dictation for challenge words. Read the sentence, say the word, have students write the word.

1. This is our <u>classroom</u>.
2. He had a happy <u>childhood</u>.

Have students check and correct their spellings, and write the words in their word study notebook.

WORD SORTS

COLLABORATE

OPEN SORT

Have students cut apart the **Spelling Word Cards BLM** in the Online Resource Book and initial the backs of each card. Have them read the words aloud with a partner. Then have partners do an **open sort**. Have them record the sort in their word study notebook.

PATTERN SORT

Complete the **pattern sort** using the key words, pointing out the /ü/ spellings. Have students use Spelling Word Cards to do their own pattern sort. A partner can compare and check their sorts.

DAY

Word Meanings

Have students copy the words below into their Writer's Notebooks. Have them figure out the spelling word that goes with each definition.

1. a bird (goose)
2. how to eat food (chew)
3. something to write notes in (notebook)
4. a stand for selling things (booth)
5. moved quickly (shook)

Challenge students to come up with clues for other spelling, review, and challenge words.

Have partners write sentences for each spelling word, leaving a blank where the word should go. Then have them trade papers and fill in the missing words.

See Phonics/Spelling Reproducibles pp. 91–96.

SPEED SORT

Have partners do a **speed sort** to see who is faster. Then have them do a word hunt in the week's reading for words with variant /ü/ vowels that create the /ü/ sound. Have them record the words in their Day 2 pattern sort in the word study notebook.

DAY

Proofread and Write

Write these sentences on the board. Have students circle and correct each misspelled word. Remind students they can use print or electronic resources to check and correct spelling.

1. I used the spon to scoop up my food to choo. (spoon, chew)
2. He set up a boothe so he kould sell his art. (booth, could)
3. The detective wrote the klews in her notebooke. (clues, notebook)
4. It is tru, I looke like my sister. (true, look)
5. My library book is do in Juli. (due, July)

Error Correction Remind students to segment the word sound by sound as they spell it. Then have students create sentences using these words to increase their familiarity with the use of these spelling patterns.

BLIND SORT

Have partners do a **blind sort**: one reads a spelling word card; the other tells under which key word it belongs. Have them take turns until both have sorted all their words. Then have students explain how they sorted the words.

DAY

5

Assess

Use the Dictation Sentences for the Posttest. Have students list misspelled words in their word study notebooks. Look for students' use of these words in their writings.

Dictation Sentences

1. Eat the soup with a <u>spoon</u>.
2. A <u>goose</u> is bigger than a duck.
3. Brenda hid in an empty <u>booth</u> on the train.
4. Kyle was full of <u>gloom</u> when his friend moved away.
5. It is <u>rude</u> to yell.
6. I can float on a rubber <u>tube</u>.
7. You library books are <u>due</u> back.
8. We need <u>clues</u> to solve the mystery!
9. Tell me a <u>true</u> story for once.
10. <u>Chew</u> your food before swallowing it.
11. How do you celebrate the Fourth of <u>July</u>?
12. Take a <u>look</u> at this picture.
13. Mr. Dean <u>shook</u> my hand.
14. My <u>notebook</u> has blue paper.
15. You <u>could</u> try the game again.

Have students self-correct the tests.

→ Build Vocabulary

OBJECTIVES

CCSS Determine the meaning of the new word formed when a known affix is added to a known word (e.g., *agreeable/ disagreeable, comfortable/ uncomfortable, care/careless, heat/ preheat*). **L.3.4b**

CCSS Use a known root word as a clue to the meaning of an unknown word with the same root (e.g., *company, companion*). **L.3.4c**

Expand vocabulary by adding inflectional endings and suffixes.

Vocabulary Words

aroma	healthful
expect	interrupted
flavorful	luscious
graceful	variety

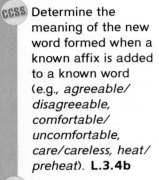

Provide sentence frames to help students practice using the different forms of this week's vocabulary words they generate on Day 2. Review verb tenses as needed.

DAY 1

Connect to Words

Practice this week's vocabulary.

1. Describe an **aroma** coming from your kitchen.
2. What do you **expect** to get on the test?
3. Tell about a **flavorful** meal you have had.
4. Describe a **graceful** dancer.
5. What **healthful** foods do you eat at lunch?
6. What can you say to someone who has **interrupted** you?
7. What desserts would you describe as **luscious**?
8. Name a **variety** of foods.

DAY 2

Expand Vocabulary

Help students generate different forms of this week's words by adding, changing, or removing inflectional endings.

- Draw a four-column chart on the board. Write *expect* in the left column. Then write *expected, expecting,* and *expectation* in the other columns. Read aloud the words and discuss the meanings.

- Have students share sentences with each form of *expect.*

- Students can fill in the chart for other words, such as *interrupt.*

- Have students copy the chart in their word study notebook.

BUILD MORE VOCABULARY

COLLABORATE

ACADEMIC VOCABULARY

Discuss important academic words.

- Display the words *contribute* and *nutrition* and discuss the meanings with students.

- Display *contribute* and *contribution.* Have partners look up and define related words.

- Write the related words on the board. Have partners ask and answer questions using the words. Repeat with *nutrition.* Elicit examples from students.

SUFFIXES *–ible, –able*

- Remind students that adding a suffix, such as *–ible* and *–able,* to a base word changes the meaning of the word. Give examples, such as *fashionable* and *visible.* Discuss the meaning of each word.

- Have partners list other words with the suffixes *–ible* and *–able.* Then ask them to write a sentence with one of the words.

- Invite partners to share their words. Have students use the suffixes and base words to discuss the meanings of the words.

DAY

Reinforce the Words

Review this week's vocabulary words. Have students orally complete each sentence stem.

1. The ____ made the soup very <u>flavorful</u>.

2. I love the <u>aroma</u> coming from the ____ when my mom cooks.

3. I didn't <u>expect</u> to ____ that movie as much as I did.

4. Are you <u>graceful</u> or clumsy when you ____?

5. My younger brother <u>interrupted</u> our ____. It was really annoying!

6. This ____ is really <u>luscious</u>! I'd like another, please.

DAY

Connect to Writing

- Have students write sentences in their word study notebooks using this week's vocabulary.

- Tell them to write sentences that provide information about the words and their meanings.

- **ELL** Provide the Day 3 sentence stems for students needing extra support.

Write About Vocabulary Have students write something they learned from this week's words in their word study notebook. For example, they might write about a favorite meal. What parts are the most *flavorful*? Does the meal end with a *luscious* dessert?

DAY
5

Word Squares

Ask students to create Word Squares for each vocabulary word.

- In the first square, students write the word. (example: *graceful*)

- In the second square, students write their own definition of the word and any related words. (example: *agile*)

- In the third square, students draw a simple illustration that will help them remember the word. (example: a dancer)

- In the fourth square, students write non-examples. (example: *clumsy*)

- Have students share their Word Squares with a partner.

ROOT WORDS

Remind students that identifying root words can help them determine the meanings of unfamiliar words.

- Display **Your Turn Practice Book** pages 153–154. Read the first page. Model using the root words to figure out the meanings of *powerful* and *inspiration*.

- For additional practice with root words, have students complete page 157.

- Students can confirm meanings in a print or online dictionary.

SHADES OF MEANING

Help students generate words related to *luscious*. Draw a synonym/antonym scale.

- Begin a discussion about the word *luscious*. Elicit synonyms and write them on the scale. Ask: *What things can you call* luscious? Discuss examples (a rich dessert) and non-examples (a plain sandwich).

- Have partners work together to add other words to the scale. Ask students to copy the words in their word study notebook.

MORPHOLOGY

Use the word *healthful* as a springboard for students to learn more words. Draw a T-chart.

- Write the word *health* in the first column. Discuss the meaning.

- In the second column, write the suffix *–ful*. Discuss the meaning and model how to use the suffix and the base word to determine the meaning of *healthful*.

- Have partners generate other words with the suffix *-ful*, such as *colorful, tasteful*.

- Tell students to use the suffix and base words to determine the meanings of the words.

→ Integrate Ideas

Close Reading Routine

Read   DOK 1–2

- Identify key ideas and details about Choices.
- Take notes and summarize.
- Use **A C T** prompts as needed.

Reread   DOK 2–3

- Analyze the text, craft, and structure.
- Use the **Close Reading Companion.**

Integrate   DOK 4

- Integrate knowledge and ideas.
- Make text-to-text connections.
- Use the Integrate lesson.
- Use *Close Reading Companion,* p. 106.

TEXT CONNECTIONS

Connect to the Essential Question

Write the essential question on the board: What choices are good for us? Divide the class into small groups. Tell students that each group will compare the information that they have learned about what choices are good for us. Model how to compare this information by using examples from this week's **Leveled Readers** and "Nail Soup," **Reading/Writing Workshop** pages 262–265.

Evaluate Text Evidence Have students review their class notes and completed graphic organizers before they begin their discussions. Encourage students to compare information from all the week's reads. Have each group pick one student to take notes. Explain that each

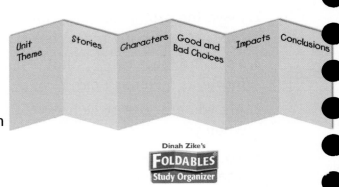

Dinah Zike's
FOLDABLES
Study Organizer

INQUIRY SPACE

LEVEL	**1**	2	3	4	5	6

Analyze the Task

PREVIEW LEVEL 1 Display Level 1 from the Narrative Perform2-ance Task. Explain to students that in Level 1 they will analyze the task and make a research plan.

❶ **Purpose and Audience** Read aloud the prompt to students. Ask: *What is the topic of the project?* (frogs) *What is the purpose, or goal, of the project?* (to tell a story about the day in the life of a frog) *Who is the audience for your presentation?* (teachers and students) *Why is it important to think about the purpose and audience for your presentation?* (It helps you decide what ideas and events to include and how long to make your presentation.)

NARRATIVE PERFORMANCE TASK

Write About: Frogs

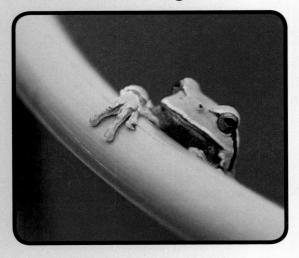

Gudella/Getty Images

OBJECTIVE

CCSS Describe characters in a story (e.g., their traits, motivations, or feelings) and explain how their actions contribute to the sequence of events. **RL.3.3**

group will use an Accordion Foldable® to record their ideas. You may wish to model how to use an Accordion Foldable® to record comparisons.

Text to Poetry

As students discuss the information from all the week's reads, have them include Hilaire Belloc's poem "The Vulture" on page 106 of the **Close Reading Companion** as a part of their discussion. Guide students to see the connections between the poem and text. Ask: *How does Belloc's poem connect to what you read this week?*

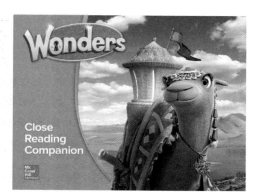

Present Ideas and Synthesize Information

When students finish their discussions, ask for a volunteer from each group to read his or her notes aloud.

OBJECTIVE

CCSS Conduct short research projects that build knowledge about a topic. **W.3.7**

❷ **Research Plan** Have students discuss what they know about frogs and what they want to find out about them. Display the **Student Model: Research Plan** slide presentation in the **Toolkit** and review it with students.

❸ **Keywords** Explain to students that *keywords* are words connected to the topic you will explore. Say: *When you type a keyword in a search engine, it creates a list of websites with that keyword.* Point out that a source containing several keywords in the title will have information about the topic. Ask students to identify keywords related to the topic of frogs. (amphibians, frogs, tadpoles, toads, endangered frogs)

ASSIGN LEVEL 1 Have students begin Level 1. Remind them that the hyperlinks on each screen will help them complete each level. You may wish to have students view the **Purpose and Audience** and **Keywords** slide presentations in the Toolkit.

→ **Approaching Level**

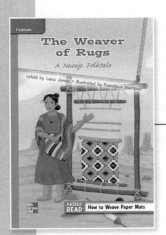

Lexile 520
TextEvaluator™ 20

 OBJECTIVES

(ccss) Ask and answer questions to demonstrate understanding of a text, referring explicitly to the text as the basis for the answers. **RL.3.1**

(ccss) Distinguish their own point of view from that of the narrator or those of the characters. **RL.3.6**

• Use root words to determine the meanings of words.

• Identify the narrator's point of view.

ACADEMIC LANGUAGE
ask, answer questions, point of view, folktale, directions, root words

Leveled Reader:
The Weaver of Rugs

Go Digital

Leveled Readers

Fill in the Graphic Organizer

Before Reading

Preview and Predict

Have students read the Essential Question. Then have them read the title and table of contents of *The Weaver of Rugs*. Have students predict how learning to weave will play a role in the story.

Review Genre: Folktale

Review with students that a folktale is a fictional story in which the main character must find a clever way to solve a problem. It also contains a lesson or message. As they preview *The Weaver of Rugs*, have students identify features of a folktale.

During Reading

Close Reading

Note Taking Have students use their graphic organizer as they read.

Page 2 *Is the narrator a character inside or someone outside the story?* (someone outside of the story) *What is the problem at the beginning of the story?* (It is too cold to go out to get food, and the Navajo people are growing weak from lack of food and warmth.)

Page 3 *What is the root word of* hopelessly? (*hope*) *There are two suffixes, -less and -ly. What does -less mean?* ("without") *The suffix -ly changes an adjective to an adverb. Define* hopelessly. ("without hope") *The narrator tells about what the women are feeling as they call out for help. What is the women's point of view at the end of this page?* (They are feeling hopeless.) *Explain how you might feel if you were in their situation.*

Pages 4–6 Reread the words of Spider Woman on page 4. *What do Spider Woman's words tell us about her?* (Possible Response: She does not like to be bothered.) *What will the women have to do in return if the Spider Woman helps them?* (They must do everything she tells them.)

Pages 7–11 *What is a question you might have about how the women are feeling on page 10? Reread page 10 to answer the question.* (Possible Question and Answer: Why are they feeling angry? They are beginning to think Spider Woman cannot help them.) **Have students ask and answer a question about their decision to leave holes in their rug.**

Pages 12–13 *How does the women's choice to leave holes in the rug affect them?* (Spider Woman sends them back to their own world.) *Why are they sad?* (They feel that they have failed to help their people.)

Pages 14–15 *Summarize to a partner how learning to weave benefits the community.* (The rugs keep the people warm and they can trade extra rugs for food and other goods.) *What is one of the lessons in this folktale?* (Learning new skills can help in unexpected ways.)

After Reading

Respond to Reading Revisit the Essential Question, and ask students to complete the Text Evidence questions on page 16.

Analytical Writing **Write About Reading** Make sure students are telling the story from Spider Woman's perspective and that the details of their story match up with the details in *The Weaver of Rugs*.

Fluency: Expression

Model Model reading page 2 with proper expression. Next, reread the page aloud, and have students read along with you.

Apply Have students practice reading with a partner.

PAIRED READ

"How to Weave Paper Mats"

Make Connections:
Write About It *Analytical Writing*

Before reading, have students note that the genre of this text is directions, which means that it instructs readers how to do something. Then discuss the Essential Question.

After reading, have students make connections between how learning new skills can help in *The Weaver of Rugs* and "How to Weave Paper Mats."

✏️ **Analytical Writing**

COMPARE TEXTS

- Have students use text evidence to compare what they learned from the folktale and directions.

Leveled Reader

Literature Circles

Ask students to conduct a literature circle using the Thinkmark questions to guide the discussion. You may wish to have a whole-class discussion on choices students have made and what happened as a result.

Level Up

Level-up lessons available online.

IF students read the `Approaching Level` fluently and answered the questions

THEN pair them with students who have proficiently read the `On Level` and have approaching-level students

- echo-read the `On Level` main selection with their partner.

- use self-stick notes to mark a detail they would like to discuss in each section.

A C T Access Complex Text

The `On Level` challenges students by including more **domain-specific words** and **complex sentence structures**.

Approaching Level

Phonics/Decoding

DECODE WORDS WITH VARIANT VOWELS /ü/ AND / u̇ /

 TIER 2

OBJECTIVES

 Decode regularly spelled one-syllable words. **RF.1.3b**

Decode words with variant vowels /ü/ and / u̇ / spelled *oo*.

 I Do Write the words *gloom* and *look* on the board and say them aloud. Explain that the variant vowels /ü/ and / u̇ / can be spelled several ways. Point to the word *gloom*. Tell students that one way to spell the variant vowel /ü/ is *oo*. Now point to the word *look*. Tell students that one way to spell the variant vowel sound / u̇ / is also *oo*. Repeat with *doom, book, took,* and *room*. Review the letters and sound for each variant vowel.

 We Do Write *food, shook, loot, foot,* and *mood* on the board. Underline the variant vowel spellings. Model decoding the first two words. Students can read the rest aloud and identify the letter and vowel sounds.

 You Do Add the words *loop, boot, nook, soot,* and *loon* to the board. Have students read each word aloud and identify the variant vowel sound. Point to the words in random order for students to read chorally.

BUILD WORDS WITH VARIANT VOWELS /ü/ AND / u̇ /

 TIER 2

OBJECTIVES

 Know and apply grade-level phonics and word analysis skills in decoding words. Decode multisyllable words. **RF.3.3c**

Build words with variant vowels /ü/ spelled *oo, ew, u_e, ue, u, ui, ou;* and / u̇ / spelled *oo, ou.*

 I Do Tell students they will be building multisyllable words with the variant vowels /ü/ and / u̇ /. Explain that these sounds have different spellings. The /ü/ can be spelled *oo, ew, u_e, ue, u, ui,* and *ou,* and the / u̇ / can be spelled *oo* and *ou.* Display these **Word-Building Cards** one at a time: *ing, less, ly, out, un.* On the board, write the following syllables: *loom, grew, rude, due, fruit, through, cook.* Model sounding out each syllable.

 We Do Have students chorally read each syllable. Repeat at varying speeds and in random order. Next, display the cards. Work with students to combine the Word-Building Cards and syllables on the board to form two-syllable words. Have students chorally read the words with the variant-vowel sounds: *looming, outgrew, rudely, undue, fruitless, throughout,* and *cookout.*

You Do Write other syllables on the board, such as *fool, re, suit, ful, foot, gloom, tune, new, ish, y, group, able, er, cook, ball.* Have students work with partners to build words using these syllables. Have partners make a list of their words.

PRACTICE WORDS WITH VARIANT VOWELS /ü/ AND /ů/

OBJECTIVES

CCSS Know and apply grade-level phonics and word analysis skills in decoding words. Decode multisyllable words. **RF.3.3c**

Use words with variant vowels /ü/ spelled *oo, ew, u_e, ue, u, ui, ou;* and /ů/ spelled *oo, ou.*

 I Do Remind students that they can use their knowledge of the variant vowels /ü/ and /ů/ to figure out how to read multisyllable words. Write *bedroom* on the board, and underline *oo.* Read the word aloud. Repeat for *corkscrew, pollute, suitcase, blueberry,* and *newspaper.* Write *scrapbook* on the board, and underline *oo.* Read the word aloud. Repeat for *couldn't.*

 We Do Write *classroom, crewcut, include, untrue, juicer,* and *childhood* on the board. Model how to decode the first word, then guide students as they read the remaining words. Help them divide each word into syllables using the syllable-scoop technique to help them read each syllable.

 You Do Afterward, point to the words in random order for students to chorally read.

ROOTS IN RELATED WORDS

OBJECTIVES

CCSS Use a known root word as a clue to the meaning of an unknown word with the same root (e.g., *company, companion*). **L.3.4c**

Decode words with related root words.

 I Do Remind students that related words share a base word known as a root word. Tell students they can use their knowledge of a root word to figure out the meaning of an unfamiliar word that has the same root. The words *textbook, bookworm, storybook,* and *booklet* are related words. They share the same root word, *book.*

 We Do Write and say the words *artist, artifact,* and *artistic.* Have students repeat the words. Model finding the root word *art* in all of the words. Give the following examples of words with the root word *star: starlight, starless, starring,* and *starfish.* With students, find the root word and decode the words, dividing multisyllable words into their syllables.

 You Do Afterward, write the words *twilight, sunlight, lightly; backseat, backache, backstage* on the board. Have students identify the common root word in each set of related words and then say each word.

ELL ENGLISH LANGUAGE LEARNERS

For the students who need **phonics, decoding,** and **fluency** practice, use scaffolding methods as necessary to ensure students understand the meaning of the words. Refer to the **Language Transfers Handbook** for phonics elements that may not transfer in students' native languages.

Approaching Level

Vocabulary

REVIEW HIGH-FREQUENCY WORDS

TIER 2

OBJECTIVES

 Use conventional spelling for high-frequency and other studied words and for adding suffixes to base words (e.g., *sitting, smiled, cries, happiness*). **L.3.2e**

Review high-frequency words.

 I Do   Use **Word Cards** 121–130. Display one word at a time, following the routine:

Display the word. Read the word. Then spell the word.

 We Do   Ask students to state the word and spell the word with you. Model using the word in a sentence, and have students repeat after you.

 You Do   Display the word. Ask students to say the word and then spell it. When completed, quickly flip through the word card set as students chorally read the words. Provide opportunities for students to use the words in speaking and writing. For example, provide sentence starters such as *The students got ____ of their work done early.* Have students write each word in their **Writer's Notebook.**

REVIEW VOCABULARY WORDS

TIER 2

OBJECTIVES

 Acquire and use accurately grade-appropriate conversational, general academic, and domain-specific words and phrases, including those that signal spatial and temporal relationships (e.g., *After dinner that night we went looking for them*). **L.3.6**

I Do   Display each **Visual Vocabulary Card** and state the word. Explain how the photograph illustrates the word. State the example sentence and repeat the word.

 We Do   Point to the word on the card and read the word with students. Ask them to repeat the word. Engage students in structured partner talk about the image as prompted on the back of the vocabulary card.

 You Do   Display each visual in random order, hiding the word. Have students match the definitions and context sentences of the words to the visuals displayed. Then ask students to complete **Approaching Reproducibles** page 151.

ANSWER CHOICE QUESTIONS

OBJECTIVES

 Demonstrate understanding of word relationships and nuances in word meanings. Identify real-life connections between words and their use (e.g., describe people who are *friendly* or *helpful*). **L.3.5b**

Answer questions to show understanding of meanings of words.

 Display the *aroma* **Visual Vocabulary Card** and say the word aloud. Model answering the question: *Do you smell or see an* aroma*?* Point out that the word *aroma* refers to a pleasant smell.

 Display the vocabulary card for *healthful*. Say the word aloud and define it. With students, answer the question: *Is a banana or candy more* healthful*?*

 Display the remaining cards one at a time, and read each question below aloud. Have students answer the questions.

Do you expect a ballet dancer or a farmer to be graceful*?*

When a speaker is interrupted*, has she stopped speaking or started speaking?*

Do you consider a muffin or a dictionary flavorful*?*

Does variety *mean that you have one choice or many choices?*

Do you eat or listen to something luscious*?*

ROOT WORDS

OBJECTIVES

 Use a known root word as a clue to the meaning of an unknown word with the same root (e.g., *company, companion*). **L.3.4c**

Use root words as clues to longer words with the same root words.

 Display the Comprehension and Fluency passage on **Approaching Reproducibles** pages 153–154. Read aloud the first page. Point to the word *powerful*. Explain to students that they can look for a root word to figure out the meaning of an unfamiliar word.

Think Aloud I see clues that might help me figure out the meaning of *powerful*. I think the root word is *power*. I know *power* means "strength" or "influence." The suffix *-ful* means "full of." From these clues, I think the turtle is full of strength or has a lot of influence.

Write the definition of the word *powerful*.

 Have students point to the word *kindness*. With students, discuss how to find and use the root word to figure out the meaning of the word. Write the definition of the word.

 Have students find the meaning of *admiration* and *disbelief* using root words as clues.

→ Approaching Level

Comprehension

FLUENCY

 OBJECTIVES
Read on-level prose and poetry orally with accuracy, appropriate rate, and expression on successive readings. **RF.3.4b**

Read fluently with good expression.

 I Do Tell students that part of reading with expression is putting an emphasis on certain words to show emotion and understanding. Read the first three paragraphs of the Comprehension and Fluency passage on **Approaching Reproducibles** pages 153–154. Remind students that reading with expression will help them understand what they are reading.

 We Do Read the rest of the page aloud, and have students repeat each sentence after you using the same expression. Explain that you emphasized certain words and phrases to show that they are important.

 You Do Have partners take turns reading sentences from the Reproducibles passage. Remind students to show emotion by emphasizing certain words. Provide corrective feedback by modeling proper fluency.

IDENTIFY THE NARRATOR

 OBJECTIVES
Distinguish their own point of view from that of the narrator or those of the characters. **RL.3.6**

Identify the narrator of a story.

 I Do Explain that sometimes a character in a story is also the narrator telling the story in his or her own words. A first-person narrator uses the pronouns *I, me,* and *my* to tell what he or she sees and does. Sometimes, the story is told by a narrator who is not a character in the story. In this case, the story is told from the third-person point of view. Display these sentences: *I tried out for the soccer team. Deanna tried out for the soccer team.* Tell students that the first sentence is by a first-person narrator who uses the pronoun *I.* The second sentence is by a third-person narrator who is not a character.

 We Do Read the first page of the Comprehension and Fluency passage in the **Approaching Reproducibles.** Ask: *Who is the fisherman's helper? Who tells us about him? Is the narrator a character in the story?* Help students identify the narrator.

 You Do Have students read the rest of the passage. They should write down details about the characters in the story. Have students explain how they know the narrator is not a character in the story.

REVIEW POINT OF VIEW

OBJECTIVES

 Distinguish their own point of view from that of the narrator or those of the characters. **RL.3.6**

Identify the narrator's point of view.

 I Do Remind students that a narrator has thoughts and feelings about the events and characters in a story. This is the narrator's point of view. Tell students to look for details that show what the narrator thinks about the characters and events in the story.

We Do Read the first page of the Comprehension and Fluency passage in the **Approaching Reproducibles** together. Pause to identify the narrator's point of view in the story. Model how to decide which details show the narrator's thoughts and feelings about characters and events in the story. *How does the fisherman's helper feel about the way the turtle is treated? Which details show his feelings? What does the narrator think about the turtle? Which details support what the narrator thinks?*

 You Do Ask students to read the rest of the selection. Have students discuss whether they would make the same choices as the fisherman's helper.

SELF-SELECTED READING

OBJECTIVES

Ask and answer questions to demonstrate understanding of a text, referring explicitly to the text as the basis for answers. **RL.3.1**

Distinguish their own point of view from that of the narrator or those of the characters. **RL.3.6**

Identify the narrator's point of view.

Read Independently

Have students choose a folktale for sustained silent reading. Tell students that a folktale usually has a lesson or message. Remind them that:

- point of view is the narrator's or characters' feelings about story events and characters. They might be different from the reader's point of view.

- as they read, students should ask themselves questions about sections in the passage they do not understand. Asking questions and rereading to find the answers will help them understand the story and its characters.

Read Purposefully

Have students record important details about the narrator's point of view in Graphic Organizer 146 as they read independently. After they finish, they can conduct a Book Talk, each telling about the book they read.

- Students should share their organizers and answer these questions: *Who is the narrator? What does the narrator think of the events and characters? Which details show what the narrator thinks?*

- They should discuss questions they asked about the folktale and share where they found answers to their questions.

On Level

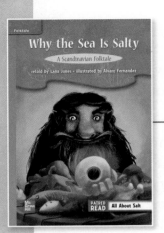

Lexile 570
TextEvaluator™ 29

___

OBJECTIVES

CCSS Ask and answer questions to demonstrate understanding of a text, referring explicitly to the text as the basis for the answers. **RL.3.1**

CCSS Distinguish their own point of view from that of the narrator or those of the characters. **RL.3.6**

• Use root words to determine the meanings of words.

• Identify the narrator's point of view.

___

ACADEMIC LANGUAGE
ask, answer questions, point of view, folktale, root words, directions

Leveled Reader:
Why the Sea Is Salty

Before Reading

Preview and Predict

Have students read the Essential Question. Then have them read the title and table of contents of *Why the Sea Is Salty*. Have students predict what lesson or message they might learn in this story.

Review Genre: Folktale

Review with students that a folktale is a fictional story in which the main character must find a clever way to solve a problem. It also contains a lesson or message. As they preview *Why the Sea Is Salty*, have students identify features of a folktale.

During Reading

Close Reading

Note Taking Have students use their graphic organizer as they read.

Pages 2–5 *Is the narrator inside or outside the story?* (outside) *Who is the narrator?* (the author of the story) *What is the poor brother's problem in the beginning of the story?* (His crops have failed and he has run out of food.) *What words show how the narrator feels about the rich brother?* (*mean and greedy*) *Why might he think this way?* (because the rich man will not help his brother)

Pages 6–7 *Define* handful *on page 6 to a partner.* ("a quantity of something that would fill a hand") *How does the root word help you define the word?* (I know that the root word is *hand,* and I can find the meaning of the suffix *–ful,* which means "full of.")

Pages 8–9 *Do you think the poor man makes the right choice by asking for the millstone?* (yes) *How can you tell?* (Hiysi says it is a wise choice. The millstone can magically give him any food his heart desires.)

Pages 10–12 *What does the rich man do when his brother tries to explain what instructions to give the millstone?* (He interrupts him.) *What does the poor man offer to do in the end?* (He offers to lend him the millstone.) *What word tells you how he feels about lending the millstone?* (*gladly*) *Talk to a partner about what you think of the two brothers.*

Go Digital

Leveled Readers

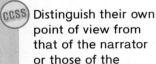

Fill in the Graphic Organizer

Pages 13–15 *What is the consequence of the rich man interrupting his brother's instructions?* (He cannot turn off the millstone.)

Summarize to a partner how this folktale explains why the sea is salty. (The rich brother never shuts down the millstone after his boat grows heavy. So the millstone continues to produce salt that fills the sea.)

After Reading

Respond to Reading Revisit the Essential Question, and ask students to complete the Text Evidence questions on page 16.

Analytical Writing **Write About Reading** Make sure students have picked a character that is already in the story to discuss a different point of view, and make sure that the students are correctly retelling the main details of the story.

Fluency: Expression

Model Model reading page 2 with proper expression. Next, reread the page aloud, and have students read along with you.

Apply Have students practice reading with a partner.

PAIRED READ

"All About Salt"

Make Connections:
Write About It *Analytical Writing*

Before reading, have students note that the genre of this text is directions, which means that it instructs readers how to do something. Then discuss the Essential Question.

After reading, have students write down and share distinctions between fact and fiction in *Why the Sea Is Salty* and "All About Salt."

Leveled Reader

✎ *Analytical Writing*

COMPARE TEXTS

- Have students use text evidence to compare what they learned from the folktale and directions.

Literature Circles

Ask students to conduct a literature circle using the Thinkmark questions to guide the discussion. You may wish to have a whole-class discussion on positive choices students have made and what happened as a result.

Level Up

Level-up lessons available online.

IF students read the On Level fluently and answered the questions

THEN pair them with students who have proficiently read the Beyond Level and have on-level students

- partner-read the Beyond Level main selection.
- list difficult words and look them up with a partner.

A C T Access Complex Text

The Beyond Level challenges students by including more **domain-specific words** and **complex sentence structures**.

On Level

Vocabulary

REVIEW VOCABULARY WORDS

OBJECTIVES

 Acquire and use accurately grade-appropriate conversational, general academic, and domain-specific words and phrases, including those that signal spatial and temporal relationships (e.g., *After dinner that night we went looking for them*). **L.3.6**

 I Do Use the **Visual Vocabulary Cards** to review key selection words *aroma, expect, flavorful, graceful, healthful, interrupted, luscious,* and *variety.* Point to each word, read it aloud, and have students chorally repeat it.

 We Do Ask these questions, and help students respond and explain their answers.
- Which *aromas* make you think of breakfast?
- How do you prepare a *healthful* meal?
- What do you *expect* to do this weekend?

 You Do Have student pairs respond to these questions and explain their answers.
- Do you like to be *interrupted* when you are speaking?
- Do you want to see a lot of *variety* when you shop for clothes?
- How do you react when you taste something that is not *flavorful?*

ROOT WORDS

OBJECTIVES

 Use a known root word as a clue to the meaning of an unknown word with the same root (e.g., *company, companion*). **L.3.4c**

 I Do Remind students that they can figure out the meaning of an unknown word by looking for its root word, which is the simplest form of a word. Use the Comprehension and Fluency passage on **Your Turn Practice Book** pages 153–154 to figure out the meaning of *powerful.*

Think Aloud I know that *power* is the root word of *powerful. Power* means "strength" or "influence." The suffix *-ful* means "full of." So, I think the turtle in the story is full of strength or has a lot of influence.

 We Do Have students continue reading the passage. When they read *inspiration,* have them figure out its definition by looking at the root word *inspire.*

 You Do As they continue to read, have students work in pairs to determine the meanings of the words *beautiful* and *calmly* using their root words.

Comprehension

REVIEW POINT OF VIEW

OBJECTIVES

 Distinguish their own point of view from that of the narrator or those of the characters. **RL.3.6**

Identify the narrator's point of view.

I Do Remind students that the narrator has thoughts and feelings about events and characters in a story. Those are the narrator's point of view. Tell students to look for details that reveal what the narrator thinks about the characters and events in the story.

We Do Have a volunteer read the first page of the Comprehension and Fluency passage on **Your Turn Practice Book** pages 153–154. Have students orally list details about how the narrator feels about the fisherman's helper, the turtle, and the events of the story.

You Do Have partners identify details that show how the narrator's feelings about the fisherman's helper change in the story. Then have students discuss what they think of the fisherman's helper's actions.

SELF-SELECTED READING

OBJECTIVES

 Ask and answer questions to demonstrate understanding of a text, referring explicitly to the text as the basis for the answer. **RL.3.1**

 Distinguish their own point of view from that of the narrator or those of the characters. **RL.3.6**

Identify the narrator's point of view.

Read Independently

Have students choose a folktale for sustained silent reading. Remind students that a folktale usually has a message or lesson.

- Before they read, have students preview the book, reading the title and viewing the front and back cover.

- As students read, remind them to ask questions about sections they do not understand and reread to find the answers.

Read Purposefully

Encourage students to read different folktales from various cultures.

- As students read, have them fill in key details about the narrator's point of view in **Graphic Organizer 146.**

- They can use their organizers to help them identify the narrator and summarize his or her point of view of the characters and events.

- Have students share questions they asked and answered about their folktale.

→ Beyond Level

Leveled Reader:
Finn MacCool and the Salmon of Knowledge

Go
Digital

Lexile 780
TextEvaluator 39

Leveled Readers

OBJECTIVES

 CCSS Ask and answer questions to demonstrate understanding of a text, referring explicitly to the text as the basis for the answers. **RL.3.1**

CCSS Distinguish their own point of view from that of the narrator or those of the characters. **RL.3.6**

• Use root words to determine the meanings of words.

• Identify the narrator's point of view.

ACADEMIC LANGUAGE

ask, answer questions, point of view, folktale, directions, root words

Before Reading

Preview and Predict

Have students read the Essential Question. Then have them read the title and table of contents of *Finn MacCool and the Salmon of Knowledge*. Have students predict what lesson or message they might learn in this story.

Review Genre: Folktale

Review with students that a folktale is a fictional story in which the main character must find a clever way to solve a problem. It also contains a lesson or message. As they preview *Finn MacCool and the Salmon of Knowledge*, have students identify features of a folktale.

During Reading

Close Reading

Note Taking Ask students to use their graphic organizer as they read.

Pages 2–5 *Who is the narrator of the story?* (the author) *What is his point of view of how Finn gained wisdom?* (He thinks we are not the ones to decide why or how the hero made his choices.) *What is Finn's problem in the beginning of the story?* (He does not have wisdom, nor can he tell a story or sing a song.)

Pages 6–8 *What makes Finn a difficult student to teach?* (He has too much energy. He would rather be out hunting or playing.) *Ask a partner a question about Chapter 2. Then together find the answer in the text.*

Pages 9–11 *What is the root word of* flavorful *on page 9, and how does it help you define the word?* (*Flavor* means "the way something tastes;" 'ful means "full of;" so *flavorful* means "full of flavor.")
What directives does Finnegas give Finn about how to prepare the salmon? Why? (Finn is to keep the fish from blistering because the knowledge that Finnegas is looking for might leak out of a popped blister; and Finn is not to eat any part of the fish for the same reason.)

Fill in the Graphic Organizer

Pages 12–15 *What are the consequences of Finn tasting of the fish?* (He gains all of the knowledge and there is none left for anyone else.) *What does it mean that to seek knowledge Finn has* only to place his thumb in his mouth? (Possible Response: It reminds him of his special wisdom.)

Talk to a partner about whether or not you agree with the narrator when, before telling Finn's story, he says that we are not to decide the reasons for Finn's choices.

After Reading

Respond to Reading Revisit the Essential Question, and ask students to complete the Text Evidence questions on page 16.

Analytical Writing **Write About Reading** Make sure students write the story from Finnegas's point of view and that their story matches up with the main details from the story or the part of the story the character is in.

Fluency: Expression

Model Model reading page 4 with proper expression. Next, reread the page aloud, and have students read along with you.

Apply Have students practice reading with a partner.

PAIRED READ

Leveled Reader

"Brain Food"

Make Connections: Write About It *Analytical Writing*

Before reading, have students note that the genre of this text is directions, which means that it instructs readers how to do something. Then discuss the Essential Question.

After reading, have students write about connections between the effects of the fish in *Finn MacCool and the Salmon of Knowledge* and "Brain Food."

Analytical Writing

COMPARE TEXTS

- Have students use text evidence to compare what they learned from the folktale and directions.

Literature Circles

Ask students to conduct a literature circle using the Thinkmark questions to guide the discussion. You may wish to have a whole-class discussion on the choices students have made and what happened as a result.

Gifted and Talented

Synthesize Challenge students to use one or more of the characters from *Finn MacCool and the Salmon of Wisdom* to write a fictional story that explains something in nature. Have students choose a natural phenomenon and explain how it occurred. Students can include new characters in their story. Ask volunteers to share their stories with the class.

→ **Beyond Level**

Vocabulary

REVIEW DOMAIN-SPECIFIC WORDS

OBJECTIVES

 Produce simple, compound, and complex sentences. **L.3.1i**

Review and use domain-specific vocabulary words.

Model Use the **Visual Vocabulary Cards** to review the meanings of the words *flavorful* and *luscious*. Write sentences on the board using the words.

Write the words *wisdom* and *studies* on the board, and discuss their definitions with students. Then help students write sentences using these words.

Apply Have students work in pairs to discuss the definitions of the words *nutritious* and *energy*. Then have partners write sentences using the words.

ROOT WORDS

OBJECTIVES

 Use a known root word as a clue to the meaning of an unknown word with the same root. (e.g., *company*, *companion*). **L.3.4c**

Model Read aloud the first page of the Comprehension and Fluency passage on **Beyond Reproducibles** pages 153–154.

Think Aloud I want to know what the word *powerful* means. I know that the root word of *powerful* is *power*. *Power* means "strength" or "influence." I also know that the suffix *-ful* means "full of." So I can guess that the turtle in the story is full of strength or has a lot of influence.

With students, read the rest of the page. Help them figure out the meaning of *inspiration* using the root word *inspire*.

Apply Have pairs of students read the rest of the passage. Have them use root words to determine the meanings of *kindness*, *disbelief*, *admiration*, and *appreciation*.

 Analyze Using a dictionary, have partners explain the differences between *inspiration*, *expire*, and *perspire*. Explain to students that the Latin root of *inspire* is *spir*, which means "to breathe." Provide students with definitions for the Latin affixes: *per-* means "through," *ex-* means "out of" or "from," *-in* means "in," *-ation* means "action."

Comprehension

REVIEW POINT OF VIEW

OBJECTIVES

 Distinguish their own point of view from that of the narrator or those of the characters. **RL.3.6**

Identify the narrator's point of view.

 Model Remind students that a narrator has thoughts or feelings about events and characters in a story. This is the narrator's point of view. He or she expresses a point of view by describing what a character says, does, and thinks.

Have students read the first page of the Comprehension and Fluency passage of **Beyond Reproducibles** pages 153–154. Ask open-ended questions to facilitate discussion, such as *What is the narrator's point of view of the turtle? Of the fisherman's helper? Which details show the point of view?* Students should support their responses with details from the text.

Apply Have students identify important details about the narrator's point of view as they independently fill in **Graphic Organizer 146**. Have partners use their work to determine how the narrator's feelings about the fisherman's helper change in the story. Then have students discuss what they think of the fisherman's helper's actions.

SELF-SELECTED READING

OBJECTIVES

 Ask and answer questions to demonstrate understanding of a text, referring explicitly to the text as the basis for the answer. **RL.3.1**

 Distinguish their own point of view from that of the narrator or those of the characters. **RL.3.6**

Identify the narrator's point of view.

Read Independently

Have students choose a folktale for sustained silent reading. Remind students that a folktale is a short story that has a problem for the character to solve. It usually has a message or lesson.

- As students read, have them fill in **Graphic Organizer 146**.
- Remind them to ask questions if they do not understand something they have read. Tell students to reread a section to find the answers.

Read Purposefully

Encourage students to keep a reading journal. Ask them to read different folktales from various cultures.

- Students can write summaries of the folktales in their journals.
- Have students share their reactions to the books with classmates.

 Independent Study Challenge students to discuss how their folktales relate to the weekly theme of making good choices. Ask students to compare the message or lesson in each folktale.

→ English Language Learners

Reading/Writing Workshop

 OBJECTIVES
Distinguish their own point of view from that of the narrator or those of the characters. **RL.3.6**

• Ask and answer questions to increase understanding of a text.

• Use root words to determine the meanings of words.

LANGUAGE OBJECTIVE

Identify the narrator's point of view.

ACADEMIC LANGUAGE
ask, answer questions, point of view, root words, suffix, folktale

Shared Read
Nail Soup

Go Digital

View "Nail Soup"

Before Reading

Build Background

Read the Essential Question: What choices are good for us?

• Explain the meaning of the Essential Question. Show pictures of a bowl of cereal or oatmeal with a banana and a frosted donut to the class. *What is your choice of breakfast? Which choice is better for your health?*

• **Model an answer:** *The donut looks tasty, but I know that the cereal is better for me. It will give me a healthy start to the day.*

• Ask students a question that ties the Essential Question to their own background knowledge: *Think about a choice you made today. It could be about doing your homework or what to have for lunch. Work with a partner to come up with a list of reasons about why you made good choices.* Call on several pairs to show their lists.

During Reading

Interactive-Question Response

• Ask questions that help students understand the meaning of the text after each paragraph.

• Reinforce the meanings of key vocabulary.

• Ask students questions that require them to use key vocabulary.

• Reinforce strategies and skills of the week by modeling.

Page 263

Paragraph 1

Reread paragraph 1 to find out who the characters are and what the setting is, or where the story takes place. *We are introduced to two characters, a boy and his Papa.*

Describe the setting. (There is a road, and around are fields with vegetables.)

Paragraphs 2–3

Explain and Model Asking and Answering Questions *When I read a story for the first time, I may have questions about what happened. I wonder why Papa is knocking on the farmhouse door. Let's look at what we can find in the story to answer the question. What problem does the narrator, the boy, have?* (He is hungry.) *How does he think his father can help?* (His father will find them a meal.) *The father knocks on the door to find or ask for food. Let's read on to find out what happens.*

Paragraph 6

Explain and Model Root Words *A root word is the smallest form of a word. The root of* flavorful *is* flavor. Flavor *means "taste." Demonstrate the meaning of the word. The suffix, -ful, means "full of." Use this information to figure out what* flavorful *means.* ("full of taste or flavor")

Paragraph 7

Papa asks for a cup of water to make soup with a nail. Do the husband and wife believe that nail soup is possible? (no) *Have students point to* overwhelmed *in the story.* Overwhelmed *means "was stronger than."*

What does the author mean by saying the husband's "curiosity overwhelmed him"? (His curiosity was stronger than his doubts. He wants to see if Papa can make nail soup.)

Page 264

Paragraph 1

Papa begins to make the nail soup. What does the nail look like? (It is long and crooked.)

What does graceful *mean?* ("full of grace") *Demonstrate a graceful motion with a partner.*

Paragraph 3

Model Point of View *The boy is the narrator of this story. What words give the boy's point of view of his father?* (clever, charming)

Paragraph 4

How does Papa get more water for the soup? (He says it is impolite for him to eat alone.)

Page 265

Paragraphs 1–2

Have students choral-read the paragraphs. Have students point to the word *interrupted. What does* interrupted *mean?* Have students demonstrate.

Paragraph 7

How does Papa fool the man and woman into making a delicious soup? (He gets them to give some of their food to make the soup.) *What did the man and woman learn because of the soup?* (They can all eat well if they share.) *Discuss how you think they will act differently in the future.*

After Reading

Make Connections

- Review the Essential Question: What choices are good for us?
- Make text connections.
- Have students complete the **ELL Reproducibles** pages 153–155.

English Language Learners

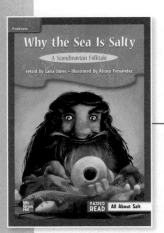

Lexile 510
TextEvaluator™ 11

OBJECTIVES
(CCSS) Distinguish their own point of view from that of the narrator or those of the characters. **RL.3.6**

• Ask and answer questions to increase understanding of a text.

• Use root words to determine the meanings of words.

LANGUAGE OBJECTIVE
Identify the narrator's point of view.

ACADEMIC LANGUAGE
ask, answer questions, point of view, folktale, root words, directions

Leveled Reader:
Why the Sea Is Salty

Before Reading

Preview

• Read the Essential Question: What choices are good for us?

• Refer to Smart Choices: *Which choice is better for your health?*

• Preview *Why the Sea Is Salty* and "All About Salt": *Let's read about salt and the ways we have learned about it.*

Vocabulary

Use the **Visual Vocabulary Cards** to preteach the ELL vocabulary: *grinding, preserve.* Use the routine found on the cards. Point out the cognate: *preservar.*

During Reading

Interactive Question-Response

Note Taking Have students use the graphic organizer on **ELL Reproducibles** page 152 as you read. Ask the following questions after reading each section. Use visuals or pictures to define key vocabulary.

Pages 2–5 *The narrator is not a character in the story. The narrator of this story is the author. What is her point of view of the two brothers?* (The rich brother is mean, and the poor brother is kind.) *What is the poor brother's problem in the beginning of the story?* (His crops have failed, and he has no more food.) *Does his brother give him food?* (no) *Ask a question about what the brother does instead, then look for the answer in the story.* (Possible Question and Answer: What does the rich man decide to do? He decides to teach his brother a lesson.) *Talk to a partner about what you think of the rich brother's actions so far.*

Pages 6–7 *On page 6, Hiysi says he is going to give* something *to the poor man.* Thing *is the root word. Some means "that is not known." So Hiysi is going to give the man a thing but does not tell what the thing is right away. What does Hiysi offer the poor man?* (gold, jewels)

Pages 8–9 *Do you think the poor man makes the right choice by asking for the millstone?* (yes) *How can you tell?* Have students choral read the first two sentences of what Hiysi says on page 9. *How is the millstone magical?* (It can give you any food you want.)

Go Digital

Leveled Readers

Details
↓
Point of View

Fill in the Graphic Organizer

Pages 10–12 *On page 12, the rich man interrupts his brother while he is speaking. What was the brother trying to tell him?* (Possible Response: He was trying to tell him how the millstone works.)

Pages 13–15 *What mistake does the rich man realize he has made?* (He did not get the directions for how to use the millstone.) *What are the consequences?* (He cannot stop the millstone. That is how the sea becomes salty.)

After Reading

Respond to Reading Help students complete the graphic organizer. Revisit the Essential Question. Have student pairs summarize and answer the Text Evidence questions. Support students as necessary, and review all responses as a group.

Write About Reading Make sure the students tell the story from the rich man's point of view and that it matches up with the original story.

Fluency: Expression

Model Model reading page 2 with proper expression. Next, reread the page aloud, and have students read along with you.

Apply Have students practice reading with a partner.

PAIRED READ

"All About Salt"

Make Connections: Write About It *Analytical Writing*

Before reading, have students note that the genre of this text is directions, which means that it instructs readers how to do something. Then discuss the Essential Question.

After reading, have students write about distinctions between fact and fiction in *Why the Sea Is Salty* and "All About Salt."

Leveled Reader

Analytical Writing

COMPARE TEXTS

• Have students use text evidence to compare what they learned from the folktale and directions.

Literature Circles

Ask students to conduct a literature circle using the Thinkmark questions to guide the discussion. You may wish to have a whole-class discussion on positive choices students have made and what happened as a result.

Level Up

Level-up lessons available online.

IF students read the **ELL Level** fluently and answered the questions

THEN pair them with students who have proficiently read **On Level** and have ELL students

• echo-read the **On Level** main selection with their partner.

• list difficult words and discuss them with their partner.

A C T Access Complex Text

The **On Level** challenges students by including more **domain-specific words** and **complex sentence structures**.

→ English Language Learners

Vocabulary

PRETEACH VOCABULARY

OBJECTIVES

CCSS Acquire and use accurately grade-appropriate conversational, general academic, and domain-specific words and phrases, including those that signal spatial and temporal relationships (e.g., *After dinner that night we went looking for them*). **L.3.6**

LANGUAGE OBJECTIVE

Use vocabulary words.

 Preteach vocabulary from "Nail Soup," following the Vocabulary Routine on the **Visual Vocabulary Cards** for words *aroma, expect, variety, healthful, luscious, interrupted, graceful,* and *flavorful.*

 After completing the Vocabulary Routine for each word, point to the word on the Visual Vocabulary Card, and read the word with students. Have students repeat the word.

 Have students work with a partner to define three words and draw pictures that show what each word means. Have pairs read their definitions aloud.

Beginning	Intermediate	Advanced/High
Help students write the definitions correctly and read them aloud.	Have students write the definitions using complete sentences.	Challenge students to write five definitions using complete sentences.

REVIEW VOCABULARY

OBJECTIVES

CCSS Acquire and use accurately grade-appropriate conversational, general academic, and domain-specific words and phrases, including those that signal spatial and temporal relationships. **L.3.6**

LANGUAGE OBJECTIVE

Use vocabulary words.

 Review vocabulary words from the previous week. The words can be reviewed over a few days. Read each word aloud pointing to the word on the **Visual Vocabulary Card**. Have students repeat after you. Act out two of the words using gestures or actions.

 Have students guess the definitions of the words you have acted out. Give students additional clues. Write their responses on the board.

 In pairs, have students think of ways to act out three or more words. Help them with the definitions, and suggest appropriate gestures or actions. Then have them act out the meaning of the words for the class.

Beginning	Intermediate	Advanced/High
Help students think of ways to act out two words.	Have students act out three or more words.	Have students act out each word.

ROOT WORDS

CCSS

OBJECTIVES

Use a known root word as a clue to the meaning of an unknown word with the same root (e.g., *company, companion*). **L.3.4c**

LANGUAGE OBJECTIVE

Determine the meaning of words using their root words.

 I Do Read aloud page 263 of "Nail Soup" while students follow along. Point to the word *flavorful*. Explain that root words can help them figure out the meaning of a word they do not know, such as *flavorful*. Remind students that a root word is the simplest form of a word.

Think Aloud I am not sure what *flavorful* means, but the root word *flavor* can help me figure out the meaning. I know that *flavor* means "taste." I also know that *-ful* means "full of." According to the text, people really liked the soup. From these clues, I think *flavorful* means "tasty."

We Do Have students point to the word *graceful* on page 264. Find the root word with students. Write the definition of the word on the board.

You Do In pairs, have students write a definition for *healthful* on page 265 using the root word.

Beginning	Intermediate	Advanced/High
Help students find the word and write its meaning using its root word and suffix.	Have students find the word and define it using a complete sentence.	Have students define the word and use it in a sentence.

ADDITIONAL VOCABULARY

CCSS

OBJECTIVES

Produce simple, compound, and complex sentences. **L.3.1i**

Discuss concept and high-frequency words.

LANGUAGE OBJECTIVE

Use concept and high-frequency words.

 I Do List academic language and high-frequency words from "Nail Soup": *nutritious, vegetables;* and *Why the Sea Is Salty: amount, me, more, my.* Define each word for students: *A healthful meal is* nutritious.

We Do Model using the word *more* for students in a sentence: *The cook put* more *vegetables in the soup. The artist wants to use* more *colors in her painting.* Next, provide sentence frames and complete them with students: *We had _____ than one tropical fish to choose from at the pet store.*

 You Do Have pairs make up questions using the words *me, more,* or *my* and share them with the class.

Beginning	Intermediate	Advanced/High
Help students write a sentence using *me, more,* or *my*.	Have students write sentences using *me, more,* and *my*.	Have students write sentences using all of the words.

English Language Learners
Writing/Spelling

WRITING TRAIT: SHOW FEELINGS

OBJECTIVES

 Use dialogue and descriptions of actions, thoughts, and feelings to develop experiences and events or show the response of characters to situations. **W.3.3b**

Include details that show feelings.

LANGUAGE OBJECTIVE

Include details that show feelings.

 I Do Explain that good writers use their own voice in writing. It can be by describing characters' feelings. Read the Student Model passage aloud as students follow along. Identify details that show the couple's feelings.

 We Do Read aloud a passage from "Nail Soup" as students follow along. Help them find details that show how Erik feels. Remind students to use their voice when writing to show how they feel.

 You Do Have students write three sentences about a choice they have made that makes them proud. Tell them to use their own voice to show how they feel about their choice. Edit students' writing, and have them revise.

Beginning	Intermediate	Advanced/High
Have students copy the edited sentences.	Have students revise, adding details that show their feelings.	Have students revise to add details showing feelings and edit for errors.

SPELL WORDS WITH VARIANT VOWELS

OBJECTIVES

 Use spelling patterns and generalizations (e.g., word families, position-based spellings, syllable patterns, ending rules, meaningful word parts) in writing words. **L.3.2f**

LANGUAGE OBJECTIVE

Spell words with variant vowels /ü/: oo, ew, u_e, ue, u, ui, ou; and /ů/: oo, ou.

 I Do Read aloud the Spelling Words on page T34, modeling variant vowels /ü/ and /ů/. Explain that variant vowel /ü/ can be spelled oo, ew, u_e, ue, u, ui, and ou. Variant vowel /ů/ can be spelled oo and ou.

 We Do Read the Dictation Sentences on page T35 aloud for students. With each sentence, read the underlined word slowly, segmenting it into syllables. Have students repeat after you and write the word.

 You Do Display the words. Have students exchange their list with a partner to check the spelling and write the words correctly.

Beginning	Intermediate	Advanced/High
Have students copy the words with correct spelling and say the words aloud.	Have students circle the variant-vowel spellings in their corrected words.	After students correct their words, have them write sentences with six words.

Grammar

LINKING VERBS

OBJECTIVES

 Explain the function of nouns, pronouns, verbs, adjectives, and adverbs in general and their functions in particular sentences. **L.3.1a**

 Form and use regular and irregular verbs. **L.3.1d**

Use linking verbs.

LANGUAGE OBJECTIVE

Write sentences.

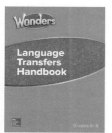

Language Transfers Handbook

The verb *to be* can be omitted with adjectives and prepositional phrases in Cantonese, Hmong, and Vietnamese. Students speaking these languages may say "They very happy together." Model correct usage in additional examples, and have students repeat.

I Do Remind students that an action verb tells what the subject of a sentence does. Write the sentence on the board, pointing out the action verb: *Allison* studies *for the test*. Tell students that a linking verb does not show action. A linking verb connects the subject to a noun or an adjective in the predicate. It tells what the subject is or is like. Explain that the most common linking verb is *to be*. Forms of *to be* are *am, is, are, was*, and *were*. Write the following sentence on the board, pointing out the linking verb: *Allison* is *my classmate*. Remind students that a linking verb must agree with its subject. The verbs *am, is*, and *was* go with singular nouns: *I* am *surprised*. The verbs *are* and *were* go with plural nouns: *We* were *surprised*.

We Do Write the sentences below on the board. Have a volunteer correct the linking verbs that do not agree with the subjects.

> The sisters was on vacation in Australia.
>
> Brendan and Molly is ready for school.
>
> We am preparing food for the party.
>
> I are ready to clean my room.

You Do Have pairs study the pictures in "Nail Soup" and come up with three sentences describing characters, objects, or places in the pictures using linking verbs. Students should include at least one example of a singular and plural subject and make sure each linking verb agrees with its subject.

Beginning	Intermediate	Advanced/High
Describe one picture in "Nail Soup" to students, using linking verbs in simple sentences. Ask: *What do you see?* Help them write the sentences.	Have students describe two pictures in "Nail Soup" using linking verbs in their descriptions. Have students use complete sentences.	Have students discuss all of the pictures in "Nail Soup" using linking verbs. Have them add descriptive words to their sentences.

For extra support, have students complete the activities in the **Grammar Practice Reproducibles** during the week, using the routine below:

- Explain the grammar skill.
- Model the first activity in the Grammar Practice Reproducibles.
- Have the whole group complete the next couple of activities, then the rest with a partner.
- Review the activities with correct answers.

PROGRESS MONITORING

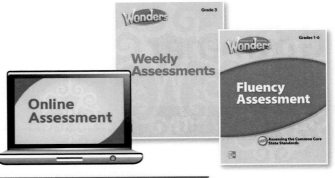

Unit 4 Week 1 Formal Assessment	Standards Covered	Component for Assessment
Text Evidence	RL.3.1	• *Selection Test* • *Weekly Assessment* • *Approaching-Level Weekly Assessment*
Point of View	RL.3.6	• *Weekly Assessment* • *Approaching-Level Weekly Assessment*
Root Words	L.3.4c	• *Selection Test* • *Weekly Assessment* • *Approaching-Level Weekly Assessment*
Writing About Text	W.3.8	*Weekly Assessment*

Unit 4 Week 1 Informal Assessment	Standards Covered	Component for Assessment
Research/Listening/ Collaborating	SL.3.1d, SL.3.2, SL.3.3	• *RWW* • *Teacher's Edition*
Oral Reading Fluency (ORF) Fluency Goal: 82–102 words correct per minute (WCPM) Accuracy Rate Goal: 95% or higher	RF.3.4a, RF.3.4b, RF.3.4c	*Fluency Assessment*

Using Assessment Results

Weekly Assessments Skills and Fluency	If . . .	Then . . .
COMPREHENSION	Students score below 70% . . .	. . . assign Lessons 37–39 on Point of View from the *Tier 2 Comprehension Intervention online PDFs*.
VOCABULARY	Students score below 70% . . .	. . . assign Lesson 155 on Roots from the *Tier 2 Vocabulary Intervention online PDFs*.
WRITING	Students score below "3" on constructed response . . .	. . . assign Lessons 37–39 and/or Write About Reading Lesson 194 from the *Tier 2 Comprehension Intervention online PDFs*.
FLUENCY	Students have a WCPM score of 75–81 . . .	. . . assign a lesson from Section 1,7,8,9 or 10 of the *Tier 2 Fluency Intervention online PDFs*.
	Students have a WCPM score of 0–74 . . .	. . . assign a lesson from Sections 2–6 of the *Tier 2 Fluency Intervention online PDFs*.

Using Weekly Data

Check your data Dashboard to verify assessment results and guide grouping decisions.

Data-Driven Recommendations

Response to Intervention

Use the appropriate sections of the *Placement and Diagnostic Assessment* as well as students' assessment results to designate students requiring:

 Intervention Online PDFs

 WonderWorks Intervention Program

Build Knowledge
Skills and Talents

 Essential Question:
How can you use what you know to help others?

Teach and Model
Close Reading and Writing

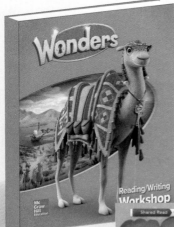

Reading/Writing Workshop

"The Impossible Pet Show," 276–279
Genre Realistic Fiction **Lexile** 600 ETS *TextEvaluator* 37

Practice and Apply
Close Reading and Writing

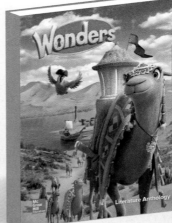

Literature Anthology

The Talented Clementine, 300–317
Genre Realistic Fiction **Lexile** 660 ETS *TextEvaluator* 36

Clementine and the Family Meeting, 320–325
Genre Realistic Fiction **Lexile** 630 ETS *TextEvaluator* 39

Differentiated Texts

APPROACHING
Lexile 470
ETS *TextEvaluator* 22

ON LEVEL
Lexile 530
ETS *TextEvaluator* 28

BEYOND
Lexile 700
ETS *TextEvaluator* 41

ELL
Lexile 440
ETS *TextEvaluator* 17

Leveled Readers

Extended Complex Texts

Stone Fox
Genre Fiction
Lexile 550

Make Way for Dyamonde Daniel
Genre Fiction
Lexile 620

Classroom Library

Student Outcomes

Close Reading of Complex Text
- Cite relevant evidence from text
- Identify point of view
- Ask and answer questions

RL.3.1, RL.3.6, SL.3.1c

Writing

Write to Sources
- Draw evidence from literature
- Write opinion texts
- Conduct extended research on frogs

Writing Process
- Draft and Revise a Fictional Narrative

W.3.1a, W.3.8, W.3.10

Speaking and Listening
- Engage in collaborative discussions about skills and talents
- Paraphrase portions of "Dancing *La Raspa*"
- Present information on skills and talents

SL.3.1c, SL.3.2, SL.3.3

Language Development

Conventions
- Use contractions with *not*

Vocabulary Acquisition
- Acquire and use academic vocabulary

achievement	apologized	attention	audience
confidence	embarrassed	realized	talents

- Use prefixes as clues to the meaning of a word

L.3.2f, L.3.4b, L.3.6, RL.3.4

Foundational Skills

Phonics/Word Study
- Plural words
- Vowel team syllables

Spelling Words

years	twins	trays	states	ashes
foxes	inches	flies	cities	ponies
bunches	alleys	lunches	cherries	daisies

Fluency
- Phrasing

RF.3.3c, RF.3.4a, RF.3.4b, RF.3.4c

Professional Development
- See lessons in action in real classrooms.
- Get expert advice on instructional practices.
- Collaborate with other teachers.
- Access PLC Resources.

Go Digital! www.connected.mcgraw-hill.com.

INSTRUCTIONAL PATH

1 ## Talk About Skills and Talents

Guide students in collaborative conversations.

Discuss the essential question: *How can you use what you know to help others?*

Develop academic language.

Listen to "Dancing *La Raspa*" and discuss the story.

2

Read "The Impossible Pet Show"

Model close reading with a short complex text.

Read

"The Impossible Pet Show" to learn how a boy discovers his hidden talent by trying something new, citing text evidence to answer text-dependent questions.

Reread

"The Impossible Pet Show" to analyze text, craft, and structure, citing text evidence.

3 ## Write About "The Impossible Pet Show"

Model writing to a source.

Analyze a short response student model.

Use text evidence from close reading to write to a source.

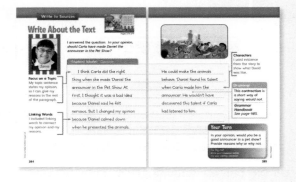

4 Read and Write About *The Talented Clementine*

Practice and apply close reading of the anchor text.

The Talented Clementine to learn how Clementine finds her special talent.

Reread

The Talented Clementine and use text evidence to understand how the author uses text, craft, and structure to develop a deeper understanding of the story.

Write a short response about *The Talented Clementine.*

Integrate

Information about the plot, setting, and theme in the two stories..

Write to Two Sources, citing text evidence from *The Talented Clementine* and "Clementine and the Family Meeting"

5 Independent Partner Work

Gradual release of support to independent work.

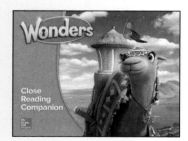

- Text-Dependent Questions
- Scaffolded Partner Work
  Talk with a Partner
  Cite Text Evidence
  Complete a sentence frame.
- Guided Text Annotation

6 Integrate Knowledge and Ideas

Connect Texts

Text to Text Discuss how each of the texts answers the question: How can you use what you know to help others?

Text to Photography Compare and contrast the talents of the characters in the texts read and the people in the photograph.

Performance Task

Evaluate sources about frogs.

Write to Sources

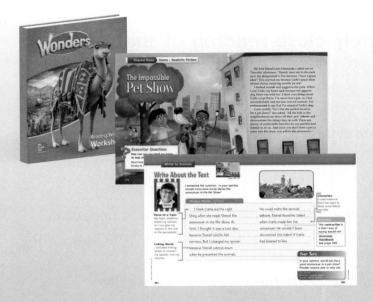

Day 1 and Day 2

Build Writing Fluency

- Quick write on "The Impossible Pet Show," p. T92

Write to a Source

- Analyze a student model, p. T92

- Write about "The Impossible Pet Show," p. T93

- Apply Writing Trait: Develop Characters, p. T92

- Apply Grammar Skill: Contractions with *Not,* p. T93

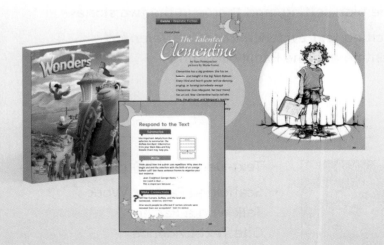

Day 3

Write to a Source

- Write about *The Talented Clementine,* independent practice, p. T89T

- Provide scaffolded instruction to meet student needs, p. T94

Day 4 and Day 5

Write to Two Sources

- Analyze a student model, pp. T94–T95

- Write to compare *The Talented Clementine* with "Clementine and the Family Meeting," p. T95

Writing Process

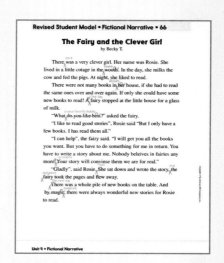

Go Digital

Writer's Workspace

Genre Writing: Narrative Text/Poetry

Fictional Narrative

Draft

- Discuss the student draft model
- Students write their drafts

Revise

- Discuss the revised student model
- Students revise their drafts

Revised Student Model

Student Draft

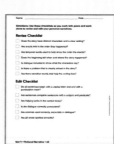

Revise Checklist

Grammar and Spelling Resources

Online PDFs

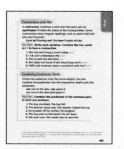

Reading/Writing Workshop Grammar Handbook p. 485

Online Spelling and Grammar Games

Grammar Practice, pp. 81–85

Phonics/Spelling Practice, pp. 97–102

SUGGESTED LESSON PLAN

READING		DAY 1	DAY 2
Teach, Model and Apply 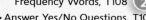 Reading/Writing Workshop	Core	**Introduce the Concept** T74–T74 **Vocabulary** T78–T79 **Close Reading** "The Impossible Pet Show," T80–T81	**Close Reading** "The Impossible Pet Show," T80–T81 **Strategy** Ask and Answer Questions, T82–T83 **Skill** Point of View, T84–T85 **Vocabulary Strategy** Prefixes, T88–T89
	Options	**Listening Comprehension** T76–T77	**Genre** Realistic Fiction, T86–T87

LANGUAGE ARTS			
Writing **Grammar** **Spelling** **Build Vocabulary**	Core	**Grammar** Contractions with *Not*, T96 **Spelling** Plural Words, T98 **Build Vocabulary** T100	**Write About the Text** Model Note-Taking and Write to a Prompt, T92–T93 **Grammar** Contractions with *Not*, T96 **Build Vocabulary** T100
	Options	**Write About the Text** Writing Fluency, T92 **Genre Writing** Fictional Narrative: Draft, T346	**Genre Writing** Fictional Narrative: Teach the Draft Minilesson, T346 **Spelling** Plural Words, T98

Writing Process: Narrative Fictional Narrative, T344-T349   Use with Weeks 1–3

Whole Group

Differentiated Instruction Use your data dashboard to determine each student's needs. Then select instructional support options throughout the week.

Small Group

APPROACHING LEVEL

Leveled Reader
Every Picture Tells a Story, T104–T105
"Hidden Treasure," T105
Literature Circles, T105

Phonics/Decoding
Decode Plural Words with -s, T106
Build Plural Words with -s, -es, T106
Practice Plural Words with -s, -es, T107
Syllables with Vowel Teams, T107

Vocabulary
• Review High-Frequency Words, T108
• Answer Yes/No Questions, T109
• Preteach Vocabulary, T124
• Review High-Frequency Words, T108

Comprehension
• Identify Point of View, T110
• Review Narrator's Point of View, T111
• Self-Selected Reading, T111

Fluency
Phrasing, T110

ON LEVEL

Leveled Reader
A Chef in the Family, T112–T113
"The Perfect Sandwich," T113
Literature Circles, T113

Vocabulary
Review Vocabulary Words, T114
Prefixes *un-, non-, im-, pre-*, T114

Comprehension
• Identify Point of View, T110
• Review Narrator's Point of View, T111
• Self-Selected Reading, T110

DAY 3	DAY 4	DAY 5
Close Reading *The Talented Clementine*, T89A–T89T	**Fluency** T91 **Close Reading** *Clementine and the Family Meeting*, T89U–T89V **Integrate Ideas** Inquiry Space, T102–T103	**Integrate Ideas** T102–T103 • Text Connections • Inquiry Space **Weekly Assessment**
Phonics/Decoding T90–T91 • Plural Words • Syllables with Vowel Teams, T91	**Close Reading** *The Talented Clementine*, T89A–T89T	
Grammar Contractions with *Not*, T97	**Write About Two Texts** Model Note-Taking and Taking Notes, T95	**Write About Two Texts** Analyze Student Model and Write to the Prompt, T96 **Spelling** Plural Words, T99
Write About the Text T94 **Genre Writing** Fictional Narrative: Teach the Draft, T347 **Spelling** Plural Words, T99 **Build Vocabulary** T101	**Genre Writing** Fictional Narrative: Teach the Revise Minilesson, T347 **Grammar** Contractions with *Not*, T99 **Spelling** Plural Words, T99 **Build Vocabulary** T101	**Genre Writing** Fictional Narrative: Peer Conferences, T348 **Grammar** Contractions with *Not*, T99 **Build Vocabulary** T101

Writing Process: Narrative Fictional Narrative, T344–T349 Use with Weeks 1–3

BEYOND LEVEL

Leveled Reader
Stepping Forward, T116–T117
"Rigel to the Rescue," T117
Literature Circles, T117

Vocabulary
• Review Domain-Specific Words, T118
• Prefixes *un-, non-, im-, pre-*, T118

Comprehension
Review Narrator's Point of View, T119
• Self-Selected Reading, T119
• Independent Study, T119

Gifted and Talented

ENGLISH LANGUAGE LEARNERS

Shared Read
"The Impossible Pet Show,
"T120–T121

Leveled Reader
A Chef in the Family,
T122–T123
"The Perfect Sandwich,"
T123
Literature Circles, T123

Phonics/Decoding
Build Plural Words with *-s, -es*, T106
Practice Plural Words with *-s, -es*, T107
Syllables with Vowel Teams, T107

Vocabulary
• Preteach Vocabulary, T124
• Review High-Frequency Words, T108
Review Vacabulary, T124
Prefixes *un-, non-, im-, pre-*, T125
Additional Vocabulary, T125

Spelling
Spell Plural Words with *-s, -es*, T126

Writing
Writing Trait: Ideas, T126

Grammar
Contractions with *Not*, T127

DIFFERENTIATE TO ACCELERATE

 Scaffold to **A**ccess **C**omplex **T**ext

IF the text complexity of a particular selection is too difficult for students

THEN see the references noted in the chart below for scaffolded instruction to help students Access Complex Text.

Qualitative / Quantitative
Reader and Task
TEXT COMPLEXITY

	Reading/Writing Workshop	Literature Anthology	Leveled Readers		Classroom Library

			Approach · On Level · Beyond · ELL		
Quantitative	**"The Impossible Pet Show"** Lexile 600 *TextEvaluator*™ 37	***The Talented Clementine*** Lexile 660 *TextEvaluator*™ 36 **"Clementine and the Family Meeting"** Lexile 630 *TextEvaluator*™ 39	**Approaching Level** Lexile 470 *TextEvaluator*™ 22 **Beyond Level** Lexile 700 *TextEvaluator*™ 41	**On Level** Lexile 530 *TextEvaluator*™ 28 **ELL** Lexile 440 *TextEvaluator*™ 14	***Stone Fox*** Lexile 550 ***Make Way for Dyamonde Daniel*** Lexile 620
Qualitative	**What Makes the Text Complex?** • **Specific Vocabulary** Figurative Language T81 • **Connection of Ideas** Infer T83 **A C T** *See Scaffolded Instruction in Teacher's Edition T81 and T83.*	**What Makes the Text Complex?** • **Organization Problems** T89Q • **Connection of Ideas** Make Inferences T89C, T89G, T89W; Theme T89Y • **Sentence Structure** T89I, T89M • **Prior Knowledge** New Terms T89K • **Genre** Realistic Fiction T89A, T89E, T89U • **Specific Vocabulary** Context Clues T89V **A C T** *See Scaffolded Instruction in Teacher's Edition T89A–T89Z.*	**What Makes the Text Complex?** • **Specific Vocabulary** • **Sentence Structure** • **Connection of Ideas** • **Genre** **A C T** *See Level Up lessons online for Leveled Readers.*		**What Makes the Text Complex?** • **Genre** • **Specific Vocabulary** • **Prior Knowledge** • **Sentence Structure** • **Organization** • **Purpose** • **Connection of Ideas** **A C T** *See Scaffolded Instruction in Teacher's Edition T360–T361.*
Reader and Task	The Introduce the Concept lesson on pages T74–T75 will help determine the reader's knowledge and engagement in the weekly concept. See pages T80–T89 and T102–T103 for questions and tasks for this text.	The Introduce the Concept lesson on pages T74–T75 will help determine the reader's knowledge and engagement in the weekly concept. See pages T89A–T89Z and T102–T103 for questions and tasks for this text.	The Introduce the Concept lesson on pages T74–T75 will help determine the reader's knowledge and engagement in the weekly concept. See pages T104–T105, T112–T113, T116–T117, T122–T123, and T102–T103 for questions and tasks for this text.		The Introduce the Concept lesson on pages T74–T75 will help determine the reader's knowledge and engagement in the weekly concept. See pages T360–T361 for questions and tasks for this text.

Monitor and *Differentiate*

 **Quick Check**

To differentiate instruction, use the Quick Checks to assess students' needs and select the appropriate small group instruction focus.

Comprehension Strategy Ask and Answer Questions T83

Comprehension Skill Point of View T85

Genre Realistic Fiction T87

Vocabulary Strategy Prefixes T89

Phonics/Fluency Plural Words, Phrasing T91

If No →	Approaching Level	**Reteach** T104–T111
	ELL	**Develop** T120–T127
If Yes →	On Level	**Review** T112–T115
	Beyond Level	**Extend** T116–T119

Using Weekly Data

Check your data Dashboard to verify assessment results and guide grouping decisions.

Level Up with Leveled Readers

IF students can read their leveled text fluently and answer comprehension questions

THEN work with the next level up to accelerate students' reading with more complex text.

Stepping Forward — **Beyond** T113

A Chef in the Family — **On Level**

Every Picture Tells a Story — **Approaching** T105

A Chef in the Family — **ELL** T123

ELL ENGLISH LANGUAGE LEARNERS

Small Group Instruction

Use the ELL small group lessons in the Wonders Teacher's Edition to provide focused instruction.

Language Development
Vocabulary preteaching and review, additional vocabulary building, and vocabulary strategy lessons, pp. T124–T125

Close Reading
Interactive Question-Response routines for scaffolded text-dependent questioning for reading and rereading the Shared Read and Leveled Reader, pp. T120–T123

Writing
Focus on the weekly writing trait, grammar skills, and spelling words, pp. T126–T127

Additional ELL Support

Use *Reading Wonders for English Learners* for ELD instruction that connects to the core.

Language Development
Ample opportunities for discussions, and scaffolded language support

Close Reading
Companion Worktexts for guided support in annotating text and citing text evidence. Differentiated Texts about the weekly concept.

Writing
Scaffolded instruction for writing to sources and revising student models

Reading Wonders for ELLs Teacher Edition and Companion Worktexts

→ Introduce the Concept

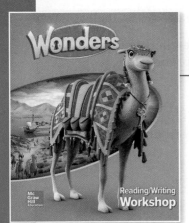

Reading/Writing Workshop

OBJECTIVES

CCSS Ask questions to check understanding of information presented, stay on topic, and link their comments to the remarks of others. **SL.3.1c**

CCSS Determine the main ideas and supporting details of a text read aloud or information presented in diverse media and formats, including visually, quantitatively, and orally. **SL.3.2**

ACADEMIC LANGUAGE

• *confidence, achievement*

• Cognate: *confianza*

MINILESSON 10 Mins

Build Background

ESSENTIAL QUESTION

How can you use what you know to help others?

Have students read the Essential Question on page 272 of the **Reading/Writing Workshop**. Explain to students that using your talents to help others can help you build *confidence*, or a belief in yourself.

Discuss the photograph of a man teaching a boy how to play basketball. Focus on how the man is sharing his skill to help the boy learn something new. Learning a new or difficult skill can be quite an *achievement*. An *achievement* is something done successfully.

• Everyone has a talent or skill that they can share with others.

• When we share our talents, we can help others, and it can be fun.

Talk About It

COLLABORATE

Ask: *How is the man in the photograph helping the boy build confidence? Why is it important to use our talents to help others?* Have students discuss in pairs or groups.

• Model using the concept web to generate words and phrases about talents. Add students' contributions.

• Have partners continue the discussion by sharing what they have learned about talents. They can complete the Concept Webs, generating additional related words and phrases.

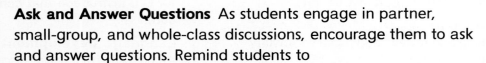

Collaborative Conversations

Ask and Answer Questions As students engage in partner, small-group, and whole-class discussions, encourage them to ask and answer questions. Remind students to

• ask questions to clarify ideas or comments they do not understand.

• wait a few seconds after asking a question, to give others a chance to think before responding.

• answer questions thoughtfully with complete ideas, not one-word answers.

Go Digital

Discuss the Concept

Watch Video

Use Graphic Organizer

Weekly Concept Skills and Talents

? Essential Question
How can you use what you know to help others?

Go Digital!

USE YOUR SKILLS

We all have skills and talents. We might be artistic or smart. We might be good at sports or music.

► We can use our talents to help others.
► Our skills and talents also make us feel good about ourselves.

Talk About It

Write words you have learned about using your talents. Talk with a partner about ways to helps others.

Talents

272   273

READING/WRITING WORKSHOP, *pp. 272–273*

ELL ENGLISH LANGUAGE LEARNERS SCAFFOLD

Beginning	Intermediate	Advanced/High
Use Visuals Point to the photograph. Say: *One of this man's talents is basketball. Talents are things you are good at.* Help students complete the sentence frame. *One of my talents is ____.* Remind them that *talents* in Spanish is *talentos.* Have students ask a partner a question about his or her talent.	**Describe** Remind students that sharing their talents can help them build confidence. Say: *What talents can you share with others? How does this help you build confidence?* Elicit details to develop students' responses.	**Discuss** Have partners discuss different talents that people have and how those talents can help them build confidence. Ask questions to help them elaborate. *What talents do you have? How can you use your talents to build confidence?*

GRAPHIC ORGANIZER 62

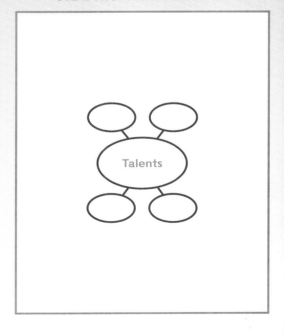

Talents

→ Listening Comprehension

MINILESSON
10 Mins

Interactive Read Aloud

OBJECTIVES

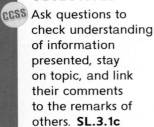
CCSS Ask questions to check understanding of information presented, stay on topic, and link their comments to the remarks of others. **SL.3.1c**

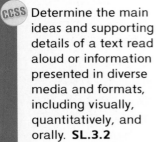
CCSS Determine the main ideas and supporting details of a text read aloud or information presented in diverse media and formats, including visually, quantitatively, and orally. **SL.3.2**

- Listen for a purpose.
- Identify characteristics of realistic fiction.

ACADEMIC LANGUAGE
realistic fiction, ask and answer questions

Connect to Concept: Skills and Talents

Tell students that we can use what we know to help others. Let students know that you will be reading aloud a passage about two sisters who share their talents. As students listen, have them think about how the passage answers the essential question.

Preview Genre: Realistic Fiction

Explain that the story you will read aloud is realistic fiction. Discuss features of realistic fiction:

- has characters with believable human characteristics
- includes a realistic setting and story events that could happen in real life
- shows life as it could be lived today

Preview Comprehension: Ask and Answer Questions

Point out that readers can ask questions as they read to help them better understand the characters and what they do. When reading a story, it is helpful to ask, "Why did this character say or do that? Would I behave in the same way?"

Use the Think Alouds on page T77 to model the strategy.

Respond to Reading

Think Aloud Clouds Display Think Aloud Master 1: *I wonder. . .* to reinforce how you used the Ask and Answer Questions strategy to understand content.

Genre Features With students, discuss the elements of the Read Aloud that let them know it is realistic fiction. Ask them to think about other texts that you have read aloud or they have read independently that were realistic fiction stories.

Summarize Have students determine the main ideas and supporting details of the article "Dancing *La Raspa.*" Then, have students briefly retell the story in their own words.

Go Digital

View Illustrations

Model Think Alouds

Fill in Genre Chart

Dancing *La Raspa*

"What's this?" asked Reina, holding a flyer that fell from her little sister's backpack. "A school talent show! What will you do?"

Carisa shook her head. "Nothing," she said. "I don't have a talent." **1**

"That's not true," said Reina. "You have many talents! For one thing, you're an amazing artist. I wish I could paint like you." All through the apartment their mother had hung dozens of Carisa's paintings that showed a sunny village in Mexico. When they first moved to California, Carisa began painting to help her family remember their old life in the beautiful seaside village of Mazunte.

Carisa laughed. "I don't think I could win a talent show by sitting on stage painting a picture of sea turtles on the beach!"

"What about a dance?" asked Reina. "I could teach you a traditional Mexican folk dance! You share your talent with me by giving me paintings, so let me share my talent with you!" **2**

"I don't know," said Carisa. But Reina wouldn't take no for an answer. Every evening Reina taught Carisa the dance steps for La Raspa. "I like the way my feet sound when they brush the floor," said Carisa.

"Yes, like a rasp!" explained Reina. "Remember the scraping noise when Señor Ruiz made strawberry raspadas for us at the beach?" How could Carisa forget the delicious snow cones? "When you dance, pretend you are making raspadas with your feet," suggested Reina.

The night of the talent show, Carisa was nervous, but ready. Her mother had given her a beautiful white dress trimmed in red and gold that swirled around her. The audience clapped wildly at the end of Carisa's colorful dance. Backstage, the two sisters hugged. Carisa knew that it wasn't important whether she won the talent show or not. Her prize was her kind and generous sister. **3**

1 Think Aloud As I read I can **ask and answer questions** to help me understand the characters. "Is it true that Carisa does not have a talent?" I will keep reading to find out.

2 Think Aloud As I continue to read, I can **answer** my earlier **question** as I learn that Carisa's talent is painting. Now I will **ask** the **question**, "Will Reina teach Carisa to dance?"

3 Think Aloud After reading this paragraph, I can **answer** my last **question.** "Yes, Reina teaches Carisa the La Raspa dance." As I think about the talent show, I can **ask,** "What are my talents? What would I perform for a talent show?"

Yellow Dog Productions/Digital Vision/Getty Images

→ Vocabulary

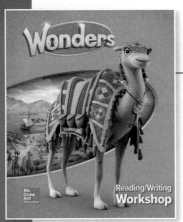

Reading/Writing Workshop

OBJECTIVES

CCSS Determine the meaning of words and phrases as they are used in a text, distinguishing literal from nonliteral language. **RL.3.4**

CCSS Acquire and use accurately grade-appropriate conversational, general academic, and domain specific words and phrases, including those that signal spatial and temporal relationships (e.g., *After dinner that night we went looking for them*). **L.3.6**

ACADEMIC LANGUAGE

• achievement, confidence

• Cognate: *confianza*

 MINILESSON 10 Mins

Words in Context

Model the Routine

Introduce each vocabulary word using the Vocabulary Routine found on the Visual Vocabulary Cards.

Visual Vocabulary Cards

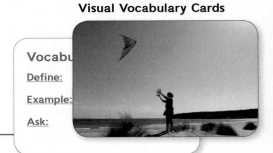

Vocabu

Define:

Example:

Ask:

> **Vocabulary Routine**
>
> <u>Define:</u> An **achievement** is something that you accomplish.
>
> <u>Example:</u> It is a big **achievement** to fly a kite on a very windy day.
>
> <u>Ask:</u> What is your biggest *achievement?*

Definitions

- **apologized** — If you **apologized**, you said you were sorry.
- **attention** — When you give something your **attention**, you watch, listen, or concentrate on it.
  Cognate: *atención*
- **audience** — An **audience** is a group of people gathered to hear or see something.
  Cognate: *audiencia*
- **confidence** — When you have **confidence**, you have trust or faith in something or someone.
- **embarrassed** — When you feel **embarrassed**, you feel shy, uncomfortable, or ashamed.
- **realized** — If you **realized** something, you understood it completely.
- **talents** — **Talents** are natural abilities or skills.
  Cognate: *talentos*

Talk About It

COLLABORATE

Have students work with a partner and look at each picture and discuss the definition of each word. Then have students pick three words and write questions for their partner to answer.

Go Digital

achievement

Use Visual Glossary

Words to Know

Vocabulary

Use the picture and the sentence to talk with a partner about each word.

achievement It is a big **achievement** to fly a kite on a very windy day.

What is your biggest achievement?

apologized Kate **apologized** for breaking the dish.

When have you apologized for doing something?

attention It is important to pay **attention** to directions.

What is something else you should pay attention to?

audience The **audience** clapped and cheered at the end of the play.

When have you been part of an audience?

confidence Jody read her report calmly and with **confidence**.

What does it mean to have confidence?

embarrassed Tia was **embarrassed** when she forgot her lines in the play.

What was something that made you feel embarrassed?

realized My soccer team celebrated when we **realized** we had won the game.

Describe a time when you realized something.

talents One of Lila's **talents** is playing the violin.

What talents do you have?

Your Turn

COLLABORATE

Pick three words. Write three questions for your partner to answer.

Go Digital! *Use the online visual glossary*

274

275

READING/WRITING WORKSHOP, *pp. 274–275*

ELL ENGLISH LANGUAGE LEARNERS SCAFFOLD

Beginning

Use Visuals Point to the picture for *confidence*. Say: *Jody has confidence that she will give a good speech.* Pantomime having confidence. Invite students to use gestures to demonstrate confidence. Then, have them complete the sentence frame: *When I have ____ , I am sure I will succeed.*

Intermediate

Describe Pantomime having confidence. Say: *Think about a time when you had confidence.* Have students complete the sentence frame: *I had confidence when ____.* Elicit details to develop students' responses.

Advanced/High

Discuss Ask: *What talent or skill do you have that gives you confidence?* Have partners discuss what gives them confidence. Have students write a short sentence and then share their sentences with the class.

ON-LEVEL PRACTICE BOOK p. 161

achievement	attention	confidence	apologized
talents	audience	realized	embarrassed

Use the context clues in each sentence to help you decide which vocabulary word fits best in the blank.

Madeleine had many ____talents____ , such as singing and dancing. However, she liked acting the most. There was nothing she enjoyed more than being on stage in front of an ____audience____ and performing in a play. If all went well, the lead role in the school play would surely be hers. Getting the part would be a great ____achievement____ .

On the day of the audition, Madeleine was ready. She knew her lines by heart and had a lot of ____confidence____ that she would get the lead role.

"I'm so excited!" said her best friend, Helen. "I can't wait to be in the play!"

"I want the lead role," said Madeleine. She got up on stage for the audition. Somehow, she couldn't remember her lines! Madeleine's face turned red, she started sweating, and she felt more ____embarrassed____ than ever before. She said she was sorry and ____apologized____ to her teacher. "I don't remember my lines," said Madeleine. She quickly walked off the stage.

"What's the matter?" asked Helen.

"I forgot my lines!" said Madeleine. "Now I won't be in the play! I wish no one had been watching me or paying ____attention____ at all."

"Everyone knows you're talented," said Helen. "You just made one mistake. It's okay. I think that you will still be in the play no matter what."

Madeleine understood what Helen meant. She ____realized____ it would be fun to be on stage with her best friend Helen, even if she didn't get the lead role.

APPROACHING p. 161	BEYOND p. 161	ELL p. 161

Shared Read › Genre • Realistic Fiction

The Impossible Pet Show

My best friend Carla Hernandez called me on Thursday afternoon. "Daniel, meet me in the park near the playground in five minutes. I have a great idea!" This worried me because Carla's great ideas almost always mean big trouble for me!

I dashed outside and jogged to the park. When I saw Carla, my heart sank because her gigantic dog Perro was with her. I liked everything about Carla *except* Perro. I've never had a pet, so I feel uncomfortable and nervous around animals. I'm **embarrassed** to say that I'm afraid of Carla's dog.

Carla smiled. "Isn't this the perfect location for a pet show?" she asked. "All the kids in the neighborhood can show off their pets' **talents** and demonstrate the things they do well. There are plenty of comfortable benches for our parents and friends to sit on. And since you don't have a pet to enter into the show, you will be the announcer."

? Essential Question

How can you use what you know to help others?

Read how Daniel uses what he knows to save a pet show.

276 | 277

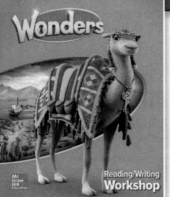

Reading/Writing Workshop

ELL

See pages T120–T121 for Interactive Question-Response routine for the Shared Read.

READING/WRITING WORKSHOP, *pp. 276–277*

Shared Read

CLOSE READING

Lexile 600   *TextEvaluator*™ 37

Close Reading Routine

Read   DOK 1–2

• Identify key ideas and details about Skills and Talents.
• Take notes and summarize.
• Use prompts as needed.

Reread   DOK 2–3

• Analyze the text, craft, and structure.
• Use the Reread minilessons.

Integrate   DOK 4

• Integrate knowledge and ideas.
• Make text-to-text connections.
• Use the Integrate lesson.

Read

Connect to Concept: Skills and Talents Tell students they will read about a boy who discovers his hidden talent by trying something new.

Note Taking Read page 277 together. As you read, model how to take notes. *I will think about the Essential Question as I read and note key ideas and details.* Encourage students to note words they don't understand and questions they have.

Paragraph 2: Read the paragraph together. Ask: *What questions do you have about story events?* Model using details to ask and answer questions.

I read that Daniel's heart sank when he saw Perro. I ask: *Why does he not like Perro?* I read that Daniel has never had a pet, so animals make him uncomfortable. This helps me answer my question.

"I'm sorry," I **apologized**, "but that's impossible! Crowds make me nervous and unsure. Besides, I don't like animals, remember?"

"That's nonsense," said Carla. "There's nothing to be concerned about because you'll be great!"

Just then, Perro leaped up, slobbered all over me, and almost knocked me down. "Yuck. Down, Perro! Stay!" I shouted. Perro sat as still as a statue. "Wow, you're good at that," said Carla. "Now let's get started because we have a lot to do."

By Saturday morning I had practiced announcing each pet's act a hundred times. My stomach was doing flip flops by the time the **audience** arrived. The size of the crowd made me feel even more anxious.

When the show began, I gulped and announced the first pet. It was a parakeet named Butter whose talent was walking back and forth on a wire. When Butter finished, everyone clapped and cheered. So far, everything was perfect, and I was beginning to feel calmer and more relaxed. I **realized** that being an announcer wasn't so bad after all.

Then it was Carla and Perro's turn.

"Sit, Perro," she said, but Perro didn't sit.

Perro was not paying **attention** to Carla. He was too interested in watching Jack's bunnies jump in and out of their boxes. Suddenly, Perro leaped at the bunnies who hopped toward Mandy and knocked over her hamster's cage. Pudgy, the hamster, escaped and began running around in circles while Kyle's dog, Jake, howled. This was a disaster, and I had to do something.

"Sit!" I shouted at Perro. "Quiet!" I ordered Jake. "Stay!" I yelled. Everyone – kids and pets – stopped and stared at me. Even the audience froze.

"Daniel, that was incredible," said Carla. "You got the pets to settle down. That's quite an **achievement**."

Sadly, that was the end of our pet show. But now I have more **confidence** when I have to speak in front of people. And even though I am still nervous around animals, Perro and I have become great friends. And I've discovered my talent, too.

PET SHOW TODAY

Make Connections

How did Daniel use what he knows to help others? ESSENTIAL QUESTION

Discuss whether you would like to take part in a pet show, and why. TEXT TO SELF

READING/WRITING WORKSHOP, *pp. 278–279*

Paragraph 3: Model how to use details to identify realistic fiction. Ask: *What happens in this story that could happen in real life?*

Two details I see are that Daniel and Carla meet at an ordinary park and that Carla talks like a real person would. I know the story is realistic fiction because the events in it could happen in real life.

Make Connections COLLABORATE

Essential Question Encourage students to work with a partner to discuss how Daniel used what he knows to help others. Use these sentence frames to focus discussion:

Before the show, Daniel was . . .
During the show he . . .

A C T Access Complex Text

▶ **Specific Vocabulary**

Help students understand figurative language.

- Point out "my heart sank" on page 277. Explain that we use the heart as a metaphor for feelings. *Did his heart really sink? What does this phrase mean?* (No. He became sad.)

- Discuss the phrase "my stomach was doing flip flops" on page 278. *What does this phrase mean?* (He was nervous.) Build understanding by using similar phrases, such as "butterflies in my stomach."

→ Comprehension Strategy

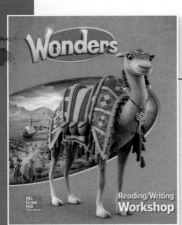

Reading/Writing Workshop

OBJECTIVES

CCSS Ask and answer questions to demonstrate understanding of a text, referring explicitly to the text as the basis for the answers. **RL.3.1**

CCSS Ask questions to check understanding of information presented, stay on topic, and link their comments to the remarks of others. **SL.3.1c**

ACADEMIC LANGUAGE

ask and answer questions

Ask and Answer Questions

1 Explain

Explain to students that as they read, they may come across a part they do not understand. Remind them that they can ask questions about what is happening in the story and then look for answers in the text.

- Good readers think of questions about the text as they read.

- When reading fiction, students can ask *who, what, when, where, why,* and *how* questions to help them understand what is happening in the story.

- Students should look for details in the text to help them answer their questions.

- When they do not find an answer to a question, they can reread the text.

Point out that asking and answering questions about a story will help them understand it better.

2 Model Close Reading: Text Evidence

Model how asking and answering questions can help students understand why Carla's great ideas often mean trouble for Daniel. Reread paragraphs 2 and 3 on page 277 of "The Impossible Pet Show."

3 Guided Practice of Close Reading

Have students work in pairs to answer the example question, "Why does Daniel think being an announcer is not so bad?" Direct students to reread page 278. Partners can reread to make sure they understand that, because the pet show is going well, Daniel starts to like being an announcer. Have partners come up with more questions about other sections in "The Impossible Pet Show" and then work together to find the answers.

Go Digital

View "The Impossible Pet Show"

Comprehension Strategy

Ask and Answer Questions

Stop and ask yourself questions about "The Impossible Pet Show" as you read. Then look for story details to answer your questions.

 Find Text Evidence

Reread page 277. Ask a question about what is happening. Then read again to find the answer.

> page 277
>
> I dashed outside and jogged to the park. When I saw Carla, my heart sank because her gigantic dog Perro was with her. I liked everything about Carla except Perro. I've never had a pet, so I feel uncomfortable and nervous around animals. I'm embarrassed to say that I'm afraid of Carla's dog.
> Carla smiled. "Isn't this the perfect location for a pet show?" she asked. "All the kids in the neighborhood can show off their pets' **talents** and demonstrate the things they do well. There are plenty of comfortable benches for our parents and friends to sit on. And since you don't have a pet to enter into the show, you will be the announcer."

I have a question. Why are Carla's ideas trouble for Daniel? Daniel is uncomfortable around pets. Carla asks him to help at the pet show. Carla's ideas are trouble because she is asking Daniel to do something he is not comfortable doing.

Your Turn

Reread "The Impossible Pet Show." Think of a question. You might ask: Why does Daniel think being an announcer isn't so bad? Reread page 278 to find the answer.

280

Marcin Piwowarski

READING/WRITING WORKSHOP, *p. 280*

A C T Access Complex Text

▶ Connection of Ideas

Tell students that sometimes the answers to their questions may be implied by the text. Tell them that they can draw inferences to help answer the questions that they have.

- Ask: *What is Daniel's talent?* (He is good at giving directions; he is a good announcer.)

- *What details from the text support your answer?* (Everyone stops and listens when Daniel is speaking. I think this is because Daniel has a talent for giving directions and being in charge.)

 Monitor and *Differentiate*

 Quick Check

Do students ask and answer questions to improve understanding of the text?

⬇

Small Group Instruction

If No →	Approaching Level	Reteach p. T104
	ELL	Develop p. T120
If Yes →	On Level	Review p. T112
	Beyond Level	Extend p. T116

ON-LEVEL PRACTICE BOOK pp. 163–164

Read the passage. Use the ask and answer questions strategy to tell about the most important details of the passage.

Painting From Memory

Few people know of Damyang, South Korea, but I think it is
12 impossible to find a place more beautiful. It is known for its bamboo
25 forests. When I was younger, I spent much time in the forests
37 painting pictures of the bamboo. Painting is one of my talents.
48 I lived in Damyang until last year when my family moved to
60 New York. My mother, a scientist, was asked to come work here.
72 "There are no bamboo forests in New York," I said. "There is
84 nothing to paint in New York."
90 "Bae," she said, "that is nonsense. You will find many things
101 to see and paint there. You will see."
109 I was unsure. "But I will miss home," I said.
119 "Then you must paint pictures of your favorite places," she
129 said. "They will make you feel at home even in New York."
141 So when we moved, I brought my forest paintings with me.
152 New York was not easy at first, because I knew no one and spoke
166 only imperfect English. Yet I didn't feel homesick when I looked at
178 my paintings of home. I soon found friends at school, too. Like me,
191 they were artists, and we now paint in a group after school.
203 Last month someone moved into the apartment next to my
213 family's. "Come, Bae," said my mother. "Let's welcome our
222 neighbor." We crossed the hall and knocked on the door. An old
234 woman who looked kind yet unhappy answered.

APPROACHING	BEYOND	ELL
pp. 163–164	pp. 163–164	pp. 163–164

→ # Comprehension Skill

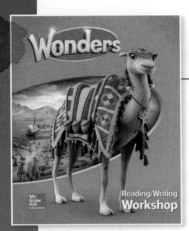

Reading/Writing Workshop

OBJECTIVES

CCSS Ask and answer questions to demonstrate understanding of a text, referring explicitly to the text as the basis for the answers. **RL.3.1**

CCSS Distinguish their own point of view from that of the narrator or those of the characters. **RL.3.6**

ACADEMIC LANGUAGE

• *point of view, narrator*

• Cognate: *narrador*

 Point of View
MINILESSON 10 Mins

1 Explain

Explain to students that fiction is often told from the point of view of the narrator or one of the characters telling the story. The point of view is what the narrator thinks about the story's events or other characters. In "The Impossible Pet Show," Daniel is the narrator.

- Good readers identify the narrator by asking, "Who is telling the story?"

- To find the narrator's point of view, students should look for details that show the narrator's thoughts.

- Students can then distinguish their own point of view on the same topic from that of the narrator.

2 Model Close Reading: Text Evidence

Identify details from "The Impossible Pet Show" that help determine the narrator's point of view. Then model using the details written on the graphic organizer to determine Daniel's point of view.

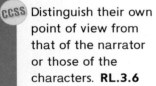 **Write About Reading: Summary** Model for students how to use the notes from the graphic organizer to write a summary of what Daniel thinks about animals.

3 Guided Practice of Close Reading

 Have students work in pairs to complete a graphic organizer for the narrator's point of view about being an announcer. Remind them to look for details that show how the narrator thinks. Then have them tell if they agree with the narrator's point of view.

 Write About Reading: Summary Have pairs work together to write a summary of "The Impossible Pet Show." Remind them to identify the narrator's point of view and distinguish their own point of view from that of the narrator.

Go Digital

Present the Lesson

SKILLS TRACE

POINT OF VIEW

Introduce Unit 2 Week 5

Review Unit 4 Weeks 1, 2, 6; Unit 5 Weeks 1, 2; Unit 6 Week 5

Assess Units 2, 4, 5, 6

Comprehension Skill

Point of View

Point of view is what a narrator thinks about other characters or events in a story. Look for details that show what the narrator thinks. Use them to figure out the point of view.

Find Text Evidence

I read on page 277 that animals make Daniel nervous and uncomfortable. This will help me figure out what Daniel's point of view is about being an announcer for the pet show.

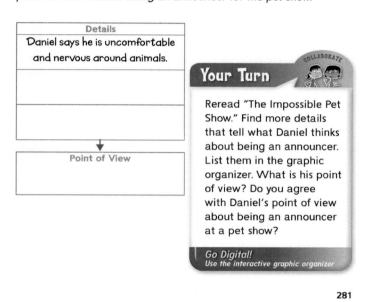

Details
Daniel says he is uncomfortable and nervous around animals.

↓

Point of View

Your Turn

COLLABORATE

Reread "The Impossible Pet Show." Find more details that tell what Daniel thinks about being an announcer. List them in the graphic organizer. What is his point of view? Do you agree with Daniel's point of view about being an announcer at a pet show?

Go Digital!
Use the interactive graphic organizer

281

READING/WRITING WORKSHOP, *p. 281*

ENGLISH LANGUAGE LEARNERS SCAFFOLD

Beginning

Demonstrate Understanding Reread paragraph 4 on page 278. Ask after each sentence: *What is this sentence about? Is Daniel nervous or calm?* Help students describe the narrator's point of view. *The narrator is feeling ____.*

Intermediate

Describe Reread page 278. Ask: *What is Daniel thinking? How do his thoughts change? Explain to a partner.* Then have partners describe Daniel's point of view. *Daniel thinks ____.*

Advanced/High

Discuss Have students work with a partner to identify Daniel's point of view. Make sure students use details from the text to support their answers. Ask questions to develop their responses. *What does Daniel think about being the announcer for the pet show?*

Monitor and *Differentiate*

✓ Quick Check

Do students understand the narrator's point of view? Do they distinguish their own point of view on the topic from that of the narrator?

↓

Small Group Instruction

If No → | Approaching Level | Reteach p. T111
| ELL | Develop p. T121

If Yes → | On Level | Review p. T115
| Beyond Level | Extend p. T119

ON-LEVEL PRACTICE BOOK pp. 163–165

A. Reread the passage and answer the questions.
Possible responses provided.

1. **What is Bae's point of view in the third paragraph about moving to New York?**
   Bae thinks that he will miss his home because there is nothing to paint in New York.

2. **How have Bae's feelings about moving to New York changed in the eighth paragraph?**
   Bae's paintings help him feel better. He is happy to have found friends who also like to paint.

3. **Give one detail from the passage that helps you figure out why Bae wants to help Varvara.**
   Bae wants to help Varvara because he has been in her situation and missed his home so much that it hurt.

B. Work with a partner. Read the passage aloud. Pay attention to phrasing. Stop after one minute. Fill out the chart.

	Words Read	–	Number of Errors	=	Words Correct Score
First Read		–		=	
Second Read		–		=	

APPROACHING pp. 163–165	BEYOND pp. 163–165	ELL pp. 163–165

COMPREHENSION SKILL **T85**

Genre: Literature

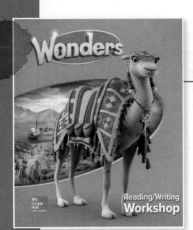

Reading/Writing Workshop

ACADEMIC LANGUAGE
- *fiction, dialogue, realistic, illustrations*
- Cognates: *ficción, diálogo, realista, ilustraciones*

Go Digital

MINILESSON 10 Mins — Realistic Fiction

1 Explain

Share with students the following key characteristics of **realistic fiction**.

- Realistic fiction is a type of fiction, or made-up story.
- The events could happen in real life, and the characters act and talk like people in real life. The setting might be a real place, but the story is not based on history.
- It includes dialogue, which tells readers exactly what the characters say when they talk to each other.
- Students can use the story's illustrations to help them better understand the characters, setting, and events.
- It might be written in the form of a series with the same character but with different settings and themes.

2 Model Close Reading: Text Evidence

Model identifying characteristics that show "The Impossible Pet Show" is realistic fiction. Point out that the setting is a city park. The dialogue shows the story is realistic fiction because the characters talk the way people talk in real life. Point out how the illustrations contribute to what is conveyed by the words in the story.

3 Guided Practice of Close Reading

Have students work with partners to find two events in "The Impossible Pet Show" that could happen in real life. Partners should discuss why these events identify the story as realistic fiction. They should point out how the illustrations give readers more information or details about what happens in the story. Then have them share their work with the class.

Discuss with students realistic fiction books they have read, including series books. Have them name a series they know and talk about the characters, plots, and settings. Ask how the books in the series are alike and different. Encourage students to give specific details.

Present the Lesson

Genre Literature

Realistic Fiction

"The Impossible Pet Show" is realistic fiction.

Realistic fiction:
- Is a made-up story that could really happen
- Has dialogue and illustrations
- May be part of a longer book with chapters or part of a series about the same characters

 Find Text Evidence

I can tell that "The Impossible Pet Show" is realistic fiction. The characters talk and act like real people. The events are made up, but they could really happen.

page 278

"I'm sorry," I apologized, "but that's impossible! Crowds make me nervous and unsure. Besides, I don't like animals, remember?"

"That's nonsense," said Carla. "There's nothing to be concerned about because you'll be great!"

Just then, Perro leaped up, slobbered all over me, and almost knocked me down. "Yuck. Down, Perro! Stay!" I shouted. Perro sat as still as a statue. "Wow, you're good at that," said Carla. "Now let's get started because we have a lot to do."

By Saturday morning I had practiced announcing each pet's act a hundred times. My stomach was doing flip flops by the time the audience arrived. The size of the crowd made me feel even more anxious.

When the show began, I gulped and announced the first pet. It was a parakeet named Butter whose talent was walking back and forth on a wire. When Butter finished, everyone clapped and cheered. So far, everything was perfect, and I was beginning to feel calmer and more relaxed. I realized that being an announcer wasn't so bad after all.

Dialogue Dialogue is what the characters say to each other.

Illustrations Illustrations give more information or details about the characters and setting in the story.

Your Turn COLLABORATE

Reread "The Impossible Pet Show." Find two events that help you figure out this is realistic fiction.

282

READING/WRITING WORKSHOP, *p. 282*

Monitor and *Differentiate*

 Quick Check

Do students identify characteristics of realistic fiction?

Small Group Instruction

If No →	Approaching Level	Reteach p. T104
	ELL	Develop p. T122
If Yes →	On Level	Review p. T112
	Beyond Level	Extend p. T116

ENGLISH LANGUAGE LEARNERS SCAFFOLD

Beginning	**Intermediate**	**Advanced/High**
Use Visuals Point to the illustration on page 278. Ask: *What do you see in the illustration?* (a city park, animals, people) Now reread the first two paragraphs on page 278. Point to the quotation marks and explain that this is dialogue. Here, Daniel and Carla are talking. Point out the words that help us know who is speaking.	**Describe** Have students reread paragraph 1 on page 278. Explain that dialogue is usually found in quotation marks. Ask: *How can you tell who is speaking?* Then have students reread the first 3 paragraphs on page 279. Ask: *What parts of the illustrations on pages 278–279 help us better understand what we just read?*	**Discuss** Have partners discuss the dialogue and illustrations on page 278–279 and how they contribute, or add, to the story. Monitor conversations, and correct the meaning of students' responses as needed.

ON-LEVEL PRACTICE BOOK p. 166

Class by the Pond

Fumiko's class was about to have a quiz about the life cycle of a frog. She was surprised that her class was so worried. She knew lots about frogs since she often watched them by the school pond. Then she had an idea.

"Can we have class by the pond tomorrow?" Fumiko asked as she pointed out the window.

"Why do you ask?" replied Ms. McNally.

"The frog eggs are starting to hatch. Maybe going to the pond and studying the tadpoles will help us learn more about them," Fumiko said.

Answer the questions about the text.

1. How do you know this is realistic fiction?
   It tells a made-up story that could really happen.

2. Why do you think the author uses dialogue?
   Possible response: To show how the characters talk like real people.

3. What text feature is included? How does it help show that the text is realistic fiction?
   Illustration; Possible response: It shows a realistic setting.

APPROACHING p. 166	BEYOND p. 166	ELL p. 166

→ Vocabulary Strategy

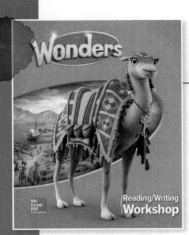

Reading/Writing Workshop

OBJECTIVES

CCSS Determine the meaning of the new word formed when a known affix is added to a known word (e.g., *agreeable/ disagreeable, comfortable/ uncomfortable, care/ careless, heat/ preheat*). **L.3.4b**

ACADEMIC LANGUAGE

• *prefixes, definition*

• Cognates: *prefijos, definición*

MINILESSON 10 Mins

Prefixes

1 Explain

Explain to students that a prefix is a word part added to the beginning of a word. Prefixes change the meaning of a word.

• Readers can determine the meaning of a new word by looking for prefixes.

• The prefixes *un-, non-,* and *im-* mean "not" or "opposite of."

• The prefix *pre-* means "before."

2 Model Close Reading: Text Evidence

Model using prefixes on page 278 to determine the meaning of *unsure*.

3 Guided Practice of Close Reading

Have students work in pairs to determine the meanings of the words *uncomfortable, impossible,* and *nonsense* in "The Impossible Pet Show." Encourage partners to use prefixes to help them determine each word's definition.

Go Digital

Present the Lesson

Vocabulary Strategy

Prefixes

A prefix is a word part added to the beginning of a word. A prefix changes the word's meaning. The prefixes *un-, non-,* and *im-* mean "not" or "opposite of." The prefix *pre-* means "before."

 Find Text Evidence

On page 278, I see the word unsure. *It has the root word* sure *and the prefix* un-. *I know that* sure *means "certain" and the prefix* un- *means "not." The word* unsure *must mean "not certain."*

Crowds make me nervous and unsure.

Your Turn

Use the prefixes in each word to figure out its meaning.
uncomfortable, *page 277*
impossible, *page 278*
nonsense, *page 278*

283

READING/WRITING WORKSHOP, *p. 283*

 **Monitor and** *Differentiate*

 Quick Check

Do students recognize that prefixes change the meaning of a word? Do they understand the meanings of various prefixes?

Small Group Instruction

If No →	Approaching Level	Reteach p. T109
	ELL	Develop p. T125
If Yes →	On Level	Review p. T114
	Beyond Level	Extend p. T118

ENGLISH LANGUAGE LEARNERS SCAFFOLD

Beginning

Understand Write the words *impossible* and *nonsense* on the board. Tell students that *impossible* in Spanish is *imposible.* Underline the root word in each word. Say: Im- *and* non- *mean "not" or "opposite of."* Help students define the root word and then the word with the prefix. Use the words in sentences, and help students replace them with words they know.

Intermediate

Practice Write the words *possible* and *sense* on the board and define each. Remind students that prefixes change the meaning of a word. Say: Im- *and* non- *mean "not" or "opposite of."* Guide students to add the prefixes to the root words to create the words *impossible* and *nonsense.* Then, have them use each word in a sentence.

Advanced/High

Comprehend Write the words *possible* and *nonsense* on the board. Remind students that prefixes change the meaning of a word. Say: Im- *and* non- *mean "not" or "opposite of."* Add the prefixes to the words. Have partners write example sentences for each word that show understanding of the word.

ON-LEVEL PRACTICE BOOK p. 167

Add the prefix *pre-, un-, im-,* or *non-* to the words in the box below. Then complete the sentences with the new words.

pre heat	*un* sure	*im* possible
un bearable	*non* sense	*im* perfect

1. Without my coat on, I find the cold weather is ___unbearable___

2. He was ___unsure___ of how to answer the question because he did not study.

3. This riddle is ___nonsense___! I don't understand it at all.

4. Some people said training an elephant was ___impossible___, but she said that it could be done.

5. I will ___preheat___ the oven before baking the pie.

6. The beautiful diamond had a small scratch on it that made it ___imperfect___

APPROACHING p. 167	BEYOND p. 167	ELL p. 167

The Talented Clementine

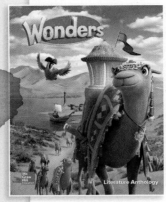

Literature Anthology

*Complex sentence structure places this selection above TextEvaluator range. Content is grade-level appropriate.

Text Complexity Range

Lexile

420 ▲ 820
660

TextEvaluator™

2 35 ▲
*36

What makes this text complex?

▶ **Genre**
▶ **Connection of Ideas**
▶ **Sentence Structure**
▶ **Prior Knowledge**
▶ **Organization**

Close Reading Routine

Read — DOK 1–2

- Identify key ideas and details about skills and talents.
- Take notes and summarize.
- Use **A C T** prompts as needed.

Reread — DOK 2–3

- Analyze the text, craft, and structure.
- Use *Close Reading Companion,* pp. 107–109.

Integrate — DOK 4

- Integrate knowledge and ideas.
- Make text-to-text connections.
- Use the Integrate lesson.

Genre • Realistic Fiction

Excerpt from

The Talented Clementine

by Sara Pennypacker
pictures by Marla Frazee

Clementine has a big problem. She has no **talents**, and tonight is the big Talent-Palooza. Every third and fourth grader will be dancing, singing, or turning cartwheels—except Clementine. Even Margaret, her best friend, has an act. Now Clementine has to tell Mrs. Rice, the principal, and Margaret's teacher why she won't be performing. What can Clementine say? For once, she is completely out of ideas.

①

 Essential Question

How can you use what you know to help others?

Read about how Clementine finds her special talent.

Go Digital!

The Talented Clementine © 2007 by Sara Pennypacker, Illustrated by Marla Frazee © 2007. Reprinted by Permission of Disney-Hyperion, an imprint of Disney Book Group LLC. All Rights Reserved. British Commonwealth Rights: The Talented Clementine by Sara Pennypacker. © 2007

300

 Access Complex Text

▶ Genre

Point out that this story is an excerpt, or part, of a larger book of realistic fiction.

- Explain that page 300 is an introduction to the excerpt, which means that it explains events and ideas discussed before the excerpt begins. The introduction is provided to give readers enough background to understand the excerpt.

301

LITERATURE ANTHOLOGY, *pp. 300–301*

Read

Tell students they will be reading about how Clementine found her special talent while helping with a school talent show. Ask students to predict how the selection will help them answer the Essential Question.

Note Taking: Use the Graphic Organizer

Remind students to take notes as they read. Have them fill in the graphic organizer on **Your Turn Practice Book** page 162. Ask them to record details related to point of view for each section. They can also note words they don't understand and questions they have.

1 Text Features: Introduction

What pronoun refers to the main character, Clementine, in the introduction? (she) What is the point of view of the text? (third-person) What is happening "tonight" in the story? (Talent-Palooza) What do you think Talent-Palooza is? (It is a talent show put on by the third and fourth graders.) Who is Margaret? (Clementine's best friend) What other characters are in the story? (Mrs. Rice, the principal, and Margaret's teacher)

Remind students that characters in realistic fiction often have a problem to overcome.

- *According to the introduction on page 300, what is Clementine's problem?* (She has no talents, and no act for the Talent-Palooza.)

- *Do you really believe that Clementine has no talents?* (No. The title tells us that this is not true.)

ELL Point out that *talent* and *talento* are cognates, and model the meaning of *an act.* Say: *Some students dance in the show. They have a dancing act. Some students sing. Clementine does not sing or dance. She has no act because she has no talents.*

- *Does Clementine have an act?* (no) *Why does she have no act?* (She thinks she has no talents.)

Read

2 Skill: Point of View

Who is the narrator? (Clementine) What details contain pronouns that show she is the narrator? ("*I* tried to hide . . . *I* went over there . . . when *I* get embarrassed") Based on the text, what are Clementine's feelings? (Clementine is embarrassed because she says that when she is embarrassed, her face turns red. One of the fourth graders is teasing her about her red face, so she must be embarrassed.) Add the details and her feelings to the chart.

Details
She wants to hide from Margaret's teacher and Mrs. Rice.
She whispers that she doesn't have an act.
She is embarrassed when the others learn she has no talents.

↓

Point of View
Clementine believes she has no talents and is embarrassed not to have an act.

2 When I walked into the auditorium, I saw Margaret's teacher and Mrs. Rice sitting at the side of the stage on tall director's chairs. I tried to hide, but Margaret's teacher saw me. She looked down at her clipboard and frowned. Then she yelled so loud all the kids in the auditorium stopped what they were doing to listen.

"Clementine, I don't seem to have you listed here. No matter, we'll fit you in. What's your act?"

I went over there and whispered in her ear that I didn't have one. I hoped the kids watching thought I was saying I couldn't choose one because I had too many talents.

"What do you mean, you don't have one?" Margaret's teacher yelled, even though I was right there.

Okay, fine. Maybe she didn't yell it. But all the kids were listening so hard, they heard anyway.

"Hey, Clementine," one of the fourth graders called out. "Your face looks like it's burning up! Maybe that could be your act!"

STOP AND CHECK

Ask and Answer Questions Why does Clementine whisper in the teacher's ear? Reread page 302 to find the answer.

302

A C T Access Complex Text

▶ Connection of Ideas

Help students make inferences about Margaret's teacher and how Clementine feels about her.

- *Clementine says "Margaret's teacher" instead of using the teacher's actual name. What impression does that give you of the way Clementine feels about Margaret's teacher?*

(She is not friendly with Margaret's teacher and feels that the teacher is not a friendly to her.)

- *Why do you think Clementine says "Margaret's teacher yelled" when she didn't actually yell?* (Clementine is upset that Margaret's teacher let the other kids know her secret, despite the fact that Clementine whispered it to her.)

About a million kids laughed, even though he was N-O-T, *not* funny. But he was right—when I get **embarrassed** my face gets red and hot. So I didn't yell anything back to him. I just stood there with my red, hot face hanging down.

Mrs. Rice called me over. "Come sit beside me, Clementine," she said. "You can keep me company during the rehearsal."

303

LITERATURE ANTHOLOGY, *pp. 302–303*

STOP AND CHECK

Ask and Answer Questions Why does Clementine whisper in the teacher's ear? Reread page 302 to find the answer.

Teacher Think Aloud Asking questions about details in the story and then rereading to find the answers will help me understand Clementine's point of view. For example, why does Clementine whisper in the teacher's ear? I read how Clementine wants to hide from Margaret's teacher and Mrs. Rice. She is embarrassed to tell them why she is not performing. But Margaret's teacher sees Clementine enter the auditorium and yells out to her. She asks, "What's your act?" Now the teacher has gotten everyone's attention, and all the kids in the auditorium have stopped what they are doing to listen. Clementine must feel even more embarrassed telling them she has no talents in front of all the other kids. She whispers in Margaret's teacher's ear so the other kids cannot hear her say that she has no act.

Build Vocabulary page 303
  rehearsal: a practice of a show

ELL Review first-person subject pronouns by modeling. Say: *I walk to school every day. We go outside for recess.* Have students complete sentence frames using the pronoun *I*, and then help them identify Clementine as the character who tells the story.

- *When ____ get embarrassed, my face gets red and hot.*

- *____ just stood there with my red, hot face hanging down.*

- *Why is Clementine's face red and hot?* (She is embarrassed.) *Is Clementine telling this story?* (yes)

Read

3 Skill: Point of View

What detail tells why Clementine doesn't want to sit between the adults? (The kids will know she has no talents.) Why does she pile mats in front of the stage? (She knows the Doozies will fall off.) What happens after they check the kids for broken bones? (She sees something else with her "amazing corner-eyes.") What is Clementine's point of view from these details? (She still thinks she has no talents, but she knows what to do before the Doozies take the stage.) Add this information to your chart.

Details
Clementine has to sit and watch the rehearsal.
She piles tumbling mats in front of the stage to keep the cartwheelers safe.
She notices something else that needs her attention.

Point of View
She thinks she has no talents but she watches the rehearsal closely and knows how to help.

3 So I had to sit in between Mrs. Rice and Margaret's teacher, right there at the side of the stage where all the kids could see me and know that I had no talents.

The first act was called A Dozen Doozie Cartwheelers. Twelve kids lined up, six on each side of the stage.

"Wait!" I yelled. I ran into the gym and dragged a tumbling mat back into the auditorium. I placed it on the floor in front of the stage. Then I got some of the Dozen Doozies to help me. Pretty soon we had all the mats piled up.

304

A C T Access Complex Text

▶ Genre

Remind students to use the illustrations to understand the text.

- *On page 304, why does Clementine think that some of the Doozies will fall off the stage?* (The stage is not very deep, and the Doozies are cartwheeling, or doing handsprings.)

- *How would the results of the act been different if the mats were not there?* (At least six of the Doozies would have fallen onto the floor. Since the floor is harder than the mats, they would have had a greater chance of hurting themselves.)

Margaret's teacher was glaring at me. She tapped her watch.

"They're going over," I explained. "No matter how they start off aiming, some of them are going over."

And they did. At least half a dozen of the Doozies went flying off the stage and right onto the mats. As soon as we got those kids back up and checked them for broken bones, I saw something else with my amazing corner-eyes. **4**

305

LITERATURE ANTHOLOGY, pp. 304–305

Read

4 Skill: Make Inferences

What does Clementine mean when she says that she sees "something else with my amazing corner-eyes"? (While helping to check the Dozen Doozies for broken bones, Clementine notices something important that no one else sees. Her "amazing corner-eyes" must be a special talent, or ability, to see all that is going on around her.) **Do you think Clementine realizes that she has a talent?** (She doesn't realize that her "amazing corner-eyes" are a talent because it is not an act she can perform in the show.)

Build Vocabulary page 305
glaring: staring in an angry way

Reread

Genre: Realistic Fiction

What details about the characters and setting are clues that the story is realistic fiction? (The kids act and talk the way kids do in real life. Margaret's teacher and Mrs. Rice are also believable characters. The story's details are realistic, such as Clementine thinking the other children now know that she has no talents when she has to sit alone with the grown-ups. The setting is a school auditorium that is familiar. The setting is not a place from long ago or in the future.)

ELL Help students point to the stage, tumbling mats, and children doing cartwheels in the illustration.

- *Where are these children doing cartwheels?* (on stage)

- *What are they falling on?* (tumbling mats)

Read

⑤ Strategy: Ask and Answer Questions

Teacher Think Aloud Clementine doesn't get to sit down again all afternoon because everybody needs her help with something. Why doesn't Clementine call her parents to tell them not to come to the show?

Prompt students to apply the strategy in a Think Aloud by rereading to answer the question. Have them turn to a partner to paraphrase what they have read.

Student Think Aloud I can reread the last three paragraphs on page 307 to find out why Clementine doesn't call her parents. When she asks to use the phone in Mrs. Rice's office, the principal tells her that it's too late to call her parents. Clementine does not realize how long she has been helping the other kids with their acts. Mrs. Rice shows Clementine the time on her watch and announces, "Take your places, people. Five minutes to showtime!" The show is about to start, so her parents must already be seated in the auditorium.

Build Vocabulary page 306
   nonsense: silly behavior
   antsy: nervous

"Stop!" I yelled. Then I ran over and grabbed a handful of crackers from one of the third graders just before they went into his mouth.

"You're up next," I reminded him. "And you're whistling 'Yankee Doodle Dandy.' No crackers!"

When I got back, Margaret's teacher gave me a look that said she was going to remember all this nonsense when I got into her grade.

But Mrs. Rice gave me a thumbs-up. "Thank you, Clementine," she said. "Those crackers could have been a problem."

And you will not believe what happened next: Margaret's teacher **apologized**!

"I'm sorry," she said. "I'm a little antsy tonight."

I wanted to stick around to hear about why she was antsy, but just then I noticed that the Super-Duper Hula-Hoopers had been Hula-Hooping for a while. I went over and asked them how long they were planning to go on.

306

A C T Access Complex Text

▶ Connection of Ideas

The author describes a series of events that demonstrate Clementine's powers of observation. Have students use these events to make inferences about Clementine.

- *Clementine stops a third grader from eating crackers. What problem could the crackers cause?* (They could make him unable to whistle.)

- *Why does Clementine ask the Hula-Hoopers how long they plan to go on?* (She sees they have been practicing for a long time and worries that their act won't have an ending.)

- *What do these events tell you about Clementine?* (She is observant. She thinks ahead.)

The girl on the right said, "I once went for five hours and thirteen minutes."

The girl on the left made a face that said, "That's nothing!"

"Well, you need to have an ending tonight," I said. "There are a lot of acts after yours." I borrowed the jump-ropers' CD player and explained about how they could Hula-Hoop to the music and then S-T-O-P, *stop* when it was over.

And I didn't even get to sit down again for the rest of the afternoon because everybody needed my help for something. Finally, after everyone had a chance to practice their acts, I went over to Mrs. Rice.

"May I go into your office and use the phone? I need to call my parents and tell them not to come." **5**

"I think it's a little late for that." Mrs. Rice showed me her watch and then called out, "Take your places, people. Five minutes to showtime!"

307

LITERATURE ANTHOLOGY, *pp. 306–307*

Author's Craft: Contrast

How does the author help you understand how Margaret's teacher and Mrs. Rice are different? (When Clementine stops the third grader from eating crackers before his whistling act, the two women have different reactions. Margaret's teacher gives a disapproving look that says she is going to remember Clementine's nonsense when she gets into her grade. Mrs. Rice shows her approval of Clementine's help by giving her a thumbs-up and thanking her. When Mrs. Rice says "those crackers could have been a problem," Margaret's teacher realizes that Clementine is being helpful. She apologizes to her by saying she is antsy.)

ELL Have volunteers demonstrate some of the acts, such as whistling and jumping rope. Model each in a sentence. *A third grader can whistle a song called "Yankee Doodle Dandy." Students jump rope to music, or with music playing.*

- *What song can one third grader whistle?* ("Yankee Doodle Dandy")
- *What act can students do to music?* (jump rope)

Read

6 Skill: Point of View

Why does Margaret's teacher thank the students? (for being in the show) What does Clementine believe the others are thinking? (Margaret's teacher is thanking everybody except for her.) What does she say to Mrs. Rice when Margaret's teacher has to leave? ("So now you have to run the whole show by yourself.") Do you think Clementine understands her part in the show? (She does not understand that she is part of the show by helping the others.) Do you think she is a part of the show? (yes)

Details
Margaret's teacher thanks the students for being part of the show.
Clementine feels that she is not part of the show.
She believes Mrs. Rice must now run the show by herself when Margaret's teacher leaves.

↓

Point of View
Clementine does not understand how she is helping to run the show.

Everybody ran to their places. I ran to the curtains and peeked out: every seat in the **audience** was filled.

308

A C T Access Complex Text

▶ Sentence Structure

Point out the colon on page 308. Help students understand how the text that follows the colon is related to the text preceding it.

- *What does Clementine do from behind the curtains?* (She peeks out.)

- *What does she see when she peeks out?* (She sees that "every seat in the audience was filled.")

- *What does the text after the colon tell the reader?* (It explains, or tells, what Clementine discovers when she peeks out from behind the curtains.)

Margaret's teacher clapped her hands for attention.

"Before we get started," she said, "I just want to thank you all for being part of the show. Each and every one of you is helping to raise money for the big school trip next spring. Except Clementine."

6

Okay, fine, she didn't actually say, "Except Clementine," but you could see everyone was thinking it.

Just then, the secretary came over and handed her a note.

7

"Oh! Oh, my goodness!" she cried. She jumped up out of her seat faster than I thought a grown-up should. "Oh, my goodness gracious, it's now! My daughter's having her baby! My first grandchild!"

"Go," said Mrs. Rice. "It's all right. We can handle the show. Just go be with your daughter."

"Oh, thank you!" Margaret's teacher said. And then she left so fast she really did lose one of her bobby pins. It didn't look like lightning, though. It just looked like a bobby pin falling to the floor.

8

"Wow," I said to Mrs. Rice. "So now you have to run the whole show by yourself."

309

LITERATURE ANTHOLOGY, pp. 308–309

Read

7 Strategy: Ask and Answer Questions

COLLABORATE

Generate a question of your own about the text and share it with a partner. For example, you might ask, why does Margaret's teacher leave before the show starts? You can reread page 309 and stop when you find the answer. (Margaret's teacher gets a note telling her that her daughter is having a baby. The baby is Margaret's teacher's first grandchild. This is so important that Mrs. Rice tells her to go and be with her daughter.)

8 Skill: Make Inferences

Why do you think Margaret's teacher has been acting antsy, and how may this affect, or change, Clementine's opinion of her? (All during rehearsal she must have been thinking about her daughter and the possibility that the baby would be born soon. Clementine sees Margaret's teacher jump out of her chair and leave so fast that she loses a bobby pin. Clementine and the reader alike now understand why she has been antsy during rehearsal.)

ELL Demonstrate the phrase *peek out* to describe Clementine in the illustration. Say: *Clementine is behind the curtains. She peeks out at the people in the audience. Every seat is filled by a person.*

- *Where is Clementine?* (behind the curtains)

- *What does she peek out at?* (the audience)

- *Is every seat filled by a person?* (yes)

Ask and Answer Questions How does Clementine feel about being the principal's assistant? Reread page 310 to find the answer. (Clementine doesn't think she can do it. She says, "Me? Oh, no. I can't!")

Read

9 Strategy: Ask and Answer Questions

Remind students to ask questions about details they are unsure of and then reread the text to find the answers. For example, how does Mrs. Rice convince Clementine to be her assistant during the talent show?

Student Think Aloud Mrs. Rice tells her that she may not always pay attention in class, but she notices "more about what's going on than anyone" Mrs. Rice knows. She then asks Clementine questions about Caleb's act to show how she knows every detail about each act. Principal Rice says, "I rest my case" and points a "no buts" finger at the empty director's chair for Clementine.

"No, not by myself," Mrs. Rice said. "I have an assistant. And that's you."

"Me? Oh, no. I can't!"

"You can. And I'm certainly not doing this alone."

"I really can't. I don't pay **attention**, remember?"

"You do pay attention, Clementine. Not always to the lesson in the classroom. But you notice more about what's going on than anyone I know. And that's exactly what I need tonight."

"I don't think this is a very good idea at all."

"Well, I do think it's a good idea. I'll prove it to you." Principal Rice called over one of the Hula-Hoopers. "Hillary, what's the second act after intermission?"

Hillary looked around. "I don't have a program," she said. "Do you want me to get you one?"

Mrs. Rice told her No thanks, then she turned to me. "Clementine, what's the second act after intermission?"

"Caleb from the fourth grade is going to burp 'The Star-Spangled Banner'," I told her.

"Does he need any props?"

"A two-liter bottle of root beer."

"How long will it take?"

"Forty-one seconds. Forty-eight if he has to stop to drink extra soda at the 'rockets' red glare' part."

310

ACT Access Complex Text

▶ Prior Knowledge

Students may be not be familiar with stage performance terms. Tell them that *intermission* is a break in the show, a *program* is a guide that lists the order of the acts, and *props* are objects, or things, used in a show.

- *What does Mrs. Rice ask Hillary?* ("... what's the second act after intermission?")

- *Why does Hillary ask if Mrs. Rice wants a program?* (She does not know the order of the acts in the show, so she offers to get Mrs. Rice a program.)

- *What prop does Caleb need?* (root beer) *Why does he use it?* (to burp "The Star-Spangled Banner")

"I rest my case," Principal Rice said. She pointed a "no buts" finger at the empty director's chair.

When a principal orders you to do something, it is impossible to refuse. Some part of you always gives in. So I climbed into the chair. **🔟**

"Open the curtains!" Principal Rice said. And the worried scribbling feeling exploded all through my body.

STOP AND CHECK

Ask and Answer Questions How does Clementine feel about being the principal's assistant? Reread page 310 to find the answer.

311

LITERATURE ANTHOLOGY, *pp. 310–311*

🔟 Vocabulary: Prefixes

Find a word in the second paragraph on page 311 that has the prefix *im-*. (impossible) How can the prefix *im-* help you figure out the meaning of *impossible*? (The prefix *im-* means "not" or "the opposite of," so the word *impossible* means "not possible.") How does Clementine explain how she becomes Mrs. Rice's assistant? (She explains how it is impossible, or not possible, to refuse "when a principal orders you to do something.")

Reread

Author's Craft: Sensory Language

Authors may use sensory language to describe how a character feels during an event in a story. How does the author use sensory language to describe how Clementine feels when Principal Rice says, "Open the curtains!"? ("The worried scribbling feeling" describes how Clementine feels when she gets nervous. "Exploded all through my body" describes how she is overwhelmed by nervousness when the show starts.)

ELL Demonstrate looking worried. Say: *Clementine helps Mrs. Rice with the show. Clementine looks worried when the show starts.* Help students point to Clementine looking worried in the illustration.

- *Who helps Mrs. Rice with the talent show?* (Clementine)

- *How does Clementine look?* (worried)
- *When does Clementine look worried?* (She looks worried when the show starts.)

Read

11 Skill: Point of View

Why does Clementine close the curtains on the twins? (So the audience will not feel sick and the janitor can clean up.) **Why does she send Sidney out?** (Clementine knows she can yell her poem standing sideways.) **What does Clementine do next?** (She closes the curtains and pulls the hoopers off stage because they have forgotten to stop.) **Do you think Clementine knows her help is important?** (She knows her help is needed and says, "you would think those kids had never had a rehearsal.") **Add this information to your chart.**

Details
Clementine closes the curtains on the O'Malley twins.
She sends Sidney out while the stage is being cleaned.
She pulls the hoopers off stage.

↓

Point of View
So many acts go wrong in the show that Clementine knows her help is needed.

Well, you would think those kids had never had a rehearsal.

First thing: all Dozen Doozies cartwheeled off the edge of the stage. Well, except for one girl, who forgot to move at all. Maria and Morris-Boris-Norris, from my class, went on next, and they cartwheeled right off the stage, too.

Nobody had to go to the emergency room, though, and the audience thought the whole thing was supposed to happen that way, so it was okay.

312

A C T Access Complex Text

▶ Sentence Structure

Help students understand what *Nobody* and *the whole thing* refer back to in the first sentence in the third paragraph on page 312.

- *Who is Clementine talking about when she says "nobody had to go to the emergency room"?* (She means none of the cartwheelers are hurt, so nobody has to go to the hospital.)

- *What does the audience believe?* (They think the whole thing was supposed to happen that way.) *What is the whole thing?* (the cartwheelers falling off the stage when they do their act)

The next act was the O'Malley twins. Lilly had convinced Willy not to do the thing with his lunch, and to play a duet on the piano with her instead. But when Lilly got up to the mike to announce the act, she got so nervous she threw up.

I looked at Willy, sitting on the piano bench. Willy does everything Lilly does. And sure enough, he was getting ready.

"Not on the piano!" I yelled. Just in time.

Then I ran over and closed the curtains quick, so the whole audience wouldn't get started, too.

11

When the janitor came running out to clean everything up, I had a good idea.

"Send Sidney out now, in front of the curtains," I told Mrs. Rice.

"Why?" she asked. "There's no microphone out there."

"That's okay. Sidney's really loud. And she's going to recite a poem so there's no cartwheeling, just standing still. Besides, she's got really skinny feet, so she can fit out there if she stands sideways."

So Sidney went onstage and stood sideways and yelled her poem. By the time she was done, the stage was all mopped clean.

Next came the Hula-Hoopers, and they completely forgot what I'd told them about stopping. The music ended, but they just kept on going. Finally, I had to close the curtains to pull them off the stage so the jump-ropers could go on.

313

LITERATURE ANTHOLOGY, *pp. 312–313*

Build Vocabulary page 313
   duet: a performance by two people

Reread   *Close Reading Companion*

Author's Craft: Humor

In realistic fiction, authors often use humor in key details to entertain readers. How does the author use humor to describe how important Clementine is to the talent show? (The author tells how something amusing goes wrong with each act and how only Clementine knows how to help. For example, she knows that Sidney can be loud and that her skinny feet will allow her to stand on stage with the curtain closed.)

ELL Point out that *piano* and *duet* are cognates (*piano, dueto*). Help students identify Lilly and Willy O'Malley in the illustration. Say: *Lilly and Willy want to play a duet on the piano.* Point out that *recite, poem,* and *audience* are cognates (*ricitar, poema,* and *audiencia*). Say: *Sidney recites a poem for the audience.*

- *Who wants to play a duet on the piano?* (Lilly and Willy)
- *Who recites a poem for the audience?* (Sidney)

Read

12 Strategy: Ask and Answer Questions

COLLABORATE

Why does Margaret freeze on stage? With a partner, paraphrase details in the text to answer the question. (Margaret freezes on stage because Alan takes a picture of her when she is not expecting it. She has explained to Clementine that the horror of not knowing if she looks perfect in a picture freezes her.)

Build Vocabulary page 314
   empathetic: understanding what someone is feeling

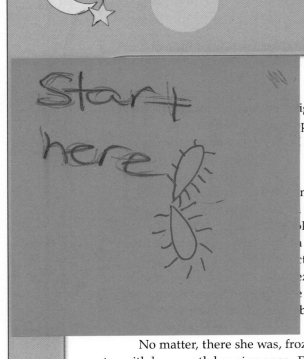

igured that if the
p at the end of
had to close the

n-stage-on-time
. But just as she
ok a picture of her
bad mistake.
ture of Margaret
ezes. She says it's
looks perfect or
because Margaret

No matter, there she was, frozen on the stage with her mouth hanging open. For one tiny second, a little part of me thought, *Good! No showing off for you tonight!*

But then my empathetic part took over.

I ran over to where Margaret could see me and waved until I got her eyes to unfreeze. I pointed **13** to my hair and pretended to brush it.

314

A C T — Access Complex Text

▶ Connection of Ideas

Help students understand that the purpose of the last paragraph of page 314 and the text on page 315 is to show how Clementine helps Margaret do her act. Help them infer the nature of Margaret's act.

• *What is Margaret able to say after Clementine pretends to brush her hair?* (She tells the audience to "first, always brush your hair.") *What does Clementine pretend to do next?* (She pretends to do up some buttons.) *What does Margaret say next?* ("Always make sure you're buttoned up right.")

Margaret nodded like a robot. She turned to the audience. "First, always brush your hair. Even if it's cut off like mine."

She looked back at me. I pretended to do up some buttons, then I pointed to my right.

"Always make sure you're buttoned up right," Margaret told the audience.

315

LITERATURE ANTHOLOGY, *pp. 314–315*

⑬ Skill: Point of View

What does a "little part" of Clementine think "for one tiny second" when Margaret is frozen on stage? ("Good! No showing off for you tonight!") Why does Clementine decide to help her friend? (The empathetic part of her takes over.) What do you think the empathetic part of Clementine is? (The part that understands how someone else feels.)

Reread

Author's Craft: Figurative Language

Authors may use a simile, or comparison using the words *like* or *as,* to help readers visualize a key detail in a story. What simile is used to describe how Margaret nods to Clementine on page 315? ("She nodded like a robot.") Why do you think Clementine compares her best friend to a robot? (Margaret is still mostly frozen on stage, so she moves like a machine.)

• *How do you know it is important to Margaret that she look her best?* (I know because Clementine has commented that she always looks perfect.) *What type of advice do you think Margaret is giving in her act?* (She is explaining how to always look your best.)

ELL Help students understand the multiple-meaning words *freeze/frozen.* Say: *Water freezes and turns to ice. Ice is frozen and does not move like water.* Demonstrate standing frozen. Have students point to Margaret frozen on stage.

• *Why does Margaret not move or talk?* (because she is frozen on stage)

Read

14 Skill: Point of View

When does Clementine know that Margaret is okay? (after they smile at each other) Why do you think Mrs. Rice compliments Clementine? (Mrs. Rice wants her to know that she is a good assistant.) What does Clementine finally realize? (She is no longer worried and is proud to be Mrs. Rice's assistant.) Does she still think that she has no talents? (No, she is confident and proud of how she uses her talents.) Do you think Clementine should feel confident and proud? (Yes, Clementine did a good job.) Add this information to your chart.

Details
She and Margaret smile to each other, and Clementine knows her best friend is okay.
Mrs. Rice compliments Clementine's ability to help the other kids.
Clementine's worried feeling is replaced with a proud feeling.

↓

Point of View
Clementine is confident and proud of her talents.

Then I lifted my foot and crossed my fingers over my sneaker.

"Never wear green sneakers!" Margaret said. "Green sneakers are the worst!" Then she shook herself, as if she'd been asleep. She went up closer to the mike.

"Wait a minute," she said. "I was just kidding about that one. You can wear any color sneakers you want. And green is the most fashionable of all."

She zoomed me a smile so huge all her teeth-bracelets sparkled like diamonds in the spotlight. I zoomed her one back—except with no teeth-bracelets because I don't have them yet. After that, Margaret was okay.

I went back and climbed up onto the director's chair, and Principal Rice gave me a huge smile, too. She leaned over and said, "I have the answer for you now, Clementine. About why you can't have a substitute. It's because there is no substitute for you. You are one of a kind!"

14 And that's when I **realized** I didn't have the worried feeling anymore. Instead, I had the proud feeling: like the sun was rising inside my chest.

316

A C T Access Complex Text

▶ Organization

Remind students how Clementine's problem in the beginning of the story is that she feels embarrassed because she believes she has no talents. Help students understand how Mrs. Rice helps Clementine gain confidence and overcome this problem.

- *On page 311, when does Clementine get a "worried scribbling feeling"?* (It begins when Mrs. Rice starts the show by saying "Open the curtains!".)

- *Why do you think she gets this feeling?* (She is not confident that she will be a good assistant.)

The proud, sun-rising feeling stayed with me all through the rest of the show. And no matter what went wrong, which was plenty, Mrs. Rice and I just fixed it.

STOP AND CHECK

Visualize Use the descriptions to visualize Clementine's actions at the end of the story. How does she feel?

317

LITERATURE ANTHOLOGY, pp. 316–317

STOP AND CHECK

Visualize Use descriptions to visualize Clementine's actions at the end of the story. How does she feel? (She feels happy and proud. She has a "proud, sun-rising feeling." She is not worried anymore even when things go wrong.)

Return to Purposes Review students' predictions about the selection. Ask them to use text evidence to answer the Essential Question. (We learn that Clementine has a talent for paying attention and learning the details of each act in the talent show. This allows her to help the other students when they have problems performing their acts.)

Reread *Close Reading Companion*

Author's Craft: Figurative Language

How does the author help you understand what Principal Rice means when she tells Clementine that she is "one of a kind"? (The author shows Clementine solving different problems, and saving the show as Mrs. Rice's assistant. So the reader can understand that Mrs. Rice is complimenting her on being such a good assistant. Mrs. Rice believes no one could do the job as well as Clementine does it.)

- *What replaces this feeling?* (She feels proud. The text says the feeling is like the sun rising inside her chest.) *Why does she realize she has this proud feeling?* (Mrs. Rice calls her one of a kind, and Clementine knows she is a good assistant.)

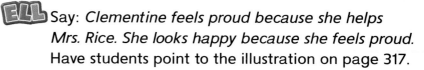 Say: *Clementine feels proud because she helps Mrs. Rice. She looks happy because she feels proud.* Have students point to the illustration on page 317.

- *Why does Clementine feel proud?* (because she helps Mrs. Rice) *Why does she look happy?* (because she is proud)

LITERATURE ANTHOLOGY **T89R**

Read

About the Author and Illustrator

Sara Pennypacker and Marla Frazee

Have students read the biographies of the author and illustrator. Ask:

- How might Sara Pennypacker's own experiences have helped her invent the characters in *The Talented Clementine*?
- How do the illustrations help you visualize the characters in the story?

Author's Purpose

To Entertain

Remind students that authors who write realistic fiction may choose to write from the first-person point of view to tell the story from a character's own words. Students may say they were entertained because it is told from the point of view of a child their age. They may also say that Clementine is a funny character and the author wanted to make readers laugh.

Reread

Author's Craft

Explain how humorous details are used to entertain the reader throughout the story. What funny details, such as rhyming or alliterative names, can you find in the story? (Dozen Doozies, Super-Duper Hula-Hoopers, Maria and Morris-Boris-Norris, Lilly and Willy O'Malley)

About the Author and Illustrator

Sara Pennypacker was shy as a girl. She loved books, art, and baseball. In fact, her dream was to play major league baseball. Sara has not yet lived her baseball dream. But she has been able to combine her other two loves. She works with books and art! First she was a watercolor painter with her own studio. After that, she started writing children's books.

Marla Frazee has written and illustrated five books. She has also illustrated many other books, including the Clementine series. Marla studied art at a college in California. Now, in addition to writing and illustrating, she shares her talents by teaching other people how to create illustrations for children's books.

Author's Purpose

Why do you think the author chose Clementine as the story's narrator?

318

LITERATURE ANTHOLOGY, *pp. 318–319*

Respond to the Text

Summarize

What are the most important events in this story? The details from your Point of View chart may help you summarize.

Details
↓
Point of View

Write

How does the author use what the characters do and say to help you understand how Clementine has changed? Use these sentence frames to focus your discussion.

The author describes Clementine . . .
She uses dialogue to tell me that her teachers . . .
I can see how Clementine has changed because the author . . .

Make Connections

How does Clementine use what she knows to help others? **ESSENTIAL QUESTION**

Why do people perform in talent shows? **TEXT TO WORLD**

319

Respond to the Text

Read

Summarize

Tell students they will use the information from their Point of View graphic organizer to summarize.

As I read *The Talented Clementine*, I collected key details and figured out the point of view in each section of the text. To summarize, I will retell, or paraphrase, the most important details.

Reread

Analyze the Text

After students summarize the selection, have them reread to develop a deeper understanding of the text and answer the questions on **Close Reading Companion** pages 107–109. For students who need support in citing text evidence, use the Reread prompts on pages T89F–T89R.

Write About the Text

Review the writing prompt and sentence frames. Remind students to use their responses from the **Close Reading Companion** to support their answers. For a full lesson on writing a response using text evidence, see page T94.

Answer: At the beginning, Clementine is embarrassed to admit that she has no talent for the show. During the show, she solves problems, and Mrs. Rice praises her. Evidence: On pages 302–303, Clementine's face turns red and she feels everyone is laughing at her. On page 316, Mrs. Rice tells Clementine she's "one of a kind!"

Integrate

Make Connections

COLLABORATE

Essential Question Answer: Clementine is observant and thinks ahead. She uses these skills to help the other kids stay safe and to keep the show going. Evidence: On pages 304–305, Clementine places mats in front of the stage before the Doozies start their act. On page 306, she stops the third grader from eating crackers before his whistling act. On pages 312–316, she helps each act as it goes on stage.

Text to World Responses may vary, but encourage students to cite text evidence from their sources.

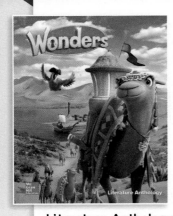

Clementine and the Family Meeting

Literature Anthology
*Complex vocabulary places this selection above TextEvaluator range. Content is grade-level appropriate.

Text Complexity Range

Lexile

420   ▲   820
630

TextEvaluator™

2   35 ▲
*39

What makes this text complex?
▶ **Genre**
▶ **Specific Vocabulary**
▶ **Connection of Ideas**

Compare Texts

As students read and reread *Clementine and the Family Meeting,* encourage them to take notes and think about the Essential Question: *How can you use what you know to help others?* Tell students to think about how this text compares with *The Talented Clementine.*

Genre • Realistic Fiction

Compare Texts
Read about how Clementine's parents help her gain **confidence** and get ready for a change.

From

Clementine
and the Family Meeting

by Sara Pennypacker
pictures by Marla Frazee

It's almost time for the family meeting at Clementine's house, and Clementine is really nervous. What did she and her little brother do this time? Did she eat too much junk food? Maybe she misplaced one of Dad's tools? Both Mom and Dad have assured her that this meeting is only about good news. But ❶ *Clementine is not so sure . . .*

320

A C T   Access Complex Text

▶ Genre

Tell students that this selection and *The Talented Clementine* are books in a series, which means that they have the same main character.

* *After reading* The Talented Clementine, *what do you think might happen at the family meeting?* (If the books are alike, something funny might happen. Clementine might learn a lesson.)

My dad called the meeting to order.

"We are a very lucky family," he said. "Very lucky."

"What's on the agenda?" I asked.

"I'm getting to that," my dad said. "Now, families change. They grow. It's hard to believe, but you're eight and a half now, and your brother's almost four."

I clapped my hands over my brother's ears. "Should we have a surprise party for him? You know what would make a great present? A gorilla!"

"His birthday's not for a few months," my mom said. "I vote we table that discussion for another time."

"Well, so what's the good thing we have to talk about tonight?" I asked.

321

LITERATURE ANTHOLOGY, *pp. 320–321*

Read

1 Skill: Make Inferences

Based on the text on page 320, do you think Clementine has gotten in trouble before? (yes) How do you know? (She asks what she and her little brother might have done "this time." Then she mentions things she might have done wrong, such as eat too much junk food or misplace one of Dad's tools.) Make an inference about Clementine's family meetings. (It is likely that her family often have meetings to talk about things she and her little brother have done wrong.)

Reread   *Close Reading Companion*

Author's Craft: Character

How does the author help the reader understand how Clementine feels about the family meeting? (The introduction says that Clementine is "really nervous" about the meeting, even though Mom and Dad say the meeting is "only about good news." The illustration on page 320 shows her staring at the note about the meeting. She looks like she is thinking hard.)

▸ Specific Vocabulary

Help students with vocabulary related to meetings.

- *The story begins when dad calls the meeting to order. What do you think that phrase means?* (starts the meeting)

- *When Clementine asks what's on the agenda, what does she want to know?* (She wants to know what the meeting will be about.)

ELL Model the term *family meeting*. Explain that when families have something important to talk about, they call, or have, a family meeting. They all meet together to talk about it.

- *What is a family meeting?* (Family members meet to talk about something important.)

Read

2 Skill: Point of View

What happens when Clementine's parents talk about an "addition" to their family? (Clementine convinces herself that the "addition" to the family is a gorilla.) **Why a gorilla?** (On page 321, Clementine suggests that a gorilla is a great birthday present for her little brother.) **What does she say to her little brother?** (She leans over and squeezes him and says, "We're getting a gorilla, after all!") **What can you tell about Clementine's point of view, based on these details?** (She hopes the family meeting is about getting a gorilla.)

My dad looked at my mom and raised his eyebrows. My mom looked back at him and smiled. She waved her palm to him like a game show host, as if to say "Show us these great prizes, Bill!"

My dad looked at my mom again, and this time he looked like he was going to cry! Not in a sad way, but in an "I can't believe how lucky I am that you're here" way. Which was nuts because my mom is *always* here.

"Families grow," he said again. "And tonight . . ." He stopped and smiled at my mom again. "Tonight, your mother and I want to talk to you about . . . an addition to our family. Our family is about to grow again."

And then finally, I figured out what he was saying! I slid Pea Pod off my lap and jumped up to give my dad and mom a hug.

"Yes! Thank you! Yes! You won't be sorry, I promise I'll take good care of it, you'll barely even notice it's here . . . Thank you!"

322

A C T Access Complex Text

▶ Connection of Ideas

After students read pages 322–323, have them reread the first two paragraphs of page 322.

- *Do Clementine's parents seem happy or sad? What makes you think so?* (They seem happy. Mom is smiling and waving like a game show host. Dad looks like he will cry because he can't believe how lucky he is.)

- *Why are Clementine's parents happy?* (The family is going to have a new baby.)

- *How does Clementine feel about having a baby brother or sister? How do you know?* (She is unhappy. She yells "No thanks!")

Cauliflower was sitting on the floor, looking between me and our parents, completely clueless, I leaned over and squeezed him hard. "We're getting a gorilla, after all!"

2

My mom fell back against her chair, laughing. "Oh, Clementine," she said. "It's definitely not a gorilla!"

I was a little tiny bit relieved. The truth is, since I got my kitten, I'm not sure I really want a gorilla anymore. That would be a really big litter box.

I studied my parents. "What is it then? A pony? We're getting a *pony?*"

My dad pulled me over to him and held my hands. "We're talking about a new baby. A brother or a sister for you two. What do you think about that?"

What I thought about that was N-O, *no thanks!* I yelled it.

3

"No thanks!" Parsnip echoed. Then he looked up at me. "No thanks what?"

323

LITERATURE ANTHOLOGY, pp. 322–323

Read

3 Ask and Answer Questions

COLLABORATE

How are *The Talented Clementine* and *Clementine and the Family Meeting* similar so far? How are they different? With a partner, write notes about how the stories compare. (In *The Talented Clementine* the setting is at Clementine's school. She is embarrassed because she doesn't have an act for the talent show. *Clementine and the Family Meeting* takes place at her house. She is upset to learn that she is going to have a new baby brother or sister. The story about the talent show has many characters, but this text is only about Clementine's family. Clementine learns that she has talents in *The Talented Clementine,* but it is too early to identify a theme in this story.)

Reread   *Close Reading Companion*

Author's Craft: Illustrations

How does the author use illustrations to help you understand how Clementine feels? (They show how Clementine changes as the story progresses. At first, she is happy. Her little brother and the kitten sit on her lap. After hearing the news, Clementine is angry and stomping her feet. The kitten and her brother have been thrown off.)

ELL Point out that *gorilla* and *gorila* are cognates. Say: *Clementine wants the family to get another animal for a pet. She wants a gorilla, or a large ape that comes from Africa.*

- *What kind of animal does Clementine want the family to get?* (a gorilla)

Read

4 Ask and Answer Questions

How do Clementine's parents try to comfort Clementine? (They tell her that life is always moving too fast and this is how life is. Her mother says, "But somehow that's just perfect. Her father says things, such as toy-truck ziti is how their family rolls.)

Reread *Close Reading Companion*

Author's Craft: Dialogue

How do you know how Clementine feels about having a new baby in the family? (The author uses dialogue to show that Clementine doesn't like the idea of the change. Clementine tells her parents, "No thanks to more people!" and explains that four is the "perfect number for a family.")

"No thanks to more people! Our family is four. There are four sides to a puzzle so we can all work on it at once. Hot dogs come in packages of eight, so we can each have two. At the playground, four is an even number for the seesaws. Four can all be together in the car. Four can be two and two sometimes, and nobody is lonely. Two kids and two grown-ups. Two boys and two girls. There are four sides to the kitchen table, so we each get one. Four is a perfect number for a family!"

While I'd been explaining all this, my brother had snuck over to his favorite cupboard and thrown all the pots and pans out, like a personal-size tornado. He was sitting inside now, crashing lids together.

I pointed to the mess in the kitchen. "Look at us! Lima Bean puts toy trucks in the ziti and we used a drill gun to stir the muffins this morning because we couldn't find the mixer and my rat is missing, which isn't my fault, and so is my hat, and maybe that *is* my fault, but how is a baby going to help with anything, that's what I want to know! It's all moving too fast and we're not ready."

"Oh, honey," my mom said. "Life is *always* moving too fast and we're *never* ready. That's how life *is*. But somehow that's just perfect." She dragged Zucchini out of the cupboard and hauled him off to get his pajamas on.

324

A C T Access Complex Text

Connection of Ideas

Have students compare and contrast themes in *The Talented Clementine* and *Clementine and the Family Meeting*.

- *What lesson does Clementine learn in* The Talented Clementine? (Everyone has talents. Clementine can use her talents to predict and solve problems.)

- *What does she learn in* Clementine and the Family Meeting? (Her home is hectic and everything is "moving too fast," but she learns that life is always too fast and things are always changing.)

- How are the themes in the two books the same? (In both books, life is unpredictable and always changing.)

"Your mother," my dad said, "is exactly right. Things are always changing—that's life. And this?" He spread his hands to the tornadoed kitchen. "Us? Toy-truck ziti, missing hats, drill-gun mixers? Well, this is how we roll, Clementine. This is how we roll."

Make Connections

How do Clementine's parents help her understand the changes in her family? ESSENTIAL QUESTION

How are the plot and setting and theme in the two stories about Clementine alike? How are they different? TEXT TO TEXT

325

LITERATURE ANTHOLOGY, pp. 324–325

Read

Summarize

Guide students to summarize the selection.

Reread

Analyze the Text

After students read and summarize, have them reread to develop a deeper understanding of the text by annotating and answering questions on pages 110–112 of the **Close Reading Companion**.

Integrate

Make Connections

Essential Question Answer: Clementine's parents say that life is always changing. Evidence: On page 324, her mother says, "Life is *always* moving too fast and we're *never* ready. That's how life *is*."

Text to Text *The Talented Clementine* takes place in a school auditorium, while "Clementine and the Family Meeting" is set at Clementine's home. In both stories, Clementine learns a lesson: in the first story, she learns how talented she is. In the second, she learns that she needs to adapt.

- **How are they different?** (In *The Talented Clementine,* she uses her talents to solve problems. In *Clementine and the Family Meeting,* there are no problems she can solve. Clementine learns that her family rolls with life's changes.)

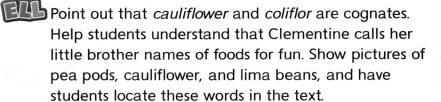 Point out that *cauliflower* and *coliflor* are cognates. Help students understand that Clementine calls her little brother names of foods for fun. Show pictures of pea pods, cauliflower, and lima beans, and have students locate these words in the text.

- *Who is Cauliflower?* (Clementine's brother) *Why does she call him Cauliflower?* (She thinks it is fun.)

→ Phonics/Fluency

 MINILESSON 20 Mins ## Plural Words

OBJECTIVES

CCSS Know and apply grade-level phonics and word analysis skills in decoding words. Decode multisyllable words. **RF.3.3c**

CCSS Read on-level text with purpose and understanding. **RF.3.4a**

Rate: 82–102 WCPM

ACADEMIC LANGUAGE
• *phrasing*
• Cognate: *fraseo*

 ELL

Refer to the sound transfers chart in the **Language Transfers Handbook** to identify sounds that do not transfer in Spanish, Cantonese, Vietnamese, Hmong, and Korean.

1 Explain

Tell students that a singular noun means "one" and a plural noun means "more than one." Point out that an -s is added to most singular nouns to make them plural. Explain that an -es is added to singular nouns that end in -s, -ss, -sh, -ch, or -x.

2 Model

Write the word *boats* on the board. Underline the -s. Model how to say the word. Repeat with the words *passes, wishes, bunches,* and *boxes.* Run your finger under each word as you sound it out.

3 Guided Practice

Write the following words on the board. Help students identify the plural ending added to each word. Guide students as they underline the plural ending and then pronounce each word.

years	states	foxes	latches
inches	classes	lunches	dishes
lashes	taxes	twins	trees

Read Multisyllabic Words

Transition to Longer Words Help students transition to reading longer plural words. Draw a T-chart. In column one write *scratch, wish, paintbrush, flower, mailbox, sandwich.* In column two, write *scratches, wishes, paintbrushes, flowers, mailboxes,* and *sandwiches.* Point to the words in the first column and underline the final letter or letters in each word. Model how to read each word and have students chorally read. Explain that the words in the second column include the plural spelling of each of the singular nouns. Have students identify the -s or -es ending in each plural word. Point to each word and have students read the words chorally. Write simple sentences using words from column two and have students read them.

Go Digital

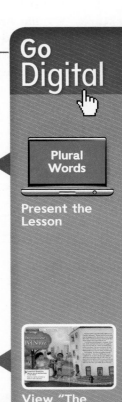

Plural Words

Present the Lesson

View "The Impossible Pet Show"

Vowel Team Syllables

1 Explain

Every syllable in a word has one vowel sound. Many vowel sounds are spelled with vowel digraphs, or teams, such as *ea, ee, ai, ie, ay, ow, ey, oe,* and *oa.*

- When two vowels appear together in a word, they work as a team to form one vowel sound.
- The vowel teams appear in the same syllable.

2 Model

Write and say the words *peaches, oatmeal, indeed,* and *afraid.* Have students repeat the words. Model dividing the words into syllables and then underlining the vowel teams.

3 Guided Practice

Write the words *flowing, mailbox, rowboat, birthday, briefcase, monkey, oboe,* and *coatrack* on the board. Have students identify the vowel team in each word and then say the words.

Phrasing

Explain/Model Explain that appropriate phrasing means grouping words to convey meaning. Tell students that paying attention to punctuation marks, such as pausing at commas and dashes and stopping at periods, is one way to read with appropriate phrasing. Remind students that reading with appropriate phrasing will help to convey meaning and understanding to the text.

Model reading the first two paragraphs of "The Impossible Pet Show" on page 277. Emphasize phrasing by pausing at the commas and stopping briefly at the periods.

Practice/Apply Divide the class into two groups and have the groups alternate reading the sentences. Remind students to use appropriate phrasing as they read and offer feedback as needed.

Daily Fluency Practice FLUENCY

Students can practice fluency using **Your Turn Practice Book.**

Can students decode plural words? Can students read multisyllabic words with vowel teams? Can students read fluently?

Small Group Instruction

If No →	Approaching Level	Reteach pp. T104, T106
	ELL	Develop p. T122
If Yes →	On Level	Review p. T122
	Beyond Level	Extend p. T116

ON-LEVEL PRACTICE BOOK p. 168

A. Read each sentence below. Circle the word that has the correct plural spelling.

1. Last summer my family visited five (states, stateses).

2. How many (lunchs, lunches) should we make for the field trip?

3. After the forest fire, the trees were reduced to (ashes, ashs).

4. We need several (trays, trayes) to clear the tables.

5. People were surprised that the (twines, twins) looked so different.

6. My puppy grew two more (inchs, inches) since his last vet visit.

B. Read each word in bold. Circle the letter that shows the word correctly divided into syllables. Then underline each vowel team in the correctly divided word.

1. teacher   a. teach / er   b. te / acher
2. explain   a. expl / ain   b. ex / plain
3. railroad   a. rail / road   b. ra / il / road
4. reaches   a. re / aches   b. reach / es
5. seeing   a. see / ing   b. se / eing

APPROACHING p. 168	BEYOND p. 168	ELL p. 168

→ Write to Sources

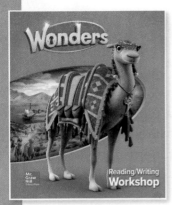

Reading/Writing Workshop

OBJECTIVES

CCSS Write narratives to develop real or imagined experiences or events using effective technique, descriptive details, and clear event sequences. Use dialogue and descriptions of actions, thoughts, and feelings to develop experiences and events or show the response of characters to situations. **W.3.3b**

ACADEMIC LANGUAGE

dialogue, narration, situations

Go Digital

U4W2 Ideas: Develop Characters

DAY 1

Writing Fluency

Write to a Prompt Provide students with the prompt: *Write about the Pet Show.* Have students share their ideas about pet shows. *What types of acts did the animals perform at the Pet Show?* When students finish sharing ideas, have them write continuously for eleven minutes in their Writer's Notebook. If students stop writing, encourage them to keep going.

 When students finish writing, have them work with a partner to compare ideas and make sure they both have a clear understanding of the story.

✎ Genre Writing

Fictional Narrative pp. T344–T349

Second Week Focus: Over the course of the week, focus on the following stages of the writing process:

Draft Distribute copies of the Student Model found online in Writer's Workspace. Teach the minilesson on dialogue. Have students review the Problem and Solution Charts they prepared in Prewrite, and write a draft.

Revise Analyze the Revised Student Model found online in Writer's Workspace. Teach the minilesson on temporal words and phrases. Have students review their partner's draft and revise their own. Distribute the Revise and Edit Checklist from Writer's Workspace to guide them.

DAY 2

Write to the Reading/Writing Workshop Text

Analyze the Prompt Read aloud the first paragraph on page 284 of the **Reading/Writing Workshop**. Ask: *What is the prompt asking?* (to state and support an opinion) Say: *Let's reread to find details and dialogue that tell us about Daniel's skills and talents. We can note text evidence.*

Analyze Text Evidence Display Graphic Organizer 33 in Writer's Workspace. Say: *Let's see how one student, Jamie, took notes to answer the prompt. She notes that Daniel says he's uncomfortable and nervous around animals.* Guide the class through the rest of Jamie's notes.

Analyze the Student Model Explain how Jamie used text evidence from her notes to write a response to the prompt.

- **Focus on a Topic** Jamie focused on the topic. She states her opinion in her topic sentence. She used text evidence from her notes to form her opinion. Trait: Ideas

- **Linking Words** Jamie used linking words to connect the ideas from her notes and the situations from the text. Trait: Sentence Fluency

- **Characters** Jamie described what Daniel was like, using evidence from the story. She mentioned that Daniel knew how to calm down the pets during the Pet Show. Jamie's details supported her opinion and help show how the author developed Daniel's character. Trait: Ideas

For additional practice with ideas and developing characters, assign **Your Turn Practice Book** page 169.

Write to Sources

Write About the Text

Pages 276-279

Jamie

I answered the question: *In your opinion, should Carla have made Daniel the announcer in the Pet Show?*

Focus on a Topic
My topic sentence states my opinion, so I can give my reasons in the rest of the paragraph.

Linking Words
I included linking words to connect my opinion and my reasons.

©Jose Luis Pelaez Inc/Blend Images LLC

284

Student Model: *Opinion*

I think Carla did the right thing when she made Daniel the announcer in the Pet Show. At first, I thought it was a bad idea because Daniel said he felt nervous. But I changed my opinion because Daniel calmed down when he presented the animals. He could make the animals behave. Daniel found his talent when Carla made him the announcer. He wouldn't have discovered this talent if Carla had listened to him.

Characters
I used evidence from the story to show what David was like.

Grammar
This **contraction** is a short way of saying *would not*.
Grammar Handbook
See page 485.

Your Turn

In your opinion, would you be a good announcer in a pet show? Provide reasons why or why not.

Go Digital!
Write your response online.
Use your editing checklist.

Marcin Piwowarski

285

READING/WRITING WORKSHOP, *pp. 284-285*

Your Turn Writing Read the Your Turn prompt on page 285 of the Reading/Writing Workshop aloud. Discuss the prompt with students. If necessary, review with students that authors use dialogue and narration to explain how characters handle situations.

Have students take notes as they look for text evidence to answer the prompt. Remind them to include the following elements as they craft their response from their notes:

- Focus on a Topic
- Linking Words
- Characters

Have students use **Grammar Handbook** page 485 in the Reading/Writing Workshop to edit for errors related to contractions.

ELL ENGLISH LANGUAGE LEARNERS SCAFFOLD

Beginning

Write Help students complete the sentence frames.
At a pet show, the announcer ____.
Pets and their owners ____.

Intermediate

Describe Ask students to complete the sentence frames. Encourage students to provide details.
A good announcer in a pet show has to be able to ____.
I would need to ____.

Advanced/High

Discuss Check for understanding. Ask: *Could you be an announcer in a pet show? What qualities would you need to have to be a good announcer?*

Write to Sources

DAY 3 For students who need support to complete the writing assignment for the Literature Anthology, provide the following instruction.

DAY 4

Write to the Literature Anthology Text

Analyze the Prompt Explain that students will write about *The Talented Clementine* on **Literature Anthology** pages 300–317. Provide the following prompt: *How does the author use what the characters do and say to help you see how Clementine has changed?* Ask: *What is the prompt asking you to do?* (to analyze the author's use of situations and dialogue)

Analyze Text Evidence Help students note evidence.

Page 302 Read the page aloud. Ask: *Why does Clementine's face turn red?* (She is embarrassed because she just had to tell Margaret's teacher that she had no talent.)

Page 313 Read the page aloud. Ask: *What happens during the show?* (The pianists throw up; the Hula-Hoopers go on too long.) *Who is the only one who helps?* (Clementine) *Why is this important?*

Encourage students to look for more text evidence about Clementine's character. Then have them craft a short response. Use the conference routine below.

Write to Two Sources

Analyze the Prompt Explain that students will compare *The Talented Clementine* and "Clementine and the Family Meeting." Provide students with the following prompt: *In your opinion, what kind of person is Clementine? Use text evidence from two sources to support your answer.* Ask: *What is the prompt asking you to do?* (to state and support an opinion about a main character) Say: *On page 314 of the Literature Anthology, I read that Margaret freezes while on stage, and Clementine helps her carry on. So in my notes, I will write:* Clementine helps Margaret get over her stage fright. *I will also note the page number and the title of the source. On page 323, Clementine yells "No thanks!" when she finds out the family is having a new baby. I will add this to my notes.*

Analyze Text Evidence Display online Graphic Organizer 34 in Writer's Workspace. Say: *Let's see how one student took notes to answer the prompt. Here are Jamie's notes.* Read through the text evidence for each selection and have students point out what Clementine is like in different situations.

Teacher Conferences

STEP 1

Talk about the strength of the writing.

You order your ideas clearly and in a way that makes it easy to read. The topic of the writing is well focused.

STEP 2

Focus on how the writer uses text evidence.

The details you have cited support your topic, but your writing would be stronger if you added more text evidence about ____.

STEP 3

Make concrete suggestions.

This section is interesting. I'd be able to understand it better if you made stronger links between ideas and situations.

DAY

5

Share the Prompt Provide the following prompt to students: *In your opinion, would it be easier to help with a talent show or baby-sit a little brother? Use text evidence from* The Talented Clementine *and "Clementine and the Family Meeting" to support your opinion.*

Find Text Evidence Have students take notes. Find text evidence and give guidance where needed. If necessary, review with students how to paraphrase. Remind them to write the page number and source of the information.

Analyze the Student Model Review the prompt and Jamie's notes from Day 4. Display the student model on page 170 of the **Your Turn Practice Book**. Explain to students that Jamie synthesized her notes to write a response to the prompt. Discuss the page together with students or have them do it independently.

Write the Response Review the prompt from Day 4 with students. Have students use their notes to craft a short response. Tell students to include the title of both sources and the following elements:

- Focus on a Topic
- Linking Words
- Characters

COLLABORATE

Share and Reflect Have students share their responses with a partner. Use the Peer Conference routine below.

Suggested Revisions

Provide specific direction to help focus young writers.

Focus on a Sentence
Read the draft and target one sentence for revision. *Rewrite this sentence by adding more supporting details to show ____.*

Focus on a Section
Underline a section that needs to be revised. *This section is confusing. Add more linking words to connect your ideas.*

Focus on a Revision Strategy
Underline a section. Have students use a specific revision strategy, such as substituting. *What the characters say is important. Try substituting some descriptions with dialogue.*

Peer Conferences

Focus peer responses on adding supporting details to explain the main idea. Provide these questions:

- Is the writing clearly focused on a topic?
- Are the ideas linked together in a logical way?
- Are there enough details to support the opinion?

Grammar: Contractions with *Not*

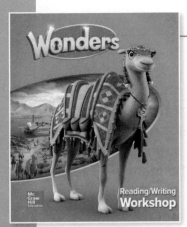

Reading/Writing Workshop

OBJECTIVES

CCSS Use spelling patterns and generalizations (e.g., *word families, position-based spellings, syllable patterns, ending rules, meaningful word parts*) in writing words. **L.3.2f**

- Use contractions with *not*
- Identify contractions and apostrophes
- Use contractions and apostrophes correctly
- Proofread sentences for mechanics and usage errors

Have each student write three short sentences using the contractions *isn't, wasn't,* and *aren't.* Students should then check a partner's sentences to be sure apostrophes are placed correctly.

DAY 1

DAILY LANGUAGE ACTIVITY

What is the name of the movie we saw last week I is going to tell my friend Beth to whach it.

(1: week?; 2: I am; 3: watch)

Introduce Contractions with *Not*

- A **contraction** is a shortened form of two words.
- An **apostrophe** takes the place of one or more letters in a contraction:
  - is not = isn't
  - was not = wasn't
- Some contractions are formed with forms of the verbs *be, do,* and *have*:
  - do not = don't
  - have not = haven't
- *Won't* is a contraction for *will not*. The spelling of the verb *will* changes.

Discuss contractions using page 485 of the Grammar Handbook.

 TALK ABOUT IT

COLLABORATE

CONTRACTION QUIZ

Partners should create five simple or compound sentences with contractions and trade sentences with another pair. One partner should read a sentence aloud; the other should identify the contraction using a question form (for example, "What is *didn't?*").

DAY 2

DAILY LANGUAGE ACTIVITY

charles hasnt played soccer in over a week. He said he wasnt feeling well

(1: Charles; 2: hasn't; 3: wasn't; 4: well.)

Review Contractions with *Not*

Review what contractions are and how to place an apostrophe in contractions.

Introduce More Contractions with *Not*

Present the following:

- A **contraction** is a shortened form of two words:
  - cannot = can't
  - are not = aren't
  - does not = doesn't
  - did not = didn't
  - has not=hasn't
- An **apostrophe** takes the place of one or more letters.

CONTRACTIONS WITH *NOT*

Ask partners to use contractions with *not* to talk about how they have used what they know to help others. Students might discuss how a friend wasn't able to do something until the student showed them how to do it.

DAY

Jerry doesnt have practice on mondays. He has practice on Wednesdays and fridays

(1: doesn't; 2: Mondays.; 3: Fridays.)

Mechanics and Usage: Using Apostrophes

- Do not confuse contractions with possessive nouns. An **apostrophe** is used with a possessive noun to show ownership:

  The *boy's* boat.
  The *family's* car.

- The words *don't, won't,* and *haven't* are contractions. They each have an **apostrophe** which shows where letters are left out.

- When spelling contractions, make sure the apostrophe is in the correct place.

Refer students to Grammar Handbook pages 485 and 503.

See Grammar Practice Reproducibles pages 81–85.

DAY

Maria hasnt been to a peting zoo. She is going to go with her friend Tyrone and his family next week

(1: hasn't; 2: petting; 3: week.)

Proofread

Have students correct errors in these sentences.

1. Lucia didnt know how to fly a kite until Dwaine teached her. (1: didn't; 2: taught)

2. Jon wasnt sure he could draw a picture of a horse without Amys' help. (1: wasn't; 2: Amy's)

3. Mr. Brown said, "I cant say this enough. write your name at the top of the test (1: can't; 2: Write; 3: test.")

4. Darnell wont be going because he did not bring his permission slip. (1: won't; 2: didn't)

Have students check their work using Grammar Handbook pages 485 and 503.

DAY 5

The ranger showed us how to camp He said to clear away rocks branches and twigs before setting up our tent.

(1: camp.; 2: rocks, branches, and)

Assess

Use the Daily Language Activity and Grammar Practice Reproducibles page 85 for assessment.

Reteach

Use Grammar Practice Reproducibles pages 81–84 and selected pages from the Grammar Handbook for reteaching. Tell students that it is important to use and understand how to use contractions correctly as they read, write, and spell.

Check students' writing for use of the skill and listen for it in their speaking. Assign Grammar Revision Assignments in their Writer's Notebooks as needed.

REPLACE THE CONTRACTION

Have groups write five sentences using contractions with *not*. Then have each student read the sentences aloud, substituting the contraction with the two words used to form it. Students should keep the long form and the contraction the same.

SAY THE CONTRACTION

Have students in small groups each write five contractions containing "not" on index cards. Students will take turns selecting a card and reading the contraction aloud, as the others guess what the main verb of the contraction is.

ACT OUT A SCENE

Have students write and reenact a scene from a story the class has read where someone uses a talent to help solve a problem. Have them use contractions and remind them to use commas and quotation marks when writing dialogue.

Spelling: Plural Words

DAY 1

DAY 2

OBJECTIVES

CCSS Use spelling patterns and generalizations (e.g., *word families, position-based spellings, syllable patterns, ending rules, meaningful word parts*) in writing words. **L.3.2f**

CCSS Consult reference materials, including beginning dictionaries, as needed to check and correct spellings. **L.3.2g**

Spelling Words

years	foxes	bunches
twins	inches	alleys
trays	flies	lunches
states	cities	cherries
ashes	ponies	daisies

Review spoon, clues, shook
Challenge heroes, libraries

Differentiated Spelling

Approaching Level

years	foxes	horses
twins	inches	ties
trays	flies	skies
states	cities	bodies
ashes	lunches	boxes

Beyond Level

trays	bunches	libraries
ashes	alleys	chimneys
foxes	cherries	eyelashes
inches	daisies	journeys
ponies	heroes	scratches

Assess Prior Knowledge

Display the spelling words. Read them aloud, drawing out and slowly enunciating the plural endings in each word.

Model for students how to spell the word *cities*. Segment the word sound by sound, then attach a spelling to each sound. Point out that the root word *city* ends in a consonant and the letter *y*, so to form its plural, you need to change the *y* to *i* and add the ending *-es*.

Demonstrate sorting the spelling words by pattern under key words *years, foxes,* and *cities.* (Write the words on index cards or the IWB.) Sort a few words. Remind them that nouns ending in *s, ss, x, ch,* or *sh* form the plural by adding *-es* to the root, as in *foxes.*

Then use the Dictation Sentences from Day 5. Say the underlined word, read the sentence, and repeat the word. Have students write the words.

Spiral Review

Review /ü/ and /u̇/ in the words *spoon, clues* and *shook.* Have students identify the *oo, ue* spelling patterns. Then have them find words in this week's readings with the same sounds. Use the Dictation Sentences below for review words. Read the sentence, say the word, and have students write the words.

1. I eat cereal with a <u>spoon</u>.
2. The detectives found <u>clues</u>.
3. The house <u>shook</u> in the storm.

Have students trade papers and check the spellings.

Challenge Words Review this week's spelling words, pointing out the plural endings. Use these Dictation Sentences for challenge words. Read the sentence, say the word, have students write the word.

1. My parents are my <u>heroes</u>.
2. There aren't many <u>libraries</u> nearby.

Have students write the words in their word study notebook.

 **WORD SORTS**

COLLABORATE

OPEN SORT

Have students cut apart the **Spelling Word Cards BLM** in the Online Resource Book and initial the backs of each card. Have them read the words aloud with a partner. Then have partners do an **open sort**. Have them record the sort in their word study notebook.

PATTERN SORT

Complete the **pattern sort** using the key words, pointing out the plural endings. Have students use Spelling Word Cards to do their own pattern sort. A partner can compare and check their sorts.

DAY

Word Meanings

Have students copy the words below into their Writer's Notebooks. Have them figure out the spelling word that goes with each definition.

1. groups of many things
   (bunches)
2. flowers (daisies)
3. animals that hunt (foxes)
4. reddish fruit (cherries)
5. sisters that look alike (twins)

Challenge students to come up with clues for spelling, review, or challenge words. Have students do a word hunt for the words in the weekly reading or other materials. They should identify the definition of the spelling word being used in context.

See Phonics/Spelling Reproducibles pp. 97–102.

SPEED SORT

Have partners do a **speed sort** to see who is faster. Then have them do a word hunt in the week's reading for plural words. Have them record the words in their Day 2 pattern sort in the word study notebook.

DAY

Proofread and Write

Write the sentences below on the board. Have students circle and correct each misspelled word. Remind students they can use print or electronic resources to check and correct spelling.

1. Many yeares had passed since the twinies were born. (years, twins)
2. They always serve cherrys at the lunchs in May. (cherries, lunches)
3. There were bunchs of foxs in that meadow. (bunches, foxes)
4. My favorite cites are in other staties. (cities, states)
5. Alleies are bad places to look for daisyes. (alleys, daisies)

Error Correction Review with students the spelling change rule when adding a plural. Have students write these words multiple times in their Writer's Notebooks.

BLIND SORT

Have partners do a **blind sort**: one reads a spelling word card; the other tells under which key word it belongs. Have them take turns until both have sorted all their words. Then have students explain how they sorted the words.

DAY

5

Assess

Use the Dictation Sentences for the Posttest. Have students list misspelled words in their word study notebooks. Look for students' use of these words in their writings.

Dictation Sentences

1. It has been two <u>years</u> since that party.
2. I had no idea you and your brother are <u>twins!</u>
3. She collected the <u>trays</u> at the end of class.
4. How many <u>states</u> are in America?
5. After the fire, all I saw were <u>ashes</u>.
6. <u>Foxes</u> can be dangerous.
7. How many <u>inches</u> are in a yard?
8. How many legs do <u>flies</u> have?
9. There are many <u>cities</u> in California.
10. I love to watch <u>ponies</u> run.
11. There are <u>bunches</u> of flowers growing in the forest.
12. Mom told me to stay away from <u>alleys</u> while walking home.
13. I planned many <u>lunches</u> for the school year.
14. I love to eat <u>cherries</u>.
15. I will buy <u>daisies</u> for my mother.

Have students self-correct the tests.

Build Vocabulary

OBJECTIVES

CCSS Determine the meaning of the new word formed when a known affix is added to a known word (e.g., *agreeable/ disagreeable, comfortable/ uncomfortable, care/careless, heat/ preheat*). **L.3.4b**

CCSS Distinguish shades of meaning among related words that describe states of mind or degrees of certainty (e.g., *knew, believed, suspected, heard, wondered*). **L.3.5c**

Vocabulary Words

achievement	confidence
apologized	embarrassed
attention	realized
audience	talents

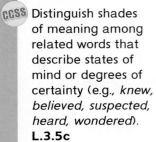

Pair students of different language proficiency levels to practice vocabulary. Have partners discuss different shades of meaning in synonyms or other words with similar meanings, such as **audience** and *gathering*.

DAY 1

Connect to Words

Practice this week's vocabulary.

1. Tell about an **achievement** you have had.
2. Have you ever **apologized** to someone?
3. Do you always pay **attention** in class?
4. How many people were in the **audience** at a recent movie?
5. How can you get more **confidence** before a test?
6. How can a person feel better after being **embarrassed**?
7. Have you ever **realized** something all of a sudden?
8. Describe some of your **talents**.

 BUILD MORE VOCABULARY

COLLABORATE

ACADEMIC VOCABULARY

Discuss important academic words.

- Display the words *achieve* and *demonstrate*.
- Define each word and discuss the meanings with students.
- Display *achieve* and *achievement*. Have partners look up and define related words.
- Write the related words on the board. Have partners ask and answer questions using the words. Repeat with *demonstrate*. Elicit examples from students.

DAY 2

Expand Vocabulary

Help students generate different forms of this week's words by adding, changing, or removing inflectional endings.

- Draw a four-column chart on the board. Write *apologize* in the left column. Then write *apologizes, apologized,* and *apology* in the other columns. Read aloud the words and discuss the meaning of each one.
- Have students share sentences with each form of *apologize*.
- Students can fill in the chart for other words, such as *realized*.
- Have students copy the chart in their word study notebook.

ROOT WORDS

Remind students that identifying root words can help them figure out the meanings of unfamiliar words.

Write *apology* and *apologize* on the board. Have students underline the root and discuss its meaning.

- Have partners identify other root words from the weekly readings. Then ask them to write a sentence with one of the words.
- Invite partners to share their words. Discuss the meanings of the words.

DAY 3

Reinforce the Words

Review this week's vocabulary words. Have students orally complete each sentence stem.

1. The <u>audience</u> cheered when the basketball team ____.

2. Tasha <u>apologized</u> to her mom for ____.

3. Horatio suddenly <u>realized</u> that he didn't have his ____ in his pocket.

4. It was hard to pay <u>attention</u> during the long ____.

5. I wasn't <u>embarrassed</u> when I ____ at the ice rink. It happens to everyone!

6. My brother has many <u>talents</u>, such as ____.

DAY 4

Connect to Writing

- Have students write sentences in their word study notebooks using this week's vocabulary.

- Tell them to write sentences that provide information about the words and their meanings.

- **ELL** Provide the Day 3 sentence stems for students needing extra support.

Write About Vocabulary Have students write something they learned from this week's words in their word study notebook. For example, they might write about putting on a *talent* show for their family and friends.

DAY 5

Word Squares

Ask students to create Word Squares for each vocabulary word.

- In the first square, students write the word. (example: *talents*)

- In the second square, students write their own definition of the word and any related words. (example: *skills*)

- In the third square, students draw a simple illustration that will help them remember the word. (example: a student playing an instrument)

- In the fourth square, students write non-examples. (example: *common*)

- Have students share their Word Squares with a partner.

PREFIXES *UN-, NON-, IM-, PRE-*

Remind students that adding a prefix to the beginning of a base word changes the meaning of the word. Remind them to use the meaning of the prefix and the base word to determine the meaning of the whole word.

- Display **Your Turn Practice Book** pages 163–164. Read the first paragraph. Model figuring out the meaning of *impossible*.

- For additional practice with prefixes, have students complete page 167. Discuss the meanings of the words.

SHADES OF MEANING

Help students generate words related to the state of mind of being *confident*. Draw a word web.

- Begin a discussion about the word *confident*. Ask: *How do you feel when you have confidence?* Write examples on the web.

- Have partners work together to add other words to the web. They may confirm meanings in a print or online dictionary.

- Ask students to copy the words in their word study notebook.

MORPHOLOGY

Use the word *realization* as a springboard for students to learn more words. Draw a T-chart.

- Write the word *realize* in the first column. Discuss the meaning.

- In the second column, write the suffix *-tion*. Model how to use the suffix and the base word to determine the meaning of *realization*.

- Have partners generate other words with the suffix *-tion*.

- Tell students to use the suffix and base words to determine the meanings of the words.

VOCABULARY **T101**

→Integrate Ideas

Close Reading Routine

Read   DOK 1–2

- Identify key ideas and details about Skills and Talents.
- Take notes and summarize.
- Use **A C T** prompts as needed.

Reread   DOK 2–3

- Analyze the text, craft, and structure.
- Use the **Close Reading Companion.**

Integrate   DOK 4

- Integrate knowledge and ideas.
- Make text-to-text connections.
- Use the Integrate lesson.
- Use *Close Reading Companion,* p. 113.

TEXT CONNECTIONS

Connect to the Essential Question

Write the essential question on the board: How can you use what you know to help others? Divide the class into small groups. Tell students that each group will compare the information that they have learned about how they can use what they know to help others. Model how to compare this information by using examples from this week's **Leveled Readers** and "The Impossible Pet Show," **Reading/Writing Workshop** pages 276–279.

Evaluate Text Evidence Have students review their class notes and completed graphic organizers before they begin their discussions. Encourage students to compare information from all the week's reads. Have each group pick one student to take notes. Explain that each group will use an Accordion

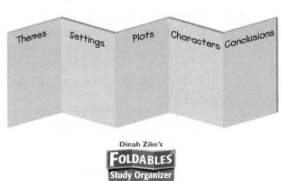

Dinah Zike's
FOLDABLES
Study Organizer

INQUIRY SPACE

LEVEL		1	**2**	3	4	5	6

NARRATIVE PERFORMANCE TASK

Write About: Frogs

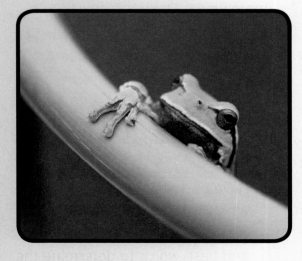

Guidello/Getty Images

Evaluate Sources

PREVIEW LEVEL 2 Display Level 2 from the Narrative Performance Task. Explain to students that in Level 2 they will be given four sources to evaluate. After reviewing the sources, they will choose the three most reliable sources to find information about their topic.

❶ **Reliable Sources** Explain to students how to decide if a source is reliable. Say: *A reliable source is one you can trust. A source is reliable when it contains information that is true.* Say: *When you look at a source, ask yourself: Does the source give facts about the topic? Is the writer someone who knows the topic well?* Remind students that a reliable source should also include information that is up-to-date and related to the topic. Show them the **Evaluate Sources** slide presentation from the **Toolkit.** Afterwards, have students summarize how to evaluate a source.

OBJECTIVE

CCSS Compare and contrast the most important points and key details presented in two texts on the same topic. **RI.3.9**

Foldable® to record their ideas. You may wish to model how to use an Accordion Foldable® to record comparisons.

Text to Photography

As students discuss the information from all the week's reads, have them include the photograph of young musicians on page 113 of the **Close Reading Companion** as a part of their discussion. Guide students to see the connections between the photograph and text. Ask: *How does the photograph connect to what you read this week?*

Present Ideas and Synthesize Information

When students finish their discussions, ask for a volunteer from each group to read his or her notes aloud.

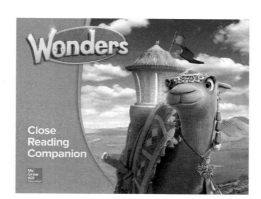

OBJECTIVE

CCSS Conduct short research projects that build knowledge about a topic. **W.3.7**

2 Skim and Scan Tell students to scan, or look over, a source to see if it contains keywords related to their topic. If it does, they can skim it to look for main ideas. Review with students the following definitions:

Skim: Read quickly for main ideas in a text.

Scan: Look quickly over a text to find keywords.

You may wish to show students the **Skim and Scan** animation from the Toolkit.

ASSIGN LEVEL 2 Have students begin Level 2 of the task. Before they evaluate the four sources, encourage students to re-watch the Evaluate Sources presentation and the Skim and Scan animation.

Approaching Level

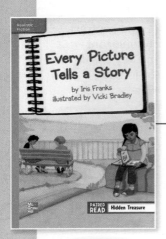

Lexile 470
TextEvaluator™ 22

___

OBJECTIVES

 Ask and answer questions to demonstrate understanding of a text, referring explicitly to the text as the basis for the answers. **RL.3.1**

Distinguish their own point of view from that of the narrator or those of the characters. **RL.3.6**

___

• Use prefixes to determine the meanings of words.
• Identify the narrator's point of view.

___

ACADEMIC LANGUAGE
ask, answer questions, point of view, realistic fiction, prefixes

Leveled Reader:
Every Picture Tells a Story

Go Digital

Before Reading

Preview and Predict

Have students read the Essential Question. Then have them read the title and table of contents of *Every Picture Tells a Story*. Have students predict how pictures will play a role in the story.

Review Genre: Realistic Fiction

Review with students that realistic fiction has characters and settings that could exist in real life. As they preview *Every Picture Tells a Story*, have students identify features of realistic fiction.

Leveled Readers

During Reading

Close Reading

Note Taking Have students use their graphic organizer as they read.

Pages 2–3 Reread the first three sentences on page 3. *Who is narrating the story?* (Lila) *Is Lila a character in the story or a person outside the story? How do you know?* (She is a character in the story because she is telling about things that have happened to her.) *How do you know that Lila's life has changed recently?* (She says that she used to live in a village, but now lives in a big city.)

Page 4 *How does Lila know the hot chocolate will taste delicious?* (Making chocolate is one of her grandmother's special talents.)

Pages 5–6 *What do we learn about Lila?* (She does not know many people. She likes to draw.) *Why does Lila draw pictures of different people around her?* (to remember their names) *Think of a question you have about one of the children Lila has drawn.* Have students ask their questions, and then work together to find the answers in the story.

Pages 7–8 *Why does Lila want to use pictures to help Lucia?* (because she does not speak English very well)

Page 9 *What is the prefix in the word* unhappy *on page 9?* (un-) *What does the prefix mean?* ("not") *Use the prefix to define* unhappy *to a partner.* (*Unhappy* means "not happy.") *Why was Lila unhappy?* (She did not want to leave the village.)

Fill in the Graphic Organizer

Pages 10–13 *What are the steps for making hot chocolate? Use time-order words for each step.* Help students find the steps in the story as needed. (First, roast cacao beans. Next, peel the skins. Then grind the cacao into a powder, heat the powder to soften it, and add sugar and spices. Last, whisk the chocolate paste into hot water.)

Pages 14–15 *Reread the last paragraph on page 15. How does Lila feel about the attention she is getting?* (embarrassed) Have students discuss how they would feel if they were in her place.

After Reading

Respond to Reading Revisit the Essential Question, and ask students to complete the Text Evidence questions on page 16.

Analytical Writing **Write About Reading** Make sure students use evidence from the text to show how the author shows Lila's point of view at the beginning of the story.

Fluency: Phrasing

Model Model reading page 9 with proper phrasing. Next, reread the page aloud, and have students read along with you.

Apply Have students practice reading with a partner.

PAIRED READ

"Hidden Treasure"

Make Connections: Write About It **Analytical Writing**

Before reading, have students note that the genre of this text is also realistic fiction. Then discuss the Essential Question.

Leveled Reader

After reading, have students write about connections between the different characters' points of view in *Every Picture Tells a Story* and "Hidden Treasure."

✏️ *Analytical Writing*

COMPARE TEXTS

- Have students use text evidence to compare the skills and talents of characters in both stories.

Literature Circles

Ask students to conduct a literature circle using the Thinkmark questions to guide the discussion. You may wish to have a whole-class discussion on students' special talents and how they could use them for the good of others.

Level Up

Level-up lessons available online.

IF students read the `Approaching Level` fluently and answered the questions

THEN pair them with students who have proficiently read the `On Level` and have approaching-level students

- echo-read the `On Level` main selection with their partner.
- use self-stick notes to mark a detail to discuss in each section.

A C T Access Complex Text

The `On Level` challenges students by including more **domain-specific words** and **complex sentence structures**.

Approaching Level

Phonics/Decoding

DECODE PLURAL WORDS WITH -s

OBJECTIVES

 Decode regularly spelled one-syllable words. **RF.1.3b**

Decode plural words with -s.

 I Do Write *dog* on the board and say it. Remind students that a singular noun means "one." Add -s to the end of the word to make *dogs*. Underline the *s*. Say the word, emphasizing the *s*. Explain that a plural noun means "more than one" and an -s is added to most singular nouns to make them plural.

 We Do Write the words *boys, bugs, girls,* and *songs* on the board. Underline the *s* in each word. Model how to decode the first word. Have students repeat. Point out that the plural is formed by adding -s. Have students read the rest of the words aloud, identifying the letter that forms the plural.

You Do Add these words to the board: *books, trees, lights,* and *states*. Have students read each word aloud and identify the letter that forms the plural. Then point to all of the words in random order for students to read chorally.

BUILD PLURAL WORDS WITH -s, -es

OBJECTIVES

 Decode multisyllable words. **RF.3.3c**

Build plural words with -s, -es.

 I Do Tell students that they will be building multisyllable plural words that are formed by adding -s or -es. Remind them that an -s is added to most singular nouns to make them plural. An -es is added to singular nouns ending in -s, -ss, -ch, -sh, or -x. Then display these **Word-Building Cards** one at a time: s, es; and write the syllables *box, nose, bench, bush, face, bus,* and *class* on the board. Model saying each syllable or sound.

 We Do Have students chorally read each syllable or sound. Repeat at varying speeds and in random order. Next, display all the Word-Building Cards and syllables. Work with students to combine the cards and syllables to form two-syllable plural nouns ending in -s or -es. Have students chorally read the words: *boxes, noses, benches, bushes, faces, buses, classes*.

 You Do Write other syllables on the board, such as *horse, glass, ash, lens, mask, switch,* and *fox* and display the Word-Building Cards s and es again. Have students work with partners to build words using these syllables. Have partners share their words with the class.

PRACTICE PLURAL WORDS WITH -s, -es

OBJECTIVES

 Decode multisyllable words. **RF.3.3c**

Decode plural nouns with -s and -es.

 I Do Remind students of the meaning of *singular* and *plural*. Write *edges* on the board and say it. Point out that the *s* at the end of the word makes it plural. *Edges* means "more than one edge." Remind students that an -s is added to most singular nouns to make them plural, and an -es is added to singular nouns ending in -s, -ss, -sh, -ch, or -x. Model decoding *foxes*.

 We Do Write the words *teachers, marbles, wishes, foxes, bosses, pitches,* and *gases* on the board. Model how to decode the first word. Then guide students as they decode the remaining words.

You Do Afterward, point to the words in random order for students to chorally read. Then have students read the words independently.

SYLLABLES WITH VOWEL TEAMS

OBJECTIVES

 Know spelling-sound correspondences for additional common vowel teams. **RF.2.3b**

 Decode multisyllable words. **RF.3.3c**

Identify vowel teams in multisyllable words.

 I Do Review that every syllable in a word has only one vowel sound. Point out that many vowel sounds are spelled with vowel digraphs, or teams, such as *ea, ee, ai, ie, ay, ow, ey, oe,* and *oa*. Explain that when two vowels appear together, they work as a team to form one vowel sound. Remind students that these vowel teams always appear in the same syllable.

 We Do Write *reaches, feeling, explain, pieces,* and *today* on the board. Say each word and have students repeat. Model dividing the words into syllables using the syllable-scoop technique. Then model underlining each word's vowel team.

 You Do Write *window, chimney, tiptoe,* and *floated* on the board. Have students say the words. Then, have students divide the words into syllables using the syllable-scoop technique and underline each word's vowel team. Ask them if they know any other words with vowel teams. Write them on the board. Point to all of the words in random order for students to read chorally.

ELL ENGLISH LANGUAGE LEARNERS

For the students who need **phonics, decoding,** and **fluency** practice, use scaffolding methods as necessary to ensure students understand the meaning of the words. Refer to the **Language Transfers Handbook** for phonics elements that may not transfer in students' native languages.

Approaching Level

Vocabulary

REVIEW HIGH-FREQUENCY WORDS

OBJECTIVES

 Use conventional spelling for high-frequency and other studied words and for adding suffixes to base words (e.g., *sitting, smiled, cries, happiness*). **L.3.2e**

Review high-frequency words.

 I Do Use **Word Cards** 131–140. Display one word at a time, following the routine:

Display the word. Read the word. Then spell the word.

 We Do Have students state the word and spell the word with you. Model using the word in a sentence, and have students repeat after you.

 You Do Display the word. Ask students to say the word and then spell it. When completed, quickly flip through the word card set as students chorally read the words. Provide opportunities for students to use the words in speaking and writing. For example, provide sentence starters such as *I have only been to the zoo ____.* Have students write each word in their **Writer's Notebook**.

REVIEW VOCABULARY WORDS

OBJECTIVES

Acquire and use accurately grade-appropriate conversational, general academic, and domain-specific words and phrases, including those that signal spatial and temporal relationships (e.g., *After dinner that night we went looking for them*). **L.3.6**

 I Do Display each **Visual Vocabulary Card** and state the word. Explain how the photograph illustrates the word. State the example sentence, and repeat the word.

 We Do Point to the word on the card and read the word with students. Ask them to repeat the word. Engage students in structured partner talk about the image as prompted on the back of the vocabulary card.

You Do Display each visual in random order, hiding the word. Have students match the definitions and context sentences of the words to the visuals displayed. Then have students complete **Approaching Reproducibles** page 161.

ANSWER YES/NO QUESTIONS

OBJECTIVES

 Demonstrate understanding of words relationships and nuances in word meanings. Identify real-life connections between words and their use (e.g., describe people who are *friendly* or *helpful*). **L.3.5b**

Answer questions to show understanding of the meanings of words.

 I Do Display the *audience* **Visual Vocabulary Card** and ask: *If you went to a concert, were you part of the* audience? Point out that the *audience* is the people who come to see or hear an event.

 We Do Display the card for *embarrassed* and ask: *If you are proud of your work, are you* embarrassed *by it?* With students, identify that *embarrassed* means someone is worried or uncomfortable about what other people think.

You Do Using the questions below, display the remaining cards one at a time, and read each question aloud. Have students answer *yes* or *no*.

If you realized *your mistake, did you understand it?*

Is an achievement *something you would celebrate?*

If you pay attention *when you read, do you follow along closely?*

If you apologized *to someone, did you say you were sorry?*

If you have confidence *in yourself, are you worried and nervous?*

If you do not cook well, is cooking one of your talents?

PREFIXES *un-, non-, im-, pre-*

OBJECTIVES

 Determine the meaning of the new word formed when a known affix is added to a known word (e.g., *agreeable/ disagreeable, comfortable/ uncomfortable, care/careless, heat/ preheat*). **L.3.4b**

Determine the meaning of unknown words with the prefixes *un-, non-, im,* and *pre-*.

I Do Display the Comprehension and Fluency passage on **Approaching Reproducibles** pages 163–164. Read paragraph 1. Point to *impossible*. Explain that it is formed by adding the prefix *im-* to *possible*. Remind students what a prefix is. Point out that *un-, non-* and *im-* mean "not" or "opposite of," and *pre-* means "before."

Think Aloud I see the prefix *im-* at the beginning of *impossible*. I know that *im-* means "not." So, I think that *impossible* means "not possible."

Write the meaning of the word from its prefix.

 We Do Ask students to point to the word *nonsense*. With students, discuss how to use the prefix to figure out the meaning of this word. Write the meaning.

 You Do Have students find the meaning of the words *unsure* and *imperfect* using each word's prefix.

Approaching Level

Comprehension

FLUENCY

 TIER 2

OBJECTIVES

CCSS Read on-level text with purpose and understanding. **RF.3.4a**

CCSS Read on-level prose and poetry orally with accuracy, appropriate rate, and expression on successive readings. **RF.3.4b**

Read fluently with appropriate phrasing.

 I Do   Explain that good readers learn to read with appropriate phrasing, which is grouping words together to convey meaning. Tell students that one way to read with appropriate phrasing is by pausing at commas and dashes and stopping at periods. Read the first two paragraphs of the Comprehension and Fluency passage on **Approaching Reproducibles** pages 163–164. Tell students to listen for your pauses at commas and stops at periods.

 We Do   Read the rest of the page aloud, and have students repeat each sentence after you using the same phrasing. Explain that you paid attention to punctuation by pausing or stopping.

 You Do   Have partners take turns reading sentences from the Reproducibles passage. Remind them to focus on their phrasing. Listen in and provide corrective feedback as needed by modeling proper fluency.

IDENTIFY POINT OF VIEW

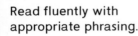 TIER 2

OBJECTIVES

CCSS Distinguish their own point of view from that of the narrator or those of the characters. **RL.3.6**

Identify point of view in a work of fiction.

 I Do   Write the topic: *Point of View*. Then write: *There is nothing to paint in New York; You will find many things to see and paint there*. Read the statements aloud. Remind students that a point of view is what someone thinks or feels. Explain that the first statement is Bae's point of view because it is what he thinks. He cannot know for sure because he has never been to New York. The second statement is Bae's mother's point of view because it is what she thinks. She thinks that once Bae gets to New York, he will find many things to paint.

 We Do   Read the first page of the Comprehension and Fluency passage in the **Approaching Reproducibles**. Ask: *What is Bae's point of view of Varvara when she answers the door?* Point out that when Bae first sees Varvara, he thinks she looks kind and unhappy, but he does not know for sure.

 You Do   Have students read the rest of the passage. After each paragraph, they should list examples of point of view. Review their examples with them. Help them explain how the characters expressed their points of view.

REVIEW NARRATOR'S POINT OF VIEW

OBJECTIVES

 Distinguish their own point of view from that of the narrator or those of the characters. **RL.3.6**

Identify the narrator's point of view.

 I Do Remind students that fiction is told from the point of view of the narrator. Explain that this is the narrator's thoughts and feelings about story events and other characters. Students can determine the narrator's point of view by looking for details that show how the narrator thinks and feels. They should also think of what their own point of view is.

 We Do Read the first paragraph of the Comprehension and Fluency passage in the **Approaching Reproducibles** together. Pause to point out details that express the narrator's point of view. Model how to decide when the narrator expresses a point of view and what this point of view is. Help students identify other examples of the narrator's point of view in the story.

You Do Have students look for statements showing the narrator's thoughts to determine the narrator's point of view on story events and characters. Have them decide if they agree or disagree with the narrator's point of view.

SELF-SELECTED READING

OBJECTIVES

 Ask and answer questions to demonstrate understanding of a text, referring explicitly to the text as the basis for answers. **RL.3.1**

 Distinguish their own point of view from that of the narrator or those of the characters. **RL.3.6**

Determine the narrator's point of view.

Read Independently

Have students choose a realistic-fiction book for sustained silent reading. Remind students that:

- the narrator's point of view is his or her thoughts and feelings about story events and other characters. They should look for details that show how the narrator thinks or feels.

- students can ask themselves questions to check their understanding about the story and reread to look for details that answer their questions.

Read Purposefully

Have students record the narrator's point of view on **Graphic Organizer 146** as they read independently. After they finish, they can conduct a Book Talk, each telling about the book they read.

- Students should share their organizers and answer these questions: *What is the narrator's point of view on story events and other characters? Which details helped you identify it? Do you agree with this point of view?*

- Students should also tell if they asked and answered any questions to help them better understand what is happening in the story.

On Level

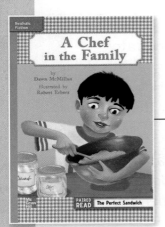

Lexile 530
TextEvaluator™ 28

OBJECTIVES

(CCSS) Ask and answer questions to demonstrate understanding of a text, referring explicitly to the text as the basis for the answers. **RL.3.1**

(CCSS) Distinguish their own point of view from that of the narrator or those of the characters. **RL.3.6**

• Use prefixes to determine the meanings of words.

• Identify the narrator's point of view.

ACADEMIC LANGUAGE
ask and answer questions, point of view, realistic fiction, prefixes

Leveled Reader:
A Chef in the Family

 Go Digital

Before Reading

Preview and Predict

Have students read the Essential Question. Then have students read the title and table of contents of *A Chef in the Family*. Have students predict how mice will play a role in the story.

Leveled Readers

Review Genre: Realistic Fiction

Review with students that realistic fiction has characters and settings that could exist in real life. As they preview *A Chef in the Family*, have students identify features of realistic fiction.

During Reading

Close Reading

Note Taking Have students use their graphic organizer as they read.

Pages 2–5 *Who is narrating the story?* (Benny) *Is Benny a character in the story or is he outside of the story?* (He is a character in the story.) *How do you know?* (He introduces himself, and the details of the story are about what he is doing.) *What is Benny's special skill?* (cooking) *How does he feel about making things?* (He is not good at making things.) *Talk to a partner about your own skills and whether you share Benny's point of view about cooking and making things.*
How does Benny incorporate his special talent into a birthday gift for his grandmother? (He adds a recipe for a cake and a special ingredient.)
Turn to a partner and ask a question about something Benny does in the first chapter. Reread if necessary to find the answer.

Pages 6–8 *How does Benny feel about all the different foods at the store?* (amazed) *Why does he have this point of view?* (because he loves food and cooking) *Why do you think Benny buys the candied fruit?* (Possible Responses: He thinks it looks pretty; he wants to buy food because he knows his grandmother loves food.)
On page 8, what does it mean when Benny's mom speaks "with confidence"? Demonstrate with a partner.

Fill in the Graphic Organizer

Pages 9–11 *What is the problem at the beginning of Chapter 3?* (Mice have gotten into all of the cake ingredients.) *Define* unhappy *on page 11 to a partner.* (*Unhappy* means *not happy.*) *How does the prefix help you define it?* (I know *un-* means "not.") *Why is Benny's mom unhappy?* (because mice got into the cake ingredients)

Pages 12–15 *Summarize to a partner how Benny uses his special talent to solve the problem.* (Benny makes a cake using other ingredients in the pantry. Since they do not have bread, he makes lettuce wraps.)

After Reading

Respond to Reading Revisit the Essential Question, and ask students to complete the Text Evidence questions on page 16.

Write About Reading Make sure students are using text evidence to explain how the author shows Benny's point of view at the end of the story.

Fluency: Phrasing

Model Model reading page 8 with proper phrasing. Next, reread the page aloud, and have students read along with you.

Apply Have students practice reading with a partner.

PAIRED READ

"The Perfect Sandwich"

Make Connections:

Write About It

Before reading, have students note that the genre of this text is also realistic fiction. Then discuss the Essential Question.

After reading, have students write about connections between how point of view helps them understand the characters in *A Chef in the Family* and "The Perfect Sandwich."

Leveled Reader

Analytical Writing

COMPARE TEXTS

- Have students use text evidence to compare the skills and talents of characters in both stories.

Literature Circles

Ask students to conduct a literature circle using the Thinkmark questions to guide the discussion. You may wish to have a whole-class discussion on students' special talents and how they could use them for the good of others.

Level Up

Level-up lessons available online.

IF students read the On Level fluently and answered the questions

THEN pair them with students who have proficiently read Beyond Level and have on-level students

- partner-read the Beyond Level main selection.
- list difficult vocabulary words and look them up with their partner.
- name two details in the text to learn more about.

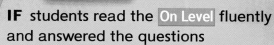

The Beyond Level challenges students by including more **domain-specific words** and **complex sentence structures**.

On Level

Vocabulary

REVIEW VOCABULARY WORDS

OBJECTIVES

 Acquire and use accurately grade-appropriate general academic and domain-specific words and phrases, including those that signal spatial and temporal relationships (e.g., *After dinner that night we went looking for them*). **L.3.6**

Review vocabulary words.

 Use the **Visual Vocabulary Cards** to review key vocabulary words *achievement, attention, apologized, confidence, embarrassed,* and *audience*. Point to each word, read it aloud, and have students chorally repeat it.

 Ask these questions, and help students respond and explain their answers.
- What is one thing you have done that you consider an *achievement*?
- How do you pay *attention* when someone is speaking to you?
- For what reason has someone *apologized* to you or someone else?

 Have students respond to these questions and explain their answers.
- When have you had *confidence* that you had done something well?
- How could you help someone from feeling *embarrassed*?
- If you are part of an *audience*, what are you doing?

PREFIXES *un-, non-, im-, pre-*

OBJECTIVES

 Determine the meaning of the new word formed when a known affix is added to a known word (e.g., *agreeable/ disagreeable, comfortable/ uncomfortable, care/careless, heat/ preheat*). **L.3.4b**

Determine the meanings of unknown words with prefixes *un-, non-, im,* and *pre-*.

 Remind students that they can use prefixes to help them determine the meaning of unknown words. Use the Comprehension and Fluency passage on **Your Turn Practice Book** pages 163–164 to model.

Think Aloud When I look at the word *impossible,* I see that the prefix *im-* has been added to the base word *possible.* I know that the prefix *im-* means "not," so *impossible* must mean "not possible."

 Have students read paragraph 4, where they will encounter *nonsense*. Have students figure out the meaning of the word by using its prefix. Point out that, like *im-,* the prefix *non-* means "not" or "opposite of."

 Have students work in pairs to determine the meaning of the words *unsure, imperfect, unhappy,* and *unbearable* as they read the rest of the selection.

Comprehension

REVIEW NARRATOR'S POINT OF VIEW

OBJECTIVES

 Distinguish their own point of view from that of the narrator or those of the characters. **RL.3.6**

Identify a narrator's point of view.

 I Do

Remind students that fiction can be told from the point of view of the narrator, which is the thoughts and feelings the narrator has about story events and other characters. To determine the narrator's point of view, students should look for details that show what the narrator feels and thinks. They can then decide if they share this point of view.

We Do

Have a volunteer read the first paragraph of the Comprehension and Fluency passage on **Your Turn Practice Book** pages 163–164. Have students orally list examples of the narrator giving a point of view, both stated and suggested. Then model finding the narrator's point of view of his homeland. With students, continue looking for details identifying the narrator's point of view on the rest of the page.

You Do

Have partners identify the narrator's point of view in the rest of the passage and explain whether or not they share this point of view.

SELF-SELECTED READING

OBJECTIVES

 Ask and answer questions to demonstrate understanding of a text, referring explicitly to the text as the basis for answers. **RL.3.1**

 Distinguish their own point of view from that of the narrator or those of the characters. **RL.3.6**

Determine the narrator's point of view.

Read Independently

Have students choose a book of realistic fiction for sustained silent reading.

- Before they read, have students preview the book, reading the title and viewing the front and back cover.

- As students read, remind them to ask questions about their story and to look for story details to answer these questions.

Read Purposefully

Encourage students to read different books in order to learn about a variety of subjects.

- As students read, they can fill in the narrator's point of view on **Graphic Organizer 146**. They can refer back to it to write a summary of the book.

- Students should share their organizers and answer these questions: *What is the narrator's point of view about story events and other characters? Which details help you identify the narrator's point of view? Do you agree with this point of view?*

- Ask students to share their reactions to the book with classmates.

→ Beyond Level

Lexile 700
TextEvaluator™ 41

OBJECTIVES

CCSS Ask and answer questions to demonstrate understanding of a text, referring explicitly to the text as the basis for the answers. **RL.3.1**

CCSS Distinguish their own point of view from that of the narrator or those of the characters. **RL.3.6**

• Use prefixes to determine the meanings of words.

• Identify the narrator's point of view.

ACADEMIC LANGUAGE

ask and answer questions, point of view, realistic fiction, prefixes

Leveled Reader:
Stepping Forward

Leveled Readers

Before Reading

Preview and Predict

Have students read the Essential Question. Then have them read the title and table of contents of *Stepping Forward*. Have students predict how someone's hobby will play a role in the story.

Review Genre: Realistic Fiction

Review with students that realistic fiction has characters and settings that could exist in real life. As they preview *Stepping Forward*, have students identify features of realistic fiction.

During Reading

Close Reading

Fill in the Graphic Organizer

Note Taking Have students use their graphic organizer as they read.

Pages 2–4 *Who is narrating the story?* (Rigel) *How do you know?* (He tells his name and talks about himself.) *What does Rigel love?* (maps) *What are Rigel's friends' point of view of his fascination with maps?* (They do not understand it.) *What is his point of view about some of his friends' hobbies?* (He finds some of their hobbies boring.) *What are those hobbies?* (fishing, computer games) *How does Rigel feel about going to school today? Why?* (He is looking forward to school because his class is going on an orienteering hike; this hike is a great way to learn how to read maps.) *Reread page 4, and discuss with a partner how each character has a different point of view of the hike. Then discuss how you would feel about going on an orienteering hike.*

Pages 5–8 *Turn to a partner and summarize the two most important things to do on the orienteering course.* (Read a map properly, and stay together.) *Why does Rigel feel embarrassed about volunteering to be the leader?* (He does not like to be the center of attention.) *Why does Kevin not want to read the map?* (He is impatient and wants to start hiking.)

Page 9 *Define* nonsense *on page 9 to a partner.* (*Nonsense* means "something that does not make sense.") *How does the prefix help you figure out the definition?* (I know that *non-* means "not.")

Pages 10–12 *How does Rigel's talent help him solve the problem his group has?* (His knowledge of maps helps him navigate an alternative route.)

Pages 13–15 *What effect do Rigel's actions have on the class the next day?* (They think he is the hero of the moment. The teacher decides to have the students study maps.) *What does Rigel learn about himself by the end of the story?* (He learns he is more confident than he thought.) *Turn to a partner and ask a question about something that happens in Chapter 4, then find the answer in the story.*

Literature Circles

Ask students to conduct a literature circle using the Thinkmark questions to guide the discussion. You may wish to have a whole-class discussion on students' special talents and how they could use them for the good of others.

After Reading

Respond to Reading Revisit the Essential Question, and ask students to complete the Text Evidence questions on page 16.

Write About Reading *Analytical Writing* Make sure students write about the hike from Kevin's point of view and that they follow the original story's sequence.

Fluency: Phrasing

Model Model reading page 2 with proper phrasing. Next, reread the page aloud, and have students read along with you.

Apply Have students practice reading with a partner.

Gifted and Talented

Synthesize Challenge students to draw a map for an orienteering hike around the classroom. Have students note three checkpoints on their maps. Have groups follow the maps around the room.

PAIRED READ

Leveled Reader

"Rigel to the Rescue"

Make Connections: Write About It *Analytical Writing*

Before reading, have students note that the genre of this text is also realistic fiction. Then discuss the Essential Question.

After reading, have students write about connections between how point of view helps you understand the characters in *Stepping Forward* and "Rigel to the Rescue."

Analytical Writing

COMPARE TEXTS

- Have students use text evidence to compare the skills and talents of characters in both stories.

Beyond Level

Vocabulary

REVIEW DOMAIN-SPECIFIC WORDS

 OBJECTIVES
Acquire and use accurately grade-appropriate general academic and domain-specific words and phrases, including those that signal spatial and temporal relationships (e.g., *After dinner that night we went looking for them*). **L.3.6**

 Model
Use the **Visual Vocabulary Cards** to review the meanings of the words *talents* and *audience*. Write social studies related sentences on the board using the words.

Write *fascination* and *skills* on the board, and discuss the meanings with students. Then help students write sentences using these words.

 Apply
Have students work in pairs to discuss the meanings of the words *practice, adventurous,* and *direction.* Then have students write sentences using the words. Challenge students to write sentences that use two of these words in each sentence.

PREFIXES *un-, non-, im-, pre-*

 OBJECTIVES
Determine the meaning of the new word formed when a known affix is added to a known word (e.g., *agreeable/ disagreeable, comfortable/ uncomfortable, care/careless, heat/ preheat*). **L.3.4b**

Determine the meaning of unknown words with prefixes *un-, non-, im,* and *pre-*.

 Model
Read aloud the first paragraph of the Comprehension and Fluency passage on **Beyond Reproducibles** pages 163–164.

Think Aloud I want to figure out the meaning of the word *impossible.* I know that it is formed by adding the prefix *im-* to *possible.* I know that the prefix *im-* means "not," so I think that *impossible* must mean "not possible."

With students, read the fourth paragraph. Help them figure out the meaning of the word *nonsense* using the word's prefix.

 Apply
Have pairs of students read the rest of the passage. Ask them to use their knowledge of prefixes to determine the meaning of the words *unsure, imperfect, unhappy,* and *unbearable.*

Write Dialogue Have students think back to this week's selections and how using what we know can help others. Have them write dialogue between two characters. One of the characters uses what he or she knows to help the other character. Encourage them to use words from this week's vocabulary, as well as words with the prefixes, *un-, non-, im-,* and *pre-.*

Comprehension

REVIEW NARRATOR'S POINT OF VIEW

OBJECTIVES

 Distinguish their own point of view from that of the narrator or those of the characters. **RL.3.6**

Identify the narrator's point of view.

Model Remind students that fiction is often told from the point of view of the narrator, which is the narrator's thoughts and feelings about the story's events and other characters. Students can look for details that show what the narrator feels or thinks to identify the narrator's point of view. They can then decide if they share this point of view.

Have students read the first paragraph of the Comprehension and Fluency passage of **Beyond Reproducibles** pages 163–164. Ask open-ended questions to facilitate discussion, such as *What is the narrator's point of view in this paragraph? Which story details show this point of view?* Students should provide text evidence to support their answers.

Apply Have students identify other details that show the narrator's point of view as they read the rest of the story. Then have them identify the narrator's point of view for the entire story. Have them tell whether or not they agree with the narrator's point of view and explain why or why not.

SELF-SELECTED READING

OBJECTIVES

 Ask and answer questions to demonstrate understanding of a text, referring explicitly to the text as the basis for answers. **RL.3.1**

 Distinguish their own point of view from that of the narrator or those of the characters. **RL.3.6**

Identify the narrator's point of view.

Read Independently

Have students choose a book of realistic fiction for sustained silent reading.

- As students read, have them fill in **Graphic Organizer 146**.
- Remind students to ask and answer questions about the story to check their understanding. They should look for answers in the story.

Read Purposefully

Encourage students to keep a reading journal. Ask them to read different books to learn about a variety of subjects.

- Students can write summaries of the books in their journals.
- Have students give the narrator's point of view, tell whether or not they agree with this point of view, and explain why or why not.

 Independent Study Challenge students to discuss how their books relate to the weekly theme of skills and talents. Have students compare some of the different ways that people's skills and talents help others. How can you use what you know to help others?

English Language Learners

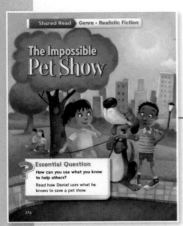

Reading/Writing Workshop

OBJECTIVES
Distinguish their own point of view from that of the narrator or those of the characters. **RL.3.6**

- Ask and answer questions to check understanding of a story.
- Use prefixes to determine the meanings of words.

LANGUAGE OBJECTIVE

Identify the narrator's point of view.

ACADEMIC LANGUAGE

- *ask and answer questions, point of view, realistic fiction, prefixes*
- Cognates: *ficción realista, prefijos*

Shared Read
The Impossible Pet Show

Before Reading

Build Background

Read the Essential Question: How can you use what you know to help others?

- Explain the meaning of the Essential Question. Make a list with students of the different things they might be good at.

- **Model an answer:** *We can use our talents to help others. Our skills and talents also make us feel good about ourselves.*

- Ask students a question that ties the Essential Question to their own background knowledge: *Turn to a partner and tell about something you are good at. Discuss or act out the talent. Can you help others with your talents?* Call on several pairs. Allow students to respond with gestures, eliciting details to develop their responses.

During Reading

Interactive-Question Response

- Ask questions that help students understand the meaning of the text after each paragraph.
- Reinforce the meanings of key vocabulary.
- Ask students questions that require them to use key vocabulary.
- Reinforce strategies and skills of the week by modeling.

Go Digital

View "The Impossible Pet Show"

Page 277

Paragraphs 1–2

Model Point of View *Daniel, a character in the story, is the narrator. The story is being told from his point of view. Look at the illustration and point to Carla, Perro, and Daniel.*

Model identifying a detail that tells about the narrator's point of view. *Daniel says he is worried about Carla's idea. Who can tell me another detail that tells about Daniel's point of view?* Continue until students have provided 2 or 3 details.

Paragraph 3

The story takes place in a park. Is a park a real place? (yes) *Do Carla and Daniel talk like real people?* (yes) Remind students that realistic fiction is a made-up story that could happen in real life, but it is not based on history. *Is "The Impossible Pet Show" realistic fiction, or is it historical fiction?* (realistic fiction)

Page 278

Paragraph 2

Explain and Model Prefixes *Adding a prefix to the beginning of a base word can change its meaning.* Point out the word *nonsense. I can see the root is* sense, *which can mean "logic." What word does* non- *look and sound like?* (no) *Non- means "no," or "opposite of."* Elicit from students that *nonsense* means "no sense." *What Daniel is saying is not logical.*

Paragraph 3

Explain and Model Asking and Answering Questions *I have a question about what Carla says. Carla says that Daniel is good at something, but I am not sure what. I will reread the paragraph to answer my question. I see that, after Daniel shouts at Perro to get down, the dog gets down and sits very still. So what does the text say Daniel is good at?* Have one student answer the question and another verify the answer. (Possible Response: He is good at getting Perro to settle down.)

Paragraph 5

When the show begins, it says that Daniel gulps. Have students point to the word *gulped.* Demonstrate and define the word, and have students gulp.

Talk to a partner about how Daniel feels and why he gulps.

Page 279

Paragraph 3

What does Perro do instead of sitting? (He leaps.) Demonstrate leaping for students and point to the illustration. *What do the rest of the animals do? Look for the action verbs.* (jump; hopped; escaped; running; howled)

Paragraph 4

What does Daniel tell the animals? (sit; quiet; stay) Point to the sentence *Even the audience froze.* Wrap your arms around yourself and shiver to demonstrate freezing. *Did the audience really freeze?* (no) Point to and read the previous sentence. *The kids stopped and stared. Did the audience stop and stare?* (yes) Have students demonstrate stopping and staring, and explain that in this context, *freeze* means "stop moving."

Have students turn to a partner and discuss their own talents. Have volunteers come up to the board and write down their talents.

After Reading

Make Connections

- Review the Essential Question: How can you use what you know to help others?
- Make text connections.
- Have students complete the **ELL Reproducibles** pages 163–165.

English Language Learners

Lexile 440
TextEvaluator™ 17

OBJECTIVES
Distinguish their own point of view from that of the narrator or those of the characters. **RL.3.6**

• Ask and answer questions to increase understanding of a text.
• Use prefixes to determine the meanings of words.

LANGUAGE OBJECTIVE
Identify the narrator's point of view.

ACADEMIC LANGUAGE
• ask and answer questions, point of view, realistic fiction, prefixes
• Cognates: *ficción realista, prefijos*

Leveled Reader:
A Chef in the Family

Leveled Readers

Go Digital

Before Reading

Preview

• Read the Essential Question: How can you use what you know to help others?

• Refer to Use Your Skills: *What are your special skills?*

• Preview *A Chef in the Family* and "The Perfect Sandwich": *Let's read about someone who wants to use his special skills.*

Vocabulary

Use the **Visual Vocabulary Cards** to preteach the ELL vocabulary: *ingredients, interesting.* Use the routine found on the cards. Point out the cognates: *ingrediente, interesante.*

During Reading

Interactive Question-Response

Note Taking Have students use the graphic organizer on **ELL Reproducibles** page 162. Ask the following questions after reading each section. Use visuals or pictures to define key vocabulary.

Pages 2–3 Read the first sentence on page 2 to students. *Who is the narrator?* (Benny) *What does he want to be?* (a chef) *On page 3, what is Benny's point of view about making a present for his grandmother? Have one student answer and another student elaborate on the answer.* (He says he is great at cooking but not so good at making things.)

Pages 4–5 *With a partner, ask a question about Benny's card when he first makes it. Then, reread page 4 to answer the question. What does Benny add to the card on page 5?* (a picture from a magazine, his own recipe for a cake)

Pages 6–7 *What is Benny's point of view of the candied fruit?* (He thinks they look like jewels.) *What does Benny believe his grandmother will think of the candied fruit?* (He believes she will like the fruit.)

Page 8 *How does Benny's mom feel about the cake she will make?* (that it will be hard to make but that Grandma will love it) *What do you think of the cake? Talk to a partner about your point of view of the cake.*

Fill in the Graphic Organizer

Pages 9–11 *What is the problem at the beginning of Chapter 3? Fill in the sentence frame:* ____ (Mice) *have gotten into the cake ingredients. Point to the word* unhappy *on page 11. The prefix* un- *means "not." Use this information to define* unhappy. Unhappy *means* ____ ("not happy"). *Now choral read the first sentence on page 11 using "not happy."*

Pages 12–15 *How does Benny solve the problem?* (He makes his own cake.) *How does his mother describe his cake?* (It is a great achievement.)

After Reading

Respond to Reading Help students complete the graphic organizer. Revisit the Essential Question. Have student pairs summarize and answer the Text Evidence questions. Support students as necessary, and review all responses as a group.

Analytical Writing **Write About Reading** Make sure the story is about Benny's cake and is told from the point of view of a mouse hiding in the kitchen.

Fluency: Phrasing

Model Model reading page 8 with proper phrasing. Next, reread the page aloud, and have students read along with you.

Apply Have students practice reading with a partner.

PAIRED READ

"The Perfect Sandwich"

Make Connections: Write About It ⟶ *Analytical Writing*

Before reading, have students note that the genre of this text is also realistic fiction. Then discuss the Essential Question.

After reading, have students write about connections between how point of view helps you understand the characters in *A Chef in the Family* and "The Perfect Sandwich."

Leveled Reader

✏️ *Analytical Writing*

COMPARE TEXTS

- Have students use text evidence to compare the skills and talents of characters in both stories.

Literature Circles

Ask students to conduct a literature circle using the Thinkmark questions to guide the discussion. You may wish to have a whole-class discussion on students' special talents and how they could use them for the good of others.

Level Up

Level-up lessons available online.

IF students read the ELL Level fluently and answered the questions

THEN pair them with students who have proficiently read On Level and have ELL students

- echo-read the On Level main selection with their partner.
- list difficult words and discuss these words with their partner.

A C T Access Complex Text

The On Level challenges students by including more **domain-specific words** and **complex sentence structures**.

English Language Learners

Vocabulary

PRETEACH VOCABULARY

OBJECTIVES

 Acquire and use accurately grade-appropriate general academic and domain-specific words and phrases, including those that signal spatial and temporal relationships (e.g., *After dinner that night we went looking for them*). **L.3.6**

LANGUAGE OBJECTIVE

Use vocabulary words.

 I Do Preteach vocabulary from "The Impossible Pet Show" following the Vocabulary Routine found on the **Visual Vocabulary Cards** for *achievement, apologized, attention, audience, confidence, embarrassed, realized,* and *talents.*

 We Do After completing the routine for each word, point to the word on the card and read the word with students. Have them repeat the word.

 You Do Have students work with a partner to use two or more words in statements or questions. Then have each pair read the sentences aloud.

Beginning	Intermediate	Advanced/High
Have students copy the sentences and read them aloud.	Have students write the sentences for two or more words.	Challenge students to write sentences for all of the words.

REVIEW VOCABULARY

OBJECTIVES

 Acquire and use accurately grade-appropriate general academic and domain-specific words and phrases, including those that signal spatial and temporal relationships. **L.3.6**

LANGUAGE OBJECTIVE

Review vocabulary words.

 I Do Review the previous week's vocabulary words over a few days. Read each word aloud and point to the word on the **Visual Vocabulary Card**. Ask students to repeat after you. Then follow the Vocabulary Routine on the back of each card.

 We Do Have students fill in sentence frames with the words *graceful, aroma,* and *flavorful.* Provide clues and act out words to help students recall the words. Have students define the words.

 You Do In pairs, have students write sentence frames for the other words. Ask them to read them aloud for the class to guess the word and use it in a sentence.

Beginning	Intermediate	Advanced/High
Help students write the sentence frames.	Have students write sentence frames on the board and read them aloud.	Have students write sentence frames and provide clues.

PREFIXES *un-, non-, im-, pre-*

OBJECTIVES

Determine the meaning of the new word formed when a known affix is added to a known word (e.g., *agreeable/ disagreeable, comfortable/ uncomfortable, care/ careless, heat/ preheat*). **L.3.4b**

LANGUAGE OBJECTIVE

Determine the meanings of unknown words with prefixes *un-, non-, im-,* and *pre-*.

 I Do
Read aloud the first paragraph of "The Impossible Pet Show" on page 278 while students follow along. After summarizing the paragraph, point to the word *unsure*. Explain that this word has the prefix *un-*. Remind students that a prefix is a word part added to the beginning of a word that changes the word's meaning. Point out that the prefixes *un-, non-,* and *im-* mean "not" or "opposite of." The prefix *pre-* means "before."

Think Aloud I do not know what *unsure* means. I see that it has the prefix *un-* added to the word *sure*. I know that sure means "certain." I also know the prefix *un-* means "not." I think *unsure* must mean "not certain."

 We Do
Have students point to the word *impossible* on page 278. Find the prefix of the word with students. Write the meaning on the board.

 You Do
Have pairs write definitions for *uncomfortable* on page 277 and *nonsense* on page 278 by using each word's prefix to determine its meaning.

Beginning	Intermediate	Advanced/High
Help students locate the words and determine their meanings.	Have students write a sentence for each word.	Have students write other words they know that have these prefixes.

ADDITIONAL VOCABULARY

OBJECTIVES

Produce simple, compound, and complex sentences. **L.3.1i**

Discuss concept and high-frequency words.

LANGUAGE OBJECTIVE

Use concept and high-frequency words.

 I Do
List and define concept and high-frequency words from "The Impossible Pet Show": *practiced, now, off;* and *A Chef in the Family: special, not.* Example: *When you have practiced something, you have done it many times.*

 We Do
Model using *special* in a sentence: *Visiting my friend who lives far away was a* special *event.* Then provide sentence frames and complete them with students: *Something* special *that I have done for a friend is ____.*

 You Do
Have pairs make up their own sentence frames and share them with the class to complete them.

Beginning	Intermediate	Advanced/High
Help students copy the sentence frames correctly and complete them.	Have students write sentence frames on the board and read them aloud.	Have students write definitions for the words they used.

English Language Learners
Writing/Spelling

WRITING TRAIT: IDEAS

 OBJECTIVES
Use dialogue and descriptions of actions, thoughts, and feelings to develop experiences and events or show the response of characters to situations. **W.3.3b**

Identify dialogue and description.

LANGUAGE OBJECTIVE
Develop ideas.

 I Do Explain that writers use dialogue and description to show a character's thoughts, feelings, and actions. Read the Student Model passage aloud as students follow along and listen for examples of dialogue and description.

 We Do Read aloud page 277 from "The Impossible Pet Show" as students follow along. Identify examples of dialogue and description. Model describing what the characters are like and what they are thinking and doing.

 You Do Have pairs write a short paragraph about two characters reacting to a situation that includes descriptions showing the characters' thoughts, feelings, and actions. Edit each paragraph. Then have students revise.

Beginning	Intermediate	Advanced/High
Have students copy the edited writing.	Have students revise to add descriptive words.	Have students revise to add dialogue and edit for errors.

SPELL PLURAL WORDS WITH -s, -es.

 OBJECTIVES
Use spelling patterns and generalizations (e.g., word families, position-based spellings, syllable patterns, ending rules, meaningful word parts) in writing words. **L.3.2f**

LANGUAGE OBJECTIVE
Spell plural words with -s and -es

 I Do Read the Spelling Words on page T98 aloud. Remind students that -s is added to most singlular nouns to make them plural. Explain that -es is added to singular nouns that end in -s, -ss, -sh, -ch, or -x to form the plural.

 We Do Read the Dictation Sentences on page T99 aloud for students. With each sentence, read the underlined word slowly. Have students repeat after you and write the word.

 You Do Display the words. Have students exchange their list with a partner to check the spelling and write the words correctly.

Beginning	Intermediate	Advanced/High
Have students copy the words with correct spelling and say the words aloud.	Have students correct the words and circle the letters that form the plural.	After students correct the words, have pairs quiz each other.

Grammar

CONTRACTIONS WITH *not*

OBJECTIVES

 Use an apostrophe to form contractions and frequently occurring possessives. **L.2.2c**

Use contractions with *not*.

LANGUAGE OBJECTIVE

Write sentences.

Language Transfers Handbook

In the Spanish language, contractions are not common and apostrophes are not used in contracted words. Therefore, Spanish-speaking students may be unfamiliar with the concept of combining words and using an apostrophe to indicate omitted letters. Give students additional practice forming contractions with the word *not*.

 Remind students that a contraction is a shortened form of two words. Point out that in a contraction, an apostrophe takes the place of one or more letters. Explain that some contractions are formed with the verbs *to be, do, have* and the word *not*. Tell students that these verbs do not usually change their spellings in a contraction with *not*. Write the following on the board: *do not/don't, is not/isn't, has not/hasn't, cannot/can't, will not/won't*. Point out that in the first three examples, an apostrophe replaces the *o* in *not* and that both the *n* and the *o* are removed in *can't*. Remind students that *won't* is a special contraction for *will not*. The spelling of the verb *will* changes.

 Write the sentences below on the board, and underline the words that will form the contraction. For each sentence, have a volunteer provide the contraction for the underlined word. Have the volunteer read the new sentence aloud and the other students echo read.

Dan is not home.	*The door will not open.*
Anna cannot find her shoes.	*The dog was not hungry.*
They do not have the book.	*She has not seen the movie.*

You Do Have students write three sentences each that have a contraction. Then have them switch papers with another student to write the words that form the contraction.

Beginning	**Intermediate**	**Advanced/High**
Help students write the sentences and the words forming each contraction. Have students read the sentences aloud after you.	Have students write their sentences on the board. Next to each sentence, have them write the letter or letters that the apostrophe replaces.	Have students write their sentences on the board. Then have them rewrite their sentences to make them mean the opposite.

For extra support, have students complete the activities in the **Grammar Practice Reproducibles** during the week, using the routine below:

* Explain the grammar skill.

* Model the first activity in the Grammar Practice Reproducibles.

* Have the whole group complete the next couple of activities, then the rest with a partner.

* Review the activities with correct answers.

PROGRESS MONITORING

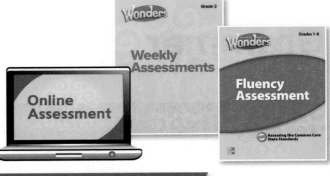

Unit 4 Week 2 Formal Assessment	Standards Covered	Component for Assessment
Text Evidence	RL.3.1	• *Selection Test* • *Weekly Assessment* • *Approaching-Level Weekly Assessment*
Point of View	RL.3.6	• *Weekly Assessment* • *Approaching-Level Weekly Assessment*
Prefixes *un-, non-, im-, pre-*	L.3.4b	• *Selection Test* • *Weekly Assessment* • *Approaching-Level Weekly Assessment*
Writing About Text	W.3.8	*Weekly Assessment*
Unit 4 Week 2 Informal Assessment	**Standards Covered**	**Component for Assessment**
Research/Listening/ Collaborating	SL.3.1d, SL.3.2, SL.3.3	• *RWW* • *Teacher's Edition*
Oral Reading Fluency (ORF) **Fluency Goal:** 82–102 words correct per minute (WCPM) **Accuracy Rate Goal:** 95% or higher	RF.3.4a, RF.3.4b, RF.3.4c	*Fluency Assessment*

Using Assessment Results

Weekly Assessments Skills and Fluency	If . . .	Then . . .
COMPREHENSION	Students score below 70% . . .	. . . assign Lessons 37–39 on Point of View from the *Tier 2 Comprehension Intervention online PDFs.*
VOCABULARY	Students score below 70% . . .	. . . assign Lesson 146 on Prefixes *un-, non-, im-, pre-* from the *Tier 2 Vocabulary Intervention online PDFs.*
WRITING	Students score below "3" on constructed response . . .	. . . assign Lessons 37–39 and/or Write About Reading Lesson 194 from the *Tier 2 Comprehension Intervention online PDFs.*
FLUENCY	Students have a WCPM score of 75–81 . . .	. . . assign a lesson from Section 1,7,8,9 or 10 of the *Tier 2 Fluency Intervention online PDFs.*
	Students have a WCPM score of 0–74 . . .	. . . assign a lesson from Sections 2–6 of the *Tier 2 Fluency Intervention online PDFs.*

Using Weekly Data

Check your data Dashboard to verify assessment results and guide grouping decisions.

Data-Driven Recommendations

Response to Intervention

Use the appropriate sections of the *Placement and Diagnostic Assessment* as well as students' assessment results to designate students requiring:

 Intervention Online PDFs

 WonderWorks Intervention Program

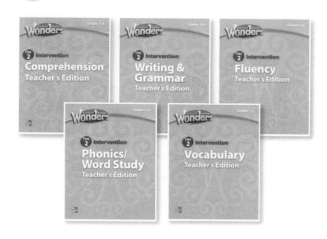

Build Knowledge
Adaptations

? Essential Question:
How do animals adapt to challenges in their habitat?

Teach and Model
Close Reading and Writing

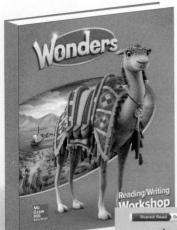

Reading/Writing Workshop

"Gray Wolf! Red Fox!" 290–293
Genre Expository Text **Lexile** 750 ETS *TextEvaluator* 17

Practice and Apply
Close Reading and Writing

Literature Anthology

Amazing Wildlife of the Mojave, 326–337
Genre Expository Text **Lexile** 720 ETS *TextEvaluator* 30

"Little Half Chick," 340–341
Genre Folktale **Lexile** 690 ETS *TextEvaluator* 21

Differentiated Texts

APPROACHING
Lexile 550
ETS *TextEvaluator* 12

ON LEVEL
Lexile 730
ETS *TextEvaluator* 20

BEYOND
Lexile 860
ETS *TextEvaluator* 22

ELL
Lexile 660
ETS *TextEvaluator* 5

Leveled Readers

Extended Complex Texts

Bat Loves the Night
Genre Informational Text
Lexile 560

Gray Wolves
Genre Informational Text
Lexile 640

Student Outcomes

Close Reading of Complex Text
- Cite relevant evidence from text
- Describe text structure: compare and contrast
- Reread

RI.3.1, RI.3.8

Writing
Write to Sources
- Draw evidence from informational text
- Write informative text
- Conduct extended research on frogs

Writing Process
- Proofread/Edit and Publish a Fictional Narrative

W.3.2a, W.3.8, W.3.10, W.4.9a

Speaking and Listening
- Engage in collaborative discussions about adaptations
- Paraphrase portions of "African Lions"
- Present information on adaptations

SL.3.1c, SL.3.2, SL.3.3

Content Knowledge
- Describe how in a particular environment, some organisms survive well, some less well, and some cannot survive.

Language Development
Conventions
- Form and use regular and irregular verbs

Vocabulary Acquisition
- Acquire and use academic vocabulary

alert	competition	environment	excellent
prefer	protection	related	shelter

- Use sentence clues to understand the meaning of a word

L.3.1d, L.3.1e, L.3.2c, L.3.4a, RI.3.4

Foundational Skills
Phonics/Word Study
- Varient vowel /ô/
- Greek and Latin roots

Spelling Words

taught	hauls	caused	paused
squawk	drawing	crawl	flawless
lawn	salt	talked	halls
water	bought	thoughtless	

Fluency
- Intonation

L.3.4c, RF.3.3b, RF.3.4a, RF.3.4b, RF.3.4c

Professional Development
- See lessons in action in real classrooms.
- Get expert advice on instructional practices.
- Collaborate with other teachers.
- Access PLC Resources.

Ken Karp/McGraw-Hill Education

Go Digital! www.connected.mcgraw-hill.com.

INSTRUCTIONAL PATH

1 Talk About Adaptations

Guide students in collaborative conversations.

Discuss the essential question: *How do animals adapt to challenges in their habitat?*

Develop academic language and domain specific vocabulary on adaptations.

Listen to "African Lions" to summarize how lions have adapted to their home on the grasslands of Africa.

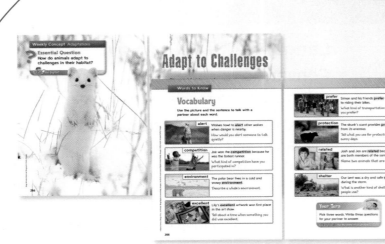

2

Read About "Gray Wolf!, Red Fox!"

Model close reading with a short complex text.

Read

"Gray Wolf!, Red Fox!" to learn how foxes and wolves adapt to challenges in their environments, citing text evidence to answer text-dependent questions.

Reread

"Gray Wolf!, Red Fox!" to analyze text, craft, and structure, citing text evidence.

3 Write About Adaptations

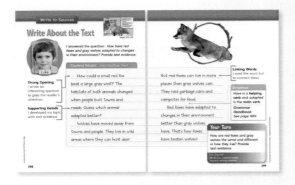

Model writing to a source.

Analyze a short response student model.

Use text evidence from close reading to write to a source.

4 Read and Write About Adaptations

Practice and apply close reading of the anchor text.

Read

Amazing Wildlife of the Mojave to learn how different animals in the Mojave Desert survive in a dry, hot place.

Reread

Amazing Wildlife of the Mojave and use text evidence to understand how the author presents information that describes how the Mojave is a lively and challenging place to live.

Write a short response about ***Amazing Wildlife of the Mojave.***

Integrate

Information about *Little Half Chick* and compare him to other animals you have read about.

Write to Two Sources, citing text evidence to compare ***Amazing Wildlife of the Mojave*** and "Little Half Chick."

5 Independent Partner Work

Gradual release of support to independent work

- Text-Dependent Questions
- Scaffolded Partner Work
  Talk with a Partner
  Cite Text Evidence
  Complete a sentence frame.
- Guided Text Annotation

6 Integrate Knowledge and Ideas

Connect Texts

Text to Text Discuss how each of the texts answers the question: How do animals adapt to challenges in their habitat?

Text to Photography Compare animal traits in the texts read and the photograph.

Performance Task

Take notes about frogs.

DEVELOPING READERS AND WRITERS

Write to Sources

Day 1 and Day 2

Build Writing Fluency

- Quick write on "Gray Wold! Red Fox!," p. T156

Write to a Source

- Analyze a student model, p. T156
- Write about "Gray Wold! Red Fox!," p. T157
- Apply Writing Trait: Strong Openings, p. T156
- Apply Grammar Skill: Main and Helping Verbs, p. T157

Day 3

Write to a Source

- Write about *Amazing Wildlife of the Mojave*, independent practice, p. T153N
- Provide scaffolded instruction to meet student needs, p. T158

Day 4 and Day 5

Write to Two Sources

- Analyze a student model, pp. T158–T159
- Write to compare *Amazing Wildlife of the Mojave* with "Little Half Chick," p. T159

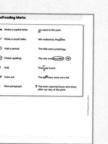

Writing Process

Go Digital

Writer's Workspace

Genre Writing: Narrative Text/Poetry

Fictional Narrative
Proofread/Edit
- Discuss the edited student model
- Review main and helping verbs

Publish
- Review options for publishing writing

Evaluate
- Use rubric and anchor papers to evaluate student writing.

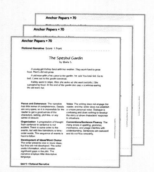

Expert Model • Fictional Narrative • 61

The Brown Seeds
By Gretchen H.

Edited Student Model

Proofreading Marks

Edit Checklist

Writing Rubric • 6/1

Fictional Narrative Rubric

Fictional Narrative: Rubric

Anchor Papers • 70

Fictional Narrative Score 1 Point

The Spiteful Garden
By Marie S.

Fictional Narrative: Anchor Papers

Grammar and Spelling Resources

Online PDFs

Verbs

Verbs: Be, Do, and Have

Reading/Writing Workshop Grammar Handbook p. 484

GRAMMonster!

Answer each question and try to drive the GRAMMonster out of his castle!

Online Spelling and Grammar Games

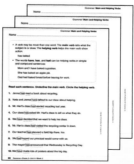

Grammar Practice, pp. 86–90

Phonics/Spelling Practice, pp. 103–108

Whole Group

READING		DAY 1	DAY 2
Teach, Model and Apply Wonders Reading/Writing Workshop	Core	**Introduce the Concept** T138–T139 **Vocabulary** Words in Context, T142–T143 **Close Reading** "Gray Wolf! Red Fox!" T144–T145	**Close Reading** "Gray Wolf! Red Fox!" T144–T145 **Strategy** Reread, T146–T147 **Skill** Compare and Contrast, T148–T149 **Vocabulary Strategy** Sentence Clues, T152–T153
	Options	**Listening Comprehension** T140–T141	**Genre** Realistic Fiction, T150–T151

LANGUAGE ARTS			
Writing **Grammar** **Spelling** **Build Vocabulary**	Core	**Grammar** Main and Helping Verbs, T160 **Spelling** Variant Vowels /ô/, T162 **Build Vocabulary** T164	**Write About the Text** Model Note-Taking and Write to a Prompt, T156–T157 **Grammar** Main and Helping Verbs, T160 **Build Vocabulary** T164
	Options	**Write About the Text** Writing Fluency, T156 **Genre Writing** Fictional Narrative: Discuss the Edited Model, T348	**Genre Writing** Fictional Narrative: Proofread/Edit, T348 **Spelling** Variant Vowels /ô/, T162

Writing Process: Narrative Fictional Narrative, T344–T349   Use with Weeks 1–3

Small Group

Differentiated Instruction Use your data dashboard to determine each student's needs. Then select instructional supports options throughout the week.

APPROACHING LEVEL

Leveled Reader
Life in a Tide Pool, T168–T169

"Bluebird and Coyote," T169

Literature Circles, T169

Phonics/Decoding
Decode Words with Variant Vowel /ô/, T170 TIER 2

Build Words with Varient Vowel /ô/, T170 TIER 2

Practice Variant Vowel /ô/, T171

Greek and Latin Roots, T171

Vocabulary
• Review High-Frequency Words, T172 TIER 2
• Identify Related Words, T173
Context Clues, T173

Comprehension
• Text Structure, T174 TIER 2
• Review Text Structure: Compare and Contrast, T175
Self-Selected Reading, T175

Fluency
Intonation, T174 TIER 2

ON LEVEL

Leveled Reader
Life in a Tide Pool, T176–T177

"Bluebird and Coyote," T177

Literature Circles, T177

Vocabulary
Review Vocabulary Words, T178
Context Clues, T178

Comprehension
Review Text Structure: Compare and Contrast, T179
Self-Selected Reading, T179

DAY 3	DAY 4	DAY 5
Close Reading *Amazing Wildlife of the Mojave,* T153A–T153N	**Fluency** T155 **Close Reading** "Little Half Chick," T153O–T153P **Integrate Ideas** Inquiry Space, T166-T167	**Integrate Ideas** T166–T167 • Text Connections • Inquiry Space **Weekly Assessment**
Phonics/Decoding T154–T155 • Variant Vowel /ô/ • Greek and Latin Roots	**Close Reading** *Amazing Wildlife of the Mojave,* T153A–T153N	

Grammar Main and Helping Verbs, T161	**Write About Two Texts** Model Note-Taking and Talking Notes, T158	**Write About Two Texts** Analyze Student Model and Write to the Prompt, T159 **Spelling** Variant Vowels /ô/, T163
Write About the Text T158 **Genre Writing** Fictional Narrative: Publish, T348 **Spelling** Variant Vowels /ô/, T163 **Build Vocabulary** T165	**Genre Writing** Fictional Narrative: Evaluate, T349 **Grammar** Main and Helping Verbs, T161 **Spelling** Variant Vowels /ô/, T165 **Build Vocabulary** T165	**Genre Writing** Fictional Narrative: Conference with Students, T349 **Grammar** Main and Helping Verbs, T161 **Build Vocabulary** T165

Writing Process **Writing Process: Narrative** Fictional Narrative, T344–T349   Use with Weeks 1–3

BEYOND LEVEL

Leveled Reader
Life in a Tide Pool, T180–T181
"Bluebird and Coyote," T177
Literature Circles, T181

Vocabulary
Review Domain-Specific Words, T182
• Context Clues, T182
• Compare and Contrast, T182

Comprehension
Review Text Structure: Compare and Contrast, T183
• Self-Selected Reading, T183
• Independent Study, T183

 Gifted and Talented

ENGLISH LANGUAGE LEARNERS

Shared Read
"Gray Wolf! Red Fox!", T184–T185

Leveled Reader
Life in a Tide Pool, T186–T187
"Bluebird and Coyote," T187
Literature Circles, T187

Phonics/Decoding
Decode Words with Variant Vowel /ô/, T170
Build Words with Variant Vowel /ô/, T170
Practice Variant Vowel /ô/, T171
Greek and Latin Roots, T171

Vocabulary
• Preteach Vocabulary, T188
• Review High-Frequency Words, T172
Review Vocabulary, T188
Context Clues, T189
Additional Vocabulary, T189

Spelling
Spell Variant Vowel /ô/, T190

Writing
Writing Trait: Organization, T190

Grammar
Main and Helping Verbs, T191

DIFFERENTIATE TO ACCELERATE

 Scaffold to **Access Complex Text**

IF the text complexity of a particular selection is too difficult for students

THEN see the references noted in the chart below for scaffolded instruction to help students Access Complex Text.

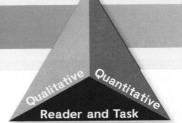
Qualitative — Quantitative
Reader and Task
TEXT COMPLEXITY

	Reading/Writing Workshop	Literature Anthology	Leveled Readers	Classroom Library
Quantitative	"Gray Wolf! Red Fox!" **Lexile** 750 *TextEvaluator™* 16	***Amazing Wildlife on the Mojave*** **Lexile** 720 *TextEvaluator™* 30 "Little Half Chick" **Lexile** 690 *TextEvaluator™* 21	**Approaching Level** **Lexile** 550 *TextEvaluator™* 12 **Beyond Level** **Lexile** 860 *TextEvaluator™* 22 **On Level** **Lexile** 730 *TextEvaluator™* 20 **ELL** **Lexile** 660 *TextEvaluator™* 5	***Bat Loves the Night*** **Lexile** 560 ***Gray Wolves*** **Lexile** 640
Qualitative	**What Makes the Text Complex?** • **Prior Knowledge** Background Knowledge T145 • **Genre** Text Features T151 **ACT** *See Scaffolded Instruction in Teacher's Edition T145 and T151.*	**What Makes the Text Complex?** • **Purpose** Main Topic T153B; Lesson T153O • **Prior Knowledge** Reptiles T153C • **Genre** Text Features T153E, T153G • **Specific Vocabulary** Context Clues T153I • **Connection of Ideas** Adaptation T153K **ACT** *See Scaffolded Instruction in Teacher's Edition T153A–T153P.*	**What Makes the Text Complex?** • **Specific Vocabulary** • **Prior Knowledge** • **Sentence Structure** • **Connection of Ideas** • **Genre** **ACT** *See Level Up lessons online for Leveled Readers.*	**What Makes the Text Complex?** • **Genre** • **Specific Vocabulary** • **Prior Knowledge** • **Sentence Structure** • **Organization** • **Purpose** • **Connection of Ideas** **ACT** *See Scaffolded Instruction in Teacher's Edition T360–T361.*
Reader and Task	The Introduce the Concept lesson on pages T138–T139 will help determine the reader's knowledge and engagement in the weekly concept. See pages T144–T153 and T166–T167 for questions and tasks for this text.	The Introduce the Concept lesson on pages T138–T139 will help determine the reader's knowledge and engagement in the weekly concept. See pages T153A–T153P and T166–T167 for questions and tasks for this text.	The Introduce the Concept lesson on pages T138–T139 will help determine the reader's knowledge and engagement in the weekly concept. See pages T168–T169, T176–T177, T180–T181, T186–T187, and T166–T167 for questions and tasks for this text.	The Introduce the Concept lesson on pages T138–T139 will help determine the reader's knowledge and engagement in the weekly concept. See pages T360–T361 for questions and tasks for this text.

Universal Access

Monitor and *Differentiate*

✓ **Quick Check**

To differentiate instruction, use the Quick Checks to assess students' needs and select the appropriate small group instruction focus.

Comprehension Strategy Reread T147

Comprehension Skill Compare and Contrast T149

Genre Expository Text T151

Vocabulary Strategy Sentence Clues T153

Phonics/Fluency Variant Vowel /ô/, Intonation T155

If No →

| Approaching Level | Reteach T168–T175 |
| ELL | Develop T184–T191 |

If Yes →

| On Level | Review T176–T179 |
| Beyond Level | Extend T180–T183 |

Using Weekly Data

Check your data Dashboard to verify assessment results and guide grouping decisions.

Level Up with Leveled Readers

IF students can read their leveled text fluently and answer comprehension questions

THEN work with the next level up to accelerate students' reading with more complex text.

Beyond

T177

On Level

Approaching

T169   T187

ELL

ELL ENGLISH LANGUAGE LEARNERS

Small Group Instruction

Use the ELL small group lessons in the Wonders Teacher's Edition to provide focused instruction.

Language Development
Vocabulary preteaching and review, additional vocabulary building, and vocabulary strategy lessons, pp. T188–T189

Close Reading
Interactive Question-Response routines for scaffolded text-dependent questioning for reading and rereading the Shared Read and Leveled Reader, pp. T184–T187

Writing
Focus on the weekly writing trait, grammar skills, and spelling words, pp. T190–T191

Additional ELL Support

Use *Reading Wonders for English Learners* for ELD instruction that connects to the core.

Language Development
Ample opportunities for discussions, and scaffolded language support

Close Reading
Companion Worktexts for guided support in annotating text and citing text evidence. Differentiated Texts about the weekly concept.

Writing
Scaffolded instruction for writing to sources and revising student models

Reading Wonders for ELLs Teacher Edition and Companion Worktexts

→ Introduce the Concept

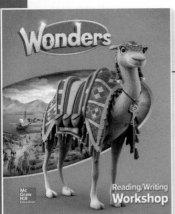

Reading/Writing Workshop

OBJECTIVES

CCSS Engage effectively in a range of collaborative discussions (one-on-one, in groups, and teacher-led) with diverse partners on grade 3 topics and texts, building on others' ideas and expressing their own clearly. Ask questions to check understanding of information presented, stay on topic, and link their comments to the remarks of others. **SL.3.1c**

ACADEMIC LANGUAGE
environment, shelter

Build Background

ESSENTIAL QUESTION
How do animals adapt to challenges in their habitat?

Have students read the Essential Question on page 286 of the **Reading/Writing Workshop**. Discuss the photos of an ermine and tell them that *adapt* means "to change over time."

- An ermine adapts to challenges in its **environment**, or the natural features of where it lives, such as the weather, type of land, and plants that grow there. Ermines are normally brown in color, but in the winter, their fur becomes denser and white. This helps ermines stay warm and also helps them blend into their environment.

- While it helps to have warm fur, ermines also need some kind of **shelter** to protect them from their environment. Ermines often seek shelter in dens or caves that are no longer used by other animals.

Talk About It

Ask: *How have ermines adapted to changes in their habitat? How have the adaptations helped them find food? How have they helped ermines survive?* Have students discuss in pairs or groups.

- Model using the Concept Web to generate words and phrases related to adaptation. Add students' contributions.

- Have partners continue the discussion by sharing what they have learned about adaptations. They can complete the Concept Web, generating additional related words and phrases.

Collaborative Conversations

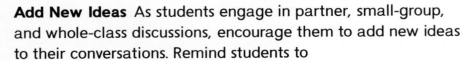

Add New Ideas As students engage in partner, small-group, and whole-class discussions, encourage them to add new ideas to their conversations. Remind students to

- stay on topic and speak in complete sentences when asked to provide additional details or clarification.

- connect their own ideas to things their peers have said.

- look for ways to connect their personal experiences or prior knowledge to the conversation.

Go Digital

Discuss the Concept

Watch Video

View Photos

Use Graphic Organizer

Assign Blast

Weekly Concept Adaptations

Essential Question
How do animals adapt to challenges in their habitat?

Go Digital!

Adapt to Challenges

This ermine's fur is brown and white in the summer. It turns white in the winter and blends in with the snowy ground. This adaptation helps ermines escape its predators.

► Ermines are also fast runners and good climbers.

► They have an excellent sense of smell.

► Adaptations help ermines survive.

Talk About It

Write words you have learned about adaptation. Talk with a partner about ways animals have adapted.

Adaptations

286

287

READING/WRITING WORKSHOP, *pp. 286–287*

Share the Blast assignment. Point out that you will discuss students' responses during the **Integrate Ideas** lesson at the end of the week.

GRAPHIC ORGANIZER 62

ENGLISH LANGUAGE LEARNERS SCAFFOLD

Beginning	Intermediate	Advanced/High
Use Visuals Point to the white ermine. *This is an ermine. What color is the ermine's fur?* (white) Point out that the white fur helps the ermine blend in. Have students echo you as you say *An ermine adapts to challenges in its environment.*	**Describe** Have students describe the ermine. Ask: *What is a challenge ermines face?* (surviving the cold winter) *How does the ermine's color help it adapt to its environment?* (It blends in with the snow.) Help students with pronunciation.	**Discuss** Ask students to describe the features that help an ermine survive. Ask questions to help them elaborate. *How does its color help it survive? How does its fur help it survive?* Have students work with a partner to discuss the ermine.

Adaptations

→ Listening Comprehension

Interactive Read Aloud

OBJECTIVES

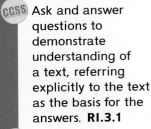 Ask and answer questions to demonstrate understanding of a text, referring explicitly to the text as the basis for the answers. **RI.3.1**

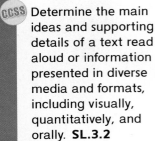 Determine the main ideas and supporting details of a text read aloud or information presented in diverse media and formats, including visually, quantitatively, and orally. **SL.3.2**

- Listen for a purpose.
- Identify characteristics of expository text.

ACADEMIC LANGUAGE
expository text, reread

Connect to Concept: Adaptations

Tell students that animals must adapt to challenges in their habitat. Let students know that they will be listening to a passage about how lions have adapted to their home on the grasslands of Africa. As students listen, have them think about how the passage answers the Essential Question.

Preview Genre: Expository Text

Explain that the story you will read aloud is expository text. Discuss features of expository text:

- informs readers about a topic
- may include photographs with captions, maps, or other graphic aids
- may use headings and subheadings to organize information

Preview Comprehension Strategy: Reread

Point out that when reading expository text, readers should reread a section of text if something does not make sense. Readers may sometimes misread a word and then go back to reread once they realize that the text seems confusing or wrong.

Use the Think Alouds on page T141 to model the strategy.

Respond to Reading

Think Aloud Clouds Display Think Aloud Master 4: *When I read ____, I had to reread. . .* to reinforce how you used the Reread strategy to understand content.

Genre Features With students, discuss the elements of the Read Aloud that let them know it is expository text. Ask them to think about other texts that you have read or they have read independently that were expository texts.

Summarize Have students determine the main ideas and details of "African Lions" and briefly retell the information in their own words.

Go Digital

View Photos

Model Think Alouds

When I read ____, I had to reread...

Genre	Features

Fill in Genre Chart

African Lions

The lion has been called "The King of the Beasts." The male lion's thick mane gives this large cat a regal look.

But did you know that the lion's mane helps keep it safe? It is an adaptation, or a special trait that helps an animal stay alive. The male lion's mane protects its soft throat from the sharp claws and teeth of other males. It also makes the lion look even larger. This helps scare away some animals that may try to attack it. **1**

Adapting to Challenges

Most African lions make their home on the open grasslands of Africa. This is where the lions can find food. The lion has found ways to adapt, or to live with the challenges of the grassland.

Lions live in groups called prides. In fact, they are the only members of the cat family to live in groups. The lions in a pride hunt together. Lions are fast runners. But they cannot run fast for a long distance. Often the female lions work with each other when hunting. They may take turns when chasing prey. They use their strong sense of smell and sharp hearing to track their next meal. **2**

The male lions in a pride work to defend their hunting range from other male lions. They also work together to keep their newborn cubs safe. The males roar loudly to scare away other animals that come too close. If the intruder is not scared by the lions' roar, then the male lions will attack. Their weapons are their sharp, pointed teeth and razor-like claws. **3**

Living and Working Together

The African lions have found ways to adapt to their home on the grasslands. By living and working together in a pride, lions can find food and protect each other.

Image Source/Getty Images

1 Think Aloud I can picture what a lion's mane looks like. I think I understand how a lion's mane keeps it safe, but I can **reread** this paragraph again to make sure.

2 Think Aloud I want to **reread** to help me understand and remember why lions live together in prides. I think this is important information.

3 Think Aloud This tells me how and why male lions protect the pride from other animals. I want to **reread** this section to make sure I understand how the male lions do this.

→ **Vocabulary**

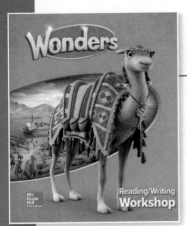

Reading/Writing Workshop

OBJECTIVES

CCSS Determine or clarify the meaning of unknown and multiple-meaning words and phrases based on grade 3 reading and content, choosing flexibly from a range of strategies. Use sentence-level context as a clue to the meaning of a word or phrase. **L.3.4a**

CCSS Determine the meaning of general academic and domain-specific words and phrases in a text relevant to a grade 3 topic or subject area. **RI.3.4**

ACADEMIC LANGUAGE
environment, shelter

 Words in Context

Model the Routine

Introduce each vocabulary word using the **Vocabulary Routine** found on the **Visual Vocabulary Cards**.

Visual Vocabulary Cards

Vocabulary Routine

Define: **Shelter** is something that covers or protects.

Example: Our tent was a dry and safe shelter during the storm.

Ask: What is another kind of shelter people use?

Definitions

- **alert**   To **alert** is to give warning.
                 Cognate: *alerta*

- **competition**   A **competition** is a situation in which people or animals are trying to be more successful than others.
                    Cognate: *competencia*

- **environment**   An **environment** is the natural features of a place.

- **excellent**   Something that is **excellent** is very good.
                  Cognate: *excelente*

- **prefer**   To **prefer** is to like better.
                  Cognate: *preferir*

- **protection**   **Protection** is when something is kept safe.
                   Cognate: *protección*

- **related**   To be **related** is to belong to the same family.

Talk About It

Have students work with a partner to look at each picture and discuss the definition of each word. Then ask students to choose three words and write questions for their partner to answer.

Go Digital

shelter

Use Visual Glossary

Words to Know

Vocabulary

Use the picture and the sentence to talk with a partner about each word.

alert
Wolves howl to **alert** other wolves when danger is nearby.

How would you alert someone to talk quietly?

competition
Joe won the **competition** because he was the fastest runner.

What kind of competition have you participated in?

environment
The polar bear lives in a cold and snowy **environment**.

Describe a whale's environment.

excellent
Lily's **excellent** artwork won first place in the art show.

Tell about a time when something you did was excellent.

288

prefer
Simon and his friends **prefer** walking to riding their bikes.

What kind of transportation do you prefer?

protection
The skunk's scent provides **protection** from its enemies.

Tell what you use for protection on sunny days.

related
Josh and Jen are **related** because they are both members of the same family.

Name two animals that are related.

shelter
Our tent was a dry and safe **shelter** during the storm.

What is another kind of shelter people use?

Your Turn COLLABORATE

Pick three words. Write three questions for your partner to answer.

Go Digital! Use the online visual glossary

289

READING/WRITING WORKSHOP, pp. 288–289

ELL ENGLISH LANGUAGE LEARNERS SCAFFOLD

Beginning

Use Visuals Look at the picture for the word *shelter*. Repeat that *shelter* provides cover and protection. Say: *Point to the shelter in the picture.* Explain that the tent is a type of shelter. Have students echo you. Help students complete the sentence frame: *Right now, the school is our ____.* (shelter)

Intermediate

Describe Have students describe the picture. Help them with pronunciation. Ask: *How does the tent provide shelter?* (It covers the people. It protects them from rain and wind.) Ask them to turn to a partner and talk about other shelters they have seen.

Advanced/High

Discuss Ask students to talk about the picture with a partner and write a definition. Then share the definition with the class. Correct and expand upon their definitions. Challenge pairs to use each vocabulary word in a sentence.

ON-LEVEL PRACTICE BOOK p. 171

| excellent | prefer | environment | shelter |
| alert | protection | related | competition |

Finish each sentence using the vocabulary word provided.
Possible responses provided.

1. (environment) A desert _is a dry environment that can be difficult to live in_

2. (prefer) When it comes to reading books, _I prefer to read stories about history_

3. (competition) Those are the two best soccer teams, _so the game should be a good competition_

4. (excellent) She lived by the beach her whole life _so she became an excellent swimmer_

5. (related) Since my sister and I look exactly alike, _it is obvious to most people we are related_

6. (protection) A turtle has a hard shell _that it uses for protection_

7. (shelter) My father and I built a doghouse _so our dog has shelter from the rain_

8. (alert) The town has a loud siren _that is used to alert people if there is a tornado_

| APPROACHING p. 171 | BEYOND p. 171 | ELL p. 171 |

Shared Read Genre • Expository

GRAY WOLF! RED FOX!

Did you ever see a photograph of a gray wolf or a red fox? Don't they look a lot like dogs? Aren't they fantastic-looking animals? Well, dogs, foxes, and wolves are all **related**. They are all members of the same family. And while gray wolves and red foxes may look alike, they are different in many ways.

LOOKS ARE EVERYTHING

The gray wolf is the largest member, or a part, of the wild dog family. An adult wolf is the size of a large dog. The red fox is smaller and weighs less. Both animals have **excellent** hearing. The red fox can even hear small animals digging holes underground.

And just take a look at those beautiful tails! The gray wolf and red fox both have long, bushy tails. The wolf's tail can be two feet long. The fox's tail is not as long but has a bright, white tip. In the winter, foxes use their thick, furry tails as **protection** from the cold.

The gray wolf and red fox are both mammals.

? Essential Question

How do animals adapt to challenges in their habitat?

Read how gray wolves and red foxes adapt to challenges.

290

291

READING/WRITING WORKSHOP, pp. 290–291

Reading/Writing Workshop

Shared Read CLOSE READING

Lexile 750   TextEvaluator™ 17

Close Reading Routine

Read DOK 1–2

• Identify key ideas and details about Adaptations.

• Take notes and summarize.

• Use **ACT** prompts as needed.

Reread DOK 2–3

• Analyze the text, craft, and structure.

• Use the Reread minilessons.

Integrate DOK 4

• Integrate knowledge and ideas.

• Make text-to-text connections.

• Use the Integrate lesson.

Read

Connect to Concept: Adaptations Tell students that they will read about how foxes and wolves adapt to their environments.

Note Taking Read page 291 together. As you read, model how to take notes. *I will think about the Essential Question as I read and note key ideas and details.* Encourage students to note words they don't understand and questions they have.

Paragraph 1: Model how to paraphrase the opening paragraph. Ask students to pay attention to the main idea. Reread the first paragraph together.

Gray wolves and red foxes look similar to dogs, and all three are members of the same animal family. Although gray wolves and red foxes look alike, they are different in many ways.

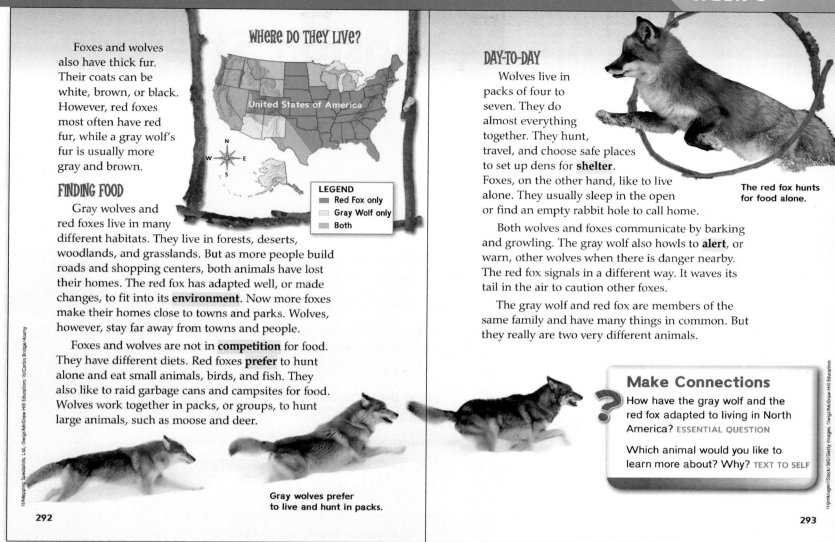

Foxes and wolves also have thick fur. Their coats can be white, brown, or black. However, red foxes most often have red fur, while a gray wolf's fur is usually more gray and brown.

FINDING FOOD

Gray wolves and red foxes live in many different habitats. They live in forests, deserts, woodlands, and grasslands. But as more people build roads and shopping centers, both animals have lost their homes. The red fox has adapted well, or made changes, to fit into its **environment**. Now more foxes make their homes close to towns and parks. Wolves, however, stay far away from towns and people.

Foxes and wolves are not in **competition** for food. They have different diets. Red foxes **prefer** to hunt alone and eat small animals, birds, and fish. They also like to raid garbage cans and campsites for food. Wolves work together in packs, or groups, to hunt large animals, such as moose and deer.

WHERE DO THEY LIVE?

United States of America

LEGEND
■ Red Fox only
□ Gray Wolf only
■ Both

Gray wolves prefer to live and hunt in packs.

292

DAY-TO-DAY

Wolves live in packs of four to seven. They do almost everything together. They hunt, travel, and choose safe places to set up dens for **shelter**. Foxes, on the other hand, like to live alone. They usually sleep in the open or find an empty rabbit hole to call home.

Both wolves and foxes communicate by barking and growling. The gray wolf also howls to **alert**, or warn, other wolves when there is danger nearby. The red fox signals in a different way. It waves its tail in the air to caution other foxes.

The gray wolf and red fox are members of the same family and have many things in common. But they really are two very different animals.

The red fox hunts for food alone.

Make Connections

How have the gray wolf and the red fox adapted to living in North America? ESSENTIAL QUESTION

Which animal would you like to learn more about? Why? TEXT TO SELF

293

READING/WRITING WORKSHOP, pp. 292–293

Paragraph 3: Reread the paragraph together. Ask: *What is a challenge that red foxes face in their environment? How do their tails help them adapt to it?* Model how to cite evidence to answer the questions.

One challenge foxes face is extreme cold in winter. They use their thick, furry tails to help keep them warm in their cold environment.

Make Connections

Essential Question Encourage students to work with a partner to talk about how the gray wolf and the red fox have adapted to living in North America. Use these sentence frames to focus discussion.

Red foxes and gray wolves are . . .
Changes in their environments have . . .

A C T Access Complex Text

▶ Prior Knowledge

Students may lack background knowledge about the difference between an animal's habitat and its environment.

- A habitat is the natural living conditions for an animal. An environment includes all parts of the area in which an animal lives.

- Even though roads and shopping centers are not natural parts of an animal's habitat, they are now part of the environment.

SHARED READ **T145**

→ Comprehension Strategy

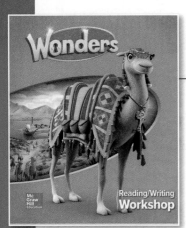

Wonders
Reading/Writing
Workshop

**Reading/Writing
Workshop**

OBJECTIVES

CCSS Ask and answer
questions to
demonstrate
understanding of a
text, referring
explicitly to the text
as the basis for the
answers. **RI.3.1**

Reread difficult
sections of text
to increase
understanding.

**ACADEMIC
LANGUAGE**
*reread, expository
text*

MINILESSON 10 Mins — Reread

1 Explain

Explain that when students read expository text, they may come
across unfamiliar ideas and facts. Remind students that they can
reread difficult sections of text to increase their understanding.

- Good readers reread something that they do not understand.

- When students come across a section of text that does not make
  sense, they can stop and reread that section. They may need to
  reread it more than once before they understand it.

- Often, students may find that rereading will improve their
  understanding of expository text.

Point out that after rereading, students can ask and answer
questions about what they have reread to help remember key facts
and ideas.

2 Model Close Reading: Text Evidence

Model how rereading can help students understand the ways that
red foxes look different from gray wolves. Reread the section "Looks
Are Everything" on page 291.

3 Guided Practice of Close Reading

Have students work in pairs to find details about how gray wolves
and red foxes are alike. Direct them to the sections "Looks Are
Everything" and "Finding Food." Partners can reread the sections and
ask and answer questions about how gray wolves and red foxes are
alike. Have partners discuss other sections of "Gray Wolf! Red Fox!"
they may want to reread.

**Go
Digital**

View "Gray Wolf!
Red Fox!"

Comprehension Strategy

Reread

Stop and think about the text as you read. Are there new facts and ideas? Do they make sense? Reread to make sure you understand.

Find Text Evidence

Do you understand how red foxes look different from gray wolves? Reread "Looks Are Everything" on page 291.

page 291

Did you ever see a photograph of a gray wolf or a red fox? Don't they look a lot like dogs? Aren't they fantastic-looking animals? Well, dogs, foxes, and wolves are all related. They are all members of the same family. And while gray wolves and red foxes may look alike, they are different in many ways.

Looks Are Everything

The gray wolf is the largest member, or a part, of the wild dog family. An adult wolf is the size of a large dog. The red fox is smaller and weighs less. Both animals have excellent hearing. The red fox can even hear small animals digging holes underground.

And just take a look at those beautiful tails! The gray wolf and red fox both have long, bushy tails. The wolf's tail can be two feet long. The fox's tail is not as long but has a bright, white tip. In the winter, foxes use their thick, furry tails as protection from the cold.

I read that gray wolves are bigger than red foxes. I also read that the color of their fur and their tails look different. Now I understand some of the ways the red fox and gray wolf look different.

Your Turn COLLABORATE

Reread the section "Looks Are Everything." Look for details about how gray wolves and red foxes are alike.

294

Darrell Gulin/Stone/Getty Images; (twrip) McGraw-Hill Companies, Inc.

READING/WRITING WORKSHOP, *p. 294*

ENGLISH LANGUAGE LEARNERS SCAFFOLD

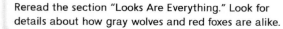

Beginning

Comprehend Help students reread the first paragraph of "Looks Are Everything" on page 291. Point out that the suffix -est in *largest* means that the wolf is the most large. The suffix -er in *smaller* means that the fox is more small than the wolf. Have students fill in the sentence frame: *The fox is ____ than the wolf.* Invite them to ask one question about the fox and the wolf.

Intermediate

Demonstrate Comprehension Have students reread the first paragraph of "Looks Are Everything" on page 291. Ask: *What is a similarity between the gray wolf and the red fox?* (They both have excellent hearing.) Have students work in pairs to come up with synonyms for *excellent.*

Advanced/High

Discuss Have students reread the first paragraph of "Looks Are Everything" on page 291. Elicit from students how the text is confusing. Ask: *Why do you think it is important to learn about how foxes and wolves adapt to their environment?* Turn to a partner and discuss.

Monitor and *Differentiate*

✓ Quick Check

Do students reread expository text that they do not understand? Do they reread it more than once if necessary?

Small Group Instruction

If No →	Approaching Level	Reteach p. T168
	ELL	Develop p. T184
If Yes →	On Level	Review p. T176
	Beyond Level	Extend p. T180

ON-LEVEL PRACTICE BOOK pp. 173–174

Read the passage. Use the reread strategy to be sure you understand what you read.

Adaptations: Grizzly and Polar Bears

Every animal has adaptations. These are special ways that a
10 body works or is made. Not all birds eat the same things. Their
23 beaks have different shapes. Some fish that live at the bottom of
35 the ocean glow in the dark. Mammals live all over the world, so
48 they need to have different skills and body shapes. Giraffes have
59 long tongues. They use them to pull leaves off the tops of trees.
72 Jackrabbits have wide feet to run across sand.
80 These things help animals be as effective as they can be. This
92 means that they can do the best job possible of finding food and
105 raising offspring. Adaptations are very important for keeping all
114 animals alive and able to reproduce, or have offspring.

123 **Similarities**
124 Mammals have adapted to live in different parts of the
134 world. Bears live all over the world. Grizzly bears live in North
146 America. Polar bears live inside the Arctic Circle. In many ways
157 they are the same. They are very large animals. They can weigh
169 more than 1,500 pounds. Both kinds of bears have toes with
180 claws they cannot retract. This means bears cannot pull their
190 claws inside. They can stand on their hind legs. They can even
202 sit up, as if they were sitting in a chair! And all bears have
216 rounded ears.

APPROACHING pp. 173–174	BEYOND pp. 173–174	ELL pp. 173–174

→ Comprehension Skill

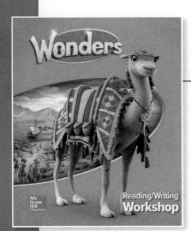

Reading/Writing Workshop

 MINILESSON 10 Mins

Text Structure: Compare and Contrast

Go Digital

Present the Lesson

1 Explain

Explain to students that they can compare and contrast two things in expository texts to understand how they are alike and different.

- To compare, students should look for ways that two things are alike. To contrast, students should look for ways two things are different.

- Students can look for signal words like *both, alike, same,* or *different* to help them compare and contrast.

2 Model Close Reading: Text Evidence

Identify the similarities and differences between gray wolves and red foxes in the second paragraph of "Looks Are Everything" on page 291. Then model using the details written on the graphic organizer to compare and contrast the two species.

 Analytical Writing **Write About Reading: Compare and Contrast** Model for students how to use the notes from the graphic organizer to write a summary of how gray wolves and red foxes are alike and different.

3 Guided Practice of Close Reading

 COLLABORATE Have students work in pairs to complete a graphic organizer for each section of "Gray Wolf! Red Fox!," going back into the text to find details that tell how gray wolves and red foxes are alike and different. Remind them to look for signal words. Discuss each section and the signal words students find as they complete the graphic organizer.

Analytical Writing **Write About Reading: Compare and Contrast** Ask pairs to work together to identify the sentences that compare and contrast gray wolves and red foxes and to write a summary of how they are alike and different. Select pairs of students to share their summaries with the class.

OBJECTIVES

CCSS Describe the logical connection between particular sentences and paragraphs in a text (e.g. comparison, cause/effect, first/second/third in a sequence). **RI.3.8**

Compare and contrast two things in an expository text.

ACADEMIC LANGUAGE
compare, contrast

SKILLS TRACE

TEXT STRUCTURE

Introduce Unit 1 Week 3

Review Unit 1 Weeks 4, 6; Unit 2 Week 6; Unit 3 Weeks 5, 6; Unit 4 Weeks 3, 4; Unit 5 Weeks 5, 6; Unit 6 Weeks 3, 4, 6

Assess Units 1, 3, 4, 5, 6

Compare and Contrast

When authors compare, they show how two things are alike. When they contrast, they tell how two things are different. Authors use signal words such as *both, alike, same,* or *different* to compare and contrast.

 Find Text Evidence

How are red foxes and gray wolves alike and different? I will reread "Gray Wolf! Red Fox!" and look for signal words.

Wolves	Both	Foxes
The wolf's tail can be two feet long	Thick fur and long, bushy tails.	A fox's tail has a bright, white tip at the end.

Your Turn

COLLABORATE

Reread "Gray Wolf! Red Fox!" Find details that tell how red foxes and gray wolves are alike and different. Add these details to your graphic organizer. What signal words helped you?

Go Digital!
Use the interactive graphic organizer

295

READING/WRITING WORKSHOP, *p. 295*

 **Monitor and *Differentiate***

✓ **Quick Check**

As students complete the graphic organizer for each section, do they compare and contrast two things? Can they identify signal words?

Small Group Instruction

If No → | Approaching Level | Reteach p. T175
| ELL | Develop p. T186
If Yes → | On Level | Review p. T179
| Beyond Level | Extend p. T183

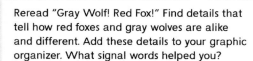 **ENGLISH LANGUAGE LEARNERS SCAFFOLD**

Beginning

Respond Orally Help students reread the second paragraph of "Looks Are Everything" on page 291. Ask after each sentence: *What did you learn about foxes' or wolves' tails in this sentence?* Have them list the details they find describing tails using a sentence frame. *Foxes' tails are ____, ____, and ____. Wolves' tails are ____, ____, and ____.*

Intermediate

Comprehend Have students reread the second paragraph of "Looks Are Everything" on page 291. Ask questions to help students compare and contrast: *What does the fox's tail look like?* (It has a bright white tip.) *What does the wolf's tail look like?* (It can be up to two feet long.) *How are the tails the same?* (They are both bushy and long.) Expand upon answers.

Advanced/High

Explain Have students reread the first and second paragraph of "Looks Are Everything" on page 291. Have students describe how foxes and wolves are alike and different. Then have them explain how they used signal words to compare and contrast.

ON-LEVEL PRACTICE BOOK pp. 173–175

A. Reread the passage and answer the questions.
Possible responses provided.

1. In the third paragraph, how does the author compare the two kinds of bears?
   The author says they both are very large, cannot retract their claws, and can stand on their hind legs.

2. In the fifth paragraph, how does the author contrast what the two kinds of bears eat?
   The author says that polar bears only eat meat but that grizzly bears are omnivorous.

3. What are some of the signal words the author uses in the text to compare and contrast?
   Some signal words used to compare in the text are *same* and *both*.
   Some signal words used to contrast in the text are *different, do not,* and *longer than.*

B. Work with a partner. Read the passage aloud. Pay attention to intonation. Stop after one minute. Fill out the chart.

	Words Read	–	Number of Errors	=	Words Correct Score
First Read		–		=	
Second Read		–		=	

| APPROACHING pp. 173–175 | BEYOND pp. 173–175 | ELL pp. 173–175 |

→ # Genre: Informational Text

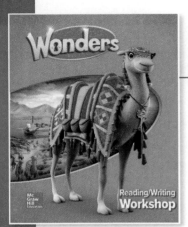

Reading/Writing Workshop

OBJECTIVES

CCSS Use information gained from illustrations (e.g., maps, photographs) and the words in a text to demonstrate understanding of the text (e.g., where, when, why, and how key events occur). **RI.3.7**

CCSS By the end of the year, read and comprehend informational texts, including history/social studies, science, and technical texts, at the high end of the grades 2–3 text complexity band independently and proficiently. **RI.3.10**

Recognize the characteristics and text features of expository text.

ACADEMIC LANGUAGE
informational text, expository text

 MINILESSON **10** Mins

Expository Text

 **Go Digital**

1 Explain

Share with students the following key characteristics of **expository text.**

- Expository text gives important facts and information about a topic. The topic may be about science.

- Expository text may include text features such as maps, photographs, and captions. However, even if a text has none of these features, it may still be an expository text.

Present the Lesson

2 Model Close Reading: Text Evidence

Model identifying and using the text features on page 292 of "Gray Wolf! Red Fox!"

Map Point out the map. Remind students that a map is a flat drawing representing a place. Ask: *What does this map show?*

Caption Point out the caption. Explain that it provides information about the photograph of wolves. Ask: *What does the caption tell you about the photograph?*

3 Guided Practice of Close Reading

 Have students work with partners to find and list more text features in "Gray Wolf! Red Fox!" Partners should discuss how the photographs and captions added to their understanding of the text. Then have them share their work with the class.

Genre Informational Text

Expository Text

"Gray Wolf! Red Fox!" is an expository text.
Expository text:
- Gives facts and information to explain a topic
- May be about science topics
- Includes text features such as a map, photographs, and captions

 Find Text Evidence

I can tell that "Gray Wolf! Red Fox!" is expository text. It explains how gray wolves and red foxes are alike and different. It includes a map, photographs, and captions.

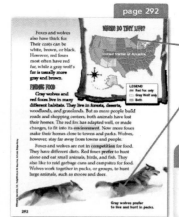

Text Features

Map A map is a flat drawing of a place. It has a key that shows what colors and symbols mean.

Caption A caption explains a photograph or illustration.

Your Turn COLLABORATE

Look at the text features in "Gray Wolf! Red Fox!." Tell your partner about something you learned.

296

READING/WRITING WORKSHOP, *p. 296*

A C T Access Complex Text

▶ **Genre**

Students may have difficulty understanding how text features such as maps relate to an expository text as a whole.

- *What does the map on page 292 tell you?* (the areas where wolves and foxes live)

- *What information does it provide that the text does not?* (It helps me to better visualize where foxes and wolves live.)

Monitor and *Differentiate*

 Quick Check

Are students able to find text features in "Gray Wolf! Red Fox!"? Can they describe what they learned from each feature?

⬇

Small Group Instruction

If No → | Approaching Level | Reteach p. T168
ELL | Develop p. T184
If Yes → | On Level | Review p. T176
Beyond Level | Extend p. T180

ON-LEVEL PRACTICE BOOK p. 176

The Monarch Migrations

Monarch butterflies live all over the United States. They migrate south each fall to warmer climates. Some fly all the way from Canada to Mexico. Monarchs migrate to adapt to changing temperatures. In the fall, temperatures in the north get cooler, and there are fewer flowers on plants. Monarchs cannot survive very cold winter weather and need flowering plants for food. They move to warm areas in the south where there is food.

Monarch butterflies west of the Rocky Mountains fly south to California. Those east of the Rocky Mountains fly south to Mexico.

Answer the questions about the text.

1. How do you know this is expository text?
   It tells facts about monarch butterflies.

2. How do the text features help the reader understand the text?
   Possible response: The map shows you how far monarchs have to travel. The caption helps explain the map.

3. Why do monarchs migrate?
   They cannot survive in cold weather and need flowering plants.

| APPROACHING p. 176 | BEYOND p. 176 | ELL p. 176 |

→ Vocabulary Strategy

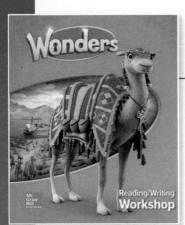

Reading/Writing Workshop

OBJECTIVES

 Determine or clarify the meaning of unknown and multiple-meaning words and phrases based on grade 3 reading and content, choosing flexibly from a range of strategies. Use sentence level context as a clue to the meaning of a word or phrase. **L.3.4a**

ACADEMIC LANGUAGE

sentence clues, context clues

SKILLS TRACE

CONTEXT CLUES: SENTENCE CLUES

Introduce Unit 1 Week 2

Review Unit 1 Week 3; Unit 4 Weeks 3, 4; Unit 5, Weeks 3, 4

Assess Units 1, 4, 5

MINILESSON 10 Mins

Context Clues

1 Explain

Remind students that they can often figure out the meaning of an unknown word by using context clues within the sentence.

- To find **sentence clues**, students can look for phrases between commas that are near the unknown word.

- Sentence clues may define or tell what the unknown word means or they may provide a further description of the word.

2 Model Close Reading: Text Evidence

Model using context clues in the first sentence of the "Looks Are Everything" section on page 291 to find the meaning of *member*.

3 Guided Practice of Close Reading

 Have students work in pairs to figure out the meanings of *adapted* and *packs* from page 292 of "Gray Wolf! Red Fox!" Encourage partners to go back into the text and use context clues within each sentence to develop each word's definition.

Use Reference Sources

Dictionaries Have students use either a print or digital dictionary to look up the precise meanings of *adapted* and *packs*. Have them confirm the definitions they developed using sentence clues, and revise their definitions if necessary. If the dictionary gives more than one meaning, have students use context to determine the correct one.

Go Digital

Present the Lesson

Vocabulary Strategy

Sentence Clues

Sentence clues are words or phrases in a sentence that help you figure out the meaning of an unfamiliar word. Sometimes clues define, or tell exactly, what a word means.

 Find Text Evidence

I'm not sure what the word member *means on page 291. I see the words "a part of" in the same sentence. This clue tells me that* member *means "a part of something."*

The gray wolf is the largest member, or a part, of the wild dog family.

James Hager/Robert Harding World Imagery/Getty Images

Your Turn

COLLABORATE

Find context clues to figure out the meanings of these words.
  adapted, *page 292*
  packs, *page 292*
Talk about the sentence clues that helped you figure out the meanings.

297

READING/WRITING WORKSHOP, *p. 297*

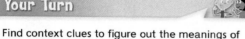

ENGLISH LANGUAGE LEARNERS SCAFFOLD

Beginning	**Intermediate**	**Advanced/High**
Explain Point out the words *adapted* and *packs* on page 292 and define them for students. Use the words in sentences, and help students replace them with words they know. Point out that *adapted* has the cognate *adaptado*.	**Describe** Point out the words *adapted* and *packs* on page 292 and define the words for students. Have them find sentence clues and talk to a partner. Then, have pairs write a sentence for each word. Elicit from students how cognates helped them understand the text.	**Discuss** Point out the words *adapted* and *packs* on page 292 and ask students to define them and use them in sentences. Have them find sentence clues and replace the words with words they know. Ask students to find cognates with a partner.

Monitor and *Differentiate*

✓ **Quick Check**

Can students identify and use sentence clues to determine the meanings of *adapted* and *packs*?

↓

Small Group Instruction

If No →	Approaching Level	Reteach p. T173
	ELL	Develop p. T189
If Yes →	On Level	Review p. T178
	Beyond Level	Extend p. T182

ON-LEVEL PRACTICE BOOK p. 177

Read each passage below. Underline the sentence clues that help you figure out the meaning of each word in bold. On the line, write the meaning of the word in bold. Possible responses provided.

1. Every animal has **adaptations**. These are special ways that its body works or is made.

   special ways the body is made

2. Adaptations are very important for keeping all animals alive and able to **reproduce**, or have offspring.

   have babies or offspring

3. Both kinds of bears have toes with claws they cannot **retract**. This means bears cannot pull their claws inside.

   pull inside

4. They also have a layer of **blubber**, or fat, over four inches thick.

   fat

5. This helps them blend in with the trees and rocks in their **environment**, or where they live.

   place where something lives

6. Grizzlies are **omnivorous**. They are just as happy eating fish as they are eating berries.

   eats both animals and plants

APPROACHING p. 177	BEYOND p. 177	ELL p. 177

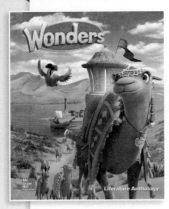

Amazing Wildlife of the Mojave

Literature Anthology

Text Complexity Range

Lexile

420 — 720 ▲ — 820

TextEvaluator™

2 — 30 ▲ — 35

What makes this text complex?
▶ **Purpose**
▶ **Prior Knowledge**
▶ **Genre**
▶ **Specific Vocabulary**
▶ **Connection of Ideas**

Close Reading Routine

Read   DOK 1–2

• Identify key ideas and details about Adaptations.
• Take notes and summarize.
• Use **A C T** prompts as needed.

Reread   DOK 2–3

• Analyze the text, craft, and structure.
• Use *Close Reading Companion,* pp. 114–116.

Integrate   DOK 4

• Integrate knowledge and ideas.
• Make text-to-text connections.
• Use the Integrate lesson.

Genre • Expository Text

Amazing Wildlife of the Mojave

By Laurence Pringle

Essential Question
How do animals adapt to challenges in their habitat?
Read about how different animals in the Mojave Desert survive in a dry, hot place.

Go Digital!

326

A C T   Access Complex Text

▶ Purpose

Remind students that the purpose of an expository text is to inform readers about a topic. Look at the title, *Amazing Wildlife of the Mojave,* the photograph on pages 326–327, and the text on page 327.

• *What do you think the author wants to inform readers about?* (how living things survive in the desert) *Can all living things survive here?* (no)

eserts are challenging places to live. They are dry and often very hot. Each year only a few inches of rain fall in the Mojave (Mo-HA-vee). It is North America's smallest desert. It lies mostly in parts of southern California and southern Nevada. The Mojave has both mountains and valleys. It includes Death Valley, the lowest and hottest place in North America.

On a car ride through the Mojave desert, you may pass by many miles of bare, dusty earth and scattered bushes. However, on a morning hike you can discover that a desert is a lively place. Birds sing. Lizards scurry after insects. Jackrabbits and roadrunners dash among the bushes and cactus plants.

327

LITERATURE ANTHOLOGY, *pp. 326–327*

Read

Tell students they will be reading about how animals and plants in the Mojave desert adapt to live in such extreme conditions. Ask students to predict how the selection will help them answer the Essential Question.

Note Taking:
Use the Graphic Organizer

Remind students to take notes as they read. Have them fill in the graphic organizer on **Your Turn Practice Book** page 172. Ask them to compare and contrast for each section. They can also note words they don't understand and questions they have.

1 Text Features: Photographs

Look at the photograph and text on pages 326–327 with a partner. What plants do you see? (desert plants, bushes) What can we learn about the desert from looking at the photo? (dry, hot, has valleys) What kinds of animals live here? (birds, lizards, insects, jackrabbits, roadrunners)

Build Vocabulary page 327
  scurry: move quickly

- *How does the author show that the wildlife of the Mojave have special traits to survive?* (The author starts with, "Deserts are challenging places to live.")

- *What do the living things in a desert have to overcome to survive there?* (the heat, little rain, bare, dusty earth)

Read

② Text Features: Maps

Turn to a partner. Use the map key to find Death Valley. In what two states is it located? (California, Nevada) What river flows through part of the desert? (Colorado) How does the map help you understand the text? (It helps me visualize the desert's size and location; makes the information about the Mojave easier to understand.)

③ Skill: Compare and Contrast

What signal word is used to introduce how lizards are the same? (all) How are lizards the same? (scaly skin; can live in hot, dry environment) How are they different? (various sizes, some eat insects and others eat plants, different methods of protection) How are the spiny lizard and chuckwalla alike and different? Add this information to your chart.

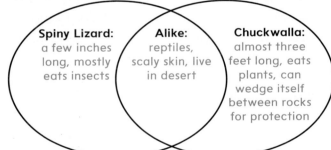

Spiny Lizard: a few inches long, mostly eats insects

Alike: reptiles, scaly skin, live in desert

Chuckwalla: almost three feet long, eats plants, can wedge itself between rocks for protection

Build Vocabulary page 328
fascinating: very interesting

A Living Place

Although it is very dry, the Mojave is a living place or environment for many fascinating animals and plants. Over many years they have changed, or adapted, so they live very well in a dry, hot environment. They do this in different ways. In the Mojave you might see several kinds of lizards. They are all **related**. All lizards are reptiles. Reptiles all have scaly skin. However, they are different in many ways. The desert spiny lizard, for example, is only a few inches long. Most of its food is insects.

This hawk looks out for food from the top of a yucca palm.

The name Mojave means "alongside water." It comes from the Mojave people. They were Native Americans who once lived along the Lower Colorado River. The river flows through part of the Mojave desert.

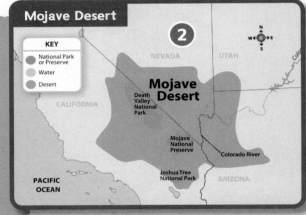

Mojave Desert

KEY
- National Park or Preserve
- Water
- Desert

NEVADA UTAH
CALIFORNIA
Death Valley National Park
Mojave Desert
Mojave National Preserve
Colorado River
Joshua Tree National Park
PACIFIC OCEAN
ARIZONA

328

A C T Access Complex Text

▶ Prior Knowledge

Tell students they should think about what they know about reptiles to better understand the desert and the types of animals that are able to live there. Explain that reptiles are cold-blooded. They breathe with their lungs. Most reptiles lay shelled eggs. There are over 6,000 species of reptiles.

- *What are some examples of reptiles?* (lizards, snakes, turtles, iguanas, chameleons)
- *What is something that all reptiles have in common?* (scaly skin)

The chuckwalla is very different. It can grow to almost three feet long. This big lizard eats leaves, flowers, and fruit of plants. It also has a special way of protecting itself. If a chuckwalla senses danger, it quickly hides in a crack between rocks. Then it gulps in air, making its body fatter. It becomes tightly wedged in so that a predator cannot pull it out. ③

This chuckwalla will quickly squeeze itself between rocks if a predator comes near.

329

LITERATURE ANTHOLOGY, *pp. 328–329*

Reread   *Close Reading Companion*

Author's Craft: Descriptive Words

What words does the author use help you visualize how the chuckwalla protects itself? (*gulps, wedged*) How do these words help you understand the chuckwalla's actions? (The author uses descriptive words and phrases to help me understand the animal's actions. The verb *gulps* helps me visualize the chuckwalla taking in large amounts of air. *Wedged in* helps me visualize the chuckwalla filling up a very small space.)

Author's Craft: Text Structure

Authors can begin comparisons and contrasts by using signal words. What word can you find on page 328 that signals a contrast? (however) What is the author contrasting? (The author is contrasting what lizards have in common with their many differences.)

ELL Students may have difficulty identifying the features of a lizard.

- Have students point to and identify the lizard on page 329. Then have them point out and label what they see. (claws, scales, mouth, throat, eyes)

- *Lizards are a type of ____.* (reptile) *The chuckwalla is a type of ____.* (lizard)

Read

4 Skill: Compare and Contrast

What do all desert animals need to survive? (water) Compare the way a large mammal, such as a coyote, gets its water with the way a small lizard might get its water. Add this information to your chart.

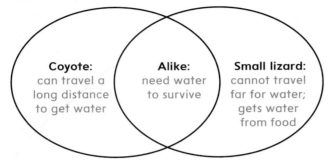

Coyote: can travel a long distance to get water

Alike: need water to survive

Small lizard: cannot travel far for water; gets water from food

STOP AND CHECK

Reread What are some different ways that animals in the Mojave get the water?

Teacher Think Aloud To learn how animals in the desert get water, I can look at the photographs and read the captions. I can reread that some animals have to travel a long distance to get water, while others get water from the food they eat.

Getting Water in the Desert

4 Animals get water in different ways in the Mojave. Coyotes, bobcats, and other large mammals can travel a long distance for a drink. So can some birds. Small lizards, snakes, and mice are different. They cannot travel far. They might **prefer** to drink from a stream or even a puddle, but these are rare treats in a desert. They find water in different ways. They get some from tiny drops of dew that form overnight on plants or stones. Their main source of water is the food they eat. Flowers, seeds, and leaves contain water. The bodies of insects, scorpions, and other animals are all at least half water. Some desert animals get most or all of the water they need simply by eating food.

STOP AND CHECK

Reread What are some different ways that animals in the Mojave get water? Reread to find the answer.

This coyote can travel far to find water.

330

A C T Access Complex Text

▶ Genre

Point out the ways students can follow the information that is presented. The headings tell the reader the topic of each section. The captions explain what is happening in the photographs and provide additional information.

- *How do coyotes get water?* (Coyotes can travel far distances to find water.)

- *How does the caption and photograph on page 331 show the importance of an animal's color in the desert?* (An animal's color helps it hide from its predators.)

Light-colored fur helps this kangaroo rat hide from predators.

Robert Shantz/Alamy

Light Colors Help

People who live in or visit deserts often wear light-colored clothes. This is smart because dark colors take in, or absorb, Sun energy, while light colors reflect it. You can avoid overheating by wearing light colors. Desert animals do the same by being light-colored. **5**

Being light-colored can help animals in another way. In the Mojave, the land is often colored tan, gray, and light brown. Pale mice, insects, or lizards are hard to see against this background. This gives the animals some **protection** from predators that try to catch and eat them.

Not all desert animals are light-colored. In some parts of the Mojave, mice and lizards are much darker. They are different because they live among rocks and soil that are black or dark brown. In those places, darker colors help them hide and survive. **6**

331

LITERATURE ANTHOLOGY, pp. 330–331

Read

⑤ Vocabulary: Context Clues

What clues in the surrounding sentence can help you determine the meaning of the word *absorb*? (*take in* means the same thing; the opposite of *absorb* is "to reflect.")

⑥ Strategy: Ask and Answer Questions

COLLABORATE

Generate questions of your own about the text and discuss them with a partner. For example, how would we want to dress if we spent a day in the desert? (in light colors) What colors would help us to blend in with the desert? (tan, gray, light brown)

Reread   *Close Reading Companion*

Author's Craft: Text Structure

How does the author help you understand how light-colored and dark-colored animals survive in the desert? (In the section called "Light-Colors Help," the author talks about how light colors help animals survive. But the last paragraph describes dark-colored animals and how their color helps them. This helps me understand that not all desert animals have the same features.)

CONNECT TO CONTENT
ADAPTATION AND THE FOOD CHAIN

Plants and animals must adapt to survive. The food chain keeps all of the plants and animals connected. They need each other to survive. In the selection, students read about how some animals get water from plants. These animals cannot travel far to get the water they need, so they drink from the dew on plants. Other animals get water from the animals they eat.

STEM

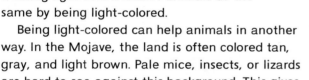

ELL Have students list the ways animals in the desert get the water they need to survive. Point out the image of the coyote getting water from the stream on page 330.

- *How does this animal get water?* (travels far to find water)

- *Is it easy to find water in the desert?* (no)

Read

7 Skill: Compare and Contrast

What is one way desert animals are alike? (They all find ways to avoid the midday heat.) Do all animals handle the heat the same way? (no) How does a scorpion avoid the heat? (It hides in shady places or "stilts.") How do snakes and lizards avoid the heat? (They crawl up into bushes.) Choose two desert animals to compare and contrast, and add this information to your chart.

Scorpions: hide in shady places; able to stilt

Alike: find ways to avoid midday heat

Snakes and Lizards: crawl up into bushes

STOP AND CHECK

Reread How do scorpions avoid the heat? (They usually hide in shady places. Scorpions can stand tall on their legs, or "stilt.")

Build Vocabulary page 332
  surface: the place on which the animals rest, such as the ground

Escaping the Heat

7   Desert animals are all alike in one way. They find ways to avoid midday heat. Different animals do this in different ways. Most of them rest during the hottest time of day. They are active in cooler times, such as mornings, evenings, or at night.

Different animals avoid heat in different ways. Scorpions usually hide in shady places. However, if a scorpion must be out in daytime, it can stand tall on its legs. This is called "stilting." It keeps the scorpion's body from touching the hot surface. A snake, of course, cannot "stilt" because it has no legs! On a hot day some snakes and lizards crawl up into bushes. There, the air is cooler than on the hot soil surface.

STOP AND CHECK

Reread How do scorpions avoid the heat? Reread to find the answer.

A scorpion uses its legs to raise its body above the hot ground.

332

A C T Access Complex Text

▶ Genre

Remind students to connect the photographs and other text features with what they are reading.

• Have students connect the photo of the scorpion with the text on page 332. (I can see the legs of the scorpion that help it to stand tall and avoid the heat of the day.)

• *How is the photograph of the jackrabbit connected to the text on page 333?* (The text describes the large ears of the jackrabbit. Looking at the photograph helps me understand how the jackrabbit's large ears help it stay cool.)

A jackrabbit's long ears help it stay cool.

Most desert animals also **(8)** escape the heat by seeking shelter under bushes, rocks, and other shady places. Black-tailed jackrabbits sprawl in the shade. They lose body heat by panting or breathing rapidly. Heat is also given off from many tiny blood vessels in their large ears.

333

LITERATURE ANTHOLOGY, pp. 332–333

Read

8 Strategy: Reread
COLLABORATE

Teacher Think Aloud There is information about scorpions, snakes, and black-tailed jackrabbits. How can we remember how the animals are alike and how they are different?

Prompt students to apply the strategy in a Think Aloud by rereading to remember facts and ideas and better understand the text. Have them turn to a partner to explain what they have reread.

Student Think Aloud I can reread the section about how each animal is able to escape the heat of the desert. Scorpions are able to stand to keep their body from touching the hot ground. A snake is able to use its body to crawl to a higher place. Jackrabbits can breathe quickly to lose the heat from their body. Their large ears also help them to keep cool. Each animal has special ways to escape the heat.

Build Vocabulary page 333
 sprawl: to lie spread out on the ground

ELL Point out the animals in the photographs. Have students point to and identify the parts of the animal that help it to survive in the desert.

- Read the captions with the students. *Are desert animals the same?* (no) *Some animals adapt to stay _____.* (cool)

- Ask students what they do to stay cool.

Read

9 Skill: Compare and Contrast

What is a reason many desert animals use underground burrows? (for protection from extreme temperatures) Compare and contrast how burrows protect animals during the day and during the night. (During the day, burrows shield animals from the hot sun. At night, when the desert can get cold, burrows help keep animals warm.)

10 Skill: Make Inferences

Use what you know about tortoises to make inferences about why desert tortoises spend so much of their lives in burrows. (The selection says that many animals burrow underground to stay cool. I also know that tortoises are very slow and cannot defend themselves well, so it seems like spending their lives in burrows is a good way for desert tortoises to protect themselves from the heat and from predators.)

Build Vocabulary page 334
abandoned: left empty

Cool and Safe Underground

9 Many desert animals seek the coolness of underground burrows. The afternoon soil temperature may be as hot as 140 degrees F! Just a foot or two underground, the temperature might be 85 degrees. Burrows protect animals from heat and also from cold. Desert nights are often chilly. Winter snow sometimes falls in the Mojave.

10 Desert tortoises spend most of their lives in burrows they dig. They come out in the spring to eat plant leaves, flowers, and fruit. Because their burrows are big and often several feet long, there is room for other animals too. A tortoise burrow is an **excellent** hiding and resting place for kangaroo rats, rabbits, snakes, lizards, owls, and other small desert creatures. Some join a sleeping tortoise. Others use an abandoned burrow.

These owl chicks make a comfortable home in this abandoned burrow.

334

A C T Access Complex Text

▶ Specific Vocabulary

Review strategies for finding the meaning of an unfamiliar word, such as using context clues. Point out the word *burrows* on page 334.

- *What context clues help you to figure out what a burrow is?* ("a foot or two underground" and "in burrows they dig")

- Have students define *burrow*. (A *burrow* is "a hole dug in the ground by an animal.")

- *Why are burrows so important for desert animals?* (Burrows can protect animals from the heat and the cold and they are good places for hiding and resting.)

The hard shell of a desert tortoise protects it from predators.

Some desert animals also use their hideouts in a different way. In the evening, scorpions wait just inside their shelters for their next meal. A lizard, beetle, or even another scorpion might pass by. These moving animals make ground vibrations that scorpions can feel. The vibrations **alert** scorpions that an animal is nearby. Some scorpions can sense vibrations in the air caused by a flying insect. They can reach out and grab a low-flying moth! **11**

335

NPS Photo by Stacy Manson

LITERATURE ANTHOLOGY, *pp. 334–335*

Read

11 Strategy: Reread
COLLABORATE

Reread pages 334–335. Turn to your partner and tell in your own words why animals might need to be careful when hiding in burrows.

Student Think Aloud I can reread to remember that animals move to burrows to stay cool during the day and to stay safe and warm at night. But the burrows can be dangerous. They might find a predator already inside, using the burrow too. Some animals hide just inside and wait for prey to pass by, then pop out to eat them. So animals must still be very careful when they use burrows to stay safe.

Reread

Author's Craft: Word Choice

Authors choose specific words to give the reader extra information. The author switches from using *burrow* to *hideout*. Why do you think the author made this choice? (This section discusses the way scorpions catch their prey. The word *hideout* is appropriate because it is often used to describe a secret place where people go to hide. Scorpions use hideouts to hide and wait for their next meal.)

ELL Demonstrate for students the feeling of a vibration. Have students list or act out different types of vibrations. *Can you feel a vibration?* (yes) Then have them complete sentence frames with the word *vibrations*.

• _____ can help animals in the desert catch food.

The desert iguana's skin turns pale in the afternoon to help it stay cool.

Read

⑫ Skill: Compare and Contrast

What is another problem desert animals face? (warming up after a cool night) How do desert iguanas warm up and cool off? (change color) How do roadrunners warm up? (They turn their backs toward the sun and raise their body feathers. Their skin is black, which absorbs the sun's energy.) Add this information to your chart.

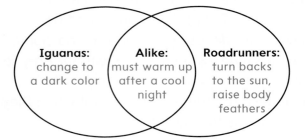

| Iguanas: change to a dark color | Alike: must warm up after a cool night | Roadrunners: turn backs to the sun, raise body feathers |

STOP AND CHECK

Ask and Answer Questions Why do desert iguanas change color? (They change color for warming and cooling. As the day gets hotter, their skin turns white to reflect the sun. As the day becomes cooler, their skin darkens to absorb the heat.)

Build Vocabulary page 336
    absorb: soak in, as water or warmth

Morning Warmth

Desert animals have many different ways to avoid overheating. Sometimes, however, they need to get warm! At night, the desert air is quite cool. By dawn, some animals need to warm up. Lizards and snakes crawl to a sunny place. They turn their bodies toward ⑫ the Sun to raise their body temperature.

Desert iguanas have an amazing ability for warming and also for cooling. They change color! In the morning, their skin is dark. This helps them absorb heat from the Sun. Then the day gets hotter and hotter. By early afternoon the iguanas' skin has turned white, reflecting sunlight. Then, as the air becomes cooler in the evening, their skin darkens again.

The desert iguana's skin is dark in the morning. This helps the animal warm up.

STOP AND CHECK

Ask and Answer Questions Why do desert iguanas change color? Reread the page to find the answer.

336

A C T   Access Complex Text

▶ Connection of Ideas

Remind students that they learned about how animals have to adapt to the heat of the desert (pages 332–333), and about how animals have to adapt to the cold (pages 336–337).

• Have students reread the last paragraph on page 336. *What do iguanas do when it is too warm?* (As the day gets hotter, they turn white to reflect

the sunlight.) *What else can iguanas do to stay cool?* (hide in the shade)

• *What happens to an iguana's skin as the air gets cool in the evening?* (It gets dark.)

• *How does this help the iguana get warm?* (In the morning, the dark skin helps it absorb heat from the sun.)

Like iguanas, some birds need to warm their bodies after a chilly night. Roadrunners turn their backs toward the Sun and raise their body feathers. Their skin is black. It absorbs Sun energy. When warm enough, roadrunners join in the **competition** for food. They dash to hunt for lizards and small snakes.

This roadrunner cools off in the shade of a tree.

Roadrunners live very well in deserts. Like all the other Mojave animals, they are wonderfully adapted to thrive in a dry, hot environment. So are scorpions, jackrabbits, chuckwallas, and tortoises. They all make the Mojave a lively, fascinating place.

After warming up, this roadrunner is ready to run fast to catch its prey.

337

LITERATURE ANTHOLOGY, *pp. 336–337*

Read

Return to Purposes Review students' predictions and purposes for reading. Ask them to answer the Essential Question. (Animals have different ways of adapting to challenges in their habitat. Some animals have adapted their physical features and characteristics to survive and some have adapted to the environment around them to survive.)

Reread   *Close Reading Companion*

Author's Craft: Descriptive Words

Reread pages 336–337. How does the author feel about the desert iguana's ability to change color? How can you tell? (The author is impressed by the skill; he calls it an *amazing ability.*) How does the author describe how the roadrunner is adapted to live in the desert? (*wonderfully*) Why does the author include these descriptions? (to emphasize that these abilities and adaptations are special and out of the ordinary)

ELL Have students draw pictures of an iguana to show how it changes colors throughout the day.

- *Why does it change from a dark color to white from morning to afternoon?* (The afternoon is when the sun is the strongest. It is very hot.)

- *When is its skin dark again?* (at night)

Read

About the Author

Laurence Pringle

Have students read the biography of the author. Ask:

- What do many of Laurence Pringle's books have in common?
- How did he discover his love for nature?

Author's Purpose

To Inform

Remind students that authors who write to inform present the reader with information and examples. Students may say that the author wanted to inform readers about the special qualities of the animals of the Mojave to help spread his love of nature to others.

Reread

Author's Craft

The author's point of view is how he or she thinks about a subject. In *Amazing Wildlife of the Mojave,* the author describes how deserts are challenging places to live. The author also states that the Mojave is a lively, fascinating place. These points are supported by the details and images in the text. What examples of the author's point of view can you find in the selection?

About the Author

Growing up, **Laurence Pringle** loved to explore the outdoors—tramping through the woods, splashing through ponds and streams, and fishing in the ocean. His other strong interest was reading, so writing about nature made perfect sense. Among his other books are *Snakes! Strange and Wonderful, Come to the Ocean's Edge,* and *A Dragon in the Sky: The Story of a Green Darner Dragonfly.* When he's not writing, he still enjoys hiking and fishing.

Author's Purpose

Why do you think the author calls the animals of the Mojave "amazing"?

338

LITERATURE ANTHOLOGY, *pp. 338–339*

Respond to the Text

Summarize

How have different animals in the Mojave adapted to the challenges in their habitat? Information from your Venn Diagram may help you summarize.

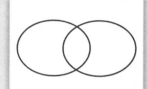

Write

How do you know how the author feels about the wildlife in the Mojave desert? Use these sentence frames to organize your text evidence.

The author says that living in the desert is . . .
He tells about how the animals . . .
This helps me know that he feels . . .

Make Connections

Describe how one of the animals in the selection has adapted to its environment. ESSENTIAL QUESTION

How do animals in cities or towns adapt to their habitat? TEXT TO WORLD

339

Make Connections

Essential Question Responses will vary, depending on the animal the student chooses to describe, but students should cite text evidence, including page numbers, to support their responses.

Text to World Responses will vary, but encourage students to do research online and cite text evidence from their sources.

Respond to the Text

Read

Summarize

Tell students they will use the information from their Compare and Contrast Charts to summarize. *As I read Amazing Wildlife of the Mojave, I learned about animals with varied ways of adapting to the extreme conditions of the desert environment. To summarize, I will reword the most important details.*

Reread

Analyze the Text

After students summarize the selection, have them reread to develop a deeper understanding of the text and answer the questions on **Close Reading Companion** pages 114–116. For students who need support in citing text evidence, use the Reread prompts on pages T153D–T153M.

Write About the Text

Review the writing prompt and sentence frames. Remind students to use their responses from the **Close Reading Companion** to support their answers. For a full lesson on writing a response using text evidence, see page T158.

<u>Answer:</u> The author thinks that desert animals are fascinating in their adaptations and abilities to live in such a hot, dry environment. <u>Evidence:</u> On page 328, he says desert animals are fascinating. On page 336, he says the desert iguana has an "amazing ability for warming and . . . cooling." On page 337, he says that roadrunners are "wonderfully adapted to thrive in a dry, hot environment."

Literature Anthology

"Little Half Chick"

Text Complexity Range

Lexile

420 ——————▲—————— 820
690

TextEvaluator™

2 ——————▲—————— 35
21

What makes this text complex?
▶ **Purpose**

Compare Texts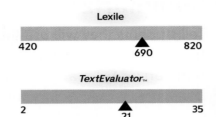

As students read and reread "Little Half Chick," encourage them to take notes and think about the Essential Question: *How do animals adapt to challenges in their environment?* Tell students to think about how this text compares with *Amazing Wildlife of the Mojave.*

Read

1 Skill: Theme

What challenges did Little Half Chick face? (He has one leg, one wing, and one eye.) What is the lesson of the story? (Always help those in need because you may need help yourself.)

Reread　　*Close Reading Companion*

Author's Craft: Description

What words and phrases help you visualize how Little Half Chick escapes the cook's pot of water? (The verbs "grabbed" and "plunged" and the phrases "refused to burn" and "refused to boil" help me picture the events. I can picture how wind carries the chick "to the top of the highest tower.".)

Genre · Folktale

Compare Texts
Read about Little Half Chick. Find out how he adapts to life in the city.

Little Half Chick

Once in Mexico, an unusual chick hatched. He had only one eye, one wing, and one leg. He was named Little Half Chick. He quickly learned to hop faster on one leg than most chickens could walk on two. He was a curious and adventurous chick and soon grew tired of his barnyard **environment**. One day he decided to hop to Mexico City to meet the mayor.

Along the way, he hopped by a stream blocked with weeds. "Could you clear these weeds away so my water can run freely?" the stream gurgled. Little Half Chick helped the stream. Then he hopped on.

Illustration: Christiane Beauregard

340

 **A C T**　**A**ccess **C**omplex **T**ext

▶ **Purpose**

Remind students that folktales teach a lesson.

* *Why do the water, the fire, and the wind help Little Half Chick?* (He helped them.)

* *How do these events support the lesson stated at the end of the story?* (They show that we all need help, and if you help others, they will help you.)

It started to rain. A small fire on the side of the road crackled, "Please give me **shelter** from this rain, or I will go out!" Little Half Chick stretched out his wing to protect the fire until the rain stopped.

Further down the road Little Half Chick met a wind that was tangled in a prickly bush. "Please untangle me," it whispered. Little Half Chick untangled the wind. Then he hopped on to Mexico City.

Little Half Chick did not meet the mayor. He met the mayor's cook. She grabbed him, plunged him into a pot of water, and lit a fire. However, the fire and the water remembered Little Half Chick's kindness. The fire refused to burn, and the water refused to boil. Then, the grateful wind picked him up and carried him safely to the top of the highest tower in Mexico City.

Little Half Chick became a weather vane. His flat body told everyone below the direction the wind blew. And he learned this lesson: Always help someone in need because you don't know when you'll need help.

Make Connections

Explain how Little Half Chick adapted to his new habitat. ESSENTIAL QUESTION

Compare Little Half Chick to other animals you have read about. TEXT TO TEXT

341

LITERATURE ANTHOLOGY, *pp. 340–341*

Read

Summarize

Guide students to summarize the selection.

Reread

Analyze the Text

After students read and summarize, have them reread to develop a deeper understanding of the text by annotating and answering questions on pages 117–119 of the **Close Reading Companion**.

Integrate

Make Connections

Essential Question <u>Answer:</u> Little Half Chick adapted by exploring and helping those he met along the way. He became a helpful part of Mexico City by turning into a weather vane. <u>Evidence:</u> On page 340, the chick cleared weeds from the steam. On page 341, he protected fire from rain and untangled the wind. Finally, he accepted the job of being a weather vane.

Text to Text Responses may vary, but encourage students to cite text evidence.

ELL Have students point to the image of Little Half Chick.

- Identify and label what made Little Half Chick different from the other chickens. (He only had one eye, one wing, and one leg.)

- *Did these challenges stop Little Half Chick from doing what he wanted?* (no) *How did he walk?* (He hopped.) Have students demonstrate *hopping*.

Phonics/Fluency

 MINILESSON 20 Mins

Variant Vowel /ô/

OBJECTIVES

CCSS Use a known root word as a clue to the meaning of an unknown word with the same root (e.g., *company, companion*). **L.3.4c**

CCSS Create engaging audio recordings of stories or poems that demonstrate fluid reading at an understandable pace; add visual displays when appropriate to emphasize or enhance certain facts or details. **SL.3.5**

Rate: 82–102 WCPM

ACADEMIC LANGUAGE
• *intonation*
• Cognate: *entonación*

 ELL

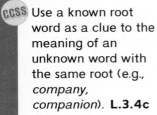 Refer to the sound transfers chart in the **Language Transfers Handbook** to identify sounds that do not transfer in Spanish, Cantonese, Vietnamese, Hmong, and Korean.

1 Explain

Display the *Straw* **Sound-Spelling Card** for the variant vowel /ô/. Point out that this vowel sound can be spelled in several different ways. Discuss each spelling for /ô/ and provide a sample word for each, for example: *aw* as in *straw*; *au* as in *haul*; *al* as in *salt* and *walk*; *all* as in *ball*; *ough* as in *bought*; *wa* as in *water*.

2 Model

Write the sample words *straw, haul, salt, walk, ball,* and *bought* on the board. Underline the spelling for the variant vowel /ô/ in each word. Model how to blend the words. Run your finger under each word as you sound it out.

3 Guided Practice

Write the following list of words on the board. Help students identify the variant-vowel spelling in each word. Guide students as they underline the spelling for /ô/ and then pronounce each word.

brought	caused	halt	halls	small
lawn	stalk	thought	raw	pause

Read Multisyllabic Words

Transition to Longer Words Help students transition to reading longer words with the variant vowel /ô/. Draw a T-chart on the board. In the first column write *thought, straw, cause, draw, awe,* and *walk*. In the second column, write *thoughtless, strawberry, because, drawing, awesome,* and *sidewalk*. Point to the first column and have students chorally read the words. Underline the variant-vowel spelling for /ô/ in each word.

Explain that the words in the second column include a word part with a spelling for /ô/. Have students underline the variant-vowel spelling for /ô/ in each word. Point to each word in random order and have students read the words chorally.

For practice decoding variant words in context, assign the decodable passages on **Teacher's Resource Book** page 31.

 **Go Digital**

 Variant Vowels

Present the Lesson

View "Gray Wolf! Red Fox!"

Greek and Latin Roots

1 Explain

Many English words come from the Greek or Latin language. Learning Greek and Latin roots can help readers figure out the meanings of unfamiliar words.

- The word part *-graph* comes from a Greek word that means "something written." The word *photograph* means "written picture."

- The word part *aud-* comes from a Latin word that means "to hear or listen." The word *audience* means "a group of listeners."

2 Model

Write and say the words *auditorium* and *biography*. Have students repeat. Underline the roots *aud-* and *-graph* and model defining each word.

3 Guided Practice

Write the words *audition, calligraphy,* and *autograph* on the board. Help students say each word and use the root to define each word.

Intonation

Explain/Model Explain that intonation means changing the tone of your voice to stress important words or sentences and express meaning. Point out that readers use punctuation clues, such as question marks, to help them use appropriate intonation.

Model reading page 291 of "Gray Wolf! Red Fox!". Point out how the tone of your voice changed as you read the questions in the first paragraph.

Practice/Apply Have students create audio recordings of the passage to demonstrate fluid reading. Remind students to use appropriate intonation. Offer opportunities for students to listen to their recordings. Provide feedback as needed.

Daily Fluency Practice

Students can practice fluency using **Your Turn Practice Book**.

Monitor and *Differentiate*

 Quick Check

Can students decode words with the variant vowel /ô/? Can students use Greek and Latin roots to determine the meanings of words? Can students read fluently?

Small Group Instruction

If No → Approaching Level	Reteach pp. T168, T170
	ELL	Develop p. T186
If Yes → On Level	Review p. T176
	Beyond Level	Extend p. T180

ON-LEVEL PRACTICE BOOK p. 178

A. Read each word in the box and listen for the vowel sound. Then write each word under the correct heading.

chalk	halt	small	crawl
thought	stalk	brought	lawn
caused	malt	halls	paused

aw as in *straw*	*alt* as in *salt*	*all* as in *ball*
crawl	halt	small
lawn	malt	halls

au as in *haul*	*alk* as in *walk*	*ough* as in *bought*
caused	chalk	thought
paused	stalk	brought

B. Read each sentence and underline the word with the root *graph* or *aud*. Then write the word on the line and circle the root.

1. The president's <u>autograph</u> is very valuable. _autograph_
2. The <u>audience</u> clapped after the great performance. _audience_
3. I read a <u>biography</u> about a famous astronaut. _biography_
4. She had a great <u>audition</u> and won the lead role. _audition_
5. I read a <u>graphic</u> novel about a family from outer space. _graphic_

APPROACHING p. 178	BEYOND p. 178	ELL p. 178

→ Write to Sources

Reading/Writing Workshop

OBJECTIVES

CCSS Write informative/ explanatory texts to examine a topic and convey ideas and information clearly. Introduce a topic and group related information together; include illustrations when useful to aiding comprehension. **W.3.2a**

ACADEMIC LANGUAGE

opening, fact, topic, purpose

Go Digital

U4W3 Organization: Strong Openings

DAY 1

Writing Fluency

Write to a Prompt Provide students with the prompt: *Write about some challenges red foxes and gray wolves face in their environments.* Have students share their ideas about the challenges to these animals. *How have humans caused challenges for red foxes and gray wolves?* When students finish sharing ideas, have them write continuously for eleven minutes in their Writer's Notebook. If students stop writing, encourage them to keep going.

 When students finish writing, have them work with a partner to compare ideas and make sure that they both have a clear understanding of the topic.

Writing Process Genre Writing

Fictional Narrative pp. T344–T349

Third Week Focus: Over the course of the week, focus on the following stages of the writing process:

Edit Analyze the Student Model found online at Writer's Workspace. Have students use the Edit questions on the Revise and Edit Checklist to guide them as they review and edit their drafts on their own.

Publish For the final presentation of their fictional narratives, have students choose a format for publishing.

Evaluate Distribute the Student Rubric found online at Writer's Workspace to students. Have students set writing goals to prepare for a Teacher conference.

DAY 2

Write to the Reading/Writing Workshop Text

Analyze the Prompt Read aloud the first paragraph on page 298 of the **Reading/ Writing Workshop**. Ask: *What is the prompt asking?* (to explain how red foxes and gray wolves have adapted to changes in their environment) Say: *Let's reread to find information about how the animals have adapted. We can note text evidence.*

Analyze Text Evidence Display Graphic Organizer 35 in Writer's Workspace. *Say: Let's see how one student, Luke, took notes to answer the prompt. He notes that foxes use their tails to protect them from the cold.* Guide the class through the rest of Luke's notes.

Analyze the Student Model Explain how Luke used text evidence from his notes to write a response to the prompt.

- **Strong Opening** Grabbing the reader's attention with an interesting question is a great way to write a strong opening. Luke does this with his question, "How could a small red fox beat a large gray wolf?" Trait: Organization

- **Supporting Details** Luke supports his topic only with facts and details that connect directly to that main idea. Trait: Ideas

- **Linking Words** Luke connects his thoughts by starting a sentence with "But," which signals a contrasting idea. Trait: Sentence Fluency

For additional practice with organization and strong openings, assign **Your Turn Practice Book** page 179.

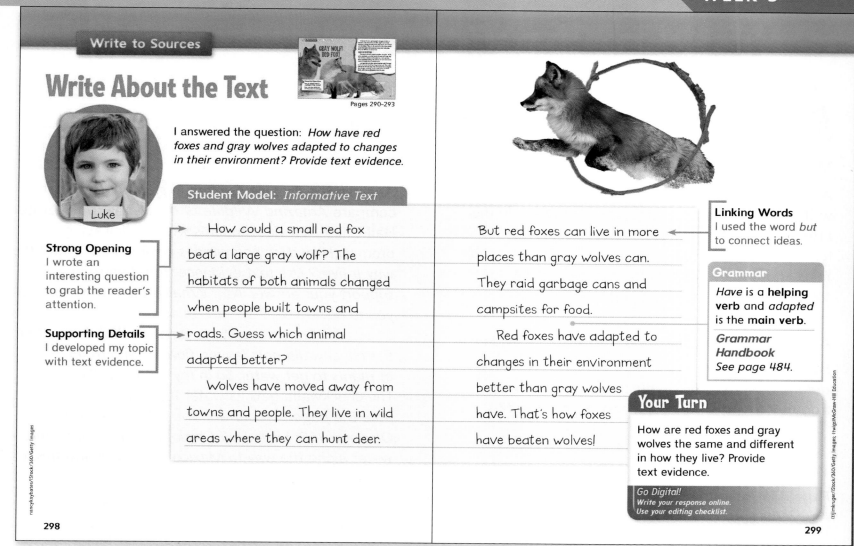

Write to Sources

Write About the Text

Pages 290-293

Luke

I answered the question: *How have red foxes and gray wolves adapted to changes in their environment? Provide text evidence.*

Student Model: *Informative Text*

Strong Opening
I wrote an interesting question to grab the reader's attention.

Supporting Details
I developed my topic with text evidence.

How could a small red fox beat a large gray wolf? The habitats of both animals changed when people built towns and roads. Guess which animal adapted better?

Wolves have moved away from towns and people. They live in wild areas where they can hunt deer.

But red foxes can live in more places than gray wolves can. They raid garbage cans and campsites for food.

Red foxes have adapted to changes in their environment better than gray wolves have. That's how foxes have beaten wolves!

Linking Words
I used the word *but* to connect ideas.

Grammar
Have is a **helping verb** and *adapted* is the **main verb**.

Grammar Handbook
See page 484.

Your Turn
How are red foxes and gray wolves the same and different in how they live? Provide text evidence.

Go Digital!
Write your response online. Use your editing checklist.

298

299

READING/WRITING WORKSHOP, *pp. 298-299*

Your Turn Writing Read the Your Turn prompt on p. 299 of the Reading/Writing Workshop aloud. Discuss the prompt with students. If necessary, review with students that authors use strong openings to state their topic and set their purpose for writing.

Have students take notes as they look for the text evidence to answer the prompt. Remind them to include the following elements as they craft their response from their notes:

- Stong Opening
- Supporting Details
- Linking Words

Have students use the **Grammar Handbook** on page 484 in the Reading/Writing Workshop to edit for errors in helping verbs and main verbs.

ENGLISH LANGUAGE LEARNERS SCAFFOLD

ELL

Beginning

Write Help students complete the sentence frames.
Red foxes are ____.
Gray wolves are ____.

Intermediate

Describe Ask students to complete the sentence frames. Encourage students to provide details.
Red foxes prefer to ____, while gray foxes are more likely to ____.

Advanced/High

Discuss Check for understanding. Ask: *Are wolves and red foxes members of the same family? Could wolves and red foxes live and hunt together?*

Write to Sources

DAY 3

For students who need support to complete the writing assignment for the Literature Anthology, provide the following instruction.

DAY 4

Write to the Literature Anthology Text

Analyze the Prompt Explain that students will write about *Amazing Wildlife of the Mojave* in the **Literature Anthology,** pages 326–338. Provide the following prompt: *How do you know how the author feels about the wildlife in the Mojave desert?* Ask: *What is the prompt asking you to do?* (to analyze the author's point of view)

Analyze Text Evidence Help students note evidence.

Pages 328–329 Read the pages aloud. Ask: *What details show that the plants and animals have adapted to the desert's extreme environment?* (The Mojave is very dry and hot; the lizards that live there have adapted to their conditions in different ways.) *Why is this important?*

Page 336 Read the text and study the photographs. Ask: *What ability does the author say is "amazing"?* (the desert iguana's ability to change color to warm or cool itself)

Encourage students to look for more text evidence about the author's point of view. Then have them craft a short response. Use the conference routine below.

Write to Two Sources

Analyze the Prompt Explain to students they will compare *Amazing Wildlife of the Mojave* and "Little Half Chick." Provide students with the following prompt: *How does an animal's environment affect the way it lives? Use text evidence from two sources to support your answer.* Ask: *What is the prompt asking you to do?* (to explain how an animal's environment affects the way it lives) Say: *On page 329, I read that the chuckwalla eats leaves, flowers, and fruits of plants to get water. So in my notes I will write:* The chuckwalla gets its water from plants. *I will also note the page number and the title of the source. On page 340, Little Half Chick helps fire, wind, and water along the way to Mexico City. I will add this to my notes.*

Analyze Text Evidence Display online Graphic Organizer 36 in Writer's Workspace. Say: *Let's see how one student took notes to answer the prompt. Here are Luke's notes.* Read through the text evidence for each selection and have students point out details about animals' environments.

Teacher Conferences

STEP 1

Talk about the strengths of the writing.

The opening paragraph clearly states the main idea and identifies the writer's point of view. It tells me what the passage will be about.

STEP 2

Focus on how the writer uses text evidence.

Your topic sentence is very strong, but you need to add more details from the text to support it. Be sure your evidence is relevant to the topic.

STEP 3

Make concrete suggestions.

The first part of your opening is interesting. I have learned more about ____. Be sure to grab the reader's attention and also state your topic clearly.

DAY

5

Share the Prompt Provide the following prompt to students: *How are these two stories about animals in the desert the same and different? Use text evidence from both* Amazing Wildlife of the Mojave *and "Little Half Chick" to support your answer.*

Find Text Evidence Have students take notes. Find text evidence and give guidance where needed. If necessary, review with students how to paraphrase. Remind them to write the page number and source of the information.

Analyze the Student Model Review the prompt and Luke's notes from Day 4. Display the student model on page 180 of the **Your Turn Practice Book**. Explain to students that Luke synthesized his notes to write a response to the prompt. Discuss the page together with students or have them do it independently.

Write the Response Review the prompt from Day 4 with students. Remind them that they took notes on this prompt on Day 4. Have students use their notes to craft a short response. Tell students to include the titles of both sources and the following elements:

- Strong Opening
- Supporting Details
- Linking Words

Share and Reflect Have students share their responses with a partner. Use the Peer Conference routine below.

Suggested Revisions

Provide specific direction to help focus young writers.

Focus on a Sentence
Read the draft and target one sentence for revision. *Rewrite this sentence to add another relevant supporting detail.*

Focus on a Section
Underline a section that needs to be revised. *This section is interesting. I want to know more about ____. Provide more details to help me better understand your ideas.*

Focus on a Revision Strategy
Underline a section. Have students use a specific revision strategy, such as linking ideas. *You've included good details. Try using more linking words and phrases to connect your ideas.*

Peer Conferences

Focus peer response on writing a strong opening that grabs attention and includes a clear topic. Ask these questions:

- Does the introduction grab your attention?
- Are the details relevant to the topic?
- Are the ideas connected with linking words and phrases?

→ Grammar: Main and Helping Verbs

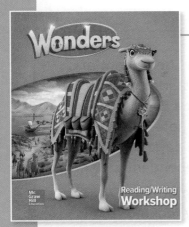

Reading/Writing Workshop

OBJECTIVES

CCSS Form and use regular and irregular verbs. **L.3.1d**

CCSS Form and use the simple (e.g., *I walked; I walk; I will walk*) verb tenses. **L.3.1e**

CCSS Use commas and quotation marks in dialogue. **L.3.2c**

- Distinguish main and helping verbs
- Capitalize and punctuate dialogue correctly
- Proofread sentences for mechanics and usage errors

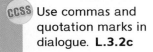

Have students write three sentences using helping verbs. Help them check each sentence to be sure the helping verb agrees with the subject of the sentence.

DAY 1

DAILY LANGUAGE ACTIVITY

Fred hasnt seen his pet turtle since this morning. His sister said she seen it craling under the couch.

(1: hasn't; 2: saw; 3: crawling)

Introduce Main and Helping Verbs

- Sometimes a verb may be more than one word. The main verb tells what the subject is or does. The helping verb helps the main verb show action.

- **Have**, **has**, and **had** can be helping verbs. Helping verbs must agree with the subject in simple and compound sentences:

    Lee and I **have decided** to join the tennis team.

    Marley **had examined** the plant's roots, and Bryan **had removed** its dry leaves.

Discuss verbs using page 484 of the Grammar Handbook.

DAY 2

DAILY LANGUAGE ACTIVITY

The fox has grow longer fur since we last saw him It is now winter and the long fur keep's him warm.

(1: grown; 2: him.; 3: keeps)

Review Main and Helping Verbs

Review main and helping verbs. *Have, has,* and *had* are helping verbs.

Introduce More Helping Verbs

Present the following:

- The verb forms of **be** can also act as helping verbs. **Is, are, am, was, were**, and **will** can be helping verbs:

    The kittens **are playing** with the yarn.

- The helping verb must agree with the subject of the sentence in simple and compound sentences:

    The kitten **is playing** with the yarn.

 TALK ABOUT IT

COLLABORATE

USE HELPING VERBS

Ask partners to form and use main and helping verbs to talk about how animals adapt to their habitat. They might discuss how desert animals come out at night to avoid the heat. As they talk, students should listen to be sure they use main and helping verbs.

DESCRIBE THE SCENE

Have students cut out pictures from a magazine showing animals in their natural habitats and spread them out on the table. As students look at pictures, have them take turns describing the animals in the pictures and what they are doing using main and helping verbs.

DAY 3

Monkeys are great tree climers. They have thums that help them grab a hold of tree trunk's when they climb.
(1: climbers; 2: thumbs; 3: trunks)

Mechanics and Usage: Commas and Quotation Marks in Dialogue

- **Quotation marks** show that someone is speaking. They come at the beginning and end of the speaker's exact words.
- Begin a quotation with a capital letter. **Commas** and periods appear inside quotation marks.
- If the end of a quotation comes at the end of a sentence, use a period, question mark, or exclamation mark to end it.
- If the sentence continues after a quotation, use a comma to close.

As students write, refer them to Grammar Handbook pages 484 and 504.

See Grammar Practice Reproducibles pages 86–90.

DAY 4

We went to bills farm. He taght us to ride horses and said, always bring carrots. They are a horse's favorite treat."
(1: Bill's; 2: taught; 3: "Always)

Proofread

Have students correct errors in these sentences.

1. They was riding bicycles in the park (1: were; 2: park.)
2. The pet shop owner said, put the goldfish in a bowl with fresh water. (1: "Put; 2: water.")
3. randall was here yesterday" said Susan. (1: "Randall; 2: yesterday,")
4. Jerry noticed his friend was coming fast down the hill when he said, terry look out for the tree! (1: "Terry,; 2: tree!")

Have students check their work using Grammar Handbook pages 484, 501, and 504.

DAY 5

Doctor Lee said I must drink fluids. He said, "since you're sick, it's important that you drink plenty of juice. (1: Dr. Lee; 2: "Since; 3: juice.")

Assess

Use the Daily Language Activity and Grammar Practice Reproducibles page 90 for assessment.

Reteach

Use Grammar Practice Reproducibles pages 86–89 and selected pages from the Grammar Handbook for additional reteaching. Remind students it is important to use main and helping verbs correctly as they read, write, and speak.

Check students' writing for use of the skill and listen for it in their speaking. Assign Grammar Revision Assignments in their Writer's Notebooks as needed.

ROLE-PLAY A SCENE

Have students reenact a favorite scene from a story the class has read about animals adapting to challenges in their habitat. As students role play, be sure they use many main and helping verbs. As other students watch, have them listen for the verbs.

HELPING VERB QUIZ

Partners should create five sentences with main and helping verbs and trade sentences with another pair. One partner should read a sentence aloud; the other should identify the main and helping verb using a question form (for example, "What is *will walk*?").

WRITE SENTENCES

Have groups each write five main verbs and five helping verbs on cards and place them in two piles. Students will take turns selecting a card from each pile and saying aloud the main and helping verbs, as the others use the main and helping verb in a sentence.

Spelling: Variant Vowels /ô/

DAY 1

DAY 2

OBJECTIVES

CCSS Use spelling patterns and generalizations (e.g., *word families, position-based spellings, syllable patterns, ending rules, meaningful word parts*) in writing words. **L.3.2f**

CCSS Consult reference materials, including beginning dictionaries, as needed to check and correct spellings. **L.3.2g**

Spelling Words

taught	drawing	talked
hauls	crawl	halls
caused	flawless	water
paused	lawn	bought
squawk	salt	
thoughtless		

Review inches, cities, cherries
Challenge walrus, autumn

Differentiated Spelling

Approaching Level

taught	halls	crawl
hauls	small	draw
caused	ball	walk
salt	lawn	water
halt	raw	bought

Beyond Level

taught	salt	flawless
hauls	stalk	scrawny
squawk	halted	walrus
paused	smallness	thoughtless
fault	crawl	sought

Assess Prior Knowledge

Display the spelling words. Read them aloud, drawing out and slowly enunciating the /ô/ sounds in each word.

Model for students how to spell the word *lawn*. Segment the word sound by sound, then attach a spelling to each sound. Point out that aw is one way to spell the /ô/ sound.

Demonstrate sorting the spelling words by pattern under key words *taught, lawn,* and *salt.* (Write the words on index cards or the IWB.) Sort a few words. Remind them that /ô/ can be spelled aw, *au, a,* and *ou* as in *bought.*

Then use the Dictation Sentences from Day 5. Say the underlined word, read the sentence, and repeat the word. Have students write the words.

Spiral Review

Review plurals in the words *inches, cities,* and *cherries*. Have students find words in this week's readings with the same plural spellings. Use the Dictation Sentences below for the review words. Read the sentence, say the word, and have students write the words.

1. Tam grew two <u>inches</u> last year.
2. Manuel has visited three <u>cities</u>.
3. He made the pie with <u>cherries</u>.

Have students trade papers and check the spellings.

Challenge Words Review this week's spelling words, pointing out the /ô/ spellings. Use these Dictation Sentences for challenge words. Read the sentence, say the word, have students write the word.

1. A <u>walrus</u> has long tusks.
2. <u>Autumn</u> comes after summer.

Have students write the words in their word study notebook.

 WORD SORTS

COLLABORATE

OPEN SORT

Have students cut apart the **Spelling Word Cards BLM** in the Online Resource Book and initial the backs of each card. Have them read the words aloud with a partner. Then have partners do an **open sort**. Have them record the sort in their word study notebook.

PATTERN SORT

Complete the **pattern sort** using the key words, pointing out the /ô/ spellings. Have students use Spelling Word Cards to do their own pattern sort. A partner can compare and check their sorts.

DAY 3

Alphabetizing

Display *taught, halls, talked, hauls.* Model how to alphabetize to the third letter.

Say: *Look at the first two letters.* Decide which ones come first in the alphabet. If the first and second letters are the same, go to the third letter.

Put the words in ABC order: *halls, hauls, talked, taught.* Explain that it is necessary to go to the third letter to alphabetize *halls* and *hauls,* since the beginning letters *ha* are the same, and *l* comes before *u.*

Have students alphabetize *caused, crawl, water,* and *walrus* to the second or third letter as needed (caused, crawl, walrus, water) and write them in their Writer's Notebooks.

See Phonics/Spelling Reproducibles pp. 103–108.

SPEED SORT

Have partners do a **speed sort** to see who is fastest. Then have them do a word hunt in the week's reading for words with the /ô/ sound. Have them record the words in their Day 2 pattern sort in the word study notebook.

DAY 4

Proofread and Write

Write these sentences on the board. Have students circle and correct each misspelled word. Remind students they can use print or electronic resources to check and correct spelling.

1. The artist tawght painting and drauing. (taught, drawing)

2. The chef pawsed and added more sault to the pot. (paused, salt)

3. He cralled through a small door and onto the laun. (crawled, lawn)

4. The hawls are filled with students in awtumn. (halls, autumn)

5. A large branch fell with a crack, which cawsed a nearby bird to squak. (caused, squawk)

Error Correction Remind students that the *ou* spelling does not always spell /ô/, such as in *found, amount, tough,* and *enough.*

BLIND SORT

Have partners do a **blind sort**: one reads a spelling word card; the other tells under which key word it belongs. Have them take turns until both have sorted all their words. Then have students explain how they sorted the words.

DAY 5

Assess

Use the Dictation Sentences for the Posttest. Have students list misspelled words in their word study notebooks. Look for students' use of these words in their writings.

Dictation Sentences

1. Who <u>taught</u> you how to cook?
2. The man <u>hauls</u> heavy boxes.
3. The heavy rain <u>caused</u> a flood.
4. We <u>paused</u> for five minutes.
5. The birds each made a loud <u>squawk</u>.
6. The <u>drawing</u> was made with crayons.
7. The baby can <u>crawl</u> now.
8. The shiny new bike was <u>flawless</u>.
9. Who will mow the <u>lawn</u>?
10. The soup needs <u>salt</u> and pepper.
11. Everyone <u>talked</u> about the movie.
12. The <u>halls</u> at school are long.
13. Danica drank the <u>water</u> with ice.
14. I <u>bought</u> a new book.
15. Teddy apologized for his <u>thoughtless</u> actions.

Have students self-correct the tests.

→ Build Vocabulary

DAY 1

OBJECTIVES

CCSS Use sentence-level context as a clue to the meaning of a word or phrase. **L.3.4a**

CCSS Determine the meaning of the new word formed when a known affix is added to a known word (e.g., *agreeable/ disagreeable, comfortable/ uncomfortable, care/careless, heat/ preheat*). **L.3.4b**

Expand vocabulary by adding inflectional endings, prefixes, and suffixes.

Connect to Words

Practice this week's vocabulary.

1. How does an alarm **alert** you to a possible danger?
2. Describe a **competition**.
3. What animals live in a desert **environment**?
4. Describe an **excellent** book.
5. Do you **prefer** action movies or comedies?
6. Where do animals go for **protection** during the winter?
7. What animals are **related** to mice?
8. What **shelter** is in a forest?

DAY 2

Expand Vocabulary

Help students generate different forms of this week's words by adding, changing, or removing inflectional endings.

- Draw a four-column chart. Write *prefer* in the left column. Then write *prefers, preferred,* and *preference* in the other columns. Read aloud the words and discuss the meaning of each one.

- Have students share sentences with each form of *prefer*.

- Students can fill in the chart for other words, such as *alert*.

- Have students copy the chart in their word study notebook.

Vocabulary Words

alert	prefer
competition	protection
environment	related
excellent	shelter

ELL

Have partners practice using other academic vocabulary terms from the week, such as *contrast* and *shelter* precisely while speaking and writing. They should discuss any synonyms or antonyms they know for these words and shades of meaning differences.

BUILD MORE VOCABULARY

COLLABORATE

ACADEMIC VOCABULARY

Discuss important academic words.

- Display the terms *environment* and *adapt*.

- Define each word and discuss the meanings with students.

- Display *environment* and *environmental*. Have partners look up and define related words.

- Write the related words on the board. Have partners ask and answer questions using the words. Repeat with *adapt*. Elicit examples from students.

PREFIXES *UN-, NON-, IM-, PRE-*   *Review*

- Remind students that adding a prefix to a base word changes its meaning. Write examples such as *undo, nonsense, improper,* and *preview*. Have students circle the prefixes and discuss the meanings. Ask: *How does adding this prefix change the meaning of the word?*

- Have partners identify other words with these prefixes. Invite partners to share their words. Have students use the prefixes and base words to discuss the meanings of the words.

DAY 3

Reinforce the Words

Review this week's vocabulary words. Have students orally complete each sentence stem.

1. Are dogs and _____ related?

2. It is important to alert a teacher if _____.

3. Have you ever seen a _____ competition?

4. Do you prefer ice cream or _____?

5. There is an excellent _____ at the theater right now.

6. Smaller animals need to find protection from _____animals.

DAY 4

Connect to Writing

- Have students write sentences in their word study notebooks using this week's vocabulary.

- Tell them to write sentences that provide information about the words and their meanings.

- Provide the Day 3 sentence stems for students needing extra support.

Write About Vocabulary Have students write something they learned from this week's words in their word study notebook. For example, they might write about an *environment* they find interesting. What kinds of plants, animals, and *shelter* does it have?

DAY 5

Word Squares

Ask students to create Word Squares for each vocabulary word.

- In the first square, students write the word. (example: *shelter*)

- In the second square, students write their own definition of the word and any related words. (example: *home*)

- In the third square, students draw a simple illustration that will help them remember the word. (example: a bird in a nest)

- In the fourth square, students write non-examples. (example: *open space*)

- Have students share their Word Squares with a partner.

SENTENCE CLUES

Remind students to look for definitions or restatements of an unfamiliar word within a sentence.

- Display **Your Turn Practice Book** pages 173–174. Read the first two paragraphs. Model figuring out the meanings of *adaptations* and *reproduce*.

- For additional practice with sentence clues, have students complete page 177.

- Discuss the sentence clues that students identified.

SHADES OF MEANING

Help students generate words related to *protection*. Draw a web.

- Begin a discussion about the word *protection*. Elicit synonyms such as *safety* and *security* and add them to the web. Ask: *When do people and animals need protection? Where can they find it?* Write examples on the board.

- Have partners work together to add other words to the web. They may confirm meanings in a print or online dictionary.

- Ask students to copy the words in their word study notebook.

MORPHOLOGY

Use the word *competition* as a springboard for students to learn more words. Draw a T-chart.

- Write *compete* in the first column. Discuss the meaning.

- In the second column, write the suffix *-tion*. Discuss the meaning and model how to use the suffix and the base word to determine the meaning of *competition*.

- Have partners generate other words with the suffix *-tion,* such as *action* and *deletion*.

- Tell students to use the suffix and base words to determine the meanings of the words.

→Integrate Ideas

Close Reading Routine

Read   DOK 1–2

- Identify key ideas and details about Adaptations.
- Take notes and summarize.
- Use prompts as needed.

Reread   DOK 2–3

- Analyze the text, craft, and structure.
- Use the **Close Reading Companion.**

Integrate   DOK 4

- Integrate knowledge and ideas.
- Make text-to-text connections.
- Use the Integrate lesson.
- Use *Close Reading Companion,* p. 120.

TEXT CONNECTIONS

Connect to the Essential Question

Write the essential question on the board: How do animals adapt to challenges in their habitat? Divide the class into small groups. Tell students that each group will compare the information that they have learned about how animals adapt to challenges in their environment. Model how to compare this information by using examples from this week's **Leveled Readers** and "Gray Wolf! Red Fox!," **Reading/Writing Workshop** pages 290–293.

Evaluate Text Evidence Have students review their class notes and completed graphic organizers before they begin their discussions. Encourage students to compare information from all the week's reads. Have each group pick one student to take notes. Explain that each group will use a Three-Tab Foldable® to record their ideas. You may wish to model how to use a Three-Tab Foldable® to record comparisons.

Dinah Zike's
FOLDABLES
Study Organizer

INQUIRY SPACE

| LEVEL | | 1 | 2 | **3** | 4 | 5 | 6 |

Take Notes

PREVIEW LEVEL 3 Display Level 3 of the Narrative Performance Task. Tell students that in this level they will take notes from the sources they have chosen. Explain to them that taking notes as they research will help them remember what they learn about frogs. Have students review the questions that they wrote in the "What I Want to Find Out" section of their research plans. These questions will provide their purpose for reading. Tell students that they will use information from their research in their stories. Research will help them describe the setting and characters. It will also give them ideas for a story about a day in the life of a frog.

❶ Paraphrasing Help students understand the importance of paraphrasing. Say: *Paraphrasing means to retell something in your own words.* Explain that paraphrasing will help them understand what they read. Share the **Paraphrase** animation from the **Toolkit** with students.

NARRATIVE PERFORMANCE TASK

Write About: Frogs

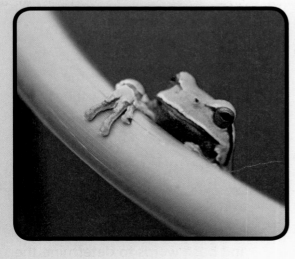

Gudella/Getty Images

Text to Media

CCSS **OBJECTIVE**
Compare and contrast the most important points and key details presented in two texts on the same topic. **RI.3.9**

Post Online Remind students to discuss their responses to the Blast along with information from all the week's reads. Tell students to include the photograph of the sea cucumber crab on page 120 of the **Close Reading Companion** as a part of their discussion. Guide students to see the connections among media, the photograph, and text. Ask: *How does the Blast connect to what you read this week? To the photograph?*

Present Ideas and Synthesize Information

When students finish their discussions, ask for a volunteer from each group to read his or her notes aloud.

OBJECTIVE
Recall information from experiences or gather information from print and digital sources; take brief notes on sources and sort evidence into provided categories. **W.3.8**

❷ **Taking Notes** Tell students to remember these tips when they take notes:

- Write down the big ideas.

- Sort the information into categories that relate to the topic, such as information on what frogs look like, what frogs eat, where they live, and possible dangers to the survival of frogs.

- Write in short phrases, not complete sentences.

- Write down the source and the page number or URL where you found the information.

Show students the **Take Notes (Print Sources)** animation from the Toolkit.

ASSIGN LEVEL 3 Have students begin Level 3. Remind them to record their source information. You may wish to have students watch the Paraphrase and Take Notes (Print Sources) animations again.

→ Approaching Level

Lexile 550
TextEvaluator™ 12

OBJECTIVES

Describe the logical connection between particular sentences and paragraphs in a text (e.g. comparison, cause/effect, sequence). **RI.3.8**

• Compare and contrast two things in an expository text.

• Reread to increase understanding of a text.

• Use definitions and restatements as context clues to determine the meanings of words.

ACADEMIC LANGUAGE

reread, compare, contrast, expository, context clues, folktale

Leveled Reader:
Life in a Tide Pool

Before Reading

Preview and Predict

Have students review the Essential Question. Then have students read the title and table of contents of *Life in a Tide Pool* and then make two predictions about what life is like in a tide pool. Have partners share their predictions.

Review Genre: Expository

Review with students that expository text explains about a topic. It includes text features like photographs, captions, labels, and diagrams. As they preview *Life in a Tide Pool*, have students identify features of expository text.

During Reading

Close Reading

Note Taking Have students use their graphic organizer as they read.

Page 2 Have students point to the photo. Read the caption. *What sentences in the main text connect to the caption text?* (the first two sentences in paragraph 2)

Page 3 *We read that a tide pool is a habitat for many plants and animals. What is a* habitat*? Look for a definition and a restatement of the word in the text.* ("where a plant or animal lives;" "a plant or animal's environment")

Pages 4–5 *Look at the diagram on page 5. What animals live in the splash zone?* (limpets, periwinkles) *What is another zone where limpets can also live?* (high tide zone)

Page 6 *How do the labels and the photo help you better understand the main text?* (I can better understand what the sea anemones look like depending on whether the tide pool is full of water or not.)

Pages 7–8 *Reread page 8, then turn to a partner and summarize a sea hare's adaptations that help it survive.* (A sea hare can shrink its body to hide between rocks and protect itself. Its colors help it blend in, and if a predator comes close, it can shoot out purple ink.)

Go Digital

Leveled Readers

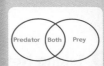

Fill in the Graphic Organizer

Pages 9–11 *On page 9, what word signals that sea urchins and sea stars are being compared?* (same) *How are sea urchins and sea stars the same?* (They both have many sticky tube feet.) *How are they different?* (Sea urchins only eat plants. Sea stars eat other animals.)

Pages 12–14 *How does a sea star catch prey?* (It has suction cups to move on rocks and sticky feet to open shells.) *What should you do if you go visit a tide pool?* (be careful; leave it as you found it)

After Reading

Respond to Reading Revisit the Essential Question, and ask students to complete the Text Evidence questions on page 15.

Analytical Writing **Write About Reading** Have students work with a partner to write a paragraph comparing and contrasting the octopus on page 13 with another animal in the text using text evidence.

Fluency: Accuracy and Phrasing

Model Model reading page 2 with accuracy and proper phrasing. Next, reread the page aloud, and have students read along with you.

Apply Have students practice reading with a partner.

PAIRED READ

"Bluebird and Coyote"

Make Connections:
Write About It *Analytical Writing*

Before reading, have students note that the genre of this text is a folktale, which is a fictional tale that sometimes explains something about science. Then discuss the Essential Question.

After reading, have students write about connections between how animals adapt to challenges in their environment in *Life in a Tide Pool* and "Bluebird and Coyote."

Leveled Reader

Literature Circles

Ask students to conduct a literature circle using the Thinkmark questions to guide the discussion. You may wish to have a whole-class discussion on how animals in their community have adapted to challenges in their habitats.

Level Up

Level-up lessons available online.

IF students read the `Approaching Level` fluently and answered the questions

THEN pair them with students who have proficiently read `On Level` and have approaching level students

• echo-read the `On Level` main selection with their partner.

• use self-stick notes to mark a new detail to discuss in each section.

A C T Access Complex Text

The `On Level` challenges students by including more **domain-specific words** and **complex sentence structures**.

FOCUS ON SCIENCE

Students can extend their knowledge of how to compare and contrast tide pool animals by completing the science activity on page 20. **STEM**

Approaching Level

Phonics/Decoding

DECODE WORDS WITH VARIANT VOWEL /ô/

TIER 2

OBJECTIVES

 Know spelling-sound correspondences for additional common vowel teams. **RF.2.3b**

Decode words with variant-vowel /ô/ spellings.

 I Do Display the **Sound-Spelling Card** for the word *straw*. Point out that the vowel sound in *straw* can be spelled several different ways. In this word, it is spelled *aw*. Review the variant-vowel spelling and sound with *caw, law,* and *gnaw*.

 We Do Write *raw, lawn, fawn, small,* and *flaw* on the board. Model how to decode each word. Underline the letters making the /ô/ sound in each word and model blending. Then run your finger under each word as you sound it out. Have students sound out the words with you.

 You Do Add these words to the board: *jaw, draw,* and *dawn*. Have students read each word aloud and identify its vowel sound. Then point to the words in random order for students to read chorally. Repeat several times.

BUILD WORDS WITH VARIANT VOWEL /ô/

TIER 2

OBJECTIVES

 Know and apply grade-level phonics and word analysis skills in decoding words. Decode multisyllable words. **RF.3.3c**

Build words with variant-vowel /ô/ spellings.

 I Do Tell students that they will be building multisyllable words using variant-vowel /ô/ spellings. Remind students that this vowel sound can be spelled *au, aw, al, all,* and *ough*. Next, display these **Word-Building Cards** one at a time: *au, al, in,* and *ful*. Then write these syllables on the board: *thor, aw, most, stall,* and *thought*. Model sounding out each syllable.

 We Do Have students chorally read each syllable. Repeat at varying speeds and in random order. Next, display all the cards and syllables. Work with students to combine the Word-Building Cards and syllables to form multisyllable words with variant-vowel /ô/ spellings. Have students chorally read the words: *author, awful, almost, install,* and *thoughtful*.

 You Do Write other syllables on the board, such as *laun, awe, wal, fall, cough, dry, some, nut,* and *ing*. Have students work with partners to build words using these syllables. Then have partners share the words they built and make a class list.

PRACTICE VARIANT VOWEL /ô/

OBJECTIVES

CCSS Know spelling-sound correspondences for additional common vowel teams. **RF.2.3b**

Decode words with variant-vowel /ô/ spellings.

 I Do Remind students that the vowel sound in *dawn* is made by the letters *aw*. The variant vowel /ô/ can also be made by the letter combinations *au, al, all, ough*. On the board, write *launch, false, mall, sought*. Read the words aloud. Now write *wasp* and explain that, when a *w* comes before *a*, the vowel can also be pronounced /ô/. Read the word aloud.

 We Do Write the words *faucet, awkward, alright, hallway, prebought,* and *waterfall* on the board. Model how to decode the first word, then guide students as they decode the remaining words. Remind students that different spellings can be used to make the same vowel sounds.

 You Do Point to the words in random order for students to chorally read.

GREEK AND LATIN ROOTS

OBJECTIVES

CCSS Use common, grade-appropriate Greek and Latin affixes and roots as clues to the meaning of a word (e.g., *telegraph, photograph, autograph*). **L.4.4b**

Decode words with Greek and Latin roots.

 I Do Review that many English words come from either the Greek or Latin language. The root word, or word part, *aud* comes from a Latin word that means "to hear." The word *audience* means "a group of listeners." The root word *graph* comes from a Greek word that means "written." The word *autograph* means "self-written." The root word *tele* comes from a Greek word that means "far off." The word *telescope* means "to see far off."

 We Do Write the words *audible, geography,* and *telecommute* on the board. Say each word and have students repeat. Underline the Greek or Latin root in each word. Help students figure out the meaning of each word based on its root word. Read the list out loud again and have students echo read.

 You Do On the board, write *audiobook, graphite,* and *televised*. Have students determine the meaning of each word using its Greek or Latin root. Then point to the words in random order for students to chorally read.

ELL ENGLISH LANGUAGE LEARNERS

For the students who need **phonics**, **decoding**, and **fluency** practice, use scaffolding methods as necessary to ensure students understand the meaning of the words. Refer to the **Language Transfers Handbook** for phonics elements that may not transfer in students' native languages.

Approaching Level

Vocabulary

REVIEW HIGH-FREQUENCY WORDS

 TIER 2

OBJECTIVES

 Use conventional spelling for high-frequency and other studied words and for adding suffixes to base words (e.g., *sitting, smiled, cries, happiness*). **L.3.2e**

Review high-frequency words.

 I Do Use **Word Cards** 141–150. Display one word at a time, following the routine:

Display the word. Read the word. Then spell the word.

 We Do Have students state the word and spell the word with you. Model using the word in a sentence, and have students repeat after you.

 You Do Display the word. Have students say the word then spell it. When completed, quickly flip through the word card set as students chorally read the words. Provide opportunities for students to use the words in speaking and writing. For example, provide sentence starters such as *I can help by holding the door _____*. Have students write each word in their **Writer's Notebook**.

REVIEW VOCABULARY WORDS

TIER 2

OBJECTIVES

 Acquire and use accurately grade-appropriate conversational, general academic, and domain-specific words and phrases, including those that signal spatial and temporal relationships. **L.3.6**

Review vocabulary words.

 I Do Display each **Visual Vocabulary Card** and state the word. Explain how the photograph illustrates the word. State the example sentence, and repeat the word.

 We Do Point to the word on the Visual Vocabulary Card, and read the word with students. Have them repeat the word. Engage students in structured partner talk about the image as prompted on the back of the Visual Vocabulary Card.

 You Do Display each visual in random order, hiding the word. Have students match the definitions and context sentences of the words to the visuals displayed. Then have students complete **Approaching Reproducibles** page 171.

IDENTIFY RELATED WORDS

OBJECTIVES

CCSS Demonstrate understanding of word relationships and nuances in word meanings. Identify real-life connections between words and their use (e.g., describe people who are *friendly* or *helpful*). **L.3.5b**

Identify words that are related in meanings.

 I Do Display the *shelter* **Visual Vocabulary Card** and say aloud the word set *shelter, dwelling, wilderness*. Point out that the word *dwelling* means almost the same thing as *shelter*.

 We Do Display the vocabulary card for the word *alert*. Say aloud the word set *alert, ignore, notify*. With students, identify the word that means close to the same thing as the vocabulary word *alert,* and discuss why.

 You Do Using the word sets below, display the remaining cards one at a time, saying aloud each word set. Ask students to identify the word in each set that has the closest meaning to each vocabulary word.

competition, contest, cooperation   *environment, surroundings, story*

excellent, substandard, first-rate   *prefer, favor, dislike*

protection, security, danger   *related, different, kindred*

CONTEXT CLUES

OBJECTIVES

CCSS Use sentence level context as a clue to the meaning of a word or phrase. **L.3.4a**

Use definitions and restatements as clues to the meanings of unknown words.

 I Do Display the Comprehension and Fluency passage on **Approaching Reproducibles** pages 173–174. Read aloud the first paragraph. Point to the sentence *Every animal has adaptations*. Explain to students that they can look for sentence or context clues to find the meaning of the word *adaptations*.

Think Aloud I do not know what *adaptations* means. I can see whether a definition or further information about the word has been given. The next sentence says *These are special ways that its body works or is made*. So *adaptations* refers to the special ways a body works or is made.

Write the meaning of the word *adaptations*.

 We Do Ask students to point to the sentence *They can stand on their hind, or back legs*. With students, discuss how to determine the meaning of *hind* using the definition within the sentence. Write the meaning of the word.

 You Do Have students use sentence and context clues to find the meanings of the words *effective, retract,* and *environment* in the rest of the passage.

Approaching Level

Comprehension

FLUENCY

 TIER 2

OBJECTIVES

 Read on-level prose and poetry orally with accuracy, appropriate rate, and expression on successive readings. **RF.3.4b**

Read fluently with appropriate intonation.

 I Do Explain that intonation means changing the tone of your voice to stress important words or sentences to express meaning. Point out that readers use punctuation clues such as exclamation points to help them use proper intonation. Read paragraph 3 of the Comprehension and Fluency passage on **Approaching Reproducibles** pages 173–174. Point out how the tone of your voice changed as you read the exclamatory sentence.

 We Do Read the rest of the page aloud, and have students repeat each sentence after you using the same intonation. Explain that you stressed certain words and phrases to express meaning.

 You Do Have partners take turns reading sentences from the Reproducibles passage. Remind them to focus on their intonation. Listen in and provide corrective feedback as needed by modeling proper fluency.

TEXT STRUCTURE

TIER 2

OBJECTIVES

Describe the logical connection between particular sentences and paragraphs in a text (e.g., comparison, cause/effect, first/second/third in a sequence). **RI.3.8**

Examine similarities and differences.

 I Do Write the topic *Bears* on the board. Underneath, write *Grizzly Bears* and *Polar Bears*. Explain that the text is structured to give first the similarities and then the differences between these two types of bears. Write two columns on the board labeled *Similarities* and *Differences*. Tell students that they will help find information to put in these columns as they read.

 We Do Read the first page of the Comprehension and Fluency passage in the **Approaching Reproducibles**. Ask: *What are similarities?* Point out that the first page is structured to compare the grizzly and polar bears, showing how they are similar, or alike. Ask, *How are these bears alike?* Note similarities in the appropriate column. Discuss why the author would choose to first write about the ways the bears are alike.

 You Do Have students read the rest of the passage. After they finish, they should work to fill in the *Differences* column on the board. Review the similarities and differences between grizzly bears and polar bears with students.

REVIEW TEXT STRUCTURE: COMPARE AND CONTRAST

OBJECTIVES

CCSS Describe the logical connection between particular sentences and paragraphs in a text (e.g., comparison, cause/effect, first/second/third in a sequence). **RI.3.8**

Compare and contrast two things in expository text.

 I Do Remind students that an author might structure a text by comparing and contrasting two things, or showing how those two things are alike and different. Students can look for signal words like *both, alike, same,* or *different* to help them find how the things are alike and different.

 We Do Read the first page of the Comprehension and Fluency passage in **Approaching Reproducibles** together. Pause to point out similarities that may be comparisons in the text. Model how to decide which two things are being compared and how. Then, work with students to determine what those comparisons are by referring to the text.

 You Do Have students work in small groups to come up with a list of comparisons and contrasts in the Reproducibles passage. Make sure they are comparing or contrasting the bears using evidence from the text.

SELF-SELECTED READING

OBJECTIVES

CCSS Describe the logical connection between particular sentences and paragraphs in a text (e.g., comparison, cause/effect, first/second/third in a sequence). **RI.3.8**

• Compare and contrast two things in expository text.
• Reread to increase comprehension.

Read Independently

Have students choose an expository text that compares and contrasts things for sustained silent reading. Remind students that:

• they should look for signal words like *both, alike, same,* or *different* to help them find similarities and differences.

• if they have trouble understanding something, they can reread a paragraph or section.

Read Purposefully

Have students record the similarities and differences in the text on **Graphic Organizer 66** as they read independently. After they finish, they can conduct a Book Talk, each telling about the book they read.

• Students should share their organizers and answer this question: *What was one comparison and one contrast you read about?*

• They should also tell the group if there were any sections they reread to increase their understanding.

On Level

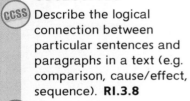

Lexile 730
TextEvaluator™ 20

OBJECTIVES

(CCSS) Describe the logical connection between particular sentences and paragraphs in a text (e.g. comparison, cause/effect, sequence). **RI.3.8**

(CCSS) Use information gained from illustrations (e.g., maps, photographs) and the words in a text to demonstrate understanding of the text (e.g., where, when, why, and how key events occur). **RI.3.7**

- Compare and contrast two things in an expository text.
- Reread to increase understanding of a text.
- Use context clues to determine the meanings of words.

ACADEMIC LANGUAGE

reread, compare, contrast, expository, context clues, folktale

Leveled Reader:
Life in a Tide Pool

Go Digital

Before Reading

Preview and Predict

Have students read the Essential Question. Have them preview the text by reading the title and table of contents of *Life in a Tide Pool* and then make two predictions about what kind of animals and plants live in a tide pool. Have partners share their predictions.

Leveled Readers

Review Genre: Expository

Review with students that expository text explains about a topic. It includes text features like photographs, captions, labels, and diagrams. As they preview *Life in a Tide Pool*, have students identify features of expository text.

During Reading

Close Reading

Note Taking Have students use their graphic organizer as they read.

Pages 2–3 *Why are animals' lives in tide pools always changing?* (The water in tide pools goes in and out.) *Point to the word* habitat *on page 3. Use context clues to find the meaning of* habitat. ("A habitat is a place where a plant or an animal lives.") *Does this sentence define or restate the word?* (It defines it.) *What is a restatement of the word?* (*environment*)

Pages 4–5 *Turn to a partner and find some animals that live in multiple tidal zones by looking at the Intertidal Zone Map on page 5.* (mussels, barnacles, snails, limpets) *How does the map help you find this information more easily?* (the illustrations and labels)

Pages 6–8 *Summarize how a sea anemone adapts to challenges in its environment.* (When the sea anemone is covered in water, it can use its tentacles to catch fish; when the water recedes, the anemone retracts its tentacles so they will not dry out in the sun; a sucker disk keeps the sea anemone attached to a rock so it will not be washed away.)

Reread page 8, and then turn to a partner to explain something that you were able to better understand by rereading.

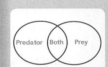

Fill in the Graphic Organizer

Pages 9–11 *Compare and contrast sea urchins and sea stars. List one way they are different and one way they are similar.* (Sea urchins and sea stars are similar because they both have hundreds of sticky feet. They are different because sea urchins only eat plants.) *What words signal that the author was comparing and contrasting?* (same, like, unlike)

Pages 12–14 *How can people help animals survive in a tide pool?* (People can be careful not to harm animals in tide pools and to leave them as they found them.)

After Reading

Respond to Reading Revisit the Essential Question, and ask students to complete the Text Evidence questions on page 15.

Analytical Writing **Write About Reading** Have students work with a partner to write a short paragraph comparing the octopus on page 13 with another animal in the text using evidence from the text.

Fluency: Accuracy and Phrasing

Model Model reading page 2 with accuracy and proper phrasing. Next, reread the page aloud, and have students read along with you.

Apply Have students practice reading with a partner.

PAIRED READ

"Bluebird and Coyote"

Make Connections: Write About It *Analytical Writing*

Leveled Reader

Before reading, have students note that the genre of this text is a folktale, which is a fictional tale that sometimes explains something about science. Then discuss the Essential Question.

After reading, have students write about connections between how animals adapt to challenges in their environment in *Life in a Tide Pool* and "Bluebird and Coyote."

FOCUS ON SCIENCE

Students can extend their knowledge of how to compare and contrast tide pool animals by completing the science activity on page 20. **STEM**

Literature Circles

Ask students to conduct a literature circle using the Thinkmark questions to guide the discussion. You may wish to have a whole-class discussion on how animals in their community have adapted to challenges in their habitat.

Level Up

Level-up lessons available online.

IF students read the On Level fluently and answered the questions

THEN pair them with students who have proficiently read Beyond Level and have on-level students

• partner-read the Beyond Level main selection.

• list difficult vocabulary words and look them up with a partner.

A C T Access Complex Text

The Beyond Level challenges students by including more **domain-specific words** and **complex sentence structures**.

On Level

Vocabulary

REVIEW VOCABULARY WORDS

 OBJECTIVES

Acquire and use accurately grade-appropriate conversational, general academic, and domain-specific words and phrases, including those that signal spatial and temporal relationships (e.g., *After dinner that night we went looking for them*). **L.3.6**

Review vocabulary words.

 I Do Use the **Visual Vocabulary Cards** to review key vocabulary words *related, protection, excellent, alert, prefer,* and *competition*. Point to each word, read it aloud, and have students chorally repeat it.

 We Do Ask these questions and help students respond and explain their answers.

- Who are two people to whom you are *related*?
- What is one item you could use for *protection* from cold weather?
- What makes your favorite book or movie *excellent*?

 You Do Have students respond to these questions and explain their answers.

- How might a dog *alert* you if someone has knocked on a door?
- How do you *prefer* to travel, by skateboard or bicycle? Why?
- What is a *competition* you have watched or participated in?

CONTEXT CLUES

 OBJECTIVES

Use sentence level context as a clue to the meaning of a word or phrase. **L.3.4a**

Use definitions and restatements as clues to the meanings of unknown words.

 I Do Remind students that they can use sentence and context clues to help them determine the meaning of unknown words. They can look for definitions or restatements of words. Use the Comprehension and Fluency passage on **Your Turn Practice Book** pages 173–174 to model.

Think Aloud I want to know what the word *adaptations* means. I can look for more information about adaptations in the surrounding sentences. The next sentence says that *these are ways that its body works or is made*. It is referring to the word *adaptations*, so *adaptations* are the ways an animal's body works or is made.

 We Do Have students reread paragraph 1 to encounter the word *effective*. Have them figure out the meaning of the word using sentence or context clues.

 You Do Have students work in pairs to determine the meanings of *retract, blubber, environment,* and *omnivorous* as they read the rest of the selection.

Comprehension

REVIEW TEXT STRUCTURE: COMPARE AND CONTRAST

OBJECTIVES

Describe the logical connection between particular sentences and paragraphs in a text (e.g., comparison, cause/effect, first/second/third in a sequence). **RI.3.8**

Compare and contrast two things in expository text.

 Remind students that they can compare and contrast two things in an expository text to understand how they are alike and different. Point out that to compare, students should look for ways two things are alike. To contrast, students should figure out ways they are different. Signal words such as *both*, *alike*, *same*, or *different* can help them compare and contrast.

 Have a volunteer read paragraph 3 sentences 1–6 of the Comprehension and Fluency passage on **Your Turn Practice Book** pages 173–174. Have students list details that show how two types of bears are different and alike. Then model how to compare and contrast the bears. With students, find how the bears are compared and contrasted on the rest of the page.

You Do Have partners read the rest of the passage and write a list of ways in which the two types of bears are alike and different. Remind students to use text evidence when they compile their lists.

SELF-SELECTED READING

OBJECTIVES

Describe the logical connection between particular sentences and paragraphs in a text (e.g., comparison, cause/effect, first/second/third in a sequence). **RI.3.8**

• Compare and contrast two things in expository text.

• Reread text to increase understanding.

Read Independently

Have students choose a book of expository text comparing and contrasting two or more things for sustained silent reading.

• Before they read, have students preview the book, reading the title and looking for any text features that tell more about the book.

• As students read, ask them to stop and think about any information in the text that is unclear. Tell them to reread sections of the text to confirm that all of the information makes sense.

Read Purposefully

Encourage students to read different books in order to learn about a variety of subjects.

• As students read, they can fill in **Graphic Organizer 66**.

• Students can refer back to their graphic organizers to write a summary of the book.

• Ask students to share their reactions to the book with classmates. Have them tell about any sections of the text they reread and how it helped increase their understanding.

Beyond Level

Lexile 860
TextEvaluator™ 22

OBJECTIVES

CCSS Describe the logical connection between particular sentences and paragraphs in a text (e.g. comparison, cause/effect, sequence). **RI.3.8**

CCSS Use information gained from illustrations (e.g., maps, photographs) and the words in a text to demonstrate understanding of the text (e.g., where, when, why, and how key events occur). **RI.3.7**

- Compare and contrast two things in an expository text.
- Reread to increase understanding of a text.
- Use context clues to determine the meanings of words.

ACADEMIC LANGUAGE
reread, compare, contrast, expository, context clues, folktale

Leveled Reader:
Life in a Tide Pool

Leveled Readers

Before Reading

Preview and Predict

Have students review the Essential Question. Then have students read the title and table of contents of *Life in a Tide Pool* and make two predictions about what life is like in a tide pool. Have partners share their predictions.

Review Genre: Expository

Review with students that expository text explains about a topic. It includes text features like headings, photographs, captions, sidebars, labels, and diagrams. As they preview *Life in a Tide Pool*, have students identify features of expository text.

During Reading

Close Reading

Note Taking Have students use their graphic organizer as they read.

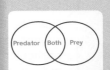
Fill in the Graphic Organizer

Pages 2–5 *For what word in the second paragraph on page 3 are we given context clues to understand its meaning?* (habitat) *Is habitat defined or restated?* (defined) *Use the context clue to define the word to a partner.* (*Habitat* means "the type of environment in which plants or animals naturally live.") *What type of habitat are tide pools?* (coastal)

What text feature gives us more information about high tide and low tide? (the sidebar on page 4) *What is the difference between high and low tide?* (High tide is when a rising tide reaches its maximum height. Low tide is the lowest level of a tide.) *How does the Intertidal Zone Map on page 5 help you understand the main text?* (It shows pictures and labels of what animals can survive in the different tidal zones, which helps me better understand the text.) *Using the map, what can you say about what zone limpets live in?* (They live in the mid, high tide, and splash zones.) *What other animals live in more than one zone?* (barnacles, mussels, snails)

Pages 6–8 *Turn to a partner and summarize a sea hare's adaptations that help it survive.* (A sea hare's color allows it to blend into its surroundings. If a predator comes too close, it can shoot out purple ink to blind it.)

Pages 9–11 *Compare and contrast sea urchins and sea stars. Tell what words signal that they are being compared or contrasted.* (Sea urchins and sea stars both have hundreds of sticky tube feet. Unlike sea stars, urchins eat only plants. Signal words to compare and contrast are: *same, like* and *unlike.*)

Pages 12–14 *Reread page 14, and then explain what message the author wants us to remember.* (It is important to leave tide pools as you found them.)

After Reading

Respond to Reading Revisit the Essential Question. Have student pairs summarize and answer the Text Evidence questions.

Analytical Writing **Write About Reading** Have students work with a partner to write a short paragraph comparing the octopus on page 13 with another animal in the text using text evidence.

Fluency: Accuracy and Phrasing

Model Model reading page 2 with accuracy and proper phrasing. Next, reread the page aloud, and have students read along with you.

Apply Have students practice reading with a partner.

PAIRED READ

"Bluebird and Coyote"

Make Connections:
Write About It · *Analytical Writing*

Leveled Reader

Before reading, have students note that the genre of this text is a folktale, which is a fictional tale that explains something about science. Then discuss the Essential Question.

After reading, have students write about connections between how animals adapt to challenges in their environment in *Life in a Tide Pool* and "Bluebird and Coyote."

FOCUS ON SCIENCE

Students can extend their knowledge of how to compare and contrast tide pool animals by completing the science activity on page 20. **STEM**

Literature Circles

Ask students to conduct a literature circle using the Thinkmark questions to guide the discussion. You may wish to have a whole-class discussion on how animals in their community have adapted to challenges in their habitats.

Gifted and Talented

Synthesize Challenge students to discover more about one of the animals in the text. Students can do additional research about the animal in which they are interested. Have them write a profile of the animal that includes its life cycle, habitat, eating habits, and adaptations. Have volunteers share their profiles with the class.

Beyond Level

Vocabulary

REVIEW DOMAIN-SPECIFIC WORDS

OBJECTIVES

 Produce simple, compound, and complex sentences. **L.3.1i**

Review and discuss domain-specific vocabulary words.

 Model Use the **Visual Vocabulary Cards** to review the meaning of the words *protection* and *alert*. Write science-related sentences on the board using the words.

Write *predator* and *conceal* on the board, and discuss the meanings with students. Then help students write sentences using these words.

 Apply Have students work in pairs to discuss the meanings of the words *habitat, survive,* and *prey*. Then have them write sentences using the words. Challenge students to write sentences that use two of the words in each sentence.

CONTEXT CLUES

OBJECTIVES

 Use sentence level context as a clue to the meaning of a word or phrase. **L.3.4a**

Use definitions and restatements as clues to the meanings of unknown words.

Model Read aloud the first paragraph of the Comprehension and Fluency passage on **Beyond Reproducibles** pages 173–174.

Think Aloud I see more information about the word *adaptations* in the sentence following the one in which the word appears. It says that they are ways that an animal's body is *specially made. Adaptations* must refer to the various skills and body shapes animal have.

Help students figure out the meaning of *effective* using sentence clues.

 Apply Have pairs of students read the rest of the passage. Have them find sentence or context clues to determine the meanings of the words *retract, blubber, environment,* and *omnivorous*.

 Compare and Contrast Have students think of two animals to research. They should use classroom resources to write a report that compares and contrasts the animals. Encourage them to use this week's vocabulary words and language signaling how the animals are alike and different, and include artwork. Have them present their reports to the class.

Comprehension

REVIEW TEXT STRUCTURE: COMPARE AND CONTRAST

OBJECTIVES

 Describe the logical connection between particular sentences and paragraphs in a text (e.g., comparison, cause/effect, first/second/third in a sequence). **RI.3.8**

Compare and contrast two things in expository text.

 Model Remind students that they can compare and contrast two things in an expository text to understand how they are alike and different. Explain that when they compare two things, they look for ways they are alike. When they contrast two things, they try to figure out how they are different. Point out that students can look for signal words such as *alike, both, same* or *different* to help them compare and contrast.

Have students read the first paragraph of the Comprehension and Fluency passage of **Beyond Reproducibles** pages 173–174. Ask open-ended questions to facilitate discussion, such as *Which details show how the two types of bears are alike? Which details show how the two types of bears are different?* Students should provide text evidence to support their answers.

Apply Have students identify other comparing and contrasting details as they read the rest of the text. Remind students to use evidence from the text.

SELF-SELECTED READING

OBJECTIVES

 Describe the logical connection between particular sentences and paragraphs in a text (e.g., comparison, cause/effect, first/second/third in a sequence). **RI.3.8**

• Compare and contrast two things in expository text.
• Reread to increase understanding.

Read Independently

Have students choose an expository text comparing and contrasting two or more things for sustained silent reading.

- As students read, have them fill in **Graphic Organizer 66**.
- Remind them them to reread difficult sections of the text.

Read Purposefully

Encourage students to keep a reading journal. Ask them to read different types of expository texts to learn about a variety of subjects.

- Students can write summaries of the texts in their journals.
- Have students give their reactions to the texts to their classmates. Have them tell how the things they read about were compared and contrasted.

 Independent Study Challenge students to discuss how what they have been reading relates to the weekly theme of adaptations. Have students compare some of the different adaptations animals have to survive. How do animals adapt to challenges in their habitat?

→ English Language Learners

Reading/Writing Workshop

OBJECTIVES

 Describe the logical connection between particular sentences and paragraphs in a text (e.g. comparison, cause/effect, sequence). **RI.3.8**

• Reread text to check for understanding.

• Use definitions and restatements as context clues to determine the meanings of words.

LANGUAGE OBJECTIVE

Compare and contrast at least two things in a text.

ACADEMIC LANGUAGE

• *reread, context clues, compare, contrast, expository, define, restate*

• Cognates: *comparar, contraste, expositivo*

Shared Read
Gray Wolf! Red Fox!

View "Gray Wolf! Red Fox!"

Before Reading

Build Background

Read the Essential Question: How do animals adapt to challenges in their habitat?

• Explain the meaning of the Essential Question, including the vocabulary in the question: *Adapt means "to change." Challenges are difficult situations or obstacles. Habitat means "a place where a plant or animal lives."*

• **Model an answer:** *Ermines have adapted to challenges in their habitat. Their fur becomes thicker and turns white in the winter. This protects them by keeping them warm and helping them hide in the snow.*

• Ask students a question that ties the Essential Question to their own background knowledge: *Cold weather can be a challenge for many animals. Turn to a partner and think of another animal that has adapted to cold weather; talk about how it has adapted.* Call on several pairs to answer.

During Reading

Interactive-Question Response

• Ask questions that help students understand the meaning of the text after each paragraph.

• Reinforce the meanings of key vocabulary words by providing meanings embedded in the questions.

• Ask students questions that require them to use key vocabulary.

• Reinforce strategies and skills of the week by modeling.

Page 291

Paragraph 1
Explain and Model Context Clues *Sometimes an author will define or restate a difficult word in the text. The word* related *is defined in the next sentence by the phrase "members of the same family."*

 Who are you related to?

Looks Are Everything

Paragraph 2
Read the heading "Looks Are Everything." *What do you think this section will be about?* (how the animals look)

Model Compare and Contrast *The wolf and fox are both from the same dog family. This is a comparison. Look at the picture on page 290, and reread paragraph 2 to find how they are different.* Have students fill in the sentence frame: *The fox is _____* (smaller) *than the wolf.*

Paragraph 3
Explain and Model Rereading *When we reread, we may learn information we did not notice the first time.* Have students choral read the paragraph. *How does a fox's tail protect the fox?* (The tail keeps the fox warm.) *What challenge in the environment makes a fox's tail important?* (cold winter weather)

Page 292

Point to the map. What does it show? (the different environments wolves and foxes live in)

Finding Food

Paragraph 1
Look for a clue to the meaning of adapted *in the same sentence.* ("made changes") *Notice how "made changes" is framed by commas; this means it is defining the word* adapted. Have students fill in the sentence frame: *Adapted means "_____."*

Paragraph 2
How do red foxes find food? Reread this paragraph to find the answer. (They raid garbage cans and campsites.)

 Compare and contrast what foxes and wolves eat.
Ask further questions to prompt them: *What do both foxes and wolves eat?* (small animals) *What do wolves eat that foxes do not?* (large animals) *What do foxes eat that wolves do not?* (birds, fish, food in garbage cans)

Page 293

Paragraph 1
What type of group does a wolf live in? (a pack of four to seven)

Do you think wolves or foxes are more social animals? Why? Encourage students to use vocabulary words in their responses. (Wolves are more social. They live and hunt in groups. Foxes prefer to be alone.)

Paragraph 2
 Wolves and foxes communicate by barking and growling. What other noises have you heard animals make? Ask students to imitate other animal sounds they have heard, and have partners name them.

After Reading

Make Connections
- Review the Essential Question: How do animals adapt to challenges in their habitat?
- Make text connections.
- Have students complete the **ELL Reproducibles** pages 173–175.

English Language Learners

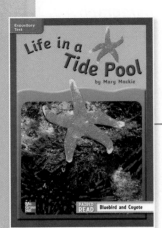

Lexile 660
TextEvaluator 5

___

 **Go Digital**

Leveled Reader:
Life in a Tide Pool

Before Reading

Preview

• Read the Essential Question: How do animals adapt to challenges in their habitat?

• Refer to Adapt to Challenges: *What are some challenges in this animal's environment?*

• Preview *Life in a Tide Pool* and "Bluebird and Coyote": *Let's read about how animals have special features that help them survive in tough environments.*

Vocabulary

Use the **Visual Vocabulary Cards** to preteach the ELL vocabulary: *tide, zone.* Use the routine found on the cards. Point out the cognate: *zona.*

Leveled Readers

During Reading

Interactive Question-Response

Note Taking Have students use the graphic organizer in **ELL Reproducibles** page 172. Use the following questions after you read each section. Use visuals or pictures to define key vocabulary.

Pages 2–3 *What sentence on page 2 explains what a tide pool is?* (*When the water goes out, it leaves small pools of water behind.*) Have students choral read the sentence. *What lives in tide pools?* (animals and plants)

Pages 4–5 *Look at the Intertidal Zone Map on page 5. Point to the splash zone. What lives there?* (limpets, periwinkles) *Work with a partner to name one thing that lives in each zone.*

Pages 6–7 *Look at the photo on page 6. What special adaptations does a sea anemone have?* (long tentacles; sucker disks) *How does the sea anemone use these features?* (to catch fish; to stick to rocks)

Page 8 *What adaptations does the sea hare have?* Have one student answer the question and another elaborate on the answer. (It can shoot purple ink at predators; its color is like a rock so it can hide.)

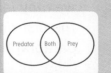
Fill in the Graphic Organizer

Page 9 *How are sea urchins and sea stars the same?* (in the same family; have the same type of feet) *How are they different? Sea urchins eat _____* (plants)*, but sea stars eat _____* (other animals).

Pages 10–11 *What is the sidebar on page 11 about?* (a special glue) *How do sand-castle worms use this glue?* (to build their homes)

Pages 12–14 *Reread page 14. Then turn to a partner to explain why it is important for us to be careful at a tide pool.* (so animals will not get hurt)

After Reading

Respond to Reading Help students complete the graphic organizer. Have student pairs summarize and answer the Text Evidence questions. Review all responses as a group.

Analytical Writing **Write About Reading** Have students work with a partner to write a short paragraph comparing the octopus on page 13 with another animal in the text using text evidence.

Fluency: Accuracy and Phrasing

Model Model reading page 2 with accuracy and proper phrasing. Next, reread the page aloud, and have students read along with you.

Apply Have students practice reading with a partner.

PAIRED READ

Leveled Reader

"Bluebird and Coyote"

Make Connections:
Write About It *Analytical Writing*

Before reading, have students note that the genre of this text is a folktale, which is a tale that might explain something about science. Then discuss the Essential Question.

After reading, have students write about connections between how animals adapt to challenges in their habitats in *Life in a Tide Pool* and "Bluebird and Coyote."

FOCUS ON SCIENCE

Students can extend their knowledge of how to compare and contrast tide pool animals by completing the science activity on page 20. **STEM**

Literature Circles

Ask students to conduct a literature circle using the Thinkmark questions to guide the discussion. You may wish to have a whole-class discussion on how animals in their community have adapted to challenges in their habitats.

Level Up

Level-up lessons available online.

IF students read the **ELL Level** fluently and answered the questions

THEN pair them with students who have proficiently read **On Level** and have ELL students

• echo-read the **On Level** main selection with their partner.

• list difficult words and discuss them with their partner.

A C T Access Complex Text

The **On Level** challenges students by including more **domain-specific words** and **complex sentence structures**.

English Language Learners
Vocabulary

PRETEACH VOCABULARY

OBJECTIVES

 Produce simple, compound, and complex sentences. **L.3.1i**

Preteach vocabulary words.

LANGUAGE OBJECTIVE

Use vocabulary words in sentences.

I Do Preteach vocabulary from "Gray Wolf! Red Fox!" following the Vocabulary Routine on the **Visual Vocabulary Cards** for words *alert, competition, environment, excellent, prefer, protection, related,* and *shelter.*

We Do After completing the routine for each word, point to the word on the card, and read the word with students. Have students repeat the word.

You Do Have student pairs write sentence frames for three words. Have them exchange the frames with another pair to complete.

Beginning	Intermediate	Advanced/High
Help students write their sentence frames correctly and read them aloud.	Have students write three sentence frames and a synonym for one sentence.	Challenge students to write four frames and give a synonym for each one.

REVIEW VOCABULARY

OBJECTIVES

 Acquire and use accurately grade-appropriate conversational, general academic, and domain-specific words and phrases, including those that signal spatial and temporal relationships (e.g., *After dinner that night we went looking for them*). **L.3.6**

LANGUAGE OBJECTIVE

Use vocabulary words.

I Do Review vocabulary words from the previous week. The words can be reviewed over a few days. Read each word aloud pointing to the word on the **Visual Vocabulary Card**. Have students repeat after you. Act out three of the words using gestures or actions.

We Do Have students guess the definitions of the words you acted out. Give them additional clues, including synonyms or antonyms.

You Do In pairs, have students think of ways to act out three words. Help students with the definitions, and suggest appropriate gestures or actions. Then have them act out the meaning of the words for the class.

Beginning	Intermediate	Advanced/High
Help students write the definitions correctly and read them aloud.	Help students think of ways to act out three of the words.	Have students come up with ways to act out each word.

CONTEXT CLUES

OBJECTIVES

 Use information gained from the illustrations (e.g., maps, photographs) and the words in a text to demonstrate understanding of the text (e.g., where, when, why, and how key events occur). **RI.3.7**

 Use sentence-level context as a clue to the meaning of a word or phrase. **L.3.4a**

LANGUAGE OBJECTIVE

Use definitions and restatements as clues to the meanings of unknown words.

 I Do Read aloud paragraph 1 of "Gray Wolf! Red Fox!" on page 291 while students follow along. Point to the word *related*. Explain that context clues are words or phrases that help you figure out the meaning of a word you do not know. Point out that a sentence might even define the word.

Think Aloud I am not sure what the word *related* means. I can look for clues in the surrounding sentences. The next sentence says that these animals are members of the same family. This tells me that *related* means "connected and part of the same family."

 We Do Have students point to the word *member* on page 291. Guide them as they figure out the meaning of the word using sentence clues. Write the definition of the word on the board.

You Do Have student pairs define *adapted* on page 292 using sentence clues. Have them write a sentence using the word to describe a fox or wolf in one of the photos from "Gray Wolf! Red Fox!"

Beginning	Intermediate	Advanced/High
Help students find the word and write a basic definition for it.	Have students find the word and define it using a complete sentence.	Have students write sentences using *related, member,* and *adapted.*

ADDITIONAL VOCABULARY

OBJECTIVES

 Produce simple, compound, and complex sentences. **L.3.1i**

Discuss concept and high-frequency words.

LANGUAGE OBJECTIVE

Use concept and high-frequency words.

 I Do List academic language and high-frequency words from "Gray Wolf! Red Fox!": *fur, hunt, other;* and *Life in a Tide Pool: survival, over, people.* Define each word for students: Fur *is an animal's coat of hair.*

 We Do Model using the words for students in sentences: *Tony is coming* over *at three o'clock.* Next, write *yes/no* questions and help students answer the questions: *Have you ever walked* over *to a friend's house?*

 You Do Have pairs make up their own *yes/no* question using the word *people.* Have students answer the question.

Beginning	Intermediate	Advanced/High
Help students write and copy the question correctly.	Have students write questions for three of the words and share with the class.	Challenge students to write questions for all of the words and share with the class.

English Language Learners
Writing/Spelling

WRITING TRAIT: ORGANIZATION

 OBJECTIVES
Introduce a topic and group related information together; include illustrations when useful to aiding comprehension. **W.3.2a**

Clearly introduce a topic.

LANGUAGE OBJECTIVE
Add a strong opening to writing.

 I Do Remind students that a strong opening can get readers' attention. For informational text, writers clearly state their topic and let readers know why they are writing. Read the Student Model passage aloud as students follow. Point out questions in the passage that make up the strong opening.

 We Do Read aloud the opening passage of "Gray Wolf! Red Fox!" Have students focus on the questions the author asks and identify the topic.

You Do Have students write a paragraph about a favorite animal. Tell them to use facts and questions to grab readers' attention and clearly state their topic. Edit students' writing, then have them revise and check word order.

Beginning	Intermediate	Advanced/High
Have students work with a partner to write a three-sentence paragraph.	Have students work independently to write a three-sentence paragraph.	Have students work independently to write a five-sentence paragraph.

SPELL VARIANT VOWEL /ô/

OBJECTIVES
Use spelling patterns and generalizations (e.g., word families, position-based spellings, syllable patterns, ending rules, meaningful word parts) in writing words. **L.3.2f**

LANGUAGE OBJECTIVE
Spell words with variant-vowel /ô/.

 I Do Read aloud the Spelling Words on page T162, modeling the pronunciation of each word. Point out that the variant vowel /ô/ can be spelled *au*, *aw*, *al*, *all*, *ough*, and *wa*. Have students repeat the words.

 We Do Read the Dictation Sentences on page T163 aloud for students. With each sentence, read the underlined word slowly, modeling proper pronunciation. Have students repeat after you and write the word.

 You Do Display the words. Have partners exchange their lists to check the spelling and write the words correctly.

Beginning	Intermediate	Advanced/High
Help students copy the words with correct spelling and say the words aloud.	Have students circle the variant-vowel spellings in their corrected words.	After students have corrected their words, have pairs quiz each other.

Grammar

MAIN AND HELPING VERBS

OBJECTIVES

 Explain the function of nouns, pronouns, verbs, adjectives, and adverbs in general and their functions in particular sentences. **L.3.1a**

Identify main and helping verbs.

LANGUAGE OBJECTIVE

Write sentences.

Language Transfers Handbook

In Hmong and Khmer, verb forms do not change to indicate the number of the subject in the primary language. Therefore, students who speak these languages might have trouble with making helping verbs agree with the subject. Give students additional practice selecting the correct form of helping verbs in written sentences.

 Remind students that a verb can have more than one part in a sentence. Sometimes helping verbs are used to help the main verb show action. Write on the board: *Rose has learned to speak another language.* Remind students that the main verb *learned* tells what the subject is or does. Next, point to and circle the helping verb *has*. Tell students that the word *has* helps the main verb show action. Explain that *have, has,* and *had* are forms of the helping verb *to have.* Forms of the verb *to be* can also act as helping verbs, such as *is, are, am, was, were,* and *will.* Write on the board: *The wolf is hunting for food.* Underline the main verb *hunting* and circle the helping verb *is.* Tell students that helping verbs must agree with the subject.

 Write the sentences below on the board. Have student volunteers choose a helping verb or a main verb to complete each sentence.

> We _____ visited the Grand Canyon twice.
>
> Olivia _____ choosing another coat.
>
> They are _____ the play.

You Do Have students study the pictures in "Gray Wolf! Red Fox" and discuss ways gray wolves and red foxes survive when the weather is very cold. Next, ask students: When the weather has gotten bad, what changes have you made? Have students write three sentences using helping verbs.

Beginning	Intermediate	Advanced/High
Help students write about one way they have prepared for bad weather using a helping verb.	Have students write about two ways they have prepared for bad weather using helping verbs. Have them use complete sentences.	Have students write about three ways they have prepared for bad weather using helping verbs and adding descriptive words.

For extra support, have students complete the activities in the **Grammar Practice Reproducibles** during the week, using the routine below:

- Explain the grammar skill.
- Model the first activity in the Grammar Practice Reproducibles.
- Have the whole group complete the next couple of activities, then the rest with a partner.
- Review the activities with correct answers.

PROGRESS MONITORING

Unit 4 Week 3 Formal Assessment	Standards Covered	Component for Assessment
Text Evidence	RI.3.1	• *Selection Test* • *Weekly Assessment* • *Approaching-Level Weekly Assessment*
Structure: Compare and Contrast	RI.3.8	• *Weekly Assessment* • *Approaching-Level Weekly Assessment*
Context Clues: Sentence Clues	L.3.4a	• *Selection Test* • *Weekly Assessment* • *Approaching-Level Weekly Assessment*
Writing About Text	W.3.8	*Weekly Assessment*

Unit 4 Week 3 Informal Assessment	Standards Covered	Component for Assessment
Research/Listening/ Collaborating	SL.3.1d, SL.3.2, SL.3.3	• *RWW* • *Teacher's Edition*
Oral Reading Fluency (ORF) **Fluency Goal:** 82–102 words correct per minute (WCPM) **Accuracy Rate Goal:** 95% or higher	RF.3.4a, RF.3.4b, RF.3.4c	*Fluency Assessment*

Using Assessment Results

Weekly Assessments Skills and Fluency	If . . .	Then . . .
COMPREHENSION	Students score below 70% . . .	. . . assign Lessons 79–81 on Text Structure: Compare and Contrast from the *Tier 2 Comprehension Intervention online PDFs.*
VOCABULARY	Students score below 70% . . .	. . . assign Lesson 134 on Using Sentence Clues from the *Tier 2 Vocabulary Intervention online PDFs.*
WRITING	Students score below "3" on constructed response . . .	. . . assign Lessons 79–81 and/or Write About Reading Lesson 200 from the *Tier 2 Comprehension Intervention online PDFs.*
FLUENCY	Students have a WCPM score of 75–81 . . .	. . . assign a lesson from Section 1, 7, 8, 9 or 10 of the *Tier 2 Fluency Intervention online PDFs.*
	Students have a WCPM score of 0–74 . . .	. . . assign a lesson from Sections 2–6 of the *Tier 2 Fluency Intervention online PDFs.*

Using Weekly Data

Check your data Dashboard to verify assessment results and guide grouping decisions.

Data-Driven Recommendations

Response to Intervention

Use the appropriate sections of the *Placement and Diagnostic Assessment* as well as students' assessment results to designate students requiring:

 Intervention Online PDFs

 WonderWorks Intervention Program

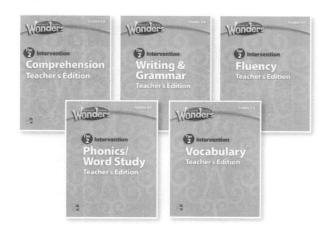

Build Knowledge
Flight

? **Essential Question:**
How are people able to fly?

Teach and Model
Close Reading and Writing

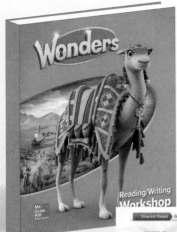

Reading/Writing Workshop

"Firsts in Flight," 304–307
Genre Expository Text **Lexile** 750 ETS *TextEvaluator* 27

Practice and Apply
Close Reading and Writing

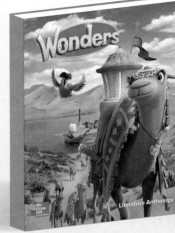

Literature Anthology

Hot Air Balloons, 342–355
Genre Expository Text **Lexile** 680 ETS *TextEvaluator* 12

"Bellerophon and Pegasus," 358–359
Genre Myth Text **Lexile** 640 ETS *TextEvaluator* 20

Differentiated Texts

APPROACHING
Lexile 600
ETS *TextEvaluator* 21

ON LEVEL
Lexile 690
ETS *TextEvaluator* 31

BEYOND
Lexile 770
ETS *TextEvaluator* 32

ELL
Lexile 670
ETS *TextEvaluator* 18

Leveled Readers

Extended Complex Texts

Bat Loves the Night
Genre Informational Text
Lexile 560

Gray Wolves
Genre Informational Text
Lexile 640

Classroom Library

Student Outcomes

Close Reading of Complex Text
- Cite relevant evidence from text
- Describe text structure; cause and effect
- Reread

RI.3.1, RI.3.3, RI.3.8

Writing

Write to Sources
- Draw evidence from informational text
- Write informative text
- Conduct extended research on frogs

Writing Process
- Prewrite a Poem

W.3.3a, W.3.8, W.3.10, W.4.9b

Speaking and Listening
- Engage in collaborative discussions about flight
- Paraphrase portions of "Fly Like a Bird"
- Present information on flight

SL.3.1b, SL.3.1d, SL.3.2, SL.3.3

Content Knowledge
- Learn that forces that do not sum to zero can cause changes in speed or direction.

Language Development

Conventions
- Produce simple, compound, and complex sentences

Vocabulary Acquisition
- Acquire and use academic vocabulary

controlled	direction	flight	impossible
launch	motion	passengers	popular

- Demonstrate understanding of multiple-meaning words

L.3.1h, L.3.1i, L.3.4a, RI.3.4

Foundational Skills

Phonics/Word Study
- Homophones
- *r*-Controlled vowels

Spelling Words

sale	sail	beet	beat
rode	road	rowed	its
it's	your	you're	their
they're	peace	piece	

Fluency
- Accuracy

RF.3.3d, RF3.4a, RF.3.4b, RF.3.4c

Professional Develoicon over textpment
- See lessons in action in real classrooms.
- Get expert advice on instructional practices.
- Collaborate with other teachers.
- Access PLC Resources.

Go Digital! www.connected.mcgraw-hill.com.

INSTRUCTIONAL PATH

1 Talk About Flying

Guide students in collaborative conversations.

Discuss the essential question: *How are people able to fly?*

Develop academic language and domain specific vocabulary on flying.

Listen to "Fly Like a Bird" to summarize a passage about different ways people can fly using wind energy.

2 Read "Firsts in Flight"

Model close reading with a short complex text.

Read

"Firsts in Flight" to learn about the Wright brothers and other inventors who worked to make flight possible, citing text evidence to answer text-dependent questions.

Reread

"Firsts in Flight" to analyze text, craft, and structure, citing text evidence.

3 Write About Flying

Model writing to a source.

Analyze a short response student model.

Use text evidence from close reading to write to a source.

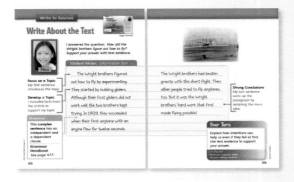

4 Read and Write About Flying

Practice and apply close reading of the anchor text.

Read

Hot Air Balloons to learn what it's like to fly in a hot air balloon.

Reread

Hot Air Balloons and use text evidence to understand how the author presents information about hot air balloons and how it would feel to ride one.

Write a short response about *Hot Air Balloons*.

Integrate

Information about air travel with other stories you have read.

Write to Two Sources, citing text evidence from *Hot Air Balloons* and "Bellerophon and Pegasus."

5 Independent Partner Work

Gradual release of support to independent work

- Text-Dependent Questions
- Scaffolded Partner Work
  Talk with a Partner
  Cite Text Evidence
  Complete a sentence frame.
- Guided Text Annotation

6 Integrate Knowledge and Ideas

Connect Texts

Text to Text Discuss how each of the texts answers the question: How are people able to fly?

Text to Photography Compare the reasons why people want to fly in the texts read and the photograph.

Performance Task

Prewrite and draft.

DEVELOPING READERS AND WRITERS

Write to Sources

Day 1 and Day 2
Build Writing Fluency
- Quick write on "Firsts in Flight," p. T220

Write to a Source
- Analyze a student model, p. T220
- Write about "Firsts in Flight," p. T221
- Apply Writing Trait: Strong Conclusions, p. T220
- Apply Grammar Skill: Complex Sentences, p. T221

Day 3
Write to a Source
- Write about *Hot Air Balloons*, independent practice, p. T217P
- Provide scaffolded instruction to meet student needs, p. T222

Day 4 and Day 5
Write to Two Sources
- Analyze a student model, pp. T222–T223
- Write to compare *Hot Air Balloons* with "Bellerophon and Pegasus," p. T223

Writing Process

Go Digital

Writer's Workspace

Genre Writing: Narrative Text/Poetry

Poetry
Expert Model

- Discuss features of narrative writing
- Discuss the expert model

Prewrite

- Discuss purpose and audience
- Plan the topic

Expert Model • Poetry • 71

The Contest
By Maggie D.

My sister and I share a room to ourselves.
It's a hideous work of art
Her books were falling off the shelves,
Her posters were crumbling apart.
My things were scattered across the floor.
They sat in a monstrous mound.
Her socks were tangled and leaked from her drawer.
My clothes lounged all around.

My mother was exhausted with seeing the mess,
So we put together our master plan.
We had a contest to see who could clean the best,
And on the count of three we began.
We rushed around and picked up a ton
Of clothes, books, and art supplies.
I finished first, but we both really won,
When we learned a clean room is the prize.

Unit 4 • Poetry

Expert Model

Features of a Poem

Model Graphic Organizer

Graphic Organizer

Grammar and Spelling Resources

Online PDFs

Reading/Writing Workshop Grammar Handbook p. 477

Online Spelling and Grammar Games

Grammar Practice, pp. 91–95

Phonics/Spelling Practice, pp. 109–114

SUGGESTED LESSON PLAN

READING		DAY 1	DAY 2
Teach, Model and Apply	Core	**Introduce the Concept** T138–T139 **Vocabulary** T206–T207 **Close Reading** "Firsts in Flight," T208–T209	**Close Reading** "Firsts in Flights," T208–T209 **Strategy** Reread, T210–T211 **Skill** Cause and Effect, T212–T213 **Vocabulary Strategy** Multiple-Meaning Words, T216–T217
	Options	**Listening Comprehension** T204–T205	**Genre** Expository Text, T214–T215

LANGUAGE ARTS			
Writing **Grammar** **Spelling** **Build Vocabulary**	Core	**Grammar** Complex Sentences, T224 **Spelling** Homophones, T226 **Build Vocabulary** T228	**Write About the Text** Model Note-Taking and Write to a Prompt, T220–T221 **Grammar** Complex Sentences, T224 **Build Vocabulary** T228
	Options	**Write About the Text** Writing Fluency, T220 **Genre Writing** Poetry: Read Like a Writer, T350	**Genre Writing** Poetry: Discuss the Expert Model, T351 **Spelling** Homophones, T226

Writing Process: Narrative Poetry, T350–T355   Use with Weeks 4–6

Differentiated Instruction Use your data dashboard to determine each student's needs. Then select instructional support options throughout the week.

APPROACHING LEVEL

Leveled Reader
The Future of Flights, T232–T233

"The Cloak of Feathers," T233

Literature Circles, T233

Phonics/Decoding
Long-Vowel Spellings, T234
Build Homophones, T234
Practice Homophones, T235
r-Controlled Vowel Syllables, T235

Vocabulary
• Review High-Frequency Words, T236
• Identify Related Words, T237
Multiple-Meaning Words, T237

Comprehension
• Text Structure, T238
• Review Text Structure: Cause and Effect, T239
Self-Selected Reading, T239

Fluency
Accuracy and Phrasing, T238

ON LEVEL

Leveled Reader
The Future of Flight, T240–T241

"The Cloak of Feathers," T241

Literature Circles, T241

Vocabulary
Review Vocabulary Words, T242
Multiple-Meaning Words, T242

Comprehension
Review Text Structure: Cause and Effect, T243
Self-Selected Reading, T243

DAY 3	DAY 4	DAY 5
Close Reading *Hot Air Balloons,* T217A–T217O	**Fluency** T219 **Close Reading** "Bellerophon and Pegasus," T217Q–T217R **Integrate Ideas** Inquiry Space, T230–T231	**Integrate Ideas** T230–T231 • Text Connections • Inquiry Space **Weekly Assessment**
Phonics/Decoding T218–T219 • Homophones • *r*-Controlled Vowel Syllables	**Close Reading** *Hot Air Balloons,* T217A–T217O	
Grammar Complex Sentences, T225	**Write About Two Texts** Model Note-Taking and Taking Notes, T222	**Write About Two Texts** Analyze Student Model and Write to the Prompt, T223 **Spelling** Homophones, T227
Write About the Text T221 **Genre Writing** Poetry: Prewrite, T351 **Spelling** Homophones, T227 **Build Vocabulary** T229	**Genre Writing** Poetry: Teach the Prewrite Minilesson, T351 **Grammar** Complex Sentences, T225 **Spelling** Homophones, T227 **Build Vocabulary** T229	**Genre Writing** Poetry: Choose Your Topic, T351 **Grammar** Complex Sentences, T225 **Build Vocabulary** T229

Literature Anthology

 Writing Process

Writing Process: Narrative Poetry, T350–T355   Use with Weeks 4–6

BEYOND LEVEL

Leveled Reader
The Future of Flight,
T244–T245
"The Cloak of Feathers,"
T245
Literature Circles, T245

Vocabulary
Review Domain-Specific Words, T246
• Multiple-Meaning Words, T246
• Analyze, T246

Gifted and Talented

Comprehension
Review Text Structure: Cause and Effect, T247
• Self-Selected Reading, T247
• Independent Study, T247

ENGLISH LANGUAGE LEARNERS

Shared Read
"Firsts in Flight," T248–T249

Leveled Reader
The Future of Flights,
T250–T251
"The Cloak of Feathers," T251
Literature Circles, T251

Phonics/Decoding
Long Vowel Spellings, T234
Build Homophones, T234
Practice Homophones, T235
r-Controlled Vowel Syllables, T235

Vocabulary
• Preteach Vocabulary, T252
• Review High-Frequency Words, T236
Review Vocabulary, T252
Multiple-Meaning Words, T253
Additional Vocabulary, T189

Spelling
Spell Homophones, T254

Writing
Writing Trait: Organization, T254

Grammar
Complex Sentences, T255

DIFFERENTIATE TO ACCELERATE

 Scaffold to **A**ccess **C**omplex **T**ext

 IF ▶ the text complexity of a particular selection is too difficult for students

▶ **THEN** ▶ see the references noted in the chart below for scaffolded instruction to help students Access Complex Text.

Qualitative · Quantitative
Reader and Task
TEXT COMPLEXITY

	Reading/Writing Workshop	Literature Anthology	Leveled Readers		Classroom Library

Quantitative	**"Firsts in Flight"** Lexile 750 *TextEvaluator™* 27	**Hot Air Balloons** Lexile 680 *TextEvaluator™* 12	**Approaching Level** Lexile 600 *TextEvaluator™* 21	**On Level** Lexile 690 *TextEvaluator™* 31	**Bat Loves the Night** Lexile 560
		"Belleraphon and Pegasus" Lexile 640 *TextEvaluator™* 20	**Beyond Level** Lexile 770 *TextEvaluator™* 32	**ELL** Lexile 670 *TextEvaluator™* 18	**Gray Wolves** Lexile 640
Qualitative	**What Makes the Text Complex?** • **Connection of Ideas** Generalize T209 • **Sentence Structure** T217 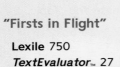 *See Scaffolded Instruction in Teacher's Edition T209 and T217.*	**What Makes the Text Complex?** • **Purpose** Key Details T217C • **Organization** Cause and Effect T217M–T217N • **Specific Vocabulary** Context Clues T217G, T217I • **Genre** Text Features T217B, T217E; Myths T217R • **Prior Knowledge** Greek Myths T217Q • **Connection of Ideas** Cause and Effect T217K **A C T** *See Scaffolded Instruction in Teacher's Edition T217A–T217R.*	**What Makes the Text Complex?** • **Specific Vocabulary** • **Prior Knowledge** • **Sentence Structure** • **Connection of Ideas** • **Genre** **A C T** *See Level Up lessons online for Leveled Readers.*		**What Makes the Text Complex?** • **Genre** • **Specific Vocabulary** • **Prior Knowledge** • **Sentence Structure** • **Organization** • **Purpose** • **Connection of Ideas** **A C T** *See Scaffolded Instruction in Teacher's Edition T360–T361.*
Reader and Task	The Introduce the Concept lesson on pages T202–T203 will help determine the reader's knowledge and engagement in the weekly concept. See pages T208–T217 and T230–T231 for questions and tasks for this text.	The Introduce the Concept lesson on pages T202–T203 will help determine the reader's knowledge and engagement in the weekly concept. See pages T217A–T217R and T230–T231 for questions and tasks for this text.	The Introduce the Concept lesson on pages T202–T203 will help determine the reader's knowledge and engagement in the weekly concept. See pages T232–T233, T240–T241, T244–T245, T250–T251, and T230–T231 for questions and tasks for this text.		The Introduce the Concept lesson on pages T202–T203 will help determine the reader's knowledge and engagement in the weekly concept. See pages T360–T361 for questions and tasks for this text.

Monitor and *Differentiate*

✓ Quick Check

To differentiate instruction, use the Quick Checks to assess students' needs and select the appropriate small group instruction focus.

Comprehension Strategy Reread T211

Comprehension Skill Cause and Effect T213

Genre Expository Text T215

Vocabulary Strategy Multiple-Meaning Words T217

Phonics/Fluency Homophones, Accuracy and Phrasing T219

If No →

| Approaching Level | **Reteach** T232–T239 |
| ELL | **Develop** T248–T255 |

If Yes →

| On Level | **Review** T240–T243 |
| Beyond Level | **Extend** T244–T247 |

Using Weekly Data

Check your data Dashboard to verify assessment results and guide grouping decisions.

Level Up with Leveled Readers

IF → students can read their leveled text fluently and answer comprehension questions

THEN → work with the next level up to accelerate students' reading with more complex text.

Beyond

T49

On Level

Approaching T41   T59   ELL

ELL ENGLISH LANGUAGE LEARNERS

Small Group Instruction

Use the ELL small group lessons in the Wonders Teacher's Edition to provide focused instruction.

Language Development
Vocabulary preteaching and review, additional vocabulary building, and vocabulary strategy lessons, pp. T252–T253

Close Reading
Interactive Question-Response routines for scaffolded text-dependent questioning for reading and rereading the Shared Read and Leveled Reader, pp. T248–T251

Writing
Focus on the weekly writing trait, grammar skills, and spelling words, pp. T254–T255

Additional ELL Support

Use *Reading Wonders for English Learners* for ELD instruction that connects to the core.

Language Development
Ample opportunities for discussions, and scaffolded language support

Close Reading
Companion Worktexts for guided support in annotating text and citing text evidence. Differentiated Texts about the weekly concept.

Reading Wonders for ELLs Teacher Edition and Companion Worktexts

Writing
Scaffolded instruction for writing to sources and revising student models

(→) Introduce the Concept

Reading/Writing Workshop

OBJECTIVES

CCSS Follow agreed upon rules for discussions (e.g., gaining the floor in respectful ways, listening to others with care, speaking one at a time about the topics and texts under discussion). **SL.3.1b**

Build background knowledge on flight.

ACADEMIC LANGUAGE

flight, motion

 Build Background

ESSENTIAL QUESTION

How are people able to fly?

Have students read the Essential Question on page 300 of the **Reading/Writing Workshop**.

Discuss the photograph of the man in the glider on pages 300 and 301. Draw attention to the fact that he cannot fly by himself and is using a machine that uses energy to help him stay in the air and fly.

- Because we cannot fly by ourselves, **flight** has been the dream of humans for ages.

- Building a machine that could stay in the air while in **motion** was difficult. It took inventors many tries before they did it successfully.

Talk About It

Ask: *Why do people fly? How are people today able to fly? What kinds of machines do they use?* Have students discuss in pairs or groups.

- Model using the Concept Web to generate words and phrases related to flight. Add students' contributions.

- Have partners continue the discussion by sharing what they have learned about flight. They can complete the Concept Webs, generating additional related words and phrases.

Collaborative Conversations

Take Turns Talking As students engage in partner, small-group, and whole-class discussions, encourage them to follow discussion rules by taking turns speaking. Remind students to

- wait for a person to finish before they speak. They should not speak over others.

- quietly raise their hand to let others know they would like a turn to speak.

- ask others in the groups to share their opinions so that all students have a chance to share.

- speak in complete sentences when responding to a request for details or clarification.

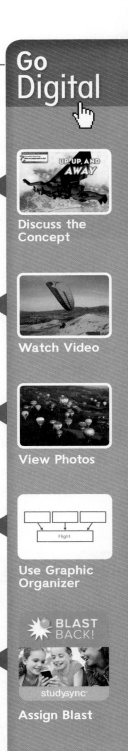

Go Digital

Discuss the Concept

Watch Video

View Photos

Use Graphic Organizer

BLAST BACK!

studysync

Assign Blast

Weekly Concept Flight

? Essential Question
How are people able to fly?

Go Digital!

UP, UP, AND AWAY

People have wanted to fly for hundreds of years. Thanks to many inventors, there are lots of ways they can!

▶ People can cross the country in tiny planes, huge passenger jets, or colorful hot air balloons.

▶ Helicopters take small groups from here to there.

▶ And some adventurers fly solo high above the Earth.

Talk About It

Write words about flight. Talk about how people have learned to fly.

Flight

300   301

READING/WRITING WORKSHOP, *pp. 300–301*

Share the Blast assignment. Point out that you will discuss students' responses during the **Integrate Ideas** lesson at the end of the week.

GRAPHIC ORGANIZER 111

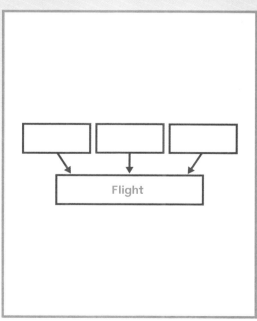

Flight

ELL ENGLISH LANGUAGE LEARNERS SCAFFOLD

Beginning	Intermediate	Advanced/High
Use Visuals Point to the picture of the man in the glider on page 300. Ask: *What is this man doing?* (flying) *Is he flying by himself?* (no) *People use machines to help them fly. We will find out how people made the first flying machines.*	**Describe** Ask: *How is this man able to fly?* (He is using a glider.) *People had to invent machines to help them fly.* Ask students to think of other aircraft people use to fly. Allow students ample time to respond.	**Discuss** Ask students: *What are some different kinds of flying machines?* (airplane, helicopter, hot air balloon, etc.) Discuss how the different kinds of machines work. Have students name things in nature that fly using similar principles.

→ Listening Comprehension

MINILESSON
10 Mins

Interactive Read Aloud

OBJECTIVES

CCSS Determine the main ideas and supporting details of a text read aloud or information presented in diverse media and formats, including visually, quantitatively, and orally. **SL.3.2**

- Listen for a purpose.
- Identify characteristics of expository text.

ACADEMIC LANGUAGE

expository text, reread

Connect to Concept: Flight

Tell students that people have always longed to fly like birds. Let students know that you will be reading aloud a passage about different ways people can fly using wind energy. Explain that their purpose in listening is to gain information.

View Photos

Preview Genre: Expository Text

Explain that the passage you will read aloud is expository text. Discuss features of expository text:

- includes accounts of actual persons, living things, situations, or events
- may explain how something works or why
- explains a topic by presenting facts

Preview Comprehension Strategy: Reread

Explain that when reading expository text, it is helpful to reread a section of text if a word or concept is complex or unfamiliar to the reader. If a topic is difficult, students can use the reread strategy to help them monitor what they read.

Use the Think Alouds on page T205 to model the strategy.

Respond to Reading

Think Aloud Clouds Display Think Aloud Master 4: *When I read _____, I had to reread. . .* to reinforce how you used the reread strategy to understand content.

Genre Features With students, discuss the elements of the Read Aloud that let them know it is expository text. Ask them to think about other texts that you have read aloud or they have read independently that were expository text.

Summarize Have students determine the main ideas and details of the article "Fly Like a Bird." Then have them restate the article's most important information in their own words.

When I read _____, I had to reread...

Model Think Alouds

Genre	Features

Fill in Genre Chart

Fly Like a Bird

Think about seeing a bird fly across the sky. Its wings help it lift and soar higher and higher. Humans have often wanted to fly like birds. The airplane is one way that people can fly. But what if people want to fly without machines?

Hang Glider

A hang glider looks like a large wing. It has a hollow frame covered in a strong, but lightweight fabric. The pilot is strapped into a harness under the frame. A control bar helps the pilot steer through the air. To launch, a pilot may run down a hill. Or the pilot may run to the edge of a cliff and then jump. The reason for running is to allow the wind to catch under the wing and lift the hang glider up. To land, the pilot leans forward on the control bar. This helps guide the hang glider slowly down. The pilot touches down, feet first, and then runs until he or she can safely stop. A soft, sandy beach is a good place for hang gliders to land. **1**

Parasailing

Parasailing is floating or flying over water while wearing a parachute. The parachute is attached to a boat by a strong rope. As the boat picks up speed, wind catches under the parachute and opens it up. The person strapped to the parachute is lifted higher and higher. **2**

Gliding

Have you ever made a paper airplane? A glider flies in much the same way a paper airplane flies. Air currents lift the glider up and keep it aloft. A glider may look similar to a traditional airplane, but there's no engine. To launch, a glider is often towed behind another plane by a cable. Once the glider catches an air current, the cable is removed. To land, the pilot rides an air current down to an open, flat area. **3**

Birds make flying look easy. But hang gliding, parasailing, and flying a glider are dangerous activities. People must be trained to use the equipment and learn many safety rules in order to stay safe in the air and when landing.

1 **Think Aloud** I think I understand how a hang glider flies, but I can **reread** this paragraph again to make sure that I didn't miss any important details.

2 **Think Aloud** I know what a parachute looks like, but I didn't know that a parachute could be used this way. I want to **reread** this section to make sure I understand parasailing.

3 **Think Aloud** I've made paper airplanes before so this helps me think about how gliders fly. I think I will **reread** this section though to make sure I understand how a glider is launched.

Stockbroker/SuperStock

→ Vocabulary

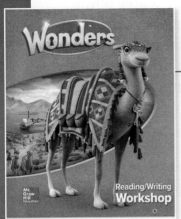

Reading/Writing Workshop

Wonders
Mc Graw Hill Education
Reading/Writing Workshop

OBJECTIVES

CCSS Determine the meaning of general academic and domain-specific words and phrases in a text relevant to a grade 3 topic or subject area. **RI.3.4**

CCSS Use sentence-level context as a clue to the meaning of a word or phrase. **L.3.4a**

ACADEMIC LANGUAGE

flight, motion

MINILESSON **10** Mins

Words in Context

Model the Routine

Introduce each vocabulary word using the Vocabulary Routine found on the Visual Vocabulary Cards.

Visual Vocabulary Cards

Vocabu...
Define:
Example:
Ask:

Vocabulary Routine

Define: If something is **controlled**, it is adjusted or moved by something else.

Example: Tom controlled his toy boat's movements from the shore.

Ask: What is something you have *controlled* at home?

Definitions

- **direction**   Something's **direction** is the line or course it moves along.
  Cognate: *dirección*
- **flight**   **Flight** is the act of flying.
- **impossible**   When something is **impossible**, it can't be done.
  Cognate: *imposible*
- **launched**   When something is **launched**, it is put into motion.
- **motion**   Something that is in **motion** is moving.
- **passenger**   A **passenger** is a person who travels in a vehicle.
  Cognate: *pasajero*
- **popular**   When something is **popular**, it is liked by many people.

Talk About It

Have students work with a partner and look at each picture and discuss the definition of each word. Then ask students to choose three words and write questions for their partner to answer.

Go Digital

controlled

Use Visual Glossary

Words to Know

Vocabulary

Use the picture and the sentence to talk with a partner about each word.

controlled — Tom **controlled** his toy boat's movements from the shore.

What is something you have controlled at home?

direction — The sign showed us which **direction** to go.

Point in the direction of the door.

flight — The first airplane **flight** took place many years ago.

Where would you like to go on an airplane flight?

impossible — Crossing this river is **impossible**, so we will have to go a different way.

Name something that is impossible to do.

launched — The space shuttle was **launched** and soared toward space.

What other things can be launched?

motion — Julie enjoys the **motion** of the swing.

What kinds of motion do you like?

passenger — Denise likes being a **passenger** in the car.

When was the last time you were a passenger?

popular — Soccer is the most **popular** sport at our school.

Tell about a popular sport at your school.

Your Turn

COLLABORATE

Pick three words. Write three questions for your partner to answer.

Go Digital! Use the online visual glossary

302   303

READING/WRITING WORKSHOP, *pp. 302–303*

ELL ENGLISH LANGUAGE LEARNERS SCAFFOLD

Beginning

Use Visuals Have students look at the picture for *controlled*. Ask students: *Did the boat move by itself?* (no) *Who moved the boat?* (the boy) *The boy controlled the boat.* Have students repeat after you.

Intermediate

Demonstrate Comprehension Ask: *What is the boy doing with this boat?* (He is moving it from far away.) *The boat did not move by itself. The boy controlled the boat.* Help students create new sentences with the frame: _____ *controlled the* _____.

Advanced/High

Discuss Have students work with a partner to define the word *controlled*. Then ask students for examples of other things that are controlled. Challenge pairs to present their examples in complete sentences. Correct students' responses as needed.

ON-LEVEL PRACTICE BOOK p. 181

| passenger | launched | direction | flight |
| impossible | popular | controlled | motion |

Use a word from the box to answer each question. Then use the word in a sentence.

1. What word might describe a famous actor? popular; Spaghetti is the most *popular* food in our cafeteria.

2. What do you call a person who rides the bus? passenger; Every *passenger* in my mother's car must wear a seatbelt.

3. What is another word for *movement*? motion; You should never change seats when a car is in *motion*.

4. What word describes something that cannot be done? impossible; People used to think it was *impossible* to go to the moon.

5. What did the pilot do when he flew the plane? controlled; I *controlled* my toy car with a special remote.

6. What is another word for *the line something moves along*? direction; I wanted to find her house, but I wasn't sure which *direction* to go.

7. What is another word for *put something into motion*? launched; My mom and I built two small rockets and *launched* them into the sky.

8. Which word describes the movement of a bird through the air? flight; The *flight* from coast to coast is very long.

| APPROACHING p. 181 | BEYOND p. 181 | ELL p. 181 |

Shared Read · Genre • Expository

Firsts in Flight

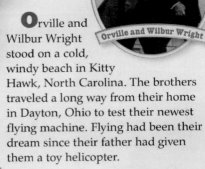

Orville and Wilbur Wright

Orville and Wilbur Wright stood on a cold, windy beach in Kitty Hawk, North Carolina. The brothers traveled a long way from their home in Dayton, Ohio to test their newest flying machine. Flying had been their dream since their father had given them a toy helicopter.

The Wright brothers owned a bicycle shop in Dayton. In addition to selling, building, and repairing bicycles, they built flying machines. They flew the first one in 1899. However, the winds weren't strong enough to keep the machine in **motion**. So they looked for a place where the winds were stronger. As a result, they chose Kitty Hawk. It was not only windy there, but the sandy beaches made for soft landings.

? Essential Question

How are people able to fly?

Read about how inventors learned how to fly.

On December 17, 1903, the *Wright Flyer* flew for 12 seconds at Kitty Hawk.

304 305

READING/WRITING WORKSHOP, pp. 304–305

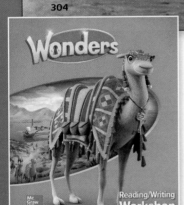

Wonders

Reading/Writing Workshop

ELL

See pages T248–T249 for Interactive Question-Response routine for the Shared Read.

Shared Read

Close Reading Routine

Read DOK 1–2

- Identify key ideas and details about Flight.
- Take notes and summarize.
- Use (A C T) prompts as needed.

Reread DOK 2–3

- Analyze the text, craft, and structure.
- Use the Reread minilessons.

Integrate DOK 4

- Integrate knowledge and ideas.
- Make text-to-text connections.
- Use the Integrate lesson.

Lexile 750 TextEvaluator™ 27

Read

Connect to Concept: Flight Tell students they will read about the Wright Brothers and others who made flight possible.

Note Taking Read page 305 together. Model how to take notes. *I will think about the Essential Question as I read and note key ideas and details.* Encourage students to note words they don't understand and questions they have.

Paragraphs 1 and 2: Reread the paragraphs with students. Ask: *How did the Wright brothers' first flying machine move? How does the text use cause and effect to explain why they had to move?*

The Wright brothers were in Kitty Hawk but lived in Ohio. The flyer needed wind to move. The Wright brothers had to find a place with stronger winds.

Because their first **flight** was not successful, the Wright brothers learned a lot about flying. As a result, they built a better glider with bigger wings in 1900. This glider did not work very well either. The brothers did not give up. That's why they experimented with a new glider in 1902. Then in 1903, they built the *Wright Flyer*, their first airplane with an engine.

Flying Firsts

By December 17, the brothers were ready to test the *Wright Flyer*. Orville started up the engines to power the plane. He **controlled** the plane, while Wilbur watched from the ground. The *Flyer* was **launched** into the sky. The plane moved in an upward **direction**, and the flight lasted twelve seconds. The Wright brothers had conquered gravity and unlocked the secrets of flying.

Orville and Wilbur kept improving their planes, and their flights became longer. Soon, other people tried to fly airplanes.

Alberto Santos-Dumont was the third man in the world to fly a plane with an engine.

Will It Fly?

Do an experiment on flying using paper airplanes.

Materials needed:
- pencil - paper - ruler

Directions:
1. With a partner, fold two paper airplanes. Make the wing sizes different in each plane.
2. Gently throw one plane.
3. Measure and record how far the paper plane flew.
4. Take turns throwing the plane four more times. Each time, measure and record how far it flies.
5. Repeat the experiment with the other airplane.
6. Compare the plane's flights. Then discuss what you learned about flight.

306

Alberto Santos-Dumont was an inventor and pilot from Brazil. In 1906, he made the first official flight in front of an audience. The next year, the French pilot, Henri Farman, took along a **passenger** in his plane. They flew for one minute and fourteen seconds.

Better Flying Machines

Because of these flights, airplane research became **popular** with inventors. Before long, better planes were traveling longer distances. In 1909, a French pilot flew an airplane across the English Channel. This plane was very different from the Wright brothers' plane. The new plane had only one long wing across its body. It looked a lot like today's airplanes.

This is what an airplane looked like in 1930.

Soon inventors began building airplanes that could carry more people. By 1920, several new companies offered passengers the chance to fly. Humans had done the **impossible**. They had figured out how to fly.

Make Connections

How did the Wright brothers help people fly? ESSENTIAL QUESTION

Tell what you know about airplanes. Discuss other ways to fly. TEXT TO SELF

307

READING/WRITING WORKSHOP, *pp. 306–307*

"Better Flying Machines": Ask: *How did advances in flight lead to planes traveling longer distances?*

After reading, I know that advances in flight made research popular with inventors. This research led to the invention of airplanes that could fly longer distances and carry more people.

Make Connections

COLLABORATE

Essential Question Encourage students to discuss with a partner how the Wright brothers helped people fly. Ask them to cite text evidence. Use these sentence frames to focus discussion:

I read that the Wright brothers . . .
Their invention . . .

A C T Access Complex Text

▶ **Connection of Ideas**

Lead students to see that inventors meet challenges by testing an idea or an invention and using the results to improve their work.

- *Why did the Wright Brothers keep experimenting with different gliders?* (They wanted to use what they learned to make their gliders fly better.)

- *What did the Wright brothers do after they tested their first plane with an engine?* (They kept improving their planes.)

- *How do experiments help us, even when they fail?* (The results help us improve our work.)

→ Comprehension Strategy

 Reread

MINILESSON
10 Mins

**Reading/Writing
Workshop**

OBJECTIVES

CCSS Ask and answer
questions to
demonstrate
understanding of a
text, referring
explicitly to the text
as the basis for the
answers. **RI.3.1**

Students will reread
to strengthen
comprehension.

**ACADEMIC
LANGUAGE**

reread

1 Explain

Explain to students that when they read something they don't
understand in a text, they should go back and read it a second time.

- When they encounter unclear or difficult text, students can stop
  and reread that section. They may need to reread text more than
  once before they understand it.

- Students should ask themselves which parts of the text they
  don't understand, so they can focus their reading on specific
  words and phrases.

- Often, students may find that rereading will improve their
  understanding of expository texts.

2 Model Close Reading: Text Evidence

Model how rereading can help you understand what the Wright
brothers learned from their unsuccessful flights. Reread page 306
of "Firsts in Flight."

3 Guided Practice of Close Reading

Have students work in pairs to explain how other inventors used
the Wright brothers' ideas. Direct them to reread pages 306–307.
Have partners refer directly to the text for information about other
inventors' accomplishments, noting how they resemble and differ
from those of the Wright brothers.

**Go
Digital**

**View "Firsts in
Flight"**

Comprehension Strategy

Reread

Stop and think as you read. Does the text make sense? Reread to make sure you understand.

 Find Text Evidence

Do you understand what the Wright brothers learned from their unsuccessful flights? Reread page 306.

page 306

Because their first flight was not successful, the Wright brothers learned a lot about flying. As a result, they built a better glider with bigger wings in 1900. This glider did not work very well either. The brothers did not give up. That's why they experimented with a new glider in 1902. Then in 1903, they built the *Wright Flyer*, their first airplane with an engine.

Flying Firsts

By December 17, the brothers were ready to test the *Wright Flyer*. Orville started up the engines to power the plane. He controlled the plane, while Wilbur watched from the ground. The *Flyer* was launched into the sky. The plane moved in an upward direction, and the flight lasted twelve

I read that the Wright brothers' first flight was not successful. But they learned a lot about flying. Then they built a better glider with bigger wings. Now I understand why their unsuccessful flights were important.

©Heritage Images/Corbis

Your Turn

How did other inventors use the Wright brothers' ideas? Reread pages 306 and 307.

308

READING/WRITING WORKSHOP, *p. 308*

 ENGLISH LANGUAGE LEARNERS SCAFFOLD

Beginning	Intermediate	Advanced/High
Understand Help students reread the first paragraph on page 306. Point out difficult words or phrases such as *successful, did not give up,* and *engine.* Define them for students, and then guide them in connecting these words and phrases to text elements and ideas in the story. For example, ask: *What did the Wright brothers do after their first flight?* (kept trying)	**Recognize** Have students reread the first paragraph on page 306. Ask: *What did the Wright brothers do after their first flight?* (They kept trying to make a plane that would fly.) Explain that this is important because we learn that they had many failures but kept trying anyway and did not give up.	**Discuss** Have students reread the first paragraph on page 306. Elicit from students why this text is important. Ask: *Why is it important to know about the Wright brothers' failures? Turn to a partner and explain.*

 **Monitor and *Differentiate***

 Quick Check

Do students reread expository text that they do not understand? Do they reread it more than once if necessary?

↓

Small Group Instruction

If No → | Approaching Level | Reteach p. T232
| ELL | Develop p. T248

If Yes → | On Level | Review p. T240
| Beyond Level | Extend p. T244

ON-LEVEL PRACTICE BOOK pp. 183–184

Read the passage. Use the reread strategy to be sure you understand what you read.

History of Human Flight

Wanting to Fly Like Birds

5   Humans have always wanted to fly. But it took a long time
17   for them to learn how to do it. At first, they tried to copy birds.
32   They made wings out of wood. They attached the wings to their
44   arms and tried to fly. But birds and humans do not have the
57   same muscles. So the wings did not work.
65   The first big step toward human flight was the kite. The kite
77   was first made in China in 400 b.c. Some used kites for fun.
90   Others used them to test the weather. Some people wanted
101 to make flying objects that could carry people. So they made
111 balloons and gliders.

114 **Hot Air Balloons**

117   The first hot air balloon was a silk bag. The bag was filled with
131   smoke from a fire. The hot air made the balloon lighter than the
145   air around it. Because of this, the bag rose into the sky. People
158   attached a basket to the bag. Soon, they began to use it to travel.

171   **Gliders**

172   The next big step in human flight was the glider. A glider does
185   not float like a balloon. It falls to earth. But it falls so slowly that
200   it stays in the air a long time. Gliders are easier to control than
214   balloons. With gliders people could fly where they wanted.

| APPROACHING pp. 183–184 | BEYOND pp. 183–184 | ELL pp. 183–184 |

→ Comprehension Skill

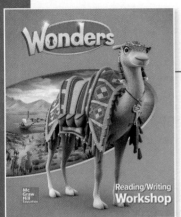

Reading/Writing Workshop

MINILESSON
10 Mins

Text Structure: Cause and Effect

Go Digital

1 Explain

Explain that history is a sequence of events. One event causes another event to happen, which in turn leads to another event. We use **cause and effect** to describe how one event leads to another.

- A cause is why something happens. An effect is the thing that happens as a result.
- To help identify causes and effects, students should look for signal words like *so, because of, as a result,* or *due to.*

Cause and effect form the sequence of an expository text by demonstrating how one event leads to another.

2 Model Close Reading: Text Evidence

Point out the second paragraph on page 305, and model identifying the effect of the weak winds in Dayton. Point out the use of the signal word *so* in the following sentence: *So they looked for a place where the winds were stronger.*

 Analytical Writing **Write About Reading: Summary** Model for students how to use the notes from the graphic organizer to summarize the sequence of the Wright brothers' journey from Dayton, Ohio, to Kitty Hawk, North Carolina, emphasizing causes and their effects.

3 Guided Practice of Close Reading

 Have students work in pairs to complete the graphic organizer for "Firsts in Flight," rereading the text to identify the sequence of events and to describe the relationships between the events in the text using causes and effects. Remind students to look for signal words that can help readers identify cause and effect.

 Analytical Writing **Write About Reading: Summary** Ask pairs to write a summary of "Firsts in Flight" using their graphic organizers. Have students include connections between the sentences and paragraphs in the text. Select pairs of students to share their summaries with the class.

Present the Lesson

OBJECTIVES

CCSS Describe the relationship between a series of historical events, scientific ideas or concepts, or steps in technical procedures in a text, using language that pertains to time, sequence, and cause/effect. **RI.3.3**

CCSS Describe the logical connection between particular sentences and paragraphs in a text (e.g., comparison, cause/effect, first/second/third in a sequence). **RI.3.8**

SKILLS TRACE

TEXT STRUCTURE

Introduce Unit 1 Week 3

Review Unit 1 Weeks 4, 6; Unit 2 Week 6; Unit 3 Weeks 5, 6; Unit 4 Weeks 3, 4; Unit 5 Weeks 5, 6; Unit 6 Weeks 3, 4, 6

Assess Units 1, 3, 4, 5, 6

Comprehension Skill

Cause and Effect

A cause is why something happens. An effect is what happens. They happen in time order. Signal words, such as *so, as a result,* and *because* help you find causes and effects.

 Find Text Evidence

On page 305 I read that the Wrights had to find a windier place to fly. This is the effect. Now I can find the cause. The wind wasn't strong enough. The signal word so helped me find the cause and effect.

Cause		Effect
First	→	So the brothers found a place where the winds were stronger.
The winds weren't strong enough.		
Next	→	
Then	→	
Finally	→	

Your Turn
COLLABORATE

Reread "Firsts in Flight." Use signal words to help you find more causes and effects. Make sure they are in time order. Fill in the graphic organizer.

Go Digital!
Use the interactive graphic organizer

309

READING/WRITING WORKSHOP, *p. 309*

ENGLISH LANGUAGE LEARNERS SCAFFOLD

ELL

Beginning

Explain To help students understand the concept, demonstrate simple cause-effect relationships, such as blowing a pencil or piece of paper from a desk onto the floor. Use the sentence frame ___ is the cause; ___ is the effect. Then relate the concept to the text: *The ___ causes a kite to fly.* (*wind*)

Intermediate

Demonstrate Comprehension Ask students: *What does a kite need to fly?* (Kites need wind.) *A glider is like a kite. It needs wind. Can you fly a kite without wind?* (no) *Dayton had no wind. So the Wright brothers had to go somewhere else to use the glider. No wind is the cause. Going somewhere else is the effect.*

Advanced/High

Discuss Have students find the cause-and-effect relationship in the second paragraph on page 305. Then have them explain how they identified the cause and the effect using signal words.

Monitor and *Differentiate*

 Quick Check

Can students fill in the graphic organizer with the causes and effects that form the text's sequence?

↓

Small Group Instruction

If No →	Approaching Level	Reteach p. T238
	ELL	Develop p. T248
If Yes →	On Level	Review p. T243
	Beyond Level	Extend p. T247

ON-LEVEL PRACTICE BOOK pp. 183–185

A. Reread the passage and answer the questions.
Possible responses provided.

1. When people made wings out of wood, why did they not work?
They did not work because birds and humans do not have the same muscles.

2. According to paragraph 2, why did people make balloons and gliders?
They made balloons and gliders because they wanted to make flying objects that could carry people.

3. According to the section "Hot Air Balloons," what caused the silk bags to rise into the sky?
They rose into the sky because they were filled with smoke, which made the balloon lighter than the air around it.

4. What was the effect of the Wright brothers reading Octave Chanute's book?
They became convinced that they could make a flying machine.

B. Work with a partner. Read the passage aloud. Pay attention to accuracy and phrasing. Stop after one minute. Fill out the chart.

	Words Read	–	Number of Errors	=	Words Correct Score
First Read		–		=	
Second Read		–		=	

APPROACHING pp. 183–185	BEYOND pp. 183–185	ELL pp. 183–185

Genre: Informational Text

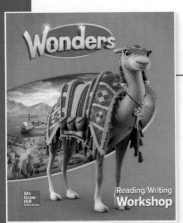

Reading/Writing Workshop

OBJECTIVES

CCSS Use text features and search tools (e.g., key words, sidebars, hyperlinks) to locate information relevant to a given topic efficiently. **RI.3.5**

CCSS Use information gained from illustrations (e.g., maps, photographs) and the words in a text to demonstrate understanding of the text (e.g., where, when, why, and how key events occur). **RI.3.7**

Recognize the characteristics and text features of expository text.

ACADEMIC LANGUAGE

• *expository*

• Cognate: *expositivo*

Expository Text

1 Explain

Explain to students that "Firsts in Flight" is an **expository text**.

- Expository text often presents causes and their effects in sequence.

- It gives facts and information to explain a topic.

- It includes text features such as headings, photographs, or sidebars.

The selection "Firsts in Flight" introduces readers to the early history of flight by presenting important achievements in chronological sequence.

2 Model Close Reading: Text Evidence

Model identifying and using the text feature on page 306 of "Firsts in Flight." Explain to students how the text features in the selection help you figure out that the text is expository.

Sidebar Point out the science experiment at the bottom of page 306. Explain that this experiment helps readers understand the testing process that early airplane inventors used.

3 Guided Practice of Close Reading

 Have pairs look at the text features in "Firsts in Flight." Partners should discuss the information they learned from each feature. Then have them share their work with the class.

Go Digital

Present the Lesson

Genre **Informational Text**

Expository Text

"Firsts in Flight" is an expository text. **Expository text:**
- May present causes and their effects in sequence
- May explain a science topic
- Includes text features such as headings, photographs, or sidebars

Find Text Evidence

I can tell that "Firsts in Flight" is an expository text. It gives facts and information about how people first started flying. It includes headings, photographs with captions, and a sidebar.

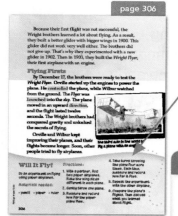
page 306

Text Features

Sidebar A sidebar gives more information about a topic. Sometimes a sidebar can be a science experiment or directions showing how to do something.

Your Turn

Look at the text features in "Firsts in Flight." Tell your partner something you learned.

310

READING/WRITING WORKSHOP, *p. 310*

✓ Quick Check

Are students able to identify expository text features in "Firsts in Flight"?

⬇

Small Group Instruction

If No →	Approaching Level	Reteach p. T232
	ELL	Develop p. T248
If Yes →	On Level	Review p. T240
	Beyond Level	Extend p. T244

ENGLISH LANGUAGE LEARNERS SCAFFOLD

ELL

Beginning

Use Visuals Point to the sidebar on page 306. Explain that sidebars usually give interesting information related to the main topic. Read the first paragraph, and explain that the sidebar explains an experiment with paper airplanes to find which plane will fly the best. Invite students to describe the sidebar in their own words, with your guidance as needed.

Intermediate

Describe Point to the sidebar. Explain that sidebars usually give us interesting information related to the main topic. Ask: *What do we learn about in this sidebar?* (how to do experiments using paper airplanes) Give students ample time to answer the question.

Advanced/High

Discuss Explain that sidebars usually give us interesting information related to the main topic. Have students talk to a partner about what they learn in this sidebar and how it gives them a better understanding of the work the Wright brothers did.

ON-LEVEL PRACTICE BOOK p. 186

How Rockets Move

A rocket is filled with fuel. When the fuel burns, gas leaves the back of the rocket. This gas moves at a very high speed. It has a lot of force. The rocket then moves forward using a basic law of nature. This law says that every action has an equal and opposite reaction. This means that the force of the moving gas has an opposite reaction. When the gas leaves the back of the rocket, it pushes the rocket in the opposite direction. This makes the rocket move forward at a very high speed.

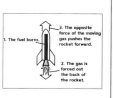
1. The fuel burns.
2. The gas is forced out the back of the rocket.
3. The opposite force of the moving gas pushes the rocket forward.

Answer the questions about the text.

1. What topic does this expository text tell about?
   It tells facts about how rockets move.

2. What text feature does this text include?
   sidebar/diagram

3. How does the text feature help you understand the text?
   Possible response: The arrows show how the gas moves the rocket.

APPROACHING p. 186	BEYOND p. 186	ELL p. 186

→ # Vocabulary Strategy

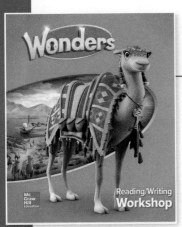

Reading/Writing Workshop

OBJECTIVES

CCSS Use sentence level context as a clue to the meaning of a word or phrase. **L.3.4a**

Use context to determine how a word with multiple meanings is being used in a sentence.

ACADEMIC LANGUAGE

multiple-meaning word

SKILLS TRACE

MULTIPLE-MEANING WORDS

Introduce Unit 1 Week 5

Review Unit 2 Week 1; Unit 4 Weeks 4, 5; Unit 5 Week 1

Assess Units 1, 4

MINILESSON 10 Mins — Context Clues

1 Explain

Explain to students that some words can be used in different ways, even when they are spelled the same and pronounced the same.

- Students should be able to distinguish **multiple-meaning words** from homophones and homonyms. A word can mean something entirely different even if it is spelled the same and pronounced the same way.

- To figure out a word's meaning, students can reread the sentence and note whether it is used as a verb, noun, adjective, or adverb.

2 Model Close Reading: Text Evidence

Model how to figure out the meaning of *well* in the sentence "This glider did not work very well either" on page 306. Use context clues in the first two sentences of the first paragraph to show that the meaning of *well* is "in a good way."

3 Guided Practice of Close Reading

Have students work in pairs to determine the meanings of *seconds* and *fly* using context clues. Have students share their answers.

> ## Use Reference Sources
>
> **Digital Dictionary** Have students check an online dictionary to clarify and compare the meanings they find there for *seconds* and *fly* with the meanings they came up with using context clues. If necessary, have students use a print dictionary or glossary to find the words. Remind students that *seconds* and *fly* have multiple meanings.
>
> Review a dictionary entry for the word *seconds*. Discuss each meaning and example sentence. Then have students review the meanings and example sentences for *fly*. Ask students to choose the meanings closest to those used in the selection for each word.

Go Digital

Present the Lesson

Vocabulary Strategy

Multiple-Meaning Words

Multiple-meaning words have more than one meaning. Find other words in the sentence to help you figure out the correct meaning of a multiple-meaning word.

 Find Text Evidence

On page 306, I know well *can mean "a deep hole with water in it" or "in a good way." The context clue* work *helps me figure out what* well *means in this sentence. I think* well *means "in a good way." The glider did not work in a good way.*

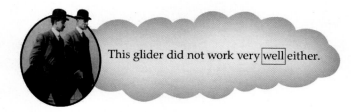

This glider did not work very well either.

Everett Collection/SuperStock

Your Turn

Find context clues. Use them to figure out the meaning of each word.
seconds, *page 306*
fly, *page 307*

311

READING/WRITING WORKSHOP, *p. 311*

A C T Access Complex Text

▶ Sentence Structure

Help students decide if *shop* is being used as a noun or a verb in "The Wright Brothers owned a bicycle *shop* in Dayton" on page 305.

- *Is* shop *a thing or an action in this sentence?* (It is a thing.) *What is the action verb in the sentence?* (owned) *Who in the sentence did the owning?* (The Wright Brothers)

- *In this sentence,* They *is the subject of the sentence.* Owned *is the predicate.* Shop, *a noun, is the object of the verb. It is what the Wright brothers owned.*

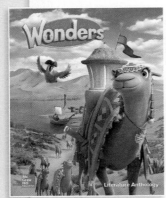

Hot Air Balloons

Literature Anthology

Text Complexity Range

Lexile

420   ▲   820
      680

TextEvaluator™

2   ▲   35
    12

What makes this text complex?
▷ **Genre**
▷ **Purpose**
▷ **Organization**
▷ **Specific Vocabulary**
▷ **Connection of Ideas**

Close Reading Routine

Read	DOK 1–2

- Identify key ideas and details about flight.
- Take notes and summarize.
- Use **A C T** prompts as needed.

Reread	DOK 2–3

- Analyze the text, craft, and structure.
- Use *Close Reading Companion,* pp. 121–123.

Integrate	DOK 4

- Integrate knowledge and ideas.
- Make text-to-text connections.
- Use the Integrate lesson.

Genre • Expository Text

Reprinted from Hot Air Balloons by Dana Meachen Rau with permission of Marshall Cavendish.

Essential Question
How are people able to fly?
Read to find out what it's like
to fly in a hot air balloon.

Go Digital!

342

A C T Access Complex Text

▷ Genre

Point out that the photographs in a nonfiction text can also give information.

- *What is the green in the photograph?* (trees and grass)

- *What else can you see?* (mountains, houses)

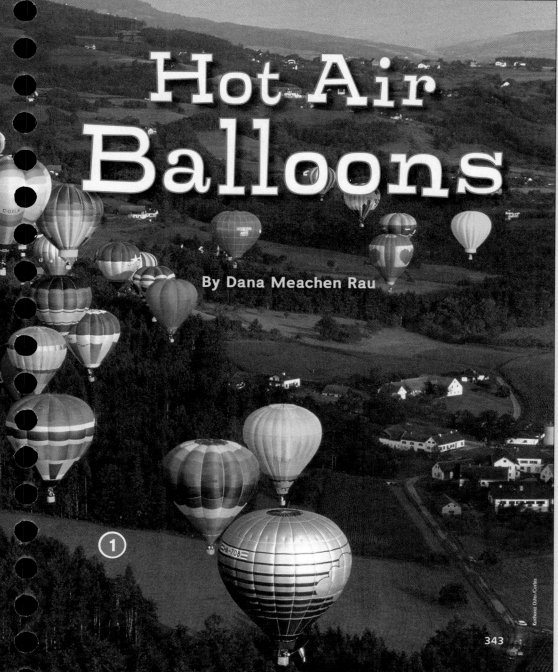

Hot Air Balloons

By Dana Meachen Rau

①

343

LITERATURE ANTHOLOGY, pp. 342–343

Ask students to read the title and the headings, and to preview the illustrations. Have a student read aloud the Essential Question. Ask them to predict how the selection will help them answer the Essential Question.

Note Taking:
Use the Graphic Organizer

Remind students to take notes as they read. Have them fill in the graphic organizer on **Your Turn Practice Book** page 182. Ask them to record the main idea and key details of each section. They can also note words they don't understand and questions they have.

① **Text Features: Photographs**

Look at the photograph on pages 342–343. Turn to a partner and talk about what you see. What is in the air? (hot air balloons) What does the photograph teach you about hot air balloons? (It shows what they look like, how big they are, how high they fly, what kind of view they offer, and that they are sometimes flown in large groups.)

- *What is helping the balloons stay in the air?* (the wind)

- *Based on the photograph, do people ride these balloons? How do you know?* (People ride hot air balloons. You can see people sitting in the baskets under the balloons.)

Read

2 Skill: Cause and Effect

On page 344, what events cause the balloon to take off? (A strong fan is used to blow up the balloon. A burner heats the air inside the balloon. The balloon overcomes gravity and rises from the ground.) **Add these events to your graphic organizer.**

Cause	➡	Effect
First: A strong fan is aimed into the opening of the huge balloon.	➡	The bag starts to grow into a balloon.
Next: A burner heats the air in the balloon.	➡	The balloon rises above the houses and trees.

3 Use Text Features: Captions

COLLABORATE

Turn to a partner and look at the photographs and the description of each. What information can you learn about balloons from the captions on pages 344 and 345 that is not in the main text? (The burner heats the air so that it becomes lighter. The balloon can then rise. The reader can also see what a bird's-eye view looks like when the balloon is the air.)

Build Vocabulary page 344

fabric: woven cloth

inflates: fills with air

Ready for Take Off

2   It is early morning. People unload a huge colorful bag in an open field. They turn on a strong fan. They aim it into the opening of the bag. The bag starts to grow. It's a balloon! But it isn't the kind of balloon you get at a birthday party. This balloon is taller than sixteen men!

  Suddenly, fire roars into the balloon. It starts to rise. People climb into the basket under the balloon while others hold it steady. Then the balloon takes off, carrying its **passengers** into the sky. They float higher than the houses, higher than the trees, up to where the birds fly.

  Can you imagine what it would be like to float so high? Cars would look like tiny dots. You'd be able to see for miles. The wind would be your guide. What would it feel like to ride with the wind?

Hot air is lighter than cool air. A burner heats the air in a balloon so it will rise from the ground.

The fabric of a balloon slowly inflates until it is full.

© A3609 Daniel Karmann/dpa/Corbis (r) Carl & Ann Purcell/Corbis

344

A C T   Access Complex Text

▶ Purpose

Because page 344 is written in narrative form, students may not realize that this text gives key details about how a hot air balloon is launched. Help students focus on these details. Remind them to use text features such as photos and captions.

- *Look at the first paragraph on page 344. Why do the people need a fan?* (to blow up the balloon)

- *How does fire help the balloon fly?* (Fire heats the air. Since hot air is lighter than cold air, the balloon rises.)

Balloon riders get a bird's-eye view.

③

345

LITERATURE ANTHOLOGY, pp. 344-345

Reread *Close Reading Companion*

Author's Craft: Imagery

Reread the first paragraph of page 344. How does the author help you visualize what a balloon launch is like? (The author sets a scene, as if it were happening now. Readers can visualize a huge and colorful bag that gets bigger and becomes a balloon.)

Author's Craft: Word Choice

Authors choose descriptive words to add stronger meaning to a sentence and help the readers better understand what they are reading. Reread the second paragraph on page 344. Why is *roars into* a better word choice than *goes into*? (You can hear and imagine the word *roar* and the fire entering the balloon. *Roar* makes the fire seem like a living creature.)

ELL Point out the top of the balloon on page 345.

* Say it with me: *hot air balloon*

* Read the caption with students. *What do birds see when they fly?* (top of houses, cars, trees) *Is this what you see in a hot air balloon?* (Yes)

Read

4 Skill: Cause and Effect

What historical events had an effect on ballooning? (kite flying, stories, drawings, lighting a fire under paper and silk)
What was the effect of the Montgolfier experiment? (the first hot air balloon) What clue word shows us the cause and its effect? (So) Add these sequence of events and the effects to your graphic organizer.

Cause	→	Effect
First: People throughout history have always wanted to fly.	→	The Chinese fly kites, Greeks tell stories of flying, and people draw pictures.
Next: The Montgolfier brothers experiment with fire and paper.	→	The hot smoke makes the paper float and rise.
Then: The brothers make a balloon out of paper and silk.	→	The first hot air balloon has a successful flight.
Now:	→	

Jean-Pierre Blanchard crossed the English Channel from England to France in a balloon.

346

A C T Access Complex Text

▶ Genre

Remind students that when they read expository text, they can get information from text and features such as headings, illustrations, and captions. Help students connect the features and text on page 347.

- *What do the two illustrations on page 347 have in common?* (They show two ideas people in history had about how to fly.)

- *How do the illustrations help you understand the text under the heading "Ballooning History"?* (They show what the first paragraph describes: ideas people in history had about how to fly.)

- *What do these illustrations have to do with the history of balloons?* (Balloons are another idea that people had about how to fly.)

Ballooning History

Throughout history, people have wondered what it would be like to fly. The Chinese watched their kites move with the wind. The Greeks told stories of men who made wings to help them fly. People drew pictures of flying machines. But flying seemed **impossible**.

In the late 1700s in France, the Montgolfier [mont-GOL-fee-ay] brothers noticed something about paper and fire. If paper got too close to the flames, it burned. But they saw that if the paper was above the fire, the hot smoke seemed to make it float and rise. So in 1783 they made a balloon out of paper and silk. They lit a fire under it. People were amazed when the Montgolfier brothers sent a sheep, a duck, and a rooster as passengers in this first hot air balloon. The animals had a successful flight. Soon after, two men rode in a Montgolfier balloon. They traveled more than 5 miles for 25 minutes.

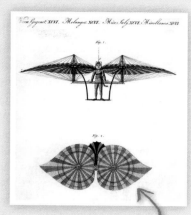

Early inventors drew pictures of unbelievable flying machines.

Greek stories tell of Daedalus and his son Icarus, who made their own flying wings.

347

LITERATURE ANTHOLOGY, pp. 346–347

Read

5 Strategy: Reread

Teacher Think Aloud I know that when I read nonfiction text, I can get information from different features on the page. To make sure I understand the details of how balloons travel, I can reread the text and look at the illustrations and their captions. I can reread the first paragraph on page 347 and retell in my own words that many people tried to fly. The pictures show the different ways that they tried. I can look again on page 347 to see that in 1783, the first balloon was made in France. The image on page 346 shows a successful balloon flight.

ELL Students may have difficulty with the concept of ballooning. Explain that ballooning is the act of riding in a hot air balloon.

- Demonstrate floating and rising for students. Then have students point to and identify the image of ballooning.

- *What happens when fire is lit under the balloon?* (It rises.)

Read

6 Skill: Cause and Effect

Look on pages 348–349 to find what caused ballooning to become popular, and the effect of the first airplane flight. Add these events to the graphic organizer.

Cause	→	Effect
First: People throughout history have always wanted to fly.	→	The Chinese fly kites, Greeks tell stories of flying, and people draw pictures.
Next: The Montgolfier brothers experiment with fire and paper.	→	The hot smoke makes the paper float and rise.
Then: The brothers make a balloon out of paper and silk.	→	The first hot air balloon has a successful flight.

Cause	→	Effect
Then: Jean-Pierre Blanchard flies a gas balloon over the English Channel and in America.	→	Ballooning becomes very popular.
Now: In the early 1900s, the Wright Brothers fly the first airplane.	→	People ride airplanes for travel.

Build Vocabulary page 348

scout: to observe and analyze a situation before taking action

Other French people made balloons filled with a **gas** called hydrogen. Hydrogen can rise like hot air does. In 1785 Jean-Pierre Blanchard flew a gas balloon over the English Channel, a waterway between England and France. He also flew the first balloon in America. George Washington watched Blanchard's balloon **launch** in 1793 from Pennsylvania on its way to New Jersey.

Ballooning became very **popular**. Pilots tried flying balloons higher and farther than ever before. People found uses for balloons during war. Balloons could carry messages. They could spy from the sky.

Soldiers used balloons to scout out the battlefield.

The stiff framework of an airship helped the balloon keep its shape.

(t) Corbis (b) The Print Collector/HIP/The Image Works

348

A C T Access Complex Text

▶ Specific Vocabulary

Point out the word *spy* in the last sentence on page 348.

- *Identify context clues to figure out what the word* spy *means.* (uses for balloons during war, from the sky)

- *What made balloons perfect for spying?* (They were up in the sky, and made it possible for people to see things they could not see on land.)

The Wright brothers' first airplane gave people another way to travel the sky.

By the early 1900s, **airships** flew in the sky. An airship had a gas-filled balloon with a frame to give it a sausage shape. The basket in which people rode, called the gondola, was enclosed and often very large. It also had an **engine** and **propellers**. Pilots could steer these new types of balloons in the direction they wished to go. Some airships were used in war. Others were used for travel and the gondolas looked like fancy hotels inside.

In the early 1900s, the Wright brothers also flew the first airplane. After that, people rode airplanes for travel instead.

But people didn't forget about balloons. They built gas balloons that could study the weather and even travel around the world. In 1960, modern hot air balloons were developed by Ed Yost, and were later used for sport. Today, people join hot air balloon clubs. Teams hold balloon races. Passengers take rides in the sky to see the beautiful land below.

STOP AND CHECK

Reread Why were airships better than hot air balloons? Reread page 349 to find the answer.

349

LITERATURE ANTHOLOGY, pp. 348–349

STOP AND CHECK

Reread How were airships better than hot air balloons?

Teacher Think Aloud There is information about airships in the first paragraph of page 349. How can we tell that they were better than hot air balloons?

Prompt students to apply the strategy in a Think Aloud by first rereading and then retelling the text in their own words. Have them reread with a partner.

Student Think Aloud I can reread to see that the airship had an engine and propeller. Airships were better because pilots could steer them in the direction they wanted. Airships could be used for war and travel.

Reread

Author's Craft: Text Structure

The word *but* is used to signal a change in what the author is stating. How does the author use *but* in the last paragraph on page 349? (The author describes changes in flying, yet wants to tell the reader that people still use hot air balloons.)

CONNECT TO CONTENT
FORCES OF GRAVITY

A balloon rises when it is filled with hot air because hot air is lighter than cold air. Without the force of gravity, the hot air balloon would continue to rise and would not be able to return to the ground. The force of the air pushing up on the balloon and the force of gravity pulling down on the balloon keeps the balloon in the air at a normal height. The balloon comes down to the ground when the hot air inside of the balloon is let out.

STEM

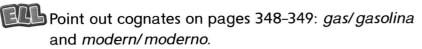

Point out cognates on pages 348–349: *gas/ gasolina* and *modern/ moderno*.

- Point out the different ways people would fly. (balloons, airship, airplane)

- *Do we still use hot air balloons today?* (yes) *How else can we fly?* (airplanes, helicopters)

Read

STOP AND CHECK

Reread What causes a balloon to rise in the air? Reread page 351 to find the answer. Turn to a partner and tell in your own words how balloons leave the ground.

Student Think Aloud I will reread page 351 to find out what causes a balloon to rise in the air. I read that physics can help us understand how things move. The burner makes the air inside a balloon hotter and lighter than the air outside the balloon. Since hot air is lighter than cold air, the hot air rises and the balloon can take off.

7 Skill: Cause and Effect

The words *so* and *because* are usually signal words to help show the relationships between causes and effects. What is the effect of heating the air inside the balloon? (The balloon rises.)

The burner heats the air inside the envelope to inflate the balloon.

350

A C T Access Complex Text

▶ Specific Vocabulary

Review with students that authors often provide definitions or restatements in the surrounding sentences to clarify the meanings of unfamiliar words.

- Point out the word *physics* on page 351. *What does* physics *mean?* (a science that helps us understand how things move) Have a volunteer read aloud the sentence that defines *physics*.

- Identify context clues to figure out the meaning of *valve* using the image and the caption on page 351. (a tool that lets hot air out)

At a balloon festival many balloons take off at the same time and fill the sky with color.

The parachute valve in the top of a balloon lets out hot air.

How Hot Air Balloons Work

The science called **physics** helps us understand how hot air balloons rise in the sky. Physics is the science of how things move.

Air is all around you. You can't see it. But you can feel it when the wind blows. Air also has **weight**. Hot air is light. Cold air is heavy. That means that hot air rises up in the sky. Cold air sits closer to the ground.

7 A hot air balloon works because the hot air trapped inside the balloon is lighter than the cold air outside the balloon. So the balloon rises up into the sky!

> **STOP AND CHECK**
>
> Reread What causes a balloon to rise in the air? Reread page 351 to find the answer.

351

(t) Kevin Fleming/Corbis (b) Jason Todd/Photonica/Getty Images

LITERATURE ANTHOLOGY, *pp. 350–351*

Reread

Genre: Nonfiction

COLLABORATE

The purpose of nonfiction text is often to explain something. What does the author explain on pages 350–351? (How hot air balloons work.) Turn to a partner and talk about the features of nonfiction you notice on pages 350–351. How do they help you understand the text? (The heading tells you what the section is about. The photographs and captions help you to picture the information that is described in the text. These images show us that the events actually happened, and how.)

Build Vocabulary page 351

valve: a device that opens and closes to let air or liquid flow through

ELL Have students use the photograph on page 350 to identify and label the parts of the balloon that helps it to fly. Then demonstrate the terms *light* and *heavy* by using your desk and a piece of paper as examples.

Hot air is ____ (light).

Cold air is ____ (heavy).

Read

8 Vocabulary: Multiple-Meaning Words

What word in the first and second paragraphs is a multiple-meaning word? (envelope) What is its meaning in the selection? (the big balloon) What other meaning does it have? (paper that is used to hold a letter)

9 Skill: Cause and Effect

What causes the balloon to sink toward the ground? (The pilot pulls a cord.) Then what happens? (The parachute valve opens and some of the hot air is let out. The balloon stops rising. As more hot air is let out, the balloon comes down.)

Crowds wait for the big launch.

Sean Cayton/The Image Works

352

8 The big balloon is called an envelope. Most envelopes are larger on the top and narrower on the bottom. They come in all colors. The envelope is made out of strong, light cloth called nylon.

Just like a paper envelope holds a letter, the balloon envelope holds the hot air. Pilots heat the air in the balloon with a burner. The burner sends out a huge flame into the envelope. When the balloon is full of hot air, it starts lifting off the ground.

A basket hangs below the burner. This basket carries the pilot and the passengers. The basket is light, but strong enough to carry several people. Some baskets can carry up to twenty passengers at a time if the balloon is big enough to lift them.

A C T Access Complex Text

▶ Connection of Ideas

Students may have difficulty understanding how a hot air balloon rises and falls.

- *Reread the last paragraph on page 352. What is the relationship between the amount of hot air in a balloon and the weight that the balloon can lift into the air?* (The more hot air a balloon holds, the more weight it can lift in the air.)

- *How does letting out hot air make the balloon sink?* (Since there is less hot air, the balloon cannot keep the same weight in the air.)

When the pilot wants the balloon to go up, he fires up the burner. This can be very loud. The flame grows bigger. It heats the air in the envelope so the balloon will rise. **9**

When the pilot wants the balloon to go down, he pulls a cord that lets out some of the hot air. The cord opens the parachute valve. The parachute valve is a cut-out circle of nylon in the top of the balloon. The balloon stops rising. As more hot air escapes, the balloon sinks toward the ground.

A basket hangs below the balloon to hold passengers.

353

LITERATURE ANTHOLOGY, *pp. 352–353*

10 **Skill: Make Inferences**

What would happen if there were a hole in the envelope? Use text evidence to support your inference. (Paragraph 1 says the flame heats the air in the envelope. The heated air lifts the balloon. If the hot air escapes, the envelope would not be able to hold the hot air.) Would the balloon be able to lift off the ground? (No)

Reread   *Close Reading Companion*

Text Structure: Sequence

How does the way the author organizes the text help you understand how a pilot flies a hot air balloon? (The author explains the process in sequence, step by step: how a pilot fills the envelope of a hot air balloon with hot air, and how the pilot makes the balloon rise and sink.)

ELL Demonstrate the way a hot air balloon works by using a balloon or drawing pictures on the board. Show students what happens as you start taking some of the air out of the balloon. Use the phrases *air escapes, stops rising,* and *sinks toward the ground.*

• Have students use the phrases to complete the following sentence frames:

The ____ (air escapes) *from the balloon.*

The balloon ____ (stops rising/sinks toward the ground).

Read

11 **Vocabulary: Multiple-Meaning Words**

What word in the second paragraph is a multiple-meaning word? (current) What is its meaning in the selection? (path of wind) What other meaning does it have? (right now, today, modern)

12 **Ask and Answer Questions**

Generate a question of your own about the text and share it with a partner. For example, you might ask, "Why is it so important for pilots to check the weather before ballooning?" To find the answer, reread page 354. (Pilots need help from the wind to move the balloon. Too much wind and dark, cloudy weather can be dangerous. It needs to be a clear and calm day to balloon.)

Up to the Wind

You turn your handlebars to steer your bike. But a pilot can't steer a balloon. He can make it fly higher or lower, but he can't make it go from side to side. He needs some help from the wind.

Wind moves in different directions. Wind might be moving one way high in the sky. It might be moving another way lower in the sky. **11** These paths of wind are called **currents**. A pilot uses these currents to move the balloon from place to place. He moves the balloon up and down with the burner and parachute valve. When he finds a current going in the **direction** he wants to go, he lets the balloon ride the wind right or left.

Balloon pilots use wind currents to push them in the direction they want to go.

354

A C T Access Complex Text

▶ Organization

Review with students that one way authors organize information is by cause and effect and time order. Looking for signal words, such as *because* and *so*, can help readers recognize causes and effects and put important events in order.

• How do currents affect how the balloon moves?

(The pilot uses the currents to move the balloon in the right direction.)

• *What causes pilots to always check the weather?* (Pilots cannot control how the balloon moves, and need to make sure the wind is calm and the air is cool.)

Pilots can't control how fast or how slow the balloon moves. That's **controlled** by the wind. But too much wind can be dangerous. It can tear the balloon or send it in the wrong direction.

So pilots always check the weather. A day with clear skies and not too much wind is best for ballooning. They often launch right after the sun comes up when the wind is calm and the air is cool. They can also launch in the evening, but must land before the sun sets.

Balloons don't usually land in the same place they started. A pilot talks to his crew on the ground with a radio. They look for a safe place to set the balloon down. The crew meets the balloon when it lands. They will let the air out of the balloon and pack it up again.

Riding a hot air balloon is an adventure. Where will the wind take you?

STOP AND CHECK

Summarize How does the wind cause a hot air balloon to fly? Tell what you learned on pages 354 and 355.

LITERATURE ANTHOLOGY, *pp. 354–355*

STOP AND CHECK

Summarize **How does the wind affect a hot air balloon flight?** (The pilot must use the wind currents to control the direction the balloon travels. Wind can also be dangerous. It can tear the balloon, or make it go in the wrong direction.)

Return to Purposes Review students' predictions and purposes for reading. Ask them to use text evidence to answer the Essential Question. (To fly in a hot-air balloon, pilots take off by filling the balloon with hot air from a burner. They can't steer the balloon, so they float with the wind. People can enjoy the ride by sitting in the basket below the balloon and floating above the land.)

Reread   *Close Reading Companion*

Author's Craft: Direction Words

How does the author use words and phrases to help you see how hot air balloons move? (The phrase *ride the wind* helps me picture the way the balloons move. The author uses direction words, such as *higher or lower, side to side, up and down, right or left* to tell how pilots use wind currents to push hot air balloons in the direction they want to go.)

- Why is hot air ballooning always an adventure? (The pilot and passengers need to follow the wind to move.)

ELL Point out that *adventure* is a cognate (*aventura*). Work with students to make a list of *adventures*. Then have them circle the *adventures* they have experienced.

- *Have you been hot air ballooning? Would you like to go hot air ballooning? Why is hot air ballooning an adventure?* (It is exciting, scary, and fun.)

Read

About the Author

Dana Meachen Rau

Have students read the biography of the author. Ask:

- Why do you think Dana Meachen Rau chose to write about hot air balloons?
- How do the photographs and captions help the reader to better understand what Dana Meachen Rau is describing?

Author's Purpose

To Inform

Review with students that when authors write to inform, they may include photographs, diagrams, and captions to explain the topic. The author used the captions to give the reader additional information about hot air balloons and the history of flying.

Reread

Author's Craft

Explain that authors describe events by adding details that help the reader better understand and picture the information. These details also make the text more interesting. What descriptive details in the selection can you find that helps you to visualize the way the balloon works? (On page 344, the author describes how a hot air balloon gets ready for takeoff by re-creating the scene.)

About the Author

As a child, **Dana Meachen Rau** drew pictures everywhere. She illustrated the family's mailbox and the walls of their garage! Then her father brought her big stacks of paper so she could write and draw on them. That was the beginning of Dana's love for writing. Today, she has written more than 200 books for children and young adults. Besides fiction stories, Dana has written nonfiction books on many topics such as nature, cooking, and science. She continues to write every day.

Author's Purpose

The author uses many photographs and captions in *Hot Air Balloons*. How do these text features help you understand what you read?

356

LITERATURE ANTHOLOGY, *pp. 356–357*

Respond to the Text

Summarize

Tell the important ideas
and details that you
learned about hot air
balloons. The details from
your Cause and Effect
chart may help you
summarize.

Cause	→	Effect
First	→	
Next	→	
Then	→	
Finally	→	

Write

How does the way the author organizes the text in
this selection help you understand how people are
able to fly? Use these sentence frames to focus your
discussion.

> The author helps me understand how hot air
> balloons fly by . . .
> She also uses words and phrases to . . .
> The way the text is organized helps me . . .

Make Connections

Why do you think people like to ride in hot air
balloons? **ESSENTIAL QUESTION**

In what ways are hot air balloons a good way to fly?
In what ways are they not so good? **TEXT TO WORLD**

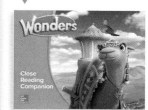
©Kelly Harriger/Corbis

357

Integrate

Make Connections
COLLABORATE

Essential Question <u>Answer:</u> People like to experience the
adventure of flying and they like to see what the land looks
like from high up in the sky. Some people enjoy being in
balloon races. <u>Evidence:</u> On page 347, I read that people
have dreamed of flying throughout history. On page 349, I
read that teams race balloons, and that passengers ride in
balloons to see the beautiful land below.

Text to World Responses will vary, but encourage students
to cite text evidence.

Respond to the Text

Read

Summarize

Tell students they will use the information from
their Cause and Effect Chart to summarize. As
I read *Hot Air Balloons,* I collected key details
and figured out the cause and effect of each
section. To summarize, I will paraphrase, or
reword, the most important details.

Reread

Analyze the Text

After students summarize
the selection, have them
reread to develop a
deeper understanding of the text and answer
the questions on **Close Reading Companion**
pages 121–123. For students who need support
in citing text evidence, use the Reread
prompts on pages T217C–T217L.

Write About the Text

Review the writing prompt and sentence
frames. Remind students to use responses from
the **Close Reading Companion** to support
their answers. For a full lesson on writing a
response using text evidence, see page T222.

<u>Answer:</u> The author explains the science
behind the balloons' ability to rise and
stay afloat. She describes the process as a
sequence. <u>Evidence:</u> On pages 344 and 345,
the text provides descriptive details of the
balloon being filled with hot air and floating
in the air. On 354, I learned how pilots use air
currents to carry the balloon in the direction
they want to go.

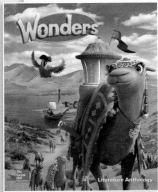

"Bellerophon and Pegasus"

Literature Anthology

Text Complexity Range

Lexile

420 ▲ 820
640

TextEvaluator™

2 ▲ 35
20

What makes this text complex?
▶ **Prior Knowledge**
▶ **Genre**

Compare Texts

As students read and reread "Bellerophon and Pegasus," encourage them to take notes and think about the Essential Question: *How are people able to fly?* Tell students to think about how this text compares with *Hot Air Balloons*.

1 **Skill: Cause and Effect**

How did Pegasus help Bellerophon to defeat the Chimera? (They flew above the monster so it could not catch them. Then Bellerophon swung his sword three times until the monster fell.)

Reread   *Close Reading Companion*
▼
Author's Craft: Word Choice

How does the author help you visualize how Bellerophon and Pegasus defeat the Chimera? (The author uses action verbs, such as *roared, hissed, shook, shot, flew, swooping, lunged, missed, swung,* and *fell* to help me visualize each character's part in the battle.)

Genre · Myth

Compare Texts
Read about how a hero finds a way to fly.

Bellerophon and Pegasus
A Greek Myth

Bellerophon (buh-LAIR-uh-fawn) lived long ago in Greece. He wanted to marry King Iobates's (ee-oh-BAH-tees-ez) daughter. But the king wanted to test Bellerophon first. He commanded him to defeat the Chimera (kigh-MIR-uh), a terrible monster. It had a lion's head, a goat's head, and a giant snake for a tail. It was attacking helpless people across the kingdom.

Bellerophon worried about his task. How could one man stop the Chimera? He asked the goddess Athena for help. In a dream, she showed him where to find the flying horse Pegasus.

358

A C T Access Complex Text

▶ **Prior Knowledge**

In Greek mythology, Athena was the goddess of wisdom and war victory. Athena helped Bellerophon with a strategy that would help him defeat the terrible monster. She gave him the golden bridle, a harness used on horses. He used it to capture Pegasus, so Pegasus would help him.

Bellerophon woke up from the dream holding a golden bridle. It shone as brightly as the sun!

Bellerophon caught Pegasus with the golden bridle and leaped onto the creature's back. Pegasus snorted and stamped his hooves. He stretched his mighty wings with a strong **motion**. Then he carried his new master up, up, up, into the sky. They were in **flight**!

Bellerophon and Pegasus soared and circled above the countryside as they hunted the Chimera. At last they found the dreadful beast.

The monster's heads roared and hissed so loudly that the ground shook. Fire shot from the monster's mouths. Pegasus flew swiftly around the Chimera, swooping down and away. Again and again the monster lunged at the flying horse and his rider. Each time it missed them. Bellerophon swung his sword with all his might, three times. The monster fell.

Bellerophon and Pegasus flew back to King Iobates. To prove his victory, Bellerophon brought King Iobates a strand of lion's mane, a snake's scale, and a goat's horn from the Chimera.

At last King Iobates agreed to let Bellerophon marry his daughter. Everyone in the kingdom was invited to the wedding feast. And Pegasus got a golden bucket filled with the finest oats in the land.

1

Make Connections

? Why was Bellerophon able to fly?
ESSENTIAL QUESTION

Compare flying in this myth with other stories you have read. TEXT TO TEXT

359

LITERATURE ANTHOLOGY, *pp. 358–359*

Read

Summarize

Guide students to summarize the selection.

Reread

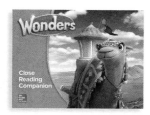

Analyze the Text

After students read and summarize, have them reread to develop a deeper understanding of the text by annotating and answering questions on pages 124–126 of the **Close Reading Companion.**

Integrate

Make Connections

Essential Question Answer: Bellerophon was able to fly because he caught Pegasus, a flying horse, and jumped onto his back. Evidence: On page 358, the goddess Athena showed Bellerophon in a dream where to find Pegasus. On page 359, Bellerophon captured Pegasus with the bridle and leaped onto his back. Then Pegasus flew into the air, carrying Bellerophon.

Text to Text Responses may vary, but encourage students to cite text evidence from other texts they've read.

▶ Genre

Explain to students that this text is a myth, a made-up story that explains why things are the way they are. These stories usually include characters with supernatural qualities.

- *Where does this myth take place?* (Greece)
- *Which characters have supernatural qualities?* (Pegasus, the Chimera, Athena)

ELL Have students look at the image of the Chimera.

- *What animals can you see?* (lion, goat, snake)
- *Was Bellerophon worried?* (yes) *Who would help him?* (Pegasus)

→ Phonics/Fluency

MINILESSON 20 Mins ## Homophones

Go Digital

Homophones

Present the Lesson

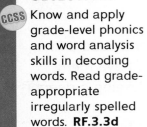

Firsts in Flight

View "Firsts in Flight"

OBJECTIVES

CCSS Know and apply grade-level phonics and word analysis skills in decoding words. Read grade-appropriate irregularly spelled words. **RF.3.3d**

CCSS Read on-level prose and poetry orally with accuracy, appropriate rate, and expression on successive readings. **RF.3.4b**

Rate: 82–102 WCPM

ACADEMIC LANGUAGE

accuracy

Refer to the sound transfers chart in the **Language Transfers Handbook** to identify sounds that do not transfer in Spanish, Cantonese, Vietnamese, Hmong, and Korean.

1 Explain

Tell students that words that sound alike but are spelled differently and have different meanings are called *homophones*.

2 Model

Write the sentence *I blew the blue horn.* on the board and then read it aloud. Underline *blew* and *blue*. Model how to say each word. Tell students that these words are homophones. Point out the different spellings and then give a meaning for each word.

3 Guided Practice

Display these sentences. Help students identify the homophones in each sentence. Guide students as they underline the homophones and give the meaning of each word. Identify words with irregular spellings (*ate, to, two, weight, write, your*).

Jon ate supper at eight o'clock.

We rowed the canoe to the bank and hauled it onto the road.

I will write my name on the right side of the paper.

Two of my friends will go to the store, too.

I will wait while you check the weight of the fruit.

You're going to be surprised when you see your gift!

Read Multisyllabic Words

Transition to Longer Words Help students transition to reading longer homophones. Draw a T-chart on the board.
In the first column write *aloud, sealing, flower, weather,* and *higher*. In the second column, write *allowed, ceiling, flour, whether,* and *hire*. Explain that the words in columns 1 and 2 are homophones.

Point to the first column and have students chorally read the words. Ask students to use each word in a sentence. Repeat with the words in the second column. Point out the homophones with irregular spellings. Have students add them to the word wall.

r-Controlled Vowel Syllables

1 Explain

When a vowel is followed by the letter *r*, the *r* changes the vowel's sound.

* In a word that has more than one syllable, both the vowel and the letter *r* appear in the same syllable because they act as a team to make the vowel sound.

2 Model

Write and say the words *person, purple,* and *sunburn.* Have students repeat the words. Underline the *r*-controlled vowel in each word. Model drawing a line to divide each word into syllables: *per/son, pur/ple, sun/burn.*

3 Guided Practice

Write the words *hammer, garlic, artist, turtle, report, charming, corner,* and *restore* on the board. Have students read each word. Guide students to underline the *r*-controlled vowel in each word and then divide each word into syllables.

Accuracy

Explain/Model Explain that reading with accuracy means saying each word correctly and not leaving out any words or sentences. Using knowledge of sounds and spellings and the context can help readers accurately pronounce unfamiliar or irregularly spelled words.

Model accuracy by reading page 305 of "Firsts in Flight." Point out the importance of correctly pronouncing the names of places and dates.

Practice/Apply Have student partners take turns reading sentences aloud with accuracy. Help students improve their accuracy by guiding them as they read any unfamiliar or irregularly spelled words.

Daily Fluency Practice **FLUENCY**

Students can practice fluency using **Your Turn Practice Book.**

Monitor and *Differentiate*

 Quick Check

Can students identify words that are homophones? Can students read words with *r*-controlled vowel syllables? Can students read fluently?

Small Group Instruction

If No →	Approaching Level	Reteach pp. T232, T234
	ELL	Develop p. T250
If Yes →	On Level	Review p. T240
	Beyond Level	Extend p. T244

ON-LEVEL PRACTICE BOOK p. 188

A. Circle the correct homophone to complete each sentence. Write the word on the line.

1. I think ___your___ report was very interesting.
   (your)   you're

2. We slowly ___rowed___ the canoe down the river.
   road   (rowed)

3. Do you think ___they're___ going to be here on time?
   their   (they're)

4. I found the missing ___piece___ of the jigsaw puzzle.
   (piece)   peace

5. I plan to buy the game once it goes on ___sale___.
   sail   (sale)

B. Read the words in each row. Underline the word that has an *r*-controlled vowel syllable. Then circle the two letters that make the *r*-controlled vowel sound.

1. people   really   per(son)
2. sh(ar)pen   slowing   safety
3. willow   w(or)king   waiting
4. h(or)ses   homemade   hopeful
5. sudden   sprouting   surprise

| APPROACHING p. 188 | BEYOND p. 188 | ELL p. 188 |

→ Write to Sources

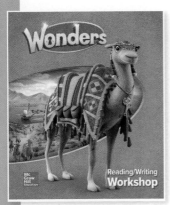

Wonders
Reading/Writing Workshop

Reading/Writing Workshop

OBJECTIVES

CCSS Write informative/explanatory texts to examine a topic and convey ideas and information clearly. Provide a concluding statement or section. **W.3.2d**

ACADEMIC LANGUAGE

conclusion, author's purpose, main idea, summarized

Go Digital

U4W4 Organization: Strong Conclusions

DAY 1

Writing Fluency

Write to a Prompt Provide students with the prompt: *Write about Orville and Wilbur Wright.* Have students share their ideas. *What did Orville and Wilbur Wright build?* When students finish sharing ideas, have them write continuously for eleven minutes in their Writer's Notebook. If students stop writing, encourage them to keep going.

 When students finish writing, have them work with a partner to compare ideas and make sure that they both have a clear understanding of the topic.

Genre Writing

Poetry pp. T350–T355

Fourth Week Focus: Over the course of the week, focus on the following stages of the writing process:

Expert Model Discuss the Expert Model found online at Writer's Workspace. Work with students to identify the features of poetry.

Prewrite Teach the minilesson on ideas. Analyze the Model Graphic Organizer found online at Writer's Workspace. Provide blank Graphic Organizers found online at Writer's Workspace, and have students use the organizers to brainstorm ideas for their own poems.

DAY 2

Write to the Reading/Writing Workshop Text

Analyze the Prompt Read aloud the first paragraph on page 304 of the **Reading/Writing Workshop**. Ask: *What is the prompt asking?* (to explain how the Wright brothers helped people fly) Say: *Let's reread to find details about the Wright brothers' experiments. We can note text evidence.*

Analyze Text Evidence Display Graphic Organizer 37 in Writer's Workspace. Say: *Let's see how one student, Mina, took notes to answer the prompt. She notes that the Wright brothers had dreamed of flying since their father gave them a toy helicopter.* Guide the class through the rest of Mina's notes.

Analyze the Student Model Explain how Mina used text evidence from her notes to write a response to the prompt.

- **Focus on a Topic** The topic is the main idea or subject of the writing. Mina introduces her topic in the first sentence. Trait: Ideas

- **Develop a Topic** Writers develop their topics through supporting details. Mina used facts from "Firsts in Flight" to develop her topic. Compare the text evidence in Mina's notes with the details in her writing. Trait: Ideas

- **Strong Conclusion** A good conclusion often restates the most important idea. Mina's conclusion clearly states how the Wright brothers helped people fly. Trait: Organization

For additional practice with organization and strong conclusions, assign **Your Turn Practice Book** page 189.

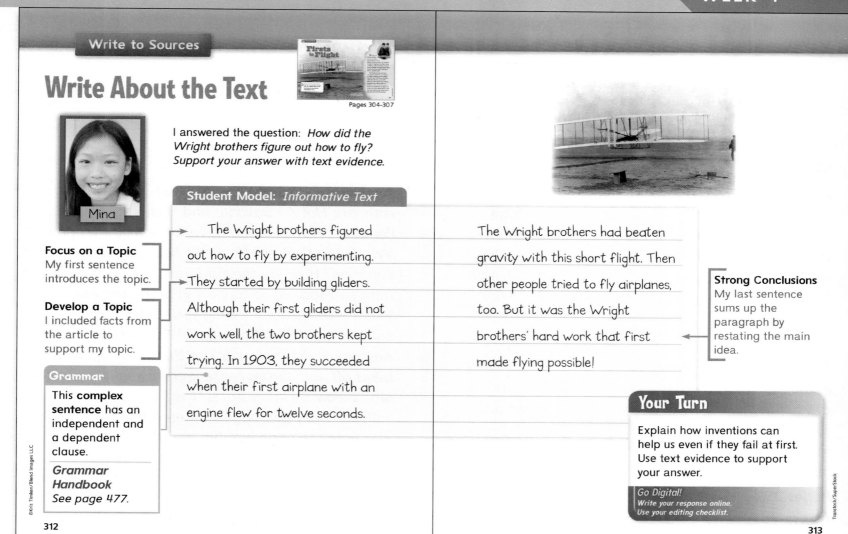

Write to Sources

Write About the Text

Firsts in Flight
Pages 304–307

Mina

I answered the question: *How did the Wright brothers figure out how to fly? Support your answer with text evidence.*

Student Model: *Informative Text*

Focus on a Topic
My first sentence introduces the topic.

Develop a Topic
I included facts from the article to support my topic.

Grammar
This **complex sentence** has an independent and a dependent clause.

Grammar Handbook
See page 477.

The Wright brothers figured out how to fly by experimenting. They started by building gliders. Although their first gliders did not work well, the two brothers kept trying. In 1903, they succeeded when their first airplane with an engine flew for twelve seconds.

The Wright brothers had beaten gravity with this short flight. Then other people tried to fly airplanes, too. But it was the Wright brothers' hard work that first made flying possible!

Strong Conclusions
My last sentence sums up the paragraph by restating the main idea.

Your Turn

Explain how inventions can help us even if they fail at first. Use text evidence to support your answer.

Go Digital!
Write your response online.
Use your editing checklist.

312
313

READING/WRITING WORKSHOP, *pp. 312–313*

Your Turn Writing Read the Your Turn prompt on page 313 of the Reading/Writing Workshop aloud. Discuss the prompt with students. If necessary, remind students that good conclusions often restate the author's purpose and summarize main ideas.

Have students take notes as they look for text evidence to answer the prompt. Remind them to include the following elements as they craft their response from their notes:

• Focus on a Topic

• Develop a Topic

• Strong Conclusions

Have students use **Grammar Handbook** page 477 in the Reading/Writing Workshop to edit for errors in complex sentences.

ELL ENGLISH LANGUAGE LEARNERS SCAFFOLD

Beginning

Write Help students complete the sentence frames.
The Wright brothers dreamed of _____.
Their first model _____.

Intermediate

Describe Ask students to complete the sentence frames. Encourage students to provide details.
At first the Wright brothers' invention _____, but they tried again and _____.

Advanced/High

Discuss Check for understanding. Ask: *What did you learn about the process of inventing? How can experimentation lead to progress?*

Write to Sources

DAY 3 For students who need support to complete the writing assignment for the Literature Anthology, provide the following instruction.

DAY 4

Write to the Literature Anthology Text

Analyze the Prompt Explain that students will write about *Hot Air Balloons* on **Literature Anthology** pages 342–355. Provide the following prompt: *How does the way the author organizes the text in this selection help you understand how people are able to fly?* Ask: *What is the prompt asking you to do?* (to analyze and explain the author's use of text structure to inform the reader)

Analyze Text Evidence Help students note evidence.

Page 349 Read this page aloud. Ask: *How is the development of the hot air balloon presented and explained?* (The author tells about early flying machines that used some of the principles found in hot air balloons.)

Pages 352–353 Read these pages. Ask: *How is the text on these pages organized?* (The author uses sequential steps in a process to describe how the hot air balloon functions.) *Why is this important?*

Encourage students to look for more text evidence. Then have them craft a short response. Use the Teacher Conference routine below.

Write to Two Sources

Analyze the Prompt Explain that students will compare *Hot Air Balloons* and "Bellerophon and Pegasus." Provide students with the following prompt: *What do a flying horse and a hot air balloon have in common? How are they different? Use text evidence from two sources to support your answer.* Ask: *What is the prompt asking you to do?* (to compare and contrast) Say: *On page 349 of the Literature Anthology, the text mentions that the hot air balloon takes off and carries passengers to see the beautiful land below. So in my notes, I will write:* Hot air balloons carry passengers for entertainment. *I will also note the page number and the title of the source. On page 359, the text tells me that Pegasus carried Bellerophon over the land in search of the Chimera. I will add this to my notes.*

Analyze Text Evidence Display online Graphic Organizer 38 in Writer's Workspace. Say: *Let's see how one student took notes to answer the prompt. Here are Mina's notes.* Read through the text evidence for each selection and have students compare and contrast a flying horse and a hot air balloon.

Teacher Conferences

STEP 1

Talk about the strengths of the writing.

The introduction builds interest. The topic sentence is clearly written and makes me want to read more.

STEP 2

Focus on how the writer uses text evidence.

The topic you developed is broad enough and interesting. I would understand it more fully if you presented more text evidence about ____.

STEP 3

Make concrete suggestions.

Try rewriting the conclusion to make it stronger and to more clearly restate your main idea.

DAY

5

Share the Prompt Provide the following prompt to students: *Explain the possible risks of flying. Use text evidence from* Hot Air Balloons *and "Bellerophon and Pegasus" to support your answer.*

Find Text Evidence Have students take notes. Find text evidence and give guidance where needed. If necessary, review with students how to paraphrase. Remind them to write the page number and source of the information.

Analyze the Student Model Review the prompt and Mina's notes from Day 4. Display the student model on page 190 of the **Your Turn Practice Book**. Explain to students that Mina synthesized her notes to write a response to the prompt. Discuss the page together with students or have them do it independently.

Write the Response Review the prompt from Day 4 with students. Have students use their notes to craft a short response. Tell students to include the title of both sources and the following elements:

- Focus on a Topic
- Develop a Topic
- Strong Conclusion

COLLABORATE

Share and Reflect Have students share their responses with a partner. Use the Peer Conference routine below.

Suggested Revisions

Provide specific direction to help focus young writers.

Focus on a Sentence
Read the draft and target one sentence for revision. *Rewrite this sentence and add details that explain _____.*

Focus on a Section
Underline a section that needs to be revised. *Your first paragraph could use more focus. State your topic clearly.*

Focus on a Revision Strategy
Underline a section. Have students use a specific revision strategy, such as rearranging. *The events are presented slightly out of order. Rewrite to rearrange them into a sequence that makes better sense.*

Peer Conferences

Focus peer responses on developing a topic to a satisfactory conclusion. Provide these questions:

- Is the focus of the topic clear and straightforward?
- Is the topic developed with logical examples and text evidence?
- Does the conclusion restate the topic sentence?

→ Grammar: Complex Sentences

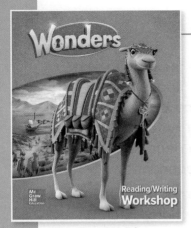

Reading/Writing Workshop

OBJECTIVES

 Use coordinating and subordinating conjunctions. **L.3.1h**

 Produce simple, compound, and complex sentences. **L.3.1i**

- Produce complex sentences
- Identify and use subordinating and coordinating conjunctions
- Capitalize and punctuate simple, compound, and complex sentences correctly

Pair students of different proficiency levels for the Talk About It activities. Partners should practice using academic terms such as *independent clause, dependent clause,* and *subordinating conjunction* precisely while speaking and writing.

DAY 1

DAILY LANGUAGE ACTIVITY

The dog was diging a hole. He were making a hole for the bones he collectted all week.
(1: digging; 2: was; 3: collected)

Introduce Complex Sentences

- A **simple sentence** has one **independent clause.** It can stand alone.

- A **compound sentence** has two or more independent clauses:
    Grandpa drove us home, and we slept in the car.

- **Complex sentences** include an independent clause and one or more dependent clauses. A **dependent clause** cannot stand alone, and often begins with words such as *before* or *when:*
    He helped *when* he fixed my bike.

Discuss sentences using pages 476–477 of the Grammar Handbook.

DAY 2

DAILY LANGUAGE ACTIVITY

The airplane left before we could get onbored. We was late because we didnt set the alarm clock.
(1: onboard: 2: were; 3: didn't)

Review Sentences

Ask students to write a simple, compound, and complex sentence.

Introduce Subordinating Conjunctions

Present the following:

- Dependent clauses cannot stand alone as a sentence and are introduced by subordinating conjunctions.

- Some **subordinating conjunctions** are *after, because, if, unless, while, until, when,* and *before:*
    Our friends searched the back of the house *while* we searched the front.

 TALK ABOUT IT

COLLABORATE

COMPLEX & COMPOUND SENTENCES

Ask partners to use complex & compound sentences to talk about airplanes. Students might discuss the Wright brothers' early attempts at flying. Have students listen for coordinating conjunctions in their compound sentences.

USING CONJUNCTIONS

Have groups write five sentences about how people are able to fly using subordinating conjunctions. Have each student read a sentence aloud, substituting a new subordinating conjunction in each. Students should keep the meaning of the sentence the same.

DAY

Mechanics and Usage: Using Commas in Sentences

- Use a **comma** and a coordinating conjunction when you combine independent clauses in a compound sentence. Place a **comma** before *and, or,* or *but* in a compound sentence.

- If a complex sentence begins with an independent clause, a comma is usually not needed.

- When beginning a complex sentence with a dependent clause, separate the dependent clause from the independent clause with a comma.

As students write, refer them to Grammar Handbook pages 474, 476, and 477.

See Grammar Practice Reproducibles pages 91–95.

DAY

Proofread

Have students correct errors in these sentences.

1. She loves grapes but she doesnt like raisins.
   (1: grapes,;2: doesn't)

2. Because vivian is fast she will be the first one to run the race. (1: Vivian; 2: fast, she)

3. the mouse scurried away, after the door slammed closed. (1: The; 2: away after)

4. Ice covered the road and the bus had to go slow (1: road, and; 2: slow.)

Have students check their work using Grammar Handbook pages 474, 476, 477, and 485.

DAY 5

Assess

Use the Daily Language Activity and Grammar Practice Reproducibles page 95 for assessment.

Reteach

Use Grammar Practice Reproducibles pages 91–94 and the Grammar Handbook for reteaching. Tell students it is important to use commas and subordinating conjunctions in complex sentences correctly as they read, speak, and write.

Check students' writing for use of the skill and listen for it in their speaking. Assign Grammar Revision Assignments in their Writer's Notebooks as needed.

PLAY CHARADES

Have students in small groups each write five compound and complex sentences using conjunctions. Students will take turns selecting and acting out the sentence, as others guess what the sentence is.

SENTENCE QUESTION QUIZ

Partners can create five complex sentences that begin with dependent clauses and trade them with another pair. One partner will read a sentence aloud; the other can identify the dependent and the independent clauses in the sentence using a question form.

ROLE-PLAY A SCENE

Have students reenact a favorite scene from a story the class has read about how people are able to fly. As students role-play, be sure they use many complex sentences that contain conjunctions. As other students watch, have them listen for the conjunctions.

Spelling: Homophones

DAY 1

DAY 2

OBJECTIVES

CCSS Use spelling patterns and generalizations (e.g., *word families, position-based spellings, syllable patterns, ending rules, meaningful word parts*) in writing words. **L.3.2f**

CCSS Consult reference materials, including beginning dictionaries, as needed to check and correct spellings. **L.3.2g**

Spelling Words

sale	road	you're
sail	rowed	their
beet	its	they're
beat	it's	peace
rode	your	piece

Review taught, talked, bought
Challenge seen, scene

Differentiated Spelling

Approaching Level

sale	road	it's
sail	two	your
beet	to	you're
beat	too	see
rode	its	sea

Beyond Level

its	they're	scene
it's	their	flea
your	peace	flee
you're	piece	weight
there	seen	wait

Assess Prior Knowledge

Display the spelling words. Read them aloud. Model for students how to spell the word *rowed*. Segment the word sound by sound, and then attach a spelling to each sound.

Remind them that homophones are words that sound the same but have different meanings. Sometimes they can be spelled similarly, but not always.

Demonstrate sorting the spelling words into pairs beginning with the words *sail* and *sale*. (Write the words on index cards or the IWB.) Pair a few more words.

Then use the Dictation Sentences from Day 5. Say the underlined word, read the sentence, and repeat the word. Have students write the words.

Spiral Review

Review the variant vowel /ô/. Write *taught, talked,* and *bought* on the board. Have students identify the vowel team in each word. Use the Dictation Sentences below for the review words. Read the sentence, say the word, and have students write the words.

1. The teacher <u>taught</u> us the math lesson.
2. I <u>talked</u> on the phone with my grandmother.
3. We <u>bought</u> fruit for the picnic.

Have students trade papers and check the spellings.

Challenge Words Review this week's spelling words, pointing out the homophone pairs. Use these Dictation Sentences for challenge words. Read the sentence, say the word, have students write the word.

1. Have you <u>seen</u> Tom?
2. I liked the first <u>scene</u> of the play.

Have students write the words in their word study notebook.

WORD SORTS

COLLABORATE

OPEN SORT

Have students cut apart the **Spelling Word Cards BLM** in the Online Resource Book and initial the backs of each card. Have them read the words aloud with a partner. Then have partners do an **open sort**. Have them record the sort in their word study notebook.

PATTERN SORT

Complete the **pattern sort** using the key words, pointing out the homophone pairs. Have students use Spelling Word Cards to do their own pattern sort. A partner can compare and check their sorts.

DAY 3

Word Meanings

Have students copy the words below into their Writer's Notebooks. Have them figure out the spelling word that goes with each definition.

1. a large piece of cloth on a boat (sail)
2. a type of vegetable (beet)
3. a path that cars travel on (road)
4. the contraction for *it* and *is* (it's)
5. one part of a whole thing (piece)

Challenge students to come up with other sentences for spelling words, review words, or challenge words. Have students do a word hunt for the words in weekly reading or other materials. They should identify the definition of the spelling word being used in context.

See Phonics/Spelling Reproducibles pp. 109–114.

DAY 4

Proofread and Write

Write the sentences on the board. Have students circle and correct each misspelled word. Remind students that they can use print or electronic resources to check and correct spelling.

1. The rode was bumpy. (road)
2. Hand me you're coat. (your)
3. I want a peace of cake. (piece)
4. There's a big sail at the store. (sale)
5. I don't want to eat that beat. (beet)

Error Correction Remind students that to correctly spell a homophone, they must think about the sentence context and then choose the right spelling. Help students generate mnemonics and other hints to remember problem words. (e.g., *"I" like a piece of cake.*)

DAY 5

Assess

Use the Dictation Sentences for the Posttest. Have students list misspelled words in their word study notebooks. Look for students' use of these words in their writings.

Dictation Sentences

1. We had a bake <u>sale</u> in school.
2. The boat has a <u>sail</u>.
3. <u>Beet</u> soup is red.
4. Norah <u>beat</u> Kate in the race.
5. Sue <u>rode</u> on a donkey.
6. We drove on the dirt <u>road</u>.
7. Have you ever <u>rowed</u> a boat?
8. The dog wagged <u>its</u> tail.
9. <u>It's</u> time to go home.
10. The zoo needs <u>your</u> dollar.
11. <u>You're</u> on time for the show.
12. <u>Their</u> feet were sore from running.
13. <u>They're</u> helping the animals.
14. The baby needs <u>peace</u> and quiet.
15. I ate a <u>piece</u> of an apple.

Have students self-correct the tests.

SPEED SORT

Have partners do a **speed sort** to see who is fastest. Then have them do a word hunt in the week's reading for words that are homophones. Have them record the words in their Day 2 pattern sort in the word study notebook.

BLIND SORT

Have partners do a **blind sort**: one reads a spelling word card; the other tells under which key word it belongs. Have them take turns until both have sorted all their words. Then have students explain how they sorted the words.

→ Build Vocabulary

DAY 1

DAY 2

OBJECTIVES

CCSS Use sentence-level context as a clue to the meaning of a word or phrase. **L.3.4a**

CCSS Acquire and use accurately grade-appropriate conversational, general academic, and domain-specific words and phrases, including those that signal spatial and temporal relationships (e.g., *After dinner that night we went looking for them*). **L.3.6**

Expand vocabulary by adding inflectional endings and suffixes.

Vocabulary Words

controlled	launch
direction	motion
flight	passengers
impossible	popular

Have partners practice using this week's words in an oral presentation, such as a brief retelling of a selection or a description of a character, event, or scientific process. Help them plan their presentations.

Connect to Words

Practice this week's vocabulary.

1. How is a hot air balloon **controlled**?
2. How can you find out which **direction** the wind is blowing?
3. Have you ever been on a long **flight**?
4. Describe an **impossible** task.
5. What things can we **launch** into the air?
6. What sets a car in **motion**?
7. Describe a vehicle that can fit a lot of **passengers**.
8. Name a **popular** movie.

Expand Vocabulary

Help students generate different forms of this week's words by adding, changing, or removing inflectional endings.

- Draw a four-column chart. Write *control* in the left column. Then write *controlled, controls,* and *controlling* in the other columns. Read aloud the words and discuss the meanings.

- Have students share sentences with each form of *control*.

- Students can fill in the chart for other words, such as *direction*.

- Have students copy the chart in their word study notebook.

 BUILD MORE VOCABULARY

COLLABORATE

ACADEMIC VOCABULARY

Discuss important academic words.

- Display the terms *inventor* and *experiment*.

- Define each word and discuss the meanings with students.

- Display *invent* and *inventor*. Have partners look up and define related words.

- Write the related words on the board. Have partners ask and answer questions using the words. Repeat with *experiment*. Elicit examples from students.

SENTENCE CLUES

- Remind students to look for definitions or restatements of an unfamiliar word within a sentence. Write an example, such as: *We watched the rocket launch, or take off into the air.* Model how to find the meaning of *launch*.

- Have partners use sentence clues to find the meanings of unfamiliar words from the weekly readings. Invite partners to share their words. Discuss the meanings of the words.

DAY

Reinforce the Words

Review this week's vocabulary words. Have students orally complete each sentence stem.

1. My mom said it was <u>impossible</u> to get a _____ score on every test, which made me feel better.

2. He <u>controlled</u> the _____ by pushing the handle.

3. There are _____ <u>passengers</u> on this crowded bus!

4. We all run in the _____ <u>direction</u> during gym class.

5. We watched the _____ <u>launch</u> on television.

6. I think it's a <u>popular</u> movie because _____.

DAY

Connect to Writing

- Have students write sentences in their word study notebooks using this week's vocabulary.

- Tell them to write sentences that provide information about the words and their meanings.

- **ELL** Provide the Day 3 sentence stems for students needing extra support.

Write About Vocabulary Have students write something they learned from this week's words in their word study notebook. For example, they might write about what it would be like to be a *passenger* on a hot air balloon *flight*.

DAY 5

Word Squares

Ask students to create Word Squares for each vocabulary word.

- In the first square, students write the word. (example: *flight*)

- In the second square, students write their own definition of the word and any related words. (examples: *trip, voyage*)

- In the third square, students draw an illustration that will help them remember the word. (example: an airplane in flight)

- In the fourth square, students write non-examples. (examples: *land, stay*)

- Have students share their Word Squares with a partner.

CONTEXT CLUES

Remind students to look for context clues to help determine the correct meaning of multiple meaning words.

- Display **Your Turn Practice Book** pages 183–184. Read the first paragraph. Model figuring out the meanings of *fly* and *copy*.

- For additional practice with context clues, have students complete page 187.

- Students can confirm meanings in a print or online dictionary.

SHADES OF MEANING

Help students generate words related to *impossible*. Draw a synonym/antonym scale.

- Begin a discussion about the word *impossible*. Elicit synonyms and write them on the scale.

- Ask students to generate antonyms. Discuss where each word should fall on the scale.

- Have partners work together to add other words to the scale. They can confirm meanings in a print or online dictionary.

- Ask students to copy the words in their word study notebook.

MORPHOLOGY

Use the word *impossible* as a springboard for students to learn more words. Draw a T-chart.

- Write the word *possible* in the first column.

- In the second column, write the prefix *im-*. Model how to use the prefix and the base word to determine the meaning of *impossible*.

- Have partners generate other words with the prefix *im-*.

- Tell students to use the suffix and base words to determine the meanings of the words.

→ Integrate Ideas

Close Reading Routine

Read   DOK 1–2

- Identify key ideas and details about Flight.
- Take notes and summarize.
- Use **A C T** prompts as needed.

Reread   DOK 2–3

- Analyze the text, craft, and structure.
- Use the **Close Reading Companion.**

Integrate   DOK 4

- Integrate knowledge and ideas.
- Make text-to-text connections.
- Use the Integrate lesson.
- Use *Close Reading Companion,* p. 127.

TEXT CONNECTIONS

Connect to the Essential Question

Write the essential question on the board: How are people able to fly? Divide the class into small groups. Tell students that each group will compare the information that they have learned about how people are able to fly. Model how to compare this information by using examples from this week's **Leveled Readers** and "Firsts in Flight," **Reading/Writing Workshop** pages 304–307.

Evaluate Text Evidence Have students review their class notes and completed graphic organizers before they begin their discussions. Encourage students to compare information from all the week's reads. Have each

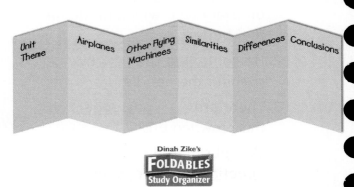

Dinah Zike's
FOLDABLES
Study Organizer

NARRATIVE PERFORMANCE TASK

Write About: Frogs

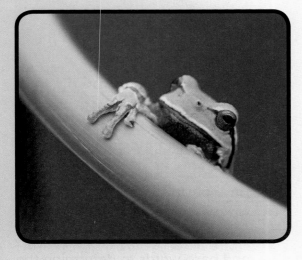

Gudella/Getty Images

INQUIRY SPACE

| LEVEL | | | 1 | 2 | 3 | 4 | 5 | 6 |

Make a Story Map

PREVIEW LEVEL 4 Display Level 4 of the Narrative Performance Task to students. Explain to them that in this level they will use their notes to create a story map for their story about frogs.

❶ **Organize Your Notes** Model for students how to organize notes. Say: *I am writing a story about a day in the life of a young dolphin calf. Most of my notes are about how dolphin calves spend time with their mothers, where dolphins live, and dangers to dolphins. I will put all the notes about dolphin calves and their mothers together. Then I will do the same thing with my notes about where dolphins live and dangers to dolphins.* You may wish to show students the **Organize Notes** animation from the **Toolkit.**

OBJECTIVE

CCSS Compare and contrast the most important points and key details presented in two texts on the same topic. **RI.3.9**

group pick one student to take notes. Explain that each group will use an Accordion Foldable® to record their ideas. You may wish to model how to use an Accordion Foldable® to record comparisons.

Text to Media

Post Online Remind students to discuss their responses to the Blast along with information from all the week's reads. Tell students to include the photograph of the big wave surfer on page 127 of the **Close Reading Companion** as a part of their discussion. Guide students to see the connections among media, the photograph, and text. Ask: *How does the Blast connect to what you read this week? To the photograph?*

Present Ideas and Synthesize Information

When students finish their discussions, ask for a volunteer from each group to read his or her notes aloud.

OBJECTIVES

CCSS Write narratives to develop real or imagined experiences or events using effective technique, descriptive details, and clear event sequences. **W.3.3**

CCSS Establish a situation and introduce a narrator and/ or characters; organize an event sequence that unfolds naturally. **W.3.2a**

 Make a Story Map Tell students that a story map shows the details and important events of a story. Encourage them to use their notes to think about the details on which they want to base their story. Tell students that they will write information about the setting, characters, and plot in a story map. Say: *A story map shows the details that I should include in my story and how to arrange them.* Display and discuss with the class the **Student Model: Story Map** from the Toolkit.

 Draft Display the **Student Model: Draft** from the Toolkit. Point out how the writer began the story. Say: *The writer introduced a character and the setting at the beginning of the story.* Ask: *Where is the plot introduced?* Discuss with students how they might improve it. Then have them identify the characters, setting, and plot in the draft.

ASSIGN LEVEL 4 Have students begin Level 4 by reviewing their notes. You may wish to have students watch the **Story Map to Draft** animation before they start writing.

→ Approaching Level

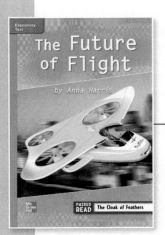

Lexile 600
TextEvaluator™ 21

OBJECTIVES

Describe the logical connection between particular sentences and paragraphs in a text (e.g. comparison, cause/effect, first/ second/third in a sequence). **RI.3.8**

- Identify cause-and-effect relationships.
- Reread to increase understanding of a text.
- Use context as a clue to determine how a word with multiple meanings is used in a text.

ACADEMIC LANGUAGE

reread, cause, effect, expository, multiple-meaning words, myth

Leveled Reader:
The Future of Flight

Before Reading

Preview and Predict

Have students read the Essential Question. Then have them preview the text by reading the title and table of contents of *The Future of Flight*. Have students make two predictions about what they will learn from the text. Have partners share their predictions.

Review Genre: Expository

Review with students that expository text explains about a topic. It includes text features like maps and charts. As they preview *The Future of Flight*, have students identify features of expository text.

During Reading

Close Reading

Note Taking Have students use their graphic organizer as they read.

Pages 2–3 *Do jetpacks exist today? Explain.* (Yes, they do; some kinds of jetpacks have been made and can be flown 30 minutes at a time.) *Look at the picture on page 3. How does it help you better understand the main text?* (I see the two joysticks used to control the jetpack.)

Pages 4–5 *Describe what scientists are studying at the myCopter project.* (They are studying very small aircraft.) *What would the aircraft be like, and how would it work? Find the details by rereading pages 4 and 5.* (It would be like a small flying car; it would be controlled by computers.)

Pages 6–7 *The aircraft NASA built in 2001 was very fast. Explain the cause.* (It had a scramjet engine.) *How fast did it go?* (7,000 MPH)

Pages 8–9 *The word* catch *on page 8 has multiple meanings. It can mean "the act of taking" or "a problem." Which definition fits in this case?* ("a problem") *What catch, or problem, is the author talking about?* (The planes will not be ready until 2050.) *What does the chart on page 9 show?* (travel times around the world now and in the future) *Turn to a partner and tell what effect flying faster might have on our lives.*

Go Digital

Leveled Readers

Fill in the Graphic Organizer

Pages 10–11 *Reread page 11, then turn to a partner to summarize how the spaceship gets off the ground and into space.* (A plane carries it down the runway and lifts it 50,000 feet into the sky, then lets go of it. The spaceship's engines fire, and the spaceship blasts into space.)

Pages 12–14 *Is the pull of gravity as strong 68 miles away from Earth as it is on Earth?* (no) *What will be the effect on passengers of a spaceship?* (They will float around inside the plane for five minutes.)

After Reading

Respond to Reading Revisit the Essential Question, and help students complete the Text Evidence questions on page 15.

Write About Reading *Analytical Writing* Have students work with a partner to write a short paragraph about why people build new aircraft. Make sure students include examples from the text.

Fluency: Accuracy and Phrasing

Model Model reading page 2 with accuracy and proper phrasing. Next, reread the page aloud, and have students read along with you.

Apply Have students practice reading with a partner.

PAIRED READ

Leveled Reader

"The Cloak of Feathers"

Make Connections: Write About It *Analytical Writing*

Before reading, have students note that the genre of this text is a myth, which is a fictional tale that might explain why something is the way it is. Then discuss the Essential Question.

After reading, have students write about connections between how people fly in *The Future of Flight* and "The Cloak of Feathers."

FOCUS ON SCIENCE

Students can extend their knowledge of motion by completing the science activity on page 20. **STEM**

Literature Circles

Ask students to conduct a literature circle using the Thinkmark questions to guide the discussion. You may wish to have a whole-class discussion on how students would use the flying technology in the text.

Level Up

Level-up lessons available online.

IF students read the Approaching Level fluently and answered the questions

THEN pair them with students who have proficiently read On Level and have approaching-level students

• echo-read the On Level main selection with their partner.

• use self-stick notes to mark a new detail to discuss in each section.

A C T Access Complex Text

The On Level challenges students by including more **domain-specific words** and **complex sentence structures**.

→ Approaching Level

Phonics/Decoding

LONG-VOWEL SPELLINGS

OBJECTIVES

 Decode regularly spelled one-syllable words. **RF.1.3b**

Decode words with long-vowel spellings.

 I Do Remind students that each vowel sound has different spellings. Review the long-vowel sounds. On the board, write *rode/road*. Read the words aloud. Underline the long-*o* spellings. Point out that these words both have the long-*o* sound but are spelled differently. Repeat with *sail/sale*.

 We Do Write *beat/beet, mite/might, hew/hue* on the board. Model how to decode the first two words. Say the long-vowel sound, then underline the long-vowel spellings. Have students sound out the rest of the words with you after you say the long-vowel sound and spelling for each.

 You Do Add these words to the board: *meet/meat, ate/eight, sea/see, write/right, grown/groan*. Have students read each word aloud, and say the long-vowel sound and how the vowel is spelled. Then point to the words in random order for students to read chorally. Repeat several times.

BUILD HOMOPHONES

OBJECTIVES

 Know and apply grade-level phonics and word analysis skills in decoding words. Decode multisyllable words. **RF.3.3c**

Build and define homophones.

 I Do Tell students they will be building multisyllable words to make homophones. Remind them that homophones are words that sound alike, but are spelled differently and mean different things. Display these **Word-Building Cards**: *al, low, ed, a, er, less, on,* and *en*. Then write these syllables on the board: *loud, weath,* and *wheth*. Model sounding out each syllable.

 We Do Have students chorally read each syllable. Repeat at varying speeds and in random order. Next, display all the cards and syllables. Work with students to combine the Word-Building Cards and the syllables to form two-syllable homophones. Have students read the words: *allowed, aloud, weather, whether, lesson,* and *lessen,* and then help them define each word.

 You Do Write other syllables on the board, such as *ceil, seal, ing, board, bord, er, symb, cymb, al,* and *ol*. Have students work with partners to build homophones using these syllables. Then have partners share the words and define them.

PRACTICE HOMOPHONES

OBJECTIVES

 Know and apply grade-level phonics and word analysis skills in decoding words. Decode multisyllable words. **RF.3.3c**

Decode and define homophones.

 I Do Remind students that homophones are words that sound alike but are spelled differently and mean different things. Write the words *piece* and *peace* on the board. Then read the words aloud. Point out that the words sound the same even though they are spelled differently. Explain the meaning of each word.

 We Do Write the words *higher, hire, flower, flour, bolder,* and *boulder* on the board. Model how to decode the first word, then guide students as they read the remaining words. Point out that different spellings can be used to make the same vowel sounds. Help students define each word.

You Do Have students chorally read the words. Have individuals define them.

r-CONTROLLED VOWEL SYLLABLES

OBJECTIVES

 Know and apply grade-level phonics and word analysis skills in decoding words. Decode multisyllable words. **RF.3.3c**

Decode words with *r*-controlled vowel syllables.

 I Do Review that when a vowel is followed by the letter *r*, the *r* changes the vowel's sound. In a word that has more than one syllable, both the vowel and the letter *r* must appear in the same syllable. They act as a team and cannot be broken up.

We Do Write *sharing, yardwork, nearly, bearable, perfect, Thursday, ignore* on the board. Say each word and have students repeat. Underline the *r*-controlled vowel in each word. Model drawing a line to divide each word into syllables: *shar/ing, yard/work, near/ly, bear/a/ble, per/fect, Thurs/day, ig/nore*. Read the list out loud again, having students chorally read with you.

 You Do Afterward, write the words *stairwell, nowhere, career, whirlwind, artwork,* and *seashore* on the board. Have students break each word into syllables. Then point to the words in random order for students to chorally read.

ENGLISH LANGUAGE LEARNERS

For the students who need **phonics, decoding,** and **fluency** practice, use scaffolding methods as necessary to ensure students understand the meaning of the words. Refer to the **Language Transfers Handbook** for phonics elements that may not transfer in students' native languages.

Approaching Level

Vocabulary

REVIEW HIGH-FREQUENCY WORDS

 TIER 2

OBJECTIVES

 Use conventional spelling for high-frequency and other studied words and for adding suffixes to base words (e.g., *sitting, smiled, cries, happiness*). **L.3.2e**

Review high-frequency words.

I Do Use **Word Cards** 151–160. Display one word at a time, following the routine:

Display the word. Read the word. Then spell the word.

We Do Have students state the word and spell the word with you. Model using the word in a sentence, and have students repeat after you.

You Do Display the word. Have students say the word then spell it. When completed, quickly flip through the word card set as students chorally read the words. Provide opportunities for students to use the words in speaking and writing. For example, provide sentence starters such as *My favorite game to _____ is _____.* Have students write each word in their **Writer's Notebook**.

REVIEW VOCABULARY WORDS

 TIER 2

OBJECTIVES

 Acquire and use accurately grade-appropriate conversational, general academic, and domain-specific words and phrases, including those that signal spatial and temporal relationships (e.g., *After dinner that night we went looking for them*). **L.3.6**

Review vocabulary words.

I Do Display each **Visual Vocabulary Card** and state the word. Explain how the photograph illustrates the word. State the example sentence and repeat the word.

We Do Point to the word on the card and read the word with students. Ask them to repeat the word. Engage students in structured partner talk about the image as prompted on the back of the vocabulary card.

You Do Display each visual in random order, hiding the word. Have students match the definitions and context sentences of the words to the visuals displayed. Then ask students to complete **Approaching Reproducibles** page 181.

IDENTIFY RELATED WORDS

OBJECTIVES

CCSS Demonstrate understanding of word relationships and nuances in word meanings. Identify real-life connections between words and their use (e.g., describe people who are *friendly* or *helpful*). **L.3.5b**

Identify words that have related meanings.

 I Do Display the **Visual Vocabulary Card** for *controlled,* and then say aloud the word set *controlled, moved, released.* Point out that the word *released* does not belong and explain why.

 We Do Display the vocabulary card for the word *direction.* Say aloud the word set *direction, disorder, course.* With students, identify the word that does not belong and discuss why.

 You Do Using the word sets below, display the remaining cards one at a time, saying each word set. Then, have students identify the words that do not belong.

flight, soaring, strolling	*impossible, unthinkable, doable*
launched, settled, fired	*motion, stillness, movement*
passenger, traveler, driver	*popular, favorite, unknown*

MULTIPLE-MEANING WORDS

OBJECTIVES

CCSS Use sentence level context as a clue to the meaning of a word or phrase. **L.3.4a**

Determine the meaning of multiple-meaning words using context clues.

 I Do Display the Comprehension and Fluency passage on **Approaching Reproducibles** pages 183–184. Read aloud the first paragraph. Point to the sentence *Humans have always wanted to fly.* Explain to students that *fly* is a multiple-meaning word.

Think Aloud I know that *fly* is a noun meaning "a small flying insect" and a verb meaning "to move through the air." In this sentence, *fly* is being used as a verb. The context clues do not seem to show that insects are being discussed. So I think that here *fly* means "to move through the air."

Write the meaning of the multiple-meaning word.

 We Do Have students point to the sentence *At first, they tried to copy birds.* With students, discuss how to determine which meaning of *copy* is being used here. Write the meaning of the multiple-meaning word.

 You Do Have students find the meaning of multiple-meaning words *rose* and *worked* by noting each word's part of speech and using context clues.

Approaching Level

Comprehension

FLUENCY

OBJECTIVES

Read on-level prose and poetry orally with accuracy, appropriate rate, and expression on successive readings. **RF.3.4b**

Read fluently with accuracy and appropriate phrasing.

I Do Explain that reading a selection with accuracy means saying each word correctly and not leaving out any words or sentences. Appropriate phrasing means grouping words for emphasis and to convey meaning. Read the first paragraph of the Comprehension and Fluency passage on **Approaching Reproducibles** pages 183–184. Emphasize reading slowly and accurately as well as grouping phrases by pausing at commas and stopping at periods.

We Do Read the rest of the page aloud, and have students repeat each sentence after you using the same phrasing. Explain that you grouped certain words and phrases together to show meaning.

You Do Have partners take turns reading sentences from the Approaching Reproducibles passage. Remind students to focus on their accuracy. Listen in and provide corrective feedback as needed by modeling proper fluency.

TEXT STRUCTURE

OBJECTIVES

Describe the relationship between a series of historical events, scientific ideas or concepts, or steps in technical procedures in a text, using language that pertains to time, sequence, and cause/effect. **RI.3.3**

Examine text structure.

I Do Write the topic *Trying to Fly* on the board. Then write *copied birds, kites, hot air balloons, gliders*. Explain that the text is structured so that related events are in historical order. Over the centuries, humans tried many things to be able to fly. Explain that the attempts at flying are in sequence. First, they tried copying birds. Then kites were invented.

We Do Read the first page of the Comprehension and Fluency passage in the **Approaching Reproducibles**. Ask: *What is the structure of the text? How did people learn to fly?* Explain that these events are related and in historical order. Help students identify how these events are related. Discuss why the author would choose to order the events this way.

You Do Have students read the rest of the passage. After each paragraph, they should write down the order in which things happened. Review their lists with them and help them explain why the order of events is important.

REVIEW TEXT STRUCTURE: CAUSE AND EFFECT

OBJECTIVES

CCSS Describe the logical connection between particular sentences and paragraphs in a text (e.g., comparison, cause/effect, first/second/third in a sequence). **RI.3.8**

Identify cause-and-effect relationships.

 I Do Remind students that text structure is a way that authors organize a text. Cause and effect is one kind of text structure that shows how and why things happen in time order. A *cause* is why something happens. An *effect* is what happens. Students can look for words and phrases that indicate cause and effect such as *because, so,* and *as a result.*

 We Do Read the first paragraph of the Comprehension and Fluency passage in **Approaching Reproducibles** together. Pause to point out events that may be effects in the text. Model how to decide which effects have identifiable causes. Then, work with students to determine what those causes are by referring to the text.

 You Do Have students work in pairs or small groups to come up with a cause-and-effect sequence for "History of Human Flight" in the Approaching Reproducibles. Make sure they are using words and phrases explaining cause and effect as well as listing events in the correct sequence.

SELF-SELECTED READING

OBJECTIVES

CCSS Describe the logical connection between particular sentences and paragraphs in a text (e.g., comparison, cause/effect, first/second/third in a sequence). **RI.3.8**

• Identify cause-and-effect relationships.
• Reread difficult sections in a text to increase understanding.

Read Independently

Have students choose an expository text discussing historical events for sustained silent reading. Remind students that:

• they should look at how events are related and what events are causes and what are effects.
• if they have trouble finding the cause of an effect, they should reread a paragraph or section to look for more information.

Read Purposefully

Have students record the causes and effects in the text on **Graphic Organizer 143** as they read independently. After they finish, they can conduct a Book Talk, each telling about the book they read.

• Students should share their organizers and answer these questions: *What was one cause you read about? What was its effect?*
• They should also tell the group if there were any sections they reread to increase their understanding.

On Level

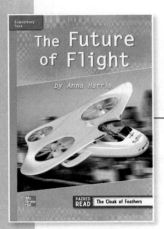

Lexile 690
TextEvaluator™ 31

OBJECTIVES

Describe the logical connection between particular sentences and paragraphs in a text (e.g. comparison, cause/effect, first/second/third in a sequence). **RI.3.8**

- Identify cause-and-effect relationships.
- Reread text to increase understanding.
- Use context as a clue to determine how a word with multiple meanings is used in a text.

ACADEMIC LANGUAGE

reread, cause, effect, expository, multiple-meaning words, myth

Leveled Reader:
The Future of Flight

| Before Reading |

Preview and Predict

Have students read the Essential Question. Have them preview the text by reading the title and table of contents of *The Future of Flight* and then make two predictions about what they will learn from the text. Have partners share their predictions.

Leveled Readers

Review Genre: Expository

Review with students that expository text explains about a topic. It includes text features like maps and charts. As they preview *The Future of Flight*, have students identify features of expository text.

| During Reading |

Close Reading

Note Taking Have students use their graphic organizer as they read.

Pages 2–3 *Explain the cause-and-effect relationship between two events in the first paragraph on page 3.* (The engine burns fuel and air which causes hot air to be forced out of the exhaust. As a result, the jetpack wearer is thrust upward.)

Fill in the Graphic Organizer

Pages 4–5 *Turn to a partner and define the multiple-meaning word* safe *as it is used on page 5.* (*Safe* means "that is not dangerous.") *What else can* safe *mean?* (*Safe* can also mean "a place to keep and protect valuables.") *How do experts plan on making the myCopter aircraft safe? Reread page 5 to find the answer.* (They would build aircraft that would fly in small groups; the aircraft would send signals to each other to stay at a safe distance; the aircraft would be controlled by computers.)

Pages 6–9 *Why were scramjet aircraft never flown by pilots and never carried passengers?* (because it was too dangerous) *How does the chart on page 9 help you understand the text?* (The main text talks about jets currently going 500-600 MPH and future jets traveling at 3,000 MPH. It shows how much shorter travel times will be in the future.) *According to the chart, how long will it take to get from London to Tokyo in the future?* (2 hours)

Pages 10–14 *How does the photograph on page 11 help you better understand the main text?* (It shows the plane that helps the spaceship get off the ground.)

Reread page 12, then explain the effect of gravity on passengers of a spacecraft 68 miles above Earth. (Gravity is not as strong, so passengers will float around on the plane for about five minutes.)

After Reading

Respond to Reading Revisit the Essential Question, and ask students to complete the Text Evidence questions on page 15.

Analytical Writing **Write About Reading** Have students work with a partner to write a short paragraph about why people build new aircraft. Make sure students use text evidence and words signaling a cause-and-effect relationship between events.

Fluency: Accuracy and Phrasing

Model Model reading page 2 with accuracy and proper phrasing. Next, reread the page aloud, and have students read along with you.

Apply Have students practice reading with a partner.

PAIRED READ

"The Cloak of Feathers"

Make Connections:
Write About It *Analytical Writing*

Before reading, have students note that the genre of this text is a myth, which is a fictional tale that might explain why something is the way it is. Then discuss the Essential Question.

After reading, have students write about connections between how people fly in *The Future of Flight* and "The Cloak of Feathers."

Leveled Reader

🧪 **FOCUS ON SCIENCE**

Students can extend their knowledge of forces and motion by completing the science activity on page 20.
STEM

Literature Circles

Ask students to conduct a literature circle using the Thinkmark questions to guide the discussion. You may wish to have a whole-class discussion on how students would use the flying technology in the text.

Level Up

Level-up lessons available online.

IF students read the On Level fluently and answered the questions

THEN pair them with students who have proficiently read Beyond Level and have on-level students

• partner-read the Beyond Level main selection.

• name two details in the text that they want to learn more about.

A C T Access Complex Text

The Beyond Level challenges students by including more **domain-specific words** and **complex sentence structures**.

On Level

Vocabulary

REVIEW VOCABULARY WORDS

 OBJECTIVES
Acquire and use accurately grade-appropriate conversational, general academic, and domain-specific words and phrases, including those that signal spatial and temporal relationships (e.g., *After dinner that night we went looking for them*). **L.3.6**

Review vocabulary words.

 I Do

Use the **Visual Vocabulary Cards** to review key vocabulary words *controlled, direction, impossible, launched, passenger,* and *popular.* Point to each word, read it aloud, and have students chorally repeat it.

 We Do

Ask these questions, and help students respond and explain their answers.
- Which can be *controlled*: an airplane or the weather?
- Which has to follow the same *direction* every time: a boat or a train?
- When something is said to be *impossible,* is it hard or easy to do?

 You Do

Have students respond to the questions below and explain their answers.
- Is something *launched* into space in a rocket or a glider?
- Who is a *passenger* on a school bus: the driver or a student?
- What is a more *popular* way to travel today: by horse or by car?

MULTIPLE-MEANING WORDS

OBJECTIVES
Use sentence level context as a clue to the meaning of a word or phrase. **L.3.4a**

Determine the meanings of multiple-meaning words using context clues.

 I Do

Review what multiple-meaning words are. To model, use *Humans have always wanted to fly* in paragraph 1 in the Comprehension and Fluency passage on **Your Turn Practice Book** pages 183–184.

Think Aloud I know that *fly* can be a noun or a verb. In this sentence, *fly* is a verb and the context clues relate to flying in the air. Therefore, in this sentence, *fly* means "to move through the air."

 We Do

Have students read the third sentence, where they encounter *copy.* Have them determine the meaning of this multiple-meaning word by noting the part of speech and using context clues.

 You Do

Have students work in pairs to determine the meanings of multiple-meaning words *rose, power,* and *worked* as they read the rest of the selection.

Comprehension

REVIEW TEXT STRUCTURE: CAUSE AND EFFECT

OBJECTIVES

Describe the logical connection between particular sentences and paragraphs in a text (e.g., comparison, cause/effect, first/second/third in a sequence). **RI.3.8**

Identify cause-and-effect relationships.

Remind students that authors can structure a text using cause and effect to show how and why things happen. Explain that an effect is what happens and a cause is why it happens. Texts that use cause and effect are usually structured so that causes happen before effects. Explain that words and phrases such as *because, so,* and *as a result* can indicate cause-and-effect relationships.

Have a volunteer read the first paragraph of the Comprehension and Fluency passage on **Your Turn Practice Book** pages 183–184. Have students orally list events in the paragraph, and help them explain how the events relate to each other as causes and effects. Model how to determine how the causes and effects are sequenced and how they are connected. Then, work with students to identify the causes and effects in the next paragraph.

Have partners identify the causes and effects in the rest of the passage. Remind them that the effect of one cause may be the cause of another effect.

SELF-SELECTED READING

OBJECTIVES

Describe the logical connection between particular sentences and paragraphs in a text (e.g., comparison, cause/effect, first/second/third in a sequence). **RI.3.8**

- Identify cause-and-effect relationships.
- Reread difficult sections in a text to increase understanding.

Read Independently

Have students choose an expository text that discusses historical events for sustained silent reading.

- Before they read, have students preview the book, reading the title, viewing the front and back cover, and noting text features such as headings, photographs, and sidebars.
- As students read, remind them to reread difficult sections to increase their understanding.

Read Purposefully

Encourage students to read different texts in order to learn about a variety of subjects.

- As students read, have them fill in **Graphic Organizer 143**.
- They can use this organizer to help them write a summary of the text.
- Ask students to share their reactions to the text with classmates.

→ Beyond Level

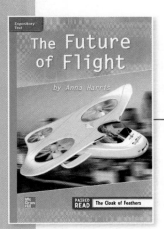

Lexile 770
TextEvaluator™ 32

OBJECTIVES

 Describe the logical connection between particular sentences and paragraphs in a text (e.g. comparison, cause/effect, first/second/third in a sequence). **RI.3.8**

- Identify cause-and-effect relationships.
- Reread text to increase understanding.
- Use context as a clue to determine how a word with multiple meanings is used in a text.

ACADEMIC LANGUAGE

reread, cause, effect, expository, multiple-meaning words, myth

Leveled Reader:
The Future of Flight

Before Reading

Preview and Predict

Have students review the Essential Question. Then have them preview the text by reading the title and table of contents of *The Future of Flight*. Have students make two predictions about what they will learn and share their predictions with a partner.

Review Genre: Expository

Review with students that expository text explains about a topic. It includes text features like charts and maps. As they preview *The Future of Flight*, have students identify features of expository text.

During Reading

Close Reading

Note Taking Have students use their graphic organizer as they read.

Pages 2–5 *Why do you think the author begins Chapter 1 with a series of questions?* (It makes the reader start to think about the topic.) *What does the multiple-meaning word* safe *mean on page 5?* ("not dangerous") *How do you know?* (It is an adjective, and, in the first paragraph on page 5, the author asks how the aircraft will avoid crashing into each other. This means the author is talking about the safety of the aircraft.) *What else can it mean?* ("a place to keep and protect valuables")

Pages 6–7 *Summarize how a scramjet engine is different from a normal rocket engine.* (*It uses oxygen from the outside instead of the oxygen carried on board, which is how a rocket engine works.*) *What does it mean to travel at Mach 4? Reread page 7 to find the answer.* (to travel at 3,000 MPH, which is four times the speed of sound)

Pages 8–9 *How does the diagram on page 8 help you better understand the main text?* (It shows the three types of engines. It also shows the hydrogen and oxygen tanks, which are what the scramjet and rocket engines will burn.) *What will be one effect of two of the engines burning hydrogen and oxygen?* (The plane will not pollute the planet as much.)

Go Digital

Leveled Readers

Fill in the Graphic Organizer

Pages 10–14 *How does* SpaceShipTwo *make it into the sky? What is the effect of the rocket engines on the spaceship firing up? Explain your answer to a partner.* (A plane called the *WhiteKnightTwo* or VSS *Enterprise* carries the spaceship down a runway then lifts it 50,000 feet into the sky. The spaceship is released and its rocket engines fire up, which cause it to blast into sub-space.)

After Reading

Respond to Reading Revisit the Essential Question, and ask students to complete the Text Evidence questions on page 15.

Analytical Writing **Write About Reading** Have students work with a partner to write a paragraph about why people build new aircraft and effects of new types of air travel. Make sure students use words that signal cause and effect.

Fluency: Accuracy and Phrasing

Model Model reading page 2 with accuracy and proper phrasing. Next, reread the page aloud, and have students read along with you.

Apply Have students practice reading with a partner.

PAIRED READ

Leveled Reader

"The Cloak of Feathers"

Make Connections: Write About It *Analytical Writing*

Before reading, have students note that the genre of this text is a myth, which is a fictional tale that might explain why something is the way it is. Then discuss the Essential Question.

After reading, have students write about connections between how people fly in *The Future of Flight* and "The Cloak of Feathers."

 FOCUS ON SCIENCE

Students can extend their knowledge of forces and motion by completing the science activity on page 20. **STEM**

Literature Circles

Ask students to conduct a literature circle using the Thinkmark questions to guide the discussion. You may wish to have a whole-class discussion on how students would use the flying technology in the text.

Gifted and Talented

Synthesize Challenge students to create their own flying machine. Have them draw a picture or describe the machine and write a short paragraph telling about its purpose and where it would fly. Students may do additional research or build on ideas from *The Future of Flight*. Have student volunteers share their ideas with the class.

Beyond Level

Vocabulary

REVIEW DOMAIN-SPECIFIC WORDS

OBJECTIVES

CCSS Produce simple, compound, and complex sentences. **L.3.1i**

Review and discuss domain-specific vocabulary words.

Model Use the **Visual Vocabulary Cards** to review the meanings of the words *direction* and *controlled*. Write science-related sentences on the board using the words.

Write the words *launched, materials,* and *devices* on the board, and discuss the meaning of each word with students. Then help students write sentences using these words.

Apply Have students work in pairs to review the meanings of the words *aircraft, engine,* and *ignite.* Then have partners write sentences using the words.

MULTIPLE-MEANING WORDS

OBJECTIVES

CCSS Use sentence level context as a clue to the meaning of a word or phrase. **L.3.4a**

Determine the meanings of multiple-meaning words using context clues.

Model Read aloud the first paragraph of the Comprehension and Fluency passage on **Beyond Reproducibles** pages 183–184.

Think Aloud I read the sentence *Human beings have always wanted to fly.* I know that the word *fly* can either be a noun meaning "a flying insect" or a verb meaning "to move through the air." Here *fly* is used as a verb, and the context clues indicate that it means "to move through the air."

With students, read the first paragraph again. Help them figure out the meaning of the multiple-meaning word *copy* in the third sentence.

Apply Have pairs of students read the rest of the passage and determine the meanings of multiple-meaning words such as *work, step,* and *power.*

 Analyze Using the passage "History of Human Flight," have partners compare and contrast the way a bird flies with one way that humans fly. Have them use reference materials as needed. Encourage them to also use artwork to depict the two types of flight.

Comprehension

REVIEW TEXT STRUCTURE: CAUSE AND EFFECT

OBJECTIVES

 Describe the logical connection between particular sentences and paragraphs in a text (e.g., comparison, cause/effect, first/second/third in a sequence). **RI.3.8**

Identify cause-and-effect relationships.

 Model Remind students that authors use cause and effect to structure the text in a time-order sequence. Explain that a cause is why things happen, and an effect is what happens. Point out that sometimes an author will use a series of cause-and-effect relationships in sequence. In this case, an effect in one relationship will act as the cause in another.

Have students read the first paragraph of the Comprehension and Fluency passage of **Beyond Reproducibles** pages 183–184. Ask open-ended questions to facilitate discussion, such as *How does the author use cause and effect in this paragraph?* and *What happened when people tried to use wings to fly?* Students should support their responses with text evidence.

Apply Have students identify the causes and effects in the rest of the passage as they independently fill in **Graphic Organizer 143**. Then have partners use their work to describe the sequence of the whole passage.

SELF-SELECTED READING

OBJECTIVES

 Describe the logical connection between particular sentences and paragraphs in a text (e.g., comparison, cause/effect, first/second/third in a sequence). **RI.3.8**

- Identify cause-and-effect relationships.
- Reread difficult sections in a text to increase understanding.

Read Independently

Have students choose an expository text discussing historical events for sustained silent reading.

- As students read, have them fill in **Graphic Organizer 143**.
- Remind them to reread difficult sections of the text to increase their understanding.

Read Purposefully

Encourage students to keep a reading journal. Have them read different texts in order to learn about a variety of subjects.

- Students can write summaries of the texts in their journals.
- Ask students to share their reactions to the texts with classmates.

 Independent Study Challenge students to discuss how what they have read relates to the weekly theme of flight. Have students compare the causes and effects they have read about. *How did the causes and effects relate to each other?*

→ English Language Learners

Reading/Writing Workshop

___

OBJECTIVES
(CCSS) Describe the logical connection between particular sentences and paragraphs in a text (e.g. comparison, cause/effect, first/second/third in a sequence). **RI.3.8**

• Reread text to increase understanding.

• Identify the meaning of a multiple-meaning word within a text.

___

LANGUAGE OBJECTIVE

Identify cause-and-effect relationships.

___

ACADEMIC LANGUAGE

• cause, effect, expository, multiple-meaning words

• Cognates: causa, efecto, expositivo

Shared Read
Firsts in Flight

Before Reading

Build Background

Read the Essential Question: How are people able to fly?

• Explain the meaning of the Essential Question. Explain how *fly* means "to move in the air." Show the class a photograph of an airplane, and have students describe the photograph.

• **Model an answer:** *One way people can fly is in an airplane. There are many other ways people can fly.*

• Ask students a question that ties the Essential Question to their own background knowledge: *Talk with a partner about other ways people can fly. Think about aircraft you have seen in the sky or in different types of media, such as on television or in books.* Call on several pairs.

During Reading

Interactive-Question Response

• Ask questions that help students understand the meaning of the text after each paragraph.

• Reinforce the meanings of key vocabulary.

• Ask students questions that require them to use key vocabulary.

• Reinforce strategies and skills of the week by modeling.

Go Digital

View "Firsts in Flight"

Page 305

Look at the picture and caption in the upper-right corner. Who are these men? (Orville and Wilbur Wright) *These brothers dreamed of flying.*

Paragraph 1

Explain and Model Rereading *When I read, I wonder why flying was the brothers' dream. I reread to see if I can find more information, and I see that when the brothers were little, their father gave them a toy helicopter.*

Why would a toy helicopter make the brothers dream of flying? (Possible Response: They wanted to fly too.)

Paragraph 2

Where did the brothers build their flying machines? (in their bicycle shop)

Model Cause and Effect *The brothers needed to fly their planes in a place where the winds were strong enough. This is a cause. The phrase* as a result *is a clue to figuring out the effect in the text. Have students find the phrase in the text. What is the effect?* (The brothers chose Kitty Hawk.) *Why was Kitty Hawk a good place to fly planes?* (It was windy; the sandy beach allowed soft landings.)

Page 306

Paragraph 1

Was the brothers' first flight successful? (no) *How did this experience help the brothers learn?* (They built a better glider with bigger wings.)

Flying Firsts

Read the heading. Can you predict what this section will be about? (The brothers will try new ways of flying.)

Paragraph 1

Explain and Model Multiple-Meaning Words *Some words have more than one meaning. Have students choral read the last sentence. Here the word* unlocked *means "discovered." What else can* unlocked *mean?* ("opened something")

Look at the experiment at the bottom of the page. What materials do you need? (pencil, paper, ruler) *What do you measure in this experiment?* (how far the paper airplanes fly) *What is different about each plane?* (the wing size)

Page 307

Paragraph 1

We learn about Alberto Santos-Dumont, an inventor and pilot from Brazil. What did he do? Have one student answer the question and another elaborate on the answer. (He made the first official flight in front of an audience.)

Better Flying Machines

How have airplanes improved over time? (travel longer distances; carry more people)

Look at the picture of the plane in 1930. Think of a plane you have seen. How is it similar to this plane from the past? How is it different?

After Reading

Make Connections

- Review the Essential Question: How are people able to fly?
- Make text connections.
- Have students complete the **ELL Reproducibles** pages 183–185.

English Language Learners

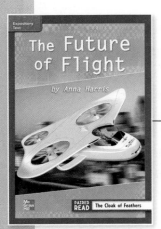

Lexile 670
TextEvaluator 18

OBJECTIVES

CCSS Describe the logical connection between particular sentences and paragraphs in a text (e.g. comparison, cause/effect, first/second/third in a sequence). **RI.3.8**

• Reread text to increase understanding.
• Determine meaning of multiple-meaning words.

LANGUAGE OBJECTIVE

Identify cause-and-effect relationships.

ACADEMIC LANGUAGE
cause, effect, expository, myth

Leveled Reader:
The Future of Flight

Go Digital

Before Reading

Preview

• Read the Essential Question: How are people able to fly?
• Refer to Up, Up, and Away: *What is this person using to fly?*
• Preview *The Future of Flight* and "The Cloak of Feathers": *Let's read how people can fly.*

Leveled Readers

Vocabulary

Use the **Visual Vocabulary Cards** to preteach the ELL vocabulary: *experts, explore, future, possible.* Use the routine found on the cards. Point out the cognates: *expertos, explorar, futuro, posible.*

During Reading

Interactive Question-Response

Note Taking Have students use their graphic organizer in **ELL Reproducibles** page 182. Use the following questions after you read each section. Use visuals or pictures to define key vocabulary.

Pages 2–3 *What is the effect of hot air forced out of a jetpack?* Have one student answer the question and another verify the answer. (The person wearing the jetpack is thrust into the air.)

Page 4 *A group of scientists is studying very small aircraft. What do the scientists want to know? Reread to answer the question.* (They want to know we can use it in the future.)

Page 5 *How could people fly the tiny aircraft safely?* (Aircraft would fly together and send out signals to each other; they would be controlled by a computer.)

Pages 6–8 *The word* trip *can mean "journey" or "to stumble and fall." Can an aircraft stumble and fall?* (no) *So here it means ____* (journey).

Page 9 *What does the chart on page 9 show?* (travel times today and in the future) *According to the chart, how long will it take to get from London to Tokyo in the future?* (2 hours) *Ask a partner another question about the chart.*

Fill in the Graphic Organizer

Pages 10–11 *What causes the spaceship to fly into space?* (the rocket engines firing up)

Pages 12–14 *What is the pull of gravity like when objects are far away from Earth? Reread page 12.* (not very strong) *What happens when people are in spaceships far away from Earth?* (They float.)

After Reading

Respond to Reading Help students complete the graphic organizer. Revisit the Essential Question. Have student pairs summarize and answer the Text Evidence questions. Support students as necessary, and review all responses as a group.

Analytical Writing **Write About Reading** Have students work with a partner to write a short paragraph about why people build new aircraft. Have students use words to signal the effects of new types of aircraft to air travel.

Fluency: Accuracy and Phrasing

Model Model reading page 2 with accuracy and proper phrasing. Next, reread the page aloud, and have students read along with you.

Apply Have students practice reading with a partner.

PAIRED READ

"The Cloak of Feathers"

Make Connections: Write About It *Analytical Writing*

Before reading, have students note that the genre of this text is a myth, which is a fictional tale that might explain why something is the way it is. Then discuss the Essential Question.

After reading, have students write about connections between how people fly in *The Future of Flight* and "The Cloak of Feathers."

Leveled Reader

🧪 **FOCUS ON SCIENCE**

Students can extend their knowledge of forces and motion by completing the science activity on page 20. **STEM**

Literature Circles

Ask students to conduct a literature circle using the Thinkmark questions to guide the discussion. You may wish to have a whole-class discussion on how students would use the flying technology in the text.

Level Up

Level-up lessons available online.

IF students read the **ELL Level** fluently and answered the questions

THEN pair them with students who have proficiently read **On Level** and have ELL students

- echo-read the **On Level** main selection with their partner.

- list difficult words and discuss them with their partner.

A C T Access Complex Text

The **On Level** challenges students by including more **domain-specific words** and **complex sentence structures**.

→ English Language Learners
Vocabulary

PRETEACH VOCABULARY

OBJECTIVES

 Acquire and use accurately grade-appropriate conversational, general academic, and domain-specific words and phrases, including those that signal spatial and temporal relationships (e.g., *After dinner that night we went looking for them*). **L.3.6**

LANGUAGE OBJECTIVE

Use vocabulary words.

 Preteach vocabulary from "Firsts in Flight" following the Vocabulary Routine on the **Visual Vocabulary Cards** for words *motion, flight, controlled, launched, direction, passenger, popular,* and *impossible.*

 After completing the Vocabulary Routine for each word, point to the word on the Visual Vocabulary Card and read the word with students. Have students repeat the word.

 Have students work with a partner to write short definitions for some of the words. Then have each pair read their definitions aloud.

Beginning	Intermediate	Advanced/High
Help students write two definitions correctly and read them aloud.	Have students write four definitions and read them aloud, including the part of speech for each word.	Challenge students to write a short definition for each word, including its part of speech.

REVIEW VOCABULARY

OBJECTIVES

 Acquire and use accurately grade-appropriate conversational, general academic, and domain-specific words and phrases including those that signal spatial and temporal relationships (e.g., *After dinner that night we went looking for them*). **L.3.6**

LANGUAGE OBJECTIVE

Use vocabulary words.

 Review the previous week's vocabulary words. They can be reviewed over a few days. Read each word aloud, pointing to the word on the **Visual Vocabulary Card**. Have students repeat after you. Then follow the Vocabulary Routine on the back of each card.

 Randomly select a Visual Vocabulary Card. Ask a volunteer to use the word in a sentence. Repeat with each card.

 In pairs, have students come up with ways to act out two or more words. Help students with multiple-meaning words, and suggest appropriate actions. Then have them act out the word meanings for the class.

Beginning	Intermediate	Advanced/High
Help students by acting out one word with them. Suggest actions for them.	Have students act out two or more word meanings.	Have students act out four or more words and define each word.

MULTIPLE-MEANING WORDS

OBJECTIVES

Use sentence-level context as a clue to the meaning of a word or phrase. **L.3.4a**

LANGUAGE OBJECTIVE

Determine the meanings of multiple-meaning words using context clues.

 I Do Read aloud the first paragraph of page 305 in "Firsts in Flight" while students follow along. Point to the sentence *Flying had been their dream since their father had given them a toy helicopter.* Explain that some words are spelled the same and sound the same but have different meanings. The word *dream* in this sentence is a multiple-meaning word.

Think Aloud I know that *dream* can mean "thoughts or images that a person has while asleep" and "a hope or ambition to do something." The context clues tell me that the Wright brothers are testing a flying machine, so I think that their *dream* is the hope of learning to fly.

We Do Point to the sentence *The Wright brothers owned a bicycle shop in Dayton* in the next paragraph. Help students determine the meaning of the multiple-meaning word *shop* in this sentence.

You Do In pairs, have students write the meaning of the word *landings* as it is used at the bottom of page 305 using context clues.

Beginning	Intermediate	Advanced/High
Help students use context clues to write a definition for *landings*.	Have students use context clues to write definitions for all three words.	Have students define all three words and use each in a complete sentence.

ADDITIONAL VOCABULARY

OBJECTIVES

Produce simple, compound, and complex sentences. **L.3.1i**

Discuss concept and high-frequency words.

LANGUAGE OBJECTIVE

Use concept and high-frequency words.

 I Do List concept and high-frequency words from "Firsts in Flight": *experimented, place;* and *The Future of Flight: aircraft, signals, put.* Define each word for students: *An* aircraft *is a machine that flies.*

 We Do Model using the words for students in a sentence: *This looks like a good* place *to play ball.* Then provide sentence frames, and complete them with students: *I think you need a better* place *to put your ___.*

 You Do Have pairs write a sentence using each word and share the completed sentences with the class.

Beginning	Intermediate	Advanced/High
Help students write the sentences correctly and complete them.	Provide sentence starters for students, if necessary.	After students share their sentences, have them define each word.

English Language Learners
Writing/Spelling

WRITING TRAIT: ORGANIZATION

 OBJECTIVES
Provide a concluding statement or section. **W.3.2d**

Identify concluding statements.

LANGUAGE OBJECTIVE
Write a strong conclusion on a single topic.

 I Do Explain that good writers use strong conclusions to help the reader understand the author's purpose. For informational text, the main idea may be restated in the conclusion. Read the Student Model passage aloud as students follow along, and identify the concluding statement.

 We Do Read aloud the passage "Better Flying Machines" on page 307 from "Firsts in Flight" as students follow along. Identify the concluding statement of each paragraph. Have students repeat the sentences chorally.

 You Do Have pairs write sentences on the topic of friendship with a strong conclusion. Tell them to restate their main ideas in the last sentence. Edit each pair's writing. Then ask students to revise.

Beginning	Intermediate	Advanced/High
Help students copy the edited sentences.	Have students revise, using words and phrases to show conclusion.	Have students revise to make a strong conclusion and edit for errors.

SPELL HOMOPHONES

 OBJECTIVES
Use conventional spelling for high-frequency and other studied words and for adding suffixes to base words (e.g., *sitting, smiled, cries, happiness*). **L.3.2e**

LANGUAGE OBJECTIVE
Spell homophones.

 I Do Read aloud the Spelling Words on page T226, modeling the pronunciation of each word. Point out that while the words sound the same, they have different meanings and spellings. Have students repeat the words.

 We Do Read the Dictation Sentences on page T227 aloud for students. With each sentence, read the underlined word slowly, modeling proper pronunciation. Have students repeat after you and write the word.

 You Do Display the words. Have students exchange their lists with partners to check the spelling and write the words correctly.

Beginning	Intermediate	Advanced/High
Help students copy the words with correct spelling and say the words aloud.	After students have corrected their words, have pairs quiz each other.	After students have corrected their words, have them define them.

Grammar

COMPLEX SENTENCES

OBJECTIVES

 Produce simple, compound, and complex sentences. **L.3.1i**

Identify complex sentences.

LANGUAGE OBJECTIVE

Write sentences.

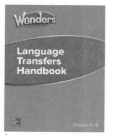

Language Transfers Handbook

Speakers of Cantonese, Haitian Creole, Hmong, Korean, and Khmer should have a transferable understanding of clauses, but they may have difficulties with subject-verb agreement. Reinforce the use of -s in present tense, third-person form by helping students form sentences using the third-person form.

 I Do

Remind students that a complex sentence includes an independent clause and one or more dependent clauses. An independent clause can stand alone as a sentence, but a dependent clause cannot. Dependent clauses often begin with a connecting word such as *before, when,* or *because.* Write on the board: *I have to do my homework before I can play any games.* This is a complex sentence because it has both an independent and a dependent clause. Tell students that *I have to do my homework* is the independent clause. The dependent clause is *before I can play any games* because it could not be a complete sentence by itself.

 We Do

Write the complex sentences below on the board. Review simple and complex sentences with students. Ask volunteers to name the independent and dependent clauses for each sentence. Then read the completed sentences aloud for students to repeat.

> *We can finish the baseball game after the rainstorm ends.*

> *The mayor was a lawyer before she ran for office.*

> *Audrey and Laura can go on the field trip because their parents signed their permission slips.*

 You Do

Have students pairs write three sentences. One writes three independent clauses. The other writes three dependent clauses. Then have students match their independent clauses to their dependent clauses to make complex sentences. Have students read their sentences aloud.

Beginning	Intermediate	Advanced/High
Help students write both kinds of clauses. Read the sentences aloud for students to repeat after you.	Ask students to write three related sentences about the same topic and identify the different kinds of clauses in each.	Have students write three related sentences about the same topic and combine them into one paragraph.

For extra support, have students complete the activities in the **Grammar Practice Reproducibles** during the week, using the routine below:

- Explain the grammar skill.
- Model the first activity in the Grammar Practice Reproducibles.
- Have the whole group complete the next couple of activities, then the rest with a partner.
- Review the activities with correct answers.

PROGRESS MONITORING

Unit 4 Week 4 Formal Assessment	Standards Covered	Component for Assessment
Text Evidence	RI.3.1	• *Selection Test* • *Weekly Assessment* • *Approaching-Level Weekly Assessment*
Text Structure: Cause and Effect	RI.3.3	• *Weekly Assessment* • *Approaching-Level Weekly Assessment*
Multiple-Meaning Words	L.3.4a	• *Selection Test* • *Weekly Assessment* • *Approaching-Level Weekly Assessment*
Writing About Text	W.3.8	*Weekly Assessment*
Unit 4 Week 4 Informal Assessment	**Standards Covered**	**Component for Assessment**
Research/Listening/ Collaborating	SL.3.1d, SL.3.2, SL.3.3	• *RWW* • *Teacher's Edition*
Oral Reading Fluency (ORF) **Fluency Goal:** 82–102 words correct per minute (WCPM) **Accuracy Rate Goal:** 95% or higher	RF.3.4a, RF.3.4b, RF.3.4c	*Fluency Assessment*

Using Assessment Results

Weekly Assessments Skills and Fluency	If . . .	Then . . .
COMPREHENSION	Students score below 70% . . .	. . . assign Lessons 76–78 on Text Structure: Cause and Effect from the *Tier 2 Comprehension Intervention online PDFs*.
VOCABULARY	Students score below 70% . . .	. . . assign Lesson 138 on Using Homograph Clues from the *Tier 2 Vocabulary Intervention online PDFs*.
WRITING	Students score below "3" on constructed response . . .	. . . assign Lessons 76–78 and/or Write About Reading Lesson 200 from the *Tier 2 Comprehension Intervention online PDFs*.
FLUENCY	Students have a WCPM score of 75–81 . . .	. . . assign a lesson from Section 1, 7, 8, 9 or 10 of the *Tier 2 Fluency Intervention online PDFs*.
	Students have a WCPM score of 0–74 . . .	. . . assign a lesson from Sections 2–6 of the *Tier 2 Fluency Intervention online PDFs*.

Using Weekly Data

Check your data Dashboard to verify assessment results and guide grouping decisions.

Data-Driven Recommendations

Response to Intervention

Use the appropriate sections of the *Placement and Diagnostic Assessment* as well as students' assessment results to designate students requiring:

 Intervention Online PDFs

 WonderWorks Intervention Program

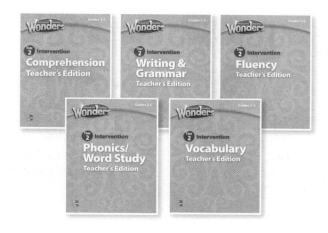

Build Knowledge
Inspiration

? Essential Question:
How can others inspire us?

Teach and Model
Close Reading and Writing

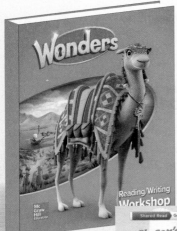

**Reading/Writing
Workshop**

"Ginger's Fingers," "The Giant,"
"Captain's Log," 318–321
Genre Narrative and Free Verse **Lexile** N/A
ETS *TextEvaluator* N/A

Practice and Apply
Close Reading and Writing

Literature Anthology

*"The Winningest Woman of the Iditarod Dog
Sled Race,"* 360–362
Genre Poetry **Lexile** N/A **ETS** *TextEvaluator* N/A

"Narcissa," 364–365
Genre Poetry **Lexile** N/A **ETS** *TextEvaluator* N/A

Differentiated Texts

APPROACHING
Lexile 480
ETS *TextEvaluator* 36

ON LEVEL
Lexile 590
ETS *TextEvaluator* 25

BEYOND
Lexile 700
ETS *TextEvaluator* 33

ELL
Lexile 510
ETS *TextEvaluator* 36

Leveled Readers

Extended Complex Texts

Stone Fox
Genre Fiction
Lexile 550

**Make Way for
Dyamonde Daniel**
Genre Fiction
Lexile 620

Classroom Library

Student Outcomes

Close Reading of Complex Text
- Cite relevant evidence from text
- Determine theme
- Identify repetition and rhyme

RL.3.2

Writing

Write to Sources
- Draw evidence from literature
- Write narrative texts
- Conduct extended research on frogs

Writing Process
- Draft and Revise a Poem

W.3.3d, W.3.8, W.3.10, W.4.9a

Speaking and Listening
- Engage in collaborative discussions about inspiration
- Paraphrase portions of "My Grandpa"
- Present information on inspiration

SL.3.1b, SL.3.1d, SL.3.2, SL.3.3

Language Development

Conventions
- Form and use regular and irregular verbs

Vocabulary Acquisition
- Acquire and use academic vocabulary

  adventurous   courageous   extremely   weird
- Demonstrate understanding of metaphor

L.3.1d, L.3.1f, L.3.5a, L.3.5b, RL.3.4

Foundational Skills

Phonics/Word Study
- Soft *c* and *g*
- Words with -*er* and -*est*

Spelling Words

pounce	placed	dice	price	space
mice	office	wage	age	gyms
giant	changes	message	pages	cents

Fluency
- Expression

RF.3.3c, RF.3.4a, RF.3.4b, RF.3.4c

Ken Karp/McGraw-Hill Education

Professional Development
- See lessons in action in real classrooms.
- Get expert advice on instructional practices.
- Collaborate with other teachers.
- Access PLC Resources.

Go Digital! www.connected.mcgraw-hill.com.

INSTRUCTIONAL PATH

1 Talk About Inspiration

Guide students in collaborative conversations.

Discuss the essential question: *How can others inspire us?*

Develop academic language.

Listen to "My Grandpa" and discuss the poem.

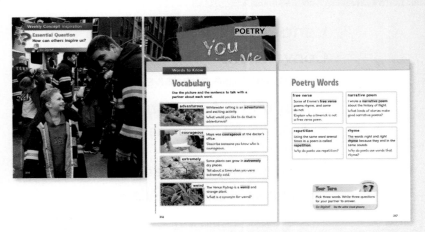

2 Read Poetry

Model close reading with a short complex text.

Read

"Ginger's Fingers," "The Giant," and **"Captain's Log"** to learn about people who inspire others, citing text evidence to answer text-dependent questions.

Reread

"Ginger's Fingers," "The Giant," and **"Captain's Log"** to analyze text, craft, and structure, citing text evidence.

Write About Poetry

3 Model writing to a source.

Analyze a short response student model.

Use text evidence from close reading to write to a source.

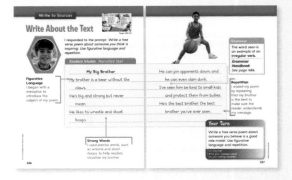

4 Read and Write About Poetry

Practice and apply close reading of the anchor text.

Read

"The Winningest Woman of the Iditarod Dog Sled Race" and "The Brave Ones" to learn about courage and bravery.

Reread

"The Winningest Woman of the Iditarod Dog Sled Race" and "The Brave Ones" and use text evidence to understand how the poets use text, craft, and structure to develop a deeper understanding of the poems.

Write a short response about the poems.

Integrate

Information about how the two women in the poems are alike and different.

Write to Two Sources, citing text evidence from poetry.

5 Independent Partner Work

Gradual release of support to independent work.

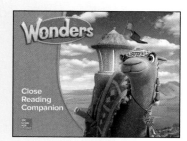

- Text-Dependent Questions
- Scaffolded Partner Work
  Talk with a Partner
  Cite Text Evidence
  Complete a sentence frame.
- Guided Text Annotation

6 Integrate Knowledge and Ideas

Connect Texts

Text to Text Discuss how each of the texts answers the question: How can others inspire us?

Text to Photography Compare similarities in the themes of the poems read and the photograph.

Performance Task

Revise and edit.

Write to Sources

Day 1 and Day 2

Build Writing Fluency

- Quick write on "Ginger's Fingers," p. T284

Write to a Source

- Analyze a student model, p. T284

- Write about "Ginger's Fingers," p. T285

- Apply Writing Trait: Strong Words, p. T284

- Apply Grammar Skill: Irregular Verbs, p. T285

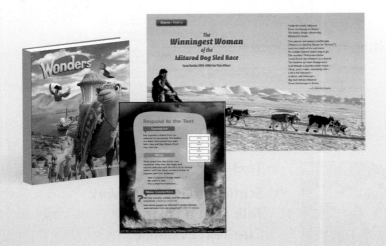

Day 3

Write to a Source

- Write about "The Winningest Woman of the Iditarod Dog Sted Race," independent practice, p. T281D

- Provide scaffolded instruction to meet student needs, p. T286

Day 4 and Day 5

Write to Two Sources

- Analyze a student model, pp. T286–T287

- Write to compare "The Winningest Woman of the Iditarod Dog Sted Race" with "Narcissa," p. T287

WEEK 4: PREWRITE | **WEEK 5: DRAFT AND REVISE** | **WEEK 6: PROOFREAD/EDIT, PUBLISH, EVALUATE**

Writing Process

Go Digital

Writer's Workspace

Genre Writing: Narrative Text/Poetry

Poetry

Draft

- Discuss the student draft model
- Students write their drafts

Revise

- Discuss the revised student model
- Students revise their drafts

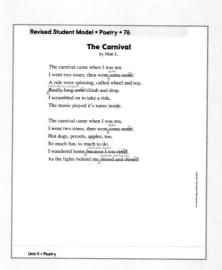

Revised Student Model

Student Draft Poetry

Revised Checklist

Grammar and Spelling Resources

Online PDFs

Reading/Writing Workshop Grammar Handbook p. 486

Online Spelling and Grammar Games

Grammar Practice, pp. 96–100

Phonics/Spelling Practice, pp. 115–120

SUGGESTED LESSON PLAN

Whole Group

READING		DAY 1	DAY 2
Teach, Model and Apply Reading/Writing Workshop	Core	**Introduce the Concept** T266–T267 **Vocabulary** T270–T271 **Close Reading** "Ginger's Fingers," "The Giant," and "Captain's Log," T272–T273	**Close Reading** "Ginger's Fingers," "The Giant," and "Captain's Log," T272–T273 **Skill** Theme, T276–T277 **Literary Element** Repetition and Rhyme, T278–T279 **Vocabulary Strategy** Metaphors, T280–T281
	Options	**Listening Comprehension** T268–T269	**Genre** Narrative and Free Verse, T274–T275

LANGUAGE ARTS			
Writing **Grammar** **Spelling** **Build Vocabulary**	Core	**Grammar** Irregular Verbs, T288 **Spelling** Soft c and g, T290 **Build Vocabulary** T292	**Write About the Text** Model Note-Taking, Write to a Prompt, T284–T285 **Grammar** Irregular Verbs, T288 **Build Vocabulary** T292
	Options	**Write About the Text** Writing Fluency, T284 **Genre Writing** Poetry and Draft, T352	**Genre Writing** Poetry: Teach the Draft Minilesson, T352 **Spelling** Soft c and g, T292

Writing Process: Narrative Poetry, T350–T355   Use with Weeks 4–6

Small Group

Differentiated Instruction Use your data dashboard to determine each student's needs. Then select instructional support options throughout the week.

APPROACHING LEVEL

Leveled Reader
A Speech to Remember, T296–T297

"Let the Lion Roar," T297

Literature Circles, T297

Phonics/Decoding
Decode Words with Soft c, T298 **TIER 2**
Practice Words with Soft c and g, T299
Words with -er and -est, T299

Vocabulary
• Review High-Frequency Words, T300 **TIER 2**
• Answer Choice Questions, T301
Metaphors, T301

Comprehension
• Identify Key Details, T302 **TIER 2**
• Review Theme, T303
Self-Selected Reading, T303

Fluency
Expression, T302 **TIER 2**

ON LEVEL

Leveled Reader
Melanie's Mission, T304–T305

"In the Land of Lions," T305

Literature Circles, T305

Vocabulary
Review Vocabulary Words, T306
Metaphors, T306

Comprehension
Review Theme, T311
Selected Self-Read, T311

DAY 3	DAY 4	DAY 5
Close Reading "The Winningest Woman of the Iditarod Dog Sled Race" and "The Brave Ones," T281A–T281D	**Fluency** T283 **Close Reading** "Narcissa," T281E–T281F **Integrate Ideas** Inquiry Space, T294–T295	**Integrate Ideas** T294–T295 • Text Connections • Inquiry Space **Weekly Assessment**
Phonics/Decoding T282–T283 • Soft *c* and *g*, T282 • Words with -*er* and -*est*, T283	**Close Reading** "The Winningest Woman of the Iditarod Dog Sled Race" and "The Brave Ones," T281A–T281D	
Grammar Irregular Verbs, T291	**Write About Two Texts** Model Note-Taking and Taking Notes, T286	**Write About Two Texts** Analyze Student Model and Write to the Prompt, T287 **Spelling** Soft *c* and *g*, T291
Write About the Text T286 **Genre Writing** Poetry: Teach the Draft Minilesson, T353 **Spelling** Soft *c* and *g*, T293 **Build Vocabulary** T293	**Genre Writing** Poetry: Teach the Revise Minilesson, T353 **Grammar** Irregular Verbs, T291 **Spelling** Soft *c* and *g*, T293 **Build Vocabulary** T293	**Genre Writing** Poetry: Peer Conferences, T353 **Grammar** Irregular Verbs, T291 **Build Vocabulary** T293

Writing Process: Narrative Poetry, T350–T355   Use with Weeks 4–6

BEYOND LEVEL

Leveled Reader
In the Running, T308–T309
"Everybody's Surfing," T309
Literature Circles, T309

Vocabulary
Review Domain-Specific Words, T310
• Metaphors, T310
• Shades of Meaning, T310

Gifted and Talented

Comprehension
Review Theme, T311
• Self-Selected Reading, T311
• Independent Study, T311

ENGLISH LANGUAGE LEARNERS

Shared Read
"Ginger's Fingers," "The Giant," and "Captain's Log," T312-T313

Leveled Reader
Melanie's Mission, T314–T315
"The Greedy Puppy," T315
Literature Circles, T315

Phonics/Decoding
Decode Words with Soft *c*, T298
Build Words with Soft *c* and *g*, T298
Practice Words with Soft *c* and *g*, T299
Words with -*er*, and -*est*, T299

Vocabulary
• Preteach Vocabulary, T316
• Review High-Frequency Words, T300
Review Vocabulary, T316
Metaphors, T317
Additional Vocabulary, T317

Spelling
Spell Words with Soft *c* and *g*, T318

Writing
Writing Trait: Word Choice, T318

Grammar
Irregular Verbs, T319

DIFFERENTIATE TO ACCELERATE

 Scaffold to **A**ccess **C**omplex **T**ext

IF	the text complexity of a particular selection is too difficult for students

THEN	see the references noted in the chart below for scaffolded instruction to help students Access Complex Text.

Qualitative | Quantitative
Reader and Task
TEXT COMPLEXITY

	Reading/Writing Workshop	Literature Anthology	Leveled Readers		Classroom Library

Quantitative

Reading/Writing Workshop

"Ginger's Fingers"

Lexile N/A
TextEvaluator™ N/A

Literature Anthology

"The Winningest Woman of the Iditorod Dog Sled Race"

Lexile N/A
TextEvaluator™ N/A

"Narcissa"

Lexile N/A
TextEvaluator™ N/A

Leveled Readers

Approaching Level

Lexile 480
TextEvaluator™ 36

Beyond Level

Lexile 700
TextEvaluator™ 33

On Level

Lexile 590
TextEvaluator™ 25

ELL

Lexile 510
TextEvaluator™ 36

Classroom Library

Stone Fox

Lexile 550

Make Way for Dyamonde Daniel

Lexile 620

Qualitative

What Makes the Text Complex?

- **Specific Vocabulary** Figurative Language T273 Metaphor T281

 See Scaffolded Instruction in Teacher's Edition T273 and T281.

What Makes the Text Complex?

- **Genre** Narrative Poetry T281A–T281B
- **Organization** Sequence T281C
- **Connection of Ideas** Inference T281E–T281F

ACT *See Scaffolded Instruction in Teacher's Edition T281A–T281F.*

What Makes the Text Complex?

- Specific Vocabulary
- Prior Knowledge
- Sentence Structure
- Connection of Ideas
- Genre

ACT *See Level Up lessons online for Leveled Readers.*

What Makes the Text Complex?

- Genre
- Specific Vocabulary
- Prior Knowledge
- Sentence Structure
- Organization
- Purpose
- Connection of Ideas

ACT *See Scaffolded Instruction in Teacher's Edition T360–T361.*

Reader and Task

The Introduce the Concept lesson on pages T266–T267 will help determine the reader's knowledge and engagement in the weekly concept. See pages T270–T281 and T294–T295 for questions and tasks for this text.

The Introduce the Concept lesson on pages T266–T267 will help determine the reader's knowledge and engagement in the weekly concept. See pages T281A–T281F and T294–T295 for questions and tasks for this text.

The Introduce the Concept lesson on pages T266–T267 will help determine the reader's knowledge and engagement in the weekly concept. See pages T296–T297, T304–T305, T308–T309, T314–T315, and T294–T295 for questions and tasks for this text.

The Introduce the Concept lesson on pages T266–T267 will help determine the reader's knowledge and engagement in the weekly concept. See pages T360–T361 for questions and tasks for this text.

GoDigital! www.connected.mcgraw-hill.com

Monitor and *Differentiate*

✓ Quick Check

To differentiate instruction, use the Quick Checks to assess students' needs and select the appropriate small group instruction focus.

Genre Narrative and Free Verse T275
Comprehension Skill Theme T277
Literary Elements Repetition and Rhyme T279
Vocabulary Strategy Metaphor T281
Phonics/Fluency Soft *c* and *g*, Expression T283

If No → | Approaching Level | **Reteach** T296–T303
| ELL | **Develop** T312–T319
If Yes → | On Level | **Review** T304–T307
| Beyond Level | **Extend** T308–T311

Using Weekly Data

Check your data Dashboard to verify assessment results and guide grouping decisions.

Level Up with Leveled Readers

IF students can read their leveled text fluently and answer comprehension questions

THEN work with the next level up to accelerate students' reading with more complex text.

Beyond T305
On Level T297 T315
Approaching ELL

Small Group Instruction

Use the ELL small group lessons in the Wonders Teacher's Edition to provide focused instruction.

Language Development
Vocabulary preteaching and review, additional vocabulary building, and vocabulary strategy lessons, pp. T316–T317

Close Reading
Interactive Question-Response routines for scaffolded text-dependent questioning for reading and rereading the Shared Read and Leveled Reader, pp. T312–T315

Writing
Focus on the weekly writing trait, grammar skills, and spelling words, pp. T318–T319

Additional ELL Support

Use *Reading Wonders for English Learners* for ELD instruction that connects to the core.

Language Development
Ample opportunities for discussions, and scaffolded language support

Close Reading
Companion Worktexts for guided support in annotating text and citing text evidence. Differentiated Texts about the weekly concept.

Writing
Scaffolded instruction for writing to sources and revising student models

Reading Wonders for ELLs Teacher Edition and Companion Worktexts

→ Introduce the Concept

Reading/Writing Workshop

OBJECTIVES

CCSS Engage effectively in a range of collaborative discussions (one-on-one, in groups, and teacher-led) with diverse partners on grade 3 topics and texts, building on others' ideas and expressing their own clearly. Follow agreed-upon rules for discussions (e.g., gaining the floor in respectful ways, listening to others with care, speaking one at a time about the topics and texts under discussion). **SL.3.1b**

Build background knowledge on inspiration.

ACADEMIC LANGUAGE
• *adventurous, courageous*
• Cognate: *aventurero*

MINILESSON 10 Mins

Build Background

ESSENTIAL QUESTION
How can others inspire us?

Have students read the Essential Question on page 314 of the **Reading/Writing Workshop**. Discuss the meaning of *inspire* with students.

Discuss the photograph of Danny and the firefighters. Focus on how people can inspire others.

• Danny talked to the firefighters and learned all about their **adventurous** jobs. They inspired him to become a firefighter, too.

• People who are **courageous**, or brave, and helpful can inspire us.

• When we feel inspired, we want to help others too.

Talk About It

Ask: *Do you know any courageous people who inspire you? Why do they inspire you? What are you inspired to do?* Have students discuss in pairs or groups.

• Model using the Concept Web to generate words and phrases related to inspiration. Add students' contributions.

• Have partners continue the discussion by describing how we are inspired by others. Partners can talk about the people who inspire them in their everyday lives.

Collaborative Conversations

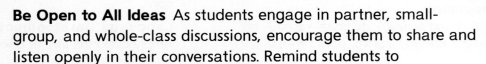

Be Open to All Ideas As students engage in partner, small-group, and whole-class discussions, encourage them to share and listen openly in their conversations. Remind students to

• be aware that all ideas, questions, or comments are important and should be heard.

• ask a question if something is unclear.

• respect the opinions of others.

• offer opinions, even if they are different from others' viewpoints.

Go Digital

Discuss the Concept

Watch Video

Use Graphic Organizer

Essential Question
How can others inspire us?

Go Digital!

POETRY

You Inspire Me

Danny talked to the firefighters in his neighborhood. He learned all about what they do. Danny thinks they are brave heroes. He wants to be a firefighter, too.

▶ People who are courageous and helpful inspire us.

▶ When we feel inspired, we want to help others, too.

Talk About It

Talk with a partner about how we are inspired by others. Write words about inspiration.

Inspiration

314   315

READING/WRITING WORKSHOP, *pp. 314–315*

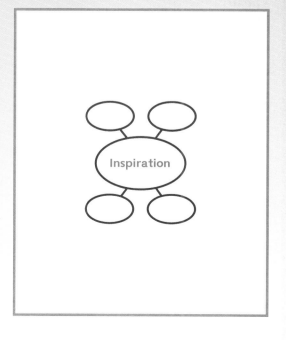

GRAPHIC ORGANIZER 62

Inspiration

ELL ENGLISH LANGUAGE LEARNERS SCAFFOLD

Beginning	Intermediate	Advanced/High
Use Visuals Point to the boy in the picture. Say: *The firefighters inspire Danny. He wants to be a firefighter.* Ask students: *Who inspires you?* Invite volunteers to list people who might inspire others. Give students ample time to respond.	**Describe** Have students describe the photograph. Ask: *Who is someone who inspires you? Why?* Elicit details to develop their responses. Encourage students to use Academic Language in their responses.	**Discuss** Have students work in pairs. Ask: *How can others inspire us? Who inspires you?* Encourage them to use Academic Language in their responses. Correct their answers for meaning as needed.

→ Listening Comprehension

 MINILESSON 10 Mins

Interactive Read Aloud

OBJECTIVES

CCSS Ask and answer questions to demonstrate understanding of a text, referring explicitly to the text as the basis for the answers. **RL.3.1**

CCSS Determine the main ideas and supporting details of a text read aloud or information presented in diverse media and formats, including visually, quantitatively, and orally. **SL.3.2**

• Listen for a purpose.
• Identify characteristics of poetry.

ACADEMIC LANGUAGE
• *poetry, reread*
• Cognate: *poesía*

Connect to Concept: Inspiration

Tell students that people are often inspired by others. Let students know that they will be listening to a poem about a boy who is inspired by an important person in his life—his grandfather. As students listen, have them think about how the poem answers the Essential Question.

Preview Genre: Poetry

Explain that the selection you will read aloud is a free-verse poem. Discuss features of poetry:

• may contain rhythmic patterns
• is written in lines and stanzas and may contain imagery, figurative language, and repetition
• expresses the thoughts and feelings of the poet

Preview Comprehension Strategy: Reread

Explain that when reading poetry, it is helpful to reread certain lines or stanzas of the poem to make sure you understand what the poet is trying to say.

Use the Think Alouds on page T269 to model the strategy.

Respond to Reading

Think Aloud Clouds Display Think Aloud Master 4: *When I read ____, I had to reread. . .* to reinforce how you used the Reread strategy to understand content.

Genre Features With students, discuss the elements of the Read Aloud that let them know it is poetry. Ask them to think about other poems that you have read or they have read independently.

Summarize Have students determine the main idea and details of the poem. Then, have students briefly retell the story in their own words.

Go Digital

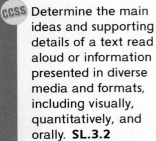
View Illustrations

Model Think Alouds

Genre	Features

Fill in Genre Chart

My Grandpa

When I was three,
my grandpa
was as tall as the tree

in the park where we used to sit
and feed the birds.
We scattered seed around
on the ground
and found
the birds fluttering around our heads
like funny, flying hats. **1**

When I was six,
my grandpa
could fix

a broken spoke, tell the best joke,
and scramble yolks
to make
the best omelet and toast
with a buttery
face that he

drew on my plate with two
raisins for eyes
and a cinnamon sugar smile. **2**

Now I am eight,
and my grandpa's
as great as the Golden Gate

Bridge, and the Statue of Liberty and Mount
Rushmore and the Grand Canyon and the
Atlantic and Pacific Oceans and all the astronauts
who ever went into space and all the explorers
who ever explored and all the presidents and
queens and kings of the entire world and even
into space and beyond.

And if you could roll all that greatness into one
big giant ball,
my grandpa is so great
that he would take me to the park
and we would play catch with it until dark. **3**

1 Think Aloud I think I'll **reread** this part again to make sure I understand what the poem is about.

2 Think Aloud This poem makes me think about some of my own experiences. I think I'll **reread** this part and think about meals I've shared with my own grandfather or other people who are important to me.

3 Think Aloud I understand that this poem is a tribute to the poet's grandfather. I think I'll **reread** the poem and think about each stage, when the poet was three, six, and eight, and what he or she was feeling at each age.

Yellow Dog Productions/Digital Vision/Getty Images

→ Vocabulary

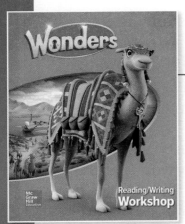

Reading/Writing Workshop

OBJECTIVES

CCSS Demonstrate understanding of word relationships and nuances in word meanings. Identify real-life connections between words and their use (e.g., describe people who are *friendly* or *helpful*). **L.3.5b**

ACADEMIC LANGUAGE
- *adventurous, courageous*
- Cognate: *aventurero*

 MINILESSON 10 Mins

Words in Context

Model the Routine

Introduce each vocabulary word using the **Vocabulary Routine** found on the **Visual Vocabulary Cards.**

Visual Vocabulary Cards

Vocabu...
Define:
Example:
Ask:

Vocabulary Routine

Define: Someone who is **adventurous** is willing to risk danger in order to have exciting or unusual experiences.

Example: Whitewater rafting is an adventurous and exciting activity.

Ask: What would you like to do that is *adventurous*?

Definitions

- **courageous**   People who are **courageous** are brave.
- **extremely**   **Extremely** means the same as "very."
- **weird**   Something that is **weird** is strange or mysterious.
- **free verse**   Some of Emma's **free verse** poems rhyme, and some do not.
- **narrative poem**   I wrote a **narrative poem** about the history of flight.
  Cognate: *poema narrativo*
- **repetition**   Using the same word several times in a poem is called **repetition**.
  Cognate: *repetición*
- **rhyme**   The words *night* and *right* **rhyme** with each other.
  Cognate: *rima*

Introduce each poetry word on page 317, and explain that students will find examples of these elements in the poems they read this week.

Talk About It

 COLLABORATE

Have partners look at each picture and definition. Have students choose three words and write questions for their partner to answer.

Go Digital

adventurous

Use Visual Glossary

Words to Know

Vocabulary

Use the picture and the sentence to talk with a partner about each word.

adventurous

Whitewater rafting is an **adventurous** and exciting activity.

What would you like to do that is adventurous?

courageous

Maya was **courageous** at the doctor's office.

Describe someone you know who is courageous.

extremely

Some plants can grow in **extremely** dry places.

Tell about a time when you were extremely cold.

weird

The Venus Flytrap is a **weird** and strange plant.

What is a synonym for weird?

316

Poetry Words

free verse

Some of Emma's **free verse** poems rhyme, and some do not.

Explain why a limerick is not a free verse poem.

narrative poem

I wrote a **narrative poem** about the history of flight.

What kinds of stories make good narrative poems?

repetition

Using the same word several times in a poem is called **repetition**.

Why do poets use repetition?

rhyme

The words *night* and *right* **rhyme** because they end in the same sounds.

Why do poets use words that rhyme?

Your Turn COLLABORATE

Pick three words. Write three questions for your partner to answer.

Go Digital! *Use the online visual glossary*

317

READING/WRITING WORKSHOP, *pp. 316–317*

ENGLISH LANGUAGE LEARNERS SCAFFOLD

Beginning

Use Visuals Say: *Let's look at the picture for* adventurous. *The people in the picture are rafting.* Act out rafting. *Rafting is an exciting activity.* Have students complete the frame: *Rafting is an ____* (adventurous) *activity.* Correct students' pronunciation as needed. Point out that *adventurous* in Spanish is *aventurero.*

Intermediate

Describe Have students describe the picture for *adventurous.* Help them pronounce the word. Ask: *What is an* adventurous *activity? Turn to a partner and discuss what* adventurous *means.* Provide the frame: *____ is an adventurous activity.* Elicit details to support students' responses. Remind students that *adventurous* in Spanish is *aventurero.*

Advanced/High

Discuss Ask students to talk about the word for *adventurous* and use the word in a sentence. Ask: *What would you like to do that is* adventurous? Have partners discuss with a partner and share their ideas with the class. Correct responses for meaning as needed.

| extremely | weird | courageous | adventurous |

Use the context clues in each sentence to help you decide which vocabulary word fits best in the blank.

Helga's Aunt Gerta invited her to go hiking. Aunt Gerta hiked all the time in the canyon near her house. She even took pictures as she hiked the trails. Helga always enjoyed looking at the photographs of trees, birds, and even _____weird_____ looking bugs that she had never seen before.

Helga was very excited about going hiking in the canyon. The last time she had done something ___adventurous___ was a nature walk she took in the field behind her house. But that was hardly as daring and exciting as a hike in a canyon. Helga remembered one of her favorite stories about a ___courageous___ explorer who had been brave enough to climb Mount Everest. The canyon wasn't exactly Mount Everest, but it was a start.

There was a knock on the door. Helga ran to answer it, with her mother close behind. It was her aunt. "Are you ready for our adventure, Helga?" asked Aunt Gerta.

"More than you know!" said Helga. "Let me grab my backpack!"

"Your backpack is on the couch," said Helga's mother. "The summer sun is already shining brightly so it will be ___extremely___ hot on the trails. I put two bottles of cold water and some apple slices in there for you."

"Thanks, Mom!" said Helga. Then she ran to join Aunt Gerta for their hiking adventure.

| APPROACHING p. 191 | BEYOND p. 191 | ELL p. 191 |

Shared Read Genre • Poetry

Ginger's Fingers

Ginger's fingers are shooting stars,
They talk of adventurous trips to Mars.
 Fingers talking without words,
 Signing when sounds can't be heard.
Ginger's fingers are ocean waves,
They talk of fish and deep sea caves.
 Fingers talking without words,
 Signing when sounds can't be heard.
Ginger's fingers are butterflies,
They talk of a honey-gold sunrise.
 Fingers talking without words,
 Signing when sounds can't be heard.

? Essential Question
How can others inspire us?
Read about different ways
that people inspire others.

318

The Giant

Dodge, dart, dash,
 Zigzag, slash!
I sizzle, SIZZLE, when I dribble,
I'm lightning on the court.
My team calls me The Giant,
Even though I'm kinda short.

The other team might laugh to see
A player tiny as a flea.

But I'm a rocket, fiery hot,
Watch me soar, SOAR, on my jump shot!

Stretching, flexing, push, push, PUSH,
My ball flies up and in—Swoosh Woosh!

I show them all
You don't need tall
To rule the ball!

319

READING/WRITING WORKSHOP, pp. 318–319

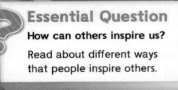

Reading/Writing Workshop

See pages T312–T313 for Interactive Question-Response routine for the Shared Read.

Shared Read

Close Reading Routine

Read DOK 1–2

• Identify key ideas and details about Inspiration.
• Take notes and summarize.
• Use **A C T** prompts as needed.

Reread DOK 2–3

• Analyze the text, craft, and structure.
• Use the Reread minilessons.

Integrate DOK 4

• Integrate knowledge and ideas.
• Make text-to-text connections.
• Use the Integrate lesson.

Read

Connect to Concept: Inspiration Tell students they will read poems about people who inspire others.

Note Taking Read page 318 together. As you read, model how to take notes. *I will think about the Essential Question as I read and note key ideas and details.* Encourage students to note words they don't understand and questions they have.

"Ginger's Fingers" Stanza 1: Ask: *What does this stanza mean?* Model how to decode the text.

The poet says that Ginger's fingers talk about trips to Mars. Her fingers are "talking without words" and are "signing," meaning that Ginger tells stories using sign language.

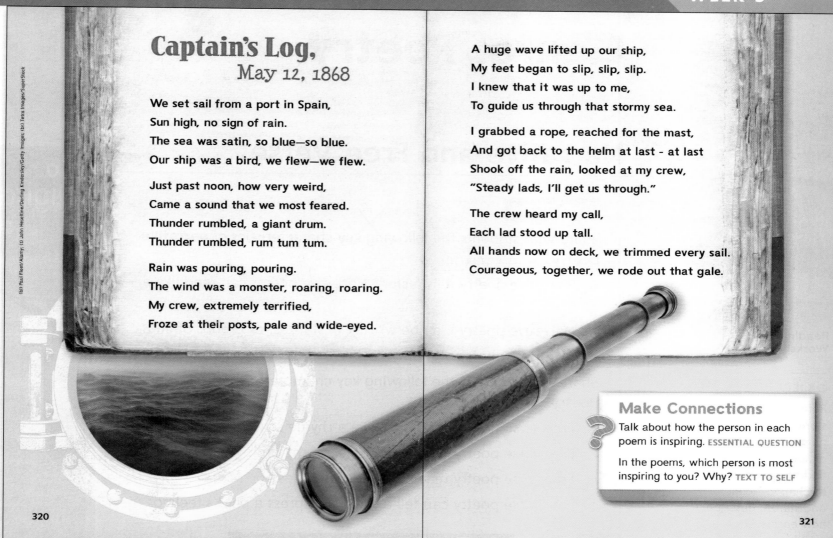

Captain's Log,
May 12, 1868

We set sail from a port in Spain,
Sun high, no sign of rain.
The sea was satin, so blue—so blue.
Our ship was a bird, we flew—we flew.

Just past noon, how very weird,
Came a sound that we most feared.
Thunder rumbled, a giant drum.
Thunder rumbled, rum tum tum.

Rain was pouring, pouring.
The wind was a monster, roaring, roaring.
My crew, extremely terrified,
Froze at their posts, pale and wide-eyed.

A huge wave lifted up our ship,
My feet began to slip, slip, slip.
I knew that it was up to me,
To guide us through that stormy sea.

I grabbed a rope, reached for the mast,
And got back to the helm at last - at last
Shook off the rain, looked at my crew,
"Steady lads, I'll get us through."

The crew heard my call,
Each lad stood up tall.
All hands now on deck, we trimmed every sail.
Courageous, together, we rode out that gale.

Make Connections

Talk about how the person in each poem is inspiring. ESSENTIAL QUESTION

In the poems, which person is most inspiring to you? Why? TEXT TO SELF

320   321

READING/WRITING WORKSHOP, *pp. 320–321*

"Captain's Log" Stanza 1: Point out the use of metaphor in the first stanza. Model how to describe the effect of the metaphors.

The metaphors help me to imagine what the start of the trip was like. Satin is very smooth, and so was the water. They traveled as swiftly as a bird.

Make Connections
COLLABORATE

Essential Question Encourage students to work with a partner to discuss how the person in each poem is inspiring. Ask them to cite text evidence. Use these sentence frames to focus discussion:

Ginger and The Giant inspire people by . . .
The Captain inspired his crew by . . .

A C T Access Complex Text

▶ **Specific Vocabulary**

Students may be unfamiliar with the poet's use of figurative language in "The Giant."

• Point out the word *sizzle* in the first stanza.

• Ask: *What is happening when something is sizzling?* (It is very hot.) *Is The Giant actually sizzling?* (no) *Why does the poet say he sizzles?* (He is hot on the court; he is playing great and can't be stopped.)

• Ask: *What other sound words does the poet use?* (swoosh, woosh) *What do they emphasize?* (the ball going in the basket)

→ Genre: Poetry

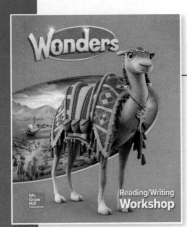

Reading/Writing Workshop

OBJECTIVES

CCSS Refer to parts of stories, dramas, and poems when writing or speaking about a text, using terms such as chapter, scene, and stanza; describe how each successive part builds on earlier sections. **RL.3.5**

CCSS By the end of the year, read and comprehend literature, including stories, dramas, and poetry, at the high end of the grades 2–3 text complexity band independently and proficiently. **RL.3.10**

Identify characteristics of narrative poetry and free verse poetry.

ACADEMIC LANGUAGE

- *narrative poetry, free verse poetry*
- Cognate: *poesía narrativa*

Narrative and Free Verse

1 Explain

Share with students the following key characteristics of **narrative poetry**:

- Narrative poetry tells a story. Narrative poems can read like a story.
- Narrative poetry may be written in stanzas, or groups of lines.
- Narrative poetry often rhymes.

Share with students the following key characteristics of **free verse poetry**:

- Free verse poetry does not have a rhyme scheme.
- Free verse poetry does not have a set rhythmic pattern.
- Free verse poetry may have irregular lines.
- Free verse poetry can tell a story or express a poet's feelings.

2 Model Close Reading: Text Evidence

Model identifying features of narrative poetry on page 320 of "Captain's Log."

3 Guided Practice of Close Reading

Have students work with partners to find elements in the text that show "The Giant" is a free verse poem. Partners should discuss what they learned from each element. Then have them share their work with the class.

Go Digital

Present the Lesson

Genre > Poetry

Narrative and Free Verse

Narrative poetry: • Tells a story. • Often has stanzas, or groups of lines. • Often rhymes.

Free verse poetry: • Does not always rhyme. • Can have stanzas with different numbers of lines. • Can tell a story or express a poet's feelings.

 Find Text Evidence

I can tell that "Captain's Log" is a narrative poem. It is a story of a ship's captain who inspires his crew during a bad storm.

> "Captain's Log" is a narrative poem that rhymes and has stanzas. It tells a story. This part describes the storm and how scared the crew on the ship was.

Your Turn

Reread "The Giant." Explain why it is a free verse poem.

322

READING/WRITING WORKSHOP, *p. 322*

Monitor and *Differentiate*

✔ Quick Check

Do students identify the elements of narrative and free verse poetry in the poems they have read?

Small Group Instruction

If No → | Approaching Level | Reteach p. T296
| ELL | Develop p. T312
If Yes → | On Level | Review p. T304
| Beyond Level | Extend p. T308

ENGLISH LANGUAGE LEARNERS SCAFFOLD

ELL

Beginning	**Intermediate**	**Advanced/High**
Clarify Reread the poem on page 320. Point out that the poem uses the form of a journal entry to tell a story. Explain that *we set sail* means that the ship left port. Clarify students' understanding as you read.	**Describe** Have students reread page 320 of "Captain's Log." Ask: *What is the poem about?* (a journey at sea) Point out why the text is difficult. The narrator is a captain on a ship from Spain in 1868, describing in his journal a storm while at sea.	**Discuss** Have partners reread page 320 of "Captain's Log." Elicit why the text is difficult. Ask: *What is the story in this poem? Turn to a partner and explain.* If necessary, ask additional questions to develop students' responses.

ON-LEVEL PRACTICE BOOK p. 195

If I Could Just Get Out of Bed

If I get out of bed, I could
    read a book about the moon
        and one about a rocket ship
           and one that tells me how to make
               a ship that flies me into space
                   to be the first kid on the moon
               if I get out of bed.

Answer the questions about the poem.

1. What makes this poem free verse?
It has no rhyming pattern.

2. Whose point of view is the poem written from?
It's written from the first-person point of view by someone who doesn't want to get out of bed.

3. What event is the speaker in the poem describing?
The speaker is describing all of the things that could happen once he or she gets out of bed.

APPROACHING p. 195	BEYOND p. 195	ELL p. 195

→ Comprehension Skill

 MINILESSON **10** Mins

Theme

Reading/Writing Workshop

OBJECTIVES

CCSS Recount stories, including fables, folktales, and myths from diverse cultures; determine the central message, lesson, or moral and explain how it is conveyed through key details in the text. **RL.3.2**

- Identify and classify important details.
- Find evidence in the text.

ACADEMIC LANGUAGE

- *theme, message, details, clues*
- Cognates: *tema, detalles*

SKILLS TRACE

THEME

Introduce Unit 2 Week 1

Review Unit 2 Weeks 2, 6; Unit 4 Weeks 5, 6; Unit 6 Weeks 1, 2, 6

Assess Units 2, 4, 6

1 Explain

Explain to students that the theme is the message or lesson an author wants to communicate to the reader.

- To identify the theme in a poem, students must pay attention to the characters' thoughts and actions as well as the author's choice of words and descriptions.
- Then they must think about what happens as a result of the characters' actions or what feelings the author is trying to create through the choices they have made.
- Students should ask themselves, "What message does the author want to get across to the reader?"

2 Model Close Reading: Text Evidence

Identify the details in "The Giant" on page 319 that give clues about the theme. Then model using the clues written on the graphic organizer to determine the theme of the poem.

 Write About Reading: Summary Model for students how to use the notes from the graphic organizer to write a summary of what they learned from the poem.

3 Guided Practice of Close Reading

 Have students work in pairs to complete a graphic organizer for "The Giant." Have them list more details from the poem that support the theme. Discuss the details as students complete the graphic organizer.

 Write About Reading: Summary Ask pairs to work together to write a summary of the theme of "The Giant." Students should work with the details listed in their graphic organizers. Select pairs of students to share the theme with the class.

Go Digital

Present the Lesson

Theme

The theme is the main message or lesson in a poem. The details in a poem can help you figure out the theme.

 Find Text Evidence

All the poems in this week are about inspirational people, but each poem has a different theme. I'll reread "The Giant" and look for details. I can use the details to figure out the theme.

Detail
I sizzle when I dribble and I'm lightning on the court.

↓

Detail
The other team might laugh to see a player so small.

↓

Detail

↓

Detail

↓

Theme
If you believe in yourself, you can do anything.

Your Turn COLLABORATE

Reread "The Giant." Find more details and list them in your graphic organizer. Make sure they support the theme.

Go Digital!
Use the interactive graphic organizer

323

READING/WRITING WORKSHOP, *p. 323*

 ENGLISH LANGUAGE LEARNERS SCAFFOLD

Beginning

Recognize Reread the first stanza on page 319. Ask after each line: *Is this an important detail?* Help students explain that the third and fourth lines are important details that tell about the theme. ____ *are important details that tell about the theme.* Correct pronunciation as needed.

Intermediate

Describe Reread the poem on page 319. Ask: *What is an important detail that tells about the theme? How do you know? Explain to a partner.* Then have partners describe the important detail that tells about the theme. ____ *is an important detail because* ____. Correct grammar as needed.

Advanced/High

Discuss Have students describe the details on page 319 that help them discover the theme of the poem. Ask: *Based on these details, what might be the theme of "The Giant?"* Have partners discuss how these clues support the theme. Encourage them to use vocabulary words. Provide input as needed.

 **Monitor and *Differentiate***

✓ Quick Check

Can students find and list key details that give clues about the theme? Can they determine the theme of "The Giant"?

↓

Small Group Instruction

If No →	Approaching Level	Reteach p. T303
	ELL	Develop p. T315
If Yes →	On Level	Review p. T307
	Beyond Level	Extend p. T311

ON-LEVEL PRACTICE BOOK pp. 193–194

Read the poem. Check your understanding by asking yourself what message the author wants to share.

Why I Run

	The first marathon I ever saw
6	was years ago with my grandma.
12	We stood out on the Boston streets
19	and marveled at the number of feet
26	and marveled at the number of feet.
33	The runners were a rumbling herd,
39	except for a few—like the swiftest birds
47	who shot out alone to run their races
55	with determination carved into their faces
61	with determination carved into their faces.
67	Motorboats speeding over gray water,
72	these runners would inspire anyone's daughter.
78	That was the day I made the decision—
86	the bounce in my steps clarified my vision
94	the bounce in my steps clarified my vision.
102	I went home that day and laced up my shoes
112	and although my feet started out as one big bruise
122	I've run in every Boston Marathon since
129	and now I'm so strong I don't even wince
138	and now I'm so strong I don't *ever* wince.

APPROACHING pp. 193–194	BEYOND pp. 193–194	ELL pp. 193–194

→ Literary Elements

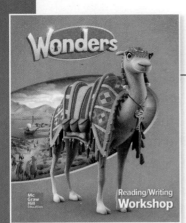

Reading/Writing Workshop

OBJECTIVES

Refer to parts of stories, dramas, and poems when writing or speaking about a text, using terms such as chapter, scene, and stanza; describe how each successive part builds on earlier sections. **RL.3.5**

Identify repetition and rhyme in poetry.

ACADEMIC LANGUAGE
• *repetition, rhyme*
• Cognate: *repetición*

 MINILESSON 10 Mins

Repetition and Rhyme

1 Explain

Explain that **repetition** is the use of repeated words and phrases in a poem.

- Repetition is used for rhythmic effect and emphasis.

- Many poets use repetition to express their ideas in interesting ways. It can also add to the emotional impact of a poem.

Explain that words **rhyme** with each other when their endings sound the same, such as *pouring* and *roaring*.

2 Model Close Reading: Text Evidence

Model identifying examples of repetition in "Captain's Log" on pages 320–321. Point out that in some lines, the repeating sounds also rhyme, giving the poem a musical quality.

3 Guided Practice of Close Reading

Have students work with partners to reread "Captain's Log." Have partners identify more examples of repetition and rhyme in the poem and describe the feelings they create. Ask volunteers to share their answers with the class.

Present the Lesson

Literary Elements

Repetition and Rhyme

Repetition means that words or phrases in a poem are repeated. A **rhyme** is two or more words that end with the same sounds, such as *pouring* and *roaring*.

 Find Text Evidence

Reread "Captain's Log" on pages 320–321. Listen for words or phrases that are repeated. Think about why the poet uses repetition.

> page 320
>
> ## Captain's Log,
> ### May 12, 1868
>
> We set sail from a port in Spain,
> Sun high, no sign of rain.
> The sea was satin, so blue—so blue.
> Our ship was a bird, we flew—we flew.

In the first stanza, the poet repeats the words so blue *and* we flew. *These words also rhyme. This repetition gives the poem a musical quality. It helps me feel the waves and how the ship moves on the sea.*

Your Turn

Reread "Captain's Log." Find examples of repetition and rhyme.

324

READING/WRITING WORKSHOP, *p. 324*

Monitor and *Differentiate*

✓ Quick Check

Can students identify examples of repetition and rhyme in "Captain's Log"?

↓

Small Group Instruction

If No → **Approaching Level** Reteach p. T297
ELL Develop p. T315
If Yes → **On Level** Review p. T305
Beyond Level Extend p. T309

 **ENGLISH LANGUAGE LEARNERS SCAFFOLD**

Beginning	Intermediate	Advanced/High
Clarify Reread the first stanza of "Captain's Log" with students, discussing the poem's main elements. Ask: *Which words have endings that sound the same?* Invite volunteers to write the words on the board. Do the same with repeated words. Correct spelling as necessary.	**Describe** Reread the first stanza of "Captain's Log" with students. Ask: *Which words repeat?* Provide the frame: ____ *and* ____ *repeat.* Ask: *Do these phrases rhyme?* Elicit details to develop students' responses.	**Discuss** Have partners reread "Captain's Log" together. Ask: *Which words and phrases are repeated? Why do you think the poet uses repetition?* Elicit details to develop students' responses, and encourage them to use Academic Language.

ON-LEVEL PRACTICE BOOK p. 196

Read the lines of the narrative poem below. Then follow the directions. Possible responses provided.

Why I Run

*Motorboats speeding over gray water,
these runners would inspire anyone's daughter.
That was the day I made the decision—
the bounce in my steps clarified my vision
the bounce in my steps clarified my vision.*

*I went home that day and laced up my shoes
and although my feet started out as one big bruise
I've run in every Boston Marathon since
and now I'm so strong I don't even wince
and now I'm so strong I don't even wince.*

1. Find two examples of rhyme in the poem. Draw boxes around the words.
2. Circle an example of repetition in the poem.
3. Write another stanza for this poem that includes repetition and rhyme.
   Answers will vary, but should include use of repetition and rhyme.

APPROACHING p. 196	BEYOND p. 196	ELL p. 196

→ Vocabulary Strategy

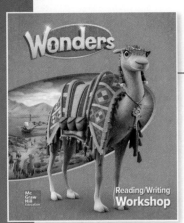

Reading/Writing Workshop

OBJECTIVES

CCSS Determine the meaning of words and phrases as they are used in a text, distinguishing literal from nonliteral language. **RL.3.4**

CCSS Demonstrate understanding of word relationships and nuances in word meanings. Distinguish the literal and nonliteral meanings of words and phrases in context (e.g., *take steps*). **L.3.5a**

ACADEMIC LANGUAGE

• *figurative language, metaphor*

• Cognate: *metáfora*

SKILLS TRACE

FIGURATIVE LANGUAGE: METAPHOR

Introduce Unit 1 Week 4

Review Unit 1 Week 5; Unit 4 Week 5

Assess Units 1, 4

MINILESSON 10 Mins

Figurative Language

1 Explain

Explain that **metaphors** compare two things that are different without using the words *like* or *as*. Metaphors are different from everyday language; they are a form of figurative language.

Sometimes authors use figurative, or nonliteral, language to help readers visualize something or to connect two separate ideas.

Students should know that metaphors do not mean exactly what they say. In the metaphor "His teeth are white pearls," the author is not saying the subject's teeth are actually pearls.

2 Model Close Reading: Text Evidence

Model identifying metaphors in "Ginger's Fingers" on page 318. Show students how to determine the meaning of the line "Ginger's fingers are shooting stars."

3 Guided Practice of Close Reading

Have students work in pairs to identify another metaphor in "Ginger's Fingers." Ask students to identify what two things are being compared and how the metaphor helps them visualize the poem.

Go Digital

Present the Lesson

Metaphor

A metaphor compares two things that are very different. It helps you picture, or visualize. "His teeth are white pearls" is a metaphor. It compares teeth to pearls. This metaphor helps me picture bright, white teeth.

 Find Text Evidence

On page 318, I read that "Ginger's fingers are shooting stars." This is a metaphor. It compares the way Ginger's fingers move and sign to shooting stars. This metaphor helps me picture Ginger's fingers moving quickly and quietly.

page 318

 Ginger's fingers are shooting stars,
They talk of adventurous trips to Mars.
Fingers talking without words,
Signing when sounds can't be heard.

Your Turn

Reread the poem "Ginger's Fingers." Find another metaphor. What two things are compared? Talk about how the metaphor helps you visualize.

Diverse Images/Universal Images Group /Getty Images

325

READING/WRITING WORKSHOP, *p. 325*

A C T Access Complex Text

▶ Specific Vocabulary

Students may have difficulty understanding metaphors. Have students read the third stanza in "Captain's Log" on page 320 and identify the metaphor. ("The wind was a monster")

- *How do you know this is a metaphor?* (It compares unlike things: the wind and a monster.)

- *How is the wind like a monster?* (The wind sounds like a monster. It can throw things around the way a giant monster might.)

Monitor and *Differentiate*

 Quick Check

Are students able to find an example of metaphors in "Ginger's Fingers"?

⬇

Small Group Instruction

If No → | Approaching Level | Reteach p. T301
        | ELL | Develop p. T317
If Yes → | On Level | Review p. T306
        | Beyond Level | Extend p. T310

ON-LEVEL PRACTICE BOOK p. 197

Read each passage. Find the metaphor and write it on the line. Then write the two things that are being compared.

1. The runners were a rumbling herd,
   except for a few—
   runners were a rumbling herd; runners and a herd of animals

2. Motorboats speeding over gray water,
   these runners would inspire anyone's daughter.
   motorboats speeding over gray water/these runners; motorboats and runners

3. I went home that day and laced up my shoes
   and although my feet started out as one big bruise
   my feet started out as one big bruise; feet and a bruise

| APPROACHING p. 197 | BEYOND p. 197 | ELL p. 197 |

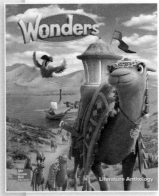

Literature Anthology

Lexile and TextEvaluator scores are not provided for non-prose selections, such as poetry and drama.

"The Winningest Woman of the Iditarod Dog Sled Race" and "The Brave Ones"

Text Complexity Range

Lexile

420   820

TextEvaluator™

2   35

NP Non-Prose*

What makes this text complex?
▸ **Genre**
▸ **Organization**

Close Reading Routine

| Read | DOK 1–2 |

- Identify key ideas and details about inspiration.
- Take notes and summarize.
- Use **A C T** prompts as needed.

| Reread | DOK 2–3 |

- Analyze the text, craft, and structure.
- Use *Close Reading Companion,* pp. 128–129.

| Integrate | DOK 4 |

- Integrate knowledge and ideas.
- Make text-to-text connections.
- Use the Integrate lesson.

The **Winningest Woman** of the **Iditarod Dog Sled Race**

Susan Butcher (1956–2006) Four-Time Winner

Essential Question

How can others inspire us?

Read about people who are courageous.

▸ *Go Digital!*

360

A C T Access Complex Text

▸ **Genre**

Help students recognize that although "The Winningest Woman of the Iditarod Dog Sled Race" is a poem, it shares many of the same elements as narrative fiction, including characters, setting, and a plot.

I rode the whole Iditarod
From Anchorage to Nome!
The husky sleigh, eleven day
Iditarod to Nome.

Two moose can cause a traffic jam.
(There is no word in Moose for *"Scram!"*)
And over trails of ice and snow,
No musher knows which way to go.
The weather? Forty-two below
Could freeze the whiskers in a beard!
The huskies up front disappeared
And though it sounds a little weird—
Okay, you're right, extremely odd—
I did I *did* Iditarod— **1**
A bitter cold Iditarod—
My sled slid the Iditarod
From Anchorage to Nome.

—*J. Patrick Lewis*

361

LITERATURE ANTHOLOGY, *pp. 360–361*

From The Fantastic 5 & 10¢ Store: A Rebus Adventure. Copyright © 2010 by J. Patrick Lewis. Used with permission of Chronicle Books LLC, San Francisco. Photo: Michio Hoshino/Minden Pictures.

Essential Question Ask a student to read aloud the Essential Question. Have students discuss how the poems will help them answer the question.

**Note Taking:
Use the Graphic Organizer** *Analytical Writing*

Remind students to take notes as they read. Have them fill in the graphic organizer on **Your Turn Practice Book** page 192 to record the theme in each poem.

1 Skill: Theme

What is the theme in "The Winningest Woman of the Iditarod Dog Sled Race"? (People can do things that seem difficult or impossible.) What details support the theme? (No musher knows which way to go; forty-two below; I did, I *did* Iditarod.)

Reread *Close Reading Companion*

Author's Craft: Figurative Language

How does the poet help you understand how the narrator feels about finishing the Iditarod? (The narrator repeats "I rode the whole Iditarod/From Anchorage to Nome" in different ways, to show how proud and amazed she must feel.)

- *Who is the main character?* (Susan Butcher)
- *What is the setting?* (from Anchorage to Nome)
- *What problem does Susan Butcher have?* (She has to face challenging conditions to run the race.)

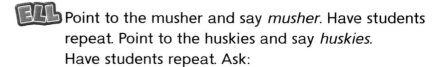 Point to the musher and say *musher*. Have students repeat. Point to the huskies and say *huskies*. Have students repeat. Ask:

- *What are huskies?* (dogs) *What do they pull?* (a sled)
- Guide students to complete this frame: The Iditarod is _____ (a dog sled race).

Read

2 Skill: Theme

What is the theme of this poem? (Firefighters are brave.) What details help you identify the theme? (we come in a hurry; we don't have much time; we are the brave ones who save)

Reread   *Close Reading Companion*

Literary Elements: Repetition

How does the poet's use of repetition help you visualize what it is like to fight a fire? (Repeating words and phrases, such as *hoses, we come in a hurry, fire, smoke, we are the brave ones who save,* emphasizes important words and actions. It also gives the poem a rushed, breathless rhythm to match the pace of the firefighters.)

The Brave Ones

We hear the bell clanging
we come in a hurry
we come with our ladders and hoses
our hoses
we come in a hurry
to fight the fire
the furious fire
to smother the smoke
the smoke
we don't have much time
we climb, we spray
we are the brave ones who save
who save
2 we are the brave ones who save

—*Eloise Greenfield*

362

LITERATURE ANTHOLOGY, *pp. 362–363*

A C T Access Complex Text

▶ Organization

Point out the use of sequence, rhythm, and repetition to capture the process of fighting a fire.

- *What starts the sequence of events?* (The firefighters hear the bell clanging.) *What do the firefighters do next?* (They come with their ladders and hoses to fight the fire.) *What do they do after they arrive?* (They climb and they spray.)

ELL Use sequence words to retell what firefighters do. Say: *First, firefighters hear the bell clanging. Then they come with ladders and hoses. Next, they climb and spray.* Have students repeat each step after you. Then have them retell or demonstrate what firefighters do.

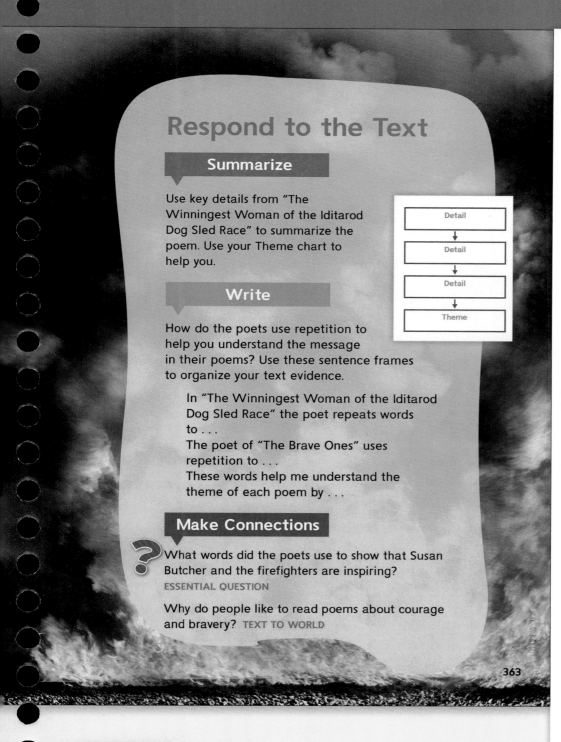

Respond to the Text

Summarize

Use key details from "The Winningest Woman of the Iditarod Dog Sled Race" to summarize the poem. Use your Theme chart to help you.

Detail
↓
Detail
↓
Detail
↓
Theme

Write

How do the poets use repetition to help you understand the message in their poems? Use these sentence frames to organize your text evidence.

In "The Winningest Woman of the Iditarod Dog Sled Race" the poet repeats words to . . .
The poet of "The Brave Ones" uses repetition to . . .
These words help me understand the theme of each poem by . . .

Make Connections

 What words did the poets use to show that Susan Butcher and the firefighters are inspiring?
ESSENTIAL QUESTION

Why do people like to read poems about courage and bravery? TEXT TO WORLD

363

Make Connections

Essential Question <u>Answer:</u> The first poem includes *winningest, bitter cold,* and *I did I did Iditarod.* The second poem includes *hurry, furious fire,* and *brave ones.* <u>Evidence:</u> Inspiring words are found in each title and in each poem. Words describe the difficulties of racing the Iditarod. Words describe the speed and bravery of firefighters.

Text to World Answers may vary, but encourage students to cite text evidence from their sources.

Respond to the Text

Read

Summarize

Tell students they will use details from their Theme Chart to summarize each poem. As I read each poem, I wrote down details. I can use these details to summarize what each poem is about.

Reread

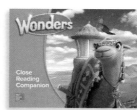

Analyze the Text

After students summarize, have them reread to develop a deeper understanding of the poems by answering the questions on **Close Reading Companion** pages 128–129. For students who need support in citing text evidence, use the Reread prompts on pages T281B–T281C.

Write About the Text

Review the writing prompt and sentence frames. Remind students to use their responses from the Close Reading Companion to support their answers. For a full lesson on writing a response using text evidence, see page T286.

<u>Answer:</u> The poets use repeated words and phrases to describe action, urgency, and a strong sense of purpose. <u>Evidence:</u> In the first poem, the word *Iditarod* is repeated with different phrases, such as "eleven day," "I did I *did*" (the second *did* for extra emphasis), "bitter cold," and "sled slid" to stress time and danger. In the second poem, the poet repeats the line "we come in a hurry" to signal the firefighters' urgency and "we are the brave ones who save" to emphasize their purpose.

Literature Anthology
*Lexile and TextEvaluator scores are not provided for non-prose selections, such as poetry and drama.

"Narcissa"

Text Complexity Range

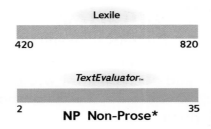

Lexile

420   820

TextEvaluator™

2   35
  NP Non-Prose*

What makes this text complex?
▶ **Connection of Ideas**

Compare Texts *Analytical Writing*

As students read and reread "Narcissa," encourage them to take notes and think about the Essential Question: *How can others inspire us?* Tell them to think about how it compares with "The Winningest Woman of the Iditarod Dog Sled Race" and "The Brave Ones."

Read

1 Ask and Answer Questions   COLLABORATE

With a partner, paraphrase what Narcissa does. (She sits in her back yard, imagining she is a queen, a wind, a nightingale.)

Reread   *Close Reading Companion*

Genre: Narrative Poem

How does the poet use descriptive words to help you visualize what Narcissa is doing? (The poet uses adjectives and rhymes.)

Reread   *Close Reading Companion*

Genre: Narrative Poem

Why does the poet repeat the phrase "as still" at the end of the poem? (The poet emphasizes that although Narcissa looks like she is not doing anything, she is doing a lot in her mind.)

Genre • Poetry

Compare Texts

Read how nature inspires a young girl to dream of great things.

364

A C T Access Complex Text

▶ Connection of Ideas

The poet does not directly state that Narcissa is daydreaming or using her imagination. Students will need to use their own experiences to make the inference.

• *What is Narcissa doing in the back yard?* (Sitting and looking at flowers)

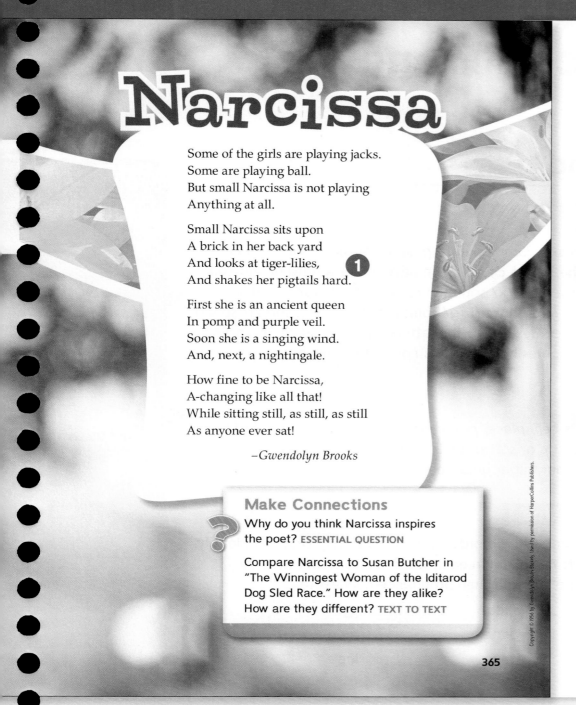

Narcissa

Some of the girls are playing jacks.
Some are playing ball.
But small Narcissa is not playing
Anything at all.

Small Narcissa sits upon
A brick in her back yard
And looks at tiger-lilies, **1**
And shakes her pigtails hard.

First she is an ancient queen
In pomp and purple veil.
Soon she is a singing wind.
And, next, a nightingale.

How fine to be Narcissa,
A-changing like all that!
While sitting still, as still, as still
As anyone ever sat!

–Gwendolyn Brooks

Make Connections

 Why do you think Narcissa inspires the poet? ESSENTIAL QUESTION

Compare Narcissa to Susan Butcher in "The Winningest Woman of the Iditarod Dog Sled Race." How are they alike? How are they different? TEXT TO TEXT

365

LITERATURE ANTHOLOGY, *pp. 364–365*

Read

Summarize

Guide students to summarize the poem.

Reread

Analyze the Text

After students read and summarize, have them reread to develop a deeper understanding of the poem by annotating and answering questions on pages 130–131 of the **Close Reading Companion**.

Integrate

Make Connections

Essential Question <u>Answer:</u> Narcissa can be anything she wants to be just through the power of her imagination. <u>Evidence:</u> In the last stanza, the poet says "how fine to be Narcissa" as she imagines being many different things.

Text to Text Narcissa and Susan Butcher both have adventures inspired by nature. Both enjoy doing things that others might not. However, Butcher had real adventures. Narcissa's adventures take place in her imagination.

- *Does Narcissa really become a queen, a wind, and a nightingale?* (no) *What is she doing?* (She is daydreaming or imagining herself as these things.)

ELL • Before reading, clarify terms such as *jacks* and *tiger lilies.*

- Say: *Narcissa is daydreaming. She is using her imagination.* Have students demonstrate daydreaming. Chorally read the stanza that tells what Narcissa imagines herself as.

→ Phonics/Fluency

MINILESSON 20 Mins

Soft *c* and *g*

Go Digital

Soft
c and g

Present the
Lesson

View
"The Giant"

OBJECTIVES

CCSS Know and apply grade-level phonics and word analysis skills in decoding words. Decode multisyllable words. **RF.3.3c**

CCSS Read on-level prose and poetry orally with accuracy, appropriate rate, and expression on successive readings. **RF.3.4b**

CCSS Create engaging audio recordings of stories or poems that demonstrate fluid reading at an understandable pace; add visual displays when appropriate to emphasize or enhance certain facts or details. **SL.3.5**

Rate: 82–102 WCPM

ACADEMIC LANGUAGE

• *expression*

• Cognate: *expresión*

ELL

Refer to the sound transfers chart in the **Language Transfers Handbook** to identify sounds that do not transfer in Spanish, Cantonese, Vietnamese, Hmong, and Korean.

1 Explain

Display the *Sun* and *Jump* **Sound-Spelling Cards** for soft *c* and *g*. Tell students that the letters *c* and *g* can have either a hard or soft sound. The letter *c* has a hard /k/ sound in *cat* and a soft /s/ sound in *circle*. The letter *g* has a hard /g/ sound in *goat* and a soft /j/ sound in *gem*. When *c* comes before the letters *i* or *e*, it usually has a /s/ sound. When *g* comes before letters *i* or *e*, it usually has a /j/ sound.

2 Model

Write the words *cell*, *place*, *price*, *age*, and *giant* on the board. Underline the soft *c* or soft *g* spelling in each word. Model how to say the words. Run your finger under each word as you sound it out.

3 Guided Practice

Write the following list of words on the board. Help students identify the soft *c* or soft *g* spelling in each word. Guide students as they underline the spelling and then pronounce each word.

since	slice	gyms
cents	page	dice
large	mice	ice

Read Multisyllabic Words

Transition to Longer Words Help students transition from reading one-syllable to multisyllabic words with the soft *c* or soft *g* spelling. Draw a T-chart. In column one write *cent*, *cell*, *gym*, *gem*, *voice*, and *charge*. In column two, write *central*, *cellular*, *gymnasium*, *gemstone*, *invoice*, and *recharge*. Point to the first column and have students chorally read the words. Underline the soft *c* or soft *g* spelling in each word. Explain that words in the second column have a syllable with a soft *c* or soft *g* spelling. Have students underline the soft spelling in each word. Point to each word and have students read the words chorally. Write simple sentences using the words and have students read them.

Words with *-er* and *-est*

1 Explain

Words that compare two people, places, or things usually end in *-er*. Words that compare three or more usually end in *-est*. For example: *I am fast. Lea is faster than I am. Kara is the fastest of us all.*

- If a word ends with a consonant and *e*, the final *e* is dropped before adding *-er* and *-est*. For example, *wide, wider, widest.*

- For some words that end with a single vowel and a consonant, double the final consonant before adding *-er* and *-est*. For example, *big, bigger, biggest.*

2 Model

Write and say the words *large, larger, largest; strange, stranger, strangest;* and *sad, sadder, saddest.* Have students repeat the words. Model identifying and underlining the *-er* or *-est* ending.

3 Guided Practice

Write the words *late, later, latest* and *cold, colder, coldest.* Guide students to underline the *-er* or *-est* ending and say each word. Then have students make up sentences using each word.

Expression

Explain/Model Reading with expression means emphasizing certain words to show emotion. Remind students that reading with expression is especially important when reading poetry because you want listeners to enjoy what you are reading.

Model reading "The Giant" on page 319. Emphasize the words *sizzle, soar, push, swoosh,* and *woosh* to convey emotion.

Practice/Apply Have students create audio recordings of the poems to demonstrate fluid reading. Remind students to use appropriate expression. Offer opportunities for students to listen to their recordings. Provide feedback as needed.

Daily Fluency Practice FLUENCY

Students can practice fluency using **Your Turn Practice Book.**

Monitor and *Differentiate*

 Quick Check

Can students decode words with the soft *c* and soft *g* spellings? Can students read words with *-er* and *-est* endings? Can students read fluently?

Small Group Instruction

If No →	Approaching Level	Reteach pp. T296, T298
	ELL	Develop p. T314
If Yes →	On Level	Review p. T304
	Beyond Level	Extend p. T308

ON-LEVEL PRACTICE BOOK p. 198

A. Read each sentence. Underline the word with the soft *c* or soft *g* sound.

1. I learned to ice skate last winter.

2. We saw giant trees in the redwood forest.

3. Mom bought celery for the salad.

4. It was fun to sing on stage last night.

5. He drew a perfect circle on his paper.

B. Read each sentence. Write the correct form of the word shown below each line. Use *-er* or *-est* to complete the sentence.

1. Oak Park is ____bigger____ than Blue Lake Park.
   big

2. Mr. Landon's house is the ____oldest____ house in our entire town.
   old

3. January is always our ____coldest____ month.
   cold

4. Who is ____younger____, you or your sister?
   young

5. I think this apple is ____sweeter____ than the one I ate yesterday.
   sweet

APPROACHING p. 198	BEYOND p. 198	ELL p. 198

→ Write to Sources

Reading/Writing Workshop

OBJECTIVES

CCSS Write narratives to develop real or imagined experiences or events using effective technique, descriptive details, and clear event sequences. Use dialogue and descriptions of actions, thoughts, and feelings to develop experiences and events or show the response of characters to situations. **W.3.3b**

ACADEMIC LANGUAGE

descriptive, specific

Go Digital

U4W5 Word Choice: Strong Words

DAY 1

Writing Fluency

Write to a Prompt Provide students with the prompt: *Write about "The Giant." Describe how the author wrote about him.* Have students share their ideas about basketball. *Why was the small player called a "giant"?* When students finish sharing ideas, have them write continuously for eleven minutes in their Writer's Notebook. If students stop writing, encourage them to keep going.

 When students finish writing have them work with a partner to compare ideas and make sure that they both have a clear understanding of the poem.

Genre Writing

Poetry pp. T350–T355

Fifth Week Focus: Over the course of the week, focus on the following stages of the writing process:

Draft Distribute copies of the Student Model found online in Writer's Workspace. Teach the minilesson on rhythm and rhyme. Have students review the Graphic Organizers they prepared in Prewrite, and write a draft.

Revise Analyze the Revised Student Model found online in Writer's Workspace. Teach the minilesson on figurative language. Have students review their partner's draft and revise their own. Distribute the Revise and Edit Checklist from Writer's Workspace to guide them.

DAY 2

Write to the Reading/Writing Workshop Text

Analyze the Prompt Read aloud the first paragraph on page 326 of the **Reading/Writing Workshop**. Ask: *What is the prompt asking?* (to write a poem in free verse) Say: *Let's reread to see how the poems are structured. We can note literary elements.*

Analyze Text Evidence Display Graphic Organizer 39 in Writer's Workspace. Say: *Let's see how one student, Juan, took notes to answer the prompt. He notes the figurative language used in the line "Ginger's fingers are ocean waves" from the poem "Ginger's Fingers."* Guide the class through the rest of Juan's notes.

Analyze the Student Model Explain how Juan used literary elements from his notes to write a response to the prompt.

- **Figurative Language** Metaphors are a form of figurative language that compares two things directly. Juan used examples of metaphors from his notes to write a metaphor in his poem. Trait: Word Choice

- **Strong Words** Juan used strong, descriptive words that show rather than tell. They help his readers visualize his brother's activities. Trait: Word Choice

- **Repetition** Juan used repetition to emphasize that he thinks his brother is the best. Ask students to compare the examples of repetition in his notes to the repetition in his writing. Trait: Organization

For additional practice with word choice and strong words, assign **Your Turn Practice Book** page 199.

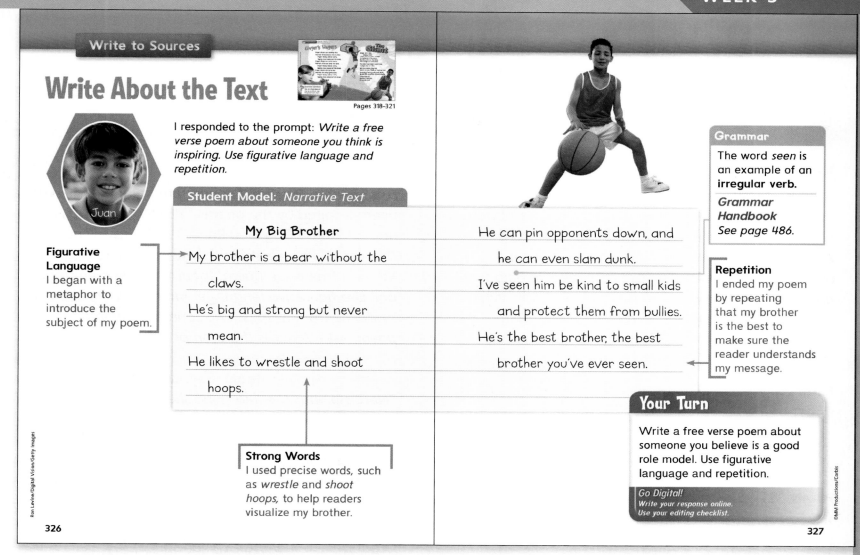

READING/WRITING WORKSHOP, *pp. 326–327*

Your Turn Writing Read the Your Turn prompt on page 327 of the Reading/Writing Workshop aloud. Discuss the prompt with students. If necessary, review with students that poets use descriptive words to paint a specific picture for the reader with their words..

Have students take notes as they look for literary elements to answer the prompt. Remind them to include the following elements as they craft their response from their notes:

- Figurative Language
- Strong Words
- Repetition

Have students use **Grammar Handbook** page 486 in the Reading/Writing Workshop to edit for errors in irregular verbs.

ENGLISH LANGUAGE LEARNERS SCAFFOLD

ELL

Beginning

Write Help students complete the sentence frames.
____ is a good role model.
This person likes to ____.

Intermediate

Describe Ask students to complete the sentence frame. Encourage students to provide details.
I think ____ is a good role model because ____.

Advanced/High

Discuss Check for understanding. Ask: *What does it mean to be a good role model? How can a role model inspire you?*

Write to Sources

DAY **3** For students who need support to complete the writing assignment for the Literature Anthology, provide the following instruction.

DAY

Write to the Literature Anthology Text

Analyze the Prompt Explain that students will write about "The Winningest Woman of the Iditarod Dog Sled Race" and "The Brave Ones" on **Literature Anthology** pages 360–362. Provide the following prompt: *How do the poets use repetition to help you understand the message in their poems?* Ask: *What is the prompt asking you to do?* (to analzye the poets' use of repetition)

Analyze Text Evidence Help students note evidence.

Page 361 Read the first stanza aloud. Ask: *What is the effect of the repeated phrase "to Nome"?* (It gives a sense of a journey and a goal. The first and third lines fill in descriptive details about the journey "to Nome.") *How does this convey the poem's message?*

Pages 361–362 Read the poems aloud. Ask: *How would you describe the action in each of the poems?* (Each poem describes vigorous action.) *Why is this important?*

Encourage students to look for more text evidence of repetition. Then have them craft a short response. Use the conference routine below.

Write to Two Sources

Analyze the Prompt Explain that students will write a poem inspired by the poems "The Winningest Woman of the Iditarod Dog Sled Race," "The Brave Ones," and "Narcissa." Provide students with the following prompt: *Write a free verse poem about a family member or pet. Use figurative language and repetition. Use text evidence from at least two sources to help craft your poem.* Ask: *What is the prompt asking you to do?* (to write a free verse poem that includes figurative language and repetition) Say: *On page 365 the poem "Narcissa" has the line "First she is an ancient queen." So in my notes, I will write:* This is an example of a metaphor. The girl isn't really a queen. *I will also note the page number and the title of the source. On page 362, the phrase "who save" is repeated to emphasize what the firefighters do. I will add this to my notes.*

Analyze Text Evidence Display online Graphic Organizer 40 in Writer's Workspace. Say: *Let's see how one student took notes to answer the prompt. Here are Juan's notes.* Read through each poem and have students point out literary elements.

Teacher Conferences

STEP 1

Talk about the strength of the writing.

You use strong words in your writing. I like how you describe the action in the poems.

STEP 2

Focus on how the writer uses text evidence.

The main idea of your writing would be stronger if you would include more text evidence, such as examples of figurative language, from the poems.

STEP 3

Make concrete suggestions.

This section is interesting. It would help me if you added some strong words to better explain how repetition is used differently in each poem.

DAY

5

Share the Prompt Provide the following prompt to students: *Write a free verse poem about someone you think is brave. Use figurative language and repetition. Use literary elements from "The Winningest Woman of the Iditarod Dog Sled Race," "The Brave Ones," and "Narcissa" to help craft your poetry.*

Find Text Evidence Have students take notes. Find literary elements and give guidance where needed. If necessary, review with students how to paraphrase. Remind them to write the page number and source of the information.

Analyze the Student Model Review the prompt and Juan's notes from Day 4. Display the student model on page 200 of the **Your Turn Practice Book**. Explain to students that Juan synthesized his notes to write a response to the prompt. Discuss the page together with students or have them do it independently.

Write the Response Review the prompt from Day 4 with students. Have students use their notes to craft a short response. Tell students to include the title of all sources and the following elements:

* Figurative Language
* Strong Words
* Repetition

COLLABORATE

Share and Reflect Have students share their responses with a partner. Use the Peer Conference routine below.

Suggested Revisions

Provide specific direction to help focus young writers.

Focus on a Sentence
Read the draft and target one sentence for revision. *Rewrite this sentence by adding strong words that tell ____.*

Focus on a Section
Underline a section that needs to be revised. *Add strong verbs and adjectives to strengthen your main points.*

Focus on a Revision Strategy
Underline a section. Have students use a specific revision strategy, such as adding. *Add figurative language in this section to describe the actions of Susan and the firefighters.*

Peer Conferences

Focus peer responses on using strong words and figurative language. Provide these questions:

* Does the poem use figurative language in an interesting way?
* Did the poet use strong words and descriptions?
* Did the poet include repetition?

→ Grammar: Irregular Verbs

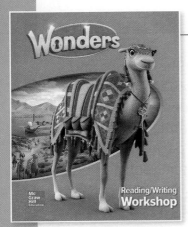

Reading/Writing Workshop

 OBJECTIVES

CCSS Form and use regular and irregular verbs. **L.3.1d**

CCSS Ensure subject-verb and pronoun-antecedent agreement. **L.3.1f**

- Distinguish irregular verbs
- Identify when to use certain forms of irregular verbs
- Use verbs and irregular verbs correctly
- Proofread sentences for mechanics and usage errors

Ask students to write sentences using the irregular verbs see, go, and say. Review the sentences together. Ask volunteers to change each sentence to the past tense, using the correct form of the irregular verb.

DAY 1

DAILY LANGUAGE ACTIVITY

My sister helps me fix the tires on my bike. Because it was flat.

(1: helped; 2: tire; 3: bike, because)

Introduce Irregular Verbs

Present the following:

- Not all verbs add -ed to form the past tense:

  I **saw** James yesterday.

- An **irregular verb** has a special spelling for the past tense. Some irregular verbs are: *come/came, do/did, say/said, go/went, eat/ate,* and *sing/sang:*

  We **ate** pasta last night. We will **eat** steak tonight.
  The choir **sang** this morning. They will **sing** again tonight.

Have partners discuss irregular verbs using page 486 of the Grammar Handbook in **Reading/Writing Workshop**.

DAY 2

DAILY LANGUAGE ACTIVITY

I draw a picture for my aunt, and give it to her. She hanged it on the wall.

(1: drew; 2: gave; 3: hung)

Review Irregular Verbs

Remind students that all verbs do not end in -ed to show past tense. Review some irregular verbs with students.

Introduce Forms with *Have* and *Do*

- Some irregular verbs have a special spelling when used with the helping verbs *have, has, had, does, did,* or *do:*

  Sam **has gone** home.

- Subjects and helping verbs must always agree in simple and compound sentences:

  He had beaten me at the game.

 TALK ABOUT IT

COLLABORATE

SENTENCES AND VERBS

Pair students together and have them write five sentences using the present tense of an irregular verb. Students should take turns reading their sentences aloud. The other partner should name the irregular verb and then create a sentence using the past-tense form.

FORM SENTENCES

Have partners each write three helping verbs and three irregular verbs. Have them take turns selecting a helping verb and an irregular verb and forming a sentence that includes both verbs and read them aloud.

DAY

I dont think we're in kansas anymore said Dorothy.
(1: "I; 2: don't; 3: Kansas;
4: anymore,")

Mechanics and Usage: Correct Verb Forms

- Irregular verbs have a special spelling to show that an action happened in the past.
- Some verbs have a special spelling when used with *have, has, had, does, did,* or *do.*
- Irregular past-tense verbs must agree with their subjects.

As students write, refer them to Grammar Handbook page 484.

DAY

Many great painters lived, during the renaissance. It must has been exciting to live than. (1: lived;
2: Renaissance.; 3: have; 4: then.)

Proofread

Have students correct errors in these sentences.

1. I had saw Jane yesterday.
   (1: saw)

2. We begun to worry when you didn't comed home on time.
   (1: began; 2: come)

3. Sally broked her mom's lamp. She sayed she was sorry.
   (1: broke; 2: said)

4. I has been forgived. (1: have; 2: forgiven.)

Have students check their work using Grammar Handbook page 486 on irregular verbs.

DAY 5

Monas house are the last one on the block. Its white with green shudders.
(1: Mona's; 2: is; 3: It's; 4: shutters.)

Assess

Use the Daily Language Activity and Grammar Practice Reproducibles page 100 for assessment.

Reteach

Use Grammar Practice Reproducibles pages 96–99 and selected pages from the Grammar Handbook for reteaching. Remind students that it is important to use irregular verbs correctly, checking for subject-verb agreement in simple and compound sentences as they read, write, and speak.

Check students' writing for use of the skill and listen for it in their speaking. Assign Grammar Revision Assignments in their Writer's Notebooks as needed.

See Grammar Practice Reproducibles pages 96–100.

NAME THE IRREGULAR VERB

Have students in small groups each write down the present-tense of five irregular verbs on separate cards. Each student will take a turn drawing a card and forming the past-tense form of the verb.

USING IRREGULAR VERBS

Have groups cut pictures from magazines that show people meeting challenges. Have students take turns choosing one picture at a time. Students will describe each image using a sentence that contains an irregular verb.

IRREGULAR VERB QUIZ

Partners should write five sentences with irregular verbs and trade sentences with another pair of students. One partner should read a sentence aloud and the other should identify the irregular verb by using it in a question form.

Spelling: Soft *c* and *g*

OBJECTIVES

CCSS Use spelling patterns and generalizations (e.g., *word families, position-based spellings, syllable patterns, ending rules, meaningful word parts*) in writing words. **L.3.2f**

CCSS Consult reference materials, including beginning dictionaries, as needed to check and correct spellings. **L.3.2g**

Spelling Words

pounce	placed	dice
cents	price	space
mice	office	wage
age	gyms	giant
changes	message	pages

Review your, road, peace
Challenge giraffe, peaceful

Differentiated Spelling

Approaching Level

cell	placed	since
price	slice	space
mice	cents	gems
age	gyms	giant
pages	village	large

Beyond Level

peaceful	pounce	office
placed	cents	citizen
officer	Egypt	pages
changes	gently	message
garage	cabbage	giant

DAY 1

Assess Prior Knowledge

Display the spelling words. Read them aloud, heavily enunciating the soft *c* and *g* sounds.

Point out the spelling pattern in *cents*. Say the word; point out that *cents* follows a spelling pattern for soft *c*.

Demonstrate sorting the spelling words by pattern under key words *dice* and *wage*. (Write the words on index cards or the IWB.) Sort a few words by their soft *c* and *g* sounds. Point out that when the letters *c* and *g* are followed by the vowel *e*, they usually have a soft sound.

Then use the Dictation Sentences from Day 5. Say the underlined word, read the sentence, and repeat the word. Have students write the words.

DAY 2

Spiral Review

Review homophones with the words *your, road,* and *peace*. Use the Dictation Sentences below for the review words. Read the sentence, say the word, and have students write the words.

1. Davin looked under the couch for <u>your</u> car keys.
2. This <u>road</u> was smooth and freshly paved.
3. After the long fight, all they wanted was <u>peace</u>.

Have partners check the spellings.

Challenge Words Review the spelling words, pointing out the soft *c* and *g* spellings and sounds. Use these Dictation Sentences for challenge words. Read the sentence, say the word, have students write the word.

1. The <u>giraffe</u> lives at the zoo.
2. Let's have a <u>peaceful</u> ball game today.

Have students write the words in their word study notebook.

COLLABORATE

OPEN SORT

Have students cut apart the **Spelling Word Cards BLM** in the Online Resource Book and initial the backs of each card. Have them read the words aloud with a partner. Then have partners do an **open sort**. Have them record the sort in their word study notebook.

PATTERN SORT

Complete the **pattern sort** using the key words, pointing out the soft *c* and *g* spellings. Have students use Spelling Word Cards to do their own pattern sort. A partner can compare and check their sorts.

DAY

Word Meanings

Have students copy the words below into their Writer's Notebooks. Have them figure out the spelling word that goes with each definition.

1. building or room for working (office)
2. pieces of paper in a book (pages)
3. another name for pennies (cents)
4. how old a person is (age)
5. what something costs (price)

Challenge students to come up with defintions for other spelling, review, and challenge words.

See Phonics/Spelling Reproducibles pp. 115–120.

DAY

Proofread and Write

Write these sentences on the board. Have students circle and correct each misspelled word. Remind students that they can use print or electronic resources to check and correct spelling.

1. The prise is four dollars and fifty scents. (price, cents)
2. We went to play dyce after dinner tonight. (dice)
3. The stamp costs ten sents. (cents)
4. This book has fifty pags. (pages)

Error Correction Some students may continue to use the more common spellings for /s/ and /j/. Provide additional reading and writing practice with soft *c* and *g* words.

DAY 5

Assess

Use the Dictation Sentences for the Posttest. Have students list misspelled words in their word study notebooks. Look for students' use of these words in their writings.

Dictation Sentences

1. The tiger hid in the bush, preparing to <u>pounce</u>.
2. We <u>placed</u> the dirty dishes in the sink.
3. The board game came with <u>dice</u>.
4. Give me fifty <u>cents</u>, please.
5. What is the <u>price</u> of this book?
6. Rockets travel in <u>space</u>.
7. The field <u>mice</u> ate our wheat.
8. His <u>office</u> has a hardwood desk.
9. The job paid a good <u>wage</u>.
10. What is your <u>age</u>?
11. We like going to new <u>gyms</u>.
12. He is as tall as a <u>giant</u>.
13. Tim <u>changes</u> his clothes after school.
14. I'll give her the <u>message</u>.
15. How many <u>pages</u> have you read?

Have students self-correct the tests.

SPEED SORT

Have partners do a **speed sort** to see who is faster. Then have partners write sentences for each spelling word, leaving blanks where the words should go. Then have them trade papers and write the missing words.

BLIND SORT

Have partners do a **blind sort**: one reads a spelling word card; the other tells under which key word it belongs. Have them take turns until both have sorted all their words. Then have students explain how they sorted the words.

Build Vocabulary

OBJECTIVES

CCSS Determine the meaning of words and phrases as they are used in a text, distinguishing literal from nonliteral language. **RL.3.4**

CCSS Use sentence-level context as a clue to the meaning of a word or phrase. **L.3.4a**

CCSS Distinguish the literal and nonliteral meanings of words and phrases in context (e.g., *take steps*). **L.3.5a**

Expand vocabulary by adding inflectional endings and suffixes.

Vocabulary Words

adventurous	extremely
courageous	weird

Have students of different language proficiency levels work together on the Build More Vocabulary activities. Partners should help each other choose language appropriate to the setting and task. For example, they should identify words that are better for talking on the playground than writing.

 DAY 1

Connect to Words

Practice this week's vocabulary words.

1. Tell about a time you felt **adventurous**.

2. Why is it sometimes difficult to be **courageous**?

3. What can you say when you want to be **extremely** polite?

4. Describe a book or movie that is a little **weird**.

DAY 2

Expand Vocabulary

Help students generate different forms of this week's words by adding, changing, or removing inflectional endings.

- Draw a three-column chart on the board. Write *adventurous* in the left column. Then write *adventure* and *adventures* in the other columns. Read aloud the words and discuss the meanings.

- Have students share sentences with each form of *adventure*.

- Students can fill in the chart for other words, such as *courageous*.

- Have students copy the chart in their word study notebook.

 # BUILD MORE VOCABULARY

COLLABORATE

ACADEMIC VOCABULARY

Discuss important academic words.

- Display the terms *assist* and *motivate* and discuss the meanings.

- Display *assist* and *assistance*. Have partners look up and define related words.

- Write the related words on the board. Have partners ask and answer questions using the words. Repeat with *motivate*. Elicit examples from students.

MULTIPLE-MEANING WORDS

- Review multiple-meaning words with students. Write an example on the board, such as: "A bat flew out of the chimney. She swung her bat at the ball." Discuss the different meanings of *bat*.

- Have partners list other multiple-meaning words using the weekly reading selections or a dictionary.

- Show several student examples on the board and discuss the meanings as a class.

DAY

Reinforce the Words

Review this week's vocabulary words. Have students orally complete each sentence stem.

1. The coach was <u>extremely</u> _____ after winning the championship.
2. <u>Weird</u> sounds came from the deserted old _____.
3. Sarah is an <u>adventurous</u> girl who likes to _____.
4. Sam felt <u>courageous</u> when he _____.

DAY

Connect to Writing

- Have students write sentences in their word study notebooks using this week's vocabulary.
- Tell them to write sentences that provide information about the words and their meanings.
- **ELL** Provide the Day 3 sentence stems for students needing extra support.

Write About Vocabulary Have students write something they learned from this week's words in their word study notebook. For example, they might write about a real or imaginary person who is *adventurous* or *courageous*.

DAY

Word Squares

Ask students to create Word Squares for each vocabulary word.

- In the first square, students write the word. (example: *adventurous*)
- In the second square, students write their own definition of the word and any related words. (examples: *brave, active*)
- In the third square, students draw a simple illustration that will help them remember the word. (example: mountain climbers)
- In the fourth square, students write non-examples. (example: *timid*)

METAPHOR

Remind students that a metaphor is a type of figurative language with a non-literal meaning.

- Display **Your Turn Practice Book** pages 193–194. Read the first two stanzas. Model figuring out the meanings of the metaphors.
- For additional practice with metaphors, have students complete page 197.
- Discuss the literal and nonliteral meanings of the metaphors.

SHADES OF MEANING

Help students generate words related to *courageous*. Draw a synonym/antonym scale.

- Discuss the word *courageous* and synonyms, such as *brave* and *fearless*. Write the words on the scale.
- Ask follow-up questions such as: *What is the opposite of courageous?* (scared, fearful) Write the words on the scale.
- Ask students to copy the words in their word study notebook.

MORPHOLOGY

Use the word *adventurous* as a springboard for students to learn more words. Draw a T-chart.

- Write the word *adventure* in the first column. Discuss the meaning with students.
- In the second column, write the suffix *–ous*. Discuss how adding this suffix changes the spelling and meaning of the word.
- Elicit other words with the suffix *–ous*, such as *courageous, outrageous*.
- Discuss the meanings of the words.

→ Integrate Ideas

Close Reading Routine

Read   DOK 1–2

- Identify key ideas and details about inspiration.
- Take notes and summarize.
- Use $\textcircled{A}\textcircled{C}\textcircled{T}$ prompts as needed.

Reread   DOK 2–3

- Analyze the text, craft, and structure.
- Use the **Close Reading Companion.**

Integrate   DOK 4

- Integrate knowledge and ideas.
- Make text-to-text connections.
- Use the **Integrate** lesson.
- Use *Close Reading Companion,* p. 132.

TEXT CONNECTIONS

Connect to the Essential Question

Write the essential question on the board: How can others inspire us? Divide the class into small groups. Tell students that each group will compare the information that they have learned about how people can inspire us. Model how to compare this information by using examples from this week's **Leveled Readers** and "Ginger's Fingers," "The Giant," and "Captain's Log, May 12, 1868," **Reading/Writing Workshop** pages 318–321.

Evaluate Text Evidence Have students review their class notes and completed graphic organizers before they begin their discussions. Encourage students to compare information from all the week's reads. Have each group pick one student to take notes. Explain that each group will use an Accordion Foldable® to record their ideas. You may wish to model how to use an Accordion Foldable® to record comparisons.

Dinah Zike's
FOLDABLES
Study Organizer

NARRATIVE PERFORMANCE TASK

Write About: Frogs

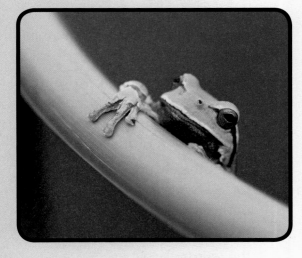

Gudella/Getty Images

INQUIRY SPACE

LEVEL			1	2	3	4	5	6

Revise and Edit

PREVIEW LEVEL 5 Display Level 5 of the Narrative Performance Task to students. Tell them that in this level they will discuss their draft with a partner, revise and edit it, and write a final draft.

❶ Peer Conferences Review with students the routine for peer review of writing. They should:

- Listen carefully as the writer reads his or her work aloud. Begin each review by saying what he or she liked about the draft.
- Ask questions that will help the writer think more about the draft.
- Make a suggestion that will make the draft stronger.

Display the **Peer Conference Checklist** from the **Toolkit.** You may also wish to show students the **Collaborative Conversations: Peer Conferencing** video.

OBJECTIVE

CCSS Refer to parts of stories, dramas, and poems when writing or speaking about a text, using terms such as chapter, scene, and stanza; describe how each successive part builds on earlier sections. **RL.3.5**

Text to Photography

As students discuss the information from all the week's reads, have them include the photograph on page 132 of the **Close Reading Companion** as a part of their discussion. Guide students to see the connections between the photograph and text. Ask: *How does the photograph connect to what you read this week?*

Present Ideas and Synthesize Information

When students finish their discussions, ask for a volunteer from each group to read his or her notes aloud.

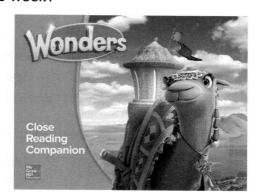

OBJECTIVES

CCSS With guidance and support from peers and adults, develop and strengthen writing as needed by planning, revising, and editing. **W.3.5**

CCSS Come to discussions prepared, having read or studied required material; explicitly draw on that preparation and other information known about the topic to explore ideas under discussion. **SL.3.1a**

❷ **Revise and Edit** Display the **Revised Student Model** from the Toolkit. Discuss the revisions that the student made to the draft. Remind students that to revise a draft they should: add details and descriptions to help the reader picture the characters and setting; remove extra words or ideas to make the story clearer; replace words that were used too many times; rearrange words and sentences to make the plot of the story easier to understand.

Display to students the **Edited Student Model** from the Toolkit. Discuss the edits the student made to the draft. Remind students that to edit a draft they should check for misspelled words, incorrect punctuation, and grammar mistakes.

❸ **Proofread** Tell students that it is important to proofread their final drafts. Explain that they should be reading their final draft to find errors that must be corrected.

ASSIGN LEVEL 5 Assign partners, and have students begin Level 5. Circulate as students have peer conferences, and make suggestions as needed. You may wish to have students watch the Collaborative Conversations: Peer Conferencing video again.

Approaching Level

Lexile 480
TextEvaluator 36

OBJECTIVES

CCSS Recount stories, including fables, folktales, and myths from diverse cultures; determine the central message, lesson, or moral and explain how it is conveyed through key details in the text. **RL.3.2**

• Reread text to check understanding.
• Identify the theme of a story.
• Determine the meanings of metaphors.

ACADEMIC LANGUAGE
reread, theme, realistic fiction, metaphor, poem

Leveled Reader:
A Speech to Remember

Go Digital

Before Reading

Preview and Predict

Have students read the Essential Question. Then have them read the title and table of contents of *A Speech to Remember* and predict what the story is about. Have partners share their predictions.

Leveled Readers

Review Genre: Realistic Fiction

Review with students that realistic fiction is a type of fiction that includes characters, settings, and events that could exist or happen in real life. As they preview *A Speech to Remember*, have students identify features of realistic fiction.

During Reading

Close Reading

Note Taking Have students use their graphic organizer as they read.

Fill in the Graphic Organizer

Pages 2–3 My stomach is in knots *on page 2 is a metaphor. What is a knot?* (something that is tied up) *Would your stomach feel good or bad if it really was in knots?* (bad) *Why would the narrator's stomach feel like it is in knots?* (She is scared.) *What other clues does the author give about the narrator being scared?* (My legs feel heavy; my head feels light; I want to run away.) *What is she scared of?* (giving a speech)

Pages 4–5 *Tell a partner how Della learned to be less scared when singing in public. You can reread page 5 to help you answer the question.* (Della took a sip of water and some deep breaths before singing. Every time she took a deep breath, she felt that she got rid of some fear.)

Pages 6–9 *What is the problem in the beginning of Chapter 2?* (Della forgets the words to the song.) *On page 8, Della says she was on a roller coaster. Was she really on a roller coaster?* (no) *This is a metaphor. What does this metaphor mean? Think about how you might feel on a roller coaster.* (She is both afraid and excited.) *What happens to Marnie, who is the narrator of the story, and Marnie's speech as she is going on stage?* (She trips, and the pages fly everywhere.)

Pages 10–12 *What is the problem with the narrator's speech?* (The last page is missing.) *Make a prediction about what will happen next.*

Pages 13–15 *How did Della inspire Marnie?* (Della showed Marnie how to be afraid but still go on.) *What lesson does the author teach us about what to do when we are afraid or nervous about something? Think about the words to Marnie's song.* (*Do not stop, just breathe, and keep going.*) *The theme of the story is about overcoming what?* (your fears)

After Reading

Respond to Reading Revisit the Essential Question, and ask students to complete the Text Evidence questions on page 16.

Analytical Writing **Write About Reading** Have students work with a partner to write a paragraph about the details the author uses to describe how Marnie feels during the story. Students should use details from the text.

Fluency: Expression

Model Model reading page 4 with expression. Next, reread the page aloud, and have students read along with you.

Apply Have students practice reading with a partner.

PAIRED READ

"Let the Lion Roar"

Make Connections:
Write About It **Analytical Writing**

Before reading, have students note that the genre of this text is a poem, which is a style of writing that often has a rhythm and does not follow the same rules as prose. Then discuss the Essential Question.

After reading, have students write about connections between how people are inspired by others in "Let the Lion Roar" and *A Speech to Remember*.

Leveled Reader

FOCUS ON LITERARY ELEMENTS

Students can extend their knowledge of poetry by completing the literary elements activity on page 20.

Literature Circles

Ask students to conduct a literature circle using the Thinkmark questions to guide the discussion. You may wish to have a whole-class discussion about people who have inspired students, making connections to characters from both stories.

Level Up

Level-up lessons available online.

IF students read the Approaching Level fluently and answered the questions

THEN pair them with students who have proficiently read the On Level and have approaching-level students.

• echo-read the On Level main selection with their partner.

• use self-stick notes to mark a detail to discuss in each section.

Access **C**omplex **T**ext

The On Level challenges students by including more **domain-specific words** and **complex sentence structures**.

→ **Approaching Level**

Phonics/Decoding

DECODE WORDS WITH SOFT c

TIER 2

OBJECTIVES

 Know and apply grade-level phonics and word analysis skills in decoding words. Decode multisyllable words. **RF.3.3c**

Decode words with soft c.

 I Do Explain to students that the letter c can have either a hard or soft sound. The letter c makes the hard /k/ in cat and soft /s/ in circle. Remind students that when c comes before the letters i or e, it is usually pronounced /s/. Write cell, place, and price on the board and read the words aloud. Underline the c in each word. Say the words again, emphasizing the /s/.

 We Do Write cent, since, and price on the board. Model how to decode the first word. Have students identify the /s/ made by the letter c in the first word. Students can read the rest aloud and identify the /s/ in each.

 You Do Add these words to the board: slice, space, and mice. Have students read each word aloud and identify the soft c sound. Then point to the words in random order for students to read chorally. Repeat several times.

BUILD WORDS WITH SOFT c AND g

TIER 2

OBJECTIVES

 Know and apply grade-level phonics and word analysis skills in decoding words. Decode multisyllable words. **RF.3.3c**

Build words with soft c and g.

 I Do Tell students that they will be building multisyllable words with soft c and g spellings. Remind students that the letter c has a hard /k/ in cat and a soft /s/ in circle; the letter g has a hard /g/ in goat and a soft /j/ in gem. Display these **Word-Building Cards** one at a time: cent, er, dan, gi. Then write these syllables on the board: cer, ger, ant. Model sounding out each syllable.

 We Do Have students chorally read each syllable. Repeat at varying speeds and in random order. Next, display all the cards and syllables. Work with students to combine the Word-Building Cards and the syllables to form two-syllable words with soft c and g sounds. Have students chorally read the words: center, dancer, danger, giant.

 You Do Write other syllables on the board, such as per, cy, lar, gen, cent, cle, gest, and tle. Have students work with partners to build words using these syllables. Then have partners share the words they built and make a class list.

PRACTICE WORDS WITH SOFT *c* AND *g*

OBJECTIVES

CCSS Know and apply grade-level phonics and word analysis skills in decoding words. Decode multisyllable words. **RF.3.3c**

Decode words with soft *c* and *g*.

 I Do Remind students that *c* and *g* can have either a hard or soft sound. When *c* comes before *i* or *e*, it usually makes the soft /s/. When *g* comes before *i* or *e*, it usually makes the soft /j/. Write *city* and *giraffe* on the board. Then read the words aloud. Point out that the *i* after *c* and *g* makes the letters soft.

 We Do Write *cereal, office, cider, agent, village, engine* on the board. Model how to decode *cereal,* then guide students as they decode the remaining words. Help them identify the soft *c* and *g* sound-spellings in each word and underline them. Draw lines between syllables to help students decode.

 You Do Point to the words in random order for students to chorally read.

WORDS WITH *-er* AND *-est*

OBJECTIVES

CCSS Form and use comparative and superlative adjectives and adverbs, and choose between them depending on what is to be modified. **L.3.1g**

Add word endings *-er* and *-est*.

 I Do Remind students that words comparing two people, places, or things usually end in *-er*. Words comparing three or more people, places, or things usually end in *-est*. If a word ends with a consonant + *e*, the final *e* is dropped before adding *-er* and *-est* (*large, larger, largest*). For some words ending with a single vowel and a consonant, double the final consonant before adding *-er* and *-est* (*big, bigger, biggest*).

 We Do Write *loud* and *wet* on the board. Say each word and have students repeat. Model doubling the final consonant and adding *-er* then *-est*. Read the words in their new forms as students sound out each word with you.

 You Do Next write the words *strange* and *mad* on the board. Have students add the endings *-er* and *-est* to each word. Write the new forms on the board. Then point to the words in random order for students to chorally read.

ELL ENGLISH LANGUAGE LEARNERS

For the students who need **phonics**, **decoding**, and **fluency** practice, use scaffolding methods as necessary to ensure students understand the meaning of the words. Refer to the **Language Transfers Handbook** for phonics elements that may not transfer in students' native languages.

Approaching Level

Vocabulary

REVIEW HIGH-FREQUENCY WORDS

 TIER **2**

OBJECTIVES

CCSS Use conventional spelling for high-frequency and other studied words and for adding suffixes to base words (e.g., *sitting, smiled, cries, happiness*). **L.3.2e**

Review high-frequency words.

 I Do Use **Word Cards** 121–160. Display one word at a time, following the routine:

Display the word. Read the word. Then spell the word.

 We Do Ask students to state the word and spell the word with you. Model using the word in a sentence, and have students repeat after you.

You Do Display the word. Ask students to say the word then spell it. When completed, quickly flip through the word card set as students chorally read the words. Provide opportunities for students to use the words in speaking and writing. For example, provide sentence starters such as *The highest ____ I have ever counted to is ____*. Ask students to write each word in their **Writer's Notebook**.

REVIEW VOCABULARY WORDS

TIER **2**

OBJECTIVES

CCSS Acquire and use accurately grade-appropriate conversational, general academic, and domain-specific words and phrases, including those that signal spatial and temporal relationships. **L.3.6**

Review vocabulary words.

  I Do Display each **Visual Vocabulary Card** and state the word. Explain how the photograph illustrates the word. State the example sentence and repeat the word.

 We Do Point to the word on the card and read the word with students. Ask them to repeat the word. Engage students in structured partner talk about the image as prompted on the back of the vocabulary card.

 You Do Display each visual in random order, hiding the word. Have students match the definitions and context sentences of the words to the visuals displayed. Then ask students to complete **Approaching Reproducibles** page 191.

ANSWER CHOICE QUESTIONS

OBJECTIVES

CCSS Identify real-life connections between words and their use (e.g., describe people who are *friendly* or *helpful*). **L.3.5b**

Answer questions to demonstrate understanding of the meanings of words.

 I Do Display the *adventurous* **Visual Vocabulary Card** and ask the question: *Which activity is more* adventurous: *mountain climbing or watching TV?* Point out that mountain climbing is a more *adventurous* activity.

 We Do Display the vocabulary card for the word *courageous.* Ask: *How can someone be* courageous *by helping others?* With students, identify ways that helping others can be *courageous,* and discuss why.

 You Do Display the remaining cards one at a time, asking each question below. Ask students to choose the best answer.

If a place is extremely *cold, is it very cold or mildly cold?*

Does a poem written in free verse *always rhyme?*

What does a poem need to be a narrative poem?

Does a poem use repetition *if every word is used only once?*

Do the words "kite" and "night" rhyme *with each other?*

METAPHORS

OBJECTIVES

CCSS Distinguish the literal and nonliteral meanings of words and phrases in context (e.g., *take steps*). **L.3.5a**

Determine the meaning of metaphors.

 I Do Display the Comprehension and Fluency passage on **Approaching Reproducibles** page 193. Read aloud the first and second stanzas. Point to *The runners were a rumbling herd*. Explain that a metaphor compares two things that are different.

Think Aloud The word *herd* is often used to describe a group of large animals, and large animals can rumble the ground when they move. This metaphor compares the runners to a herd of large animals and helps me picture them moving in a large group.

Write the meaning of the metaphor.

 We Do With students, discuss how to determine the meaning of the metaphor *who shot out alone.*

 You Do Have students find the meanings of *with determination carved into their faces* and *Motor boats speeding over grey water* from the passage.

Approaching Level

Comprehension

 FLUENCY

TIER 2

OBJECTIVES

 Read on-level prose and poetry orally with accuracy, appropriate rate, and expression on successive readings. **RF.3.4b**

Read fluently with expression.

I Do Review that part of reading a selection with expression is emphasizing certain words or phrases to show emotion and understanding. Read the first stanza of the Comprehension and Fluency passage on **Approaching Reproducibles** page 193. Tell students to listen for when your tone helps to express meaning in the text. Model appropriate expression by emphasizing certain words and phrases.

We Do Read the rest of the poem aloud, and have students repeat each sentence after you using the same expression. Explain how you emphasized certain words and phrases to show emotion and understanding.

You Do Have partners take turns reading sentences from the Approaching Reproducibles poem. Remind them to focus on their expression. Provide corrective feedback as needed by modeling proper fluency.

IDENTIFY KEY DETAILS

TIER 2

OBJECTIVES

Recount stories, including fables, folktales, and myths from diverse cultures; determine the central message, lesson, or moral and explain how it is conveyed through key details in the text. **RL.3.2**

Identify key details.

I Do Write the name of the poem, "Why I Run." Then write: *marveled at the number of feet; these runners would inspire anyone's daughter; That was the day I made the decision.* Explain that all of these details relate to the title of the poem. Tell students that paying close attention to details like these can help them figure out the message of a poem.

We Do Read the first stanza of the Comprehension and Fluency passage in the **Approaching Reproducibles**. Ask: *So far, what details help explain why the narrator runs?* Tell students that the narrator will give details throughout the poem to explain why she runs. Discuss why these details are key.

You Do Have students read the rest of the poem. After each stanza, they should write down the details that seem key. Review their lists with them and help them explain why the details they chose are key. Then have them use these details to determine why the narrator runs.

REVIEW THEME

OBJECTIVES

 Recount stories, including fables, folktales, and myths from diverse cultures; determine the central message, lesson, or moral and explain how it is conveyed through key details in the text. **RL.3.2**

Identify the theme of the poem.

 I Do Remind students that poems often have a message for the reader. This message is a poem's theme. To identify the theme, students should look for details in the poem that support a common message. Students can then use those details to determine the poem's central message, lesson, or moral. This will be the poem's theme.

We Do Read the first stanza of the Comprehension and Fluency passage in the **Approaching Reproducibles** together. Pause to point out key details in each line. Model how to consider what all the key details have in common, or how they are connected, and how the theme might relate to these details. Then, work with students to identify key details in each remaining stanza in the poem.

You Do Have students use the key details of each stanza to come up with the theme of the whole poem.

SELF-SELECTED READING

OBJECTIVES

 Recount stories, including fables, folktales, and myths from diverse cultures; determine the central message, lesson, or moral and explain how it is conveyed through key details in the text. **RL.3.2**

• Identify the theme of the poem.

• Reread difficult sections to increase understanding.

Read Independently

Have students choose a poem for sustained silent reading. Remind students that:

• the poem probably has a central message or theme. As they read, students should look for key details that will help them determine the theme of the poem.

• if they have trouble figuring out the theme, they should reread difficult sections to see if they missed key details.

Read Purposefully

Have students record key details relating to the theme on **Graphic Organizer 148** as they read independently. After they finish, they can conduct a Book Talk, each telling about the poem they read.

• Students should share their graphic organizers and answer this question: *What was the theme or central message of this poem?*

• They should also tell the group if there were any parts that they reread to help increase their understanding of the poem.

On Level

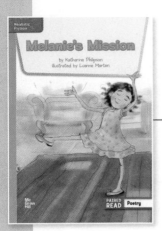

Lexile 590
TextEvaluator 25

OBJECTIVES

 Recount stories, including fables, folktales, and myths from diverse cultures; determine the central message, lesson, or moral and explain how it is conveyed through key details in the text. **RL.3.2**

- Reread text to check understanding.
- Determine the theme of a story.
- Determine the meanings of metaphors.

ACADEMIC LANGUAGE
reread, theme, realistic fiction, metaphor, poem

Leveled Reader:
Melanie's Mission

Before Reading

Preview and Predict

Have students read the Essential Question. Have them read the title and table of contents of *Melanie's Mission* and predict what this story is about. Have partners share their predictions.

Review Genre: Realistic Fiction

Review with students that realistic fiction is a type of fiction that includes characters, settings, and events that could exist or happen in real life. As they preview *Melanie's Mission*, have students identify features of realistic fiction.

During Reading

Close Reading

Note Taking Have students use their graphic organizer as they read.

Pages 2–4 *What do you learn about Melanie on page 2?* (I know, from the conversation she has with her mom, that she is good at tennis but does not sing as well as her mother.) *Why does Melanie think Mrs. Ortez has visitors?* (because she heard a piano playing)

Pages 5–7 *What else do we learn about Melanie? You can reread page 5 to find the answer.* (She says she is tone deaf; she likes the outdoors and is adventurous.) *What are Mrs. Ortez's beliefs about music?* (She believes everyone can find some music that touches their heart.) *How can you tell what effect Mrs. Ortez's music has on Melanie?* (The author says Melanie dances and is carried away by the rhythm.) *What is Mrs. Ortez's problem?* (She has arthritis in her hands and can hardly play the piano anymore.)

Pages 8–11 *What is "the idea" in the Chapter 2 title? Remember to reread if you are not sure.* (Melanie has the idea to hold a soiree at Mrs. Ortez's house.) *What does Melanie's father say a soiree is?* (an evening of music and conversation) *Reread pages 10 and 11, and then explain what the soiree involves.* (There is food, music, and games.)

Go Digital

Leveled Readers

Fill in the Graphic Organizer

Page 12 *Find the metaphor on page 12. Look for two very different things being compared.* (Della's *stomach was one huge butterfly, fluttering and swooping.*) *When might you feel like butterflies are fluttering and swooping in your stomach?* (if you are excited or nervous)

Pages 13–15 *Discuss the meaning of the metaphor* Mrs Ortez has the heart of a lion. *How does Mrs. Ortez inspire Melanie?* (She shows bravery by playing the piano in spite of her pain.) *Turn to a partner and summarize the theme of the story.* (Be brave even when things are hard.)

After Reading

Respond to Reading Revisit the Essential Question, and ask students to complete the Text Evidence questions on page 16.

Analytical Writing **Write About Reading** Have students work with a partner to write a paragraph about the message of the story using details from the story.

Fluency: Expression

Model Model reading page 4 with expression. Next, reread the page aloud, and have students read along with you.

Apply Have students practice reading with a partner.

PAIRED READ

"In the Land of Lions"

Make Connections:
Write About It ✏ *Analytical Writing*

Leveled Reader

Before reading, have students note that the genre of this text is a poem, which is a style of writing that often has a rhythm and does not follow the same rules as prose. Then discuss the Essential Question.

After reading, have students write about connections between how people are inspired by others in "In the Land of Lions" and *Melanie's Mission*.

FOCUS ON LITERARY ELEMENTS

Students can extend their knowledge of poetry by completing the literary elements activity on page 20.

Literature Circles

Ask students to conduct a literature circle using the Thinkmark questions to guide the discussion. You may wish to have a whole-class discussion on people who inspire students and why they inspire them.

Level Up

Level-up lessons available online.

IF students read the On Level fluently and answered the questions

THEN pair them with students who have proficiently read the Beyond Level and have on-level students

• partner-read the Beyond Level main selection.

• name two details in the text that they want to learn more about.

A C T Access Complex Text

The Beyond Level challenges students by including more **domain-specific words** and **complex sentence structures**.

On Level

Vocabulary

REVIEW VOCABULARY WORDS

OBJECTIVES
Acquire and use accurately grade-appropriate conversational, general academic, and domain-specific words and phrases, including those that signal spatial and temporal relationships. **L.3.6**

Review vocabulary words.

 Use the **Visual Vocabulary Cards** to review key vocabulary words *weird, extremely,* and poetry terms *free verse, narrative poem, repetition, rhyme.* Point to each word, read it aloud, and have students chorally repeat it.

 Ask these questions and help students respond and explain their answers.

- When have you been *extremely* happy about something?
- What kinds of animals could be called *weird*?
- Can a *free verse* poem rhyme at all?

 Have students respond to these questions and explain their answers.

- What has to be in a poem for it to be a *narrative poem*?
- What is an example of *repetition* in a song you like?
- What does it mean when two words *rhyme* with each other?

METAPHORS

OBJECTIVES
Distinguish the literal and nonliteral meanings of words and phrases in context (e.g., *take steps*). **L.3.5a**

Determine the meanings of metaphors.

 Remind students that a metaphor compares two things that are very different. Use the Comprehension and Fluency passage on **Your Turn Practice Book** page 193 to model.

Think Aloud I want to know the meaning of the metaphor: *The runners were a rumbling herd.* The word *herd* is used to describe a group of large animals, which can rumble the ground when they move. Runners are being compared to a rumbling herd because they are so loud as they run.

 Have students read on and encounter *like the swiftest birds who shot out alone.* Have students figure out the meaning of this metaphor.

 Have partners determine the meanings of *determination carved into their faces, motor boats speeding over grey water,* and *my feet started out as one big bruise* as they read the rest of the poem.

Comprehension

REVIEW THEME

OBJECTIVES

CCSS Recount stories, including fables, folktales, and myths from diverse cultures; determine the central message, lesson, or moral and explain how it is conveyed through key details in the text. **RL.3.2**

Identify the theme of a poem.

 I Do Remind students that the theme is the central message, lesson, or moral an author writes into a poem. Explain that to identify the theme, students should look for details in the lines of the poem. Students can recount the poem to determine the central message, lesson, or moral and explain how it is conveyed through key details in the text.

 We Do Have a volunteer read the first stanza of the Comprehension and Fluency poem on **Your Turn Practice Book** page 193. Have students orally list key details, and help them explain why they are key. Model how to decide what the details have in common or how they are connected, and how to state the theme using these details. Then, work with students to identify the key details in the next stanza.

 You Do Have partners identify the key details in each stanza in the rest of the poem. Then have them come up with the theme of the whole poem.

SELF-SELECTED READING

OBJECTIVES

CCSS Recount stories, including fables, folktales, and myths from diverse cultures; determine the central message, lesson, or moral and explain how it is conveyed through key details in the text. **RL.3.2**

• Reread difficult sections to increase understanding.
• Identify the theme of a poem.

Read Independently

Have students choose a poem for sustained silent reading.

- Before they read, have students preview the poem, reading the title and noting the line breaks and the type of poem, if appropriate.
- As students read, remind them to reread difficult sections to help increase their understanding.

Read Purposefully

Encourage students to read different types of poems.

- As students read, have them fill in the key details of the poem on **Graphic Organizer 148**.
- They can use their organizers to help them write a summary of the theme of the poem.
- Have students share with classmates any difficult sections they reread to increase understanding.

→ Beyond Level

Lexile 700
TextEvaluator™ 33

OBJECTIVES

(CCSS) Recount stories, including fables, folktales, and myths from diverse cultures; determine the central message, lesson, or moral and explain how it is conveyed through key details in the text. **RL.3.2**

• Reread text to check understanding.
• Identify the theme of a story.
• Determine the meanings of metaphors.

ACADEMIC LANGUAGE
reread, theme, realistic fiction, metaphor, poem

Leveled Reader:
In the Running

Before Reading

Preview and Predict

Have students read the Essential Question. Then have them read the title and table of contents of *In the Running* and predict what the story is about. Have partners share their predictions.

Review Genre: Realistic Fiction

Review with students that realistic fiction is a type of fiction that includes characters, settings, and events that could exist or happen in real life. As they preview *In the Running*, have students identify features of realistic fiction.

During Reading

Close Reading

Note Taking Have students use their graphic organizer as they read.

Pages 2–5 *Reread the first two pages and use evidence from the text to explain how the author characterizes Marvin.* (It says Marvin looks unenthusiastic when his mother asks him to help in the yard; it says that Marvin gets *lost in an enthralling game of Galaxy* and that he spends most of his free time in the virtual world. So Marvin does not like being outdoors and would rather be playing computer games.) *What does Marvin's mother wish?* (She wishes that he had more friends and would play a sport instead of playing computer games.) *Why does Marvin prefer playing computer games over playing a sport? Reread pages 4 and 5 if you are not sure.* (He thinks he is not good at sports. He feels like he can do anything online. He feels *adventurous and courageous*.)

Pages 6–9 *Summarize to a partner how Ben changes Marvin's attitude toward outdoor activity in Chapter 2.* (Marvin is impressed by Ben's courage and determination despite losing his legs. It makes Marvin wonder if he could run as well.) *What is Marvin's attitude when he starts to run?* (Although he is unfit, he is not going to give up just yet.)

Leveled Readers

Fill in the Graphic Organizer

Go
Digital

Pages 10–15 *Reread paragraph 2 on page 11. What is the metaphor? Explain what two things are being compared and why.* (*The course was a ribbon winding through the town.* The course and a ribbon are being compared. Just like a ribbon on a package, it winds and weaves up and down.) *Think about what Marvin has learned from Ben. What is the theme of the story?* (Do things with courage and determination even when things get hard. Do not give up.)

After Reading

Respond to Reading Revisit the Essential Question, and ask students to complete the Text Evidence questions on page 16.

Analytical Writing **Write About Reading** Have partners write a paragraph explaining the message of the story, using story details to support their answer.

Fluency: Expression

Model Model reading page 4 with expression. Next, reread the page aloud, and have students read along with you.

Apply Have students practice reading with a partner.

PAIRED READ

Leveled Reader

"Everybody's Surfing"

Make Connections: Write About It *Analytical Writing*

Before reading, have students note that the genre of this text is a poem, which often has a rhythm and does not follow the same rules as prose. Then have students discuss the Essential Question.

After reading, have students write about connections between how people are inspired by others in "Everybody's Surfing" and *In the Running*.

FOCUS ON LITERARY ELEMENTS

Students can extend their knowledge of poetry by completing the literary elements activity on page 20.

Literature Circles

Ask students to conduct a literature circle using the Thinkmark questions to guide the discussion. You may wish to have a whole-class discussion on people who inspire students and why they inspire them.

Gifted and Talented

Synthesize Challenge students to write a short essay about how someone inspired them to try something new. The person who inspired them can be someone they know or someone they have read about. Invite volunteers to share their essays with the class.

Beyond Level

Vocabulary

REVIEW DOMAIN-SPECIFIC WORDS

OBJECTIVES

 Produce simple, compound, and complex sentences. **L.3.1i**

Review vocabulary words.

Model Use the **Visual Vocabulary Cards** to review the meanings of the words *adventurous* and *courageous*. Write social studies related sentences on the board using the words.

Write the words *prosthetic, disability,* and *advantage* on the board, and discuss the meanings with students. Then help students write sentences using these words.

Apply Have students work in pairs to discuss the meanings of the words *unfit,* and *pace*. Then have partners write sentences using the words.

METAPHORS

OBJECTIVES

 Distinguish the literal and nonliteral meanings of words and phrases in context (e.g., *take steps*). **L.3.5a**

Determine the meanings of metaphors.

Model Read aloud the first two stanzas of the Comprehension and Fluency passage on **Beyond Reproducibles** page 193.

Think Aloud I want to know what *The runners were a rumbling herd* means. I know that runners and a herd are being compared. The word *herd* is used to describe a group of large animals, and large animals can rumble the ground when they move. This metaphor compares the runners to a herd of large animals and helps me picture them loudly running in a large group.

With students, read the next two lines. Help them figure out the meaning of *like the swiftest birds who shot out alone.*

Apply Have pairs of students read the rest of the poem. Have them determine the meanings of the metaphors *with determination carved into their faces, motor boats speeding over grey water,* and *my feet started out as one big bruise.*

 Shades of Meaning Using their knowledge of metaphors, have partners write their own. Remind students that metaphors compare two different things, so first they should decide on what is being compared. Encourage them to also use artwork to illustrate their metaphor.

Comprehension

REVIEW THEME

OBJECTIVES

 Recount stories, including fables, folktales, and myths from diverse cultures; determine the central message, lesson, or moral and explain how it is conveyed through key details in the text. **RL.3.2**

Identify the theme of a poerm.

 Model Remind students that the theme of a poem is the central message, lesson, or moral that an author focuses on. Explain that students can make inferences based on the details found in the text. Point out that students should look for details in the lines of the poem to identify the theme.

Have students read the first stanza of the Comprehension and Fluency passage of **Beyond Reproducibles** page 193. Ask open-ended questions to facilitate discussion, such as *What does the narrator of the poem watch? Who is she with?* Students should support their responses with details from the poem.

 Apply Have students identify key details in the rest of the passage as they independently fill in **Graphic Organizer 148**. Then have partners use their organizer to determine the theme of the whole poem.

SELF-SELECTED READING

OBJECTIVES

 Recount stories, including fables, folktales, and myths from diverse cultures; determine the central message, lesson, or moral and explain how it is conveyed through key details in the text. **RL.3.2**

• Identify the theme of a poem.

• Reread difficult sections to increase understanding.

Read Independently

Have students choose a poem for sustained silent reading.

• As students read, have them fill in **Graphic Organizer 148**.

• Remind them to reread difficult sections as necessary to help increase their understanding.

Read Purposefully

Encourage students to keep a reading journal. Ask them to read different types of poems.

• Students can write summaries of the poems in their journals.

• Ask students to share their reactions to the poems with classmates.

 Independent Study Challenge students to discuss how their poems relate to the weekly theme of inspiration. Have students compare the inspiration of the people or characters they have read about. Who inspired them? What do people do when they feel inspired?

→ English Language Learners

Shared Read

Ginger's Fingers, The Giant, Captain's Log

Shared Read Genre • Poetry

Ginger's Fingers

Ginger's fingers are shooting stars,
They talk of adventurous trips to Mars.
Fingers talking without words,
Signing when sounds can't be heard.
Ginger's fingers are ocean waves,
They talk of fish and deep sea caves.
Fingers talking without words,
Signing when sounds can't be heard.
Ginger's fingers are butterflies,
They talk of a honey-gold sunrise.
Fingers talking without words,
Signing when sounds can't be heard.

Essential Question
How can others inspire us?
Read about different ways
that people inspire others.

Reading/Writing Workshop

Go Digital

View "Ginger's Fingers," "The Giant," "Captain's Log"

Before Reading

Build Background

Read the Essential Question: How can others inspire us?

- Explain the meaning of the Essential Question. *People can inspire others to do and learn new things. To* inspire *means "to move to action."*

- **Model an answer:** *People can inspire others to do and learn new things. When someone does something that seems difficult, it can inspire others to do the same.*

- Ask students a question that ties the Essential Question to their own background knowledge: *Work with a partner to think of someone who inspires you. Discuss how that person inspires you.* Call on several pairs.

During Reading

Interactive-Question Response

- Ask questions that help students understand the meaning of the text after each paragraph.

- Reinforce the meanings of key vocabulary.

- Ask students questions that require them to use key vocabulary.

- Reinforce strategies and skills of the week by modeling.

OBJECTIVES

CCSS Refer to parts of stories, dramas, and poems when writing or speaking about a text, using terms such as chapter, scene, and stanza; describe how each successive part builds on earlier sections. **RL.3.5**

- Identify literary elements in a poem.
- Identify metaphors.

LANGUAGE OBJECTIVE

Identify the theme of a poem.

ACADEMIC LANGUAGE

- *narrative poem, theme, repetition, rhyme, metaphors*
- Cognates: *poema narrativo, tema, repetición, rima, metáfora*

Page 318

"Ginger's Fingers"

Explain and Model Metaphors Have students choral read the first line in the poem. *This is a metaphor. This means that two very different things are being compared. What is being compared?* (Ginger's fingers and shooting stars) Demonstrate how a shooting star flies through the sky. Point to the photograph, and explain that Ginger uses sign language to communicate. *Are Ginger's fingers really shooting stars?* (no) *What do her fingers look like when she is using sign language?* (shooting stars)

Explain and Model Rhyme Point to the words *stars* and *Mars,* and read them chorally with students. Remind students that words that rhyme have the same ending sounds.

What other words rhyme? (*waves/caves; butterflies/sunrise*)

Page 319

"The Giant"

Model Theme Explain what *tiny as a flea* means. *Why might the other team laugh?* (the narrator is short) *Is the narrator a good player?* (yes) *What words and phrases tell you this?* (*I'm a rocket; watch me soar; I sizzle when I dribble*) Help students complete the sentence frame: *The theme of "The Giant" is ____* (do not let others stop you from doing something you are good at).

Page 320

"Captain's Log"

Stanza 1

Point to the word *satin,* and have students chorally read the line. Explain that the ocean is being compared to satin. Tell students that *satin* is a smooth, shiny material.

Stanzas 2–3

Remind students that a narrative poem tells a story. *We know from the first stanza that the narrator is at sea.*

Help student pairs chorally read stanzas 2 and 3. *What happens at sea?* (There is a storm.)

Page 321

Draw or show a picture of a ship. Point to and then name the parts of the ship mentioned in the last three stanzas of the poem (mast, helm, sail, deck).

Stanzas 4–5

Reread the two stanzas, and act out what is happening, with students mimicking your gestures. *What does the captain need to do?* Have one student answer the question and another verify the answer. *The captain needs to ____* (get the ship through the storm).

Stanza 6

Explain and Model Rereading *The captain says the crew heard his call. How did the captain inspire the crew? Reread the last two lines if you are not sure.* Have one student answer the question and another elaborate on the answer. (to work together; to get through the storm)

After Reading

Make Connections

- Review the Essential Question: How can others inspire us?
- Make text connections.
- Have students complete the **ELL Reproducibles** pages 193–195.

→ # English Language Learners

Lexile 510
TextEvaluator™ 36

 **OBJECTIVES**
Recount stories, including fables, folktales, and myths from diverse cultures; determine the central message, lesson, or moral and explain how it is conveyed through key details in the text. **RL.3.2**

• Reread text to check understanding.

• Determine the meanings of metaphors.

LANGUAGE OBJECTIVE

Identify the theme of a story.

ACADEMIC LANGUAGE
• *reread, theme, realistic fiction, metaphor, poem*
• Cognates: *tema, ficción realista, metáfora, poema*

Leveled Reader:
Melanie's Mission

Go
Digital

Leveled Readers

Before Reading

Preview

• Read the Essential Question: How can others inspire us?

• Refer to You Inspire Me: *How might a firefighter inspire you?*

• Preview *Melanie's Mission* and "The Greedy Puppy": *Let's read about how a girl is inspired by her neighbor to try something new.*

Vocabulary

Use the **Visual Vocabulary Cards** to preteach the ELL vocabulary: *challenge, painful.* Use the routine found on the cards.

During Reading

Interactive Question-Response

Note Taking Have students use their graphic organizer on **ELL Reproducibles** page 192. Ask the following questions after reading each section. As you read, use visuals to define key vocabulary.

Pages 2–4 Have students take turns reading the dialogue between Melanie and her mother on page 2, with one student reading the first and third paragraph and another reading the second paragraph. Help students read the dialogue with expression. *Does Melanie like to play tennis?* (yes) *Can Melanie sing well?* (no)

Pages 5–7 *What does Mrs. Ortez believe about music? Fill in the sentence frame: Mrs. Ortez believes that _____* (everyone can find some music they enjoy). *How does Melanie react to Mrs. Ortez playing the piano?* (It makes her want to dance.) *Why is it hard for Mrs. Ortez to play? Reread the last paragraph on page 7 if you are not sure.* (She has arthritis in her hands, and it is very painful.)

Pages 8–11 *What is Melanie's idea?* Have one student answer the question and others elaborate on the answer by describing what activities are at the party. (to have a party at Mrs. Ortez's house; eating, playing board games, listening to music)

Fill in the Graphic Organizer

Page 12 *The phrase* stomach was one huge butterfly *on page 12 is a metaphor. It compares two things that are very different. What is a butterfly like?* (fluttering around, moving quickly) *How do you feel if your stomach is like a butterfly?* (nervous, excited)

Pages 13–15 *What challenge does Melanie face?* (playing the piano) Explain that the metaphor *Mrs. Ortez has the heart of a lion* means Mrs. Ortez is brave. *She inspired Melanie to be brave too. What is the theme of the story? Complete the sentence: It takes ____* (bravery) *to do something ____* (challenging).

After Reading

Respond to Reading Help students complete the graphic organizer. Revisit the Essential Question. Have student pairs summarize and answer the Text Evidence questions. Support students as necessary and review all responses as a group.

Analytical Writing **Write About Reading** Have partners write a paragraph about people who inspire them and explain why they inspire them.

Fluency: Expression

Model Model reading page 4 with expression. Next, reread the page aloud, and have students read along with you.

Apply Have students practice reading with a partner.

PAIRED READ

"The Greedy Puppy"

**Make Connections:
Write About It** *Analytical Writing*

Before reading, have students note that the genre of this text is a poem, which is a style of writing that often has a rhythm and does not follow the same rules as prose. Then discuss the Essential Question. After reading, have students write about connections between how people are inspired by others in "The Greedy Puppy" and *Melanie's Mission*.

Leveled Reader

FOCUS ON LITERARY ELEMENTS

Students can extend their knowledge of poetry by completing the literary elements activity on page 20.

Literature Circles

Ask students to conduct a literature circle using the Thinkmark questions to guide the discussion. You may wish to have a whole-class discussion on people who inspire students and why they inspire them.

Level Up

Level-up lessons available online.

IF students read the ELL Level and answered the questions

THEN pair them with students who have proficiently read On Level and have ELL students

- echo-read the On Level main selection with their partner.

- list difficult words or phrases and discuss them with their partner.

A C T Access Complex Text

The On Level challenges students by including more **domain-specific words** and **complex sentence structures**.

English Language Learners

Vocabulary

PRETEACH VOCABULARY

OBJECTIVES

 Acquire and use accurately grade-appropriate conversational, general academic, and domain-specific words and phrases, including those that signal spatial and temporal relationships. **L.3.6**

LANGUAGE OBJECTIVE
Use vocabulary words.

 I Do Preteach vocabulary from the poems using the Vocabulary Routine on the **Visual Vocabulary Cards** for *adventurous, courageous, extremely, weird* and poetry words *free verse, narrative poem, repetition, rhyme*.

 We Do After completing the Vocabulary Routine for each word, point to the word on the card and read it with students. Have students repeat the word.

 You Do Have students work with a partner to write short definitions for some of the words. Then have each pair read their definitions aloud.

Beginning	Intermediate	Advanced/High
Help students write two definitions correctly and read them aloud.	Have students write four definitions and read them aloud.	Have students write a short definition for each word, including parts of speech.

REVIEW VOCABULARY

OBJECTIVES

 Acquire and use accurately grade-appropriate conversational, general academic, and domain-specific words and phrases, including those that signal spatial and temporal relationships. **L.3.6**

LANGUAGE OBJECTIVE
Use vocabulary words.

 I Do Review the previous week's vocabulary words. The words can be reviewed over a few days. Read each word aloud pointing to the word on the **Visual Vocabulary Card**. Have students repeat after you. Then follow the Vocabulary Routine on the back of each card.

 We Do Randomly select a Visual Vocabulary Card. Have students give a synonym for the word and then use it in a sentence. Repeat with each card.

 You Do In pairs, have students come up with ways to act out two or more words. Then have them act out the meanings of the words for the class.

Beginning	Intermediate	Advanced/High
Help students by acting out one word meaning with them. Suggest actions for them to do.	Have students act out two or more word meanings.	Ask students to come up with ways to act out each word. Then have them define each word.

METAPHORS

OBJECTIVES

 Distinguish the literal and nonliteral meanings of words and phrases in context (e.g., take steps). **L.3.5a**

LANGUAGE OBJECTIVE

Determine the meanings of metaphors.

 I Do Read aloud the poem "Ginger's Fingers" on page 318 as students follow along. Point to the line *Ginger's fingers are ocean waves*. Explain that metaphors compare two things that are very different.

Think Aloud I think that *Ginger's fingers are ocean waves* is a metaphor comparing the movement of ocean waves to the way Ginger's fingers move as she signs. This helps me picture Ginger's fingers moving steadily and with repetition.

 We Do Have students point to *Ginger's fingers are butterflies* on page 318. Determine the meaning of the metaphor with students.

 You Do In pairs, have students determine the meaning of the metaphor *I sizzle, SIZZLE, when I dribble* on page 319.

Beginning	Intermediate	Advanced/High
Help students locate the metaphor. Help them determine what is being compared.	Ask students to locate and read aloud the metaphor. Ask them to determine its meaning.	Have students identify the metaphor. Ask them how they figured out what was being compared.

ADDITIONAL VOCABULARY

OBJECTIVES

 Use conventional spelling for high-frequency and other studied words and for adding suffixes to base words (e.g., *sitting, smiled, cries, happiness*). **L.3.2e**

Discuss concept and high-frequency words.

LANGUAGE OBJECTIVE

Use concept and high-frequency words.

 I Do List concept and high-frequency words from the Shared Read poems: *me, out, flexing, mast, helm, crew;* and *Melanie's Mission: carried along, bowed, challenge, another*. Define each word for students: Flexing *means "bending."*

 We Do Model using the words for students in sentences: *The courageous firefighters rushed to put* out *the flames.* Then provide sentence frames and complete them with students: *We went* out *at recess to play ____.*

 You Do Have pairs act out scenes related to the additional words and share them with the class.

Beginning	Intermediate	Advanced/High
Help students write a sentence about one of the scenes acted out. Help them use the vocabulary word in the sentence.	Have students write a sentence about two of the scenes acted out. Have them use the vocabulary word in each sentence.	Have students write a sentence about three of the scenes acted out. Ask them to explain how each scene relates to the vocabulary word in each sentence.

→ English Language Learners
Writing/Spelling

WRITING TRAIT: WORD CHOICE

OBJECTIVES

(CCSS) Use concrete words and phrases and sensory details to convey experiences and events precisely. **W.4.3d**

Identify strong, descriptive words.

LANGUAGE OBJECTIVE
Write using strong, descriptive words.

 Explain that good writers use strong, descriptive words to make their writing interesting and clear. Read the Student Model passage aloud as students follow along, and identify strong, descriptive words and phrases.

 Read aloud page 320 from "Captain's Log" as students follow along. Identify the strong, descriptive words such as *satin, rumbled, pouring,* and *pale,* filling in a word web as you go.

 Have pairs write sentences about a trip one of them has taken using strong, descriptive words. The sentences should help the reader visualize the trip. Edit each pair's writing, and ask students to revise.

Beginning	Intermediate	Advanced/High
Help students copy the edited sentences.	Have students revise, adding descriptive words or phrases.	Have students revise adding strong, descriptive words, and edit for errors.

SPELL WORDS WITH SOFT *c* AND *g*

OBJECTIVES

 Use spelling patterns and generalizations (e.g., word families, position-based spellings, syllable patterns, ending rules, meaningful word parts) in writing words. **L.3.2f**

LANGUAGE OBJECTIVE
Spell words with soft *c* and *g*.

 Read aloud the Spelling Words on page T290, modeling the soft *c* and *g* sounds. Point out that the letter *c* is a soft /s/ sound in *circle*, and the letter *g* is a soft /j/ sound in *gem*. Have students repeat the words.

 Read the Dictation Sentences on page T291 aloud for students. With each sentence, read the underlined word slowly, segmenting it into syllables. Have students repeat after you and write the word.

 Display the words. Have students exchange their list with a partner to check the spelling and write the words correctly.

Beginning	Intermediate	Advanced/High
Help students copy the words with correct spelling and say the words aloud.	Have students point out the soft *c* and *g* in their corrected words.	After students have corrected their words, have pairs quiz each other.

Grammar

IRREGULAR VERBS

OBJECTIVES

 Form and use regular and irregular verbs. **L.3.1d**

Use irregular verbs.

LANGUAGE OBJECTIVE

Write sentences using irregular verbs.

Language Transfers Handbook

Speakers of Cantonese, Hmong, and Korean may have problems with irregular subject-verb agreement as verb forms do not change to show the number of the subject in the native language. Use contrastive analysis as necessary to help reinforce correct subject-verb agreement in English.

 I Do Remind students that we do not add *-ed* to form the past tense of some verbs. Write on the board: *We saw a movie.* Underline *saw.* Tell students that an irregular verb has a special spelling for the past tense. Some irregular verbs are *come/came, do/did, say/said, go/went, eat/ate,* and *sing/sang.* Remind students that some irregular verbs also have a special spelling when used with the helping verbs *have, has, had* and *does, did, do.* Write on the board: *Jess had gone to the same movie last week.* Underline *had gone.* Tell students that subjects and helping verbs must always agree in both simple and compound sentences.

 We Do Write the sentences below on the board. Ask volunteers to fill in each blank with the correct form of the irregular verb in parentheses. Remind them that the subjects and verbs must agree. Then read the completed sentences aloud for students to repeat.

> We _____ (do) not have time to buy groceries yesterday.
>
> Sofia _____ (say) we had to wait an hour before we could go swimming.
>
> Reginald and I had _____ (eat) before we arrived at the game.
>
> Our team _____ (take) first place at last week's competition.
>
> If we had _____ (know) you were coming, we would have waited.

 You Do Have students work in pairs to come up with a list of irregular verbs. Have them write at least two sentences using the verbs from their list. Then have students draw pictures for each sentence and share them with the class.

Beginning	Intermediate	Advanced/High
Help students make their lists and write one sentence. Give them ideas for pictures to draw.	Ask students to write their sentences on the board. Have them give the past-tense form of each verb they used.	Have students write their sentences on the board. Ask them to explain how they determined each verb was irregular.

For extra support, have students complete the activities in the **Grammar Practice Reproducibles** during the week, using the routine below:

* Explain the grammar skill.
* Model the first activity in the Grammar Practice Reproducibles.
* Have the whole group complete the next couple of activities, then the rest with a partner.
* Review the activities with correct answers.

PROGRESS MONITORING

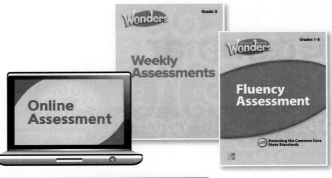

Unit 4 Week 5 Formal Assessment	Standards Covered	Component for Assessment
Text Evidence	RL.3.1	• *Selection Test* • *Weekly Assessment* • *Approaching-Level Weekly Assessment*
Poetry/Theme	RL.3.2	• *Weekly Assessment* • *Approaching-Level Weekly Assessment*
Metaphors	RL.3.4, L.3.5a	• *Selection Test* • *Weekly Assessment* • *Approaching-Level Weekly Assessment*
Writing About Text	W.3.8	*Weekly Assessment*

Unit 4 Week 5 Informal Assessment	Standards Covered	Component for Assessment
Research/Listening/ Collaborating	SL.3.1d, SL.3.2, SL.3.3	• *RWW* • *Teacher's Edition*
Oral Reading Fluency (ORF) **Fluency Goal:** 82–102 words correct per minute (WCPM) **Accuracy Rate Goal:** 95% or higher	RF.3.4a, RF.3.4b, RF.3.4c	*Fluency Assessment*

Using Assessment Results

Weekly Assessments Skills and Fluency	If . . .	Then . . .
COMPREHENSION	Students score below 70% . . .	. . . assign Lessons 34–36 on Theme from the *Tier 2 Comprehension Intervention online PDFs.*
VOCABULARY	Students score below 70% . . .	. . . assign Lesson 165 on Metaphors from the *Tier 2 Vocabulary Intervention online PDFs.*
WRITING	Students score below "3" on constructed response . . .	. . . assign Lessons 34–36 and/or Write About Reading Lesson 194 from the *Tier 2 Comprehension Intervention online PDFs.*
FLUENCY	Students have a WCPM score of 75–81 . . .	. . . assign a lesson from Section 1, 7, 8, 9 or 10 of the *Tier 2 Fluency Intervention online PDFs.*
	Students have a WCPM score of 0–74 . . .	. . . assign a lesson from Sections 2–6 of the *Tier 2 Fluency Intervention online PDFs.*

Using Weekly Data

Check your data Dashboard to verify assessment results and guide grouping decisions.

Data-Driven Recommendations

Response to Intervention

Use the appropriate sections of the *Placement and Diagnostic Assessment* as well as students' assessment results to designate students requiring:

 Intervention Online PDFs

 WonderWorks Intervention Program

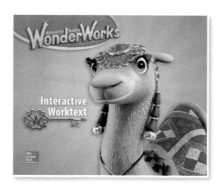

The Big Idea: *What are different ways to meet challenges?*

Student Outcomes

Close Reading of Complex Text
- Cite relevant evidence from text
- Summarize the text
- Interpret information presented visually
- Gather relevant information from digital sources
- Navigate links

RI.3.2, RI.3.5, RI.3.7

Writing
Write to Sources
- Write an opinion
- Conduct research
- Select reliable sources

Writing Process
- Edit/proofread and publish a poem
- **Celebrate** Share your writing

W.3.6, W.3.7, W.3.8

Speaking and Listening
- Paraphrase information presented digitally
- Report on a topic

SL.3.2

Foundational Skills
Fluency
- Read orally with prosody
- Read orally with accuracy
- Read orally with expression

RF.3.4a, RF.3.4b. RF.3.4c

Review and Extend

Reader's Theater

The Baker's Neighbor

Genre Play

Reading Digitally

TIME FOR KIDS "Forbidden Foods"

Go Digital!

Level Up Accelerating Progress

FROM **APPROACHING** TO **ON LEVEL**

FROM **ON LEVEL** TO **BEYOND LEVEL**

FROM **ENGLISH LANGUAGE LEARNERS** TO **ON LEVEL**

FROM **BEYOND LEVEL** TO **SELF-SELECTED TRADE BOOK**

Advanced Level Trade Book

ASSESS

Presentations

Inquiry Space
Project Presentations

Project Rubric

Writing
Narrative/Poetry Writing Presentations

Writing Rubric

Unit Assessments

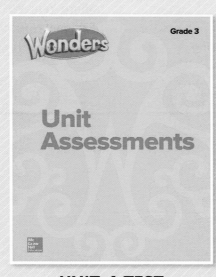

UNIT 4 TEST

FLUENCY

Evaluate Student Progress

Use the Wonders online assessment reports to evaluate student progress and help you make decisions about small group instruction and assignments.

Online Assessment

SUGGESTED LESSON PLAN

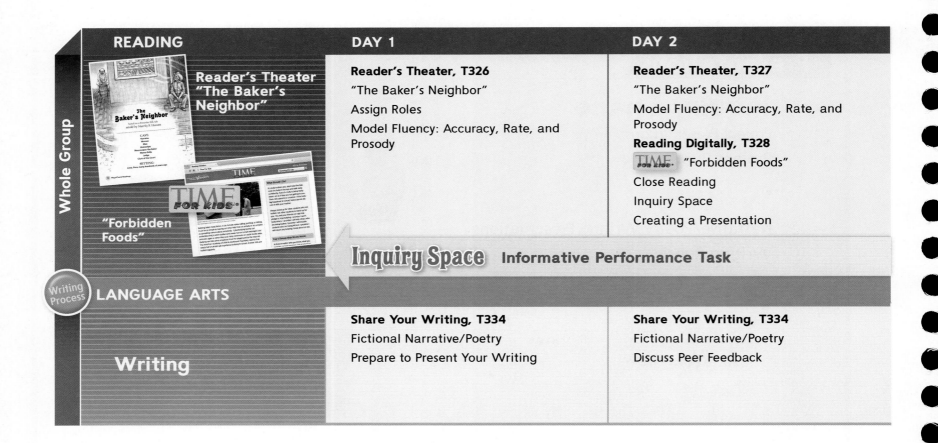

Whole Group

READING

Reader's Theater "The Baker's Neighbor"

The Baker's Neighbor

TIME FOR KIDS

"Forbidden Foods"

DAY 1

Reader's Theater, T326
"The Baker's Neighbor"
Assign Roles
Model Fluency: Accuracy, Rate, and Prosody

DAY 2

Reader's Theater, T327
"The Baker's Neighbor"
Model Fluency: Accuracy, Rate, and Prosody
Reading Digitally, T328
TIME FOR KIDS "Forbidden Foods"
Close Reading
Inquiry Space
Creating a Presentation

Inquiry Space Informative Performance Task

LANGUAGE ARTS

Writing

Writing Process

Share Your Writing, T334
Fictional Narrative/Poetry
Prepare to Present Your Writing

Share Your Writing, T334
Fictional Narrative/Poetry
Discuss Peer Feedback

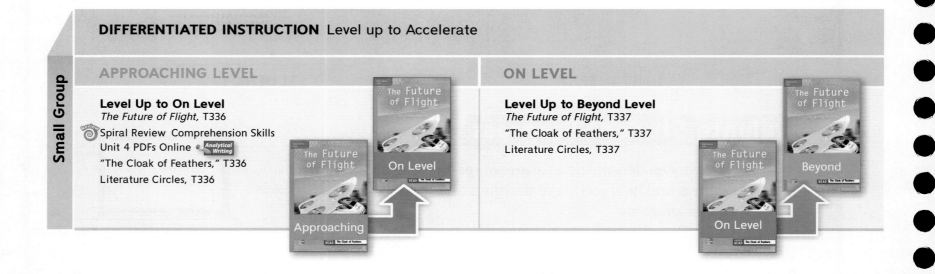

Small Group

DIFFERENTIATED INSTRUCTION Level up to Accelerate

APPROACHING LEVEL

Level Up to On Level
The Future of Flight, T336
Spiral Review Comprehension Skills
Unit 4 PDFs Online *Analytical Writing*
"The Cloak of Feathers," T336
Literature Circles, T336

ON LEVEL

Level Up to Beyond Level
The Future of Flight, T337
"The Cloak of Feathers," T337
Literature Circles, T337

DAY 3	DAY 4	DAY 5
Reading Digitally, T329	**Reader's Theater, T327**	**Inquiry Space, T330–T332**
TIME FOR KIDS. "Forbidden Foods" Analytical Writing	Performance	Presentations
Write About Reading		Wrap Up the Unit, T333
		✓ **Unit Assessment, T340–T341**

Inquiry Space Informative Performance Task

Share Your Writing, T334	**Share Your Writing, T334**	**Share Your Writing, T335**
Fictional Narrative/Poetry	Share Your Fictional Narrative/Poetry	Fictional Narrative/Poetry
Rehearse Your Presentation	Evaluate Your Presentation	Portfolio Choice

BEYOND LEVEL	ENGLISH LANGUAGE LEARNERS
Level Up to Self-Selected	**Level Up to On Level**
Trade Book, T339	*The Future of Flight,* T338
	"The Cloak of Feathers," T338
	Literature Circles, T338

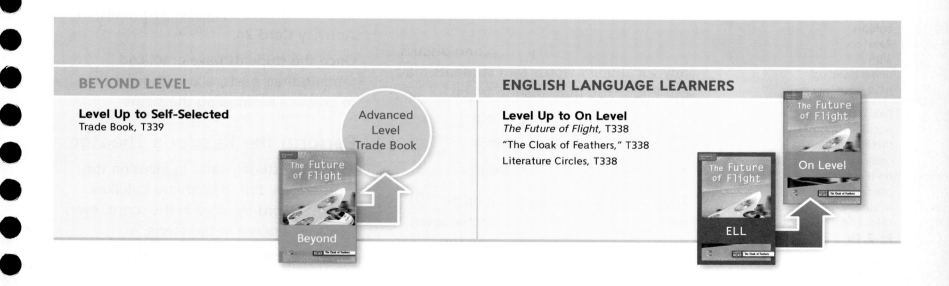

Advanced Level Trade Book

Reader's Theater

The Baker's Neighbor

Go Digital!

Teacher's Resource
PDF Online
pp. 46–55

OBJECTIVES

CCSS Read with sufficient accuracy and fluency to support comprehension. Read on-level text with purpose and understanding. **RF.3.4a**

CCSS Read with sufficient accuracy and fluency to support comprehension. Read on-level prose and poetry orally with accuracy, appropriate rate, and expression. **RF.3.4b**

Introduce the Play

Explain that *The Baker's Neighbor* is a play set in ancient Peru and based on a folktale. In the story, a baker demands gold from his neighbor as payment for his bakery's pleasing aromas. In the end, a judge decides the baker is too greedy, but does the baker really learn his lesson? Distribute scripts and the Elements of Drama handout from the **Teacher's Resource PDF Online** pages 46–55.

- Review the features of a play.
- Review the list of characters. Build background on the setting and time period, and define the roles of Atahualpa, Mancocapac, and the other characters.
- Review what students know about the features of a folktale.

Shared Reading

Model reading the play as the students follow along in their scripts.

Focus on Vocabulary Stop and discuss any vocabulary words that students may not know. You may wish to teach:

- ingredients
- annoyed
- unfortunately
- profit
- labor
- fragrant

Model Fluency As you read each part, state the name of each character, and read the part emphasizing the appropriate phrasing and expression.

Discuss Each Role

- After reading the part of the Narrator, ask students to identify what information the Narrator is giving about the play.
- After reading each character part, ask partners to note the characters' traits. Model how to find text evidence that tells about the characters.

Assign Roles

Depending on the number of students, you may wish to divide the play into two or more sections. Have different students play the eight different roles.

Practice the Play

Each day, allow students time to practice their parts in the play. Pair fluent readers with less fluent readers. Pairs can echo-read or chorally read their parts. As needed, work with less fluent readers to mark pauses in their script using one slash for a short pause and two slashes for longer pauses.

Throughout the week have students work on Reader's Theater **Workstation Activity Card 26**.

Once the students have practiced reading their parts, allow students time to practice performing the script.

Perform the Reader's Theater

- Remind students not to focus on the audience, but to continue to follow along word-by-word in the script, even if they are not in the scene.
- Lead a class discussion on the play's humor. Ask how students can use expression and exaggeration.
- Discuss what it would be like to be Atahualpa, Mancocapac, or the Judge. What are they thinking?

ACTIVITIES

THE NARRATOR IN THE SPOTLIGHT

Sometimes a play has a narrator to move the plot along. The narrator does not take part in the action of the play. Instead, the narrator stays out of the story and gives information about the characters and events.

Reread *The Baker's Neighbor* and pay attention to the Narrator's lines. Then discuss the following questions with students:

1. What does the Narrator say about the story at the beginning of the play?

2. What does the Narrator say the baker does? What does the Narrator say the baker's neighbor does?

3. How do you learn about the baker's feelings as he counts the hundred gold pieces?

IDENTIFY THEMES AS LESSONS IN FOLKTALES

Folktales are told around the world. *The Baker's Neighbor* is based on a folktale. In these stories, the main character learns a lesson. The lesson can be about love, cleverness, lying, helping people, or more.

Help students identify the theme, central message, or lesson of the play *The Baker's Neighbor*.

Have students use a graphic organizer to distinguish the plot (what happens) from the theme (the lesson the baker learns). Students can work in pairs to summarize their ideas about the play.

ENGLISH LANGUAGE LEARNERS

ELL

- Review the definitions of difficult words, including: *aroma, compliment, customers, total, splendid, absurd, court, unusual, glee,* and *glum.*

- Team a non-native speaker with a fluent reader who is also reading the part of Atahualpa. Have each reader take turns reading the lines.

- Remind students that rereading their part several times helps build fluency. Have them summarize what they are reading to check comprehension.

Reading Digitally

 OBJECTIVES

 Use text features and search tools (e.g., key words, sidebars, hyperlinks) to locate information relevant to a given topic efficiently. **RI.3.5**

Conduct short research projects that build knowledge about a topic. **W.3.7**

Forbidden Foods

Before Reading

Preview Scroll through the online article "Forbidden Foods" at www.connected.mcgraw-hill.com and have students identify text features. Review how to navigate through the article. Point out the interactive features, such as **hyperlinks**, **charts**, and **discussion boxes**. Explain that you will read the article together first and then access these features.

Close Reading Online

Take Notes Scroll back to the top and read the article aloud. As you read, ask questions to focus students on the problem of food allergies and how people are trying to solve it. Have students take notes about the problem and solutions using **Graphic Organizer 26**. After each section, have students turn to partners and paraphrase the main ideas, giving text evidence. Make sure students understand domain-specific terms, such as *allergies* and *immune system*.

Access Interactive Elements Help students access the interactive elements by clicking or rolling over each text feature. Discuss what information these elements add to the text.

Tell students they will reread parts of the article to help them answer a specific question: *What is a food allergy?* Review that they need not reread every word. Instead, they can

* **skim** by reading quickly and focusing on topic sentences, or
* **scan** by moving their eyes over the text quickly to spot key words.

Have students skim the article to find text detailing what a food allergy is. Have partners share what they find.

Navigate Links to Information Model using a hyperlink to jump to another Web page. Discuss any information on the new Web page related to the question *What is a food allergy?* Remind students that bookmarking the page allows them to return to it at another time.

WRITE ABOUT READING — Analytical Writing

Summarize Review students' graphic organizers. Model using the information to summarize "Forbidden Foods."

Ask students to write a summary of the article, stating the problem and what people can do to help. Partners should discuss their summaries.

Make Connections Have students compare what they learned about meeting challenges presented by fool allergies with what they have learned about other challenges in texts they have read in this unit.

TAKE A STAND

Food Bans

Have students state their opinion about whether or not foods, such as peanut butter, should be banned at school if someone has an allergy. Tell them they should

- clearly state their opinion and organize their ideas logically.
- support their position with precise, accurate information from the article or linked site.
- end with a concluding statement that restates their opinion.

Have students with opposing viewpoints debate one another.

RESEARCH ONLINE

Image Searches Point out that searching for images is similar to doing a key word search. Students can find images by entering key words into a search engine, plus the word *images*. Model conducting an image search related to food allergy symptoms.

Multimedia Searches Searching for multimedia resources, such as audio or video, is similar to an image search. Students can enter key words related to their topic plus the word *audio* or *video*. Explain that they can use relevant audio files or video as part of a multimedia presentation or link to them in an online article.

INDEPENDENT STUDY

Investigate

Choose a Topic Students should brainstorm questions related to the article. For example, they might ask: *How do doctors test for allergies?* Then have students choose a question to research. Help them narrow it.

Conduct Internet Research Review with students that to do an image or multimedia search, they can type key words into the search engine, plus the words *images, audio,* or *video*. Point out that they should follow the rules for Cyber Safety and only visit approved sites.

Present Have groups give an informational or persuasive presentation about allergies.

→ Integrate Ideas

NARRATIVE PERFORMANCE TASK

Write About: Frogs

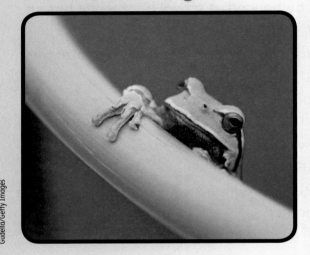

Gudella/Getty Images

Inquiry Space

LEVEL		1	2	3	4	5	**6**

Publish and Present

Display Level 6 from the Narrative Performance Task. Explain that in this level students will publish their story and plan their presentation. Review the **Presentation Plan** with students, making sure they understand how to complete it. Explain that this plan will help them think about the visuals and audio they want to include in their presentation.

1 **Add Visuals** Tell students that adding photos, illustrations, video, and props can make their presentation more interesting. Suggest that they look at their story maps from Level 4 to help them decide how the characters, setting, and events can be shown with visuals. Explain that students could have classmates act out parts of their story or that they could use video to film a scene. Suggest that they scan photos, make digital illustrations, or insert clip art. Show students the **Design Your Presentation** animation from the **Toolkit** and review key details with them.

OBJECTIVES

CCSS Ask questions to check understanding of information presented, stay on topic, and link their comments to the remarks of others. **SL.3.1c**

CCSS Explain their own ideas and understanding in light of the discussion. **SL.3.1d**

CCSS Report on a topic or text, tell a story, or recount an experience with appropriate facts and relevant, descriptive details, speaking clearly at an understandable pace. **SL.3.4**

SPEAKING

COLLABORATE

Explain to students that when they give a narrative presentation to a large audience, such as the whole class, they need to remember these strategies:

- Rehearse the presentation in front of a friend.
- Speak slowly and clearly.
- Use expression in your voice.
- Look at the people in the audience.
- Use hand gestures.

Remind students to time themselves during practice sessions to allow enough time for questions from the audience following the presentation. You may wish to show students the Presentation Checklist from the Toolkit.

2 **Add Audio** Encourage students to add audio to a presentation. Explain that they could record themselves telling their story or record classmates acting out different characters in the story. Suggest that students also use sound effects and music in their presentation. Show them the **Record and Edit Audio** animation from the Toolkit and have them retell the key points.

3 **Giving a Presentation** Ask students to think about what makes someone a good storyteller. Explain that the way someone tells a story can make it more interesting. Guide students in understanding the importance of being a good storyteller when they give their presentation. Tell them to speak slowly and clearly, use expression in their voice, look at the audience, use hand gestures, and include visuals and audio where possible. Show students the **Collaborative Conversations: Presenting** video and **Presentation Checklist** from the Toolkit and present the mini-lessons below.

ASSIGN LEVEL 6 Have students begin Level 6 by publishing their final draft. You may wish to show them the **How to Publish Your Work** PDF from the Toolkit. Then have them fill out the Presentation Plan and decide what visuals and audio they would like to add to their presentation. Have students meet in small groups or with a partner to discuss their presentation plan.

OBJECTIVES

CCSS Introduce a topic and group related information together; include illustrations when useful to aiding comprehension. **W.3.2a**

CCSS With guidance and support from adults, use technology to produce and publish writing (using keyboarding skills) as well as to interact and collaborate with others. **W.3.6**

CCSS Create engaging audio recordings of stories or poems that demonstrate fluid reading at an understandable pace; add visual displays when appropriate to emphasize or enhance certain facts or details. **SL.3.5**

LISTENING

COLLABORATE

Remind students that an effective listener

- listens carefully for details about the story, characters, and setting.
- stays focused on the speaker's story and presentation.
- listens without interrupting.
- ignores distractions.
- thinks about questions to ask after the presentation is finished.

Tell students to write down any questions that they have to ask when the speaker is finished. Discuss the presentation. Ask some students to paraphrase or summarize the key ideas of the presentation. You may show students the **Listening Checklist** from the Toolkit.

Discuss with students where else informative presentations may be given; for example, on a field trip or through an after-school activity. Point out that good listening skills can help students understand and cooperate with others in a variety of cultural settings.

OBJECTIVES

CCSS Follow agreed-upon rules for discussion (e.g., gaining the floor in respectful ways, listening to others with care, speaking one at a time about the topics and texts under discussion). **SL.3.1b**

CCSS Determine the main ideas and supporting details of a text read aloud or information presented in diverse media and formats, including visually, quantitatively, and orally. **SL.3.2**

CCSS Ask and answer questions about information from a speaker, offering appropriate elaboration and detail. **SL.3.3**

→ Integrate Ideas

Review and Evaluate

Distribute the online PDF of the checklists and rubrics. Use the following Teacher Checklist and rubric to evaluate students' research and presentations.

Student Checklist

Presenting

☑ Did you tell your story clearly?

☑ Did you include details, descriptions, and dialogue to make your story interesting?

☑ Did you look at the people in the audience when you were speaking?

☑ Did you use visuals and audio to make your presentation better?

Teacher Checklist

Assess the Presentation

☑ Spoke clearly and at an appropriate pace and volume.

☑ Used appropriate gestures.

☑ Maintained eye contact.

☑ Used appropriate visuals and technology.

Assess the Listener

☑ Listened quietly and politely.

☑ Made appropriate comments and asked clarifying questions.

☑ Responded with an open mind to different ideas.

Presentation Rubric

4 Excellent	**3** Good	**2** Fair	**1** Unsatisfactory
• presents the story clearly • includes interesting details and descriptions • includes dialogue effectively • tells an engaging story with a well-organized plot	• presents the story adequately • includes adequate details and descriptions • includes dialogue adequately • shows adequate ability to develop a plot	• attempts to present a story • may include few or vague details and descriptions • may include little or no dialogue • has difficulty developing or sequencing a plot	• may show little grasp of the narrative task • may lack a clear plot • may lack dialogue, details, and descriptions • may reflect extreme difficulty with research or presentation

Wrap Up the Unit

The Big Idea: *What are the different ways to meet challenges?*

TEXT CONNECTIONS

COLLABORATE

Connect to the Big Idea

Text to Text Write the Unit Big Idea on the board: What are the different ways to meet challenges? Divide the class into small groups. Tell students that each group will compare the information that they have learned during the course of the unit in order to answer the Big Idea question. Model how to compare this information by using examples from the **Leveled Readers** and what they have read in this unit's selections.

Collaborative Conversations Have students review their class notes and completed graphic organizers before they begin their discussions. Encourage students to compare information from all the unit's selections and the Inquiry Space presentations. Have each group pick one student to take notes. Explain

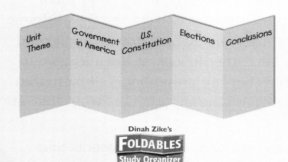

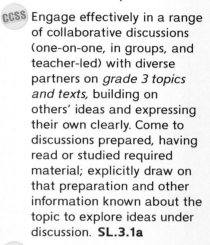
Dinah Zike's
FOLDABLES
Study Organizer

that each group will use an Accordion Foldable® to record their ideas. You may wish to model how to use an Accordion Foldable® to record comparisons of texts.

Present Ideas and Synthesize Information When students finish their discussions, ask for a volunteer from each group to read their notes aloud. After each group has presented their ideas, ask: *What are the five most important things we have learned about rising to a challenge?* Lead a class discussion and list students' ideas on the board. If there are more than five things, have students vote to narrow down the list to the top five most important things.

Building Knowledge Encourage students to continue building knowledge about the Unit Big Idea. Display the online Unit Bibliography and have students search online for articles and other resources related to the Big Idea. After each group has presented their ideas, ask: *How can overcoming challenges make us grow as people?* Lead a class discussion asking students to use the information from their charts to answer the question.

OBJECTIVES

CCSS Compare and contrast the most important points and key details presented in two texts on the same topic. **RI.3.9**

CCSS Engage effectively in a range of collaborative discussions (one-on-one, in groups, and teacher-led) with diverse partners on *grade 3 topics and texts,* building on others' ideas and expressing their own clearly. Come to discussions prepared, having read or studied required material; explicitly draw on that preparation and other information known about the topic to explore ideas under discussion. **SL.3.1a**

CCSS Explain their own ideas and understanding in light of the discussion. **SL.3.1d**

Go Digital

Research Roadmap

Resources: Research and Inquiry

Celebrate Share Your Writing

Publishing Celebrations

Giving Presentations

Now is the time for students to share one of their pieces of narrative writing or poetry that they have worked on through the unit.

You may wish to invite parents or students from other classes to the Publishing Celebrations.

Preparing for Presentations

Tell students that they will present their writing. In order to provide the best representation of their hard work, they will need to prepare.

Allow students time to rehearse their presentations. Tell them to become very familiar with the piece they will be presenting by rereading it a few times. Explain that they should find the rhythm of their work that best conveys meaning. Have them create audio recordings of their poems and stories, then listen to them for fluency and pace. They should plan not to simply read straight from their paper, but rather to look at the audience to express the feelings of what they are presenting. Tell them that the way they speak and present is as important as what they are presenting.

Students should consider any visuals or digital elements that they want to use during their presentation. Discuss a few possible options with students.

- Can they illustrate an important part of the narrative? Can they display images of what the setting looks like?

- Are there items or props that they would like to share related to the narrative or poem?

- Is there music or other audio that would accentuate the presentation of the poem that they can play?

Students can practice presenting to a partner in the classroom. They can also practice with family members at home or in front of a mirror. Share the following checklist with students to help them focus on important parts of their presentation as they rehearse. Discuss each point on the checklist.

Speaking Checklist

Review the Speaking Checklist with students as they practice.

- ☑ Have all your notes and visual aids ready.
- ☑ Stand up straight and take a few deep breaths.
- ☑ Look at the audience.
- ☑ Speak clearly and slowly, but loud enough so everyone can hear.
- ☑ Speak with rhythm and emotion.
- ☑ Emphasize your story's relevant and descriptive details.
- ☑ Use appropriate gestures.
- ☑ Display your visual aids so everyone can see them.

Vstock LLC/Getty Images

Listening to Presentations

Remind students that they will be part of the audience for other students' presentations. Review with students the following Listening Checklist.

Listening Checklist

During the Presentation

- ☑ Pay attention to how the speaker uses rhythm in the presentation.
- ☑ Take notes on what you liked about the presentation, including rhyme scheme.
- ☑ Write one question or comment you have about the presentation.
- ☑ Listen to the speaker carefully to determine the main idea.
- ☑ Do not talk during the presentation.

After the Presentation

- ☑ Only comment on the presentation when it is your turn.
- ☑ Tell why you liked the presentation.
- ☑ If someone else makes a similar comment, link your comment to his or hers.
- ☑ Ask an appropriate and detailed question about the narrative.
- ☑ Ask the speaker to elaborate on any details you did not fully understand.

Portfolio Choice

Ask students to select one finished piece of writing, as well as two revisions to include in their writing portfolio. As students consider their choices, have them use the questions below.

Published Writing

Does your writing

- clearly express feelings and ideas, using descriptive words that appeal to the senses?
- use time-order words to signal event order?
- include figurative language or dialogue?
- have few or no errors in spelling, verb tense, capitalization, or punctuation?
- appear neatly written and clearly published?

Writing Entry Revisions

Did you choose a revised entry that shows

- feelings through effective use of voice?
- strong action words?
- a strong opening, conclusion, or other organizational structure?

PORTFOLIO
Students can submit their writing to be considered for inclusion in their Digital Portfolio. Students' portfolios can be shared with parents.

Level Up Accelerating Progress

Leveled Reader

Approaching Level to On Level

The Future of Flight

Level Up Lessons also available online

Before Reading

Preview Discuss what students remember about the future of aircraft and spacecraft. Tell them they will be reading a more challenging version of *The Future of Flight*.

Vocabulary Use the **Visual Vocabulary Cards** and routine.

A C T During Reading

▶ **Specific Vocabulary** Review with students the following words that are new to this title: *thrusts, biofuel, sub-space*. Model how to use a glossary to define the words.

▶ **Connection of Ideas** Students may need help connecting and synthesizing new ideas and information. Read page 11 with students. Ask: *What is the name of the privately owned spaceship?* (SpaceshipTwo/VMS EVE) *Where does the SpaceshipTwo go after it is released by the WhiteKnightTwo?* (in sub-space) Help students synthesize new information on pages 8 and 10.

▶ **Sentence Structure** Students may need help understanding more complex sentence structures. Read the sentence aloud with the word "sense" in it on page 5. Say: *This word is important because it is in quotations. What do you think "sense" means?* ("feel") Discuss how the signals will let the aircraft know that there are others close by.

After Reading

Ask students to complete the Respond to Reading on page 15. Then have them finish the Paired Read and hold Literature Circles.

Leveled Reader

OBJECTIVES

CCSS By the end of the year, read and comprehend informational texts, including history/ social studies, science, and technical texts, at the high end of the grades 2–3 text complexity band independently and proficiently. **RI.3.10**

On Level to Beyond Level

The Future of Flight

Level Up Lessons also available online

Before Reading

Preview Discuss what students remember about the future of aircraft and spacecrafts. Tell them they will be reading a more challenging version of *The Future of Flight*.

Vocabulary Use the **Visual Vocabulary Cards** to review the vocabulary.

A C T During Reading

▶ **Specific Vocabulary** Review with students the following words that are new to this title: *swarms, ignite, accelerate*. Model how to use a glossary to find the meaning.

▶ **Sentence Structure** Students may need help understanding the use of rhetorical questions. See page 2. Read the first paragraph with students and then ask them to state what it was about. Ask: *Why is the author asking these questions?* (to get the reader to think) *What does the author want you to think about?* (space and air travel in the future) Repeat with questions on pages 3, 4, 5, 6, 10, and 13.

▶ **Connection of Ideas** Students may need help connecting and synthesizing new ideas and information. Read the second paragraph on page 4 with students. Ask: *What does the picture show?* (a MyCopter) *What is special about the MyCopters people might use in the future?* (They can be used for short trips, will take off and land like helicopters, and may be able to take off from parking spots.) Help students synthesize new information on pages 6, 7, 8 and 12.

After Reading

Ask students to complete the Respond to Reading on page 15. Then have them finish the Paired Read and hold Literature Circles.

Level Up Accelerating Progress

Leveled Reader

OBJECTIVES

CCSS By the end of the year, read and comprehend informational texts, including history/social studies, science, and technical texts, at the high end of the grades 2–3 text complexity band independently and proficiently. **RI.3.10**

English Language Learners to On Level

The Future of Flight

Level Up Lessons also available online

Before Reading

Preview Remind students that expository text gives facts about a topic. Discuss what students remember about the future of aircraft and spacecraft. Tell them they will be reading a more challenging version of *The Future of Flight*.

Vocabulary Use the **Visual Vocabulary Cards** to review the vocabulary. Use the routine found on the cards. Point out the cognates: *gravedad, orbitar, subespacio.*

A C T During Reading

▶ **Specific Vocabulary** Point out and chorally read page 11. Say: *The SpaceshipTwo needs a plane to carry it into the sky.* Point to the *WhiteKnightTwo* in the photo. *Where does the SpaceshipTwo go when the plane lets it go?* (in subspace) Point to the sky.

▶ **Sentence Structure** Read the second sentence on page 13, and write it on the board. Explain that the sentence can be simplified into two sentences. Demonstrate breaking the sentence into two sentences. Have students chorally read the new sentences: *They have built clever machines that made life easier. The machines carried people faster and farther from home.* Point out and break down other difficult sentences throughout the selection.

▶ **Connection of Ideas** Students may need help synthesizing new information and ideas. Read the first paragraph on page 8 with students. Help students find examples of biofuels. Ask: *Where does the biofuel come from?* (seaweed or algae) *Why are biofuels good for the planet?* (They will not pollute the planet as much.)

After Reading

Ask students to complete the Respond to Reading on page 15. Then have them finish the Paired Read and hold Literature Circles.

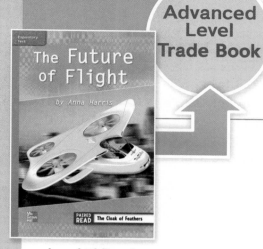

Leveled Reader

OBJECTIVES

CCSS By the end of the year, read and comprehend literature/informational text in the grades 2–3 text complexity band independently and proficiently.
RL/RI.3.10

Advanced Level Trade Book

Beyond Level
to Self-Selected Trade Book

Independent Reading

Level Up Lessons also available online

Before Reading

Together with students, identify the particular focus of their reading based on the text they choose. Students who have chosen the same title will work in groups to closely read the selection.

Close Reading

Taking Notes Assign a graphic organizer for students to use to take notes as they read. Reinforce a specific comprehension focus from the unit by choosing one of the graphic organizers that best fits the book.

Examples:

Fiction	Informational Texts
Narrator's Point of View	Main Idea and Key Details
Graphic Organizer 144	Graphic Organizer 141

Ask and Answer Questions Remind students to ask questions as they read. As students meet, have them discuss the section that they have read. They can share the questions that they noted and work together to find text evidence to support their answers. You may wish to have students write their responses to their questions.

After Reading

Write About Text

Have students work together to respond to the text using text evidence to support their writing.

Examples:

Fiction	Informational Text
What is the narrator's point of view of various characters?	Which details support the main idea of the selection?

SUMMATIVE ASSESSMENT

TESTED SKILLS

✓ COMPREHENSION:
- Point of View **RL.3.6**
- Text Structure: Compare and Contrast **RI.3.8**
- Text Structure: Cause and Effect **RI.3.8**
- Theme **RL.3.2**
- Message **RL.3.2**
- Chapter **RL.3.5**
- Headings, Photos with captions **RI.3.5**
- Illustrations **RL.3.7**
- Stanza **RL.3.5**

✓ VOCABULARY:
- Root Words **L.3.4c**
- Prefixes *un-, im-* **L.3.4b**
- Sentence Clues **L.3.4.a**
- Multiple-Meaning Words **L.3.4a**
- Metaphor **RL.3.4**

✓ ENGLISH LANGUAGE CONVENTIONS:
- Linking Verbs **L.3.1a**
- Contractions with Not **L.3.2e**
- Main and Helping Verbs **L.3.1a**
- Complex Sentences **L.3.1h**
- Irregular Verbs **L.3.1d**

✓ WRITING:
- Writing About Text **W.3.8**
- Narrative Performance Task **W.3.3a-d**

Elements of Summative Assessment

✓ Variety of Item Types
- Selected Response
- Multiple Selected Response
- Evidence-Based Selected Response
- Constructed Response
- Tech-Enhanced Items

✓ Performance-Based Task

Additional Assessment Options

Conduct assessments individually using the differentiated passages in *Fluency Assessment.* Students' expected fluency goal for this Unit is **82–102 WCPM** with an accuracy rate of 95% or higher.

Use the instructional reading level determined by the Running Record calculations for regrouping decisions. Students at Level 30 or below should be provided reteaching on specific Comprehension skills.

Using Assessment Results

Unit Assessment Skills and Fluency	If . . .	Then . . .
COMPREHENSION	Students score below 70% . . .	. . . reteach tested skills using the *Tier 2 Comprehension Intervention* online PDFs.
VOCABULARY	Students score below 70% . . .	. . . reteach tested skills using the *Tier 2 Vocabulary Intervention* online PDFs.
ENGLISH LANGUAGE CONVENTIONS	Students score below 70% . . .	. . . reteach tested skills using the *Tier 2 Writing and Grammar Intervention* online PDFs.
WRITING	Students score less than "2" on short-response items and "3" on extended constructed response items . . .	. . . reteach tested skills using appropriate lessons from the Strategies and Skills and/or Write About Reading sections in the *Tier 2 Comprehension Intervention* online PDFs.
	Students score less than "12" on the performance task . . .	. . . reteach skills using the *Tier 2 Writing and Grammar Intervention* online PDFs.
FLUENCY	Students have a WCPM score of 0–81 . . .	. . . reteach tested skills using the *Tier 2 Fluency Intervention* online PDFs.

Using Summative Data

Check online reports for this Unit Assessment as well as your data Dashboard. Use the data to assign small group instruction for students who are below the overall proficiency level for the tested skills.

Data-Driven Recommendations

Response to Intervention

Use the appropriate sections of the *Placement and Diagnostic Assessment* as well as students' assessment results to designate students requiring:

 **Intervention Online PDFs**   **WonderWorks Intervention Program**

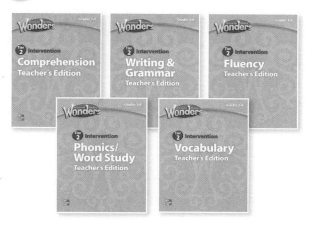

Genre Writing

Reading Extended Complex Text

Literature Anthology

Your Own Text

Program Information

Scope and Sequence

Index

(CCSS) **Correlations**

Writing Process — Genre Writing: Narrative/Poetry

Model Lesson — Reading Extended Complex Text

Program Information

Go Digital — For Additional Resources

Review Comprehension Lessons

Unit Bibliography

Word Lists

Literature and Informational Text Charts

Web Sites

Resources

www.connected.mcgraw-hill.com

NARRATIVE TEXT Fictional Narrative

EXPERT MODEL

Go Digital

Writer's Workspace

The Brown Seeds
By Gretchen H.

Stefani and her mother lived on a simple farm outside of a small kingdom. They had very little money, and Stefani had to work the farm before and after school each day. What little money they had came from the eggs and milk Stefani sold at the market in town.

One day, the king raised the taxes and demanded that Stefani's mother pay or she would lose her home. Stefani needed to work extra hard to help her mother earn the money.

The next day, while selling eggs and milk at the market, Stefani met a strange old woman sitting alone. The woman looked sad and hungry.

"Little girl," said the woman, "can you spare some milk and an egg for this tired old lady?" Stefani looked down at her basket. She would barely make any money with what she had, and her mother needed the money to save their home.

The woman looked at Stefani with pleading eyes. "I haven't eaten in days," pleaded the woman.

Stefani felt badly for the woman, but she didn't want to lose her home. She looked at the woman, who was rubbing her empty stomach. Stefani carefully picked an egg from her basket and handed it to the old woman. Then she gave the woman a small bottle of milk. The woman's face lit up with a smile. "Thank you, child. Your kindness will not be forgotten." She handed Stefani a handful of dry, brown seeds. "Take these. Plant them, water them, and wait for five days. They will grow into a tree. Dig under the tree to find your reward."

Stefani looked at the seeds in her hand, puzzled. They didn't look like much, and the woman's story seemed ridiculous. Stefani's mother would surely be angry. Stefani smiled at the old woman and walked on.

Expert Model PDF Online

OBJECTIVES

CCSS Write narratives to develop real or imagined experiences or events using effective technique, descriptive details, and clear event sequences. Establish a situation and introduce a narrator and/or characters; organize an event sequence that unfolds naturally. **W.3.3a**

ACADEMIC LANGUAGE
fictional narrative, plot, purpose, audience, sequence of events

Read Like a Writer

Tell students that there will be many times that they may be asked to write a fictional narrative, or a made-up story. They might choose to write fictional narratives for fun or they might need to write one for a classroom assignment. A fictional narrative can take a variety of forms and has limitless topics. All a writer needs is his or her own imagination. Read and discuss the features of a fictional narrative.

Provide copies of the Expert Model "The Brown Seeds" and the features of a Fictional Narrative found online in **Writer's Workspace**.

Features of a Fictional Narrative

- It is a made-up story.
- It has a beginning, middle, and end.
- It has characters, a setting, and a plot.
- It has a plot with a problem that is solved at the end.
- It includes dialogue, or the words of the people in the story.
- It uses time-order words to tell events in sequence.

Discuss the Expert Model

COLLABORATE

Use the questions below to prompt discussion of the features of fictional narratives.

- Is this a true story or is it made-up? How do you know? (This is a made-up story. The events could not happen in real life)
- What problem do the characters face in the story? (Stefani and her mother do not have enough money to pay taxes. If they cannot pay the taxes, they will lose their home.)
- Who are the characters? What is the setting? (Stefani, her mother, and the old woman are the characters; the setting is a farm outside of a kingdom)
- How do you know when the characters in the story are talking? (there are quotation marks around the words they say, or their dialogue)
- What are some words that show the sequence of events? (*One day; The next day*)

PREWRITE

Discuss and Plan

Purpose Discuss with students the purpose for writing a fictional narrative. They may write a story that is action-packed, funny, or inspirational. Or they may write a story that teaches a lesson or moral. Explain to students that fictional narratives are primarily written to entertain the reader.

Audience Have students think about who will read their fictional narratives, such as friends, family, and classmates. Ask: *How do you want your reader to feel while reading your story, and after?*

Teach the Minilesson

Sequence of Events Tell students that writers of fictional narratives often tell their story in chronological order. Characters in a story often have a problem to solve. The steps they take to solve the problem are the plot events. It's important for these events to unfold in a natural sequence so readers can better understand what is happening in the story.

Distribute copies of the Model Problem and Solution Chart found online in **Writer's Workspace**. Point out that the events in Gretchen's story unfold naturally and each step leads to another. The story's events are organized with a clear beginning, middle, and end.

ENGLISH LANGUAGE LEARNERS

Beginning

Discuss Have partners discuss examples of fictional narratives they have read and liked. Have them list what they liked about the stories.

Intermediate

Summarize Have partners work together to name each event in the Expert Model and check that the order is correct.

Advanced/High

Expand Have partners summarize the Expert Model and describe a new solution to the problem in the Expert Model.

Your Turn

Choose Your Topic Have pairs or small groups brainstorm ideas for their own fictional narratives. Have them think about a made-up setting or characters, then think of a challenge that the characters have to face. If students need help, have them think of fairy tales or fables where the characters must solve a problem. Then ask students questions to prompt thinking. Have students record their ideas in their Writer's Notebooks.

- What type of fiction stories do you like the best? What do you think are some of the challenges of writing this kind of fiction?

- Who will be the main character?

- What will be the main character's problem to solve?

Plan Provide copies of the blank Problem and Solution Chart found online in **Writer's Workspace**. Have students list the characters and the problem that they will face in the story. Encourage students to begin listing the events of the story or the steps the characters must take to solve the problem.

MODEL PROBLEM AND SOLUTION CHART

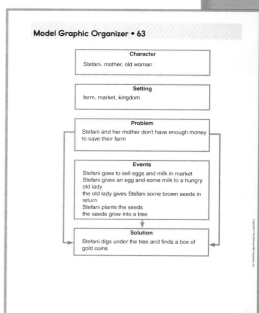

Model Graphic Organizer • 63

Character
Stefani, mother, old woman

Setting
farm, market, kingdom

Problem
Stefani and her mother don't have enough money to save their farm

Events
Stefani goes to sell eggs and milk in market
Stefani gives an egg and some milk to a hungry old lady
the old lady gives Stefani some brown seeds in return
Stefani plants the seeds
the seeds grow into a tree

Solution
Stefani digs under the tree and finds a box of gold coins

NARRATIVE TEXT Fictional Narrative

DRAFT

OBJECTIVES

CCSS Write narratives to develop real or imagined experiences or events using effective technique, descriptive details, and clear event sequences. Use dialogue and descriptions of actions, thoughts, and feelings to develop experiences and events or show the response of characters to situations. **W.3.3b**

ACADEMIC LANGUAGE
draft, dialogue, problem, solution, peer review

Discuss the Student Model

Review the features of fictional narratives. Provide copies of the Student Model found online in **Writer's Workspace** and read it aloud.

Teach the Minilesson

Dialogue Remind students that dialogue is the actual words that characters in a story speak. Tell students that dialogue is used to show how different characters communicate with each other. Dialogue can display a character's response to situations, their feelings and emotions, or their thoughts about events in the story.

Discuss with students what the dialogue in the Student Model tells about the story and the characters in the story.

Invite students to share dialogue from stories they have read.

Your Turn

Write a Draft Have students review the graphic organizers that they prepared in Prewrite to begin their drafts. Remind them to use dialogue in their drafts to show exactly what their characters say.

Go Digital

Writer's Workspace

Conferencing Routines

Teacher Conferences

STEP 1

Talk about the strengths of the writing.

You did a good job of creating realistic dialogue that helps drive the story forward.

STEP 2

Focus on how the writer uses a writing trait.

You provided some time-order words, but the sequence might be clearer if you incorporate more to clarify what is happening.

STEP 3

Make concrete suggestions for revision.

Your narrative might be stronger if you added more detail about the steps that led to the solution.

REVISE

Discuss the Revised Model

Distribute copies of the Revised Student Model found online in **Writer's Workspace**. Read the model aloud and have students note the revisions that Becky made. Use the specific revisions to show how adding details and combining sentences make the narrative more engaging.

Teach the Minilesson

Temporal Words and Phrases Remind students that good writers often use temporal words and phrases to show the sequence of events in a story. These transition words help connect the order of events. Point out that words and phrases such as *next, then, once, one day,* and *finally* are temporal words that help clarify the sequence.

Have students find revisions in the Revised Student Model where the writer added temporal words or phrases. Discuss how these revisions help clarify the story's sequence.

 **Your Turn**

Revise Have students use the **Peer Review Routine** and questions to review their partner's draft. Then have students select suggestions from the peer review to incorporate into their revisions. Provide the Revise and Edit Checklist from **Writer's Workspace** to guide them as they revise. Suggest they add words to clarify the sequence of their narratives. Circulate among students as they work and confer as needed.

REVISED STUDENT MODEL

Revised Student Model • Fictional Narrative • 66

The Fairy and the Clever Girl
by Becky T.

There was a very clever girl. Her name was Rosie. She lived in a little cotage in the woods. In the day, she milks the cow and fed the pigs. At night, she liked to read.

There were not many books in her house. if she had to read the same ones over and over again. If only she could have some new books to read! A fairy stopped at the little house for a glass of milk.

"What do you like best?" asked the fairy.

"I like to read good stories", Rosie said "But I only have a few books. I has read them all."

"I can help", the fairy said. "I will get you all the books you want. But you have to do something for me in return. You have to write a story about me. Nobody believes in fairies any more. Your story will convinse them we are for real."

"Gladly", said Rosie. She sat down and wrote the story, the fairy took the pages and flew away.

There was a whole pile of new books on the table. And by magic, there were always wonderful new stories for Rosie to read.

Peer Conferences

Review with students the routine for peer review of writing. They should listen carefully as the writer reads his or her work aloud. Begin by telling what they liked about the writing. Then ask a question that will help the writer think more about the writing. Finally, make a suggestion that will make the writing stronger.

Use these questions for peer review.

- ☑ Does the writing establish a clear problem that the characters must solve?
- ☑ Is there dialogue that shows the characters' response to situations?
- ☑ Are there temporal words that show the sequence of events?

PROOFREAD/EDIT AND PUBLISH

OBJECTIVES

CCSS With guidance and support from peers and adults, develop and strengthen writing as needed by planning, revising, and editing. **W.3.5**

CCSS With guidance and support from adults, use technology to produce and publish writing (using keyboarding skills) as well as to interact and collaborate with others. **W.3.6**

ACADEMIC LANGUAGE

proofread, edit, publish, present, evaluate, multimedia, self-evaluation, rubric

Discuss the Edited Model

Provide copies of the Edited Student Model found online in **Writer's Workspace**. Read the model aloud and have students note the editing changes that Becky made. Use the specific edits to show how editing for spelling, verb tense, and punctuation improves the fictional narrative. Have students note that Becky corrected the comma and quotation mark in the dialogue in the fifth paragraph.

Go Digital

Writer's Workspace

Your Turn

Edit Have students use the Edit questions on the Revise and Edit Checklist to guide them as they review and edit their drafts on their own. Remind them to slowly read for one type of error at a time.

Publish

For the final presentation of their fictional narratives, have students choose a format for publishing. Students may want to consider:

Print Publishing	Digital Publishing
Storybook	Writer's Workspace
Illustrated Short Story	Online Graphic Novel
Group Book of Fairy Tales	Fiction Blog

Have students handwrite, use a typewriter, or use a word-processing program to produce their writing. They should be sure to use standard margins and format their final drafts so it is easy for readers to follow the flow of the text.

Explain to students that adding visual and multimedia elements can strengthen their writing and presentation, making them more engaging for their readers and audience. Allow time for students to design and include illustrations from the story, maps of the setting, videos, audio, and other visual or multimedia elements that will enhance their personal narrative.

EDITED STUDENT MODEL

Edited Student Model • Fictional Narrative • 67

The Fairy and the Clever Girl
by Becky T.

There was a very clever girl. Her name was Rosie. She lived in a little cottage in the forest. In the day, she milked the cow and fed the pigs. At night, she liked to read.

There were not many books in the house. She had to read the same ones over and over again. If only she could have some new books to read. A fairy stopped at the little house for a glass of milk.

"What do you like best?" asked the fairy.

"I like to read good stories", Rosie said "But I only have a few books. I have read them all."

"I can help," the fairy said. "I will get you all the books you want. But you have to do something for me in return. You have to write a story about me. Nobody believes in fairies any more. Your story will convince them we are for real."

"Gladly", said Rosie. She sat down and wrote the story, the fairy took the pages and flew away.

There was a whole pile of new books on the table. And by magic there were always wonderful new stories for Rosie to read.

EVALUATE

Discuss Rubrics

Guide students as they use the Student Rubric found online in **Writer's Workspace**. Discuss how using a rubric helps them identify and focus on areas that might need further work. Work with the class to review the bulleted points on the rubric.

- **Focus and Coherence** Does the fictional narrative tell about a problem that the characters must solve?
- **Organization** Do the events in the story unfold naturally? Are the events described in a logical order?
- **Ideas and Support** Is dialogue used to show how the characters react to situations and to develop ideas?
- **Word Choice** Are temporal words used to show the order of events? Is the dialogue realistic?
- **Voice/Sentence Fluency** Does the writing sound like a real person wrote it? Do the sentences flow naturally?
- **Conventions** Are errors in grammar, spelling, punctuation, and capitalization corrected?

Writing Rubric • 69

Fictional Narrative Rubric

4 Excellent	• tells an entertaining story with a clear problem for the characters to solve • tells events in a logical and easy-to-follow order • uses detailed descriptions • uses temporal words • uses effective dialogue • includes a variety of sentences that flow • is free or almost free of errors • is easy to read, neat, and consistently formatted
3 Good	• tells an interesting story with a problem • orders events correctly • uses words that bring across details • uses dialogue well • uses some temporal words • includes a variety of complete sentences • has minor errors that do not confuse the reader • is mostly easy to read and mostly consistent
2 Fair	• tells a basic story that may have a problem, but no clear solution • includes some events out of order • uses words that do not bring across details well • displays limited or weak dialogue • uses a limited variety of sentences • makes errors that confuse the reader • is not always easy to read
1 Unsatisfactory	• does not tell a story • tells events out of order • uses few or no descriptive words • uses no dialogue • uses incomplete or run-on sentences • makes many serious errors • is difficult to read because of poor format or handwriting

Your Turn

Reflect and Set Goals After students have evaluated their own fictional narratives, tell them to reflect on their progress as writers. Encourage them to consider areas where they feel they have shown improvement, and to think about what areas need further improvement. Have them set writing goals to prepare for their conference with the teacher.

Conference with Students

Use the rubric and the Anchor Papers provided online in **Writer's Workspace** as you evaluate student writing. The Anchor Papers provide samples of papers that score from 1 to 4. These papers reflect the criteria described in the rubric. Anchor Papers offer a standard against which to judge writing.

Review with individual students the writing goals they have set. Discuss ways to achieve these goals and suggest any further areas of improvement students may need to target.

NARRATIVE TEXT Poetry

Writing Process Lesson 2

EXPERT MODEL

OBJECTIVES

CCSS Write narratives to develop real or imagined experiences or events using effective technique, descriptive details, and clear event sequences. Use dialogue and descriptions of actions, thoughts, and feelings to develop experiences and events or show the response of characters to situations. **W.3.3b**

ACADEMIC LANGUAGE

poetry, lines, stanzas, rhythm, rhyme, simile

Read Like a Writer

Tell students that one way to express their feelings and ideas in writing is to write poetry. Explain that poems can be different from other forms of writing in many ways. Poems are usually formatted differently than stories and nonfiction text. Read and discuss the features of a poem.

Provide copies of the Expert Model "The Contest" and the features of Poetry found online in **Writer's Workspace**.

Go Digital

Writer's Workspace

Features of Poetry

- It expresses feelings and ideas.
- It is often organized into lines and stanzas.
- It may use rhyme and rhythm.
- It uses figurative language, such as similes and metaphors.
- It uses descriptive words that appeal to the reader's senses.

Discuss the Expert Model

COLLABORATE

Use the questions below to prompt discussion of the features of poetry.

- **Does this piece of writing express ideas or feelings? How do you know?** (Yes; the author uses words that show how she feels and she describes the room.)

- **How is the writing organized?** (It is organized differently than a normal story. There are capital letters at the beginning of each line and sentences are broken up in different ways. The lines are grouped into two big sections.)

- **Look at the last words in each line. What do many of these words have in common?** (They rhyme.)

- **How does the writer use figurative language in the second line?** (The author uses a metaphor to describe the messy room.)

- **What details does the writer use to appeal to senses?** (The author describes the room in a scary way.)

PREWRITE

Discuss and Plan

Purpose Discuss with students the purpose for writing a poem. Some poems are written to express a feeling or emotion. Others may tell a story or express an idea. Explain to students that poems are primarily written to entertain the reader.

Audience Encourage students to think about who will be reading their poems, such as friends, family members, and classmates. Ask: *How do you want your readers to feel after they read your poem? Do you want them to laugh or do you want the poem to be more serious?*

Teach the Minilesson

Ideas Tell students that writers of poetry, or poets, include details in their poems that help readers paint a mental picture of what is being described in the poem. These details might tell how something looks, feels, tastes, smells, or makes someone feel.

Distribute copies of the Model Graphic Organizer found online in **Writer's Workspace**. Point out how Maggie used the web to organize the details of the messy room. Explain to students that each detail about the messy room could be used to make its own word web to brainstorm even more descriptive details.

ENGLISH LANGUAGE LEARNERS

Beginning

Summarize Have students work with a partner to write a summary of the Expert Model. Have them discuss how their summary differs from the poem.

Intermediate

Summarize Have students list ideas for their poem and reasons why each idea would make a good poem.

Advanced/High

Expand Have partners summarize the Expert Model and write what they think happens next. Encourage them to write in the style of the model.

Your Turn

Choose Your Topic Have students work in pairs or small groups to brainstorm ideas for their own poems. Have students decide if they want to write a poem that tells how they feel about something or if they want to express an idea. Have students think about something they feel strongly about, whether it is an important person in their lives or a favorite pet. Then ask students questions to prompt thinking. Have students record their ideas in their Writer's Notebooks.

- What was a challenging or exciting thing you have done?
- How did you feel about it? Were you happy? Excited? Scared?
- What do you remember most about it?
- What are some details about it that stand out most clearly?

Plan Provide copies of the blank Graphic Organizer found online in **Writer's Workspace**. Have students list details about the event that they chose. Encourage students to create an individual web for each detail they listed to generate descriptive details.

MODEL GRAPHIC ORGANIZER

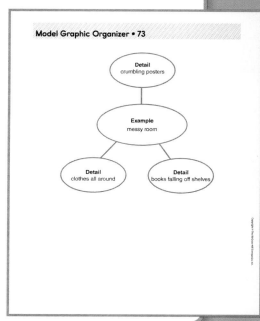

Model Graphic Organizer • 73

Detail
crumbling posters

Example
messy room

Detail
clothes all around

Detail
books falling off shelves

NARRATIVE TEXT Poetry

DRAFT

OBJECTIVES

CCSS Write narratives to develop real or imagined experiences or events using effective technique, descriptive details, and clear event sequences. Use dialogue and descriptions of actions, thoughts, and feelings to develop experiences and events or show the response of characters to situations. **W.3.3b**

ACADEMIC LANGUAGE

draft, rhythm, rhyme, peer review

Discuss the Student Model

Review the features of poetry. Provide copies of the Student Model found online in **Writer's Workspace** and read it aloud. Have students identify the features of poetry that are found in the model.

Teach the Minilesson

Rhythm and Rhyme Remind students that poems are often organized into lines and stanzas and may use rhythm and rhyme. Point out the two stanzas of the poem. Read aloud the first stanza of the poem while clapping the rhythm.

Discuss with students how the poem is separated into two stanzas and how the stanzas have a recurring rhythm.

Direct students back to the first stanza of Matt's poem. Point out how the last word in the third line rhymes with the last word in the fourth line. Repeat for the last words in the fifth and sixth lines. Have students point out how the second stanza repeats this rhyme scheme.

Your Turn

Write a Draft Have students review the graphic organizers that they prepared in Prewrite to begin their drafts. Encourage students to use a recurring rhythm and rhyme in their poems.

Go Digital

Writer's Workspace

Conferencing Routines

Teacher Conferences

STEP 1

Talk about the strengths of the writing.

You did a good job of creating a recurring rhythm in your poem.

STEP 2

Focus on how the writer uses a writing trait.

You provided descriptive words that appeal to the reader's senses, now try using stronger words or words that are more specific.

STEP 3

Make concrete suggestions for revision.

Your poem might be stronger if you included figurative language, such as a simile or metaphor, in your writing.

REVISE

Discuss the Revised Model

Distribute copies of the Revised Student Model found online in **Writer's Workspace**. Read the model aloud and have students note the revisions that Matt made. Use the specific revisions to show how adding rhyming words and figurative language can help strengthen the poem.

Teach the Minilesson

Figurative Language Remind students that poetry often includes figurative language, such as similes or metaphors, to compare two things. A simile compares two things using the words *like* or *as*. A metaphor compares two things without using *like* or *as*. Discuss with students how figurative language makes the writing more engaging.

Have students find an example of a revision in the Revised Student Model that show the writer added figurative language. Discuss how these revisions strengthen the poem.

Revise Have students use the **Peer Review Routine** and questions to review their partner's draft. Then have students select suggestions from the peer review to incorporate into their revisions. Provide the Revise and Edit Checklist from **Writer's Workspace** to guide them as they revise. Suggest they add figurative language to their poems. Circulate among students as they work and confer as needed.

COLLABORATE

REVISED STUDENT MODEL

Revised Student Model • Poetry • 76

The Carnival
by Matt L.

The carnival came when I was ten,
I went two times, then went some more.
A ride were spinning, called wheel and top,
Really long arms climb and drop.
I scrambled on to take a ride,
The music played it's tunes inside.

The carnival came when I was ten,
I went two times, then went some more.
Hot dogs, prezels, apples, too,
So much fun, to much to do.
I wandered home because I was tired.
As the lights behind me shined and shined.

Peer Conferences

Review with students the routine for peer review of writing. They should listen carefully as the writer reads his or her work aloud. Begin by telling what they liked about the writing. Then ask a question that will help the writer think more about the writing. Finally, make a suggestion that will make the writing stronger.

Use these questions for peer review.

- ☑ Does the poem express feelings or ideas?
- ☑ Is there figurative language?
- ☑ Does the poem have a rhythm? Does it use rhyming words?
- ☑ Does the poem have descriptive details that appeal to the reader's senses?

NARRATIVE TEXT Poetry

PROOFREAD/EDIT AND PUBLISH

 CCSS

OBJECTIVES

With guidance and support from peers and adults, develop and strengthen writing as needed by planning, revising, and editing. **W.3.5**

With guidance and support from adults, use technology to produce and publish writing (using keyboarding skills) as well as to interact and collaborate with others. **W.3.6**

ACADEMIC LANGUAGE

proofread, edit, publish, present, evaluate, multimedia, self-evaluation, rubric

Discuss the Edited Model

Provide copies of the Edited Student Model found online in **Writer's Workspace**. Read the model aloud and have students note the editing changes that Matt made. Use the specific edits to show how editing for spelling, verb tense, capitalization, and punctuation improves Matt's poem.

Your Turn

Edit Have students use the Edit questions on the Revise and Edit Checklist to guide them as they review and edit their drafts on their own. Tell them to read their work slowly when looking for errors, instead of skimming it or quickly glancing through it.

Publish

For the final presentation of their poems, have students choose a format for publishing. Students may want to consider:

Print Publishing	Digital Publishing
Poetry Collage	Writer's Workspace
Journal Entry	Digital Poetry Collection
Group Presentation of Poetry	Record Poetry Performances

Have students write their poems in cursive or use a computer to produce their writing. Encourage students to be creative with the way they format their poems. While they should be easy for readers to understand, their poems do not necessarily have to adhere to the same formatting as other pieces of writing. Display examples of various poetry formats to give students ideas.

Explain to students that adding visual and multimedia elements can strengthen their writing and presentation, making them more engaging for their readers and audience. Allow time for students to design and include illustrations, photos, videos, audio, and other visual or multimedia elements that will enhance their poem.

Go Digital

Writer's Workspace

EDITED STUDENT MODEL

Edited Student Model • Poetry • 77

The Carnival
by Matt L.

The carnival came when I was ten,
I went two times, then went some more.
A ride were spinning, called wheel and top,
Really long arms climb and drop.
I scrambled on to take a ride,
The music played its tunes inside.

The carnival came when I was ten,
I went two times, then went some more.
Hot dogs, prezels, apples, too.
So much fun, so much to do.
I wandered home because I was tired,
As the lights behind me shined and shined.

EVALUATE

Discuss Rubrics

Guide students as they use the Student Rubric found online in **Writer's Workspace**. Discuss how using a rubric helps them identify and focus on areas that might need further work. Work with the class to review the bulleted points on the rubric.

- **Focus and Coherence** Does the poem clearly express an idea or feelings?
- **Organization** Is the poem organized into lines and stanzas?
- **Ideas and Support** Is figurative language used to compare things or ideas?
- **Word Choice** Are strong descriptive words used to show sensory details?
- **Voice/Sentence Fluency** Is the poem's tone appropriate to the subject? Do the lines have a clear rhythm?
- **Conventions** Are errors in grammar, spelling, punctuation, and capitalization corrected?

STUDENT RUBRIC

Writing Rubric • 79

Poetry Rubric

4 Excellent	• clearly and cleverly expresses ideas or feeling • poem is organized into lines and stanzas with repeated patterns • uses strong, descriptive words that appeal to readers' senses • uses figurative language effectively • includes rhyming lines with a clear rhythm • is free or almost free of errors • is easy to read, neat, and consistently formatted
3 Good	• expresses an idea or feelings • poem is mostly organized into lines and stanzas • uses descriptive words that provide some sensory detail • uses some figurative language • includes mostly consistent rhythm and lines that rhyme • has minor errors that do not confuse the reader • is mostly easy to read and mostly consistent
2 Fair	• attempts to express ideas or feelings • includes some organization, but may be hard to follow • uses words that do not bring across descriptive details well • use of figurative language may not be clear • poem has inconsistent rhythm and rhyme • makes errors that confuse the reader • is not always easy to read
1 Unsatisfactory	• does not express ideas or feelings • poem is not organized any logical way • uses few or no descriptive words • no use of figurative language • poem has no rhythm or rhyming words • makes many serious errors • is difficult to read because of poor format or handwriting

Your Turn

COLLABORATE

Reflect and Set Goals After students have evaluated their own poems, tell them to reflect on their progress as writers. Encourage them to consider areas where they feel they have shown improvement, and to think about what areas need further improvement. Have them set writing goals to prepare for their conference with the teacher.

Conference with Students

Use the rubric and the Anchor Papers provided online in **Writer's Workspace** as you evaluate student writing. The Anchor Papers provide samples of papers that score from 1 to 4. These papers reflect the criteria described in the rubric. Anchor Papers offer a standard against which to judge writing.

Review with individual students the writing goals they have set. Discuss ways to achieve these goals and suggest any further areas of improvement students may need to target.

Close Reading Routine

Read — *What does the text say?*

Assign the Reading

Depending on the needs of your students, you can

- ask students to read the text silently
- read the text together with students
- read the text aloud

Take Notes

Students generate questions and take notes about aspects of the text that might be confusing for them. Encourage students to note

- key ideas and details
- difficult vocabulary words or phrases
- details that are not clear
- information that they do not understand

Students complete a graphic organizer to take notes on important information from the text.

Reread — *How does the author say it?*

Ask Text-Dependent Questions

Students reread shorter passages from the text and cite text evidence to answer deeper questions about craft and structure. Students should

- work with partners or small groups to talk about and identify text evidence
- generate questions about the text

Integrate — *What does the text mean?*

Students reread to integrate knowledge and ideas and make text-to-text connections. Students should

- work with partners or small groups to identify and discuss connections
- use text evidence to write a response

Use the Literature Anthology

Getting Ready

CLOSE READING OF *THE REAL STORY OF STONE SOUP,*
pages 278–295

Suggested Pacing

Days 1–3 Read
pp. 278–283
pp. 284–289
pp. 290–295

Days 4–8 Reread
pp. 278–281
pp. 282–283
pp. 284–287
pp. 288–291
pp. 292–295

Days 9–10 Integrate

Use the suggestions in the chart to assign reading of the text and to chunk the text into shorter passages for rereading.

ESSENTIAL QUESTION *What choices are good for us?*

Ask students to discuss what they have learned about making good choices.

Read *What does the text say?*

Assign the Reading

Ask students to read the text independently. You may want to have students read pages 280–281 with a partner to compare what the narrator is saying with what is happening in the illustration.

Take Notes

As students read, remind them to take notes. They can record the features of each section. They can also note words they do not understand and questions they have.

Model for students how to take notes.

Think Aloud On page 281, the narrator says he does the hardest job. The illustration doesn't show him working very hard. I wonder if the author is trying to use the illustrations to tell me something about the characters.

p. 281
Narrator says
he is hard working—
looks lazy in picture.

Use the Literature Anthology

Assign **Graphic Organizer 146** to help students take notes about the narrator's point of view.

 As students share their questions and notes, use the Access Complex Text suggestions on pages T25A–T25R to help address features about the text that students found difficult.

> **Reread** *How does the author say it?*

Analyze the Text

After students summarize the selection, have them reread to develop a deeper understanding of the text and answer the questions on **Close Reading Companion** pages 100–102. For students who need support in citing text evidence, model using the following Reread prompt:

- **Author's Craft: Character Development** Reread pages 280–281 What do the narrator's words and actions tell you about his character?

  Think Aloud The narrator says that he can "get away with" not paying the Chang brothers very much. This suggests that the narrator is not very honest or fair. He knows he should pay the brothers more but will not. The narrator also says that he is working hard. But the illustration shows that he is being lazy while the Chang brothers do all the work.

Continue using the following Reread prompts:

- **Author's Craft: Word Choice** What words does the narrator use to show his opinion of the boys?

- **Author's Craft: Character Development** What do the narrator's words and actions tell you about his character?

- **Author's Craft: Point of View** How does the author show that the narrator is wrong about how smart the boys are?

- **Author's Craft: Point of View** How do you know that the narrator has been fooled by the Chang brothers?

- **Author's Craft: Figurative Language** Explain the meanings of *onomatopoeia* and *similes*. What examples of onomatopoeia and simile do you see in the story? How do they add to the story?

Turn to a partner and use this sentence frame to talk about your opinion:

> *One difference between my idea and yours is ...*

Use text evidence to support your idea.

Write About the Text

Review the following writing prompt and sentence frames. Remind students to use their responses from the **Close Reading Companion** to support their answers. For a full lesson on writing a response using text evidence, see page T30.

> How does the author use dialogue to help you understand how the Chang brothers solved their problem? Use these sentence frames to focus your discussion.
>
> *The author uses what the narrator says to ...*
>
> *What the Chang brothers say is important because ...*
>
> *The author helps me see how they ...*

Answer: The author uses dialogue to show that the Chang brothers easily trick the narrator into thinking that it is possible to make soup out of stones. **Evidence:** On page 284, the narrator refers to the boys as foolish, but the boys tell him he has "picked out a yummy egg stone." On page 286, the illustration shows the brothers putting a real fish in the soup. On page 289, the narrator's dialogue reveals that he is entirely fooled by the brothers' trick.

Integrate   *What does the text mean?*

Essential Question

Have students respond in writing to the Essential Question using evidence from the text.

> *What choices are good for us?*

Students should use their notes and graphic organizers to cite evidence from the text to support their answer.

Model how to use notes to respond to the Essential Question:

Think Aloud I can reread the notes I took during reading to find text evidence that can help me answer the question. My notes on page 293 describe the soup and its healthful, nourishing ingredients. I can use that information in my answer. Then I will look through the rest of my notes to find additional text evidence that I can use to support my answer.

Students can work with a partner and use their notes and graphic organizer to locate evidence that can be used to answer the question. Encourage students to discuss the strength of the evidence cited and give arguments about what may be strong or weak about a particular citation.

Model Lesson: READING Extended Complex Text

Use Your Own Text

Classroom Library

Classroom Library lessons available online.

Stone Fox
Genre Realistic Fiction

Lexile 550

Bat Loves the Night
Genre Informational Text

Lexile 560

Make Way for Dyamonde Daniel
Genre Realistic Fiction

Lexile 620

Gray Wolves
Genre Informational Text

Lexile 640

or Choose from your own **Trade Books**

- Use this model with a text of your choice. Go online for title-specific Classroom Library book lessons.
- Assign reading of the text. You may wish to do this by section or chapters.
- Chunk the text into shorter important passages for rereading.
- Present an Essential Question. You may want to use the Unit Big Idea.

sync tv

Video Preview

studysync

Read | *What does the text say?*

Assign the Reading

Ask students to read the assigned sections of the text independently. For sections that are more difficult, you may read the text aloud or ask students to read with a partner. As you read, model how to take notes. Encourage students to jot down words they do not understand and any questions they have.

Ask Text-Dependent Questions

Ask students to reread a section of the text and focus on the following questions. Students should use text evidence in their answers:

Literature

- What are the plot and setting of the story?
- How would you describe the main character(s)?
- What is the theme or message of the story?

Informational Text

- What is the main idea? What are the supporting details?
- What kinds of text features does the author use?
- What is the author's point of view about the topic?

Have students write a brief summary of the section of text they read. When students finish writing, have them work with a partner to compare ideas and make sure that they both have a clear understanding of the story events or the topic.

Help students access the complex features of the text. Scaffold instruction on the following features as necessary:

- Purpose
- Genre
- Specific Vocabulary
- Sentence Structure
- Connection of Ideas
- Organization
- Prior Knowledge

Reread *How does the author say it?*

Ask Text-Dependent Questions/Generate Questions

Have students reread the same section of text as above. Then focus on the following questions. Remind students to use text evidence in their answers:

Literature

- How does the main character change from the beginning of the story to the end of the story?
- What literary elements (figurative language, flashback, symbolism) did the author use, and how effective were they?
- What other story have you read with a similar theme? How are the two stories similar? Different?

Informational Text

- How does the author organize the information in this text?
- What was the author's purpose for writing this text?
- Was the author's use of visuals (photos, graphs, diagrams, maps) effective? Why or why not?

Integrate *What does the text mean?*

Essential Question

Have students respond in writing to the Essential Question, considering the complete text. Students can work with a partner and use their notes and graphic organizer to locate evidence that can be used to answer the question.

SCOPE & SEQUENCE

FOUNDATIONAL SKILLS	K	1	2	3	4	5	6
Concepts About Print/Print Awareness							
Recognize own name							
Understand directionality (top to bottom; tracking print from left to right; return sweep, page by page)	✓						
Locate printed word on page	✓						
Develop print awareness (concept of letter, word, sentence)	✓						
Identify separate sounds in a spoken sentence	✓						
Understand that written words are represented in written language by a specific sequence of letters	✓						
Distinguish between letters, words, and sentences	✓						
Distinguish features of a sentence (first word, capitalization, ending punctuation)							
Identify and distinguish paragraphs							
Match print to speech (one-to-one correspondence)	✓						
Name uppercase and lowercase letters	✓						
Understand book handling (holding a book right-side-up, turning its pages)	✓						
Identify parts of a book (front cover, back cover, title page, table of contents); recognize that parts of a book contain information	✓						
Phonological Awareness							
Recognize and understand alliteration							
Segment sentences into correct number of words							
Identify, blend, segment syllables in words		✓					
Recognize and generate rhyming words	✓	✓					
Identify, blend, segment onset and rime	✓	✓					
Phonemic Awareness							
Count phonemes	✓	✓					
Isolate initial, medial, and final sounds	✓	✓					
Blend spoken phonemes to form words	✓	✓					
Segment spoken words into phonemes	✓	✓					
Distinguish between long- and short-vowel sounds	✓	✓					
Manipulate phonemes (addition, deletion, substitution)	✓	✓					
Phonics and Decoding/Word Recognition							
Understand the alphabetic principle	✓	✓					
Sound/letter correspondence	✓	✓	✓	✓			
Blend sounds into words, including VC, CVC, CVCe, CVVC words	✓	✓	✓	✓			
Blend common word families	✓	✓	✓	✓			

KEY	✓ = Assessed Skill Tinted panels show skills, strategies, and other teaching opportunities.

	K	1	2	3	4	5	6
Initial consonant blends		✓	✓	✓			
Final consonant blends		✓	✓	✓			
Initial and medial short vowels	✓	✓	✓	✓	✓	✓	✓
Decode one-syllable words in isolation and in context	✓	✓	✓	✓			
Decode multisyllabic words in isolation and in context using common syllabication patterns		✓	✓	✓	✓	✓	✓
Distinguish between similarly spelled words	✓	✓	✓	✓	✓	✓	✓
Monitor accuracy of decoding							
Identify and read common high-frequency words, irregularly spelled words	✓	✓	✓	✓			
Identify and read compound words, contractions			✓	✓	✓	✓	✓
Use knowledge of spelling patterns to identify syllables		✓	✓	✓	✓	✓	✓
Regular and irregular plurals	✓	✓	✓	✓	✓	✓	✓
Distinguish long and short vowels		✓	✓				
Long vowels (silent *e*, vowel teams)	✓	✓	✓	✓	✓	✓	✓
Vowel digraphs (variant vowels)		✓	✓	✓	✓	✓	✓
r-Controlled vowels		✓	✓	✓	✓	✓	✓
Hard/soft consonants		✓	✓	✓	✓	✓	✓
Initial consonant digraphs		✓	✓	✓	✓		
Medial and final consonant digraphs		✓	✓	✓	✓		
Vowel diphthongs		✓	✓	✓	✓	✓	✓
Identify and distinguish letter-sounds (initial, medial, final)	✓	✓	✓				
Silent letters		✓	✓	✓	✓	✓	✓
Schwa words				✓	✓	✓	✓
Inflectional endings		✓	✓	✓	✓	✓	✓
Triple-consonant clusters		✓	✓	✓	✓		
Unfamiliar and complex word families				✓	✓	✓	✓
Structural Analysis/Word Analysis							
Common spelling patterns (word families)		✓	✓	✓	✓	✓	✓
Common syllable patterns		✓	✓	✓	✓	✓	✓
Inflectional endings		✓	✓	✓	✓	✓	✓
Contractions		✓	✓	✓	✓	✓	✓
Compound words		✓	✓	✓	✓	✓	✓
Prefixes and suffixes		✓	✓	✓	✓	✓	✓
Root or base words			✓	✓	✓	✓	✓
Comparatives and superlatives			✓	✓	✓	✓	✓
Greek and Latin roots			✓	✓	✓	✓	✓
Fluency							
Apply letter/sound knowledge to decode phonetically regular words accurately	✓	✓	✓	✓	✓	✓	✓
Recognize high-frequency and familiar words	✓	✓	✓	✓	✓	✓	✓
Read regularly on independent and instructional levels							
Read orally with fluency from familiar texts (choral, echo, partner, Reader's Theater)							
Use appropriate rate, expression, intonation, and phrasing		✓	✓	✓	✓	✓	✓
Read with automaticity (accurately and effortlessly)		✓	✓	✓	✓	✓	✓

	K	1	2	3	4	5	6
Use punctuation cues in reading		✓	✓	✓	✓	✓	✓
Adjust reading rate to purpose, text difficulty, form, and style							
Repeated readings							
Timed readings		✓	✓	✓	✓	✓	✓
Read with purpose and understanding		✓	✓	✓	✓	✓	✓
Read orally with accuracy		✓	✓	✓	✓	✓	✓
Use context to confirm or self-correct word recognition		✓	✓	✓	✓	✓	✓

READING LITERATURE

Comprehension Strategies and Skills

	K	1	2	3	4	5	6
Read literature from a broad range of genres, cultures, and periods		✓	✓	✓	✓	✓	✓
Access complex text		✓	✓	✓	✓	✓	✓
Build background/Activate prior knowledge							
Preview and predict							
Establish and adjust purpose for reading							
Evaluate citing evidence from the text							
Ask and answer questions	✓	✓	✓	✓	✓	✓	✓
Inferences and conclusions, citing evidence from the text	✓	✓	✓	✓	✓	✓	✓
Monitor/adjust comprehension including reread, reading rate, paraphrase							
Recount/Retell	✓	✓					
Summarize			✓	✓	✓	✓	✓
Story structure (beginning, middle, end)	✓	✓	✓	✓	✓	✓	✓
Visualize							
Make connections between and across texts		✓	✓	✓	✓	✓	✓
Point of view		✓	✓	✓	✓	✓	✓
Author's purpose							
Cause and effect	✓	✓	✓	✓	✓	✓	✓
Compare and contrast (including character, setting, plot, topics)	✓	✓	✓	✓	✓	✓	✓
Classify and categorize		✓	✓				
Literature vs informational text	✓	✓	✓				
Illustrations, using	✓	✓	✓	✓			
Theme, central message, moral, lesson		✓	✓	✓	✓	✓	✓
Predictions, making/confirming	✓	✓	✓				
Problem and solution (problem/resolution)		✓	✓	✓	✓	✓	✓
Sequence of events	✓	✓	✓	✓	✓	✓	✓

Literary Elements

	K	1	2	3	4	5	6
Character	✓	✓	✓	✓	✓	✓	✓
Plot development/Events	✓	✓	✓	✓	✓	✓	✓
Setting	✓	✓	✓	✓	✓	✓	✓
Stanza				✓	✓	✓	✓
Alliteration						✓	✓
Assonance						✓	✓
Dialogue							

KEY ✓ = Assessed Skill
Tinted panels show skills, strategies, and other teaching opportunities.

	K	1	2	3	4	5	6
Foreshadowing						✔	✔
Flashback						✔	✔
Descriptive and figurative language		✔	✔	✔	✔	✔	✔
Imagery					✔	✔	✔
Meter					✔	✔	✔
Onomatopoeia							
Repetition		✔	✔	✔	✔	✔	✔
Rhyme/rhyme schemes		✔	✔	✔	✔	✔	✔
Rhythm		✔	✔				
Sensory language							
Symbolism							
Write About Text/Literary Response Discussions							
Reflect and respond to text citing text evidence		✔	✔	✔	✔	✔	✔
Connect and compare text characters, events, ideas to self, to other texts, to world							
Connect literary texts to other curriculum areas							
Identify cultural and historical elements of text							
Evaluate author's techniques, craft							
Analytical writing							
Interpret text ideas through writing, discussion, media, research							
Book report or review							
Locate, use, explain information from text features		✔	✔	✔	✔	✔	✔
Organize information to show understanding of main idea through charts, mapping							
Cite text evidence	✔	✔	✔	✔	✔	✔	✔
Author's purpose/Illustrator's purpose							
READING INFORMATIONAL TEXT							
Comprehension Strategies and Skills							
Read informational text from a broad range of topics and cultures	✔	✔	✔	✔	✔	✔	✔
Access complex text		✔	✔	✔	✔	✔	✔
Build background/Activate prior knowledge							
Preview and predict	✔	✔	✔				
Establish and adjust purpose for reading							
Evaluate citing evidence from the text							
Ask and answer questions	✔	✔	✔	✔	✔	✔	✔
Inferences and conclusions, citing evidence from the text	✔	✔	✔	✔	✔	✔	✔
Monitor and adjust comprehension including reread, adjust reading rate, paraphrase							
Recount/Retell	✔	✔					
Summarize			✔	✔	✔	✔	✔
Text structure	✔	✔	✔	✔	✔	✔	✔
Identify text features		✔	✔	✔	✔	✔	✔
Make connections between and across texts	✔	✔	✔	✔	✔	✔	✔
Author's point of view				✔	✔	✔	✔
Author's purpose		✔	✔				

	K	1	2	3	4	5	6
Cause and effect	✓	✓	✓	✓	✓	✓	✓
Compare and contrast	✓	✓	✓	✓	✓	✓	✓
Classify and categorize		✓	✓				
Illustrations and photographs, using	✓	✓	✓	✓			
Instructions/directions (written and oral)		✓	✓	✓	✓	✓	✓
Main idea and key details	✓	✓	✓	✓	✓	✓	✓
Persuasion, reasons and evidence to support points/persuasive techniques						✓	✓
Predictions, making/confirming	✓	✓					
Problem and solution		✓	✓	✓	✓	✓	✓
Sequence, chronological order of events, time order, steps in a process	✓	✓	✓	✓	✓	✓	✓

Write About Text/Write to Sources

	K	1	2	3	4	5	6
Reflect and respond to text citing text evidence		✓	✓	✓	✓	✓	✓
Connect and compare text characters, events, ideas to self, to other texts, to world							
Connect texts to other curriculum areas							
Identify cultural and historical elements of text							
Evaluate author's techniques, craft							
Analytical writing							
Read to understand and perform tasks and activities							
Interpret text ideas through writing, discussion, media, research							
Locate, use, explain information from text features		✓	✓	✓	✓	✓	✓
Organize information to show understanding of main idea through charts, mapping							
Cite text evidence		✓	✓	✓	✓	✓	✓
Author's purpose/Illustrator's purpose							

Text Features

	K	1	2	3	4	5	6
Recognize and identify text and organizational features of nonfiction texts		✓	✓	✓	✓	✓	✓
Captions and labels, headings, subheadings, endnotes, key words, bold print	✓	✓	✓	✓	✓	✓	✓
Graphics, including photographs, illustrations, maps, charts, diagrams, graphs, time lines	✓	✓	✓	✓	✓	✓	✓

Self-Selected Reading/Independent Reading

	K	1	2	3	4	5	6
Use personal criteria to choose own reading including favorite authors, genres, recommendations from others; set up a reading log							
Read a range of literature and informational text for tasks as well as for enjoyment; participate in literature circles							
Produce evidence of reading by retelling, summarizing, or paraphrasing							

Media Literacy

	K	1	2	3	4	5	6
Summarize the message or content from media message, citing text evidence							
Use graphics, illustrations to analyze and interpret information	✓	✓	✓	✓	✓	✓	✓
Identify structural features of popular media and use the features to obtain information, including digital sources				✓	✓	✓	✓
Identify reasons and evidence in visuals and media message							
Analyze media source: recognize effects of media in one's mood and emotion							
Make informed judgments about print and digital media							
Critique persuasive techniques							

KEY	✓ = Assessed Skill
	Tinted panels show skills, strategies, and other teaching opportunities.

WRITING	K	1	2	3	4	5	6
Writing Process							
Plan/prewrite/identify purpose and audience							
Draft							
Revise							
Edit/proofread							
Publish and present including using technology							
Teacher and peer feedback							
Writing Traits							
Conventions		✓	✓	✓	✓	✓	✓
Ideas		✓	✓	✓	✓	✓	✓
Organization		✓	✓	✓	✓	✓	✓
Sentence fluency		✓	✓	✓	✓	✓	✓
Voice		✓	✓	✓	✓	✓	✓
Word choice		✓	✓	✓	✓	✓	✓
Writer's Craft							
Good topic, focus on and develop topic, topic sentence			✓	✓	✓	✓	✓
Paragraph(s); sentence structure			✓	✓	✓	✓	✓
Main idea and supporting key details			✓	✓	✓	✓	✓
Unimportant details							
Relevant supporting evidence			✓	✓	✓	✓	✓
Strong opening, strong conclusion			✓	✓	✓	✓	✓
Beginning, middle, end; sequence		✓	✓	✓	✓	✓	✓
Precise words, strong words, vary words			✓	✓	✓	✓	✓
Figurative and sensory language, descriptive details							
Informal/formal language							
Mood/style/tone							
Dialogue				✓	✓	✓	✓
Transition words, transitions to multiple paragraphs				✓	✓	✓	✓
Select focus and organization		✓	✓	✓	✓	✓	✓
Points and counterpoints/Opposing claims and counterarguments							
Use reference materials (online and print dictionary, thesaurus, encyclopedia)							
Writing Applications							
Write to sources	✓	✓	✓	✓	✓	✓	✓
Personal and fictional narrative (also biographical and autobiographical)	✓	✓	✓	✓	✓	✓	✓
Variety of expressive forms including poetry	✓	✓	✓	✓	✓	✓	✓
Informative/explanatory texts	✓	✓	✓	✓	✓	✓	✓
Description	✓	✓	✓	✓			
Procedural texts		✓	✓	✓	✓	✓	✓
Opinion pieces or arguments	✓	✓	✓	✓	✓	✓	✓
Communications including technical documents		✓	✓	✓	✓	✓	✓
Research report	✓	✓	✓	✓	✓	✓	✓

	K	1	2	3	4	5	6
Responses to literature/reflection				✓	✓	✓	✓
Analytical writing							
Letters		✓	✓	✓	✓	✓	✓
Write daily and over short and extended time frames; set up writer's notebooks							

Penmanship/Handwriting

	K	1	2	3	4	5	6
Write legibly in manuscript using correct formation, directionality, and spacing							
Write legibly in cursive using correct formation, directionality, and spacing							

SPEAKING AND LISTENING

Speaking

	K	1	2	3	4	5	6
Use repetition, rhyme, and rhythm in oral texts							
Participate in classroom activities and discussions							
Collaborative conversation with peers and adults in small and large groups using formal English when appropriate							
Differentiate between formal and informal English							
Follow agreed upon rules for discussion							
Build on others' talk in conversation, adding new ideas							
Come to discussions prepared							
Describe familiar people, places, and things and add drawings as desired							
Paraphrase portions of text read alone or information presented							
Apply comprehension strategies and skills in speaking activities							
Use literal and nonliteral meanings							
Ask and answer questions about text read aloud and about media							
Stay on topic when speaking							
Use language appropriate to situation, purpose, and audience							
Use nonverbal communications such as eye contact, gestures, and props							
Use verbal communication in effective ways and improve expression in conventional language							
Retell a story, presentation, or spoken message by summarizing							
Oral presentations: focus, organizational structure, audience, purpose							
Give and follow oral directions							
Consider audience when speaking or preparing a presentation							
Recite poems, rhymes, songs							
Use complete, coherent sentences							
Organize presentations							
Deliver presentations (narrative, summaries, informative, research, opinion); add visuals							
Speak audibly (accuracy, expression, volume, pitch, rate, phrasing, modulation, enunciation)							
Create audio recordings of poems, stories, presentations							

Listening

	K	1	2	3	4	5	6
Identify musical elements in language							
Determine the purpose for listening							
Understand, follow, restate, and give oral directions							
Develop oral language and concepts							

KEY ✓ = Assessed Skill
Tinted panels show skills, strategies, and other teaching opportunities.

	K	1	2	3	4	5	6
Listen openly, responsively, attentively, and critically							
Listen to identify the points a speaker or media source makes							
Listen responsively to oral presentations (determine main idea and key details)							
Ask and answer relevant questions (for clarification to follow-up on ideas)							
Identify reasons and evidence presented by speaker							
Recall and interpret speakers' verbal/nonverbal messages, purposes, perspectives							

LANGUAGE

Vocabulary Acquisition and Use

	K	1	2	3	4	5	6
Develop oral vocabulary and choose words for effect							
Use academic language		✓	✓	✓	✓	✓	✓
Identify persons, places, things, actions		✓	✓	✓			
Classify, sort, and categorize words	✓	✓	✓	✓	✓	✓	✓
Determine or clarify the meaning of unknown words; use word walls		✓	✓	✓	✓	✓	✓
Synonyms, antonyms, and opposites		✓	✓	✓	✓	✓	✓
Use context clues such as word, sentence, paragraph, definition, example, restatement, description, comparison, cause and effect		✓	✓	✓	✓	✓	✓
Use word identification strategies		✓	✓	✓	✓	✓	✓
Unfamiliar words		✓	✓	✓	✓	✓	✓
Multiple-meaning words		✓	✓	✓	✓	✓	✓
Use print and online dictionary to locate meanings, pronunciation, derivatives, parts of speech		✓	✓	✓	✓	✓	✓
Compound words		✓	✓	✓	✓	✓	✓
Words ending in -er and -est		✓	✓	✓	✓	✓	
Root words (base words)		✓	✓	✓	✓	✓	✓
Prefixes and suffixes		✓	✓	✓	✓	✓	✓
Greek and Latin affixes and roots			✓	✓	✓	✓	✓
Denotation and connotation					✓	✓	✓
Word families		✓	✓	✓	✓	✓	✓
Inflectional endings		✓	✓	✓	✓	✓	✓
Use a print and online thesaurus			✓	✓	✓	✓	✓
Use print and online reference sources for word meaning (dictionary, glossaries)		✓	✓	✓	✓	✓	✓
Homographs				✓	✓	✓	✓
Homophones			✓	✓	✓	✓	✓
Contractions		✓	✓	✓			
Figurative language such as metaphors, similes, personification			✓	✓	✓	✓	✓
Idioms, adages, proverbs, literal and nonliteral language			✓	✓	✓	✓	✓
Analogies							
Listen to, read, discuss familiar and unfamiliar challenging text							
Identify real-life connections between words and their use							
Use acquired words and phrases to convey precise ideas							
Use vocabulary to express spatial and temporal relationships							
Identify shades of meaning in related words	✓	✓	✓	✓	✓	✓	✓
Word origins				✓	✓	✓	✓
Morphology				✓	✓	✓	✓

	K	1	2	3	4	5	6
Knowledge of Language							
Choose words, phrases, and sentences for effect							
Choose punctuation effectively							
Formal and informal language for style and tone including dialects							
Conventions of Standard English/Grammar, Mechanics, and Usage							
Sentence concepts: statements, questions, exclamations, commands		✓	✓	✓	✓	✓	✓
Complete and incomplete sentences; sentence fragments; word order		✓	✓	✓	✓	✓	✓
Compound sentences, complex sentences				✓	✓	✓	✓
Combining sentences		✓	✓	✓	✓	✓	✓
Nouns including common, proper, singular, plural, irregular plurals, possessives, abstract, concrete, collective		✓	✓	✓	✓	✓	✓
Verbs including action, helping, linking, irregular		✓	✓	✓	✓	✓	✓
Verb tenses including past, present, future, perfect, and progressive		✓	✓	✓	✓	✓	✓
Pronouns including possessive, subject and object, pronoun-verb agreement, indefinite, intensive, reciprocal, interrogative, relative; correct unclear pronouns		✓	✓	✓	✓	✓	✓
Adjectives including articles, demonstrative, proper, adjectives that compare		✓	✓	✓	✓	✓	✓
Adverbs including telling how, when, where, comparative, superlative, irregular		✓	✓	✓	✓	✓	✓
Subject, predicate; subject-verb agreement		✓	✓	✓	✓	✓	✓
Contractions		✓	✓	✓	✓	✓	✓
Conjunctions				✓	✓	✓	✓
Commas		✓	✓	✓	✓	✓	✓
Colons, semicolons, dashes, hyphens						✓	✓
Question words							
Quotation marks			✓	✓	✓	✓	✓
Prepositions and prepositional phrases, appositives		✓	✓	✓	✓	✓	✓
Independent and dependent clauses						✓	✓
Italics/underlining for emphasis and titles							
Negatives, correcting double negatives					✓	✓	✓
Abbreviations			✓	✓	✓	✓	✓
Use correct capitalization in sentences, proper nouns, titles, abbreviations		✓	✓	✓	✓	✓	✓
Use correct punctuation		✓	✓	✓	✓	✓	✓
Antecedents				✓	✓	✓	✓
Homophones and words often confused			✓	✓	✓	✓	✓
Apostrophes				✓	✓	✓	✓
Spelling							
Write irregular, high-frequency words	✓	✓	✓				
ABC order	✓	✓					
Write letters	✓	✓					
Words with short vowels	✓	✓	✓	✓	✓	✓	✓
Words with long vowels	✓	✓	✓	✓	✓	✓	✓
Words with digraphs, blends, consonant clusters, double consonants		✓	✓	✓	✓	✓	✓
Words with vowel digraphs and ambiguous vowels		✓	✓	✓	✓	✓	✓
Words with diphthongs		✓	✓	✓	✓	✓	✓

KEY   ✓ = Assessed Skill
Tinted panels show skills, strategies, and other teaching opportunities.

	K	1	2	3	4	5	6
Words with *r*-controlled vowels		✓	✓	✓	✓	✓	✓
Use conventional spelling		✓	✓	✓	✓	✓	✓
Schwa words				✓	✓	✓	✓
Words with silent letters			✓	✓	✓	✓	✓
Words with hard and soft letters			✓	✓	✓	✓	✓
Inflectional endings including plural, past tense, drop final *e* and double consonant when adding *-ed* and *-ing*, changing *y* to *i*	✓	✓	✓	✓	✓	✓	✓
Compound words		✓	✓	✓	✓	✓	✓
Homonyms/homophones			✓	✓	✓	✓	✓
Prefixes and suffixes		✓	✓	✓	✓	✓	✓
Root and base words (also spell derivatives)				✓	✓	✓	✓
Syllables: patterns, rules, accented, stressed, closed, open				✓	✓	✓	✓
Words with Greek and Latin roots						✓	✓
Words from mythology						✓	✓
Words with spelling patterns, word families	✓	✓	✓	✓	✓	✓	✓

RESEARCH AND INQUIRY

Study Skills

	K	1	2	3	4	5	6
Directions: read, write, give, follow (includes technical directions)			✓	✓	✓	✓	✓
Evaluate directions for sequence and completeness				✓	✓	✓	✓
Use library/media center							
Use parts of a book to locate information							
Interpret information from graphic aids		✓	✓	✓	✓	✓	✓
Use graphic organizers to organize information and comprehend text	✓	✓	✓	✓	✓	✓	✓
Use functional, everyday documents				✓	✓	✓	✓
Apply study strategies: skimming and scanning, note-taking, outlining							

Research Process

	K	1	2	3	4	5	6
Generate and revise topics and questions for research				✓	✓	✓	✓
Narrow focus of research, set research goals				✓	✓	✓	✓
Find and locate information using print and digital resources		✓	✓	✓	✓	✓	✓
Record information systematically (note-taking, outlining, using technology)				✓	✓	✓	✓
Develop a systematic research plan				✓	✓	✓	✓
Evaluate reliability, credibility, usefulness of sources and information						✓	✓
Use primary sources to obtain information					✓	✓	✓
Organize, synthesize, evaluate, and draw conclusions from information							
Cite and list sources of information (record basic bibliographic data)					✓	✓	✓
Demonstrate basic keyboarding skills							
Participate in and present shared research							

Technology

	K	1	2	3	4	5	6
Use computer, Internet, and other technology resources to access information							
Use text and organizational features of electronic resources such as search engines, keywords, e-mail, hyperlinks, URLs, Web pages, databases, graphics							
Use digital tools to present and publish in a variety of media formats							

INDEX

A

B

Base words. *See* **Vocabulary: base words/root words.**

Beyond Level Options,

comprehension, 1: T57, T123, T189, T255, T319, 2: T57, T123, T189, T255, 3: T57, T123, T189, T255, T319, 4: T55, T119, T183, T247, T311, 5: T55, T119, T147, T183, T247, T311, 6: T55, T119, T183, T247, T311

focus on genre, 2: T55, T121, 4: T53, T117, 6: T53

focus on literary elements, 1: T55, 2: T317, 4: T117, 6: T309

focus on science, 1: T253, 3: T187, T253, 4: T181, T245, 5: T309, 6: T133, T181, T245

focus on social studies, 1: T121, T187, T317, 2: T187, T253, 3: T317, 5: T181, T245, 6: T69

Level Up, 1: T332–T333, T345, T364–T367, 3: T51, T183, T313, 4: T339, 6: T337, T338, T339

Leveled Reader lessons, 1: T54–T55, T120–T121, T186–T187, T252–T253, T316–T317, 2: T54–T55, T120–T121, T136–T137, T186–T187, T252–T253, T316–T317, 3: T54–T55, T120–T121, T186–T187, T252–T253, T316–T317, 4: T52–T53, T116–T117, T180–T181, T244–T245, T308–T309, 5: T52–T53, T116–T117, T180–T181, T244–T245, T308–T309, 6: T52–T53, T116–T117, T180–T181, T244–T245, T308–T309

paired read, 1: T55, T121, T187, T253, T317, 2: T55, T121, T187, T253, T317, 3: T55, T121, T187, T253, T317, 4: T53, T117, T181, T245, T309, 5: T53, T117, T181, T245, T309, 6: T53, T117, T181, T245, T309

vocabulary, 1: T56, T122, T188, T254, T318, 2: T56, T122, T188, T254, T318, 3: T56, T122, T188, T254, T318, 4: T54, T118, T182, T246, T310, 5: T54, T118, T182, T246, T310, 6: T54, T118, T182, T246, T310

Bibliography, 4: T220

Biographies. *See* **Genre: informational text.**

Book, parts of. *See* **Study skills: parts of a book; Text features.**

Build background, 1: S5, S19, T10, T58, T76, T124, T142, T190, T208, T256, T274, T320, 2: T10, T58, T76, T124, T142, T190, T208, T256, T274, T334,

3: T10, T58, T76, T124, T142, T190, T208, T256, T274, T320, 4: T10–T11, T56, T74–T75, T120, T138–T139, T184, T202–T203, T248, T266, T312, 5: T10, T56, T74, T120, T138, T184, T202, T248, T266, T312, 6: T10, T56, T74, T120, T138, T184, T202, T248, T266–T267, T312, T326

C

Capitalization. *See* **Grammar.**

Captions, 5: T153M

Cause and effect. *See* **Comprehension skills: cause and effect.**

Character. *See* **Comprehension skills: character.**

Charts. *See* **Graphic Organizers: charts; Text features: charts.**

Chronological order. *See* **Comprehension skills: chronological order; Writing traits and skills: organization**

Citations. *See* **Study skills.**

Classroom Library, 1: T368–T369, 2: T368–T369 3: T368–T369 4: T360–T361, 5: T360–T361, 6: T360–T361

Close reading, 1: S19–S14, S21–S26, T16–T27, T27A–T27X, T40–T41, T42, T50, T54, T82–T93, T93A–T93X, T106–T107, T108, T116, T120, T148–T159, T159A–T159P, T172–T173, T174, T182, T186, T214–T225, T225A–T225T, T238–T239, T240, T248, T252, T282–T289, T289A–T289F, T302–T303, T304, T312, T316, T364–T369, 2: T16–T27, T27A–T27X, T40–T41, T42, T50, T54, T82–T93, T93A–T93V, T106–T107 T108, T116, T120, T148–T159, T159A–T159Z, T172–T173, T174, T182, T186, T214–T225, T225A–T225P, T238–T239, T240, T248, T252, T282–T289, T289A–T289F, T302–T303, T304, T312, T316, T364–T369, 3: T16–T27, T27A–T27Z, T40–T41, T42, T50, T54, T82–T93, T93A–T93T, T106–T107 T108, T116, T120, T148–T159, T159A–T159P, T172–T173, T174, T182, T186, T214–T225, T225A–T225N, T238–T239, T240, T248, T252, T282–T289, T289A–T289F, T302–T303, T304, T312, T316, T364–T369, 4: T16–T25, T25A–T25V, T38–T39, T40, T48, T52, T80–T89, T89A–89Z, T102–T103, T104, T112, T116, T144–T153, T153A–T153P, T166–T167, T168, T176, T180, T208–T217, T217A–T217R, T230–T231, T232, T240, T244, T272–T281, T281A–T281F, T294–T295, T296, T304, T308, T356–T361, 5: T16–T25, T25A–T25X, T38–T39, T40, T48, T52, T80–T89,

T89A–89Z, T102–T103, T104, T112, T116, T144–T153, T153A–T153P, T166–T167, T168, T176, T180, T208–T217, T217A–T217X, T230–T231, T232, T240, T244, T272–T281, T281A–T281F, T294–T295, T296, T304, T308, T356–T361, 6: T16–T25, T25A–T25T, T38–T39, T40, T48, T52, T80–T89, T89A–89X, T102–T103, T104, T112, T116, T144–T153, T153A–T153N, T166–T167, T168, T176, T180, T208–T217, T217A–T217Z, T230–T231, T232, T240, T244, T272–T281, T281A–T281F, T294–T295, T296, T304, T308, T356–T361

Collaborative conversations, 1: S6, S20, T10, T76, T142, T208, T274, T341, 2: T10, T76, T142, T208, T274, T302, 3: T10, T76, T142, T208, T274, T302, 4: T10, T74, T138, T202, T266, T295, T333, 5: T10, T74, T138, T202, T266, T333, 6: T10, T74, T138, T202, T266, T333

Colon. *See* **Grammar: punctuation.**

Commands. *See* **Grammar: sentences.**

Commas. *See* **Grammar: punctuation.**

Communication. *See* **Listening.**

Compare and contrast, 1: S23, 4: T148–T149, T174–T175, T179, T182–T183, 6: T238–T239, T243, T247

Compound sentences. *See* **Grammar: sentences.**

Compound words. *See* **Phonics/Word Study; Spelling; Vocabulary.**

Comprehension skills. *See also* **Approaching Level Options; Beyond Level Options; English Learners; On Level Options.**

author's point of view, 1: S25–S26, 2: T154–T155, T181, T185, T189, T210, T220–T221, T247, T251, T255, 5: T145, T148–T149, T157, T175, T179, T183, T212–T213, T239, T243, T247

cause and effect, 1: S23–S24, T220–T221, T247, T251, T255, 3: T88–T89, T114–T115, T101, T115, T119, T123, 4: T212–T213, T238, T239, T243, T247

character, 1: S11–S12, T22–T23, T48, T49, T53, T57, T88–T89, 3: T22–T23, T48–T49, T53, T55, T57

compare and contrast, 1: S23, 4: T148–T149, T174–T175, T179, T182–T183, 6: T238–T239, T243, T247

main idea and key details, 1: S23–S24, T284–T285, T310, T311, T315, T319, 3: T154–T155, T181, T185, T189, T220–T221, T246–T247, T251, T255, T306, T314, T318, T322, T324, T347

F

G

M

N

O

Q

R

CCSS Common Core State Standards Correlations
English Language Arts

College and Career Readiness Anchor Standards for READING

The K-5 standards on the following pages define what students should understand and be able to do by the end of each grade. They correspond to the College and Career Readiness (CCR) anchor standards below by number. The CCR and grade-specific standards are necessary complements—the former providing broad standards, the latter providing additional specificity—that together define the skills and understandings that all students must demonstrate.

Key Ideas and Details

1. Read closely to determine what the text says explicitly and to make logical inferences from it; cite specific textual evidence when writing or speaking to support conclusions drawn from the text.

2. Determine central ideas or themes of a text and analyze their development; summarize the key supporting details and ideas.

3. Analyze how and why individuals, events, and ideas develop and interact over the course of a text.

Craft and Structure

4. Interpret words and phrases as they are used in a text, including determining technical, connotative, and figurative meanings, and analyze how specific word choices shape meaning or tone.

5. Analyze the structure of texts, including how specific sentences, paragraphs, and larger portions of the text (e.g., a section, chapter, scene, or stanza) relate to each other and the whole.

6. Assess how point of view or purpose shapes the content and style of a text.

Integration of Knowledge and Ideas

7. Integrate and evaluate content presented in diverse media and formats, including visually and quantitatively, as well as in words.

8. Delineate and evaluate the argument and specific claims in a text, including the validity of the reasoning as well as the relevance and sufficiency of the evidence.

9. Analyze how two or more texts address similar themes or topics in order to build knowledge or to compare the approaches the authors take.

Range of Reading and Level of Text Complexity

10. Read and comprehend complex literary and informational texts independently and proficiently.

CCSS Common Core State Standards
English Language Arts

Grade 3

Each standard is coded in the following manner:

Strand	Grade Level	Standard
RL	3	1

Reading Standards for Literature

Key Ideas and Details		McGraw-Hill Wonders
RL.3.1	Ask and answer questions to demonstrate understanding of a text, referring explicitly to the text as the basis for the answers.	**READING/WRITING WORKSHOP:** Unit 1: 28, 29, 44, 45 **Unit 2:** 108, 109, 124 **Unit 3:** 188, 204, 205 **Unit 4:** 266, 267, 280, 281 **Unit 5:** 338, 339, 352, 353 **Unit 6:** 410, 411, 424 **LITERATURE ANTHOLOGY: Unit 1:** 29, 31, 44 **Unit 2:** 119, 141, 191 **Unit 3:** 215, 237 **Unit 4:** 297, 302, 311, 319, 363 **Unit 5:** 385, 409, 411 **Unit 6:** 477, 503 **LEVELED READERS: Unit 4, Week 1:** *The Weaver of Rugs: A Navajo Folktale* (A), *Why the Sea is Salty: A Scandinavian Folktale* (O, EL), *Finn MacCool and the Salmon of Knowledge: An Irish Folktale* (B) **Unit 4, Week 2:** *Every Picture Tells a Story* (A), *A Chef in the Family* (O, EL), *Stepping Forward* (B) **CLOSE READING COMPANION:** 1-6, 128-131, 194-197 **YOUR TURN PRACTICE BOOK:** 23-25, 163-165 **READING WORKSTATION ACTIVITY CARDS:** 19 **TEACHER'S EDITION: Unit 1:** T27H, T27X, T93F, T159G, T159I **Unit 2:** T27Q, T93I, **Unit 3:** T27V, T93J, T93R **Unit 4:** T12, T16-T19, T25D, T25F, T25H, T25N, T25T, T76, T82-T83, T89D, T89G, T89J, T89K, T89O, T89T, T89X, T89Y, T89Z, T217R, T217R **Unit 5:** T12, T16-T17, T25K, T25T, T89K, T89V **Unit 6:** T25G, T25P, T25R, T25S, T89G, T89O **www.connected.mcgraw-hill.com: RESOURCES** **Student Resources:** Comprehension Interactive Games and Activities
RL.3.2	Recount stories, including fables, folktales, and myths from diverse cultures; determine the central message, lesson, or moral and explain how it is conveyed through key details in the text.	**READING/WRITING WORKSHOP: Unit 1:** 22-27 **Unit 2:** 102-107, 118-123, 125 **Unit 4:** 318-321, 323 **Unit 5:** 338, 352 **Unit 6:** 406-409, 411, 420-423, 425 **LITERATURE ANTHOLOGY: Unit 1:** 31, 33 **Unit 2:** 119, 141, 191 **Unit 3:** 215, 237 **Unit 4:** 319, 363 **Unit 5:** 385, 411 **Unit 6:** 475, 476, 477, 481, 502, 503 **LEVELED READERS: Unit 2, Week 1:** *The Quarreling Quails* (A), *Jungle Treasures* (O, EL), *The Bear Who Stole the Chinook* (B) **Unit 2, Week 2:** *The Promise of Gold Mountain* (A), *Moving from Mexico* (O, EL), *Gustaf Goes to America* (B) **Unit 4, Week 5:** *In the Running* (A), *Melanie's Mission* (O, EL), *A Speech to Remember* (B) **Unit 6, Week 1:** *Midas and the Donkey Ears* (A), *The Naming of Athens* (O, EL), *Odysseus and King Aeolus* (B) **Unit 6, Week 2:** *The Big Storm* (A), *The Schoolhouse Blizzard* (O, EL), *The Hottest Summer* (B) **YOUR TURN PRACTICE BOOK:** 53-55, 63-65, 193-194, 253-255 **READING WORKSTATION ACTIVITY CARDS:** 6 **TEACHER'S EDITION: Unit 1:** T16-19, T24-T25, T27V-T27X, T40-T41, **Unit 2:** T12, T16-T19, T22, T24, T27C-T27E, T27K, T27L, T27M, T27Q, T27T, T78, T88, T90, T93O **Unit 3:** T12-T13, T16-T19, T24-T25, T27V, T225M-T225N **Unit 4:** T22-T23, T25R, T25T, T89T, T89Y, T217Q, T217R **Unit 5:** T22-T23, T25Q, **Unit 6:** T22-T23, T25B, T25H, T25M, T25P, T25T, T46-T47, T51, T55, T89W-T89X, T217Y-T217Z **www.connected.mcgraw-hill.com: RESOURCES** **Student Resources:** Comprehension Interactive Games and Activities **Teacher Resources:** Graphic Organizers, Interactive Read Aloud Images, Skills Review

Reading Standards for Literature

Key Ideas and Details	*McGraw-Hill Wonders*
RL.3.3 Describe characters in a story (e.g., their traits, motivations, or feelings) and explain how their actions contribute to the sequence of events.	**READING/WRITING WORKSHOP: Unit I:** 27, 29, 43, 45 **Unit 3:** 187, 189, 203, 205 **LITERATURE ANTHOLOGY: Unit I:** 31, 53 **Unit 2:** 119, 141 **Unit 3:** 215, 237 **Unit 4:** 297 **Unit 5:** 411 **Unit 6:** 477, 503, 549 **LEVELED READERS: Unit I, Week I:** *Berries, Berries, Berries* (A), *Duck's Discovery* (O, EL), *Robot Race* (B) **Unit I, Week 2:** *The Special Meal* (A), *A Row of Lamps* (O, EL), *Dragons on the Water* (B) **Unit 3, Week I:** *The Ballgame Between the Birds and the Animals: A Cherokee Folktale* (A), *King of the Birds* (O, EL), *Sheep and Pig Set Up Housekeeping* (B) **Unit 3, Week 2:** *On the Ball* (A), *Harry's Great Idea* (O, EL), *Best Friends in Business* (B) **CLOSE READING COMPANION:** I-7, 8, 10, 74-76,91, 92, 100-103, 107-112, 117-119, 130-131, 133-135,140-142,166-171, 173-178 **YOUR TURN PRACTICE BOOK:** 13-15, 103-105, 113-115 **READING WORKSTATION ACTIVITY CARDS:** I, 2, 3, 4 **TEACHER'S EDITION: Unit I:** T22, T27C, T27E–T27G, T27I, T27K, T27M, T27O, T27Q, T27S, T27V, T27X, T41, T82, T86, T93C, T93E, T93G, T93J–T93L, T93N, T93P, T93R, T93T, T107 **Unit 2:** T93C, T93K, T93M **Unit 3:** T12, T16–T18, T22, T27E–T27I, T27K–T27S, T27V, T41, T82–T89, T93C–T93P, T93R, T159Q, T159R, T225N **Unit 4:** T16–T17, T20–T21, T25C, T25G, T25K, T25T, T89E, T89T, T89X **Unit 5:** T25C, T25E, T25M, T89D, T89J **Unit 6:** T25C, T25D, T25F, T25T **www.connected.mcgraw-hill.com: RESOURCES** **Student Resources:** Comprehension Interactive Games and Activities **Teacher Resources:** Graphic Organizers, Skills Review

Craft and Structure	*McGraw-Hill Wonders*
RL.3.4 Determine the meaning of words and phrases as they are used in a text, distinguishing literal from nonliteral language.	**READING/WRITING WORKSHOP: Unit I:** 79 **Unit 2:** 127, 173 **Unit 3:** 207 **Unit 4:** 325 **Unit 6:** 427, 469 **YOUR TURN PRACTICE BOOK:** 37, 67, 97, 117, 197, 267, 297 **PHONICS/WORD STUDY ACTIVITY CARDS:** 4, 6, 8 **CLOSE READING COMPANION:** 151, 177, 195 **TEACHER'S EDITION: Unit I:** T16, T27N, T80, T93D, T93K, T93M, T93O, T224-T225, T237, T240, T245, T248 **Unit 2:** T14, T27O, T92, T93, T93C, T93E–T93F, T93K, T93L, T113, T118, T122, T125, T129, T289C, T301 **Unit 3:** T14–T16, T27Q, T80–T82, T92–T93, T93E, T93G, T104–T105 **Unit 4:** T14–T15, T25L, T36–T37, T100–T101 **Unit 5:** T14, T24–T25, T25S, T78–T79 **Unit 6:** T78, T101, T109, T114, T118, T125, T166, T281C **www.connected.mcgraw-hill.com: RESOURCES** **Student Resources:** Vocabulary Interactive Games and Activities **Teacher Resources:** Graphic Organizers
RL.3.5 Refer to parts of stories, dramas, and poems when writing or speaking about a text, using terms such as chapter, scene, and stanza; describe how each successive part builds on earlier sections.	**READING/WRITING WORKSHOP: Unit 2:** 170 **Unit 4:** 322 **Unit 6:** 412, 466 **READING WORKSTATION ACTIVITY CARDS:** 23, 24 **CLOSE READING COMPANION:** 7, I, 130, 131, 139, 198 **TEACHER'S EDITION: Unit I:** T27Q, T27S, T93R, T93T **Unit 2:** T27M, T27O, T27T, T93R, T289C, T289F **Unit 3:** T93E, T93R **Unit 4:** T89Q, T89T, T281D, T289F **Unit 6:** T25E, T25G, T25P, T29, T46, T27O, T274, T278, T281D, T281F **www.connected.mcgraw-hill.com:** Resources **Student Resources:** Comprehension Interactive Games and Activities

Reading Standards for Literature

Craft and Structure	*McGraw-Hill Wonders*
RL.3.6 Distinguish their own point of view from that of the narrator or those of the characters.	**READING/WRITING WORKSHOP: Unit 2**: 171 **Unit 4**: 267, 281 **Unit 5**: 339, 353 **Unit 6**: 467 **LITERATURE ANTHOLOGY: Unit 1**: 188–191 **Unit 4**: 278–297, 300–319, 360–363 **Unit 5**: 366–385, 390–411 **Unit 6**: 546–549 **LEVELED READERS: Unit 2, Week 5**: *Problem Solved* (A), *The Long Walk* (O, EL), *Two Up, One Down* (B) **Unit 4, Week 1**: *The Weaver of Rugs: A Navajo Folktale* (A), *Why the Sea is Salty: A Scandinavian Folktale* (O, EL), *Finn MacCool and the Salmon of Knowledge: An Irish Folktale* (B) **YOUR TURN PRACTICE BOOK:** 93–94, 153–155, 163–165, 203–205, 213–215, 293–294 **READING WORKSTATION ACTIVITY CARDS:** 5 **CLOSE READING COMPANION:** 101, 128, 198 **TEACHER'S EDITION: Unit 4**: T20–T21, T25D, T25E,T25G, T25J, T25K, T25Q, T25T, T29, T46, T47, T51, T55, T84, T89I, T89Q, T89T, T109–T111, T115, T117, T119 **Unit 5**: T20, T25T, T39, T46–T47, T51, T55, T84, T85, T89C, T89F, T89I, T89N, T89Q, T89V, T103, T111, T115, T119 **www.connected.mcgraw-hill.com: RESOURCES** **Student Resources:** Comprehension Interactive Games and Activities
Integration of Knowledge and Ideas	*McGraw-Hill Wonders*
RL.3.7 Explain how specific aspects of a text's illustrations contribute to what is conveyed by the words in a story (e.g., create mood, emphasize aspects of a character or setting).	**READING/WRITING WORKSHOP: Unit 1**: 30, 46 **Unit 3**: 206 **Unit 4**: 282 **Unit 5**: 354 **Unit 6**: 426 **LITERATURE ANTHOLOGY: Unit 4**: 281, 287, 296 **READING WORKSTATION ACTIVITY CARDS:** 7 **CLOSE READING COMPANION:** 5, 43,64, 135, 174, 179 **TEACHER'S EDITION: Unit 1**: T16, T27B, T27D, T27L, T27S, T93H **Unit 2**: T27B, T27F, T27J, T93G **Unit 3**: T28B, T27G, T27O, T93H, T108, T116 **Unit 4**: T25C, T25I, T25S, T86, T89B, T89E, T94 **Unit 5**: T25J, T25P, T86, T89L **Unit 6**: T86 **www.connected.mcgraw-hill.com: RESOURCES** **Student Resources:** Comprehension Interactive Games and Activities **Teacher Resources:** Interactive Read Aloud Images
RL.3.8 (Not applicable to literature)	**(Not applicable to literature)**
RL.3.9 Compare and contrast the themes, settings, and plots of stories written by the same author about the same or similar characters (e.g., in books from a series).	**LITERATURE ANTHOLOGY: Unit 4**: 300–325 **LEVELED READERS: Unit 1, Week 2**: *The Special Meal* (A), *A Row of Lamps* (O, EL), *Dragons on the Water* (B) **Unit 4, Week 2**: *Every Picture Tells a Story* (A), *A Chef in the Family* (O, EL), *Stepping Forward* (B) **READING WORKSTATION ACTIVITY CARDS:** 8 **TEACHER'S EDITION: Unit 1**: S14 **Unit 4**: T86, T89U, T89X, T89Y, T89Z, T102–T103, T105, T113, T117, T123 **www.connected.mcgraw-hill.com: RESOURCES** **Student Resources:** Comprehension Interactive Games and Activities
Range of Reading and Level of Text Complexity	*McGraw-Hill Wonders*
RL.3.10 By the end of the year, read and comprehend literature, including stories, dramas, and poetry, at the high end of the grades 2–3 text complexity band independently and proficiently.	**READING/WRITING WORKSHOP:** These units reflect the range of text complexity found throughout the book. **Unit 2**: 166–169 **Unit 4**: 318–321 **Unit 6**: 406–409 **LITERATURE ANTHOLOGY:** These units reflect the range of text complexity found throughout the book. **Unit 2**: 188–191 **Unit 3**: 194–215 **Unit 4**: 300–319 **Unit 5**: 366–385 **Unit 6**: 462–477, 546–549 **LEVELED READERS: Unit 1, Week 2**: *The Special Meal* (A), *A Row of Lamps* (O, EL), *Dragons on the Water* (B) **Unit 6, Week 5**: *Funny Faces* (A), *Too Many Frogs* (O, EL), *The Joke's on You* (B) **READING WORKSTATION ACTIVITY CARDS:** 27 **TEACHER'S EDITION: Unit 1**: T24, T27A, T90, T93A **Unit 3**: T24, T27A, T90, T93A, T159Q **Unit 6**: T22, T25A, T25Q, T86, T89A, T274, T281A

CORRELATIONS

Reading Standards for Informational Text

Key Ideas and Details		McGraw-Hill Wonders
RI.3.1	Ask and answer questions to demonstrate understanding of a text, referring explicitly to the text as the basis for the answers.	**READING/WRITING WORKSHOP: Unit 1:** 60, 61, 76, 77, 90, 91 **Unit 2:** 140, 141, 156, 157 **Unit 3:** 220, 221, 236, 237, 250, 251 **Unit 4:** 294, 295, 308, 309 **Unit 5:** 366, 367, 380, 381, 394, 395 **Unit 6:** 438, 439, 452, 453 **LITERATURE ANTHOLOGY: Unit 1:** 58–71 **Unit 2:** 146–167, 172–185 **Unit 3:** 240–255, 258–269 **Unit 4:** 326–339 **Unit 5:** 416–429, 432–451, 456–459 **LEVELED READERS: Unit 1, Week 3:** *Judy Baca* (A, O, EL, B) **Unit 1, Week 4:** *The Amazing Benjamin Franklin* (A, O, EL, B) **Unit 1, Week 5:** *The National Mall* (A, O, EL, B) **Unit 5, Week 3:** *Firefighting Heroes* (A, O, EL, B) **Unit 5, Week 4:** *Eunice Kennedy Shriver* (A, O, EL, B) **Unit 5, Week 5:** *The Fuel of the Future* (A, O, EL, B) **CLOSE READING COMPANION:** 15–20, 48–53, 154–159 **YOUR TURN PRACTICE BOOK:** 23–25, 33–35, 43–45, 223–225, 233–235, 243–245 **READING WORKSTATION ACTIVITY CARDS:** 19 **TEACHER'S EDITION: Unit 1:** T93V, T93W, T159D, T159I, T159P, T218, T225B, T225D–T225G, T225I–T225Q, T225T, T336 **Unit 2:** T159J, T159N, T159X, T159Y, T214, T225F **Unit 3:** T27X–T27Y, T93T, T159G, T159P, T214–T217, T225E **Unit 4:** T153F, T153K, T153N, T217M, T217P **Unit 5:** T89X–T89Y, T140–T141, T146–T147, T153D, T210–T211, T217A, T217B, T217E, T217G, T217K, T217N, T217P, T217R, T274, T328 **Unit 6:** T153I, T153L, T217J **www.connected.mcgraw-hill.com: RESOURCES** **Student Resources:** Comprehension Interactive Games and Activities **Teacher Resources:** Interactive Read Aloud Images
RI.3.2	Determine the main idea of a text; recount the key details and explain how they support the main idea.	**READING/WRITING WORKSHOP: Unit 1:** 89, 91 **Unit 3:** 219, 221, 235, 237 **LITERATURE ANTHOLOGY: Unit 1:** 91, 93, 97 **Unit 2:** 167, 185 **Unit 3:** 243, 247, 262, 265, 273 **Unit 4:** 339, 355, 357 **Unit 5:** 427, 429, 451 **Unit 6:** 517, 543 **LEVELED READERS: Unit 1, Week 5:** *The National Mall* (A, O, EL, B) **Unit 3, Week 3:** *Destination Saturn* (A, O, EL, B) **Unit 3, Week 4:** *Inspired by Nature* (A, O, EL, B) **CLOSE READING COMPANION:** 53, 56, 57, 82, 83, 103, 115, 116 **YOUR TURN PRACTICE BOOK:** 43–45, 123–125, 133–135 **READING WORKSTATION ACTIVITY CARDS:** 9 **TEACHER'S EDITION: Unit 1:** T289C, T289D, T336 **Unit 3:** T154–T155, T159C, T159E, T159G, T159I, T159K, T159M, T159P, T173, T220–T221, T225C, T225G, T225J, T225L, T239, T336 **Unit 4:** T217C, T217J, T217N **Unit 5:** T153E, T208, T328–T329 **www.connected.mcgraw-hill.com: RESOURCES** **Student Resources:** Comprehension Interactive Games and Activities **Teacher Resources:** Graphic Organizers, Interactive Read Aloud Images, Skills Review
RI.3.3	Describe the relationship between a series of historical events, scientific ideas or concepts, or steps in technical procedures in a text, using language that pertains to time, sequence, and cause/effect.	**READING/WRITING WORKSHOP: Unit 1:** 70–75, 77 **Unit 4:** 304–307, 309 **Unit 5:** 390–393, 395 **LITERATURE ANTHOLOGY: Unit 1:** 74–91, 94–97 **Unit 2:** 172–185 **Unit 4:** 342–357 **Unit 5:** 432–451, 456–459 **Unit 6:** 540, 543 **LEVELED READERS: Unit 3, Week 4:** *Inspired by Nature* (A, O, EL, B) **Unit 4, Week 4:** *Future of Flight* (A, O, EL, B) **Unit 5, Week 5:** *The Fuel of the Future* (A, O, EL, B) **YOUR TURN PRACTICE BOOK:** 33–35, 183–185, 243–244 **READING WORKSTATION ACTIVITY CARDS:** 13 **TEACHER'S EDITION: Unit 1:** T220–T221, T225C, T225G, T225L, T225P, T251, T255 **Unit 3:** T159C–T159F, T159H–T159M, T216, T225C **Unit 4:** T212–T213, T217C, T217E, T217G, T217J, T217K, T217M, T217P, T231 **Unit 5:** T153C, T153I, T217M, T217Q, T276–T277 **Unit 6:** T217K, T217M, T217P, T217Q, T217S **www.connected.mcgraw-hill.com: RESOURCES** **Student Resources:** Comprehension Interactive Games and Activities **Teacher Resources:** Graphic Organizers, Skills Review

Reading Standards for Informational Text

Craft and Structure	McGraw-Hill Wonders
RI.3.4 Determine the meaning of general academic and domain-specific words and phrases in a text relevant to a *grade 3 topic or subject area*.	**READING/WRITING WORKSHOP:** Unit 1: 50–53, 66–69, 82–85 **Unit 2:** 130–133, 146–149 **Unit 3:** 200–213, 226–229, 242–245 **Unit 4:** 286–289, 300–303 **Unit 5:** 358–361, 372–375, 386–389 **Unit 6:** 430–433, 444–447 **TEACHER'S EDITION:** Unit 1: T146, T158, T174, T212, T214, T278 **Unit 2:** T159F, T159L, T159P, T159S, T212 **Unit 3:** T27Y, T146–T148, T159I, T159O, T170–T171 **Unit 4:** T142–T143, T164–T165, T217G, T217I, T217K, T228–T229 **Unit 5:** T142–T143, T217M, T228–T229, T270 **Unit 6:** T142, T206–T207, T228–T229 **www.connected.mcgraw-hill.com: RESOURCES** **Student Resources:** Comprehension Interactive Games and Activities, Vocabulary Interactive Games and Activities **Teacher Resources:** Graphic Organizers
RI.3.5 Use text features and search tools (e.g., key words, sidebars, hyperlinks) to locate information relevant to a given topic efficiently.	**READING/WRITING WORKSHOP:** Unit 1: 78, 92 **Unit 2:** 142, 158 **Unit 3:** 222 **Unit 4:** 310 **Unit 5:** 368 **Unit 6:** 440, 454 **LITERATURE ANTHOLOGY:** Unit 3: 265, 269 **Unit 4:** 356 **Unit 6:** 517 **CLOSE READING COMPANION:** 96, 161, 181, 182 **READING WORKSTATION ACTIVITY CARDS:** 16 **TEACHER'S EDITION:** Unit 1: T156, T174, T182, T186, T190, T192, T222–T223, T336–T337 **Unit 2:** T222–T223, T225D, T336–T337 **Unit 3:** T159F, T159G, T159K, T159L, T222–T223, T225F, T225K, T336–T337, T338–T341 **Unit 4:** T217I, T217K, T217P, T328–T329 **Unit 5:** T25W, T25X, T217M, T217W, T217X, T328–T329 **Unit 6:** T142, T150, T228–T229, T328–T329 **www.connected.mcgraw-hill.com: RESOURCES** **Student Resources:** Comprehension Interactive Games and Activities, Research and Inquiry **Teacher Resources:** Research and Inquiry
RI.3.6 Distinguish their own point of view from that of the author of a text.	**READING/WRITING WORKSHOP:** Unit 2: 134–139, 141, 150–155, 156 **Unit 5:** 362–365, 367, 376–379, 381 **LITERATURE ANTHOLOGY:** Unit 2: 146–167, 172–185 **Unit 3:** 240–255, 258–269 **Unit 4:** 326–339 **Unit 5:** 416–429, 432–451, 456–459 **LEVELED READERS:** Unit 2, Week 3: *The Race for the Presidency* (A, O, EL, B) **Unit 2, Week 4:** *Protecting the Islands* (A, O, EL, B) **Unit 5, Week 3:** *Firefighting Heroes* (A, O, EL, B) **Unit 5, Week 4:** *Eunice Kennedy Shriver* (A, O, EL, B) **YOUR TURN PRACTICE BOOK:** 73–75, 83–85, 223–225, 233–235 **TEACHER'S EDITION:** Unit 2: T154–T155, T159E, T159U, T173, T220–T221, T225M, T225N, T239, T240, T246–T248, T251, T252, T255, T256, T258 **Unit 5:** T148, T149, T153C, T153J, T153K, T153N, T167, T174, T175, T179, T183, T212–T213, T217T **www.connected.mcgraw-hill.com: RESOURCES** **Student Resources:** Comprehension Interactive Games and Activities **Teacher Resources:** Graphic Organizers, Skills Review

Integration of Knowledge and Ideas	McGraw-Hill Wonders
RI.3.7 Use information gained from illustrations (e.g., maps, photographs) and the words in a text to demonstrate understanding of the text (e.g., where, when, why, and how key events occur).	**READING/WRITING WORKSHOP:** Unit 1: 54–59, 70–75 **Unit 2:** 134–139, 150–155 **Unit 3:** 214–219, 230–235 **Unit 4:** 290–293, 304–307 **Unit 5:** 362–365, 376–379 **Unit 6:** 434–437, 448–451 **LITERATURE ANTHOLOGY:** Unit 1: 57 **Unit 3:** 255, 269 **Unit 6:** 517, 543 **READING WORKSTATION ACTIVITY CARDS:** 17 **CLOSE READING COMPANION:** 49, 58, 61, 70, 81, 89, 165, 181, 187,189 **TEACHER'S EDITION:** Unit 1: T156, T222, T225B, T225E **Unit 2:** T159D, T222, T225B, T225E, T225G, T225H **Unit 3:** T159E, T159G, T159K, T159L, T159O, T222 **Unit 4:** T153B, T153C, T153G, T217B–T217E **Unit 5:** T153F, T214, T215, T217C, T217M **www.connected.mcgraw-hill.com: RESOURCES** **Teacher Resources:** Graphic Organizers, Interactive Read Aloud Images, Research and Inquiry

Reading Standards for Informational Text

Integration of Knowledge and Ideas		*McGraw-Hill Wonders*
RI.3.8	Describe the logical connection between particular sentences and paragraphs in a text (e.g., comparison, cause/effect, first/second/third in a sequence).	**READING/WRITING WORKSHOP:** **Unit 1:** 54–59, 61, 77 **Unit 3:** 246–249, 251 **Unit 4:** 290–293, 295 **Unit 6:** 434–437, 439, 448–451, 453 **LITERATURE ANTHOLOGY:** **Unit 1:** 58–71, 74–91, 94–97 **Unit 2:** 146–167, 172–185 **Unit 3:** 272–275 **Unit 4:** 326–339, 342–357 **Unit 5:** 432–451, 465–459 **Unit 6:** 506–517, 520–543 **LEVELED READERS:** **Unit 1, Week 3:** *Judy Baca* (A, O, EL, B) **Unit 1, Week 4:** *The Amazing Benjamin Franklin* (A, O, EL, B) **Unit 4, Week 3:** *Life in a Tide Pool* (A, O, EL, B) **Unit 6, Week 3:** *Reach for the Stars* (A, O, EL, B) **Unit 6, Week 4:** *African Cats* (A, O, EL, B) **YOUR TURN PRACTICE BOOK:** 23–25, 33–35, 173–175, 273–275, 283–285 **READING WORKSTATION ACTIVITY CARDS:** 10, 11, 12, 13, 14, 15 **TEACHER'S EDITION:** **Unit 1:** T154, T225C, T225G, T225L, T225M, T225P **Unit 4:** T148–T149, T153C, T153D, T153E, T153G, T212–T213, T217C, T217G **Unit 5:** T217M, T217Q, T217U, T217V **www.connected.mcgraw-hill.com: RESOURCES** **Student Resources:** Comprehension Interactive Games and Activities **Teacher Resources:** Graphic Organizers, Skills Review
RI.3.9	Compare and contrast the most important points and key details presented in two texts on the same topic.	**LEVELED READERS:** **Unit 1, Week 3:** *Judy Baca* (A, O, EL, B) **Unit 2, Week 4:** *Protecting the Islands* (A, O, EL, B) **CLOSE READING COMPANION:** 21, 28, 99, 139, 146 **READING WORKSTATION ACTIVITY CARDS:** 18, 20 **TEACHER'S EDITION:** **Unit 1:** T173, T225T, T239, T303 **Unit 2:** T107, T159Z, T173, T239, T336 **Unit 3:** T93T, T107, T159R, T173, T303 **Unit 4:** T153N, T167, T231 **Unit 5:** T103, T167, T217V, T217X, T231, T295 **Unit 6:** T39, T103, T167, T231 **www.connected.mcgraw-hill.com: RESOURCES** **Student Resources:** Comprehension Interactive Games and Activities
Range of Reading and Level of Text Complexity		*McGraw-Hill Wonders*
RI.3.10	By the end of the year, read and comprehend informational texts, including history/social studies, science, and technical texts, at the high end of the grades 2–3 text complexity band independently and proficiently.	**READING/WRITING WORKSHOP:** These units reflect the range of text complexity found throughout the book. **Unit 1:** 86–89 **Unit 2:** 134–139 **Unit 3:** 230–235 **Unit 4:** 290–293 **Unit 5:** 348–351 **Unit 6:** 448–451 **LITERATURE ANTHOLOGY:** These units reflect the range of text complexity found throughout the book. **Unit 2:** 172–185 **Unit 3:** 240–255 **Unit 4:** 326–339 **Unit 5:** 432–451 **Unit 6:** 520–543 **LEVELED READERS:** **Unit 1, Week 3:** *Judy Baca* (A, O, EL, B) **Unit 3, Week 4:** *Inspired by Nature* (A, O, EL, B) **Unit 4, Week 3:** *Life in a Tide Pool* (A, O, EL, B) **Unit 6, Week 4:** *African Cats* (A, O, EL, B) **READING WORKSTATION ACTIVITY CARDS:** 22, 27 **TEACHER'S EDITION:** **Unit 1:** T156, T222, T225A **Unit 2:** T159A, T159W, T222, T225A, T225O **Unit 3:** T93S, T156, T159A, T222, T225A **Unit 4:** T150, T153A, T214, T217A **Unit 5:** T89W–T89Z, T150, T153A, T214, T217A, T278 **Unit 6:** T150, T153A, T214 **www.connected.mcgraw-hill.com: RESOURCES** **Student Resources:** Comprehension Interactive Games and Activities

Reading Standards: Foundational Skills

There are no standards for Print Concepts (1) or Phonological Awareness (2) in Foundational Skills for Grade 3.

Phonics and Word Recognition		*McGraw-Hill Wonders*
RF.3.3	Know and apply grade-level phonics and word analysis skills in decoding words.	
RF.3.3a	Identify and know the meaning of the most common prefixes and derivational suffixes.	**READING/WRITING WORKSHOP: Unit 2:** 143, 159 **Unit 3:** 223, 253 **Unit 4:** 283 **Unit 5:** 383 **YOUR TURN PRACTICE BOOK:** 77, 87, 118, 127, 128, 138, 147, 148, 167, 218, 237, 238, 248, 258, 268, 288, 298 **PHONICS/WORD STUDY WORKSTATION ACTIVITY CARDS:** 7, 9, 12 **TEACHER'S EDITION: Unit 1:** S17, S18,S28, T105, T243 **Unit 2:** T158, T159L, T159P, T224 **Unit 3:** T95, T110, T161, T174, T177, T182, T186, T191, T192, T226, T242–T243, T262 **Unit 4:** T89L **Unit 5:** T91, T106, T107, T217E, T217T, T219, T235 **Unit 6:** T26, T107, T235, T282 **www.connected.mcgraw-hill.com: RESOURCES** **Student Resources:** Phonics Interactive Games and Activities **Teacher Resources:** Decodable Passages
RF.3.3b	Decode words with common Latin suffixes.	**READING/WRITING WORKSHOP: Unit 3:** 223, 253 **YOUR TURN PRACTICE BOOK:** 127, 128, 147, 218, 248, 268, 288 **PHONICS/WORD STUDY WORKSTATION ACTIVITY CARDS:** 9 **TEACHER'S EDITION: Unit 2:** T158, T159P, T224 **Unit 3:** T95, T110, T159N, T161, T174, T177, T182, T186, T191, T192, T226, T242–T243, T262 **Unit 4:** T89L **Unit 5:** T91, T106, T107, T217E, T217T, T219, T235 **Unit 6:** T26, T91, T107, T219, T235 **www.connected.mcgraw-hill.com: RESOURCES** **Student Resources:** Phonics Interactive Games and Activities **Teacher Resources:** Decodable Passages
RF.3.3c	Decode multisyllable words.	**READING/WRITING WORKSHOP: Unit 1:** 63 **Unit 2:** 143, 159 **Unit 3:** 223, 239, 253 **Unit 4:** 269, 283 **Unit 5:** 341, 383 **Unit 6:** 413, 441 **YOUR TURN PRACTICE BOOK:** 27, 77, 87, 88, 98, 127, 137, 138, 147, 157, 167, 168, 188, 207, 208, 228, 237, 248, 257, 268, 277, 278, 288 **PHONICS/WORD STUDY WORKSTATION ACTIVITY CARDS:** 27 **TEACHER'S EDITION: Unit 1:** T28, T44, T45, T94, T110, T111, T176 **Unit 2:** T44–T45, T110–T111, T93L, T226, T227 **Unit 3:** T44–T45, T110–T111, T176–T177, T242 **Unit 4:** T90, T91, T170–T171, T219, T234–T235 **Unit 5:** T26–T27, T42–T43, T90–T91 **Unit 6:** T42–T43, T90–T91, T106–T107, T170–T171, T234–T235 **www.connected.mcgraw-hill.com: RESOURCES** **Student Resources:** Phonics Interactive Games and Activities **Teacher Resources:** Decodable Passages
RF.3.3d	Read grade-appropriate irregularly spelled words.	**YOUR TURN PRACTICE BOOK:** 298 **PHONICS/WORD STUDY WORKSTATION ACTIVITY CARDS:** 29 **TEACHER'S EDITION: Unit 1:** S31, T226 **Unit 2:** T160, T176–T177 **Unit 3:** T161 **Unit 4:** T218 **Unit 6:** T283 **www.connected.mcgraw-hill.com: RESOURCES** **Student Resources:** Phonics Interactive Games and Activities **Teacher Resources:** Decodable Passages

CORRELATIONS

Reading Standards: Foundational Skills

Fluency		*McGraw-Hill Wonders*
RF.3.4	Read with sufficient accuracy and fluency to support comprehension.	
RF.3.4a	Read on-level text with purpose and understanding.	**READING WORKSTATION ACTIVITY CARDS:** 25, 26 **TEACHER'S EDITION: Unit 1:** T48, T53, T58, T112–T114, T161, T334–T335 **Unit 2:** T29, T48, T114, T161, T180, T227, T246, T334–T335 **Unit 3:** T46, T49, T95, T114, T161, T334–T335 **Unit 4:** T91, T110, T326–T327 **Unit 5:** T27, T91, T110, T172, T326–T327 **Unit 6:** T46, T91, T110, T174, T238, T326–T327 **www.connected.mcgraw-hill.com: RESOURCES** **Student Resources:** Fluency Interactive Games and Activities
RF.3.4b	Read on-level prose and poetry orally with accuracy, appropriate rate, and expression on successive readings.	**YOUR TURN PRACTICE BOOK:** 3–5, 63–65, 133–135, 173–175, 213–215, 263–265 **READING WORKSTATION ACTIVITY CARDS:** 25, 26 **YOUR TURN PRACTICE BOOK:** 43–45, 63–65, 113–115, 163–165, 203–205, 253–255 **TEACHER'S EDITION: Unit 1:** T29, T48, T95, T114, T127, T161, T180, T227, T246, T334–T335 **Unit 2:** T48, T114, T95, T161, T180, T291, T334–T335 **Unit 3:** T29, T114, T180, T227, T246, T291, T334–T335 **Unit 4:** T27, T46, T110, T174, T219, T238, T283, T326–T327 **Unit 5:** T46, T110, T155, T174, T219, T238, T326–T327 **Unit 6:** T46, T110, T155, T174, T238, T283, T326–T327 **www.connected.mcgraw-hill.com: RESOURCES** **Student Resources:** Fluency Interactive Games and Activities
RF.3.4c	Use context to confirm or self-correct word recognition and understanding, rereading as necessary.	**READING/WRITING WORKSHOP: Unit 1:** 31, 47, 93 **Unit 2:** 111 **Unit 3:** 191 **Unit 4:** 297, 311 **Unit 5:** 355, 369, 397 **Unit 6:** 455 **YOUR TURN PRACTICE BOOK:** 7, 17, 47, 57, 107, 177, 187, 217, 227, 247, 287 **READING WORKSTATION ACTIVITY CARDS:** 25, 26 **TEACHER'S EDITION: Unit 1:** T224, T291 **Unit 2:** T27M, T159I, T159L, T159P, T159S, T225D, T225E, T225J, T225P **Unit 3:** T27E, T27K, T27Q, T27V, T93C, T159I, T291 **Unit 4:** T89W, T217F, T217G, T217I, T217J, T217M **Unit 6:** T155 **www.connected.mcgraw-hill.com: RESOURCES** **Student Resources:** Fluency Interactive Games and Activities

College and Career Readiness Anchor Standards for WRITING

The K-5 standards on the following pages define what students should understand and be able to do by the end of each grade. They correspond to the College and Career Readiness (CCR) anchor standards below by number. The CCR and grade-specific standards are necessary complements—the former providing broad standards, the latter providing additional specificity—that together define the skills and understandings that all students must demonstrate.

Text Types and Purposes

1. Write arguments to support claims in an analysis of substantive topics or texts, using valid reasoning and relevant and sufficient evidence.

2. Write informative/explanatory texts to examine and convey complex ideas and information clearly and accurately through the effective selection, organization, and analysis of content.

3. Write narratives to develop real or imagined experiences or events using effective techniques, well-chosen details, and well-structured event sequences.

Production and Distribution of Writing

4. Produce clear and coherent writing in which the development, organization, and style are appropriate to task, purpose, and audience.

5. Develop and strengthen writing as needed by planning, revising, editing, rewriting, or trying a new approach.

6. Use technology, including the Internet, to produce and publish writing and to interact and collaborate with others.

Research to Build and Present Knowledge

7. Conduct short as well as more sustained research projects based on focused questions, demonstrating understanding of the subject under investigation.

8. Gather relevant information from multiple print and digital sources, assess the credibility and accuracy of each source, and integrate information while avoiding plagiarism.

9. Draw evidence from literary and/or informational texts to support analysis, reflection, and research.

Range of Writing

10. Write routinely over extended time frames (time for research, reflection, and revision) and shorter time frames (a single sitting or a day or two) for a range of tasks, purposes, and audiences.

CCSS Common Core State Standards
English Language Arts
Grade 3

Each standard is coded in the following manner:

Strand	Grade Level	Standard
W	3	1

Writing Standards

Text Types and Purposes	*McGraw-Hill Wonders*
W.3.1	Write opinion pieces on topics or texts, supporting a point of view with reasons.
W.3.1a Introduce the topic or text they are writing about, state an opinion, and create an organizational structure that lists reasons.	**READING/WRITING WORKSHOP: Unit 1:** 94 **Unit 2:** 128, 144 **Unit 3:** 254 **Unit 4:** 270, 284 **Unit 5:** 398 **Unit 6:** 414 **YOUR TURN PRACTICE BOOK:** 239, 249 **WRITING WORKSTATION ACTIVITY CARDS:** 13, 19 **TEACHER'S EDITION: Unit 1:** T41, T293, T294, T295 **Unit 2:** T97, T99, T107, T163, T165, T173, T175, T183, T187, T193 **Unit 3:** T107, T239, T293, T295, T359 **Unit 4:** T29, T31, T38, T93, T103 **Unit 5:** T222, T223, T285, T287, T345, T347, T350 **Unit 6:** T29, T31, T103 **www.connected.mcgraw-hill.com: RESOURCES** **Student Resources:** Writer's Workspace, Inquiry Space: Opinion Performance Task
W.3.1b Provide reasons that support the opinion.	**READING/WRITING WORKSHOP: Unit 1:** 94 **Unit 2:** 128, 144 **Unit 3:** 255 **Unit 4:** 271, 285 **Unit 5:** 398 **Unit 6:** 415 **YOUR TURN PRACTICE BOOK:** 79 **TEACHER'S EDITION: Unit 1:** T293, T294, T295 **Unit 2:** T97, T99, T163, T165, T239 **Unit 3:** T293, T295, T353 **Unit 4:** T29, T31, T39, T93, T95, T103, T167, T175, T183, T187, T193, T346 **Unit 5:** T222, T223, T285, T287, T346, T352 **Unit 6:** T29, T31 **www.connected.mcgraw-hill.com: RESOURCES** **Student Resources:** Writer's Workspace
W.3.1c Use linking words and phrases (e.g., *because, therefore, since, for example*) to connect opinion and reasons.	**READING/WRITING WORKSHOP: Unit 4:** 284 **Unit 5:** 399 **Unit 6:** 428-429 **YOUR TURN PRACTICE BOOK:** 59, 119, 269 **WRITING WORKSTATION ACTIVITY CARDS:** 7 **TEACHER'S EDITION: Unit 3:** T131, T354 **Unit 4:** T93, T95 **Unit 5:** T285, T287, T343, T353, T361 **www.connected.mcgraw-hill.com: RESOURCES** **Student Resources:** Writer's Workspace
W.3.1d Provide a concluding statement or section.	**READING/WRITING WORKSHOP: Unit 2:** 145 **YOUR TURN PRACTICE BOOK:** 139, 189 **WRITING WORKSTATION ACTIVITY CARDS:** 12 **TEACHER'S EDITION: Unit 2:** T97, T99, T163, T165 **Unit 3:** T222-T223, T361 **Unit 4:** T352 **www.connected.mcgraw-hill.com: RESOURCES** **Student Resources:** Writer's Workspace

Writing Standards

Text Types and Purposes		*McGraw-Hill Wonders*
W.3.2	Write informative/explanatory texts to examine a topic and convey ideas and information clearly.	
W.3.2a	Introduce a topic and group related information together; include illustrations when useful to aiding comprehension.	**READING/WRITING WORKSHOP:** Unit I: 64, 80 Unit 3: 224, 240 Unit 4: 298, 312 Unit 5: 370, 384, Unit 6: 442, 456 **YOUR TURN PRACTICE BOOK:** 129, 179, 229, 279 **WRITING WORKSTATION ACTIVITY CARDS:** 13, 14 **TEACHER'S EDITION: Unit I:** T41, T107, T163, T165, T173, T229, T231, T239 **Unit 2:** T41, T107, T173, T229, T231, T239, T353, T359 **Unit 3:** T41, T107, T163, T165, T173, T229, T231, T239 **Unit 4:** T157, T158–T159, T190, T221, T223 **Unit 5:** T157, T158–T159, T182, T190, T221, T223 **Unit 6:** T157, T159, T182, T190, T221, T223, T246, T345, T350-T351 **www.connected.mcgraw-hill.com: RESOURCES** **Student Resources:** Writer's Workspace, Inquiry Space: Informative Performance Task
W.3.2b	Develop the topic with facts, definitions, and details.	**READING/WRITING WORKSHOP: Unit I:** 80 **Unit 2:** 160-161 **Unit 3:** 224, 240 **Unit 4:** 298, 312 **Unit 5:** 370, 384 **Unit 6:** 442, 457 **YOUR TURN PRACTICE BOOK:** 19, 99, 299 **WRITING WORKSTATION ACTIVITY CARDS:** 2 **TEACHER'S EDITION: Unit I:** T29, T31, T98, T99 **Unit 2:** T196, T229, T231, T360 **Unit 3:** T106, T163, T165, T196, T229, T231 **Unit 4:** T157, T159, T190, T221, T223 **Unit 5:** T157, T159, T221, T223 **Unit 6:** T157, T159, T221, T223, T352 **www.connected.mcgraw-hill.com: RESOURCES** **Student Resources:** Writer's Workspace
W.3.2c	Use linking words and phrases (e.g., *also, another, and, more, but*) to connect ideas within categories of information.	**READING/WRITING WORKSHOP: Unit I:** 81 **Unit 4:** 299 **Unit 5:** 385 **YOUR TURN PRACTICE BOOK:** 39, 89 **WRITING WORKSTATION ACTIVITY CARDS:** 7 **TEACHER'S EDITION: Unit I:** T29, T31 **Unit 2:** T64, T355 **Unit 5:** T221, T223 **Unit 6:** T157, T159, T346, T352 **www.connected.mcgraw-hill.com: RESOURCES** **Student Resources:** Writer's Workspace
W.3.2d	Provide a concluding statement or section.	**READING/WRITING WORKSHOP: Unit I:** 65 **Unit 3:** 225, 241 **Unit 4:** 313 **Unit 5:** 371 **Unit 6:** 443, 457 **YOUR TURN PRACTICE BOOK:** 289 **WRITING WORKSTATION ACTIVITY CARDS:** 12 **TEACHER'S EDITION: Unit I:** T163, T165 **Unit 2:** T228-T229, T361 **Unit 3:** T163, T165, T229, T231, T262 **Unit 4:** T221, T223 **Unit 5:** T157, T159 **Unit 6:** T157, T159, T221, T223, T347 **www.connected.mcgraw-hill.com: RESOURCES** **Student Resources:** Writer's Workspace
W.3.3	Write narratives to develop real or imagined experiences or events using effective technique, descriptive details, and clear event sequences.	
W.3.3a	Establish a situation and introduce a narrator and/or characters; organize an event sequence that unfolds naturally.	**READING/WRITING WORKSHOP: Unit I:** T49 **Unit 2:** 112-113 **Unit 3:** 208 **Unit 4:** 326 **Unit 5:** 356 **Unit 6:** 428 **YOUR TURN PRACTICE BOOK:** 29, 169 **WRITING WORKSTATION ACTIVITY CARDS:** 4, 10 **TEACHER'S EDITION: Unit I:** T31, T33, T64, T97, T99, T353, T359 **Unit 2:** T262 **Unit 3:** T55, T63, T97, T99 **Unit 4:** T345 **Unit 6:** T93, T95 **www.connected.mcgraw-hill.com: RESOURCES** **Student Resources:** Writer's Workspace, Inquiry Space: Narrative Performance Task

Writing Standards

Text Types and Purposes | *McGraw-Hill Wonders*

W.3.3b	Use dialogue and descriptions of actions, thoughts, and feelings to develop experiences and events or show the response of characters to situations.	**READING/WRITING WORKSHOP: Unit I:** 32, 48 **Unit 2:** 112, 174 **Unit 3:** 192, 208 **Unit 5:** 342, 356 **Unit 6:** 429, 471 **YOUR TURN PRACTICE BOOK:** 9, 69, 169, 199, 219 **WRITING WORKSTATION ACTIVITY CARDS:** I, 3, 4 **TEACHER'S EDITION: Unit I:** T3I, T33, T97, T99, TI30, T353, T354, T360 **Unit 2:** T293, T295 **Unit 3:** T3I, T33, T97, T99 **Unit 4:** T62, TI26, T285, T287, T346, T35I, T353 **Unit 5:** TI26 **Unit 6:** T54, T93, T95, TI26, T285, T287 **www.connected.mcgraw-hill.com: RESOURCES** **Student Resources:** Writer's Workspace
W.3.3c	Use temporal words and phrases to signal event order.	**READING/WRITING WORKSHOP: Unit I:** 49 **Unit 2:** 112-113 **Unit 3:** 193, 209 **YOUR TURN PRACTICE BOOK:** 59, 119, 269 **WRITING WORKSTATION ACTIVITY CARDS:** 6 **TEACHER'S EDITION: Unit I:** T97, T99, TI63, TI65, TI96, T262, T360 **Unit 2:** T229, T23I **Unit 3:** T3I, T33, T97, T99 **Unit 6:** T93, T95 **www.connected.mcgraw-hill.com: RESOURCES** **Student Resources:** Writer's Workspace
W.3.3d	Provide a sense of closure.	**READING/WRITING WORKSHOP: Unit I:** 33 **Unit 2:** 112-113 **Unit 4:** 327 **Unit 5:** 343 **YOUR TURN PRACTICE BOOK:** 279, 289 **WRITING WORKSTATION ACTIVITY CARDS:** I2 **TEACHER'S EDITION: Unit I:** T3I, T33, T97, T99, TI63, TI65 **Unit 2:** T229, T23I, T293, T295 **Unit 3:** T3I, T33, T97, T99 **Unit 4:** T285, T287 **Unit 6:** T93, T95, T285, T287 **www.connected.mcgraw-hill.com: RESOURCES** **Student Resources:** Writer's Workspace

Production and Distribution of Writing | *McGraw-Hill Wonders*

W.3.4	With guidance and support from adults, produce writing in which the development and organization are appropriate to task and purpose. (Grade-specific expectations for writing types are defined in standards 1–3 above.)	**READING/WRITING WORKSHOP: Unit 3:** 254–255 **YOUR TURN PRACTICE BOOK:** I49 **WRITING WORKSTATION ACTIVITY CARDS:** I7, 20, 2I, 22, 23, 24, 25, 26, 27, 28, 29, 30 **TEACHER'S EDITION: Unit I:** T3I, T32, T33, T97, T98, T99, TI30, TI63, TI64, TI65, TI97, T229, T230, T23I, T293, T294, T295 **Unit 2:** T3I, T32, T33, T97, T98, T99, TI23, TI27, TI29–TI30, TI63, TI64, TI65, TI75, TI78, T229, T230, T23I, T293, T294, T295 **Unit 3:** T3I, T32, T33, T46, T6I, T93R, TI09, TII7, TI2I, TI27, TI63, TI64, TI65, T229, T230, T23I, T293, T294, T295 **Unit 4:** T25T, T29, T30, T3I, T62, T89T, T89Y, T93, T94, T95, TI26, TI57, TI58, TI59, TI90, T2I7P, T22I, T222, T223, T285, T286, T287, T238 **Unit 5:** T29, T30, T3I, T62, T93, T94, T95, TI57, TI58, TI59, TI82, T22I, T222, T223, T285, T286, T287 **Unit 6:** T29, T30, T3I, T62, T93, T94, T95, TI26, TI57, TI58, TI59, TI90, T22I, T222, T223, T266, T285, T286, T287, T328 **www.connected.mcgraw-hill.com: RESOURCES** **Student Resources:** Writer's Workspace
W.3.5	With guidance and support from peers and adults, develop and strengthen writing as needed by planning, revising, and editing. (Editing for conventions should demonstrate command of Language standards 1-3 up to and including grade 3.)	**READING/WRITING WORKSHOP: Unit I:** 33, 49, 65, 81, 95 **Unit 2:** II3, I29, I45, I6I, I75 **Unit 3:** 193, 209, 225, 24I, 255 **Unit 4:** 27I, 285, 299, 3I3, 327 **Unit 5:** 343, 357, 37I, 385, 399 **Unit 6:** 4I5, 429, 443, 457, 47I **TEACHER'S EDITION: Unit I:** 65, T353–T356, T359–T362 **Unit 2:** TI30, T262, T353–T356, T359–T362 **Unit 3:** T63, TI30, TI96, T262, T353–T356, T359–T362 **Unit 4:** T62, TI26, TI90, T345–T348, T35I–T354 **Unit 5:** T62, TI26, TI90, T254, T345–T348, T35I–T354 **Unit 6:** T62, TI26, TI90, T345–T348, T35I–T354 **www.connected.mcgraw-hill.com: RESOURCES** **Student Resources:** Writer's Workspace

Writing Standards

Production and Distribution of Writing	McGraw-Hill Wonders
W.3.6 With guidance and support from adults, use technology to produce and publish writing (using keyboarding skills) as well as to interact and collaborate with others.	**TEACHER'S EDITION:** Unit I: T302, T338–T341, T356, T362 **Unit 2:** T338–T341, T356, T362 **Unit 3:** T106, T238, T338–T341, T356, T362 **Unit 4:** T294, T330–T333, T348, T354 **Unit 5:** T330–T333, T348, T354 **Unit 6:** T102, T330–T333, T348, T354 **www.connected.mcgraw-hill.com:** RESOURCES **Student Resources:** Writer's Workspace, Inquiry Space

Research to Build and Present Knowledge	McGraw-Hill Wonders
W.3.7 Conduct short research projects that build knowledge about a topic.	**WRITING WORKSTATION ACTIVITY CARDS:** 30 **TEACHER'S EDITION:** Unit I: T40, T106, T172, T238, T338–T341 **Unit 2:** T40, T106, T172, T238, T338–T341 **Unit 3:** T40, T106, T172, T187, T238, T338–T341 **Unit 4:** T38, T102, T166, T230, T328–T329, T330–T333 **Unit 5:** T38, T102, T166, T230, T246, T330–T333 **Unit 6:** T38, T102, T328–T329, T330–T333 **www.connected.mcgraw-hill.com:** RESOURCES **Student Resources:** Research and Inquiry, Writer's Workspace **Teacher Resources:** Graphic Organizers, Research and Inquiry
W.3.8 Recall information from experiences or gather information from print and digital sources; take brief notes on sources and sort evidence into provided categories.	**WRITING WORKSTATION ACTIVITY CARDS:** 30 **TEACHER'S EDITION:** Unit I: T27B, T27C, T27G, T27I, T27O, T40, T336–T337, T338–T341 **Unit 2:** T3I, T33, T97, T99, T163, T165, T225F, T225G, T225I, T225K, T229, T23I, T238, T293, T295, T336, T338–T341 **Unit 3:** T3I, T33, T97, T99, T159G, T159K, T163, T165, T229, T23I, T293, T295, T336–T337 **Unit 4:** T25B, T25D, T25E, T25G, T25J, T25P, T25Q, T29, T3I, T89B, T93, T95, T157, T159, T22I, T223, T285, T287, T346 **Unit 5:** T38, T328–T329 **Unit 6:** T29, T3I, T93, T95, T102, T157, T159, T22I, T223, T285, T287, T328, T330–T333 **www.connected.mcgraw-hill.com:** RESOURCES **Student Resources:** Inquiry Space, Research and Inquiry, Writer's Workspace **Teacher Resources:** Graphic Organizers, Research and Inquiry
W.3.9 (Begins in grade 4)	(Begins in grade 4)

Range of Writing	McGraw-Hill Wonders
W.3.10 Write routinely over extended time frames (time for research, reflection, and revision) and shorter time frames (a single sitting or a day or two) for a range of discipline-specific tasks, purposes, and audiences.	**READING/WRITING WORKSHOP:** Unit I: 64–65 **Unit 2:** 112–113 **Unit 3:** 192–193 **Unit 4:** 298–299 **Unit 5:** 356–357 **Unit 6:** 428–429 **WRITING WORKSTATION ACTIVITY CARDS:** 20, 21, 22, 23, 24, 25, 26, 27, 28, 29, 30 **CLOSE READING COMPANION:** 3, 17,28, 30,33,36, 40, 43, 47, 51, 54, 57, 61, 63, 66, 69, 73, 76, 80, 83, 87, 90, 94, 96, 109, 116, 123, 129, 135, 142, 149, 156, 162, 168, 175, 182, 189, 195 **TEACHER'S EDITION:** Unit I: T30, T41, T43, T51, T55, T61, T64, T96, T162, T228, T292, T338–T341, T342–T363 **Unit 2:** T30, T96, T109, T117, T121, T127, T128, T130, T162, T173, T228, T292, T338–T341, T352–T363 **Unit 3:** T30, T96, T162, T196, T225L, T220, T230, T23I, T239, T24I, T249, T253, T254, T26I, T284, T338–T341, T352–T363 **Unit 4:** T95, T118, T119, T126, T158, T167, T330–T333, T344–T355 **Unit 5:** T28, T92, T156, T159, T179, T182, T190, T220, T222, T223, T231, T284, T330–T333, T344–T355 **Unit 6:** T28, T39, T62, T92, T126, T156, T190, T220, T246, T284, T330–T333, T344–T355 **www.connected.mcgraw-hill.com:** RESOURCES **Student Resources:** Inquiry Space, Research and Inquiry, Writer's Workspace **Teacher Resources:** Research and Inquiry

College and Career Readiness Anchor Standards for
SPEAKING AND LISTENING

The K-5 standards on the following pages define what students should understand and be able to do by the end of each grade. They correspond to the College and Career Readiness (CCR) anchor standards below by number. The CCR and grade-specific standards are necessary complements—the former providing broad standards, the latter providing additional specificity—that together define the skills and understandings that all students must demonstrate.

Comprehension and Collaboration
1. Prepare for and participate effectively in a range of conversations and collaborations with diverse partners, building on others' ideas and expressing their own clearly and persuasively.
2. Integrate and evaluate information presented in diverse media and formats, including visually, quantitatively, and orally.
3. Evaluate a speaker's point of view, reasoning, and use of evidence and rhetoric.

Presentation of Knowledge and Ideas
4. Present information, findings, and supporting evidence such that listeners can follow the line of reasoning and the organization, development, and style are appropriate to task, purpose, and audience.
5. Make strategic use of digital media and visual displays of data to express information and enhance understanding of presentations.
6. Adapt speech to a variety of contexts and communicative tasks, demonstrating command of formal English when indicated or appropriate.

CCSS Common Core State Standards
English Language Arts
Grade 3

Each standard is coded in the following manner:

Strand	Grade Level	Standard
SL	3	1

Speaking and Listening Standards

Comprehension and Collaboration	*McGraw-Hill Wonders*
SL.3.1	Engage effectively in a range of collaborative discussions (one-on-one, in groups, and teacher-led) with diverse partners on *grade 3 topics and texts*, building on others' ideas and expressing their own clearly.
SL.3.1a	Come to discussions prepared, having read or studied required material; explicitly draw on that preparation and other information known about the topic to explore ideas under discussion.	**READING/WRITING WORKSHOP: Unit 1:** 28, 29, 44, 45, 60, 61, 76, 77, 90, 91 **Unit 2:** 108, 109, 124, 125, 140, 141, 156, 157 **Unit 3:** 188, 189, 204, 205, 220, 221, 236, 237, 250, 251 **Unit 4:** 166, 267, 280, 281, 294, 295, 308, 309 **Unit 5:** 338, 339, 352, 353, 366, 367, 380, 381, 394, 395 **Unit 6:** 410, 411, 424, 425, 438, 439, 452, 453 **CLOSE READING COMPANION:** 1–198 **TEACHER'S EDITION: Unit 1:** T49, T53, T57, T117, T119, T123, T142, T214, T239 **Unit 2:** T117, T121, T127, T142, T220, T239, T241, T249, T253, T259 **Unit 3:** T172, T173, T175, T183, T187, T193, T208, T239, T241, T249, T253, T261 **Unit 4:** T39, T74, T82, T86, T102, T103, T167 **Unit 5:** T10, T39, T111, T115, T119, T167, T175, T179 **Unit 6:** T47, T51, T55, T103, T111, T115, T119, T175 www.connected.mcgraw-hill.com: RESOURCES **Teacher Resources:** Build Background Videos
SL.3.1b	Follow agreed-upon rules for discussions (e.g., gaining the floor in respectful ways, listening to others with care, speaking one at a time about the topics and texts under discussion).	**READING WORKSTATION ACTIVITY CARDS:** 24 **TEACHER'S EDITION: Unit 1:** T10, T76, T239 **Unit 2:** T10, T76, T162, T222 **Unit 3:** T76, T106, T107, T172, T173, T208, T209, T238, T239 **Unit 4:** T10, T38, T39, T102, T103, T202, T230, T231 **Unit 5:** T74, T103, T166, T202, T203, T266 **Unit 6:** T74, T138, T266 www.connected.mcgraw-hill.com: RESOURCES **Teacher Resources:** Build Background Videos
SL.3.1c	Ask questions to check understanding of information presented, stay on topic, and link their comments to the remarks of others.	**TEACHER'S EDITION: Unit 1:** T18, T82, T142, T218 **Unit 2:** T14, T27Q, T27W, T40, T93J, T159J, T159N, T173, T208, T340 **Unit 3:** T10, T27I, T27V, T27X–T27Z, T93J, T142, T159H **Unit 4:** T89H, T89K, T89O, T89V, T89W, T89Y, T217D, T217H, T217I, T217J, T217M, T217R, T231 **Unit 5:** T10, T231 **Unit 6:** T138 www.connected.mcgraw-hill.com: RESOURCES **Student Resources:** Research and Inquiry **Teacher Resources:** Build Background Videos, Research and Inquiry
SL.3.1d	Explain their own ideas and understanding in light of the discussion.	**CLOSE READING COMPANION:** 2, 9, 16, 23, 30, 35, 42, 49, 56, 65, 75, 82, 89, 96, 101, 108, 111, 115, 119, 122, 126, 131, 134, 141, 155, 174 **TEACHER'S EDITION: Unit 1:** T10, T76, T93B, T107, T173, T208, T222, T238, T340 **Unit 2:** T14, T27B, T27F, T27L, T27N, T27P, T27X, T41, T159J, T225E, T225J **Unit 3:** T159J, T159L, T173, T225H, T225I **Unit 4:** T25N, T25V, T39, T89H, T89O **Unit 5:** T10, T28, T102, T104, T138, T139, T167 **Unit 6:** T166, T295, T332 www.connected.mcgraw-hill.com: RESOURCES **Teacher Resources:** Build Background Videos

Speaking and Listening Standards

Comprehension and Collaboration		McGraw-Hill Wonders
SL.3.2	Determine the main ideas and supporting details of a text read aloud or information presented in diverse media and formats, including visually, quantitatively, and orally.	**CLOSE READING COMPANION:** 40, 61, 127, 132, 193 **TEACHER'S EDITION: Unit 1:** T10, T12, T30, T78, T96, T144, T162, T208, T210, T228, T336 **Unit 2:** T10, T12, T30, T78, T96, T142, T144, T159Y, T162, T208, T210, T228, T336 **Unit 3:** T10, T12, T30, T78, T96, T142, T144, T159Y, T162, T172, T208, T209, T228, T302, T340 **Unit 4:** T12–T13, T28, T74, T76, T92, T156, T204, T220, T328 **Unit 5:** T10, T12, T28, T74, T76, T92, T140, T141, T156, T202, T204, T217W, T220, T230, T328 **Unit 6:** T38, T74, T76, T138, T140, T230, T328 **CLOSE READING COMPANION:** 40, 61, 127, 132, 193 www.connected.mcgraw-hill.com: **RESOURCES** **Student Resources:** Music/Fine Arts Activities **Teacher Resources:** Interactive Read Aloud Images, Music/Fine Arts Activities
SL.3.3	Ask and answer questions about information from a speaker, offering appropriate elaboration and detail.	**TEACHER'S EDITION: Unit 1:** T340, T342–T343 **Unit 2:** T41, T238, T302, T340, T342–T343 **Unit 3:** T41, T106, T107, T172, T173, T238, T239, T340, T342–T343 **Unit 4:** T166, T332, T334–T335 **Unit 5:** T38, T332, T334–T335 **Unit 6:** T39, T332, T334–T335 www.connected.mcgraw-hill.com: **RESOURCES** **Student Resources:** Research and Inquiry **Teacher Resources:** Research and Inquiry
Presentation of Knowledge and Ideas		**McGraw-Hill Wonders**
SL.3.4	Report on a topic or text, tell a story, or recount an experience with appropriate facts and relevant, descriptive details, speaking clearly at an understandable pace.	**TEACHER'S EDITION: Unit 1:** T18, T148, T340, T342–T343 **Unit 2:** T40, T107, T340, T342–T343 **Unit 3:** T40, T239, T340, T342–T343, **Unit 4:** T38, T332, T334–T335 **Unit 5:** T292, T332, T334–T335 **Unit 6:** T167, T230, T332, T334–T335 www.connected.mcgraw-hill.com: **RESOURCES** **Student Resources:** Research and Inquiry, **Inquiry Space:** Unit 2, Collaborative Conversations Videos **Teacher Resources:** Research and Inquiry
SL.3.5	Create engaging audio recordings of stories or poems that demonstrate fluid reading at an understandable pace; add visual displays when appropriate to emphasize or enhance certain facts or details.	**TEACHER'S EDITION: Unit 1:** T238, T340 **Unit 2:** T227, T291, T340 **Unit 3:** T238, T340 **Unit 4:** T102, T155, T166, T283, T294, T332, T334–T335 **Unit 5:** T27, T332, T334–T335 **Unit 6:** T27, T102, T332, T334–T335 www.connected.mcgraw-hill.com: **RESOURCES** **Student Resources:** Research and Inquiry **Teacher Resources:** Research and Inquiry
SL.3.6	Speak in complete sentences when appropriate to task and situation in order to provide requested detail or clarification. (See grade 3 Language standards 1 and 3 for specific expectations.)	**TEACHER'S EDITION: Unit 1:** T274, T342 **Unit 2:** T142, T173, T208, T303 **Unit 3:** T41, T107, T208 **Unit 4:** T167, T202 **Unit 5:** T138, T231, T332 **Unit 6:** T74, T167, T202, T230 www.connected.mcgraw-hill.com: **RESOURCES** **Student Resources:** Grammar Interactive Games and Activities, Research and Inquiry **Teacher Resources:** Research and Inquiry

College and Career Readiness Anchor Standards for LANGUAGE

The K-5 standards on the following pages define what students should understand and be able to do by the end of each grade. They correspond to the College and Career Readiness (CCR) anchor standards below by number. The CCR and grade-specific standards are necessary complements—the former providing broad standards, the latter providing additional specificity—that together define the skills and understandings that all students must demonstrate.

Conventions of English

1. Demonstrate command of the conventions of standard English grammar and usage when writing or speaking.

2. Demonstrate command of the conventions of standard English capitalization, punctuation, and spelling when writing.

Knowledge of Language

3. Apply knowledge of language to understand how language functions in different contexts, to make effective choices for meaning or style, and to comprehend more fully when reading and listening.

Vocabulary Acquisition and Use

4. Determine or clarify the meaning of unknown and multiple-meaning words and phrases by using context clues, analyzing meaningful word parts, and consulting general and specialized reference materials, as appropriate.

5. Demonstrate understanding of figurative language, word relationships, and nuances in word meanings.

6. Acquire and use accurately a range of general academic and domain-specific words and phrases sufficient for reading, writing, speaking, and listening at the college and career readiness level; demonstrate independence in gathering vocabulary knowledge when encountering an unknown term important to comprehension or expression.

CCSS Common Core State Standards
English Language Arts
Grade 3

Each standard is coded in the following manner:

Strand	Grade Level	Standard
L	3	1

Language Standards

Conventions of English		*McGraw-Hill Wonders*
L.3.1	Demonstrate command of the conventions of standard English grammar and usage when writing or speaking.	
L.3.1a	Explain the function of nouns, pronouns, verbs, adjectives, and adverbs in general and their functions in particular sentences.	**READING/WRITING WORKSHOP: Unit 1:** 65, 80 **Unit 2:** 112–113, 175 **Unit 4:** 270, 299 **Unit 5:** 343, 357, 399 **Unit 6:** 443 **Grammar Handbook:** 478–480, 481–486, 487–490, 491–492, 493–494 **TEACHER'S EDITION: Unit 1:** T151 **Unit 2:** T32, T65, T98, T99, T131, T177, T232 **Unit 3:** T34, T64, T100, T166, T197 **Unit 4:** T32, T68, T89D, T160, T190 **Unit 5:** T32, T33, T63, T97, T98, T160, T161, T190, T224, T225 **Unit 6:** T32, T33, T63, T96, T97, T160, T161, T191, T224, T225 www.connected.mcgraw-hill.com: **RESOURCES** **Student Resources:** Grammar Interactive Games and Activities
L.3.1b	Form and use regular and irregular plural nouns.	**READING/WRITING WORKSHOP: Unit 2:** 129, 145 **Grammar Handbook:** 479–480 **YOUR TURN PRACTICE BOOK:** 38, 58 **TEACHER'S EDITION: Unit 1:** T227 **Unit 2:** T100, T130, T166–T167, T197 www.connected.mcgraw-hill.com: **RESOURCES** **Student Resources:** Grammar Interactive Games and Activities **Teacher Resources:** Music/Fine Arts Activities
L.3.1c	Use abstract nouns (e.g., *childhood*).	**READING/WRITING WORKSHOP: Grammar Handbook:** 478 **TEACHER'S EDITION: Unit 2:** T34–T35, T65 www.connected.mcgraw-hill.com: **RESOURCES** **Student Resources:** Grammar Interactive Games and Activities **Teacher Resources:** Music/Fine Arts Activities
L.3.1d	Form and use regular and irregular verbs.	**READING/WRITING WORKSHOP: Unit 3:** 193 **Unit 4:** 327 **Grammar Handbook:** 481–486 **TEACHER'S EDITION: Unit 1:** T111, T177 **Unit 4:** T32, T33, T63, T160–T161, T288–T289 www.connected.mcgraw-hill.com: **RESOURCES** **Student Resources:** Grammar Interactive Games and Activities **Teacher Resources:** Music/Fine Arts Activities
L.3.1e	Form and use the simple (e.g., *I walked; I walk; I will walk*) verb tenses.	**READING/WRITING WORKSHOP: Unit 3:** 209, 225, 241 **Grammar Handbook:** 482–483 **TEACHER'S EDITION: Unit 2:** T111, T177 **Unit 3:** T34–T35, T100, T131, T166–T167, T197, T232–T233, T263 **Unit 4:** T160, T161 www.connected.mcgraw-hill.com: **RESOURCES** **Student Resources:** Grammar Interactive Games and Activities **Teacher Resources:** Music/Fine Arts Activities
L.3.1f	Ensure subject-verb and pronoun-antecedent agreement.	**READING/WRITING WORKSHOP: Unit 5:** 371 **Grammar Handbook:** 483, 490 **TEACHER'S EDITION: Unit 2:** T151 **Unit 3:** T100, T101, T131, T166, T167, T197, T263 **Unit 4:** T32, T63, T288–T289 **Unit 5:** T32, T33, T97, T160, T161 www.connected.mcgraw-hill.com: **RESOURCES** **Student Resources:** Grammar Interactive Games and Activities

Language Standards

Conventions of English		McGraw-Hill Wonders
L.3.1g	Form and use comparative and superlative adjectives and adverbs, and choose between them depending on what is to be modified.	**READING/WRITING WORKSHOP:** Unit 6: 429, 456 Grammar Handbook: 492, 494 **TEACHER'S EDITION:** Unit 6: T96, T97, T161, T224, T225, T255 www.connected.mcgraw-hill.com: **RESOURCES** **Student Resources:** Grammar Interactive Games and Activities
L.3.1h	Use coordinating and subordinating conjunctions.	**READING/WRITING WORKSHOP:** Unit 1: 95 Unit 3: 254 **Grammar Handbook:** 476, 477 **TEACHER'S EDITION:** Unit 2: T222 Unit 4: T224–T225 www.connected.mcgraw-hill.com: **RESOURCES** **Student Resources:** Grammar Interactive Games and Activities
L.3.1i	Produce simple, compound, and complex sentences.	**READING/WRITING WORKSHOP:** Unit 1: 32, 48, 95 Unit 2: 160 Unit 3: 192, 254 Unit 4: 312 Unit 6: 415, 470 **Grammar Handbook:** 476, 477 **YOUR TURN PRACTICE BOOK:** 49, 109, 209, 259 **TEACHER'S EDITION:** Unit 1: T34, T63, T65, T100–T101, T129, T131, T166–T167, T195, T197, T232–T233, T261, T263 Unit 2: T63–T65, T260–T263 Unit 5: T30, T31, T54, Unit 6: T54, T61, T118, T125, T126, T190, T246, T253 www.connected.mcgraw-hill.com: **RESOURCES** **Student Resources:** Grammar Interactive Games and Activities
L.3.2	Demonstrate command of the conventions of standard English capitalization, punctuation, and spelling when writing.	
L.3.2a	Capitalize appropriate words in titles.	**READING/WRITING WORKSHOP:** Grammar Handbook: 498, 500 **TEACHER'S EDITION:** Unit 2: T35 Unit 3: T167, T233 Unit 5: T33, T97 www.connected.mcgraw-hill.com: **RESOURCES** **Student Resources:** Grammar Interactive Games and Activities **Teacher Resources:** Music/Fine Arts Activities
L.3.2b	Use commas in addresses.	**READING/WRITING WORKSHOP:** Grammar Handbook: 502 **TEACHER'S EDITION:** Unit 1: T356 Unit 2: T233 Unit 5: T33, T97 Unit 6: T33 www.connected.mcgraw-hill.com: **RESOURCES** **Student Resources:** Grammar Interactive Games and Activities
L.3.2c	Use commas and quotation marks in dialogue.	**READING/WRITING WORKSHOP:** Grammar Handbook: 504 **TEACHER'S EDITION:** Unit 3: T35 Unit 4: T97, T161 www.connected.mcgraw-hill.com: **RESOURCES** **Student Resources:** Grammar Interactive Games and Activities **Teacher Resources:** Music/Fine Arts Activities
L.3.2d	Form and use possessives.	**READING/WRITING WORKSHOP:** Unit 5: 385 Grammar Handbook: 480, 489 **TEACHER'S EDITION:** Unit 2: T161, T296-297, T327 Unit 4: T97 Unit 5: T224, T225, T255, T289 **YOUR TURN PRACTICE BOOK:** 78 www.connected.mcgraw-hill.com: **RESOURCES** **Student Resources:** Grammar Interactive Games and Activities **Teacher Resources:** Music/Fine Arts Activities
L.3.2e	Use conventional spelling for high-frequency and other studied words and for adding suffixes to base words (e.g., *sitting, smiled, cries, happiness*).	**YOUR TURN PRACTICE BOOK:** 18, 28, 38, 58, 68, 168, 218, 238 **PHONICS/WORD STUDY WORKSTATION ACTIVITY CARDS:** 24, 29 **TEACHER'S EDITION:** Unit 1: T46, T63, T112, T129, T178, T195, T244, T261 Unit 2: T45, T46, T112, T178, T195, T244 Unit 3: T46, T112, T130, T178 Unit 4: T44, T108, T172, T234, T254 Unit 5: T61, T98, T108, T125, T189, T236, T253 Unit 6: T44, T61, T108, T125, T170, T189, T234, T253, T302

Language Standards

Conventions of English		*McGraw-Hill Wonders*
L.3.2f	Use spelling patterns and generalizations (e.g., word families, position-based spellings, syllable patterns, ending rules, meaningful word parts) in writing words.	**READING/WRITING WORKSHOP:** Unit 4: 285 **YOUR TURN PRACTICE BOOK:** 8, 18, 28, 38, 58, 68, 168, 218, 238 **PHONICS/WORD STUDY WORKSTATION ACTIVITY CARDS:** 24 **TEACHER'S EDITION: Unit 1:** T36, T64, T102, T130, T170, T196, T166, T168, T234 **Unit 2:** T32, T65, T98, T99, T131, T177, T232 **Unit 3:** T36, T63, T102, T170, T196, T234, T300 **Unit 4:** T62, T96, T126, T190, T290 **Unit 5:** T34, T62, T98, T162, T190, T226, T254, T290 **Unit 6:** T62, T98, T126, T164, T190, T226 **www.connected.mcgraw-hill.com:** RESOURCES **Student Resources:** Grammar Interactive Games and Activities **Teacher Resources:** Music/Fine Arts Activities
L.3.2g	Consult reference materials, including beginning dictionaries, as needed to check and correct spellings.	**READING/WRITING WORKSHOP: Unit 1:** T38, T104, T170, T236, T302 **Unit 2:** T38, T104, T170, T236, T302 **Unit 3:** T38, T104, T170 **Unit 4:** T292 **Unit 5:** T36, T164, T228, T292 **Unit 6:** T36, T100, T164, T228, T292 **TEACHER'S EDITION: Unit 1:** T36, T102, T170, T234, T300 **Unit 2:** T36, T102, T170, T234, T300 **Unit 3:** T36, T102, T170 **Unit 4:** T290 **Unit 5:** T34, T164, T226, T290 **Unit 6:** T34, T98, T162, T226, T290 **www.connected.mcgraw-hill.com:** RESOURCES **Student Resources:** Grammar Interactive Games and Activities **Teacher Resources:** Music/Fine Arts Activities

Knowledge of Language		*McGraw-Hill Wonders*
L.3.3	Use knowledge of language and its conventions when writing, speaking, reading, or listening.	
L.3.3a	Choose words and phrases for effect.	**READING/WRITING WORKSHOP: Unit 1:** 32–33, 48–49 **Unit 2:** 128–129 **Unit 4:** 284–285, 326–327 **Unit 5:** 356–357 **YOUR TURN PRACTICE BOOK:** 9, 69, 169, 199, 219 **TEACHER'S EDITION: Unit 1:** T96–T99 **Unit 2:** T96–T99, T130 **Unit 4:** T284–T287 **Unit 5:** T92–T95, T102 **Unit 6:** T284–T287, T294 **www.connected.mcgraw-hill.com:** RESOURCES **Student Resources:** Writer's Workspace
L.3.3b	Recognize and observe differences between the conventions of spoken and written standard English.	**READING/WRITING WORKSHOP: Unit 3:** 255 **TEACHER'S EDITION: Unit 1:** S35, T338, T354 **Unit 2:** T106 **Unit 4:** T102 **Unit 5:** T166 **Unit 6:** T166, T330–T333 **www.connected.mcgraw-hill.com:** RESOURCES **Student Resources:** Writer's Workspace

Vocabulary Acquisition and Use		*McGraw-Hill Wonders*
L.3.4	Determine or clarify the meaning of unknown and multiple-meaning words and phrases based on *grade 3 reading and content*, choosing flexibly from a range of strategies.	
L.3.4a	Use sentence-level context as a clue to the meaning of a word or phrase.	**READING/WRITING WORKSHOP: Unit 1:** 47, 93 **Unit 2:** 111 **Unit 3:** 191 **Unit 4:** 297, 311 **Unit 5:** 355, 369, 397 **YOUR TURN PRACTICE BOOK:** 17, 47, 57, 107, 177, 187, 217, 227, 247 **PHONICS/WORD STUDY WORKSTATION ACTIVITY CARDS:** 1, 2, 5, 11, 15 **TEACHER'S EDITION: Unit 1:** T26, T27N, T41, T92, T105, T172 **Unit 2:** T93S, T216 **Unit 3:** T26–T27, T27E, T93C, T159I, T212–T213 **Unit 4:** T152, T153F, T153I, T165, T216 **Unit 5:** T14, T36, T88–T89, T152–T153, T153E, T164–T165 **Unit 6:** T216–T217, T217I, T229 **www.connected.mcgraw-hill.com:** RESOURCES **Student Resources:** Vocabulary Interactive Games and Activities
L.3.4b	Determine the meaning of the new word formed when a known affix is added to a known word (e.g., *agreeable/disagreeable, comfortable/ uncomfortable, care/careless, heat/ preheat*).	**READING/WRITING WORKSHOP: Unit 2:** 143, 159 **Unit 3:** 223, 253 **Unit 4:** 283 **Unit 5:** 383 **YOUR TURN PRACTICE BOOK:** 77, 87, 127, 147, 167, 237 **PHONICS/WORD STUDY WORKSTATION ACTIVITY CARDS:** 9, 12 **TEACHER'S EDITION: Unit 2:** T158, T171, T224–T225 **Unit 3:** T95, T158–T159, T161, T171, T226, T234, T236–T237 **Unit 4:** T88–T89, T89L, T101 **Unit 5:** T14, T101, T153K, T153L, T165, T216–T217, T229 **Unit 6:** T26, T91, T165, T219, T229 **www.connected.mcgraw-hill.com:** RESOURCES **Student Resources:** Vocabulary Interactive Games and Activities

Language Standards

Vocabulary Acquisition and Use		McGraw-Hill Wonders
L.3.4c	Use a known root word as a clue to the meaning of an unknown word with the same root (e.g., *company, companion*).	**READING/WRITING WORKSHOP:** Unit 3: 239 Unit 4: 269 Unit 5: 341 Unit 6: 413, 441 **YOUR TURN PRACTICE BOOK:** 137, 157, 158, 207, 228, 257, 258, 277 **PHONICS/WORD STUDY WORKSTATION ACTIVITY CARDS:** 10, 13 **TEACHER'S EDITION:** Unit 2: T225K, T225N Unit 3: T159N, T224–T225, T225B, T225I, T225L, T237, T240 Unit 4: T24, T25B, T25P, T25T, T27, T155 Unit 5: T24, T37, T100, T155, T171 Unit 6: T24–T25, T27, T37, T100, T152–T153, T155, T165, T228 www.connected.mcgraw-hill.com: RESOURCES **Student Resources:** Vocabulary Interactive Games and Activities
L.3.4d	Use glossaries or beginning dictionaries, both print and digital, to determine or clarify the precise meaning of key words and phrases.	**TEACHER'S EDITION:** Unit 1: S27, T26, T39, T92, T93K, T105 Unit 2: T159I, T237 Unit 3: T26, T92, T237 Unit 4: T24, T216 Unit 5: T24, T88, T89I, T152, T217O, T280 Unit 6: T88, T216 www.connected.mcgraw-hill.com: RESOURCES **Student Resources:** Vocabulary Interactive Games and Activities
L.3.5	Demonstrate understanding of word relationships and nuances in word meanings.	
L.3.5a	Distinguish the literal and nonliteral meanings of words and phrases in context (e.g., *take steps*).	**READING/WRITING WORKSHOP:** Unit 1: 79 Unit 2: 127, 173 Unit 3: 207 Unit 4: 325 Unit 6: 427, 469 **YOUR TURN PRACTICE BOOK:** 37, 67, 97, 117, 197, 267, 297 **PHONICS/WORD STUDY WORKSTATION ACTIVITY CARDS:** 4, 6, 8 **CLOSE READING COMPANION:** 151 **TEACHER'S EDITION:** Unit 1: T93M, T224, T225H, T225K, T225M, T237 Unit 2: T92, T105, T113, T118, T122 Unit 3: T38, T92–T93, T93Q, T105 Unit 4: T25L, T89G, T89P, T89W, T217G, T217I Unit 5: T89Q, T89S Unit 6: T88–T89, T101, T142, T153A–T153B, T164, T292–T293 www.connected.mcgraw-hill.com: RESOURCES **Student Resources:** Vocabulary Interactive Games and Activities
L.3.5b	Identify real-life connections between words and their use (e.g., describe people who are *friendly* or *helpful*).	**READING/WRITING WORKSHOP:** Unit 1: 20–21, 68–69 Unit 2: 116–117, 148–149 Unit 3: 196–197, 212–213 Unit 4: 288–289, 302–303 Unit 5: 346–347, 360–361 Unit 6: 418–419, 460–461 **YOUR TURN PRACTICE BOOK:** 1, 21, 41, 101, 151, 181, 211, 241, 261, 291 **TEACHER'S EDITION:** Unit 1: T47, T76, T179, T208, T212, T245 Unit 2: T47, T76, T179, T245 Unit 3: T38–T39, T113, T146, T179, T212, T245 Unit 4: T10, T14, T78, T173, T235 Unit 5: T202–T203, T228–T229, T237 Unit 6: T36–T37, T78, T142–T143, T228–T229 www.connected.mcgraw-hill.com: RESOURCES **Student Resources:** Vocabulary Interactive Games and Activities **Teacher Resources:** Build Background Videos, Graphic Organizers
L.3.5c	Distinguish shades of meaning among related words that describe states of mind or degrees of certainty (e.g., *knew, believed, suspected, heard, wondered*).	**TEACHER'S EDITION:** Unit 1: T56, T171 Unit 2: T56, T105 Unit 3: T93M, T105 Unit 4: T101 Unit 5: T101 Unit 6: T229 **CLOSE READING COMPANION:** 17 www.connected.mcgraw-hill.com: RESOURCES **Student Resources:** Vocabulary Interactive Games and Activities
L.3.6	Acquire and use accurately grade-appropriate conversational, general academic, and domain-specific words and phrases, including those that signal spatial and temporal relationships (e.g., *After dinner that night we went looking for them*).	**READING/WRITING WORKSHOP:** Unit 1: 20–21, 36–37, 52–53, 68–69, 84–85 Unit 2: 100–101, 116–117, 132–133, 148–149, 164–165 Unit 3: 180–181, 196–197, 212–213, 228–229, 244–245 Unit 4: 260–261, 274–275, 288–289, 302–303, 316–317 Unit 5: 332–333, 346–347, 360–361, 374–375, 388–389 Unit 6: 404–405, 424–425, 432–433, 446–447, 460–461 **YOUR TURN PRACTICE BOOK:** 1, 11, 51, 61, 101, 111, 151, 161, 201, 211, 251, 261 **TEACHER'S EDITION:** Unit 1: T14, T38–T39, T80, T104–T105, T146 Unit 2: T93C, T104–T105, T212 Unit 3: T13–T15, T27Y, T146–T147, T159I, T172–T173 Unit 4: T14–T15, T36–T37, T142–T143, T153I, T164–T165, T217K Unit 5: T78–T79, T100–T101, T142–143, T164–T165, T228–T229 Unit 6: T36–T37, T44, T50, T54, T61, T100–T101, T206–T207